Thinking on Thinking

Studies in Mind, Meaning, and Subjectivity

Robert M. Berchman

⁐PICKWICK *Publications* • Eugene, Oregon

THINKING ON THINKING
Studies in Mind, Meaning, and Subjectivity

Foro di Studi Avanzati Series 1

Copyright © 2021 Robert M. Berchman. All rights reserved. Except for brief quotations in critical publications or reviews, no part of this book may be reproduced in any manner without prior written permission from the publisher. Write: Permissions, Wipf and Stock Publishers, 199 W. 8th Ave., Suite 3, Eugene, OR 97401.

Pickwick Publications
An Imprint of Wipf and Stock Publishers
199 W. 8th Ave., Suite 3
Eugene, OR 97401

www.wipfandstock.com

PAPERBACK ISBN: 978-1-7252-7381-8
HARDCOVER ISBN: 978-1-7252-7382-5
EBOOK ISBN: 978-1-7252-7383-2

Cataloguing-in-Publication data:

Names: Berchman, Robert M., author.

Title: Thinking on thinking : studies in mind, meaning, and subjectivity / by Robert M. Berchman.

Description: Eugene, OR: Pickwick Publications, 2021. | Foro di Studi Avanzati Series 1. | Includes bibliographical references and index.

Identifiers: ISBN 978-1-7252-7381-8 (paperback). | ISBN 978-1-7252-7382-5 (hardcover). | ISBN 978-1-7252-7383-2 (ebook).

Subjects: LCSH: Philosophy. | Neoplatonism. | Plotinus. | Origen.

Classification: BD362 B47 2021 (print). | BD362 (ebook).

04/21/21

*Johannes D. Turner per dies faustos infaustosque
amico firmo ac fideli*

I am especially indebted to Molly, Katie and Petruchio
whose *philia*, *thumos*, and beloved "doggedness"
made this book possible.

Contents

Preface | ix
Acknowledgments | xiii
Introduction | xv
Abbreviations | xxvii

1. Distinctions | 1
2. Absolute Presuppositions | 18
3. Naming, Intentionality, and Meaning | 50
4. Limits of Thought and Language | 71
5. Identity, Relation, Modality | 87
6. Rethinking Categories | 117
7. Transcendentals and Methodological Solipsism | 145
8. In and Between Mind and Consciousness | 161
9. Touching Self-Identity and Subjectivity | 201
10. Other Minds | 227
11. A Beautiful Mind | 261
12. Aesthetics Emerging | 290
13. Fracture and Return | 319
    Conclusion: Flatland | 355

Bibliography | 371
Index of Names | 403
Index of Subjects | 415

Preface

ANYONE WHO HAS EVER attempted it will confirm that 'thinking on thinking' poses special difficulties. There is the obvious one of addressing a haunting question—is there some secret that 'thought thinking itself' uncovers but then hides? This is not a secret kept and jealously guarded, but an open metaphysical one which although grounded in the silence of 'thought thinking itself' stretches both thought and language to their limits, if not beyond. Here when we say a play, a novel or a film introduces us to an unfamiliar world, what we encounter is an impressive technical achievement or an *Erlebnis*. If transformed, however, by this encounter we undergo, in Hegel's and Gadamer's words, an *Erfahrung*.[1] A cinema conversation between Ramanujan, Hardy, and Littlewood sets the context for such an *Erfahrung*—with the question—"where are the proofs"? Here it is suggested that Aristotle's, Plotinus', and Origen's 'proofs' [*orthotes*] are aporetic thought experiments rather than dogmatic propositions and the *aporiai* they address are addressed in an ongoing series of *Problemstellungen* 'secured' [*aitias logismo*] through reasoning [*logos*]. Here we sense an act of continuity and remembrance; of distances crossed and re-crossed; and of differences between mind and consciousness mapped, then remapped. For with distances and differences not-withstanding, there remains a self-renewing capacity of 'thought thinking itself.' As a secret and a silence it speaks *out of* and *to* limits where something is found somehow apart from the language in which we know how to tell what we know. Thus with the ironic epigram—*de nobis ipsis silemus*—enquiry begins.

Some of the material in this volume has appeared in different forms in other places, but in almost every case, this collection contains a new and expanded version of research.

1. Gadamer, *Truth and Method*, 62–63, 316–20.

Chapter One "Distinctions" initially appeared in "The Language of Metaphysics Ancient and Modern," in K. Corrigan and J. D. Turner, eds., *Platonisms Ancient, Modern, and Postmodern* (Leiden: Brill Academic, 2007), 175–90.

Chapter Two "Presuppositions" is a rethinking of "Thinking on Thinking: Ultimate Presuppositions in Plotinus and Leibniz," in J. F. Finamore, Claudia D'Amico and N. Strok, eds., *Platonic Inquiries* (Westbury, UK: Prometheus Trust Press, 2017), 329–48.

Chapter Three "Naming, Intentionality, and Meaning" is a revision of "Sense Perception, and Intentionality in Brentano, Husserl, Aristotle, and Plotinus," in R. M. Berchman and J. F. Finamore, eds., *Conversations Platonic and Neoplatonic: Intellect, Soul, and Nature* (Hamburg/St. Augustine: Acadamie Verlag, 2010) 211–24 and "Intentionality and Meaning," in A. Avery-Peck, W. S. Green, G. Portion, eds., *A Legacy of Learning: Essays in Honor of Jacob Neusner* (Leiden, Brill: 2014), 137–58.

Chapter Four "The Limits of Thought, Language and Meaning" is a rethinking of three articles: "Self-Knowledge and Subjectivity in Origen," in L. Perrone, ed., *Origeniana Octava: Origene e la Tradizione Alessandrina* (Leuven: Peeters, 2004), 437–50; "Origen of Alexandria," in W. J. Abraham and F. D. Aquino, *The Oxford Handbook of the Epistemology of Theology* (Oxford: Oxford University Press, 2017), 340–53; and "Origen of Alexandria: Spheres, Squares and Other Abstract Objects," in J. F. Finamore and E. Perl, eds., *Platonic Interpretations* (Westbury, UK: Prometheus Trust Press, 2019), 30–50.

Chapter Six "Rethinking Categories" is derived from "Origen of Alexandria on the Categories: A Study in Later Platonic First Principles," in *Origeniana Quinta*, R. Daly, ed. (Leuven, 1992: Peeters), 231–52.

Chapter Seven "Transcendentals" is a rethinking of "Mapping Knowledge and Consciousness of Being: Categories as Transcendentals in Plotinus and Hegel," in J. F. Finamore and R. M. Berchman, eds., *Metaphysical Patterns in Platonism* (Dilton Marsh, UK: Prometheus Trust Press, 2007), 161–72.

Chapter Eight "In and Between Mind and Consciousness" is a reformulation of "Nous and Geist: Methodological Solipsism and Self-Identity in Plotinus and Hegel," in S. R. L. Clark and P. Vassilopoulou, eds., *Other Ways to Truth: Epistemology in Late Antique Philosophy* (New York: Palgrave MacMillan, 2008), 262–88.

Chapter Eleven "A Beautiful Mind" is a reconsideration of "A Speechless Image: Plotinus on Beauty and Truth," in M. Ciampi, A. Livi , M. A. Mendosa, and H. Seidl, eds., *Sensus Communis* Vol. 2 no. 1 [January-March] (Rome: Casa Editrice Leonardo Da Vinci, 2001), 19–30; and "Rationality and Ritual in Neoplatonism," in P. M. Gregorios, ed., *Neoplatonism and Indian Philosophy* (Albany: SUNY Press, 2002), 181–215.

Chapter Twelve "Aesthetics Emerging" uses material from "Plotinus and Kant on Beauty," in J. Bregman and M. Mineo, eds., *Neoplatonism and American Thought: Studies in Neoplatonism: Ancient and Modern* (New Orleans: University Press of the South, 2008), 193–208; and "A Speechless Image: Plotinus on Beauty and Truth," in M. Ciampi, A. Livi , M. A. Mendosa, and H. Seidl, eds., *Sensus Communis* Vol. 2 no. 1 [January-March] (Rome, Casa Editrice Leonardo Da Vinci, 2001), 19–30.

Chapter Thirteen "Fracture and Return" is a reformulation of "Aesthetics as a Philosophic Ethos: Plotinus, Foucault, and the Play of Reason," in R. Baine Harris, ed., *Neoplatonism and Contemporary Thought*. 2 vols. Studies in Neoplatonism: Ancient and Modern 10–11 (Albany: SUNY Press, 2002), 181–215.

Acknowledgments

Patrick Atherton suggested the title of this enquiry while John D. Turner and Helmut Kohlenberger encouraged research on its various topics. I greatly appreciate Frederic Schroeder, Salvatore Lavecchia, John Hendrix, and Svetla Slaveva-Griffin for their helpful critique and comments on aspects of this work. I would like to thank *Il Foro di Studi Avanzati <Gaetano Massa> Roma* for its seminars on Mind, Intentionality, and Meaning in Roma and Buenos Aires, the International Society for Neoplatonic Studies, the 'Eros and Ascent Panels' of the American Academy of Religion and Sara Ahbel-Rappe's invitation to present aspects of this research at the 2019 LSA Conference on "Why Soul Matters" at the University of Michigan.

Introduction

Intellect transcends us, everywhere it is one and
the same and each of us have the whole of it.

—Plotinus, *Enneads*, I.1.8.3

Why Thought Thinking Itself?

With Plato, Aristotle and Plotinus the proper objects of knowledge [*episteme*] were initially established with focus upon Mind [*nous*] and its activities which are 'thought thinking itself.[1] Several claims emerge from this matrix. Firstly, that mind's content and activities are non-physical, that mental states cannot be explained in terms of physical states. Secondly, that the goal of knowledge is the analysis of the structures of thought and being. Thirdly, the study of thought is to be distinguished from study of the psychological process of thinking. Fourthly, that the analysis of thought also consists of an analysis of language and fifthly, these pathways of 'thought

---

1. Aristotle, *Metaphysics*, XII.9 1074b34–35. On *nous* and *noein* see von Fritz, *Nous, Noein*, 23–85, esp. 23–43.

For a mapping of *noesis noeseos noesis* on Aristotelian grounds see, Berti, *Intellection*, 141–63; Cleary, *Aristotle, Powers that Be*, 19–64 and *Aristotle's Criticisms*, 2004, 70–97; De Koninck, *La noesis*, 215–18 and *Aristotle*, 471–515; De Filippo, *Thinking of Thinking*, 543–62; Seidl, *Begriff* and *Realistische Metaphysik*; Nyvlt, *Aristotle and Plotinus*. Also see Brinkmann, *Aristoteles' Metaphysik*; Bos, *Theology*; Barnes, Schofield, and Sorabji, *Metaphysics*, v. 3; J. Owens, *Doctrine of Being*. Plotinus, *Ennead*, I.6.8.21–27. Plotinus, *Ennead*, V.3.5.43–48. For a reading of *noesis noeseos noesis* on Plotinian criteria see Schroeder, *Conversion*, 185–95 and *Synousia*, 677–99; *Plotinus and Language*, 336–52; Bussanich, *Plotinus' Metaphysics*; Gerson, *Introspection, Self-Reflexivity*; Corrigan, *Essence and Existence*; cf. O'Meara, *Plotinus*, 40–43.

thinking itself' lead ineluctably to the questions of what are the character, dimensions and texture of rationality and understanding?

Gadamer who focuses on the 'happening" of understanding' especially as it pertains to tradition and the interpretation of works of art, literary texts and history argues a Cartesian obsession with method emerged that distorted and concealed the ontological character of Platonic and Aristotelian rationality and understanding.[2] This leads to an inability to understand what 'thinking is thinking on thinking' actually means. Many Post-Cartesian philosophers, for example, argue that without a 'foundation' or the right 'method' knowledge [*episteme*] becomes illusive, if not illusionary. Thus thought and language becomes a distorting lens for competing and shifting opinions [*doxai*] through which any knower peers in vain. What results are claims that 'thinking on thinking' is dead in the sense of what Hegel meant by the death of art; that Quine is correct that the role once played by philosophy is now fulfilled by science;[3] that Rorty is prescient when he argues the decisive and irrevocable breakup of philosophy has already occurred.[4]

But what if mind, meaning and subjectivity are not merely a biological or psychological process, or even a mere private experience, but a "sign" [*sema*], the product of an *existential* that Heidegger calls understanding, could philosophers, in an epoch where the words "Mind" and "Being" must be eliminated or bracketed altogether, still think productively of 'intellect' and 'Being'?[5] Here a more historically situated, non-algorithmic, flexible understanding of rationality, one which highlights the tacit dimension of human judgment and imagination is suggested. With *nous* guided by *noesis noeseos noesis* we may gradually deepen our understanding of what it really means to be a participant within a rationality and understanding divine and human.

Why Mind as Thinking is Thinking on Thinking?

Plato offers a powerful vision of the contemplative and synthesizing power of *nous* to be filled in by Aristotle, Plotinus and Origen as 'thinking is

---

2. Following Gadamer's ontological critique of Cartesianism who raises not only objections about the epistemological, methodological, and metaphysical claims of Cartesianism but that it is based on a misunderstanding of being and our being-in-the-world. cf. Gadamer, *Reason in the Age of Science*, 156–57.
3. Quine, *Word and Object*, 21.
4. Rorty, *Mind as Mirror*, 38–45.
5. Gersh, *Neoplatonism After Derrida*, ix.

thinking on thinking.' In the *Theatetus* Plato presents the mind and its constituents as an aviary of birds that leap into flight when our mind attempts to grasp them.[6] The birds represent functions of thought rather than memories of forms and that false judgment resides not in our perceptions or thoughts but in the fitting together of perception and thought.[7] He is thus keen to distinguish possession of knowledge from having knowledge. Someone who has caught and caged wild birds possesses them all but may not have any in hand—although he can put his hand on them.[8] Plato was also among the first to reduce *aletheia* [truth] to *orthotes* [the correctness of statements].[9] In order to have knowledge [*episteme*] true judgment must be accompanied by discourse [*logos*].[10] Moreover, since a distinction exists between simple apprehension and apprehension attended by discourse, knowledge [*episteme*] is denied to simple apprehension. Beliefs turned into knowledge are secured [*aitias logismo*] by providing foundations for them.[11]

Why Meaning and Subjectivity?

In the *Phaedrus* we encounter a vision of mind, meaning and subjectivity where human souls driving their chariots to the vault of the heavens where the true constants and unchanging patterns of being are revealed.[12] The important message this story has to teach Plotinus is that the meaning of beautiful does not lie in some realm opposed to reality but is reality itself. Moreover, beauty no longer has a fixed or normative status.[13] Once this bird is caught, *I* comprehend finally that "the beauty of a countenance is not in fixed symmetry but in light that illumines that symmetry . . . and that beauty is that which irradiates symmetry rather than asymmetry and [such] is that which truly calls out our love."[14] Here *I* and *We* complement each other. Later, Plotinus ups the ante. With commitment to the transcendence of Form as "formless form" [*eidos aneideon*] an aesthetic self emerges as self-reflexive

6. Plato, *Theatetus*, 199ab.

7. Plato, *Theatetus*, 195e; 197de.

8. Each new piece of knowledge is caught and caged but actual knowledge is putting our hands on the bird we "know" when taking it out of the cage. But we may put our hands on the wrong bird instead of the one we want thereby having false knowledge and judgment. cf. Plato, *Theatetus*, 197de and 199ab.

9. Plato, *Cratylus*, 385ac; 389a–390e.

10. Plato, *Theatetus*, 201d–202c.

11. Plato, *Theatetus*, 201d–210d.

12. Plato, *Phaedrus*, 251a–256e.

13. Schroeder, *Categories*, 129–33.

14. Plato, *Theatetus*, 1997de and 199ab; Plotinus, *Ennead*, VI.7.22–29; VI.7.22.24–26.

subjectivity.[15] The aesthetic self becomes *I* and *We* simultaneously. The point made is as with non-objective painting, properly understood *mimesis* can be applied to the self as in Mallarme's sense of pure poetry.[16] The tendency to think of the self only as an introspective subject, as mere *I* is sublated. It is alive and well not only as *I* but also as *We*. Here the Form of Beauty becomes for the aesthetic self dynamic and non-restrictive thereby opening up new horizons for understanding the meaning of what subjectivity means.

Turns and Pathways

Enquiry is divided into three parts. There is an overview of the structures of thought and being underlying 'first philosophy' metaphysics. These include epistemological, linguistic and metaphysical claims; the uses of absolute presuppositions and methodological solipsism. Types of Aristotelian-Neoplatonic rationality and understanding are tested by a series of thought experiments. Themes addressed include: intentionality and meaning; the limits of thought and language; rethinking categories and transcendentals; mind and consciousness; other minds; and the emergence of aesthetics of the self. Enquiry concludes claims that emerge from the "rationality" debates that metaphysics of "Mind" and "Being" must be eliminated or bracketed altogether.

Chapter one, "Distinctions" addresses Gadamer's insight that only since Descartes, Schleiermacher and Hegel has epistemology and history of philosophy been considered a part of theoretical philosophy. What emerges is marked differences in the language of ancient and modern metaphysics. In this situation some find it tempting to talk about "different vocabularies" or "alternative descriptions." This would not be incorrect but it also would not be illuminating—for example that Aristotle and Descartes, simply have different ways of talking about metaphysics—like with Spinoza's double-aspect theory. It is proposed a distinction between representational and realist views of language mark the divide between ancient and modern languages of metaphysics. Cartesian and post-Cartesian representationalism assumes there is an ontological and epistemological gulf between the subjective and the objective and an ocular analogy between perceiving and knowing in what has been called the "spectator" theory of knowledge erroneously traced back to Plato. Aristotelian and later Platonic realism rejects both an ontological and epistemological gap between the subjective

---

15. See Costa, *Amphoron kai Aneideon*, 69–70.

16. Mallarme, *Correspondance*, 105. This also suggests the possibility of a comparison with Derrida who offers a reading of Mallarme's *Mimique* in *The Double Session*.

and the objective and "spectator" analogies of perceiving and knowing. Thought and language map what is real and thus do not "image" objects in the world with the mere accuracy of a mirror.

Chapter two, "Absolute Presuppositions to Methodological Solipsism" focuses initially on Collingwood's and Gadamer's question and answer logic of absolute presuppositions. A general problem in metaphysics is how reality is to be understood? Collingwood claims the task of philosophical analysis is to make explicit presuppositions which are implicit in the practices of first-order sciences and the fundamental assumption that governs the study of mind involves expressions of rational rather than causal processes that cannot be accommodated within a Cartesian, Humean, Kantian or Russelarian epistemology because they cannot be reduced to relations of ideas or matters of fact. Here Collingwood shares with Gadamer the view that meaning cannot be identified with inner psychological processes. Since meaning is not a hidden psychological entity and is inter-subjectively accessible, both claim the sharing of absolute presuppositions through historical and cultural traditions over time probable. Several absolute presuppositions are mapped including the a priori/ a posteriori and analytic/synthetic distinctions, the principle of prior simplicity and the priority of the mental. Enquiry concludes with a mapping of methodological and absolute solipsism. The status of the "I" singular is suspect for Plotinus and Hegel. The first-person case of methodological solipsism can only be defended as the first-person *plural*. Eventually, every philosophical problem is *reasoned* as *our* problem. As the "I" drops out of the formulation, the possibility of a mere individuating "self-reflexivity" and "consciousness" drops out also. Once this occurs the psychological and ontological "I" no longer functions as a first principle, axiom, or premise, but merely as a methodological rule for mapping self-knowledge, self-identity and subjectivity.

Chapter three examines "Naming, Intentionality and Meaning" in Aristotle, Plotinus, Brentano and Husserl. Enquiry begins with analysis of intentionality and meaning in Aristotle followed by what each means in Plotinus. Significant differences are mapped between Aristotle and Plotinus; and Brentano and Husserl concerning intentionality and meaning. In contrast to Brentano and Husserl, Aristotle and Plotinus argue that *all* mental states are not intentional. They also propose a 'focal' theory of meaning which means that all the "senses [of 'being'] have one focus, one common element", or "a central sense", so that "all its senses can be explained in terms of substance and of the sense of 'being' that is appropriate to substance." It is in the latter context that intentionality and meaning are linked to mental causality. Abstract objects like principles [*aitiai*], causes [*archai*], and Forms [*eide/ideai*] are the sources of intentionality meaning. Enquiry closes with the observation that naming has meaning if it has intentionality.

Chapter four on "Limits of Thought and Language" examines the inadequacy of ordinary thought and language for mapping the causal structure of reality. Origen proposes that the thought and language of contemplative prayer unites human intellect, will and its affections with a spiritual world, its powers and its triune deity. He is keen to stress where conceptual and discursive thought fail 'spiritual' hearing and seeing allows access to a divine noetic realm—thus his preference for a language of 'sacred images [*agalmata*] over abstract concepts [*protaseis*] and ratiocination [*logismos*]. Origen highlights the limits of ordinary thought and language by proposing that in the *praxis* of contemplative prayer by mapping the contrast between the meaning of names and descriptions. Here he proposes the referential view that words have meaning by standing for real things. What makes the names in the Lord's Prayer meaningful is that they evince intentionality thereby offering a contemplative and ritual accompaniment that makes Christ's *epinoiai* not only real but useful ontologically and thus soteriologically.

"Identity, Relation, Modality" is the focus of chapter five. Enquiry begins by asking what does Parmenides mean by thinking and being are the same? It is proposed that Parmenides, Plato, Aristotle and Plotinus regard the identity and relation of thinking and being an *aporia* and use modal logic to parse 'that thinking and being are the same.[17] Each thinker offers a solution to this puzzle: 1] Parmenides proposes the necessity of a *numerical* identity of thinking and being on the grounds of modal logic; 2] Plato reading Parmenides claims a necessary but *qualitative* identity and *per se* relation of thinking and being; 3] Aristotle critiques Plato's reading of Parmenides to offer a necessary *pros hen* numerical identity and *a se* relation of thinking and being; and 4] Plotinus assesses Aristotle's and Plato's interpretations of Parmenides and parses a necessary *panta hen* qualitative identity and *per se* relation of thinking and being. Two key moments in analysis are: 1] a mapping of modal expressions in Parmenides' Plato's, Aristotle's and Plotinus' in the context of identity and relation of thinking and being; and 2] when the stranger from Elea [*Parmenides*] parses the two basic modes of being as motion and rest. If one does not wish to conceive of rest, one must conceive of motion, and vice

---

17. Necessity and possibility are generally used as modal modifiers. Parmenides and Aristotle are fond of necessity. cf. T. M. Robinson, *Parmenides*; Palmer, *Parmenides*; Wedin, *Parmenides*. Plato and Plotinus use the modality of the possibility of knowledge and belief are based on 'what justified true belief is' arising out of the aviary analogy of *Theaetetus*, 197de and 199a. cf. Burnyeat, *Theaetetus of Plato*, 112; Roecklin, *Plato versus Parmenides*, 174–77.

versa. Why identity, relation, and modality as well as otherness and difference are essential to being concludes enquiry.

Chapter six "Rethinking Categories" begins with the question how many meanings are implied in the simple Greek word *archai*, "principles"? In this context the categories function to determine the extent to which divinity is transferred to the lower degrees of divinity and reality. They directly map what is real and such parsings do not stumble over the ontological and epistemological gulf posited by representationalism. As a realist Origen does not approach the categories 'representationally' as conceptual and linguistic "images" [*eikona*] that indirectly represent objects in the world. Rather categories are signs [*semata*] that directly make present the objects of the world.

Starting from the qualitative identity and relation of thinking and being Origen's answer is straightforward. If Parmenides proposes the necessity of a *numerical* identity of thinking and being; while Plato reading Parmenides claims a necessary but *qualitative* identity and *per se* relation of thinking and being; then Aristotle follows with a critique of Plato's reading of Parmenides to offer a necessary *pros hen numerical* identity and *a se* relation of thinking and being; Origen parses a necessary but *qualitative* identity and *per se* relation among first principles. He argues for the substantial unity of the Father, Son, and Holy Spirit. Nonetheless, the Father is *toto caelo* distinct from all other kinds of beings and intellects. His theology treats God the Father as a necessary being who has necessary existence. In God being and essence are one, for God is the primary substance under which all that is derives being and existence. In this context the categories function to determine the extent to which divinity is transferred to the lower degrees of divinity and reality. As one moves down the degrees of reality, entities are encountered which accrue more qualifications which means that although it appears that divinity and reality share the same essence the fact is that each entity within the chain of reality evinces a distinct kind of existence. The *ousia* of God is different in kind from any other *ousia* but not separated from other *ousiai* in that God is the sole subsistent and necessary being and the source of being to a variety of subordinate beings.

Chapter seven, "Transcendentals" focuses on Plotinus' and Hegel's rethinking of the Aristotelian and Kantian categories. Both inherited Aristotelian and Kantian categories but judged them insufficient for mapping reality. Each proposed an alternate set of categories or transcendentals. Plotinus sets forth his doctrine of the categories in [*Ennead*, VI.1–3]. He attacks the Aristotelian categories on grounds that they cannot apply to both the sensible and intelligible worlds. Plotinus and Hegel propose new sets of categories on grounds that the Aristotelian and Kantian categories are insufficient to do so. On the basis of the principle of prior simplicity *transcendentals* are offered in their place. Here Plotinus rethinks Plato's five *megista gene*—being, motion, rest, identity and difference. These categories are 'transcendental' in that they go beyond Aristotle's classificatory logic that the essence of a thing is determined by its genus and specific difference.[18] Hegel rethinks them as Being, Non-Being, and Becoming. He calls them by the striking singular term—"Category" in that they 'sublate' Kant's 'transcendental' categories. Enquiry concludes with a mapping of methodological and absolute solipsism. The status of the "I" singular is suspect for Plotinus and Hegel. The first-person case of methodological solipsism can only be defended as the first-person *plural*. In methodological and absolute solipsism: "what is knowledge" is cast as "what is it for *us* to know something? Accordingly, *our* knowledge can be understood and defended only in terms of the *We* of self-reflexivity or absolute consciousness. Eventually, every philosophical problem is *reasoned* as *our* problem. Now We determine what is justifiable for us to believe or know according to the evidence which we have. As the "I" drops out of the formulation, the possibility of a mere individuating "self-reflexivity" and "consciousness" drops out also. Once this occurs the psychological and ontological "I" no longer functions as a first principle, axiom, or premise, but a methodological rule for mapping knowledge, being, self-knowledge and subjectivity.

"In and Between Mind and Consciousness" is the focus of chapter eight. Study begins with the observation that the very whisper of "consciousness" has a Cartesian ring to it. Two claims guide enquiry: firstly, although there are notions of a unified internal subject with thought, language and agency there is no word in Ancient Greek that corresponds to "consciousness" or concepts and concerns for what we now think of as consciousness characteristic of the modern reflective self; and secondly, après Descartes and Locke it is no longer puzzling to speak of mental states as internal to a mind and physical states as external to a body. It is suggested that the idea that bodies have physical properties and minds mental states has become so much a commonplace that Cartesian and post-Cartesian notions of "consciousness" [*conscientia*] are often read into Platonic and Aristotelian notions of *nous noeseos*, *sunaisthesis* and their cognates. Here there can be no appeal to other persons, to common sense, to theories or models which *I* cannot justify for myself. 'In and between' thus marks what Aristotle and Plotinus meant by self-reflexivity [*sunaisthesis*] and how it differs in kind from consciousness [*conscientia*].

---

18. Aristotle, *Topics*, VI.139a27–30.

The reasons are clear. We owe an understanding of conscious "processes" to Locke. We also owe the notion of the "mind" as a separate entity in which "processes" occur to Descartes. We owe to Leibniz's reflections on differentiation and integration claims of degrees of consciousness and explicit distinctions between perception/awareness and apperception/self-awareness. Knowledge is a question of the accuracy of the mind as 'mirror' and questions of the reliability of 'consciousness' to provide accurate reflections on its own representations becomes of paramount importance. Après Descartes, Locke and Leibniz it is no longer puzzling to speak of mental states as internal to a mind and physical states as external to a body. Thus the idea that bodies have physical properties and minds mental states has become so much a commonplace a question arises—how do we escape reading Cartesian "consciousness" [*conscientia*] into Platonic and Aristotelian notions of *nous noeseos, sunaisthesis* and their cognates—since both stress there are not two distinct substance realms in play—the mental and the physical? Our problem is if mind's images no longer point to an archetype "outside" of my mind; then the possibility that thought and language may be transparent to the world is torn asunder. We must thus opt for the raft or the pyramid.

Chapter nine "Touching and Seeing" begins with Aristotle's and Plotinus' claims that a 'transcendent' subjectivity is possible. Touching, seeing and participating with *Nous* [or the One] is what triggers awareness of a transcendent self beyond an empirical self. They also propose that with suitable discipline we can become *nous* and engage in the same kind of thinking as *Nous*. As such it is inconceivable that there are only self-conscious mental states; that perceptions are equivalent to sensations; that concepts arise from sense-data; or that mind is separate from the body. Here, Cartesian distinctions between events in non-extended and extended substance; empiricist claims that cognition is psycho-physiological; idealist proposals that thinking is apperception; and phenomenological claims that *ego* and its intended objects are an *ego cogito cogitatum* are rejected. The study concludes with what a Platonic unity of intellect with its objects the Forms and a Peripatetic *Nous* who is self-knowledge thinking itself in an absolute activity of form—but with no need of Forms at all means.

Chapter ten addresses the problem of "Other Minds." Proposals that acquisition of a 'transcendent' self beyond an empirical self is possible are well known but what is often overlooked is the role self-thought, and other minds play in such a transformation. When mind is identical with its object, it thinks itself, which guarantees self-thought. Thinking through contact and participation [touch and sight] with *Nous* [and the One] are keys to such a transformation. With this comes recognition that mind and its intentionalities are not generalizations derived from experience [psychologism]; subjective mental states with psychological properties [intuitionism]; signs or a game played with signs or a manipulation of linguistic symbols [formalism]; but conceptually independent intelligible objects [realism]. The result is the problem of other minds is a faux problem for Aristotle and Plotinus. Enquiry concludes with metaphysical and epistemological significance of such a claim.

Chapter eleven "A Beautiful Mind," examines how Plotinus reconciles several ontological and epistemological dualisms inherited from Platonic thought to propose aesthetics of the self where mind ascends to beauty in a co-ordinate series extending from the intelligible to the sensible worlds in which degrees of beauty correspond to degrees to which beauty and its images are imagined, judged and experienced by soul in its ascent to Intellect and the One. This process of ascent overcomes a 'fractured self' to create a beautiful mind in a speechless image of the One. Here a 'turn' far more profound than a defense of the metaphysical value of the plastic arts is proposed. Plotinus claims that art is a visible expression of ideal beauty. He argues that the imagination is the mental faculty through which the soul gains initial awareness of ideal beauty; and that such aesthetic awareness leads eventually to knowledge of the ideas of beauty, if not the beautiful itself, in sensible beautiful things. The arts thus become a means for the soul to reverse a situation of misfortune her descent into corporeality. Through the arts and the aesthetic imagination the self regains awareness of its intelligible origins and begins its ascent from sensibility to intelligibility to the One.

Chapter twelve "Aesthetics Emerging" examines the roles judgment, imagination, and taste has in Plotinus' and Kant's aesthetics. It also casts light on how Plotinus and Kant use aesthetic judgment, imagination, [and taste] to reconcile several ontological and epistemological dualisms inherited from Platonic thought. Inherent in this uneasiness with dualisms is an awareness of the limitations of thinking and language to formulate an adequate mapping of reality or being. Failure to formulate in language the relation between language and being results in a turn to aesthetics—not as a language of propositional and discursive sayings but of non-propositional and non-discursive images and silences. A leading theme of this whole story is Plotinus' and Kant's concepts of aesthetic subjectivity. In the end it is about the joining of heaven and earth in self-reflexivity [*sunaisthesis; Ich Denke*] where the dangerously long distance between being and becoming, consciousness and unconsciousness, is overcome through the aesthetics. As a result a new aesthetics of self-reflexivity emerges whose purpose is to heal the fractured, disparate self.

"Fracture and Return" is the theme of chapter thirteen. Two conceptual moments in a history of subjectivity within the "horizon" of aesthetics is mapped. The first recaptures definitions of art, aesthetics, and the soul at the close of antiquity in Plotinus. The second parses definitions of subjectivity where they have been most strongly formulated in our present age with Kant and Foucault. A single focus, consequently, and four problematics define enquiry. The human subject is the focus. The problematics are the specter of the isolated subject, the relation between art and truth, the notion that we construct our ontological and axiological positions by recourse to an aesthetics of the soul and of the self, and most importantly for this study, the value both Plotinus and Foucault see in art and aesthetics for the overcoming of the fallenness and isolation of the self in later antiquity and later modernity.

"Traces or Flatland" addresses contemporary physicalist and post-modern critiques of 'first philosophy by considering a story about a square living in a two dimensional world who one day is enlightened by a sphere about the possibility of a three-dimensional world.[19] It is proposed that Aristotle, Plotinus and Origen are spheres in a three-dimensional world in conversation with modern and post-modern squares. As spheres they ask squares to think as spheres. Once inside 'thinking on thinking' squares may grasp that raft and pyramid are complementary and that there are logical interconnections between beliefs similar to planks in a raft and to bricks in the structure of a pyramid—if for no other reason than they share marks of the mental.[20] Enquiry concludes by mapping why 'thinking on thinking' cannot be explained by mind, matter, or a mind-matter dualism alone but by thought, language and their intentionalities;[21] by holenmermism that the whole is present *as*

19. Abbott, *Flatland*, 47–65.

20. Sosa, *Raft and Pyramid*, 3–25. Marks of the mental include [but are not exhaustive of]: 1] non-spatiality [having a non-spatial space or element]; 2] an ability to exist separately from bodies; 3] an inability to be identified with any object "in the world; 4] an ability to know itself incorrigibly ["privileged access"]; 5] an ability to grasp universals; 6] an ability to sustain relations ["intentionality"]; 7] an ability to use language; 8] an ability to act freely; and 9] an ability to form part of a social group. See, Feigl, *Mental and Physical*.

21. A theory that posits mental events and processes where 'mental' means exhibiting intentionality. Aristotle's divine *nous* thinking itself [*kai estin he noesis noeseos noesis*] is complete and self-sufficient and that from which nothing is wanting. cf. Aristotle, *Metaphysics*, XII.9.1074b33–35. Plotinus's doctrine that every form in *Nous* contains every other form by the interiority of their relation to other Forms is based on claims that each Form is all the other Forms and each mind is identical [qualitatively] with each and every Form because the multiplicity of intellect is not spatially articulated: "Intellect and the intelligible substance; each individual Idea is not other than Intellect, but each is Intellect. And Intellect as a whole is all the Forms, and each

whole in each part;[22] and by synechism that reality cannot be identified with physical existence [or actuality] alone but also comprises real mental identities and relations, necessities and possibilities.[23]

Robert M. Berchman
Roma/Latzio/Italia and Salem/SC/USA
February 2021

---

individual Form is an individual intellect . . . we must assume that the real beings have their place in the thinking subject." cf. Plotinus, *Ennead*, V.9.8.1–5; 10–12. cf. V.V.1.19–43; V.8.3.30–34; V.9.6; V.9.8.3–7.

22. Holenmermism [that 'the whole is in the part']: is based on the notion that exclusion is always posterior to inclusion. This theory arose out of attempts to think of the divine mind as unitary in its internal aspects, relations and differentiations without being sundered in to its parts. cf. Hedley, *Iconic Imagination*, 134–35. Aristotle's claim that 'the whole is in the part' is: " . . . is the sort of principle that constitutes the nature of each . . . all must at least come to be dissolved into their elements . . . in which all share for the good of the whole." cf. Aristotle, *Metaphysics*, XII.10.1075a23–26. Aristotle also claims the perfection of divine *nous* thinking itself [*kai estin he noesis noeseos noesis*] includes knowledge of other forms including forms in nature—for to be perfect is to be complete and self-sufficient and "that from which nothing is wanting . . . what is true of each particular is true of the whole as such—the whole is that of which nothing is outside." cf. Aristotle, *Physics*, III.6.207a8–15; *Metaphysics*, XII.9.1074b33–35; *Metaphysics*, XII.8.1074b33–35; XII.10.1075b21–24. cf. Berti, *Intellection*, 1978, 141–63. Plotinus argues that while a distinction can be drawn between what a thing is and the unity which makes it what it is: "all are bound together by the one [VI.9.2.20] . . . it is by the one that all beings are beings" traced to its external cause in the "uniform" [VI.9.5.27] nature of *Nous* and finally to the One itself." cf. Corrigan, *Essence and Existence*, 109–10.

23. Synechism [Greek > *suneches*]: is based on claims that reality is not merely mind, matter, or a mind-matter dualism and cannot be identified with existence [potentiality] but comprises actual [objective] possibilities where space and time are eternal. Aristotle proposes that although there is a formal difference between Intellect's act of thinking and its object, this does not amount to a material difference as long as the object can exist self-sufficiently without any matter. In the case of divine *nous* its *noesis* as an act of self-contemplation comprises the interiority of its relations to the whole of reality. In 'thinking itself' nothing is wanting and existence is an actual possibility. See *Metaphysics*, XII.8.1074b33–35; XII.10.1075b21–24. cf. De Konnick, *La Noesis*, 474–515. Plotinus argues that every Form in *Nous* contains every other Form by the interiority of its relations to the other Forms [V.5.1.19–43]. Given the relation of a superior model to an inferior image [V.8.4.3–11], intelligible Form is reflected in the sensible world. The Forms in their mutual reflection are like images [*algamata*]. [V.8.4.42–43]. Also see *Enneads* V.8.3.30–34; V.9.6; V.9.8.3–7. cf. Schroeder, 344–46; Trouillard, *Logic*, 125–38.

Abbreviations

Abbreviations are from S. Schwertner, *Internationales Abkürzungsverzeichnis für Theologie und Grenzgebiete*, Berlin/New York 19932 supplemented by the *Journal of Biblical Literature* guidelines, the *Oxford Classical Dictionary*, and Liddell Scott Jones (LSJ).

AA	*Articles on Aristotle* [Barnes and Schofield, Sorabji [eds.]
ABG	Archiv für Begriffsgeschichte
ACA	Ancient Commentators on Aristotle
ACW	Ancient Christian Writers
AGP	*Archiv für Geschichte der Philosophie*
AJP	*American Journal of Philology*
AMP	Ancient and Medieval Philosophy
ANRW	*Aufsteig und Niedergang der Römischen Welt*
AP	*Ancient Philosophy*
APQ	*American Philosophical Quarterly*
BACAP	Boston Area Colloquium in Ancient Philosophy
BETL	Bibliotheca Ephemeridum theologicarum Lovaniensium
BICSSup	Bulletin of the Institute for Classical Studies Supplement
BJPS	*British Journal for the Philosophy of Science*
BLE	*Bulletin Litteraires Ecclestique*

CAG	*Commentaria in Aristotelem Graeca*, Berlin
CLT	Contemporary Literary Theory
CPBB	*Cognitive Psychology in Brain and Behavioural Sciences*
CP	Collected Papers of Charles Sanders Peirce
CQ	*Classical Quarterly*
Diels	*Doxographici Graeci*, Diels.
DIONYSIUS	*Dionysius*
DK	Diels/Kranz
EP	Les Etudes philosophiques
FL	Foundations of Language
GCS	Die Griechischen Christlischen Schriftsteller der ersten Jahrhunderten
HERMES	Hermes
HSCP	*Harvard Studies in Classical Philology*
HTR	*Harvard Theological Review*
IPQ	*International Philosophical Quarterly*
JBL	*Journal of Biblical Literature*
JHP	*Journal of the History of Philosophy*
JP	*Journal of Philosophy*
JSRS	*Journal of the School of Religious Studies*
JTS	*Journal of Theological Studies*
LANGUAGES	*Languages*
LCL	Loeb Classical Library
LPP	La parola del passato
METHEXIS	*Methexis*
MNEM	*Memnosyne*
MONIST	*The Monist*
MSP	Midwest Studies in Philosophy
OECT	Oxford Early Christian Texts
OSAP	Oxford Studies in Ancient Philosophy

PA	*Philosophia Antiqua*
PAPA	*Proceedings of the American Philosophical Association*
PAPS	*Proceedings of the American Philosophical Society*
PAS	*Proceedings of the Aristotelian Society*
PBA	*Proceedings of the British Academy*
PBAQAP	*Proceedings of the Boston Area Colloquium in Ancient Philosophy*
PG	Patrologia Graeca [Migne]
PGL	Patristic Greek Lexicon
PHRONESIS	*Phronesis*
PI	Philosophia Christi
PL	Patrologia Latina [Migne]
PQ	*Philosophical Quarterly*
PR	*Philosophical Review*
PS	*Philosophical Studies*
PSYCHE	*Psyche*
PT	*Philosophical Topics*
REG	*Revue des Etudes Grecques*
RIP	*Revue Internationale de Philosophie*
Rhein. Mus.	*Rheinisches Museum*
RHR	*Revue de Histoire des Religions*
RM	*Review of Metaphysics*
SA	Studia Antiqua
SAGPN	*Society for Ancient Greek Philosophy Newsletter*
SC	Sources chretiennes
SNAM	*Studies in Neoplatonism: Ancient and Modern*
SJP	*Southern Journal of Philosophy*
SPNPT	*Studies in Platonism, Neoplatonism and the Platonic Tradition*

SVF	Stoicorum Veterum Fragmenta [von Arnim]
TAPS	*Transactions of the American Philosophical Society*
TI	Theological Investigations
TPIMS	Toronto Pontifical Institute of Medieval Studies
VC	*Vigiliae Christianae*
ZAC	*Zeitschrift fuer Antike und Christentum*
ZPF	*Zeitschrift fuer philosophische Forschung*

1

Distinctions: Epistemology, Language, Metaphysics

> The older metaphysic had in this respect a loftier conception of thought than that which has become current in more modern times. For the older metaphysic laid down as fundamental that which by thinking is known of and in things, that alone is what is really true in them ... Thus this older metaphysic stands for the view that thinking and the determination of thinking are not something foreign to the objects of thought, but are rather the very essence of those objects.
>
> —G. W. F Hegel, *Science of Logic*, Introduction

Précis

THIS STUDY HAS AN odd ring to it. Not only are the words *episteme* and *logos* ancient but taken apart, the reality designated by these words are as well—whether rendered as thought, knowledge, science, understanding, contemplation or as language, speech, explanation. Both words precede the idea of *episteme* and *logos* conjunctively—or epistemology après Descartes.[1] Moreover, it has been only since Schleiermacher and Hegel that history of epistemology and metaphysics has been a part of theoretical philosophy.[2]

1. Gadamer, *Reason in the Age of Science*, 151–55.
2. Gadamer, *Heidegger's Ways*, 153. Andronicus and Aquinas understood the term meta physics to refer to the chronological and pedagogical order of Aristotle's writings of readings studied after physics. Misread by later medieval commentators metaphysics became the science beyond the physical. cf. Veldsman, *Science-Religion Debate*, 7.

If Gadamer's claims are valid, a fundamental question emerges: what is the language of ancient metaphysics?[3] In this situation some find it tempting to talk about "different vocabularies" or "alternative descriptions." This would not be incorrect but it also would not be illuminating—for example that Plato, Aristotle, Origen, Plotinus, Descartes, Locke, Hume, Kant, Hegel, and Husserl simply have different ways of talking about metaphysics—like Spinoza's double-aspect theory. But a more fundamental question is "different descriptions of *what*?" With "different vocabularies" or "alternative descriptions" how can we be sure that ancient and modern philosophers share the same or similar meanings about entities or concepts?

That they likely do not is based on a distinction between modern representational and ancient realist views of language.[4] Representationalism assumes there is an ontological and epistemological gulf between the subjective and the objective and an ocular analogy between perceiving and knowing in what has been called the "spectator" theory of knowledge erroneously traced back to Plato.[5] Realism assumes neither an ontological nor an epistemological gap between the subjective and the objective nor a metaphorical analogy between perceiving and knowing as in a "spectator" theory of knowledge. Thought and language maps what is real. They do not "image" objects in the world with the mere accuracy of a mirror.[6]

I. Family Resemblance and the Language of Metaphysics

Wittgenstein may provide a way out of this impasse. He opens the *Philosophical Investigations* with a quotation from the *Confessions* where Augustine notes that he learned to understand the speech of his elders by understanding which objects were signified by the different words.[7] Wittgenstein suggests (incorrectly) that Augustine presents a picture theory of language, that language is a *naming-game*. In this context language is mastered by learning the names of different things. A consequence of such

---

3. Consequently, what existed before was a chronicling erudition that did not serve the function of establishing philosophical foundations. The situation with Aristotle admittedly was different. He built doxography into his lectures with very definite "first philosophy" intentions—until it became a distinct branch of scholarly work in ancient pedagogy—a genre still fashionable among scholars today.

4. See Waugh and Wilkinson, *Beauty*, 221–37, esp. 221–23.

5. Contemporary philosophers who employ representational language include Rorty, *Objectivism, Relativism, Truth* and *Mirror of Nature*, 157–59; McDowell, *Knowledge and the Internal*, 877–93.

6. Kennedy, *Language and Meaning*, 78; Detienne, *Masters of Truth*, 72–75.

7. Wittgenstein, *Philosophical Investigations*, I.1.

gaming is that specific words have an essential meaning—as signifier to what is signified. Wittgenstein rejects this notion because it exalts one use of language at the expense of a whole host of other possible uses. In its place, he invokes the analogy of language games.[8] That there is no one feature or set of features that is common to what epistemological realists call a universal or the essence of the form game. Rather what linguistically exists is a complicated pattern or network of similarities overlapping and crisscrossing. Thus when philosophers use terms and concepts they employ them with various meanings which shares overlapping similarities. Wittgenstein refers to these similarities as 'family resemblances.'[9]

This might be a useful metaphor for understanding the language of metaphysics. If valid, there are no entities, terms, or concepts that are in every case of a philosopher's use of one of them that refer to exactly the same set of properties. If this claim is also valid, then what Plato proposes in the aporetic dialogues, that the definition of a term is necessarily linked with what that term names, becomes problematic. We may have no choice but to conclude that: 1) terms and concepts employed within the language of metaphysics are of the family-resemblance type not the naming or correspondence type; and 2) there is no private language of metaphysics.

II. The Language of Metaphysics

Although Plato, Aristotle, Origen, Plotinus, Descartes, Kant, Hegel, and Husserl have little difficulty with the notion of a method of knowing the truth about reality prior to and untouchable by material or empirical science, and a pre-analytic and later an analytic distinction between intuitions and concepts, they have different metaphysical vocabularies. Intellect, mind, consciousness, self-consciousness, reality, truth, being and substance are understood differently by ancient and modern philosophers. This remains the case even when sensory intuitions are identified as the source of contingent truths and concepts considered as the source of the knowledge of necessary truths.

A reason for this is that Descartes' invention of the *Cogito* or mind as consciousness and self-consciousness—his coalescence of internal mental beliefs and sensations into what becomes Locke's ideas—gave modern philosophers new ground to stand on.[10] Descartes' *Cogito* was not just a

---

8. Wittgenstein, *Philosophical Investigations*, I.47.
9. Wittgenstein, *Philosophical Investigations*, I.66.
10. See, Descartes, *Meditationes*, I-II; Locke, *An Essay Concerning Human Understanding*, 101–5.

matter of exclusion but of a confrontation, even of a union he might argue, of earlier realist notions of intellect with later representationalist and phenomenological concepts of mind as a mirror of consciousness and self-consciousness. Also what Descartes did through his radical treatment of doubt, was to call into question the totality of the intelligible world in its legitimacy. Thus after Descartes and Locke there appears little metaphysical vocabulary ancient and modern philosophers share isomorphic ally, although one can, in Wittgenstein's terminology, discern certain patterns or concepts as family resemblances.

Among the boundaries between the language of ancient and modern metaphysics is the privileging of either causal explanation or justification for "theory of knowledge" and the "foundations of knowledge." For Plato, Aristotle, Origen, and Plotinus, truths are certain because of their causes. Descartes, Kant, Hegel, and Husserl, think of truth as "certainty" as a matter of relation of ideas and the constitutive activity of consciousness rather than of relation to an object known. Plato, Aristotle, Origen and Plotinus wanted to get behind reasons to causes, beyond argument to compulsion from the object known. That point was reached when intellect "saw" or "touched" *ousia*. For Descartes, it was a matter of turning the *Cogito* from confused inner representations to clear and distinct ones. With Locke, it was a matter of reversing Descartes' directions and seeing "singular presentations to sense" as to what should "grip us."[11] In nuce, "no more useful inquiry can be proposed than that which seeks to determine the nature and scope of human knowledge."[12] Now it is wondered if the external world exists except as idea.

In nuce, ancient and modern metaphysical vocabularies divide on the distinction between what is "given" by Intellect and what is "added by the mind" as a rational reconstruction, a construction of reason, or phenomenological reduction. While Aristotle's *Nous* "touches" reality and Origen's *Logos* and Plotinus' *Nous* "picture" the certainty and truth of *ousia* as cause, Descartes' *Cogito* "represents" and "images" the fidelity of both *res cogitans* and *res materia* on inner reasoning alone. It would not have occurred to Plato, Aristotle, Origen and Plotinus to look for foundations for knowledge through the Cartesian metaphors of reasoning, representing, and imaging clear and distinct ideas or through Locke's metaphors of representing and imaging sense perceptions. What Plato, Aristotle, Origen, and Plotinus wanted to have as an object of knowledge is precisely what is not Descartes' representation and Locke's appearance.[13] It is this

---

11. Locke, *Essay Concerning Human Understanding*, II.21.6.
12. Descartes, *Rules for the Direction of the Mind*, VIII.
13. The confusion between phenomenalism and phenomenology is one of the most

'actual self-givenness' or access to realities in mind, consciousness and self-consciousness that unites Aristotelian and Neoplatonic approaches to mind and language. There is an actual interface of mind and reality at the levels of intellection and consciousness.

Summary: It was precisely this Cartesian and Lockean "turn" that seemed even to Kant, Hegel, and Husserl, as nothing but a lack of clarity and of coherence. Indeed, so greatly had the task of metaphysics been deflated between Descartes, Locke and Hume, that idealists and phenomenologists claimed that a return to reality and truth was only possible through transcendental or phenomenological reduction. In such reduction they claimed they stood shoulder to shoulder with Plato and Aristotle (they knew of Plotinus hardly at all). Do Plato, Aristotle, and Plotinus share this transcendental or phenomenological vocabulary with Kant, Hegel, and Husserl? The full story of the splendors and miseries of rationalism, empiricism, idealism and phenomenology is far beyond the scope of this study. The story I want to begin to tell is why a shared language of metaphysics between these ancient and modern philosophers is unlikely, and if a common vocabulary is wanting, why claims that Plato, Aristotle, and Plotinus are idealists or phenomenologists, read from these perspectives, should be undertaken with extreme caution.

III. Representationalism and Phenomenalism

Aristotle claims that *Nous* is mind, intellect, thought, and insight as contemplation (*theoria*). Moreover, *Nous* is also logically separable, even though nothing else about the soul is. *Nous* is also immaterial and it has the power to receive the form of the universal from the particular. It takes it on itself without becoming particular.[14] Here, as T. H. Greene notes, Aristotle makes two advances on Plato and the *Posterior Analytics*: the first is toward a discovery of holism and of the concrete universal; the second is an appreciation of the difference between sensation and intelligent consciousness of sensation.[15]

---

wide-spread mistakes that require correction. What phenomenalism holds is that we have access only to phenomena, not to real things, whether real things or Kantian things-in-themselves or Moore's experiences. Here Hegel and Husserl are not classified as phenomenalists although there are phenomenalist 'tendencies' as we shall see each exhibits. On the difference between phenomenology and phenomenalism see, Hintikka, *The phenomenological dimension* 78–105, esp. 83–84.

14. Aristotle, *Metaphysics*, XII, 1072a-1073b; *De Anima*, III.5, 430a10-25.
15. See, Green, *Collected Works*, 52–91.

Aristotle's metaphor of knowing general truths by internalizing universals, and that there is a difference between sensation and intellection are foundational, not only for the Aristotelian and Neoplatonic traditions of *Nous* metaphysics, but for a variety of modern traditions as well. The power of *nous poietikos* is the precursor of Bacon's "mind of man" and Descartes' distinction between thinking and extended substance. All these traditions inherit the claim that in a certain sort of knowledge that contemplates universals there resides truth. Locke and Hume rejected Aristotle's metaphor of knowing while Kant, Hegel, and Husserl appropriated it but with a thoroughly modern condition. Any notion of a difference between sensation and intelligent consciousness of sensation was read in the context of Descartes' *Cogito*. Mind is a mirror that images reality. Thus intelligent consciousness of sensation is representational and self-consciousness is phenomenal.

Gadamer and Philipse have noted that Aristotle's and Plotinus' mind-as-intellect model was initially challenged in the seventeenth century by the ontological revolution of mechanics.[16] The corpuscular or atomistic ontology implies a deep gap between perceptual appearance and physical reality. Consequently, Descartes and Locke come to deny phenomenal or secondary qualities, such as color and sound, to the particles whose mechanical behavior accounts for these qualities. Thus, if atoms or corpuscles lack color, then objects assembled from particles also lack color. Physical reality is very different from its perceptual appearances, because it lacks secondary qualities. This incompatibility thesis leads to representative theories of perception. Since phenomenal qualities do not exist in nature, they exist only in the perceiving mind, as Descartes argued, or the organism, as Locke and Hume argued. This results in the claim that secondary qualities are direct objects of perceptual consciousness, which results in the proposal that the primary data of sensation are really immanent in consciousness, and the mind or organism, once stimulated, projects these *qualia* into objects by a mental mechanism of perception or judgment.

In the wake of Descartes and Locke, Berkeley and Hume suggest further that there are no universals, that they are a *flatus vocis*. A way around such a claim might be Aristotle's inference concerning the separable, immaterial character of *Nous*. Here knowledge is not the possession of accurate representations of an object but rather *nous* becoming identical with an object. Intellect is both eye and mirror in one. The retinal image itself is the for which the intellect becomes all things. This is a rather different metaphor

---

16. See, Gadamer, *Reason*, 156–157; Philipse, *Transcendental Idealism*, 292–97.

than the Cartesian spectator model where the *Cogito* inspects images modeled on the metaphor of retinal images.[17]

In the shadow of these ontological and epistemological revolutions, Plato's, Aristotle's and Plotinus' realist models may strike most moderns as hopelessly quaint, while Descartes' and Locke's representative model might impress them as uncannily familiar. Between the quaint and familiar, however, arises a series of problems in philosophy of mind that require reflection. The key issue is not whether, as Rorty argues, that Aristotle and Plotinus lacked a concept of mind, or even of a mind separable from the body. Rather it was impossible for Plato, Aristotle and Plotinus, as it was not for Descartes, Berkeley, Locke, Hume, Kant, and Husserl, to divide "conscious states" from events in an "external world."[18] As we know, this division begins with Descartes who used thought or consciousness to cover all forms of doubting, understanding, willing, refusing, imagining, dreaming, and feeling.[19] Once Descartes defined thinking so inclusively, it was a short step to Locke's, Kant's, and Husserl's uses of "idea" in ways which have no equivalent in Plato, Aristotle, and Plotinus.[20]

An idea for Descartes is whatsoever object of understanding that is thought. Hume puts it more bluntly—"everything that appears to the mind is a noting but a perception."[21] This modern "turn" highlights another crucial distinction or gap. Once mind is defined so inclusively by Descartes and his heirs, it becomes "consciousness" and later "self-consciousness." However *Nous* is translated as Mind or Intellect, there is no equivalent in Aristotle or Plotinus for either "consciousness" or "self-consciousness." In this sense, Intellect's reflexivity (*sunaisthesis*) cannot be translated as consciousness. *Nous* is a `We Intellect,' capable of noetic reflexivity. It is not an `I Intellect,' a Self or a Subject who knows only its internal mental states or the conditions for the possibility of them. In brief, Descartes' *Cogito*, Kant's, Hegel's, and Husserl's *Bewusstsein* and *Selbst-Bewusstsein* are thoroughly modern conceptions. They signify a constituting mental activity, one in which mind is no longer synonymous with *Nous* and the activity of *noesis*.

It is inconceivable for Plato, Aristotle, and Plotinus that there are "purely" conscious mental states as Descartes proposed—that mental states are distinct from perceptions, and that mind and body are distinct substances; or as Locke suggested: that perceptions are equivalent to sensations and that

17. See, Rorty, *Mirror of Nature*, 45.
18. Rorty, *Mirror of Nature*, 47.
19. Descartes, *Meditation*, II.
20. See, A. Kenny, *Descartes*, 226.
21. Hume, *Treatise*, I.4.2.

ideas cover both sense-data and concepts. Once Descartes' and Locke's "consciousness" is admitted, Plato's, Aristotle's and Plotinus' distinction between reason-as-grasp-of-universals, and the living body which perceives sensation and motion, is lost. In its place it is claimed by Descartes and Locke that consciousness or thinking covers both sense and intellect. From here it is a short step to the rationalist and empiricist "conscious" distinctions between an event in non-extended and extended substance, and to the claims that the real world must be psychological; or to those transcendental idealists and phenomenological idealists who "self-consciously" claim that the real world is mentally constituted, and that intentionality is sufficient to unite the *ego cogito cogitatum*—the *ego* and its intended objects.

Moreover, another crucial difference is lost. Once it is proposed by rationalists that mind is consciousness, by empiricists that mind is sensation, by idealists that mind is constitutionally self-consciousness, or by phenomenologists that mind is intentional, the conflicting notions of indubitability associated with intellect are also lost. If mind is intellect, as Aristotle and Plotinus argue, then only what has eternity cannot be doubted. Now eternality is known with certainty solely through *Noein*—which encompasses all the activities of the *Nous,* the *Ideai,* and *Logos.* Specifically, they propose, reason-as-grasp-of-universals alone are indubitable. Doubt, however, is possible about everything particular. Here the crucial point is that indubitability is solely a criterion of mind or intellect, wherein the lines between confusion and clarity, dubitability and indubitability, and the mind and body all coincide. In their varying ways they all agree that "conscious states" or "states of consciousness" which are events in an inner life cannot be cannot be distinguished from events in an "external world."

Briefly, what Plato, Aristotle, and Plotinus are largely innocent of are modern notions of inner representations or impressions. As a result what they avoid is the empiricist confusion between a mechanistic account of the operations of the mind and the 'grounding of our claims to knowledge. This is what T. H. Green calls:

> The fundamental confusion, on which all empirical psychology rests, between two essentially distinct questions—one metaphysical, What is the simplest element of knowledge? The other physiological, What are the conditions in the individual human organism in virtue of which it becomes a vehicle of knowledge?[22]

Thus, Locke and Hume propose that the simplest element of knowledge is inner representations or impressions and that the mind is like a

---

22. Greene, *Collected Works,* 19.

wax tablet or *tabula rasa* upon which objects make impressions. Consequently, the mind is made to think by some impression upon it, or some impulse given to it by contiguous bodies. In a quasi-mechanical way our immaterial tablets or minds are dented by the material world. These representations help us know what we are entitled to believe. However, the imprinting is of less interest than the observation of the imprint—which is the activity of seeing -as-knowing.

For Plato, Aristotle, and Plotinus knowledge is, to varying degrees, the identity of the mind with the object known. However, Locke and Hume do not have this possibility available. Since impressions were representations, they needed a faculty which is aware of representations. Moreover, they needed a faculty that judged representations rather than had them. The rub is they could not postulate such a "nousing" faculty in the quasi-machine they hoped to describe. To do so would be to introduce a ghost in the machine.

But there is an obvious tension between thought and matter in the cerebral tablet that persists nonetheless. Green, reflecting on Locke's "ideas of reflection" says:

> Locke disguises the difficulty from himself and his reader by constantly shifting both the receptive subject and the impressive matter. We find the "tablet" perpetually receding. First it is the "outward part" or bodily organ. Then it is the brain ... Then it is the perceptive mind, which takes an impression of the sensation or has an idea of it. Finally, it is the reflective mind ...[23]

As Rorty notes, Locke (and later Hume) have a problem, which Kant calls the basic error of empiricism. How can knowledge as something which, being the simple having an idea, take place without judgement? And how can knowledge of that which results from forming justified judgements occur at all if there is no such "intellecting" faculty present? As Kant puts it the basic error is the confusion between a "succession of apprehensions within an apprehension of succession." That is to say, we have a succession of flowers and redness, and yet we synthesize these into the judgement—"flowers are red." Locke cannot explain how this happens because he models knowing on seeing representations which become, somehow, "ideas." What Kant claims is significant—only thought relates. Thus, an object of which several predicates are judged true is always a result of a "mental" synthesis undertaken by a "mind." Kant goes on to argue that the mind constitutes knowledge of phenomena, not things-in-themselves. This is the mind-as-consciousness model.

---

23. Green, *Collected Works*, 11.

However, for Plato, Aristotle and Plotinus knowledge (*episteme*) consists in the grasp of the nature (*phusis*) and rational structure (*logos*) of a thing. When used in connection with individual phenomena, *phusis* designated the cluster of stable characteristics by which we can recognize that thing and can anticipate the limits within which it can act upon other things or be acted upon by them. This concept of the nature or "what it is" of a thing plays a fundamental role in classical accounts of knowledge. In Plato's early dialogues Socrates will affirm as a general principle that we must first discover the essential nature of a thing—its *ti estin* or "what it is" before we attempt to determine what other features it might possess. Plato, Aristotle, and Plotinus will characterize knowledge in the most basic sense as grasping in thought a thing's essential nature or *ti estin*. This explains the frequency with which giving a *logos* enters into a number of proposed definitions of knowledge. The ability to explain what a thing is is the necessary condition for being said to know what it is. This is the mind-as intellect model.

Summary: What corresponds to these metaphysical distinctions are not as Descartes, Locke, and Kant argue—between kinds of "inner representations," *a posteriori* "ideas, or the *a priori* "conditions" for ideas in "inner space." But rather what correspond to these metaphysical distinctions are grades of certainty caused by a variety of objects of knowledge. For Plato, Aristotle, and Plotinus, the intellect, the various parts and/or powers of the soul, and the body are compelled by their respective objects to distinguish between contingent and necessary truths. Knowledge must get behind reasons to causes, and to the foundation of knowledge itself.

IV. Phenomenology and Phenomenological Reduction

With representationalism and phenomenalism, we leave the ancient ontological 'language-games' of "Being and Becoming," "Form and Matter, "Actuality and Potentiality," and enter the modern epistemological 'language-games' of "sense versus intellect," "clear versus confused perceptions," "simple versus complex ideas," "ideas and impressions," "concepts and intuitions." Thus as our 'modern' meditations begin, we want to keep in view the clash between Descartes and Leibniz on the one hand, and Locke and Hume on the other. Here the question is: are perceptions reducible to concepts or are concepts reducible to perceptions? We also want to cast both eyes on Kant's transcendental "solution" to this impasse: intuitions without concepts are blind and concepts without intuitions empty. This transcendental move signals a tectonic shift from the claims of phenomenalism to those of phenomenology.

The origins of phenomenology were made possible by the notion that philosophy's core was theory of knowledge. While this notion can be traced back to Descartes' *Meditations* and Spinoza's *De Emendatione Intellectus*, it did not achieve self-consciousness until Kant's *Kritik der reinen Vernunft*. In his Copernican "turn," Kant transcendentally distinguished the unknowable, noumenal, *Ding-an-sich* from the knowable, phenomenal constructs of pure reason. With this move phenomenology was born.

For Kant, the term transcendental no longer signifies that which transcends our experience in the sense of providing its ground or structure. The pure forms of intuition (space and time) and the pure concepts of the understanding (such as substance and cause) constitute the conditions for the possibility of phenomenal experience. A picture of epistemology-and-metaphysics as the center of philosophy, and of metaphysics as something which emerges out of philosophy (and not vice versa) emerges in Kant's transcendental and phenomenological wake. Kant claims that the proper task of philosophy is to establish the transcendental objectivity of knowledge-claims made in the various empirical disciplines. This is done by the appropriateness of the *a priori* contributions brought to bear in perception. Briefly, the Copernican revolution was based on the notion that we can only know about objects *a priori* if we constitute them.[24] Kant argued that the objective validity of certain pure, or *a priori* intuitions and concepts, are a condition for the possibility of experience. Among the intuitions and concepts required for having experience are those of time, space, substance, and cause. In a transcendental argument concerning the conditions for the possibility of experience, it is necessary that some feature entailed by the having of experience is identified. Then it is argued that experience could not have this feature without satisfying some temporal, spatial, substantive, and causal conditions. We can only be conscious of objects constituted by the synthesizing activity of the understanding.[25]

In the Transcendental Deduction the feature of experience upon which Kant concentrates is the ability of a subject to be aware of several distinct mental states as belonging to a single substantive consciousness or Transcendental Self—the *Ich Denke*. In the Refutation of Idealism he proceeds from this premise. One is conscious of one's own existence as determined in time in that one knows the temporal order of some of one's inner states. Furthermore, the condition for the possibility of such knowledge

24. Kant, *KR.V.* B. xvii.
25. Kant, *KrV*, B130.

is the existence of objects located outside of the Self in space. If one is so conscious, this would refute the skeptical view advocated by Descartes, that one lacks the knowledge of a spatial world distinct from one's mind and inner states. If one is so conscious, this would also refute the view advocated by Locke, that qualified things are found in nature without any constitutive action of the mind.

Once Kant replaced Descartes' *Cogito* and Locke's physiology of human understanding with 'the transcendental ego'—phenomenology was birthed. In *nuce*, Husserl's notions of the Self, Subject, Consciousness, and Self-Consciousness, are robustly Kantian notions which stand in the shadow of Kant's transcendental *ego*. As we enter Husserl's phenomenological project, it is necessary to distinguish phenomenalism from phenomenology. Phenomenalism holds we have access only to phenomena not real things. Physical objects, things-in-themselves, and the objects of our experiences are unknowable in-themselves. Phenomenology maintains that everything must be based on, and traced back to what is given to the mind in direct experience. Thus for Husserl, what is given to consciousness is not mere phenomena but a phenomenological interface of consciousness and reality.[26]

Husserl's view is that beings can actually present themselves to consciousness in intuition.[27] Such an interface is achieved in phenomenological reduction. Everything in the noema is bracketed which is not given to consciousness in immediate experience. It separates what is intended from what is given and reduces what is intended to what is given. Thus in phenomenological reduction there is an overlap of consciousness and reality and what is left is a residuum, an intuition, which is directly known to consciousness.[28] Intuitions are both sensuous and non-sensuous and constitute a kind of immediate seeing or givenness to consciousness.[29] Moreover, the phenomenological residuum which survives transcendental reduction is not only an interface with reality. It is the basis of the entire constitution of our conceptual world.

What is the transcendental reduction a reduction to? As Hintikka notes, once this question is answered, it is possible to define Husserl as a realist or an idealist.[30] Although Hintikka's question is correct, his answer to this question requires refinement. In one sense, Husserl is not a realist but a phenomenological realist. His phenomenological reduction takes us "zu den Sachen," to a

---

26. I am indebted to Kern for this distinction; cf. *Kant und Husserl*, 120–24.
27. Husserl, *Ideen*, SS3.
28. Husserl, *Ideen*, SS24.
29. Husserl, *Ideen*, SS19.
30. See, Hintikka, *The Phenomenological Dimension*, 90.

layer of given objects or facts. In another sense, he is also a phenomenological idealist. The outcome of reduction leaves a residue that is partially the product of consciousness' constitutive activity. This "givenness" is the raw material that the constitutive processes of consciousness work on.

The phrase "constitutive action of the mind" is the tip-off to Husserl's view of the matter. He was committed to the transcendental mode of questioning which means there is a higher level of "transcendental intuition" that animates the pure-thing perception. Husserl called this the transcendental foundation of consciousness. Although Husserl's notion of constructivism is distinct from Berkeley's Kant's, and Hegel's, he does maintain consciousness 'constructs objects.' This does not mean that an object is causally or ontologically dependent on its own manifestations in intuition. It means that the intentional relation between a noema and its object is mediated by what is immediately given to consciousness in intuition. Thus, objects can be intended as they manifest themselves through the interface of reality and consciousness in intuition. It is in this sense that an object's manifestation is conceptually dependent and constituted by consciousness.[31]

Summary: This explains why Husserl was committed to mapping what he called the unidentifiable character (*Unausgewiesenheit*) of consciousness. His constitutional analysis of consciousness claims that any self-constitution of presence is based on the concept of constitutive accomplishment, which has as its source the transcendental *ego*. However, Husserl goes beyond Kant's claim that the mind constitutes and is regulative of reality. Husserl treats all the objects of intentional acts as having some sort of reality. Moreover, he treats phenomena as a conceptual rather than an empirical proceeding. Phenomena are subjected to a process of reduction which meant their being bracketed off from any question of their real status or their empirical attachments. Thus insofar as phenomena have a genuine character, as conscious acts or as intentional objects, lies in their essences. Essences, in turn, lend themselves to intuition and it was in this intuition of essences that phenomena are. With this an acknowledgement is implied. Husserl's phenomenology is a type of transcendental or phenomenological idealism.

---

31. Hintikka, *The Phenomenological Dimension*, 93.

V. Idealism or Realism

Are Aristotle and Plotinus idealists? Each offers occasional excursions into quasi-idealist positions.[32] The continuity between both claims is that each identifies primary being with the activity of intellection. Since Intellect (and Matter) is prior to things, it is claimed Aristotle touches upon idealism in *Metaphysics* Lambda when he claims God is at once Intellect and a substance in *noesis*. Plotinus suggests a possible link to idealism in at least three possible forms. The first is in *Ennead* III.8 where a Berkeleyan mode suggests itself. The second is in *Ennead* V.5 where a possible Hegelian trope surfaces.[33] The third occurs in things Plotinus says about the One in relation to Intellect's thinking where parallels are made with what Kant says about the unity of apperception. These idealist claims are underscored by the additional proposal that Aristotle and Plotinus share a claim to intentionality. But their commitment to realism remains primary. Each identifies primary being with the activity of intellection, proposes that mind is prior to matter and that a mind-independent reality exists.[34]

Are Aristotle and Plotinus realists? Realism is the view that: 1) there are real objects that exist independently of our knowledge or experience of them; 2) that these mental and physical objects have properties and enter into relations independently of the concepts with which we understand them, or 3) the language with which we describe them. Anti-realism is any view that rejects any one of these tenets and it includes all claims to representationalism, transcendental deduction, and phenomenology.[35] Neither Aristotle nor Plotinus rejects any of the three theses of realism. Thus, even when they take occasional excursions into quasi-idealist positions, such as Aristotle's view of God as at once an Intellect and a substance in the most primary sense and Plotinus' identification of primary being with acts of thought, this does not constitute idealism. Furthermore, neither Aristotle nor Plotinus propose any anti-realist or constructivist claims that suggest either Berkeley's immaterial, Kant's transcendental, Hegel's absolute, or Husserl's phenomenological types of idealism. Thus a return to Burnyeat is apposite who argues that not only is idealism absent from antiquity. It could not have arisen.[36] But idealism is

---

32. On the question of idealism in Greek philosophy, see Burnyeat, *Idealism in Greek Philosophy*, 3–40.

33. On idealism in Plotinus see Rappe, *Self-Knowledge and Subjectivity*, 250–74; Emilsson, *Cognition*, 217–49; Gerson, *Being and Knowing*, 107–126. On other sources for idealism in antiquity see Sorabji, 287–96.

34. On the question of idealism in Greek philosophy, see Burnyeat, 1982, 3–40.

35. Audi, *Cambridge Dictionary*, 488.

36. Burnyeat, *Idealism in Greek Philosophy*, 3–40; For a critique of Burnyeat see

a thoroughly modern phenomenon and that ancient thinkers such as Plato, Aristotle, and Plotinus are essentially realists, not rationalists, empiricists, phenomenalists, idealists, or phenomenologists.[37]

On the basis of the principle of 'family resemblance' it could be argued that ancient and modern philosophers engage in a common language of metaphysics. Aristotle's and Plotinus' primary distinction is not between two kinds of entities in inner space or two types of inner representations in the soul (*en ten psuche*) with the mind inspecting various inner pictures for indubitability.[38] Rather differences in certainty correspond to differences in the objects known. Thus they want to get behind reasons or inner-outer distinction to the causes of knowledge. However, even here there is a caveat. The constitutive activity of the subject in experience (relation being the key point) is a clear-cut modern notion. There is no ancient philosopher with any comparable viewpoint concerning such unity of apperception. This requires a constitutive thinker unknown before Kant; secondly Plato, Aristotle, and Plotinus hold to the realist notion of a mind independent reality be it Being, Ideas, Forms, Intellect, or even a hyper-reality such as the One. Second, they maintain that phenomena are real because of causes rather than mental activity, and they claim that what is "given" to intellect is distinct from what is "added by the mind" as a rational reconstruction, transcendental construction, or phenomenological reduction. Such constructivist notions had to await Descartes' *Cogito*, Spinoza's *substantia*, Locke's theory of perception, but principally Berkeley's, Kant's, and Hegel's claims that our mental activity, however differently they understood mental activity, constitutes reality itself.

Summary: In Wittgenstein's terminology, although any member of the family resembles some other member, there is no single pervading feature

---

Emilsson, *Cognition*, 217–49.

37. This does not exclude the claim that Plato, Aristotle, Plotinus, Proclus, and ps-Dionysius inspired modern idealism. cf. Beierwaltes, *Platonismus und Idealismus*; Viellard-Bacon, *Platon et L'idealisme allemand* (1770–1830), 1979.

38. Plato, *Theaetetus*, 197de: Now consider whether knowledge is a thing you can possess in that way without having it about you, like a man who has caught some wild birds . . . we might say his "has" them all the time inasmuch as he possesses them . . . but in another sense he "has" none of them though he has got control of them, now that he has made them captive in an enclosure of his own; he can take holds of them whenever he likes by catching any bird he chooses, and let them go again and it is open to do that as often as he pleases. *Theaetetus*, 199ab: when in hunting for some one kind of knowledge, as the various kinds fly about . . . so in one example he thought eleven was twelve, because he caught the knowledge of twelve, which was within him, instead of that of eleven, caught a ringdove instead of a pigeon.

marking them all as members of the same family.[39] Thus, any constructivist—be it rationalist, empiricist, idealist, or phenomenological—reading of Plato, Aristotle, and Plotinus remains less than "problematic." Aristotle and Plotinus do not share the constitutive "mind vocabularies" and "descriptions of Berkeley's immaterial, Kant's transcendental, Hegel's absolute, and Husserls' phenomenological idealisms.

Conclusion

Aristotle proposes—given the principle of prior simplicity and the existence of a mind independent immaterial intellect—which can think itself as 'thinking on thinking'- that a metaphysical system is complete. Plotinus demurs and parses a *nous* that is "one" with the Forms along with a first principle or a One prior to it. Since this One is absolutely simple and beyond intellect and being and is the principle and cause of intellect and being there exists not only a mind-independent reality but hyper-reality independent of all minds—divine, daemonic or human.

Metaphysical grounds for agreement between Aristotelians and Platonists nonetheless exist. They maintain that minds are ontologically independent of bodies and reject the claim that minds can be explained in terms of the body. Three absolute presuppositions support the "mind-vocabularies" of anti-constitutive realism. The first is the principle of prior simplicity; the second is the priority of cause to effect; and the third is the priority of the mental over the physical. These merge in Aristotle's doctrine of the absolute simplicity and priority of *Nous in Metaphysics* Lambda 7 and 9 and claims that *nous* is not a composite substance in *De Anima* III. 4-5. Conceding composition within *Nous* would necessitate a degree of potentiality which would subordinate it to the impossibility of an ultimate and simpler principle he notes:

> For if it thinks of nothing, what is there here of dignity? It is just like one who sleeps. And if it thinks, but this depends On something else, then (since that which is its substance is not The act of thinking but a potency (*alla dunamis*) it cannot be the best substance; for it is through thinking that its value belongs to it.[40]

He underscores his commitment to anti-constitutive realism by employing the absolute presupposition that a cause must be like its effect; secondly, a cause must be greater than its effect; and the third is the principle of prior

---

39. Wittgenstein, *Philosophical Investigations*, I. 65–67, 71 and 116.
40. Aristotle, *Metaphysics*, XII.9.1074b17–20.

simplicity. These come together nicely in *Ennead* VI.7.17 and V.3.15 where it is argued a cause must be like its effect even though the cause possesses the same characteristics in greater degree.[41] On the basis of these claims Plotinus argues that the One or Good is not very much like *Nous* at all:[42]

> The life of Intellect, then, is all power, and the seeing which came from the Good is the power to become all things, and the Intellect which came to be is manifest as the very totality of things. But the Good sits enthroned upon them, not that it may have a base, but that it may base the "Form" of the first "Forms," being formless itself . . . Therefore, Intellect too is a trace of the Good, but since Intellect is a Form and exists in extension and multiplicity, that Good is shapeless and formless, for this is how he makes forms.[43]

The need for the cause to be greater than effect also removes any resemblance between One and Intellect for a thing need not possess what it gives which explains why the One imparts life and form to *Nous*. Since the One is greater than life, form, intellect, and being, it is not similar to or even like Mind which possesses these activities and powers.[44]

> How then does the One make what it does not have? . . . Now it has been said that, if anything comes from the One it must be something different from it, and in being different, it is not one: for if it was, it would be that One. But if it is not one, but two, it must also necessarily be many: for it is already the same and different and qualified and all the rest.[45]

---

41. The principle of likeness and the consequences of its use are vast. cf. Lloyd, 146–56.

42. See, Sorabji, *Time, Creation, Continuum*, 315–16.

43. Plotinus, *Ennead*, VI.7.17.32–41.

44. Sorabji suggests Plotinus is indebted to Aristotle's concession to resemblance theory at *De Anima* II.5.417a18–20—which the thing affected is potentially what the agent is actually, and so becomes like it. cf. Sorabji, *Time, Creation, Continuum*, 316.

45. Plotinus, *Ennead*, V.3.15.35–41.

2

Absolute Presuppositions to Methodological Solipsism

...most men live as if their thinking were a private possession.

—Heraclitus, fr. 2.

Précis

This enquiry is parsed from two similes in the *Theaetetus* where mind is an aviary of wild birds that leap into flight when our mind attempts to grasp them.[1] Three metaphors are transposed from these similes: the birds represent functions of thought; false judgment resides in the fitting together of perception and thought;[2] and there is a kind of knowledge we may 'have' but not 'possess.'[3] Socrates is keen to distinguish possession of knowledge from having knowledge. Someone who has caught and caged wild birds possesses them all but may not have any in hand—although he can put his hands on them.[4] He argues to have knowledge is to possess true judgment accompanied

---

1. Plato, *Theaetetus*, 199ab.
2. Plato, *Theaetetus*, 195e; 197de.
3. Socrates' example is until we apply our knowledge of mathematics even if we know the number twelve, we do not "possess" the knowledge that seven plus five equals twelve. Plato, *Theaetetus*, 198d. On the contexts of this *aporia* cf. Burnyeat, *Theatetus*, 112; Roecklein, *Plato versus Parmenides*, 176–77.
4. Each new piece of knowledge is caught and caged but actual knowledge is putting our hands on the bird we "know" when taking it out of the cage. However, we may put our hands on the wrong bird instead of the one we want and thus possess false knowledge and judgment. cf. Plato, *Theatetus*, 197de and 199ab.

by discourse (*logos*);[5] and since a distinction exists between simple apprehension and apprehension attended by discourse, knowledge is denied to apprehension alone. Beliefs are thus turned into knowledge by providing secured foundations (*aitias logismo*) for which results in justified true belief.[6] Three guides aid enquiry: the first, defines what 'absolute presuppositions' are;[7] the second maps Aristotle and Plotinus on thought and language;[8] and the third parses thought, language and 'absolute presuppositions.'[9]

I. Horizons

Collingwood claims task of philosophical analysis is to make explicit the foundations of knowledge claims. He calls the presuppositions which govern forms of enquiries "absolute" in contrast to those which are relative "relative." Absolute presuppositions include terms such as "substance" and "cause" while relative presuppositions are propositions offered in answer to questions verified as true or false. Absolute presupposition are meaningful even if unverifiable and thus a heuristic principle of metaphysical investigation.[10] Collingwood's theory has generated a whirlwind of criticism on two counts.[11] Nowhere does he explicitly say what an absolute

---

5. Plato, *Theatetus*, 201d–202c.
6. Plato, *Theatetus*, 201d–210d.
7. A list of primary 'absolute presuppositions' include: 1) the principle of prior simplicity; 2) the principle that actuality precedes potentiality; 3) the principles of identity and difference; 4) the principle of continuity; 5) the principle of contradiction; 6) the principle of logical possibility; 7) the principle of causal possibility; 8) the principle of intentionality; 9) the a priori/a posteriori distinction; and 10) the analytic/synthetic distinction. From these *genera* a secondary list or *species* of 'absolute presuppositions' follow including: a) thinking and being are the same; b) the truth-knowledge distinction; c) the principle of indiscernibles; d) the reality-appearance distinction; e) the principle of abstract and concrete universals; f) the propositional-non-propositional distinction; and g) the discursive-non-discursive distinction.
8. Aristotle and Plotinus claim an isomorphism between thought, language and being. Thought and language are not: 1) generalizations from our experience (psychologism); or 2) signs or a game played with signs (formalism); but 3) conceptually independent objects (realism). Here their approaches to language anticipate Frege's (realist) and Wittgenstein's (formalist) logic of signs in that language ought to reflect the structure of the objects we know. Rather than with Derrida that language is a merely a game played with signs (formalism)—that nothing is *outside* language but that everything is *inside* language: *il n'y a pas d'hors texte*.
9. These include the priority of the mental, actuality precedes potentiality, and the simplicity, identity, difference, continuity and the *se/per se* distinctions.
10. Collingwood, *Essay*, 285–97.
11. Naugle, *Hermeneutic Tradition*, 16–21.

presupposition is;[12] and he claims ultimate presuppositions are incapable of being true or false *per se* but yet they can be right or wrong depending on the question asked.[13]

The best way to approach Collingwood's dialectic of question and answer is to understand it not as a new system of logic but a hermeneutics of question and answer where interpretation becomes possible; when a text presents a question to an interpreter; and where understanding occurs when a text is interpreted by an interpreter.[14] In such cases validity and truth must be bracketed.[15] Collingwood thus points out that "every question involves an absolute presupposition"[16] and though it may be debated whether any question that has ever been asked involved one presupposition only and no more, it can be asserted that at least directly or immediately, "any given question involves one presupposition and only one, namely that from which it (the question) directly or immediately arises. The direct or immediate presupposition itself is presupposed by other presuppositions which are themselves indirectly presupposed by the original question. The fact that something causes a certain question to arise is called the "logical efficacy" of that thing[17] and this "logical efficacy of a presupposition does not depend upon the truth of what is claimed, or even on its being true, but only on its being supposed."[18] This is important especially in the domain of the 'relative presuppositions' of metaphysics and science "in which the entertaining of a hypothesis gives rise to questions about ways in which it could be confirmed or disproved."[19]

Collingwood thus argues that 'absolute presuppositions' are concrete in the sense that every 'relative proposition' rests upon an 'absolute presupposition.'[20] Moreover, since every relative proposition answers a

12. Ketner, *Emmendation*, 20.
13. Collingwood, *Essay*, 4, 40–41.
14. Following, Gadamer, *Truth and Method*, 333; D'Oro, *Gap*, 168–78.
15. Gadamer, *Truth and Method*, 350;
16. Collingwood, *Essay*, 25.
17. Collingwood, *Essay*, 27.
18. Collingwood, *Essay*, 28.
19. Mink, *Mind, History, Dialectic*, 126.

20. Collingwood's critique of Russell's propositional logic and the theory of truth that goes with it proceeds on the grounds it dissociates question and answer. To know is to seek the answer to a question; knowledge is a process of which questioning is on one stage and answering is another. A proposition, Collingwood argues, exists only as an answer to a question; it is 'true' when it is the correct answer within a question-answer complex, i.e. when it is the answer which helps inquiry to proceed. Neither the proposition, nor its truth, exists independently of the process of inquiry, as propositional logic presupposes.

question, and every absolute question rests upon a presupposition, without which the question would not arise, absolute presuppositions are the basis for propositional thinking and thus in this sense 'absolute'.[21] If 'absolute presuppositions' do not arise out of philosophical enquiry, nor answer the kinds of questions philosophers routinely ask, but constitute the presuppositions of questioning itself—of what use are they? Collingwood's answer is straightforward. Since every relative proposition answers a question, and every question rests upon an absolute presupposition, without which questions could not arise—absolute presuppositions are the *basis* for all propositional thinking.[22] They: 1) are aporetically limited and not open to propositional verification or negation which relate invariant observational statements to unobservable entities in theoretical statements;[23] 2) are principles of explanation, not a foundation for any metaphysics;[24] 3) provide the necessary and sufficient conditions for mapping the presuppositions of knowledge and meaning in metaphysical systems;[25] and 4) are independent of the hypothetical-deductive models of propositional logic and correspondence rules of verification.[26]

---

21. Collingwood, *Essay*, 47.

22. Collingwood, *Essay*, 173.

23. To know is to seek the answer to a question; knowledge is a process of which questioning is on one stage and answering is another. A proposition exists only as an answer to a question; it is ʽtrue' when it is the correct answer within a question-answer complex, i.e. when it is the answer which helps inquiry to proceed.

24. Although Collingwood rejects the traditional Platonic-Aristotelian doctrine that metaphysics is a theory of ʽpure being' or being *qua* being, he notes that such a claim itself rests on 'ultimate presuppositions,' and is not a subject of or for propositional investigation. 'Ultimate presuppositions' are concrete in the sense that every proposition rests upon an ultimate presupposition. Here his critiques of Russell's, Carnap's and Ryle's propositional logic and the theory of truth that goes with it, which rests on the ground that logic *disassociate* question and answer rather than *associates* it, are crucial to grasping its importance.

25. Collingwood, *Essay*, 23–24.

26. Collingwood's critique of Russell's and Carnap's propositional logic and the theory of truth that goes with it, rests on the ground that logic disassociates question and answer rather than associates them, are important. In nuce, to know is to seek the answer to a question; knowledge is a process of which questioning is on one stage and answering is another. A proposition exists only as an answer to a question; it is ʽtrue' when it is the correct answer within a question-answer complex, i.e. when it is the answer which helps inquiry to proceed.

II. Absolute Presuppositions

Collingwood proposes that the meaning of a "text" can be reconstructed by uncovering the 'absolute presuppositions.' Bertoldi notes: ". . . the argument of the *Essay* (on *Metaphysics*) is that metaphysics is the science of absolute presuppositions and moreover that it is the role of the metaphysician simply to discover what absolute presuppositions are being (absolutely) presupposed in his own time, or in some time in the past. His job is not to criticize, weigh, evaluate or pass judgment on the truth or falsity of these absolute presuppositions. To try to make such judgments is to engage in a kind of 'non-sense' described as pseudo-metaphysics'".[27] Collingwood's logic of question and answer is in his own metaphor an archaeological one concerned with discovery not truth. In this sense it not a replacement for a formal class or modal logic but a hermeneutical logic concerned with understanding how questions and answers are formulated.[28] He claims that "metaphysics is the science of absolute presuppositions"[29] and "analysis which detects absolute presuppositions . . . metaphysical analysis."[30] On these grounds, he argues: "Metaphysics is the attempt to find out what absolute presuppositions have been made by this or that person or group of persons, on this or that occasion or group of occasions, in the course of this or that piece of thinking."[31]

There are several important features of Collingwood's question and answer 'logic.' First, metaphysics is the science of absolute presuppositions;[32] Secondly, an absolute presupposition is one which stands, relatively to all questions to which it is related, as a presupposition, never as an answer".[33] Thirdly, the logic of question and answer are tightly related to each other.[34] A precise answer can be drawn out only by a precise question, and conversely a precise question only elicits a precise answer. This correlation of question and answer prevents vagueness and ambiguity. Fourthly, two propositions do not contradict each other unless they are the answers to the same question.[35] Implied here is the meaning of a statement is a function of the question to which it is an answer, and thus there are no logical relations among propositions

---

27. Bertoldi, "Absolute Presuppositions," 158.
28. Collingwood, *Essay*, 27–37.
29. Collingwood, *Essay*, 41.
30. Collingwood, *Essay*, 40.
31. Collingwood, *Essay*, 47.
32. Collingwood, *Essay*, 40–41.
33. Collingwood, *Essay*, 31.
34. Collingwood, *Autobiography*, 33. Implied here is the meaning of a statement is a function of the question to which it is an answer.
35. Collingwood, *Essay*, 29.

unless they are answers to the same question. Fifthly, truth and falsity is seen not as a property of propositions as in traditional logic, but rather as a function of "complexes consisting of questions and answers."[36]

Collingwood notes an ontological distinction between relative and absolute presuppositions, and redefines the latter concept. They are in important respects themselves relative, relative to the historian who discovers them and relative to the orderly, scientific thought to which they give rise—the evidence that the historian uses to discover them. They are absolute only in the sense that they are 'obvious,' or simply 'given' for the historical agent who employs them, and absolute in the further sense that the historian can discover no evidence that will lead him beyond them. These results thus qualify and temper Collingwood's more schematic account of absolute presuppositions.[37] Here—if 'absolute presuppositions' function as "synthetic a priori" or as "a priori concepts" at the point of logical possibility, Aristotle, Plotinus, Leibniz, Hegel and Collingwood might actually agree—that thinking about thinking' is essentially thinking aporetically about 'absolute presuppositions.'[38]

Collingwood's logic of 'absolute presuppositions' carries two senses:[39] firstly, since every proposition answers a question; and secondly, every question rests upon a presupposition, without which the question would not arise, presuppositions are the basis for propositional thinking and are in this sense 'absolute or ultimate.'[40] In this dialectic of question and answer reason directs its own questions to itself with the caveat that one only understands a statement when one understands it as an answer to a question.[41] "Since every proposition answers a question, and every

36. Collingwood, *Autobiography*, 37. As Hogan notes, the logic of question and answer "is not primarily concerned with truth but rather with the process of how one comes to understand. Its goal is discovery, not proof, and as such, it supplements formal logic but does not replace it" cf. Hogan, *Collingwood*, 44.

37. Collingwood, *Essay*, 164.

38. Rubinoff, *Collingwood*, 245; Mink, *Mind, History, Dialectic*, 146. There are also a third of proposition which is neither about relations of ideas nor matters of fact but are synthetic a priori in nature expressing methodological claims rather than existentially necessary ones.

39. Collingwood, *Autobiography*, 30–31.

40. Collingwood, *Essay*, 23, 25–28.

41. Collingwood, *Essay*, 63–66. Collingwood offers a definition of the logic of ultimate presuppositions. It is aporetic and hence Socratic in its horizons: "since every proposition answers a question, and every question rests upon a presupposition, without which the question would not arise, presuppositions are the basis for propositional thinking and are in this sense 'ultimate.'" Although he rejects the traditional Platonic-Aristotelian doctrine that metaphysics is a theory of 'pure being,' which is the Archimedean point in a scale of Forms or first causes, Collingwood notes that such a

question rests upon a presupposition, without which the question would not arise, presuppositions are the basis for propositional thinking and are in this sense 'absolute or ultimate.'"[42]

What separates Aristotle and Plotinus from Collingwood is the latter's subordination of ontology to epistemology through a second order enquiry into first order forms of knowledge. What unites Aristotle, Plotinus and Collingwood is a realist animus against psychologism: conceiving logical laws as empirical laws describing mental phenomena; and the notion that thoughts are derived by abstraction from sense experience.

III. Questioning Absolute Presuppositions

Collingwood's theory of absolute presuppositions has generated a whirlwind of criticism on two counts.[43] Nowhere does he explicitly say what an absolute presupposition is;[44] and he claims ultimate presuppositions are incapable of being true or false *per se* but yet they can be right or wrong depending on the question asked.[45] Gadamer may be of help here. He suggests the best way to approach Collingwood's dialectic of question and answer is to understand it not as a new system of logic but a hermeneutics of question and answer where interpretation becomes possible.[46] In such a hermeneutics questions of the validity and truth of its "logic" are bracketed.[47]

---

claim itself rests on 'ultimate presuppositions,' and is not a subject of or for propositional investigation. 'Ultimate presuppositions,' nonetheless, are concrete in the sense that every proposition rests upon an ultimate presupposition. Here his critique of Russell's and Carnap's propositional logic and the theory of truth that goes with it, which rests on the ground that logic *disassociate* question and answer rather than *associates* it, are important. In nuce, to know is to seek the answer to a question; knowledge is a process of which questioning is on one stage and answering is another. A proposition exists only as an answer to a question; it is `true' when it is the correct answer within a question-answer complex, i.e. when it is the answer which helps inquiry to proceed. Significantly, neither the proposition, nor its truth, exists independently of the process of inquiry, as propositional logic presupposes.

42. Two *foci* merit attention: 1) while every statement or proposition answers a question, every proposition or question rests upon an 'absolute presupposition,' without which the proposition or question would not arise; and 2) while every version of a proposition or a non-proposition utters something ultimately inexpressible, every non-proposition also rests on an 'absolute presupposition.' without which the non-proposition.

43. See, Naugle, *Hermeneutic Tradition*, 16–21.
44. Ketner, *Emmendation*, 20.
45. Collingwood, *Essay*, 4; 40–41.
46. Gadamer, *Truth and Method*, 333.
47. Gadamer, *Truth and Method*, 350.

What are "absolute presuppositions then?" Collingwood points out that "every question involves an absolute presupposition"[48] and though it may be debated whether any question that has ever been asked involved one presupposition only and no more, it can be asserted that at least directly or immediately, "any given question involves one presupposition and only one, namely that from which it (the question) directly or immediately arises. The direct or immediate presupposition itself is presupposed by other presuppositions which are themselves indirectly presupposed by the original question. The fact that something causes a certain question to arise is called the "logical efficacy" of that thing[49] and this "logical efficacy of a presupposition does not depend upon the truth of what is claimed, or even on its being true, but only on its being supposed."[50] This is important especially in the domain of the 'relative presuppositions' of metaphysics and science "in which the entertaining of a hypothesis gives rise to questions about ways in which it could be confirmed or disproved."[51]

Collingwood also argues that 'absolute presuppositions' are concrete in the sense that every 'relative proposition' rests upon an 'absolute presupposition.'[52] Moreover, since every relative proposition answers a question, and every absolute question rests upon a presupposition, without which the question would not arise, absolute presuppositions are the basis for propositional thinking and thus in this sense 'absolute'.[53] If 'absolute presuppositions' do not arise out of philosophical enquiry, nor answer the kinds of questions philosophers routinely ask, but constitute the presuppositions of questioning itself—of what use are they? Collingwood's answer is straightforward. Since every relative proposition answers a question, and every question rests upon an absolute presupposition, without which questions could not arise—absolute presuppositions are the *basis* for all propositional thinking.[54]

48. Collingwood, *Essay*, 25.
49. Collingwood, *Essay*, 27.
50. Collingwood, *Essay*, 28.
51. Mink, *Mind, History, Dialectic*, 126.
52. Collingwood's critique of Russell's propositional logic and the theory of truth that goes with it proceeds on the grounds it dissociates question and answer. To know is to seek the answer to a question; knowledge is a process of which questioning is on one stage and answering is another. A proposition, Collingwood argues, exists only as an answer to a question; it is `true' when it is the correct answer within a question-answer complex, i.e. when it is the answer which helps inquiry to proceed. Neither the proposition, nor its truth, exists independently of the process of inquiry, as propositional logic presupposes.
53. Collingwood, *Essay*, 47.
54. Collingwood, *Essay*, 173.

Summary: Absolute presuppositions: 1) are aporetically limited and not open to propositional verification or negation which relate invariant observational statements to unobservable entities in theoretical statements;[55] 2) are principles of explanation, not a foundation for any metaphysics;[56] 3) provide the necessary and sufficient conditions for mapping the presuppositions of knowledge and meaning in metaphysical systems;[57] and 4) are independent of the hypothetical-deductive models of propositional logic and correspondence rules of verification.[58]

IV. Aristotle and Plotinus

Book Lambda of the *Metaphysics* begins by very bluntly pronouncing, in very cryptic language, the formula which Nicolai Hartmann celebrated as the ideal formula of any ontology:[59]

> There is a knowledge (*episteme*) that contemplates (*theorei*) being as being (*on e on*)
>
> And that which belongs to it per se (*kath'auto*).[60]

---

55. To know is to seek the answer to a question; knowledge is a process of which questioning is on one stage and answering is another. A proposition exists only as an answer to a question; it is 'true' when it is the correct answer within a question-answer complex, i.e. when it is the answer which helps inquiry to proceed.

56. Although Collingwood rejects the traditional Platonic-Aristotelian doctrine that metaphysics is a theory of 'pure being' or being *qua* being, he notes that such a claim itself rests on 'ultimate presuppositions,' and is not a subject of or for propositional investigation. 'Ultimate presuppositions' are concrete in the sense that every proposition rests upon an ultimate presupposition. Here his critiques of Russell's, Carnap's and Ryle's propositional logic and the theory of truth that goes with it, which rests on the ground that logic *disassociate* question and answer rather than *associates* it, are crucial to grasping its importance.

57. Collingwood, *Essay*, 23–24. Also see Penner, *Rationality, Ritual, Science*, 11–24. esp. 20–24.

58. See Suppe, *Structure of Scientific Theories*. Collingwood's critique of Russell's and Carnap's propositional logic and the theory of truth that goes with it, rests on the ground that logic disassociates question and answer rather than associates them, are important. In nuce, to know is to seek the answer to a question; knowledge is a process of which questioning is on one stage and answering is another. A proposition exists only as an answer to a question; it is 'true' when it is the correct answer within a question-answer complex, i.e. when it is the answer which helps inquiry to proceed.

59. N. Hartmann, *Zur Grundlegung der Ontologie*, 41–42. "Man darf sich diese Formel ohne weiteres zu eigen machen. Sie ist zwar sehr formal, abrer in ihrer Art unuebertrefflich."

60. Aristotle, *Metaphysics*, IV.1003a21–22.

Aristotle claimed that the man of *episteme* who loves wisdom (*philosophia*) was a good deal advanced over the man of mere *empeiria*.[61] This is because he already sees the differences (*diaphoras*) by virtue of *logos* and *eidos*; and thus directs his attention to universals (*katholou*) rather than to singulars. Open enough to be amazed (*thaumazein*), he then realizes that he does not know anything, and therefore everything is questionable.[62] Striving to overcome this 'agnostic' state, he is gripped by a passion for wisdom so that he might grasp more and more (*mallon*) until he can see the ultimate causes and principles;[63] and knows the causes (*aitiai*) and principles (*archai*) of things.[64]

What is the meaning of *episteme* when it contemplates? What is this particular kind of *episteme* that directs its contemplation to 'being as being'? In contradistinction to 'other sciences' we are told by Aristotle that knowledge is a wisdom (*sophia*) that treats of 'being' not in a piecemeal fashion but' as a whole' and treats of it universally.[65] But what do 'being as a whole' and a 'universal *episteme*' of being imply? It is suggested it is primary philosophy (*prote philosophia*) in this sense—an *episteme* of first causes (*ta prota aitia*) and of the principles (*archai*). The primary aim of philosophy is then established as noted more precisely by Aristotle as the searching for: "some nature (*phusis*) to which these principles and causes belong necessarily and per se."[66]

So *episteme* is described as a 'searching' aimed at knowledge about nature (*phusis*). At the same time we learn something about that nature: it is to which principles and causes belong necessarily and *per se*. What sort of nature is this? What kind of searching is it that seeks to find such a nature? What is the meaning and function of thought and language when one speaks about being (*on*) in its many ways?

The problem metaphysical realists like Aristotle and Plotinus often face is that thought and language all too often 'slips out of traction' and their isomorphic relation to reality 'loosens.' Since language constitutes what words mean, or what they refer to, their solution is to put language back into traction by mapping mind, language and meaning from the perspective of Causes and Forms, rather than first picturing things known, and then mapping sensations through the perceptual languages of Cartesian and Lockean ideas. What

---

61. Aristotle, *Metaphysics*, 981b26ff; 982a16ff.
62. Aristotle, *Metaphysics*,.982b11.
63. Aristotle, *Metaphysics*, 981b21; *De Anima*, 430a14–15.
64. Aristotle, *De Anima*, 980a23
65. Aristotle, *Metaphysics*, 981b29–982a1–3.
66. Aristotle, *Metaphysics*, IV.1003a21–22.

Aristotle and Plotinus also propose knowing is not a matter of understanding reality propositionally from the outside in an indirect perceptual, phenomenal, or in a behavioralist-linguistic way.[67]

Unlike propositional or indirect understanding, which involves perception, intuition, and ordinary propositional/discursive language, *episteme* offers a direct *presuppositional* grasp or 'touching' of reality through an ideal non-propositional/non-discursive language.[68] Here the possibility of knowledge and language are largely discussed without Descartes' explicit reflection on the problem of the subject to whom knowledge is communicated, or through whom knowledge and language comes to be where subjectivity is the key to objectivity.[69] Rather an aporetic logic of 'ultimate presuppositions' using logical as well as causal possibility is employed to map the horizons of mind, language and meaning.

It is proposed that two claims ground Aristotle's and Plotinus' take on mind and language. First, Mind (*Nous*) is capable of providing foundations in the sense that reality must be described in terms of forms or concepts of thought. It (*nous*) knows reality and truth directly while other minds know truth and reality representatively, phenomenally or phenomenologically as mirrored possibilities.[70] Secondly, each proposes that *nous* language

67. See, J. Passmore, *A Hundred Years of Philosophy*, 191. Husserl claims: `any philosophy which is worthy of the name must shake itself free of all metaphysical presuppositions; not allowing any metaphysical phantasy to distract it from a direct analysis of `essences' or `general structures.' To proceed thus is to be `phenomenological' or a `realist.' However, it should be noted that this judgment itself is not a proposition but a presupposition. Thus, much contemporary misunderstanding of what ancient metaphysics is about arise propositionally not presuppositionaly.

68. To speak any ideal language requires the language and logic of metaphor for Aristotle and Hegel, and Pythagorean mathematics for Plotinus. Since the language and logic of Aristotle's and Plotinus's Mind is propositional and predicative at the level of *Psuche*, such an ideal linguistic move for Aristotle and Plotinus only arises at the level of *Nous* or the One. Given the eliminative metaphysical status of numbers in Aristotle's and Hegel, a mathematically grounded ideal language is impossible. Although there are traces or markings of an ideal (non-mathematical), non-propositional and non-discursive language that can be spoken it is limited to metaphor and simile by Aristotle and Plotinus. An ideal language could be spoken according Wittgenstein and Russell but this is the language of modal-propositional logic alone.

69. Descartes notes: "In the matter of the cognition of facts two things alone have to be considered, ourselves who know and the objects themselves which are to be known." R. Descartes, *The Philosophical Works of Descartes*, 35.

70. Four consequences follow from such claims: *first*, Mind/Intellect can tell us what reality intentionally means; *secondly*, whatever it knows is grounded *a priori*—here because knowledge claims are causally grounded on first principles which offer the necessary requirements for grasping the invariant object(s) of knowledge and thus the necessary and sufficient conditions for all knowledge and language claims. Here Causes (*archai, aitiai*), Forms (*ideai, eide*) and Concepts (*logoi*) provide *a priori* necessary

is capable of articulating truth and reality both propositionally and non-propositionally, discursively and non-discursively.[71]

Cartesian theories of self and subjectivity turn on the *cogito* as a privileged source of knowledge where the subject (mind or ego) is a substance that endures as something self-identical. Berkeley holds that ideas (and properties) are eternally in God's mind and made perceptible to the self upon the world's creation. The self becomes with Hume a bundle of perceptions and properties, with Kant an apperceptual I, and with Husserl an absolute individuator, a source of intentionalities with a history in its own right. Ryle calls such subjectivity a category mistake[72] which ends in Wittgenstein's ironically semantic and thoroughly solipsistic I.[73] Recently, exponents of behaviorist, functionalist, and causal theories of mind currently argue that the content of mental states cannot be defined purely introspectively but rather must be specified on the basis of the physical or causal role of mental states.

Aristotle and Plotinus are largely innocent of such modern notions. It is inconceivable that there are purely self-conscious mental states, that these mental states are distinct from perceptions or that perceptions are equivalent to sensations, or that idea covers both sense-data and concepts, or for that matter that the mind is separate from the body. Once all this is

---

justifications for knowledge and language. *Thirdly*, from these claims, follows that there is a collective Mind/Intellect, distinct from individual minds and intellects. Here *We* intellect provides an *a priori* justification for *our* knowledge *of* or *about* reality. *I* mind provides an *a posteriori* justification of *my* self-awareness or consciousness. Because of the nature of the objects of *We* knowledge—causes, forms, and 'ultimate presuppositions' it is *We* not *I* consciousness that has direct access to truth and knowledge. *Fourthly*, Aristotle's, Plotinus's and Hegel's Mind/Intellect exhibits a linguistic ability to access reality directly; while Descartes', Locke's, Berkeley's, Hume's, Kant's, Husserl's, and Wittgenstein's "minds" know and speak of reality indirectly. cf. R.M. Berchman, "Language of Metaphysics," 175–90.

71. It might strike one as odd that the foundations of 'ultimate presuppositions' is in propositional-discursive form. At the levels of *Psuche*, *Nous*, and *Logos* thinking may think itself and even God or the One, but there are limits to the language of each. Aristotle, Plotinus, Leibniz and Hegel would argue even an elliptical simile or an elliptical metaphor is discursive although the first principles such discursive languages "represent" is committed non-discursively to: the pre-linguistic over the linguistic; the ontological over the conceptual; and the theoretical over the practical. In the end, these languages are natural not ideal languages—all that *Nous* and *Logos* philosophers can possibly admit for natural languages—propositional and non-propositional; discursive and non-discursive. Mathematical language functions as the only ideal language of metaphysics for Plotinus and Leibniz.

72. A category mistake is one in the logic of mental statements and concepts which lead to the metaphysical theory that the self and subjectivity is composed of two separate and distinct (though somehow related) entities). cf. Ryle, *Concept of Mind*, 19.

73. "Language is the boundary of my world"—a solipsism worthy of Pyrrho. cf. L. Wittgenstein *Tractatus*, 5.6; 5.61; 562; 5.6.32–33; *Blue Book*, 55.

admitted, the Aristotle's and Plotinus' distinction between intellect-as-grasp-of-universals, and the living body which perceives sensation and motion, is lost. In its place a new distinction emerges—that between consciousness and non-consciousness wherein consciousness or thinking covers both sense and intellect. From here it is a short step to the Cartesian distinction between an event in non-extended and extended substance, and the claims of empiricists that the real world must be psychological, of idealists that the real world must be mental, and of phenomenologists that intentionality is sufficient to unite the *ego cogito cogitatum*—an *ego* and its intended objects.

Four claims provide context for Aristotle's and Plotinus' "innocence." First, Locke, Berkeley and Hume propose that the simplest element of knowledge is inner representations or impressions and that the mind is like a wax tablet or *tabula rasa* upon which objects make impressions. Consequently, the mind is made to think by some impression upon it, or some impulse given to it by contiguous bodies. In a quasi-mechanical way our immaterial tablets or minds are dented by the material world. These representations help us know what we are entitled to believe. However, the imprinting is of less interest than the observation of the imprint—which is the activity of perception-as-knowing. Again since Aristotle and Plotinus are largely innocent of modern notions of inner representations or impressions, they avoid the empiricist confusion between a mechanical account of the operations of the mind and its grounding in perception.

This confusion is what T.H. Green calls:

> The fundamental confusion, on which all empirical psychology rests, between two essentially distinct questions—one metaphysical, what is the simplest element of knowledge? The other physiological, what are the conditions in the individual human organism in virtue of which it becomes a vehicle of knowledge?[74]

Secondly, Aristotle and Plotinus do not hold that perceptions are equivalent to sensations, or that "ideas" cover both sense-data and concepts. Once this is admitted Aristotle's and Plotinus' distinction between intellect-as-grasp-of-universals and the living body which perceives sensation and motion is lost.

Thirdly, knowledge is not the possession of accurate representations of an object but rather *nous* becoming numerically (Aristotle) of qualitatively (Plotinus) identical with its objects of thought. Here *Nous* is both mirror and eye in one. The retinal image itself is the intellect which becomes all

---

74. Green, *Collected Works*, 19.

things.[75] Thus, the key issue is not whether Aristotle and Plotinus lacked a concept of mind, or even of a mind separable from the body.[76] Rather the issue is why there is no way or need for Aristotle and Plotinus—as there was for Descartes, Berkeley, Locke, Hume, Kant and Husserl—to divide "mental states" or "mental events" from "nousing" an "external world."

Fourthly, Aristotle and Plotinus do not have to worry about an eye, or for that matter an ear, tongue, finger, or nose of the mind. Knowledge is again the identity of the mind with the object known. However, Locke and Hume do not have this possibility available. Since impressions were representations, they needed a faculty which is aware of representations. Moreover, they needed a faculty that judged representations rather than had them. The rub is they could not postulate such a "nousing" faculty in the quasi-machine they hoped to describe. To do so would be to introduce a ghost in the machine. But there an obvious tension between thought and matter in the cerebral tablet persists nonetheless. Green reflecting on Locke's "ideas of reflection" says:

> Locke disguises the difficulty from himself and his reader by constantly shifting both the receptive subject and the impressive matter. We find the "tablet" perpetually receding. First it is the "outward part" or bodily organ. Then it is the brain . . . Then it is the perceptive mind, which takes an impression of the sensation or has an idea of it. Finally, it is the reflective mind . . .[77]

If knowledge-of is construed as "having in mind" and mind is a tablet, then Locke is thinking in physiological terms. If knowledge-of is construed as a "reflective mind" and mind is an activity, then Locke is thinking in psychological terms. As Kant puts it Locke exhibits the basic error of empiricism which is confusion between a "successions of apprehensions within an apprehension of succession." That is to say, we have a succession of flowers and redness, and yet we synthesize these into the judgment—"flowers are red." Locke cannot explain how this happens because he models knowing on seeing representations which become, somehow, "ideas." What Kant claims is significant—only thought relates. An object of which several predicates are

---

75. This is a rather different metaphor than Descartes' where the *Cogito* inspects images modeled on retinal images. cf. R. Rorty, *Mirror of Nature*, 45.

76. R. Rorty, *Mirror of Nature*, 47.

77. T.H. Green, *Collected Works*, 11.

judged true is always a result of a "mental" synthesis undertaken by a "mind."[78] Aristotle and Plotinus within limits agree with Kant.[79]

Summary: Aristotle's reinterpretation of the Platonic Forms and Plotinus' rehabilitation of them allows him to claim an isomorphism between indwelling and intelligible forms which yields a structural parallelism between thinking and being—*nous* and *to on*. The notion of a separate entity in which self-conscious "processes" occur is owed to Descartes; of conscious "processes" to Locke and Hume; and degrees of consciousness, and explicit distinctions between primary/secondary properties, perception/awareness and apperception/self-awareness, to Berkeley, Leibniz, and Kant. In each case "consciousness" best fits into the accuracy of the mind as 'mirror' and questions of the reliability of 'consciousness' to provide accurate reflection on its own representations becomes of paramount importance.[80] The problem is if mind's images no longer point to an archetype "outside" of my mind; then the possibility that thought and language may be transparent to the world is torn asunder.[81] Kant's transcendental turn with having concepts determine reality *a priori* is the result of such a fundamental error. Here we encounter a "return" to Aristotle and Plotinus with the caveat that an isomorphism must obtain between specific objective features of reality and specific structures of the mind for knowledge to be possible at all—otherwise a coherent experience of the world would be impossible.[82]

---

78. See, T.H. Green, *Collected Works*, 52–91. Kant goes on to argue that the mind constitutes knowledge of phenomena, not things-in-themselves. From here it is a short step to the Cartesian distinction between an event in non-extended and extended substance, claims of empiricists that reality is perception, claims of idealists that reality is apperception, and claims by phenomenologists that intentionality is sufficient to unite the *ego cogito cogitatum* with its intended objects.

79. On the synthesizing activity of mind they concur but not when Kant goes on to argue that the mind constitutes knowledge of phenomena, not things-in-themselves. From here it is a short step to the Cartesian distinction between an event in non-extended and extended substance, claims of empiricists that reality is perception, claims of idealists that reality is apperception, and claims by phenomenologists that intentionality is sufficient to unite the *ego cogito cogitatum* with its intended objects. cf. R.M. Berchman, "The Language of Metaphysics," 184–86.

80. On consciousness in Descartes, see Judovich, *Subjectivity and Representation*.

81. Dillon, *Aisthesis noete*, 247–62.

82. Rorty, *Mirror of Nature*, 12; Hedley, *Iconic Imagination*, 11–12.

V. The Priority of the Mental

Plotinus begins *Ennead* VI.9.1.1–3 (On the Good or the One) with the 'ultimate presupposition' of *prior simplicity and identity:* It is in virtue of the one that all beings are beings, both those which are primary beings and those which are . . . to be among beings." Plotinus engages the 'ultimate presuppositions' of *difference* and *continuity* at (VI.9. 1.30–33) He claims that the soul: "which is other than the one, has its being more one in proportion to its greater and real being. It is not the one itself but incidental to it, and these things, soul and one are two, just like body and the one. And what has separate parts, like a chorus, is furthest from the One, and what is a continuous body is nearer and the soul is near still and still participates in it." Bringing the 'ultimate presuppositions' of *prior simplicity, identity, difference and continuity* together, Plotinus proposes that the soul, which is multiple, and not composed of bodily parts, (*difference*) has as an attribute of its being the "one" (*identity*) as *sumbebekos pos* (VI.9.1. 31). "Soul and one are two just like body and one. Man and the living being and rational are many parts and these many are bound together by the one" (VI.9.2.20). This claim is justified, on the basis of the ultimate presupposition of *prior simplicity*, to its cause which is the "uniform nature of Intellect, and finally to the One itself (VI.9.5.20–27).

> This multiplicity all together then, the intelligible universe,
> Is what is near to the First, and our argument says that it
> Must necessarily exist, if one says that the soul exists . . . it is
> Not the first, because it is not one nor simple, but the One is
> Simple and the principle (*arche*)of all things

The 'ultimate principle' of continuity is a key: that every stage in a process, every member of series, becomes a particular instance or derivative of the formula for that process or series which allows for procession and return. In nuce, unity and being are conceptually and really distinct for Plotinus.

Plotinus' principles of prior simplicity, actuality precedes potentiality, identity, difference, and continuity have a *Nachleben* in Leibniz who rearticulates them in terms of 'the priority of the mental. The *prior simplicity* principle: that every composite thing derives from what is simple; the "identity principle" that an *a priori* analytic explanation for everything is possible: for all the facts of experience and for the truths of intellect which means every concept can be analyzed into its ultimate or prior mathematical-logical elements, so that all 'propositions' may be reduced to 'ultimate presuppositions,' leads to the principle of *identity*, in which, not only logically and conceptually, but substantially and existentially, following the principle of *continuity*, the subject is the same as the predicate. That is to say, if all propositions are analytic, and all terms are represented in the universal language of mathematical progression in Plotinus and calculus in Leibniz, then on the basis of the 'ultimate principle' that actuality precedes potentiality, all thought and language is the substitution of equivalent symbols wherein all derived concepts arise from the connection of primitive ones and further composite concepts derive from these compositions.

Although these principles serve as the general condition of the *identity* and *continuity* of a mathematical function, Plotinus and Leibniz extended it from mind and language to reality as well. This general law (analytic *a priori*) is a device for overcoming all supposed dualisms (synthetic *a posteriori*), even the one between body and mind. *Continuity* is a continuous gradation or *scala* where every stage in a process and every member of a series becomes a particular instance or "derivative" of the *identity* formula for that process or series. Here Plotinus and Leibniz emphasize the *identity* of a general type of structure or formula, as a counterpart to emphasis on *difference* the individuality or particular value of each member embraced.

As a consequence of these 'ultimate presuppositions,' Plotinus also anticipates and influences Leibniz theories of mind and language. In Plotinus' formulation, there is a phenomenal language of metaphor and a noumenal language of mathematics. In Leibniz's formulation, there is a phenomenal language of science and a noumenal language of metaphysics. However differently nuanced their philosophy of language, each affirms the superiority of mathematical and algebraic language over empirical or ordinary language. Moreover, since both take reality as possessing an objective structure, there is only one language that truly grasps this intelligible structure—*sub species aeternitatis*: mathematics–calculus–logic is the language of metaphysics.

As Leibniz noted—it is difficult to imagine how 'matter' can become idea, much less consciousness. Since Descartes, modern discussions in philosophy of mind presuppose that reality can be divided into the mental and the physical, mental substance, material substance, and their respective properties. This Cartesian privileging of the mind or *ego* and the Kantian and Fichtean desire for an absolute epistemological foundation of consciousness lead to the most radical changes: that there is not reality or thing-in-itself beyond the reach of possible experience; to the adoption of the position to which the world itself is reduced to a mere correlate of consciousness. It is Hegel's claim—that it is exclusively the mental and consciousness that has absolute being so that all other forms of being depend on consciousness for their existence which is the dissolution of the world into absolute consciousness—where Plotinus and Leibniz refuse to go. Such claims allow Plotinus and Leibniz to transition to the 'ultimate presupposition' that actuality precedes potentiality.

V.1 Actuality Precedes Potentiality

The 'ultimate presuppositions' of prior simplicity, identity and lead to two further claims: 1) actuality precedes potentiality; and 2) the priority of mental concepts to physical facts.

In *Ennead* (I.1.8.3) Plotinus states that:

> Intellect transcends us, everywhere it is one and the same and each of us has the whole of it.

The 'ultimate presupposition' of the priority of the mental leads Plotinus to the claim actuality precedes potentiality. In *Ennead* (I.1.8.3) Plotinus states that:

> Intellect transcends us, everywhere it is one and the same and each of us has the whole of it.

At this point Plotinus once 'ultimate presuppositions' are mapped a metaphysics follows. Since mind is prior to matter and actuality precedes potentiality: 1) *Nous* provides foundations in the sense that reality must be described in terms of forms or concepts of thought; 2) Mind knows reality directly, while other minds know truth and reality representatively, phenomenally or phenomenologically as mirrored possibilities; 3) *Nous* language is capable of articulating truth and reality propositionally and non-propositionally, discursively and non-discursively; 4) Mind grasps truth directly while sensation/perception does so only indirectly in a sensationalist, phenomenalist, or phenomenological 'mirroring' of reality; 5) knowledge involves a direct *presuppositional* grasp or 'touching' of reality through an ideal non-propositional/non-discursive language; and 6) this means knowledge is not a matter of understanding reality propositionally from the outside in either an indirect perceptual, phenomenal, phenomenological or linguistic way. The mind and its *concepts* thus are not to be confused with bodily *facts*. Plotinus, following Aristotle, bequeaths to succeeding generations a *conceptual* language of metaphysics, not a *factual* language of physics when addressing issues in philosophy of mind and language. Thus the decision to utilize a language of metaphysics, rather than a language of physics to analyze the mind its properties and its states, becomes a "given" for the traditions of a *Nous* philosophy of mind. Divine *nous* precedes all others levels of reality.[83]

Neither classical Greek nor Latin has a word meaning "self," "self-awareness," "consciousness," or "self-consciousness," approximating the senses in which the term has come to be used since the time of Descartes.[84] Behind such deliberation lies one pervasively influential text—Plato's *First Alcibiades*. The Delphic passage "know thyself" proposes that the real nature of man is defined as the soul's making use of the body as an instrument for self-understanding. Plotinus follows up on this by affirming an original intimate link between soul and intellect. Mind (*nous*) is the sun, while soul is the sunlight. Moreover this connection with *nous* was not lost when *psuche* became embodied.[85] Upon this claim Plotinus builds an argument where one cannot doubt that there is continuity in the soul that makes possible the act of remembering which leads him to propose a novel theory of the "self." Here the question whether soul is a multiple or single entity in a constant state resolves itself in the need of soul to turn in on itself moving from an inferior activity to a higher potentiality—ultimately to become a *nous* which is no physical thing at all to be distinguished from the psychological experiences of embodied human subjectivity. This is not to suggest, however, that Plotinus's "double-self" (psychological and intellective) is not dualistic in a Cartesian or post-Cartesian way.[86] Whether this soul is a multiple or single entity in a constant state resolves itself in the need of the soul to turn in-on-itself and move from an inferior activity to a higher potentiality, an intellect, mind, or *nous* which is no physical thing at all.

As Leibniz noted—it is difficult to imagine how 'matter' can become idea, much less consciousness. Since Descartes, modern discussions in philosophy of mind presuppose that reality can be divided into the mental and the physical, mental substance, material substance, and their respective properties. This Cartesian privileging of the mind or ego and the Fichtean desire for an absolute epistemological foundation of consciousness lead to the most radical changes: that there is not reality or thing-in-itself beyond the reach of possible experience; to the adoption of the position to which

---

83. See Themistius, *CAG* 5.4

84. Plotinus uses the terms *auto* and *hemeis* to designate the "self" and *sunaisthesis* for "self-awareness." Consequently, one should be careful in reading modern notions of self, self-awareness, consciousness, and self-consciousness into Plotinus. cf. G. Gurtler, *IJPT*, 4 (2010) pp. 83–85.

85. Plotinus, *Enneads*, IV.3.11–12.

86. This does suggest that Plotinus's "double-self" (psychological and intellective) is dualistic in a Cartesian or post-Cartesian sense. See G. Gurtler, "Self and Consciousness," 113–30.

the world itself is reduced to a mere correlate of consciousness. It is Hegel's claim—that it is exclusively the mental and consciousness (or conscious subjectivity, the "pure" ego) that has absolute being so that all other forms of being depend on consciousness for their existence which is the dissolution of the world into consciousness—where Aristotle and Plotinus refuse to go—on the basis of both necessary and sufficient 'ultimate presuppositions' of prior simplicity; actuality precedes potentiality; the a priori/a posteriori distinction; and the analytic/synthetic distinction. Neither assent to an idealism where even the thing-in-itself is a mere rule for the synthesizing activities of consciousness so that every sort of thing is associated essentially with a certain sort of conscious experience in which it reaches a most adequate level of 'givenness.' Thus a mind-independent-reality exists—even within the context of the intentionality of mental acts and the 'givenness' of their synthesizing activity in Absolute Consciousness. Here Aristotle and Plotinus sought to do justice to the claims of a realism that physical things exist independently of *I* consciousness, even though they are grounded in a *We* Mind or Intellect of first causes and Forms.[87]

Upon a claim of 'identity and continuity' Plotinus also builds an argument where one cannot doubt that there is 'identity and continuity' in the soul that makes possible the act of remembering. Whether soul is a multiple or single entity in a constant state resolves itself in the need of the soul, on the grounds of 'prior simplicity' to turn in on itself and move from an inferior activity to a higher potentiality, an intellect, mind, or *nous* which is no physical thing at all, is to be distinguished from the psychological experiences of embodied human subjectivity. This is not to suggest, however, that Plotinus's "double-self" (psychological and intellective) is dualistic in a Cartesian or post-Cartesian way.[88] Claims of the primacy of the actual over the potential leads to the 'ultimate presuppositions' of simplicity and identity.

---

87. Although Aristotle and Plotinus conceded an "empirical" description of a human being that includes both body and soul, soul being the living vitality with powers of choice, deliberation, and emotions. Plotinus also demanded recognition of a higher un-descended soul which is no physical thing at all. This mind or intellect is to be distinguished from the "*I*" psychological experiences of a human subject. It is the true "*We*" self that contemplates intelligibles. It is now a commonplace to see Plotinus's vision of as deeply indebted to Aristotle, Alcinous, and Alexander as much as to his reading of Plato. What all are certain of: is *nous* is not a physical thing and accounts of it which make it physical even on cognitivist grounds, end curiously by leaving mental processes out of the picture. They are certain there is something mental about the mind and they are keen, on the basis of conceivability arguments, to make distinctions between mental and physical states.

88. See G. Gurtler, *IJPT*, 4 (2010) pp. 83–85.

V.2 Prior Simplicity, Identity, Difference and Continuity

Plotinus begins *Ennead* VI.9.1.1–3 (On the Good or the One) with the 'ultimate presupposition' of *prior simplicity and identity:* It is in virtue of the one that all beings are beings, both those which are primary beings and those which are . . . to be among beings." Plotinus engages the 'ultimate presuppositions' of *difference* and *continuity* at (VI.9. 1.30–33) He claims that the soul: "which is other than the one, has its being more one in proportion to its greater and real being. It is not the one itself but incidental to it, and these things, soul and one are two, just like body and the one. And what has separate parts, like a chorus, is furthest from the One, and what is a continuous body is nearer and the soul is near still and still participates in it." Bringing the 'ultimate presuppositions' of *prior simplicity, identity, difference and continuity* together, Plotinus proposes that the soul, which is multiple, and not composed of bodily parts, (*difference*) has as an attribute of its being the "one" (*identity*) as *sumbebekos pos* (VI.9.1. 31). "Soul and one are two just like body and one. Man and the living being and rational are many parts and these many are bound together by the one" (VI.9.2.20). This claim is justified, on the basis of the ultimate presupposition of *prior simplicity*, to its cause which is the "uniform nature of Intellect, and finally to the One itself (VI.9.5.20–27).

> This multiplicity all together then, the intelligible universe,
> Is what is near to the First, and our argument says that it
> Must necessarily exist, if one says that the soul exists . . . it is
> Not the first, because it is not one nor simple, but the One is
> Simple and the principle (*arche*)of all things

The 'ultimate principle' of continuity is a key: that every stage in a process, every member of series, becomes a particular instance or derivative of the formula for that process or series which allows for procession and return. In nuce, unity and being are conceptually and really distinct for Plotinus.

Whatever elements of his postulate system Leibniz may have derived from Plotinus, he deconstructed it in light of the mathematical thought of reconciling oppositions through taking them as instances of a more general type. Leibniz develops the concept of unity in *Monadology 1, 2* and 5, by not only on the basis of '*prior simplicity*' but also on the basis of '*identity*' and '*difference*' as individuality and uniqueness. Each 'ultimate presupposition' is linked to the principle of 'continuity'—or *the identity of indiscernibles* (if two things have absolutely nothing which distinguishes them from each other, they are identical or the same thing). The claim that substances are simple implies that material objects are not real, that monads lack spatial extension, that they are minds with mental states, and that reality consists solely of non-spatial monads and their mental states: "for there is no way in which a simple substance could begin in the course of nature; since it cannot be formed by means of material compounding" only coheres on the basis of a logic of 'ultimate presuppositions.'[89]

Plotinus begins *Ennead* IX.9.1 with the statement in reference to the One that: "It is in virtue of identity that beings are beings." Leibniz further develops the concept of unity in the *Monadology* 2 as not only simplicity but as individuality and uniqueness, which he establishes with the principle of the identity of indiscernibles (if two things have absolutely nothing which distinguishes them from each other, they are identical or the same thing). The claim that substances are simple implies that material objects are not real, that monads lack spatial extension, that they are minds with mental states, and that reality consists solely of non-spatial monads and their mental states: "for there is no way in which a simple substance could begin in the course of nature; since it cannot be formed by means of compounding."[90] Hegel places identity (unity), A=A within the context of the mediated synthesis of subject and object; subjectivity and objectivity where "(if) all being is ultimately thought, (then) the Absolute idea is destined to become thought." Here whatever being there might be thought is not yet thought, not yet mediated in the synthesizing activity of the Idea. The clearest statement of this claim emerges in Hegel's Preface to the *Philosophy of Law*: the real is the rational and the rational is real."[91]

Claims that thinking and speaking thus start with the immediate fact of ideas, rather than with things known through ideas lead to a most

---

89. Leibniz, *Monadology*, 1, 2, and 5.

90. Leibniz, *Monadology*, 5.

91. The principle of Identity A=A is reformulated by Fichte as I=I and Schelling claims that as the indifference of subject and object. Since being precedes all antithesis, it cannot constitute their identity; it can only be the absolute in-difference of both. Indifference is not a product of antithesis, nor are antitheses implicitly contained in it. Being is the groundless. Schelling's idea of the groundless finds its echo in Heidegger's claim in *Of Human Freedom* that there must be a being before all basis (ground) and before all existence, before any duality at all. Heidegger's "turn" is to question the principle of identity as a principle of thinking at all. He concludes that the principle of identity presupposes the meaning of identity itself—a principle of thought must be a principle of Being—a fundamental characteristic of the Being of beings. A=A has become A is (transitively) A, and the "is" now takes on the meaning of belonging-together (*Mitsein*): interpreting Parmenides' statement that thought and being are the same as Being belongs together with thought into the same. cf. M. Heidegger, *Identity and Difference*, J. Stambaugh, Introduction, 10–11.

damaging point about empiricism: to pass from object to sensation to idea without shedding light on the process or activity whereby the material object generates thought is to falter in the face of mind, intellect, or consciousness. Moreover, if mind is the only reality directly known; then matter as all that affects our senses is known only indirectly through mind as well; thus, it seems unreasonable to reduce the directly known to the indirectly known, or mind to matter. In these contexts, Locke's formulation *Nihil est in intellectu nisi quod prius fuerit in sensu* (there is nothing in the mind except what was first in the senses) was questioned by Leibniz, on behalf of Aristotle, Plotinus and later Hegel. His playful answer—*nisi ipse intellectus* (except in the mind itself) is again to the point.[92] Why, in addition to the various sensory and muscular motions, is there an *awareness* of these motions; moreover, if all is matter in motion, why should not the nervous system, through sensation and response, attend to everything called knowledge, and not be bothered by mind? Here Plotinus, and Leibniz saw clearly that if we begin with matter and rise through levels of organic life to man, we shall be tempted by the logic of continuity to interpret mind as material. Indeed, each claims, however distinctly, that matter is known to us only through mind; only mind and language are known directly.

Claims that thinking and speaking start with the immediate fact of ideas, rather than with things known through ideas lead to a most damaging point about materialism or physicalism: to pass from object to sensation to idea without shedding light on the process or activity whereby the material object generates thought is to falter in the face of mind, intellect, or consciousness. Moreover, if mind is the only reality directly known; then matter as all that affects our senses is known only indirectly through mind as well; thus, it seems unreasonable to reduce the directly known to the indirectly known, or mind to matter.

Bringing the 'absolute presuppositions' of identity, difference and continuity together, Plotinus proposes that the soul, which is multiple, and not composed of bodily parts, (difference) has as an attribute of its being the "one" (identity) as *sumbebekos pos* (VI.9.1. 31). According to the principles of continuity and identity:

> Soul and one are two just like body and one. Man and the living being and rational are many parts and these many are bound together by the one.[93]

92. Leibniz, *New Essays*, II.1.

93 Plotinus, *Ennead*, VI.9.2.20. As a one and many, identity at the level of *Nous* is perspectival. It is not the kind of numerical or one to one unity as proposed in Leibniz's Law.

This claim is justified on the basis of the ultimate presuppositions of prior simplicity, identity and difference, and continuity to its cause which is the "uniform nature of Intellect, and finally to the One itself. This 'priority' claim establishes the 'ultimate presupposition' of the priority of the mental to the physical:

> This multiplicity all together then, the intelligible universe,
> Is what is near to the First, and our argument says that it
> Must necessarily exist, if one says that the soul exists . . . it is
> Not the first, because it is not one nor simple, but the One is
> Simple and the principle (arche) of all things. Now that which
> is prior . . .[94]

We have come full circle. In the Aristotelian sense, being as unity is directly known or 'touched' in *Nous*. In the Plotinian sense, being as unity is indirectly known or 'touched' by *Nous*.[95] Both notions bring us to *a se/per se* distinction.

V. 3 A *Se* and *Per Se* Distinction

An early example of the *se/per* se distinction surfaces in *Metaphysics* XII.9 where *Nous* is defined as absolute simplicity and actuality—*a se*[96] and thinks itself as thinking on thinking.[97] Act and content are different in form but the same in content. There is no distinction within *noesis noeseos*; there is no gap between act and concept, there is no potentiality otherwise Mind would be dependent upon a higher, more actual divine principle and power.[98] Plotinus offers another example of the *a se/per se* distinction with reference to the One based on the principle of prior simplicity in (V.4.1.5–15). Another quickly follows:

> But it must be single, if it is to be seen in others. unless one were
> to say that it has existence by being with the others. But then it
> would not be simple . . . for what is not capable of being simple

---

94. Plotinus, *Ennead*, VI.9.5.20–27.

95. R.M. Berchman, "Of Hunting Doves and Pigeons," 38–42.

96. This distinction is based on *ens a se* (Latin—"a being from itself") or a being that is completely independent and self-sufficient. The Latin term *aseitas* is formed from the prepositional phrase in ens a se thus translated into English as aseity. Since every *per se* contingent being depends on a *necessary* being for its existence and is not self-sufficient, only God could be *ens a se* or self-sufficient.

97. Aristotle, *Metaphysics*, XII.91074b33–35.

98. For this reading see, Nyvlt, *Aristotle and Plotinus*, 2012, 97–130; cf. De Koninck, "La Noesis," 215–18; *Aristotle on God*, 474–515.

will not exist, and if there is no simple, what is made up of many parts will not exist.[99]

Aristotle's and Plotinus' versions of an aseity argument emerge when an Intellect/Being or a One beyond being and intellect as *ens a se* are postulated[100] Aristotle's Mind and Plotinus' One are completely self-sufficient and independent *a se*—but in a *per se* relation with other beings.[101] As an *ens a se*, *Nous* and the One are 'from itself,' not *ens ex se* 'out of itself.' They do not depend on any necessary property *a se* or contingent property *per se*. Their identity is *numerical*, not *qualitative*, and if there are any changes to *a se* identity, it is a mere Cambridge change.

Aristotle's *Nous* in relation to other beings is necessary (*a se*) not contingent (*per se*). His version of the aseity argument (based on an early version of the indispensability argument) has the following form:[102]

1. Intellect's existence is either necessary or logically impossible.

2. It is not impossible for Intellect to exist *a se* (i.e., there is no contradiction in assuming that Intellect exists *a se*).

Therefore: Intellect exists necessarily *a se*.

---

99. Plotinus, *Ennead*, V.6.3.10–15.

100. From the term *aseitas* derived from the prepositional phrase *ens a se*. A primary being *ens a se* is the greatest conceivable being. If a primary being *ens a se* depended upon itself, it would cause itself to exist which is a logical contradiction. Thus *per se* relations are Cambridge properties where Intellect and the One exhibit reciprocal independence *a se*. cf. Wolterstorff, 263–65.

101. Aristotle, *Categories*, XII. 14a30–45, 14b11–24; Plotinus, VI.8.8.12–15, 11.32. cf. O'Meara, *Plotinus*, 68–71; J. Bussanich, *Plotinus' Metaphysics*, 38–65.

102. The Quine-Putnam indispensability argument has attracted a great deal of contemporary attention, in part because many see it as the best argument for mathematical realism (or platonism). Thus anti-realists about mathematical entities (or nominalists) need to identify where the Quine-Putnam argument goes wrong. Many platonists, on the other hand, rely very heavily on this argument to justify their belief in mathematical entities. The argument places nominalists who wish to be realist about other theoretical entities of science (quarks, electrons, black holes and such) in a particularly difficult position. For typically they accept something quite like the Quine-Putnam argument as justification for realism about quarks and black holes. This is what Quine calls holding a "double standard" with regard to ontology.) The indispensability argument also offers a good argument for metaphysical realism for it places physicalists, who are realists about the existence of the theoretical entities of physics, to consider the existence of the theoretical entities of metaphysics (Ideas, first causes and principles, minds, God and such) as real. To consider the Quine-Putnam argument as justification for realism about quarks and electrons but not about Ideas and first causes, would involve another "double standard" with regard to ontology.

This argument depends on *Nous* being *numerically* identical with itself, *a se* and *a priori*. Possible worlds, sets, relations, numbers and properties are also abstract objects in this sense. But is it possible for an *a priori* necessary abstract object to exist *a se*? If so Aristotle's argument exhibits the form:

1. *Nous's* existence as an abstract entity is either necessary or logically impossible.
2. It is not impossible for *Nous* as an abstract entity to exist necessarily *a se*.

Therefore, *Nous* exists as an abstract entity necessarily *a se*.

3. It is impossible for *Nous* to exist *a se* unless it is uncreated and independent of any other thinking and being object *a se or per se*.
4. *Nous* is independent of any other thinking and being object *a se* or *per se*.

Therefore, *Nous* exists as an abstract entity *a se*.

One of the key problems that remain is the tenet of the *numerical* identity of *Nous* in *a se* relation to its own thoughts. If we reject 1 we are faced with the option of nominalism and a descent into a loss of sovereignty. The denial of 2 raises the problem of ultimacy. *Nous* appears to be denied the role as ultimate principle. The dismissal of 3 and 4 raises the problem of dependency.[103] How can *Nous* be *a se* if it is in relation *per se* of or to anything?[104]

Plotinus thus proposes that Aristotle's *Nous* is really a *nous noeseos per se* which limit its sovereignty as an ultimate principle and suggest dependency on something prior and simpler—the One.[105] Thus his version of the aseity argument has the form:

1. Intellect's existence is either necessary or logically impossible.
2. It is not impossible for *Nous* to exist *per se* (there is no contradiction in assuming that *Nous* exists).

Therefore, Intellect exists *per se*.

3. The existence of an abstract entity *per se* is either necessarily or logically impossible without the existence of the One *a se*.

---

103. D. Hedley, *Iconic Imagination*, 133–137.
104. Gould, "Abstract Objects," 305–18.
105. Plotinus, *Ennead*, V.9.5–8.

4. It is impossible for *Intellect* to exist *per se* without the existence of an *a se* abstract entity—the One.

Therefore, Intellect exists contingently *per se* and the One necessarily *a se*.

A (modal) version of Anselm's ontological argument emerges from the *a se/per se* distinction.[106] It is based on conceiving God as an *ens a se* from itself and not *ex a se* out of itself. An entity *ens a se* does not depend on itself for its own existence because it is dependent on absolutely nothing. If it depended on itself, it would cause itself to exist which is a contradiction if causality is taken as transitive, asymmetric and irreflexive. On this basis Plantinga offers a modal version of Anselm's use of Aristotle to justify the existence of God who is *a se* and *necessary*.

1. God's existence is either necessary or logically impossible.
2. It is not impossible for God to exist (i.e., there is no contradiction in assuming that God exists).

Therefore: God exists necessarily *a se*.
A second version unfolds:

1. First principles, first causes, Nous or the One's existence is either necessary or logically impossible.
2. It is not impossible for them to exist *a se* (there is no contradiction in assuming that first principles, first causes, *Nous* or the One exists).

Therefore, they exist necessarily *a se*.
To this argument form Aristotle and Plotinus add:

3. The existence of abstract entities *per se* (Forms etc.) is either necessary or logically impossible without the existence of abstract entities *a se*.
4. It is not impossible for Forms etc. to exist *per se* without the necessary existence of abstract entities *a se*.

Therefore, *Nous*, God and the One exist necessarily and numerically—*a se*.

---

106. Anselm, *Proslogion*, 3. cf. Plantinga, *Does God Have a Nature?* p. 5; Malcolm, *Anselm's Ontological Arguments*, pp.143–145

V.4 Propositional and Discursive Distinctions

Plotinus and Origen place restrictions on the applicability of logical, epistemological and ontological criteria to first principles.[107] Although they retain the status of a principle or power, the One and God the Father cannot be captured in propositional or discursive form.[108] The result of such limits Plotinus suggests is the silence of contemplation.[109]

Plotinus notes:

> Since to say it (the One) is a cause is to
> Predicate an attribute not of it, but of us,
> In that we have something from it, (it) which exists in itself.
> But he who speaks accurately should not say it or it exists
> But we circle around it on the outside as it were, wishing to
> Communicate our impressions, sometimes coming near,
> sometimes falling back on account of the dilemmas that
> surround it.[110]

Thus how can one say anything about the unsayable? A distinction thus comes into play between propositional and discursive processes and no distinction between implication and inference. Specifically, each propose that the One and God the Father are above conceptual thought in two ways: a) intellection (intuitive-atemporal) and b) ratiocination (discursive-temporal). Soul possesses a and b, *Nous* and Logos possess only a, and the One and God the Father possesses neither.

> How do we speak about it? . . . But we do not say it
> Nor do we have knowledge or thought about it. How
> Then do we speak about if, if we do not have it? Or if
> We do not possess it by means of knowledge, do we
> Not have it at all?[111]

A second distinction between ordinary and ideal language also emerges.

---

107. Gersh, *Platonism After Derrida*, 2006, 72–80; Schroeder, Avocatio, 2012, 147–60.

108. Plotinus, *Enneads*, V.1.9.7–9; V.1.11.4–7; V.6.5.1–6; V.5.1.6–25; VI.7.1.29–43; VI.7.38. 1–9; V.3.10. 39–51. Origen, *On Prayer*, IX.2; XXI,2;XXVII.9.

109. Manchester, *Syntax*, 72–86.

110. Plotinus, *Ennead*, VI.9.3.49–55. For analysis of the circle image in Plotinus see Manchester, *Syntax*, 80–83.

111. Ibid. V.3.14.1–6.

> But like those who are inspired and become (divinely) possessed ... from this they are acquire a sense of the mover, being different from thus do we appear to relate to it.[112]

Origen's metaphysics and epistemology also presuppose absolute presuppositions such as prior simplicity; the priority of the mental; the irreducibility of the mental to the physical; actuality precedes potentiality; identity, relation and difference; the principle of continuity; holenmermism and synechism. The application of these presuppositions is framed in two ways. He is a metaphysical 'realist' who as early as the *Peri Archon* claims there is an *episteme* that contemplates first principles and an epistemological 'foundationalist' who construes the justification of knowledge non-inferentially on the basis of causal conditions. Here Origen proposes since knowledge (*episteme*) contemplates being as being categorically,[113] the *concept* and *act* of self-contemplation are telescoped into a *pros hen* unity.[114] However, human thought and language is limited. Ordinary propositional thought and discursive language cannot grasp first principles directly.[115]

Origen's argument is straightforward: since the human mind cannot conceptually think of or speak about God the Father at all in ordinary language, it grasps hold of the Father through the Son in the ideal language of contemplative prayer. This whole schema is set out by Origen when he parses God the Father as an absolutely simple and unknown first principle inexpressible through ordinary language and Logos as a one-in-many and known first principle who reveals his being and the Father's in the *praxis* of contemplative prayer.

> The Father is purely and simply one, is absolutely simple,
> Whereas there is multiplicity in our Saviour ... he was one but
> For this reason became many as well.[116]

When God the Father (Being-Intellect or the first One) is 'displayed' or 'shown' non-propositionally and non-discursively in contemplative prayer it retains its causal intelligibility to human consciousness.[117] Access to God the father is through contemplative prayer utilizing a '*ennoeo ton theon*' or

---

112. Ibid. II.14.8–14.
113. Origen, *PeriArch*. II.1.2 = *Philoc.* 21 = fr. 26 Koe.
114. Berchman, *Categories*, 235–44.
115. See, Sorabji, *Time, Creation, Continuum*, 137–152.
116. Origen, *CJnh*, I.20–21.
117. Berchman, *Origen*, 340–53. For parallels with Plotinus on prayer see, Alfino, *Plotinus and Non-Propositional Thought*, 273–84; D'Ancona Costa, *Amphoron kai Aneideon*, 69–113; Brisson, *Plotinus*, 443–57.

'*theoreo*' formulae. Things worth praying for have a "true and intelligible character (*ton alethinon kai noeton*).[118] In this sense, contemplative prayer is not merely many words (*polulogia*), nor merely words (*logoi*), but *Logos* revealing itself to *logos*. Through contemplative prayer a soul participates within a divine *noesis noeseos* that images first principles.[119]

> But whoever has contemplated (*ho tetheorekos*)
> The better and more divine things, which are necessary
> To Him, will obtain the objects of His contemplation
> (*on tetheoreke*), for they are known of God, and are
> known to the Father even before they are requested.[120]

This is so:

> For the eyes are lifted up from interest in
> Earthly things . . . they look beyond whatever
> Is begotten and contemplate (*ennoein*)
> God alone, and hold modest converse with
> The one who hears them. Such people afford
> The greatest benefit . . . being transformed into
> The image . . .[121]

VI. Methodological Solipsism

Any adequate understanding of the relation between mind, meaning and subjectivity must begin rather modestly with the questions: what is consciousness, self-consciousness, indeed what is the thinking self?[122] If Collingwood is correct that philosophy is activity then the only way of promising some degree of success is to begin with a logic of 'absolute presuppositions' where every question rests upon an 'ultimate presupposition' and where logic involves dissociative rather an associative kind of thinking.[123] Aristotle

---

118. Origen, *On Prayer*, XIV.17.
119. Pepin, *Linguistique*, 91–116.
120. Origen, *On Prayer*, XXI.2.
121. Origen, *On Prayer*, IX.2.
122. Gadamer notes the distance proper to *theoria* is proximity and affinity—for the primitive meaning of *theoria* is participation in the delegation sent to a divine festival. Such viewing is not an establishing of some neutral observation but rather a showing, a sharing in an event—or a being present. cf. Gadamer, *Reason*, 17–18.
123. Aristotle states such a program and its goals are contained in the first two

grounds us here. He proposes that the pursuer of *episteme* is one who loves wisdom (*philosophia*), who sees universals (*katholou*), knows the causes (*aitiai*) of things;[124] and is open enough to be amazed (*thaumazein*) one realizes everything can be questioned.[125] Manchester captures well the sense of all this when reflecting on Iamblichus: "a Platonist can always reply that eternity is not timelessness but *paradigmatic* timelessness, so that it would be no surprise if we were to find some participation in the unity of its image ... The power of the higher time allows it to translate *Nous* into *dianoia*. Time is therefore a principle of communication."[126]

The etymology of the term *episteme* has among its content notions of knowledge, vindication and understanding.[127] Epistemology is engaged in three projects: firstly, to explain what knowledge is and how it differs from true opinion; the second is vindication where the skeptic is answered on his own terms using the assumptions he would follow;[128] and involves knowledge of causes.[129]

Conclusion

Gadamer and Collingwood propose that interpretation is not a psychological and subjective act. It is an ontological and epistemological process that occurs in a historical tradition where understanding consists of the making of latent meanings explicit through question and answer logic.[130] In their critiques of the "class" and "transcendental" logics of Aristotle and Kant, Plotinus and Hegel propose theories of 'transcendentals' that move exclusively, however differently, through the medium of what Plato called the concept—"in Ideas, through Ideas, toward Ideas."[131]

For Descartes and Kant, the *Cogito* and *Ich Denke* hold a precious place.[132] It is not only a self-evident truth, the highest principle of knowledge and a criterion of truth but the first principle of what emerges as

---

chapters of *Metaphysics*, I.2.981b29–982a3; 993a15.
124. Aristotle, *Metaphysics*, I.2.980a23.
125. Aristotle, *Metaphysics*, I.2. 982b11.
126. Manchester, *Syntax*, 66.
127. Kvanvig, *Understanding*, 175–189; Greco, *Knowledge*, 9–29.
128. Greco, *Knowledge*, 12–14.
129. Greco, *Value Problem*, 313–21.
130 Gadamer, *Truth and Method*, 369–70, 373–79; Collingwood, *Essay*, 27–37.
131. Plato, *Republic*, 511c.
132 Descartes, *Meditations*, II–III; Kant *KrV*B134.

methodological or phenomenological solipsism. Husserl ups the ante—every philosophical proposition must be justified from a first-person standpoint:

> Anyone who seriously intends to become a philosopher must "once in his life" withdraw into himself and attempt within himself, to overthrow and build anew all the sciences that up to then, he has been accepting. Philosophy—wisdom is the philosopher's quite personal affair. It must arise as his wisdom, as his self acquired knowledge tending toward universality, a knowledge for which he can answer from the beginning, and at each step, by virtue of his own absolute insights . . . All the various insights proceed, as they must, according to guiding principles that are immanent or "innate," in the pure *ego*.[133]

The privileged status of "I" is suspect for Aristotle, Plotinus and Hegel, however. Methodological solipsism can only be defended, if it can be at all, as the first-person *plural* not as a strategy that restricts the validity of certain metaphysical claims within a first person standpoint but as a strategy that makes possible the expansion of the first-person perspective into a collective one. As the "I" drops out of the formulation, the possibility of a mere individuating "self-reflexivity" and "consciousness" drops out also. Moving from *my* thoughts or mental states to *our* thoughts and mental states the psychological and ontological "I" no longer functions as a first principle, axiom, or premise. But as a methodological rule where philosophical problems are reasoned as *our* problem and where philosophical problems are justified from a first-person standpoint *ourselves*. This attempt to move from *I* to a *We* self-reflexivity or consciousness is perhaps the most fundamental and seductive theme in Hegel's notion of reconciliation (*Versoehnung*). If the task of philosophy is to show how differences, oppositions, ruptures, contrarieties, and contradictions can and must be rectified in the self-identical and self-differentiating totality of *Nous* and *Geist*, then this *aufgehoben* is helpful in addressing our next problem.

---

133 Husserl, *Cartesian Meditations*, 2–3.

3

Naming, Intentionality and Meaning

Assem para et accipe auream fabulam.

—Pliny, *Ep. ad Calvisius*, II.20

Précis

FINDING A CONTEMPORARY ANALOGUE to Aristotle's and Plotinus' notions of naming, intentionality and meaning is not easy. If one is tempted to fit Aristotle into either Brentano's and Husserl's models where the *ego* is a self-constituted subject; or Russell's, Ayer's Wittgenstein's and Ryle's where any semantic relation to an 'abstract entity' like *Nous* are suspect—much of what either propose becomes either distorted or accommodating. A way around our impasse is to map the logical framework of their naming-intentionality-meaning argument in light Parmenides' Second Fragment where a Goddess, as self-appointed interpreter of ordinary thought and language sets a snare, a fetter-in-waiting with hints of an ontological identity and relation between thinking and being reducible to an ineluctable law of being:

> Come now and I will tell you the roads alone for seeking (that) be for thinking for you could not know non-being (for it cannot be accomplished) nor could you declare it, for the same is thinking as well as being (for it is the same to think and to be).[1]

---

1. Parmenides, DK <B> fr. 2 = Proclus, 1–8: *Com. in Tim.* Diehl, v. 1, 345; 3–8: Simplicius, *Com. in Phy. Com.. Arist. Gr.* IX, 116. tr. P. Manchester.

I. Horizons

G. E. L. Owen's reading of Parmenides' Second Fragment sets the initial horizon of enquiry. He notes that "being" and "non-being" are objects that ordinary speakers attempt to distinguish. When ordinary speakers name objects all names are synonyms for being: lions exist, mermaids do not and it is this qualified answer that Parmenides rejected as looking both ways. It treats existence and non-existence as different yet identical.[2] Yet in distinguishing them they identify them. Moreover, they compound the problem by claiming if non-existent mermaids could be talked about they would be existent.[3] The proof of their existence is that if they did not exist, they could not be talked or thought about for the assignment of names to objects always involves an object to be named, and once named that object exists.[4] Here the question arises—is it in the assignment of a name to an object where falsity or non-being is produced, for the being of the object named belongs to that object?

Owen maintains ordinary speakers will say lions exist and mermaids do not and thus never assign the name mermaid to an object correctly. It is "being" that the lion and the mermaid share, for being is not a part of the objects we *name* but being is what lions and mermaids *mean*. Owen thus argues that all objects whatsoever indicate the same meaning–being, for the Eleatic problem is there is no loose "being" floating around the cosmos to be momentarily pulled out of the air and linked to "whatever can be talked or thought about." Thus ordinary speakers will say lions exist and mermaids do not—because they assume "being" belongs to the objects we *name* when it is really "being" that lions and mermaids *mean*.[5] All this brings us round in a circle but we are not quite home—yet.

Owen proposes that ordinary people and even "cosmologists" try to distinguish existence from non-existence by saying lions exist and mermaids do not—but why? Could it be 'mermaids' unlike 'lions' exist but only as images in our imagination? Or could it be that "being" a lion is unlike "being" a mermaid because lions really exist while mermaids do not. Or it could be that lions and mermaids exist because they are named as such for there is a 'real' correspondence between names and things? Or could it be lions and mermaids exist not only because *names refer* but because *naming* denotes not only *reference* and *description* but *intentionally* and *meaning*?

2. Owen, *Eleatic Questions*, 11.
3. Owen *Eleatic Questions*, 12.
4. Owen *Eleatic Questions*, 16.
5. Owen, *Eleatic Questions*, 16.

Several inferences can be drawn from Owen's naming game: 1) that in distinguishing mermaids from lions we *identify* them as "beings;" 2) that the "being" implied in any object named cannot be separated from that object and reflects the distinctive nature of that object; 3) that if non-existent mermaids are thought or talked about they exist for if they did not exist, they could not be thought or talked about; 4) that the assignment of names to objects always involves an object to be named; 5) that any object named indicates "being;" 6) once objects have meaning they exist; and 7) it is with the assignment of meaning to an object where falsity and non-being can be justified.

Our reading of naming, intentionality and meaning thus is a modification of the Owen thesis: firstly, the assignment of names to objects always involves intentionality or an object to be named; secondly, any object named has meaning because all objects once named share the property of being named; and thirdly, the property in any object named cannot be separated from that object and reflects the distinctive nature of that object. The key point is: 1) being is part of the object, the object is not part of being; 2) the being implicit in any object names cannot be intentionally separated from that object; and 3) the being an object possesses reflects its meaning.

II. Problems

Few epistemological claims are more enigmatic than: 1) "being" is a part of the object, the object is not part of "being"; and 2) that thinking, speaking and naming objects infers intentionality and meaning to objects. This point shall be returned to later on but we can name objects that have no meaning, such as with the *voces magicae* and *nomen barabares* of the *PGM, PDM, Chaldaean Oracles*, and Neoplatonic theurgical literatures. This is not meant in the limited and very meager sense of Wittgenstein's, Russell's, Ayer's and Ryle's notions of elementary propositions: where firstly, they are needed to depict the primitive states of affairs formed by the combination of simple objects; and secondly, where if a series of signs fails to express either an elementary or compound proposition, and does not affirm or deny a mathematical equation, it does not express a proposition at all. In nuce, it is non-sensical. We should not miss the point of Wittgenstein's argument here.[6] The contrast between names and descriptions on which he relies, is while what is named may also be describable, it is only the use of a name, as opposed to a description that

---

6. Wittgenstein, *Tractatus*, 2.02 to 2.0212.

guarantees the existence of what is referred to. Thus the simplicity of an object consists in being nameable in this manner.[7]

The slogan 'don't ask for its *meaning*, ask for its *use*' became popular among analytic philosophers après Wittgenstein. Another banner might be hoisted: 'don't ask for its *use*, ask for its *intentionality.*' If an object satisfies a *description* which carries with it the implication of it *intentionality*, then surely it can be *named*. If this is granted, it shows we are missing a crucial point—the contrast between *names* and *descriptions*. It is only the *intentionality* and *meaning* of a *name* as opposed to its *reference* and *description* that can be talked or thought about. Moreover, is there a difference between kinds of *naming*: the first as *reference* and *description*; and the second as *intentionality* and *meaning*?

All this again brings us again round in a circle but it does not bring us home. It might not be the case for names that only their use guarantees the existence of the objects to which they refer. Perhaps this is no more than a clumsy way of saying names should be such as to afford us security of *sense*: and this means either that they are properties for which it is required that the predicates standing for them are intelligible; or if they are individuals that they are capable of being named meaningfully and not merely described. If individuals are only described but not named they might have *sense* but they would not have *meaning*. For example, just one person answers to the wife of Socrates—Xanthippe and nothing answers to the description of the wife of Wittgenstein—but both descriptions make equally good *sense* although only the first carries has *meaning*.

We must transcend these propositions then and see them as "nonsense" to set the world aright.[8] Here a quite convenient question arises in the *Cratylus* that helps us to climb up and beyond analytical problems about elementary propositions. Socrates asks: is language natural or conventional; is there a right name for each thing or not; is there a one to one correspondence between a name and a thing; and is it how a name is used that matters?[9]

> ... that which has to be named, has to be named with something ... a name is an instrument ... what do we do when we name ... do we not give information to one another and distinguish things according to their natures? (If) so then a name is an instrument of teaching and distinguishing natures.[10]

---

7. As claimed with ethical, aesthetic and religious discourse. cf. Wittgenstein, *Tractatus*, 3.221.

8. Wittgenstein, *Tractatus*, 6.54.

9. Plato, *Cratylus*, 385ac; 389a-390e.

10. Plato, *Cratylus*, 388ac.

The slogan 'don't ask *for* its *meaning*, ask *for* its *use*' became popular après Plato and Wittgenstein. If this is granted three points require consideration. The first is the contrast between *names* and *descriptions*. The second is the difference between the *meaning* and *use*. The third is the distinction between *reference* (for) and *meaning* (about).

Aristotle is aware of all three which might suggest a contemporary semantic interpretation of the use of names—that Aristotle proposes the existence of whatever is spoken of. This is unlikely. If one attempts to fit Aristotle into Brentano's and Husserl's phenomenological, or Wittgenstein's and Ryle's semantic models much of what he proposes becomes either distorted or accommodating. If the self is self-constituted as a Descartes' *cogito*, Locke's, Berkeley's or Hume's *percipio*, Kant's transcendental *ego*, Hegel's *Geist* or Wittgenstein's and Ryle's semantic self—then any relation to *Nous* remains suspect—and Aristotle's model of an Intellect common to all naming, intentionality and meaning collapses. Aristotle's model need not fail if one replaces—'don't ask for a name's *meaning*, ask for its *use*' with—'don't ask *for* a name's *use*, ask *about* its *intentionality* and *meaning*.'[11]

III. Intentionality

It is perhaps Aristotle's achievement to have suggested that the mental points toward objects. It is also an enormous leap to claim that mind is not confined within itself, that it can go beyond itself, that it can have something else as its object other than itself, and that it can refer and be directed toward something else. The foundations of a theory of intentionality and begins in *Metaphysics* (XII.7.1072b20–23) where Aristotle claims that thought thinks itself through participation (*metalepsin*) in the object of thought:

> And thought thinks itself through participation (*metalepsin*) in the object of thought for an object of thought becomes (by the act of apprehension and thinking, so that the same: thought and object of thought, i.e. being is thought. And it actually functions when it possesses (this object).

At *Metaphysics* (XII.9.1074b34–35) Aristotle notes that all forms of cognition are intentional, that is "of something else" (*h'allou*) and only incidentally of themselves:

> ... knowledge and perception and opinion and understanding have always something else as their object ... for to be an act of thinking and to be an object of thought are not the same thing

11. Berchman, *Rationality and Ritual*, 228–31.

> ... in some cases knowledge is the object ... thought and the object of thought are not different in the case of things that do not have matter, divine thought and its object will be the same, i.e. the thinking will be one with the object of its thought.

In *De Anima* (III.2.425b26–27) he applies his account of perception to thought to say that the sensible object and the sensation of it are one in *energeia* but different in *to einai*:

> The activity of the sensible object and that of the percipient sense is one and the same activity and yet the distinction between their being remains the same.

In *De Anima* (III.5.10–25) he claims that the Active Intellect makes all things:

> Intellect in the passive sense is such because it becomes all things, but Intellect has another aspect in that it makes all things ... Intellect in this sense is separable, impassive, and unmixed, since it is essentially an activity.... Actual knowledge is identical with its object...
>
> and this alone is immortal and everlasting ... and without this nothing
>
> thinks.

If Aristotle's *identity* theory of intentionality means the mind refers is: 1) mental activity always of something other than itself; 2) are we acquainted with ourselves in the exercise of this referential function; and 3) in intending its object is mind a state or direction?

Two texts help clarify these questions. At *De Anima* (III.5. 430a 10–19) Aristotle states:

> And in fact mind as we have described it is what it is by virtue of becoming all things while there is another which is what it is by virtue of making all things: this is sort of a positive state like light; for in a sense light makes potential colors into actual ones. Mind in this sense of it is separable, impassible, unmixed since it is in its essential nature activity (for always the active is superior to the passive factor, the originating force to the matter which it forms).

At *De Anima* (III.5.430a20–25) Aristotle claims:

> Actual knowledge is identical with its object: in the individual potential knowledge is in time prior to

actual knowledge but in the universe as a whole
It is not prior even in time. Mind is not at one
time knowing and at another not. When mind
is set free from its present conditions it appears
as just what it is and nothing more: this alone is
immortal and eternal (we do not, however,
remember its former activity because while mind
in this sense is impassible, mind as passive is
destructible) and without it nothing thinks.

Aristotle appears to argue that the essence of thinking is to refer, which means our mental activity is always *of* something other than itself, and we are acquainted with ourselves and others only and always in the exercise of this referential function. The fact that active reason already knows all intelligible objects makes it possible for the passive reason to "point towards" the knowable while the active intellect intentionally displays such knowledge to the passive intellect.

IV. Two Intentionalities

There are two kinds of intentionality. *Relational* intentionality is a relation between act and object—such as Molly thinks a blue square. *Linguistic* intentionality is a feature of intentional idioms when features of objects are expressed by means of adverbial modifiers—such as Molly sees bluely. Relational accounts stress intentional acts of knowing (perception and intellection) stand in a 'focal' relation to objects known *qua* being. Linguistic accounts highlight intentionality as a feature of speech acts that can be expressed by categorical modifiers. Relational intentionality takes as its starting point the existence of an ontological relation between act and object. Linguistic intentionality takes as its starting point the existence of an idiomatic association between acts and objects of thought.

Aristotle also proposes that mind's intentionality is caused by 'mind independent 'abstract objects' such as first principles, first causes, and *Nous*. The focal/causal structure of the intentionality of mental acts can be illustrated in the following way:

(object) > act (content)

Aristotle's *Nous* in intending its object is thus not an essence so much as a state or direction. Intentionality is a pointing, extending, extending toward. Intellect is an activity of thought intentionally directed toward its objects. Thinking thus *refers* as a pointing, extending toward *prote ousia/ aitiai* or primary being (*prote ousia*). knowledge about reality is "actualized" in mind (*nous*) through intellection (*noesis*). Here one's attention is directed toward "the activity of intellect" which intentionally grasps whatever focal and causal meaning that is extraneous to it.

Brentano and Husserl propose that intentionality is constituted by mind and its objects of thought are mind-dependent (or in analytic parlance a state of affairs). Meaning is constituted self-reflexively by self-consciousness.[12] The constitutive/causal structure of the intentionality of mental acts is pictured in the following way:

act (content) > (object)

Although again mind in intending its object is not an essence so much as a state or direction, a pointing, an extending toward objects of thought, the difference is mind constitutes its objects of thought.[13]

We have examined several passages in Aristotle that imply the possibility of the intentionality of mental acts. It remains his achievement to claim that mind is not confined within itself and that it can go beyond itself. Mind *refers* which means mental activity is always *of* something other than itself, and we are acquainted with ourselves only and always in the exercise of this referential function. Here

Claims that Aristotle, Plotinus, Brentano, and Husserl share a common commitment to intentionality and meaning must be radically bracketed.[14]

Aristotle proposes thus the realist thesis intentionality discloses a mind independent meaning about reality; while Brentano and Husserl map the anti-realist thesis that mind intentionality constructs mind dependent meanings about reality. The difference between these options is not trivial. Aristotle's intentionalities are not constituted by my mind alone while Brentano and Husserl's are. If this is correct, whenever an object is described and named its meaning derives from first principles, causes and *Nous* and not from an event, an image or a sign constituted from my thoughts and memories alone.

12. This appears to be the case even if a phenomenological residuum survives bracketing. cf. Husserl, *Ideen*, I, SS 76.

13. Husserl, I, *Ideen*, SS 33.

14. Aristotle and Plotinus propose intentionalities are not constituted by my mind and the objects to which it is directed. Rather a focal theory of meaning and being grounds mind's intentionalities. In contrast, Brentano's and Husserl's intentionality stand in the shadow of Descartes' and Locke's claims that all feelings, beliefs, thoughts, imaginings are "ideas" where mind in intending its objects is not a substance and state or direction; but solely a pointing (at), aiming (at), and extending itself toward objects of consciousness. cf. Husserl, I, *Ideen* SS84.

V. Meaning

Aristotle's proposes a 'focal' or *pros hen* theory of meaning that includes claims that being (*to on; ousia*) is constituted in accordance with the logic proper to being. It is said in many senses and different beings are not said to be purely homonymous, but rather to be "related to one thing (πρός εν)" (1003a33–34). Owen translates this πρός εν formula as "focal meaning", and in his paraphrase, it means that all the "senses (of "being") have one focus, one common element," or "a central sense," so that "all its senses can be explained in terms of substance and of the sense of 'being' that is appropriate to substance." According to Owen:[15]

1. Focal meaning contradicts and replaces Aristotle's earlier views in the *Organon* and *EE* that beings differ in different categories and thus 'being' has various distinct meanings.
2. Focal meaning makes it possible for Aristotle to establish a universal science (*episteme*) of being qua being in *Meta*. Γ again which contradicts and replaces his earlier view that because beings differ, a universal science of being is impossible.

Eight theses follow from a theory of focal meaning:

1. *Episteme* is not merely an internal activity of grasping external objects in inner space, but one of an instance (*nous*) exemplifying its kind, which following Plato he called *Nous*.[16]
2. There is an *episteme* (way of thinking) that contemplates (*theorei*) being as being (*on e on*) complemented by a *phusis* (nature) to which first principles and causes belong necessarily and per se (*kath' auto*).[17]
3. Thinking is grounded in a divine intellect (*nous*) that thinks itself (*noeseos noesis*). What a thinker thinks points toward a divine intellect which is one with its object of thought.
4. If the activity of thinking (*episteme*) is a theorizing (*theorein*) that contemplates ultimate causes and first principles, then *nous* must join *episteme* in contemplation (*theorei*), for it is *nous* that apprehends the causal structure of reality that *episteme* contemplates. This also means the *episteme* that contemplates the *phusis* of 'being as being' has the character of *noesis* (intellection).

---

15. G.E.L. Owen, *Logic and Metaphysics*, 163–190. For a critique of Owen on focal meaning see, Yu, *Focal Meaning*.
16. Aristotle, *Posterior Analytics*, II.100b 5–17.
17. Aristotle, *Metaphysics*, 1003a21; 28–29.

5. Thinking has as its subject matter is a *noeton* described as an a-synthetic whole (*asuntheta*) which constitutes itself in thinking as the unity of its *noeseos* (on thinking).
6. Thinking *refers*. It is always *of* or *about* something. It involves no subject-object distinction; only a pointing, extending, or an extending toward *prote ousia/aitiai*. Indeed, the ultimate subject of whatever intentionality and meaning are *of* or *about* is primary being (*prote ousia*).
7. Thinking with intentionality and meaning is not an external thinking (of what we know other than ourselves as knowers) via images, representations, calculations, deductions or propositions. It involves no spatial difference, no mediating image or representation, no separation between knower and known, so as to turn self-knowledge into an unreliable knowledge of something else. Rather it is an internal thinking of *prote ousiai*.
8. Plotinus' claim 'reflection is illumination' results in a refinement of Aristotle's 'focal' theory of meaning. Light illuminates not only awareness of the name of an object but its meaning. Once Mind abstracts (*aphesei*) the objects of its vision (or the Forms) it meaningfully sees the One.[18]

VI. Naming to Meaning

Focal meaning raises the question what does it *mean* for something 'to be.' Aristotle uses the verb 'to be' largely in three ways: First, to refer to a single focal point and meaning—'to be' qua being in reference to a single kind of being, primary being (*prote ousia*). Secondly, necessary or primary being is a being *a se* in virtue of itself and not in virtue of its relation to other beings that cause being. Thirdly, contingent or non-primary being is a being *per se* that refers to and depends on primary being, i.e. it is a being in virtue of its relation to primary being.[19]

Second, Aristotle frequently says that "being" is ιπολλαχώς"; that "being' is said in many senses and different beings are not said to be purely homonymous, but rather to be "related to one thing (πρός εν)" (*Meta* Γ 1003a33–34). The πρός εν formula is as follows: Some things are said to be because they are substances, others because they are affections of substance, others because they are a process towards substance, or destruction or privations or qualities

---

18. Plotinus, *Ennead*, IV.5.7.16–21. For commentary see Gurtler, *Ennead* IV.4.30, 2015, 279–89.

19. Wagner, *Realism*, 51–72.

of substance, or productive or generative of substance, or of things which are relative to substance (*Meta* Γ 1003b6–10). In Γ2 when all other things are πρός εν, to being, being then becomes the primary sense of all beings (1003b 7–8). In Z4, the πρός εν of being means that being is neither homonymous nor synonymous. What it expresses is that "definition and essence in the primary and simple sense belong to substances."[20] Here analysis of essence and essential predication, which focuses on the distinction between *what* an object is, and *how* it is remains foundational.[21]

Thirdly, Owen takes Aristotle's notion of signification (σημαίνειν, "to signify") to mean the "sense" or "meaning" of being.[22] πολλαχώς signifies that a word has a "sense," a distinct "meaning" or a *significatum*. Since "being" has many *significata* and is said in many senses, *meaning* refers to the "being" words signify. It is in this sense that categories "signify" (*Cat*.4, lb26 what "things that are" (*ta onto* la20, [AQ] cf. *Topics*, 1.9, 103b27). Accordingly, the study of categories is the study of beings.[23]

Categorically there is much more going on as well. If we must discard the assumption that only simple objects can be named, we allow room for the possibility that names consist of qualities united by a relation of compresence. If a plausible reading of Aristotle—that "being" is ιτολλαχώς"; that 'being' is said in many senses and different beings are not said to be purely homonymous, but rather to be "related to one thing" (πρός εν) (*Meta* Γ 1003a33–34), names would then consist of all admissible complexes of

---

20. See Owen, *Logic and Metaphysics*, 163–90.

21. A distinction between *kath hauto* or *a se* predications (*what* universals) and *kata sumbebekos* or *per accidens* predications (*how* universals) displays what is necessary to an object; and what is not.

22. Owen, *Logic and Metaphysics*, 73. Etymologically, σημαίνειν is related to the modem word "semantics." Not surprisingly, it has been a matter of dispute how to understand Aristotle's conception of signification. While Owen's understanding (held also by Barnes, *Aristotle*, 205) tends to be intensional, Ferejohn believes that it is extensional, *Focal Meaning*,118. Kirwan suggests that "to signify" can be either "to mean", or "to denote" in different texts See Kirwan, *Aristotle*, 94. Yet Hamlyn claims that Aristotle does not have a distinction between sense and reference, Hamlyn, *Focal Meaning*, 8, 12). For Aristotle signifiers include not only names, but also verbs, phrases and sentences. cf. *Poetics*, 1456b38ff . See Irwin, *Signification*, 241–66 who concludes that Aristotle's use is unsystematic.

23. When Aristotle lists "substance," "quality," "quantity," "relation," and so on, it is often not clear whether he is talking about them as signifying categories, or as that signified rather than signifier extra-linguistic beings. As Ackrill, *Categories*, 88 remarks, "It is careless of him to speak as if it were substances (and not names of substances) that signify." Likely it is both for it is on the conception of signification that Aristotle affirms that there are as many beings as there are categories (*Meta* Δ 7,1017a 23–28). Indeed, the multi-vocity of being and the theory of categories are so closely associated that Aristotle simply calls substance, quality, quantify, etc. "categories of being."

meaning and their actual combinations. The question is what triggers a name's possible complexes and combinations into something meaningful? There is no way of solving this difficulty except by adding—if a *name* is 'categorically' intentional—it has *meaning*. It is only the *intentionality* and *meaning* of a *name*—not its *description*—that matters.

Schroeder argues Aristotle regards the informed particular as primary substance and real while Plotinus sees intelligible substance as real and the particulars that belong to a genus as secondary substance. To avoid infinite regress in predicating the Form both of the particular and the Form, Aristotle locates the Form in the particular. Plotinus preserves the transcendence of the Form by replacing the Aristotelian predication by synonymy with a system of predication solely built on Aristotle's notion of *pros hen* equivocity. The Form now becomes *eidos aneideon*—a "formless form"—an unrestricted entity.[24] The question of "what is" is always a question directed not at certain knowledge but undisclosed meaning. There is thus never closure to aporetic enquiry and every attempt at knowledge and definition emerges in transcendence where the One is the locus of focal meaning.[25]

VII. Après Aristotle and Plotinus

We have examined several passages in Aristotle and Plotinus that imply the possibility of the intentionality of mental acts. We have seen why they claim the intentionality of all mental acts—theoretical and a-theoretical; intelligible and sensible. Does this mean that Brentano and Husserl have something to say about the intentionality of consciousness that Aristotle and Plotinus could concur?

VII.1. Brentano

Brentano claims intentionality to be an irreducible feature of mental phenomena but that Aristotle was the first philosopher to propose intentionality to be a fundamental constituent of all knowing in all its variety and forms. He also argues Aristotle's *nous* never thinks without intentionality. Thus, when I think or imagine; when I judge; when I love or hate or have emotions and desires—I am conscious *of* or *about* something. Thought involves a double-relation—a relation of mind to object and a relation of object to that mind which intends it.[26] Mind or consciousness is thus not a substance, a state, but a *direction* with

---

24. Schroeder, *Categories*, 115–36.
25. Schroeder, *Hermeneutics*, 108–22.
26. For arguments against Brentano's reading of Aristotle. cf. Chrudzimski,

an intentionality that points outside itself to something else. Intentionality is an irreducible feature of mental phenomena and no physical phenomena exhibit it. In this sense: mind as "consciousness" is intentional in nature and points toward objects' in its 'intentional field;'

And has a complex *a priori* mental structure without which meaning would not be possible at all.[27]

Brentano "translates" *nous poietikos* in Aristotle as intentionality, direction, a pointing toward that activates the senses, sensation, and passive reason, which is a sort of plastic material on which active reason impresses the forms of knowable objects. In this sense, active intellect is not a medium between passive reason and its object; it is a direction and not a mere mediating relation. Active reason is a third thing which has to be taken into account of if we would understand the fact of knowledge, just as light is a third thing, besides the eye and the object which we must take account of if we would understand the fact of sight.

According to Brentano, Aristotle claims that *Nous* intentionally points at or aims at or extends toward things as phenomena. Moreover, given that intentionality is phenomenal, phenomena point outside of themselves to something else. That is, whatever they are *of* or *about* are constructed by Intellect. In brief, when phenomena are constructed by Intellect with intentionality their essences are "essentially" polyvalent—which is to say meaning depends on the intentionality of intellect as it "points towards" objects.

Thus Brentano claims that Aristotle made the bold claim that to think, judge, and desire means to think, judge, and desire *of* something.[28] Thus thinking is intentional which means that every thought, judgment, and emotion contains an intended object. Hence, any act of Intellect is characterized either by its intentional relation to an object, or that the act of intellection is the constitutive relation of intentional consciousness to its object. It shall be suggested that "intentionality" for Aristotle and Plotinus is the former, while intentionality for Brentano and Husserl is the latter—where the being of objects have no one essential meaning or value.

VII.2. Brentano and Husserl

If Aristotle and Plotinus have a theory of intentionality it not in the sense that Brentano and Husserl suppose. First, *Nous* intentionality is

---

Brentano and Aristotle.

27. See Morrison, *Degrees of Being*, 31; 27-46.

28. For claims Plotinus did not have intellectual objects of intellection see Sorabji, *Intentional Objects*, 105-14.

not constitutive of things intelligible or sensible as it is for Brentano's and Husserl's consciousness. Secondly, when *nous* touches, sees or participates with objects it intentionally displays them; it does not constitute of construct them. Thirdly, thoughts and beliefs do not have phenomenal properties arguing that Intellect knows things-in-themselves. Fourthly, pains and beliefs that do not have phenomenal or physical properties are not characterized by intentionality. The mind is not that out of which pains, beliefs, and imaginings are made.

Brentano but particularly Husserl argues differently that: 1) in intending its objects mind is not an essence/substance but a state or direction as the "act-character" of consciousness;[29] and 2) consciousness is simply intentionality—a pointing (at), an aiming (at), and extending (toward). Aristotle and Plotinus on the contrary claim that: 3) *Nous* is not merely conscious activity or a transcendental *ego*. It is a substantial intellect that cognitively points, aims, and extends toward sensibles; towards intelligibles, and towards itself as thought thinking itself;[30] and 4) when mind participates or fuses with its objects it intentionally and focally displays them rather than constitutes or constructs them.

VII.3. Aristotle and Plotinus

Mapping their theories out, Aristotle argues for a theory of intentional *identity* and Plotinus a theory of intentional *complexity*. When Aristotle's Intellect intentionally touches and sees its objects there is an identity between thinker and object. When Plotinus' Intellect sees and touches its objects there is complexity, a distinction between thinker and object. Why this is so is clear. Aristotle has no principle prior to *Nous*; Plotinus does—the One. Thus, Plotinus working from the principle of prior simplicity cannot accede to an *identity* notion of intentionality. Thus he accedes to a *complexity* theory of intentionality. Aristotle, lacking a principle of prior principality identifies the

---

29. Husserl, I, *Ideen* SS84.

30. First, *Nous* intentionality is not constitutive of things intelligible or sensible as it is for Brentano's and Husserl's consciousness. Secondly, when *nous* touches, sees or participates with objects-of-knowledge it intentionally displays them; it does not constitute of construct them. Thirdly, thoughts and beliefs do not have phenomenal properties arguing that Intellect knows things-in-themselves. Fourthly, pains and beliefs that do not have phenomenal or physical properties are not characterized by intentionality. The mind is not that out of which pains, beliefs, and imaginings are made. There remains with Aristotle and Plotinus an essence or substance whose thinking is activity, whose being is in intentionally knowing intelligible "essences" understood as universals—Ideas, Forms, and Causes—because it is an essence itself whose Intellect and activity are intentionally identical. cf. Berchman, *Thinking and Being*, 70 n. 8.

best *ousia* with the highest form of cognition, *noesis* via *energeia*.[31] For Plotinus, Intellect contains a plurality of Forms. Hence there is no absolute unity. Aristotle's *Nous*, unlike Plotinus,' is identical with *noesis* and this pure activity of thinking is the highest being, an absolute unity.

It remains Aristotle's and Plotinus' achievements to have suggested that the mental refers to an object and that object-related acts are of fundamental importance. It is an enormous leap to claim that mind is not confined within itself; that it can go beyond itself; that it can have something else as its object other than itself; and that it can refer and be directed toward something else. However, although neither share Brentano's or Husserl's hard, inclusive sense of intentionality. They do anticipate notions of intentionality that emerge in both.

VII.4. Differences: Intentional Identity and Complexity

Aristotle thus argues for a theory of intentional *identity* and Plotinus for a theory of intentional *complexity*. The reason we encounter different notions of intentionality rest upon their different assessments of the intentional activity of *Nous*: When Aristotle's Intellect intentionally touches and sees its objects there is an identity between thinker and object. When Plotinus' Intellect sees and touches its objects there is complexity, a distinction between thinker and object.

Why this is so is clear. Aristotle has no principle prior to *Nous* while Plotinus does—the One. Working from the principle of prior simplicity, Plotinus cannot accede to an *identity* notion of intentionality and offers the alternative of a *complexity* theory of intentionality. Aristotle, lacking a principle of prior principality identifies the best *ousia* with the highest form of cognition, *noesis* via *energeia*.[32] *Nous* is identical with *noesis* and this pure activity of thinking is the highest being, an absolute numerical unity, as 'thought thinking itself'. For Plotinus, Intellect contains a plurality of Forms Thus there is only a qualitative unity of Intellect and Forms when 'thought thinks itself.'

Two caveats follow from either intentionality thesis. Aristotle and Plotinus do not: 1) view all mental states and activities as intentional for emotions and pains are not *of* or *about* anything; 2) *nous*'s thoughts do not have phenomenal properties or phenomenologically appear as phenomena might appear at all; 3) its mental states and activities are not Epicurean or Stoic "images" of things physical; and 4) since its intentionalities are

---

31. Aristotle, *Metaphysics.*, XII.7.1072b8.
32. Aristotle, *Metaphysics.*, XII.7.1072b8.

non-phenomenal and non-material, it directly knows things-in-themselves. As Plotinus notes:

> One must not, then, look for the intelligibles outside, or say that they are impressions (*tupous*) of the real beings in Intellect ... one must watchfully preserve reality ... but not only the knowledge of each thing's qualities, since if we had only that we should have an image and trace of realities and not possess and live with and be fused (*sugkrathentos*) with the realities themselves—we must attribute all real existences to true Intellect.[33]

We have examined several passages in Aristotle that imply the possibility of the intentionality of mental acts. It remains his achievement to claim that mind is not confined within itself and that it can go beyond itself. If Aristotle's *identity* and Plotinus' *complexity* theory of intentionality are valid, then mind *refers* and its activities are always *of* something other than itself and we are acquainted with ourselves only and always in the exercise of the referential function of meaning. Here intentionality and focal theory of meaning go hand in hand.

Summary: Claims that Aristotle, Plotinus, Brentano, and Husserl share a common commitment to intentionality and meaning must be radically bracketed. Aristotle and Plotinus propose intentionalities are not constituted by my mind and the objects to which it is directed. Rather a focal theory of meaning and being grounds mind's intentionalities. In contrast, Brentano's and Husserl's intentionality stand in the shadow of Descartes' and Locke's claims that all feelings, beliefs, thoughts, imaginings are "ideas" where mind in intending its objects is not a substance and state or direction; but solely a pointing (at), aiming (at), and extending itself toward objects of consciousness.[34]

VIII. Realism and Anti-Realism

Modern discussions of mind, meaning and intentionality usually start off by assuming that reality is divided into the mental and the physical, that this distinction is common-sensical and intuitive.[35] Whether a proponent of a sensationalist, phenomenalist, or constitutive theory of knowledge—where concepts of intentionality and meaning surface in either rationalist,

---

33. Plotinus, *Ennead*, V.V.2.1–8.
34. Husserl, I, *Ideen* SS84.
35. See, Sosa, *Epistemology*, and *Raft and Pyramid*.

empiricist, or idealist notions of the "idea"—empiricists, rationalists, and idealists propose that mind intentionally draws "the givenness" of all objects into 'consciousness' or self-consciousness meaningfully. The intuition that the mental-physical gap is unbridgeable by empirical means; or that a mental state is *in mentis sui generis*, and thus no more like a disposition than a neuron remains—if only as a bit of *res cogitans* non-spatially associated with a bit of *res extensa*—as in Spinoza's double-aspect theory.

Such criteria of the mental can be traced back to Descartes' *Meditations*, Spinoza's *De Emendatione Intellectus*, Leibniz's *Monadology*, and Locke's *An Essay Concerning Human Understanding* but it did not achieve self-consciousness until Kant's *Kritik der reinen Vernunft*. In a Copernican "turn," Kant distinguished the unknowable, noumenal, *Ding-an-sich* with the knowable, phenomenal constructs of pure reason. The subtle but revolutionary insight is that we can only know about objects *a priori* if we constitute them. Once Kant replaced the "the physiology of the human understanding of the celebrated Mr. Locke" with transcendental psychology, not only did epistemology came of age but phenomenology was born. By and large the legacy of empiricism was to deconstruct the primacy of the idea, of form, of mind and replace it with "experience". With this there is lost the notion that mind is an essence that maps essences to be replaced by claims of what Kant and Hegel call 'phenomenological synthesis'—where knowledge is not perceptions mirroring nature but mind phenomenologically constituting nature.[36] Brentano and Husserl argue similarly. Intentionality is the "act-character" of consciousness where consciousness is constitutive.

Behind such differences lie Aristotle's and Plotinus' commitments to realism not anti-realism:[37] a thoroughly modern phenomenon that un-

---

36. Idealism requires the Copernican revolution announced by Kant in the preface to the *Critique of Pure Reason* that the human mind in relation to sensory experience (the relation being the key point) is constitutive. Kant, *KrV,* V B xvii.

Kant places outer space inside an inner space (the space of the constituting activity of the transcendental ego) claiming phenomenological certainty about inner consciousness for laws which had previously been thought to be outside consciousness. In so doing, he thus reconciled the Cartesian claim that we can have certainty only about our ideas with the fact that we already had certainty—*a priori* knowledge—about what seemed not to be ideas.

37. In such contexts, a wide ranging debate has emerged among Emilsson, Sorabji, and Burnyeat concerning realism and anti-realism in antiquity. See Emilsson, *Plotinus*, 315-20; Burnyeat, *Idealism in Greek Philosophy*, 3-40. This result of this controversy includes the claim that Plato, Aristotle, Plotinus, Proclus, and ps-Dionysius inspired modern idealism in its varieties. cf. Beierwaltes, *Platonismus und Idealismus*; Viellard-Bacon, Platon, 1979.

folds from and within Descartes' *Cogito*, Berkeley's *percipio*, and Kant's transcendental *ego*.[38]

Realism is the view that: 1) there are real objects that exist independently of our knowledge or experience of them; 2) that these mental and physical objects have properties and enter into relations independently of the concepts with which we understand them, or 3) the language with which we describe them. Anti-realism is any view that rejects any one of these tenets and includes all claims to representationalism, transcendental deduction, and phenomenology.

> If we were to frame a question to capture the realist and anti-realist position it would be:
>
> Is the truth or falsity of the statement x exists independent of mind?

One is a realist about x if one responds that x exists (or does not) independently of mind; and an anti-realist about x if one denies that x exists (or does not) independently of mind. Its medieval versions arise in debates about whether universals only exist or fail to if they have a reality independent of individuals and of our conceptual categories; or whether universals are merely features of the way in which we think about individuals, thus enjoying only a nominal reality.

Two additional questions encompass what a commitment to ontological realities entail:

> Is the truth or falsity of the statement x exists—independent of a human mind?
>
> Is the truth or falsity of the statement that x exists independent of a divine mind?
>
> One is a realist if one responds x exists (or does not) independently of a human or a divine mind.[39]

IX. Naming, Intentionality and Meaning Revisited

We return to the questions that opened this enquiry: firstly, how do we get from *naming* to *meaning*; secondly, if I intentionally think a name does meaning follow; and thirdly, can a name only be described? Ritual has its own rationality different from the logico-deductive rationality of science. Theurgy

---

38. Descartes, *Meditations*, I-II; Locke, *Essay*, 101–5.

39. For an assessment of realism and anti-realism see Insole, *Realism and Anti-Realism*, 274–89.

establishes contact with reality and operates upon it in a naming language game with a 'logic' of its own that effects entry into an intelligible world of 'abstract' objects to achieve communion with the divine.[40]

The notion of there being names for which there is no existence, non-existence or meaning is puzzling. But such seems to be the case with *voces magicae* and *nomen barabara*. But even these names should be such as to afford us security of *reference* which means either they have properties for which it is required only that they have predicates standing for them to be intelligible, or, if they are individuals—that they are capable of being named and not merely described. The problem is if they could only be described any attempt to refer to them would run the risk of failure.

If, as I think we must discard the assumption that only simple objects can be named, we allow room for the possibility that names consist of qualities united by a relation of compresence. Names would then consist of all admissible complexes of meaning including their actual combinations. The question is what triggers a name's possible complexes and combinations into meaning? I see no way of solving this difficulty except by adding—if a name satisfies intentionality or is an intentional object- then surely it has meaning. For the gap between naming and meaning must be that while what is intentionally named may also be describable; it is only the meaning of a name, as opposed to its description that guarantees the existence of what a name refers to.

Intentionality triggers meaning—which is where Aristotle's notions of naming, intentionality and meaning again come into play.

Conclusion

We have mapped a way from naming by parsing a path through intentionality to meaning. In doing so we have proposed that what makes a name meaningful is its having some intentional accompaniment. Wittgenstein's and Ryle's objections to this are first that we constantly use words meaningfully without being aware of the occurrence of any mental duplicates such as intentionality and meaning; and secondly that the "mental processes" that accompany language consist in the employment of signs which share no marks of the mental at all. Given their theories of perception, Aristotle and Plotinus would likely agree but with the caveat that mental states are not wholly reducible semantic-behavioral ones. They might even agree with

Wittgenstein that thought and language is essentially the activity of operating with signs. In the case where the thought is expressed in writing

---

40. Addey, *Divination and Theurgy*, 171–290.

we can say the activity is performed by hand; in speaking by the mouth and larynx; but what of those cases in which thought is given no overt expression? In these cases we are tempted to say the activity is performed by the mind and there we go astray if we forget or fail to realize that we are resorting to a metaphor.

Here Wittgenstein suspects a philosophical trap—and rightly so. The mind is not an agent in the same sense as the hand, nor should we suppose that in order to recognize an object or a property we need to compare it with a sample, usually a mental image which acquires its meaning from other inner accompaniments such as intentionality and meaning. Which gives rise to the philosophical question: how can one think or name what is not the case? If I think that my house is on fire when it's not on fire, the fact of its being on fire does not exist. Then how can I think it? How can we strike a match that doesn't exist? Wittgenstein's answer is put in this form: I can't strike a match that doesn't exist; but I can look for it when it doesn't exist.

All this Wittgenstein may be a bit much but his objection to intellectualism returns us to the problems addressed at the beginning of enquiry—of there being *names* for which there is no *meaning*. In answer to the first, Aristotle and Plotinus seem to argue that since a *name* is fundamental to a things essence, any name without intentionality and meaning 'does not really exist.' Naming with intentionality is 'creative,' 'life-giving,' and meaningful because the *praxis* of speaking or writing a *name* things 'calls' being into existence.[41] Thus even *voces magicae* and *nomen barbares* afford us security of *reference* and *meaning*—which means they have properties for which it is only required that they have predicates standing for them once spoken to be intelligible.

In response to the second, Iamblichus and later Platonists claim ritual exhibits rationality different in kind from that of the logico-deductive rationality of science.[42] Liturgical and theurgical rites establish contact with divine reality, operating upon it in a 'naming game' with its own 'logic' of its own. In the praxis of naming, entry into an intelligible world and achievement of communion with the divine is possible where being is part of the object; the object is not a part of "Being." Here a rather bold claim emerges. The act of *naming* is onto-genetic and through words worlds are brought into existence.

Is the mermaid thus like the lion? Is the being of the lion the same as the being of the mermaid? No—if being is a part of the objects we name;

---

41. Addey, Divination and Theurgy, 215–82; Santoprete and Hoffmann, *Langage des Dieu*; Mastrocinque, *Divinatory Kit*, 98–112. Also Tardieu, Van den Kerchove and Zago, *Nomes barbares*.

42. Berchman, *Rationality and Ritual*, 229–68.

yes—if it is being that lions and mermaids *mean*. Analogically, if *voces magicae* and *nomenes barbara* are taken—not as nonsensical utterances—then they are like the mermaid and lion—when spoken the being of their names acquires meaning.

4

Limits of Thought and Language

The limits of my language mean the limits of my world.

—Wittgenstein, *Tractatus*, 5.6.

Précis

How do the thought, language and meanings of sensation refer to 'abstract' or 'noetic' entities? Are 'seeing' and 'hearing' mere metaphors about perceptions divine or do they denote something real and tangible? There are many passages in Origen (and Plotinus) that suggest the language of 'spiritual sensation' unites intellect, will and the affections.[1] He is keen to stress where conceptual and discursive thought fail 'spiritual' hearing and seeing allows access to a divine noetic realm—thus his preference for a language of 'sacred images (*agalmata*) over abstract concepts (*protaseis*) and ratiocination (*logismos*). Consequently his claims that *gnothi seauton* and *homoiosis theo* are not generalizations derived from experience psychologism); nor subjective mental states with psychological properties (intuitionism); nor signs or a game played with signs or a manipulation of linguistic symbols (formalism); but abstract objects or conceptually independent intelligible objects (realism).[2] Since ordinary thought and speech are limited Origen

---

1. On techniques of contemplation in Plotinus and Origen see Dillon, *Transcendental Imagination*, 1986, 443–55; Schroeder, *Avocatio*, 147–60; Abraham and Aquino, *Epistemology of Theology*, Gavirlyuk and Coakley, *Spiritual Senses*.

2. There is an extensive recent historical-literary reference and scholarship on *gnothi seauton*, *homoiosis theou*, and prayer in the *corpus Origenianum*. cf. Castagno, *Origene*, 2000; Limone, *Origene*, 2018; Crouzel, *La Connaissance*, 1962; Edwards, *Origen Against Plato*; Ramelli, *Origen*, 217–63; and on the spiritual senses in general, cf. e.g. Gavirlyuk

has a sense there must be something else: firstly, an ideal language spoken by a god within (*gnothi seauton*) that causes a desire for a likeness on to God (*homoiosis theo*); whereby secondly, a transcendent subjectivity is acquired through the *praxis* of contemplative prayer. Of note is the notion of a 'self attainable' beyond an empirical self and an ideal language beyond ordinary language speakable as contemplative prayer. He an attempt to overcome the limits of thought and language in a sublation of names, descriptions and meanings mark Origen's concept of contemplative prayer.

I. Horizons

That there are limits to ordinary thought and language is a later Platonic commonplace.[3] Here Origen is informed by two notions. He follows Plato that knowledge is not merely an internal activity of grasping external objects in inner space but one of an instance of *nous* exemplifying its kind; and Aristotle's focal theory of meaning, where 'Being' is said in many senses and different beings are not said to be purely homonymous but rather to be "related to one thing" (πρός εν),[4] allows him to refer meaning to an ideal language of contemplative prayer.

In the *Theaetetus* Plato defines knowledge (*episteme*) as "true knowledge with an account (*logos*)" and claims for knowledge to be true judgment it must be accompanied by "discourse." Several meanings of the word *logos* are proposed: 1) use of language; 2) the enumeration of the parts of a thing language names; and 3) analysis of that which indicates the *differentia* of a thing named. This latter attempt to "atomize" knowledge leads Plato to surmise that the elements into which an object is analyzed may not themselves be analyzable and thus unknowable or knowable in a

---

and Coates, *Spiritual Senses*. A detailed study of the concepts from an historical, literary, and textual perspective is limited. Enquiry focuses primarily on questions in Origen's epistemology of theology, philosophy of mind, and philosophy of language.

3. Origen's notions of the limits of ordinary language likely have their origins in Plato's *Theatetus, Parmenides, Cratylus* and *Seventh Letter*. On Origen's knowledge and use of Plato's *dialogues* see Dorival, *L'Apport*, 191–194. On Origen's knowledge and use of philosophical sources see Limone, *Origene*; Castagno, *Origene*, 2000. On his use of Plato's *Cratylus*, see Gasparro, *Eguaglianza*, 313; 316.

4. Aristotle, *Metaphysics*, 1003a33–34. G.E.L Owen translates this ττρός εν formula as "focal meaning", and in his paraphrase, it means that all the "senses (of 'being') have one focus, one common element", or "a central sense", so that "all its senses can be explained in terms of substance and of the sense of 'being' that is appropriate to substance." Owen, *Logic and Metaphysics*, 168–9 and 189. On Origen's use of Aristotle's categories see Berchman, *Categories*, 231–52.

different way.⁵ Three additional arguments from the *Parmenides* also merit attention.⁶ First, is the dismissal of the notion that a form is a thought (*noema*) in our minds (*en psuchais*).⁷ Secondly, in a definition of what a complex whole is something is generally omitted for difficulties ensue as soon as we try to *say* what this something extra is for this something is entirely different from the parts already enumerated.⁸ Thirdly, in the end a complex whole cannot be fully analyzed.⁹ This leads Plato to examine the kinds of occasions when we *speak* of wholes and *naming* what is characteristic of them.¹⁰ Here Plato sets up what the later Wittgenstein notes as one of the misconceptions that triggers the idea that words are labels and that we learn language by associating words with things.¹¹ Rather two words have the same meaning if they have the same use.¹²

Three questions raised in the *Cratylus* come into play here: is language natural or conventional; is there a right name for a thing or not; and is there a one to one correspondence between a name and a thing?¹³ Central to the debate is Protagoras' claim that things do not have a permanent essence of their own and Hermogenes' assent that Protagoras is wrong.¹⁴ As he pursues enquiry into the nature of language he stresses that names are instruments used to indicate the meaning of things in reference to one another and the world:

> ... that which has to be named, has to be named with something ... a name is an instrument ... what do we do when we name ... do we not give information to one another and distinguish things according to their natures? (If) so then a name is an instrument of teaching and distinguishing natures.¹⁵

---

5. Plato, *Theaetetus*, 201d-210d. cf. Annas, 111; Cooper, 144.

6. On the *Parmenides* see Roecklein, 121-158. On unity in the Parmenides see McCabe, *Unity*, 21.

7. Plato, *Parmenides*, 132bc.

8. See Harte, *On Parts and Wholes*, 83; McCabe, *Unity*, 21.

9. See Wood, *Troubling Play*, 2.

10. Plato, *Parmenides*, 157b-159b.

11. Many words are not learned this way and even when they are, this is possible because of background conditions and practices. cf. Wittgenstein, *Philosophical Investigations*, 11, 13.

12. Ketchum, *Names*, 141 and 147.

13. Plato, *Cratylus*, 385ac; 389a-390e.

14. Plato, *Cratylus*, 386cd.

15. Plato, *Cratylus*, 388ac.

Thus it appears in the *Cratylus* that Plato continues to develop a theory of language that bears resemblance to that proposed in the *Parmenides*.[16] The elements of language stand in a one to one relation with the constituents of the world and one cannot properly construct a language unless one knows the relation and meaning of words and things.[17]

A follow up question Plato asks is whether each man has his own private language and gives names to things at his own whim.[18] Here two views of the nature of names and words are distinguished—the imitative and the functional.[19] Arguing against Heraclitus on knowledge and Protagoras on truth, Plato's Socrates argues that if there is a single correct word for each thing, or even a limited number of correct words, it is reasonable to find this correctness in the fact words *imitate* the nature of a thing which enables us to learn what it is.[20] Additionally, words have a function. They give information and so that we can make distinctions about things.[21] Here it does not matter if a word is a good or poor imitation. Rather what is important is that we know what a word *means*.[22]

16. Plato, *Cratylus*, 422a, 424c-425a.

17. Kahn, *Linguistic Relativism*, 167.

18. Plato, *Cratylus*, 385e. cf. Silverman, *Plato's Cratylus*, 28–29.

19. Plato, *Cratylus*, 385ac; 389a-390e. Frege follows up on Plato to stress the *compositionality* of language—that meaning of a sentence is a function of the meaning of its constituents and syntactic structure—arguing that identity holds between *objects* not *names* for objects or that statements are about the world not merely about linguistic signs themselves. In this sense reference does not exhaust a name's semantic function. A name's meaning is whatever it intentionally picks out; a name's sense is its 'mental image' which is inter-subjectively accessible and therefore mind independent; and a terms sense determines its meaning—meaning supervenes sense.

20. The most important point is that Plato rejects: 1) the notion that knowledge of words is prior to and more important than knowledge of things; that indirect knowledge through words would be better than direct knowledge of things; and that 2) ordinary language imitates reality at all. cf. Kahn, *Linguistic Relativism*, 1978, 157.

21. Plato, *Cratylus*, 439b-440d. cf. Schofield, *Denouemont*, 70.

22. Differences between *logismos/dianoia* and *noesis/theoria* notwithstanding, the simplest realism is an outright "Platonism" that attributes a standard model consisting of 'abstract objects' to classical theories expressed in a first-order language (i.e. a language whose quantifiers range over objects not properties). Since Aristotle logicians assume that all propositions have a subject-predicate structure. A shift occurs when Frege proposes this as a grammatical rather than a logical one. Taking his lead from mathematics he employs a distinction between function and argument: $x2 + 1$ is a function expression and any numeral replacing the variable x is the argument for that function. The number yielded is the value of that function for that argument. Frege takes "true" and "false" to be the value and referents of these sentences and defines a concept as a function which has truth value as a value. Thus true and false are considered to be 'abstract objects' akin to Plato's and Plotinus' Forms and numbers or Aristotle's and Plotinus' *Nous*. cf. G. Frege, *Foundations*, 1980.

The problem of intentionality and meaning are also taken up in the *Seventh Letter* where "Plato" distinguishes three ways for gaining knowledge of reality: word, definition, and image.[23] An example includes the case of the word circle, the definition of word "circle" and the circular image drawn or turned on a lathe. An argument unfolds that engages Origen. Conventional or ordinary language does not yield knowledge. Knowledge does not come *through* language or naming alone. Rather it comes through *nous* or a direct insight into the being of an object and then with intentionality naming what an object means.[24] It is the limits of ordinary thought and language and failure of words to adequately map reality of things that raises the question of the limits of self-knowledge and subjectivity.

Summary: This whole schema is set out nicely by Origen when he maps an ideal language of metaphysics appropriate to God and *Logos* in three ways.[25] He proposes an ideal knowledge (*episteme*) that contemplates being as being categorically.[26] He offers an ideal language (*logos*) of contemplative prayer. He maps a theory of contemplative prayer wherein the *concept* and *act* of self-reflection results in acquiring a divine transcendence beyond the limits of ordinary thought, language and its meanings.[27]

III. A God Within and Likeness to God

A.C. Lloyd and Hankey distinguish between two notions of self-knowledge: *conscientia* (consciousness) and *gnothi seauton* (god within) that may help clarify Origen's notions of 'consciousness' and 'interiority.'[28] Self-knowledge in the Platonic tradition is anchored in a *gnothi seauton* that consummates in a *homoiosis theo* (*Theaet* 176ab).[29] The crucial point to

---

23. Following Edelstein, Frede and Burnyeat deny the authenticity of Plato's *Seventh Letter*. What all agree upon, however, is a "faulty argument" in the letter that expresses the failure of words to correspond to the reality of things, Edelstein, *Seventh Letter*; Frede and Burnyeat, *The Pseudo-Platonic Seventh Letter*. For a review of Frede and Burnyeat and defense of the authenticity of *Epistle* 7 see Kahn, *Burnyeat and Frede*. This is the likely "Platonic" 'hook' that catches Origen's and Plotinus' claims concerning the epistemological and metaphysical limits of ordinary language.

24. Ps. Plato, *Seventh Letter*, 341c-345c.

25. Origen, *CJh* I.20-23.

26. Ibid. *PeriArch*. II.1.2 = *Philoc*. 21 = fr. 26 Koe.

27. See Pepin, *Linguistique*, 91-116.

28. Lloyd, *Nosce Tepsium*, 188-200; Hankey, *Knowing*, 1-18.

29. On *homoiosis theo* in Alexandrian Pythagoreanism and Origen, see G. Bostock, 465-78. For where these terms appear in Origen's works, see Castagano; Limone.

note is that subjectivity (self-reflexivity) cannot be translated as consciousness of the kind which après Descartes knows only its own internal mental states in their representational, phenomenalist or constituting activities.[30] Rather the discovery of a *logos* self-knowledge and subjectivity results in an awareness that there is a (qualitative) identity of thinking and being. Indeed, the veracity of subjectivity, subjective states, and self-knowledge rests ultimately not only on being conscious of the *causal* relationship between self or subject and first principles but on recognition of a '*gnothi seauton*' complemented by a desire for '*homoiosis theo*'.

Origen thus understands the notions of 'a god within' and achieving 'likeness unto god' in terms of a strict moral and ascetic way of life where the subject transcends its empirical self and attains a transcendent self in acts of 'soul tuning.'[31] Origen describes man as a musical instrument to emphasize the power of spiritual harmony:[32]

> ... the well-tuned instruments (*scil*. David and his sons) ... were endowed with musical agreement. Such agreement is so effective that when just two who are in accord with the divine music put a request to the Father ... he grants it.[33]

Harmony of soul is only preserved when the Good Shepherd guides the irrational impulses of the soul:[34]

> The soul if found apart from that order and harmony in which it was created by God will ... bear the penalty of its own want of cohesion.[35]

The context for soul's development assumes a fall away from unity into multiplicity and soul's return to a state of unity and harmony:

> Our Saviour wishing to save man, wished to save his body, soul and spirit and so assumed all three. At the time of the Passion they were separated. At the time of the Resurrection they were united.[36]

Both concepts imply a redemption which encompasses the cosmic and subjective in four parsings: first, a fall from unity to multiplicity;

30. Gurtler, *Self and Consciousness*, 113–130.
31. G. Bostock, *Origen*, 474–78.
32. Echoing Philo: cf. *Cher* 128.
33. Origen, *CMt* XIV 1.
34. Origen, *Hier* V.6.
35. Origen, *PArch*, II.10.5.
36. Origen, *Dial* 7. 1–16.

secondly a return to unity and harmony; thirdly, the multiplicity of creation and the fragmentation of soul; and fourthly, a need for macrocosm and microcosm to be brought back into unity and harmony. On the Cross man is sundered and in the Resurrection he is united through Christ who harmonizes the three aspects of his being:

> The three have met together in his name, and he is there among them, because they are consecrated to him, and none of the three, body, soul or spirit are opposed to him.[37]

Ultimately the principle of *homoiosis theo* is related to the issue of correlation between divine and human unity. Clement notes:

> To believe in God . . . .is to become a unit, being indissolubly united in him; and to disbelieve is to be separated, disjointed, and divided.[38]

Clement then maps assimilation to God through Pythagorean imagery.

> That Pythagorean saying was mystically uttered concerning us, that man ought to become one; for the high priest is himself one; God being one in the immutable state of the perpetual flow of good things.[39]

Origen concurs:

> God is one. He is described as one not only in number . . . but also in nature, because he never becomes anything other than himself . . . Similarly the imitator of God is himself one.[40]

He notes further that the man who separates himself from God is a one who becomes many:

> When he sins, the man who is one becomes many . . . divided into parts and fallen from a state of unity.[41]

Origen was well aware that skeptics, for example, not only denied that there could be knowledge of the external world, they also denied the possibility of self-knowledge, subjectivity Moreover they denied the epistemic certainty of a *gnothi seauton* or a *homoiosis theo tout court*. To refute these arguments, he proposes (along with other Aristotelians and Platonists) a

---

37. Origen, *CMt* XIV.3.
38. Clement, *Strom.* IV.157.2.
39. Clement, *Strom.* IV.151.3.
40. Origen, *HReL* I.4.
41. Origen, *Phil.* VIII.3.

hierarchy of increasing self-awareness: beginning from sense-perception and ending in a *gnosis* where the mind discovers not only a transcendent self beyond an empirical self, and an *episteme* beyond the limits of somatic meaning and subjectivity but additionally an ideal language beyond ordinary language—wherein *Logos* speaks us and where divine aseity mixes with human perseity through the *praxis* of contemplative prayer.

How Origen managed to convince himself that *gnothi seauton* was a unified self-reflexivity rather than a binary self-consciousness rests upon giving the thinker the extended sense of participating in a single divine property—x rather than dual intelligible and sensible properties—y/z. He could not make this qualification explicit without relying on the Aristotelian distinction between sensitive and intellective souls. He viewed (self-reflexivity) as participating in a higher *nous poietikos* which leaves 'God within' to serve as the criterion of self-knowledge, subjectivity and meaning. Origen associates mind-as-reason with an 'exterior self' and mind-as-consciousness with an 'interior self' in 'union' with Logos. Once negating its exterior self (*sarx*), the soul finds a higher (*nous-pneuma*), and interior 'gnostic' self, who as a knower of all possible objects of spiritual awareness achieves *homoiosis theo*.[42] If this is plausible, he offers an image of self-consciousness, the subject, subjective states, and self-knowledge as a kind of 'inner sense' tied to the concept of *logos* as actualized self-consciousness which occurs when the self has *gnothi seauton*, thereby experiencing *homoiosis theo*.[43]

> ... the highest good to which all nature is progressing ... is
> That the highest good is to become as far as possible like God
> ... man received the honor of God's image in his first creation
> but the perfection of God's likeness is reserved for him at the consummation.[44]

Within this context six claims come into play: 1) formal and final causality is the condition for the possibility of contemplative prayer; 2) mental states are actively reflective, and not merely passive and representational, when intentionally contemplating divinity; 3) *Logos* is a third thing as (*nous poietikos*) or 'active intellect' which as God's wisdom intentionally receives and directs human thought and speech; 4) the *logikoi*, *epinoiai*, and *theoremata* of the *Logos*-Christ are 'divine intentionalities that

---

42. Plato, *Theaetetus*, 176ab.

43. For Neoplatonic parallels to Origen's appropriation of *gnothi seauton* and *homoiosis theo* see, Schroeder, *Conversion*, 337–59; cf. Alfino, *Non-Propositional Thought*, 273–84.

44. Origen, *De Prin* III.6.1.

illuminate a soul's quest for unity with divinity;⁴⁵ 5) as love, bread and light these divine attributes intentionally direct human thought and speech toward first principles; and 6) the optimum way to 'intentionally' trigger the *logikoi, epinoiai* and *theoremata* of the *Logos*-Christ is through contemplative prayer and exegesis of Scripture.⁴⁶ There are various *epinoiai, logikoi* (*CCels.* II.24) and *theoremata* of Christ (*CJn* II.8) and each denotes *Logos* as he eternally as Christ is in the world.⁴⁷ The amount of wisdom, light, and love souls receive depends on the degree they are capable of attaining self-realization within '*theia aisthesis*.' (*HGn* I.8). Hence the *Logos* appears to different classes of souls according to their capacities. To the sick he will appear as healer, for guidance he appears as shepherd, and his appearance as Wisdom and Life is kept for the perfect for the extent to which the *Logos* is proportionate to their likeness to him.⁴⁸

Summary: Origen proposes a philosophical anthropology partially within Neopythagorean contexts. Recognition of a 'God within' triggers a desire for 'assimilation to God.' In this act a negative-affective displacement occurs where soul empties itself and achieves an *arithmos*—a joining; a putting together whose end is *homoiosis theo*:⁴⁹ The acquisition of *gnothi seauton* and

---

45. On the theological significance of the mind-language predicates of the *Logos*-Christ see, Crouzel *La Connaissance*, 1962; J. Ruis-Camps, *El dinamsimo*, 1970; Wolinski, *Le recour*, 465–94.

46. Origen, *CJn,* II.10. 64–65.

47. Five theses follow from this notion of focal meaning: (1) There is an *episteme* (way of thinking) that contemplates (*theorei*) being as being (*on e on*) complemented by a *phusis* (nature) to which first principles and causes belong necessarily and per se (*kath' auto*). 2) *Episteme* is not merely an internal activity of grasping external objects in inner space, but one of an instance (*nous*) exemplifying its kind, which following Plato he called *Nous*. (3) If the activity of human thinking (*episteme*) is a theorizing (*theorein*) that contemplates ultimate causes and first principles, then human *nous* must join *episteme* in contemplation (*theorei*), for it is *nous* that apprehends the causal structure of reality that *episteme* contemplates. This also means the *episteme* that contemplates the *phusis* of 'being as being' has the character of *noesis* (intellection). (4) Thinking is not an external thinking (of what we know other than ourselves as knowers) via images, representations, calculations, deductions or propositions. It involves no spatial difference, no mediating image or representation, no separation between knower and known, so as to turn self-knowledge into an unreliable knowledge of something else. (5) Thinking *refers*. It is always *of* or *about* something. *Noesis* involves no subject-object distinction; it is a pointing, extending, or an extending toward abstract objects (*prote ousia/aitiai*). *Aisthesis* involves a subject object-distinction; it is a pointing, extending, or an extending toward concrete objects.

48. For the theological and liturgical contexts of prayer in Origen see, Hurtardo, *Christian Worship*.

49. In the case of prayer as *arithmos*, where *ARO*, usually found in the longer form

pursuit of *homoiosis theo* results in: 1) an abandonment of an empirical self, enframed by causal possibility, confined within sense and sensibility, and limited to ordinary language; 2) the acquisition of a transcendent self, open to logical possibility; and 3) access to an ideal language (prayer) that can neither be ordinarily—'said' nor spoken of—but only 'shewn.'[50]

IV. Contemplative Prayer

The passages which map Origen's aesthetics of prayer best are those which emerge in *On Prayer* and the *Commentary on the Song of Songs*.[51] But it is in the *Homilies on Leviticus* that a very blunt claim, in rather cryptic language surfaces, that symbolizes what the contemplative *praxis* of prayer in its *pros hen* sense means:

> I think that he is said to 'chew the cud' who gives his effort to knowledge and meditates on the law of the Lord day and night.[52]

An aesthetics and language of prayer emerges in Origen, where thinking and speaking *of* first principles are contemplatively associated with sights, smells, sounds, tastes, and touch.[53] His epistemology of theology is grounded in a two-fold aesthetics of prayer which proposes not only a visual, tactile and olfactory *noesis* but also a contemplative *praxis*. This *noesis* and *praxis* of sights, smells tastes and touch become logically possible (as an *arithmos*) within prayer by contemplatively applying the categories (of substance, quantity, quality, relation place, and position).[54] Since Origen is keen to synthesize mental and physical property language to attempt a qualitative identity between mental and physical states, contemplative prayer often involves a non-propositional and non-discursive 'naming,' a noetic earthiness, wherein light, smoke, ringing, smoothness, food, drink, and sex "calls" forth an *episteme* of first principles through an aesthetics of prayer.[55]

---

of *ararisko*, the self is structurally joined to Logos and God.

50. See Hadot, *Exercises* where prayer is mapped as a spiritual exercise (*melete*).

51. Origen, *Orat*, I.1; *CCt* Pro. For studies on the spiritual senses in Origen and western Christianity see, Gavirlyuk and Coakley, *Spiritual Senses*.

52. Origen, *HomLev*, VII.6.

53. On the spiritual senses in Origen see, Rahner, *Spiritual Senses*, 1979, 81–103; Origen's concept of contemplative prayer complements well later Platonic theological-epistemological tennts.cf. I. Hadot, *Arts Liberaux*; Addey, *Divination and Theurgy*, 137–142. cf. Berchman, *Rationality and Ritual*, 184–216.

54. For the categories as applied to prayer see, Origen, *DeOr*, VI.I.

55. There is an immense bibliography on early Christian prayer and liturgy but little on prayer as *episteme* or as contemplative *praxis*. For a concise discussion of this issue

In *On Prayer*, Origen distinguishes four types of prayer according to traditional *topoi* of invention: praise, thanksgiving, confession and petition.[56] He also distinguishes between petitionary prayer for earthly and spiritual goods.[57] The highest form of prayer is a contemplative utilization of '*ennoeo ton theon*' and '*theoreo*' formulae. Things worth praying for have a "true and intelligible character (*ton alethinon kai noeton*)[58] for contemplative prayer is not merely many words (*polulogia*), nor merely words (*logoi*), but *Logos* revealing itself to *logos*.

Through contemplative prayer a soul participates within a divine *noesis noeseos*:

> But whoever has contemplated (*ho tetheorekos*)
> The better and more divine things, which are necessary
> To Him, will obtain the objects of His contemplation
> (*on tetheoreke*), for they are known of God, and are
> known to the Father even before they are requested.[59]

This is so:

> For the eyes are lifted up from interest in
> Earthly things . . . they look beyond whatever
> Is begotten and contemplate (*ennoein*)
> God alone, and hold modest converse with
> The one who hears them. Such people afford
> The greatest benefit . . . being transformed into
> The image . . .[60]

Two cases illustrate such participation.

Example I.

In the *arton epiousion* access to divine *noesis noeseos* meets two language criteria—clarity and silence. Origen's clarity is that he not only allegorically combines the image of 'heavenly bread,' or the 'bread of life' with the fourth

---

see McGuckin, 2004. For contextualizing Origen on prayer with later Platonic tropes, see Tiomkin and Dillon, *Neoplatonic Prayer*.

56. For Origen's use of rhetorical *topoi* see O'Cleirigh, *Topoi*, 277–86.
57. See, J.J. O'Meara, *Prayer*, 7.
58. Origen, *Orat*, XIV.17
59. Origen, *Orat*, XXI.2
60. Origen, *Orat*, IX.2.

line of the Lord's Prayer—"on earth as it is in heaven," but he also employs property language, and an early version of the conceivability argument, to show how a soul can contemplatively direct itself towards a union with God and *Logos*.[61] Indeed, mental and physical property languages are conflated, whenever Origen reflects on the mediatory role of Christ—"who as the "Word made flesh, comes to redeem all flesh." Indeed, since *epiousion* is a heavenly food from Jesus himself, who receives his food from the Father alone, without the intervention of any other being, 'living bread' (*epiousion*) is noetic bread, intended for noetic man (*noetos anthropos*) alone.[62] Among its many activities, it nourishes soul's rationality, the highest of which is contemplation (*theoria*).[63] Here he combines the image of a noetic *epiousion* with a mind-language unity that yields a human-divine nourishing:

> We must therefore think here of *ousia* as being the
> Same nature as bread. And just as material bread
> Which is used for the body of him who is being
> nourished enters into his substance, so the living bread
> and that which came down from heaven offered
> to the mind and soul, gives a share of its own proper power
> to him who presents himself to be nourished by it.[64]

Origen introduces a version of the 'conceivability argument' to complement his mixed-property 'language game.' Conceivability is an epistemological notion concerning what can be thought, conceived or imagined that does not involve a contradiction. Since the soul needs to contemplatively pray to attain a unity with first principles, and since the *arton epiousion* offers a way by which a soul can intentionally direct itself toward receiving the *Logos* incarnate as *epiousion*, any soul nourished, sustained and shaped by *Logos* possesses not only divine *ousia*, but a qualitative identity with divinity when soul eats the 'Word made Flesh' as noetic or "Heavenly Bread."[65] In receiving the Eucharist, soul and first principles share noetic properties

---

61. There are many examples of Origen's use of property language and the conceivability argument in his *Commentaries* and *Homilies*. cf. e.g. *Song of Songs*, III.V; XIV.III; *Exodus*, VII.4; *Judges*, VI.2; and *Ezekiel*, XIV.III.2.

62. Mentioned briefly in the Gospels and the *Didache* VIII.2, *epiousios* only generated ample discussion, in the context of contemplative prayer and meditative practice, après Origen: in Athanasius, Gregory of Nyssa, Basil, Cyril of Jerusalem, Chrysostom, Cyril of Alexandria, Damascene, and Theophylact. cf. F.H. Chase, *Lord's Prayer*, 42–58; Metzger, *Historical and Literary Studies*, 64–66.

63. Origen, *Orat*, XIII.213.

64. Origen, *Orat*, XXVII.9.

65. De Lubac, *History and Spirit*, 397–98; 406–16.

in common.[66] To support such a mixed property language game, Origen quotes Jesus' words at Jn10:30 and Jn4:32: "I have meat to eat which you do not know" . . . (and since) . . . "I and the Father are one," the *Logos*-Christ is the meat or nourishment for rational souls.[67] His notion of spiritual or noetic development unites the 'true bread' (Jn6:32) with the 'true man' (Gen1:27).[68] In nuce, Jesus as living bread is the nourishing element of the true man. By 'eating' the *epiousion*, a soul receives Christ, sharing in his divine properties. Indeed, a meeting of the soul in Christ occurs that is for Origen both culinary and reflective:[69]

> Just as the Priest does not eat food in his own house
> Or in any other place but the Holies of Holies, so my
> Savior alone eats bread (. . .) while no one is able (. . .)
> when he eats, he draws me to eat with him. I stand and
> knock (. . .)[70]

The *Logos*-Christ replies:

> The bread I will give is my flesh, which I will give
>   For the life of the soul.[71]

Referencing Ex19:5 (LXX): "you shall be to me a particular people out of all the nations," Origen also plays on the etymological similarities between and *epiousios* and *periousios* (they both derive from *ousia*).[72] He notes that while *epiousios* metaphysically denotes divine and human *ousia* uniting, *periousios* also refers to the ecclesiastical unity of the new Israel or Church (*periousios*) partaking in the *ousia* of God. God's people are made into his *periousios*—"as those abiding with the *ousia* of God and partaking of it. Here Origen emphasizes not only the *I*—but the *We* character—of the *praxis* of contemplative prayer.

---

66. Also known as Leibniz's Law: A and B are identical to one another only if they have all properties in common.
67. Origen, *Orat*, XIII.204.
68. Origen, *Orat*, XXVII.2
69. Origen, *HomEz*, XXVII.2
70. Origen, *Orat*. XIV.III.III.
71. Origen, *Orat*, XXVII.4.
72. In *Orat*, XXVII.7. Working of Mt. 6:11, imagery of alimentary 'contact' with the divine is imaged allegorically and aesthetically by Origen.

Example II.

In a fragment from a letter written by Ambrose to Origen (quoted by Jerome in *Letter 43 to Marcella*), a *praxis* of silent prayer emerges that fills out Origen's aesthetic of prayer. Counter-intuitively, categories common to Scripture and later Platonism are used, not only to define the relationship between first principles, but to map a correct contemplative practice during prayer.

Employing the categories of substance, quantity, quality, time, place, position, relation and modality, a spatio-temporal map of when and how to pray is proposed by Origen. Meals were to be accompanied by reading Scripture. Since the posture of the body images the qualities of the soul in prayer, the best way to pray while eating is to extend hands with eyes elevated. Prayer could be conducted while sitting or lying down, if the person is ill. The corner of the house should serve as a sanctuary for both individual and communal prayer. In commenting on the direction of prayer, Origen advocates facing towards the East while praying which indicates the soul is looking toward the dawn of the true Light, the Sun of justice and salvation.[73] Through the mixture of mental and physical property language, soul acquires a divine 'imagery.'

In nuce, the practice of contemplative prayer brings into consciousness images of light that allow not only for a suspension of ordinary thought and language, but a union of properties between knowing human subject and known divine object as far as that might be possible.[74] The self (in the contemplative practice of prayer) becomes aware of its "iconic" mental and physical character. As soul negates its *sarxic*-self, it affirms its *pneuma-nous* self; by negating its earthly self (*sarx*), it affirms its heavenly self (*pneuma-nous*).[75] In nuce, in the contemplative practice of prayer the choice of divest-

---

73. Light is not a mere metaphor for Origen and Plotinus. It has substantiality. Following Aristotle, they define light as incorporeal *qua* luminous. cf. Beierwaltes, *Metaphysik des Lichtes*, 334–62. cf. Schroeder, *Interior Space*.

74. Acts of prayer are conducted as a noetic-pragmatic thought experiment or an *enhorasis*. Here logical possibility, as distinct from causal possibility, is the key not only to contemplative exegesis and prayer but to the actual practice of prayer. Origen limits logical possibility to a priori and synthetic presuppositions and causal possibility to a posteriori and synthetic propositions. Since a mental state is logically possible if it does not involve a contradiction, Origen considers logically possible scenarios in any *act* of contemplative prayer.

75. The term *eikon* is scriptural (cf. LXX Gen 1:26–27). It symbolizes for Origen an earthly/heavenly; letter/spirit; flesh/spirit dichotomy based on Pauline references. For purposes of this enquiry these distinctions denote ideal/ordinary ontological, epistemic and language distinctions.

ing oneself of the old man while putting on the new man occurs.[76] Once this choice is made a heavenly self (*pneuma-nous*) enters into union with *Logos*.[77] The *praxis* of prayer is epistemically instrumental in this process. It results in a thinking away of corporeality (*sarx*) and thus a breaking up of ordinary propositional and discursive reasoning which leads to a noetic illumination based on a divine presence within (*gnothi seauton*).[78]

Summary: Prayer as a contemplative *praxis* thus really matters.[79] Its techniques achieve an 'affective displacement' that delivers the soul to its *telos*—a vision of first principles when soul intentionally thinks and speaks empirical reality away. Such a fracturing of the operations of propositional and discursive reasoning opens the embodied soul up to the divine within (*gnothi seauton*). Since the conclusions of propositional thought and discursive language, though cogent, cannot be grasped by a noetic soul within grasp of the divine. Contemplative prayer is also about *logos* accessing *Logos*. Prayer permits the flowering of *Logos* in the human *logos*. And since the relationship between thought, language and the world is ineffable, contemplative prayer is a 'showing' not a 'speaking' of divine reality.[80]

Conclusion

Although there is little evidence Origen held doctrines with affinities to Russell's theory of denotation and Wittgenstein's elementary propositions, he nonetheless works with Wittgenstein's semantic distinction between 'saying' and 'showing' where: 1) speech is associated with what should not deontically or propositionally be said; and 2) silence with what can be merely

---

76. Origen frames this shift in a Pauline context contrasting *Gen.* 1:26 with *Gen.* 1:27.

77. Origen's interpretation of relevant passages in the Introduction to the *Song of Songs* and *Gospel of John* suggest a double entrance of the Logos in the soul and the soul in Logos. Abolishment of the icon does not denote suppression of self-identity but a likeness (*homoiosis*) which does not abolish iconicity but perfects it.

78. For later Platonic parallels, see Lloyd, *Nosce Tepsium*, 188–200.

79. There are similar affective patterns in Plotinus. On the affective character of Plotinian thought experiments see, A. Smith, *Porphyry's Place* and Rappe, *Self-Knowledge and Subjectivity*, 259–66.

80. Wittgenstein's distinction between the sayable and unsayable or 'shown,' is prefigured by Origen's distinction between ordinary language (propositional-discursive) and ideal language (non-propositional-discursive), or the languages of the ordinary-sensible and ideal-intelligible worlds which correspond with literal and allegorical exegesis of Scripture. Origen, *CCt*, Preface. On the distinction between 'speaking' and 'showing' see Wittgenstein, 1998Tractatus, 2.021; 2.0211.

shown. Two questions remain: is speech reduced to silence in the *praxis* of prayer; and is whether to be silent or to speak an interpretive choice? Origen dialectically frames silence and speech as not only as interpretive but as soteriological choices. Knowing the divine is not a matter of understanding reality propositionally from the outside in an indirect perceptual, phenomenal, phenomenological or linguistic way, rather—unlike *propositional* or indirect understanding, which involves perception, intuition, and ordinary propositional thought and discursive language—non-propositional and non-discursive reasoning offer a direct *pre-suppositional* grasp or 'touching' of a divine reality through an ideal language—prayer. In the act of contemplative prayer silence is elevated above speech, while in prayerful contemplation, silence is demoted below Speech. Whether Silence is identified with thought and elevated above Speech, (following Clement of Alexandria), or whether Silence is elevated above speech identified with thought, (anticipating Gregory of Nyssa), contemplative prayer involves, as Wittgenstein says, 'remaining silent about that which cannot be said and what Heidegger calls: a "silence about silence" is difficult to apprehend.[81]

---

81. Wittgenstein, *Tractatus*, 6.4.5; 6.53–57; Heidegger, *Being and Time*, 32–34 and 227.

5

Identity, Relation, Modality

I am on the same ancient thoroughfare
that I was on that summer, on that day and hour.

—Pasternak, *Explanation*

Précis

When Kahn draws a distinction between the "existential" and "veridical" significations of the word "being"—one should take notice.[1] His thesis is straightforward: first ordinary speakers use the "existential" notion of "being" which indicates a predicational use of "to be" while the goddess employs a 'veridical' one (telling or expressing the truth); and secondly, no object can be identified that commonly refers or signifies meaning in ordinary and ideal language. The use of names in Eleatic logic and the ordinary language are incommensurable.[2] To illustrate his point a simile is proposed: if the name 'chicken coop' were to be renamed "being"—in its veridical sense as an utterance which articulates 'what is the case' or a 'true state of affairs' about the chicken in the chicken coop and the fox which has entered it— then the utterance "the fox is in the chicken coop" like "being" is an object of *reference* with *meaning*. In the case of "being"—the nature of reality or the

---

1. Kahn, *Being*, 237–61.

2. "The most obvious distinction which seems to us to be ignored in the notion of being is that between existence and predication. The logician will go further, and point out the word 'is' means one thing when it represents the existential quantifier, something else when it represents class inclusion or class membership, something else when it represents identity and so forth. Kahn, *Being*, 246.

structure of the world does not refer to any perishable object—as 'the fox in the chicken coop.' Rather it tells the truth about 'the chicken coop and the fox within it.'[3] Whether Kahn is in error to think that a veridical fox is in the chicken coop, just as a veridical being is an unchanging and eternal object and not a perishable one remains an open question.[4]

This enquiry proposes that Parmenides, Plato, Aristotle and Plotinus regard the identity and relation of thinking and being an *aporia* and use modal logic to parse 'that thinking and being are the same.'[5] Each thinker offers a solution to this puzzle: 1) Parmenides proposes the necessity of a *numerical* identity of thinking and being on the grounds of modal logic; 2) Plato reading Parmenides claims a necessary but *qualitative* identity and *per se* relation of thinking and being; 3) Aristotle critiques Plato's reading of Parmenides to offer a necessary *pros hen numerical* identity and *a se* relation of thinking and being; and 4) Plotinus assesses Aristotle's and Plato's interpretations of Parmenides and parses a necessary *panta hen* qualitative identity and *per se* relation of thinking and being.

I. Horizons

The source and origin of the association of being and knowing is a fragment of Parmenides' poem preserved by Clement of Alexandria.[6] Interpretations of fragment (3) are notoriously contentious but its place in the context of Parmenides' poem is that it is a continuation of fragment (2).[7] Here our nets are cast broadly in an attempt to map the goddesses' argument 'that thinking and being are the same.' It is proposed Parmenides poses the question of 'the identity of thinking and being' in at least five possible ways: 1) as a problem

---

3. Kahn, *Being*, 237.

4. However, Owen's question—is the "being" of the lion the same as the "being" of the mermaid; and his answer—not if "being" is the object *named* rather than the object *meant* remains helpful. If "being" is part of the object and the object is not part of "being"; then the "being" implicit in any object *named* cannot be separated from what that object *means* remains another vexing problem. cf. Owen, *Eleatic Questions*, 16.

5. Necessity and possibility are generally used as modal modifiers. Parmenides and Aristotle are fond of necessity. cf. T.M. Robinson, *Parmenides*, 1975; Palmer, *Parmenides*, 2009; Wedin, *Parmenides*. Plato and Plotinus use the modality of the possibility of knowledge and belief are based on 'what justified true belief is' arising out of the aviary analogy of *Theaetetus*, 197de and 199a. cf. Burnyeat, *Theaetetus of Plato*, 112; Roecklin, *Plato versus Parmenides*, 174-177.

6. Clement, *Stromata*, U440.12.

7. Taran, *Parmenides*, 41-44; Roecklein, *Plato versus Parmenides*, 13-36.

in philosophy of mind;[8] 2) as a problem in philosophy of language;[9] 3) as a problem in physicalism;[10] 4) as a problem in philosophy of time;[11] and 5) as a problem in ontological monism;[12] It is the second and fifth of these options that guide enquiry. Here: 1) what does Parmenides mean by the words 'thinking[13] and being[14] are the same';[15] 2) how many meanings do the

8. Raven, *Pythagoreans and Eleatics*, 23; Cornford, *Plato and Parmenides*, 29,33. Taran, *Parmenides*, 37–38; Mourelatos, *Parmenides*, 1970, 90; Barnes, 155, 163; Owen, 9, 15–16;

9. Kahn, *The Greek Verb 'To Be'*, 700–701, 705; *Linguistic Relativism*, 33–35; *Being in Parmenides and Plato*, 237; Furth, *A Philosophical Hero*, 242–43, 249; Morelatos, *Pre-Socratics*, 48–49; Curd, *Eleatic Monism*, 231–32.

10. Burnet, *Early Greek Philosophy*, 178; Popper, *Parmenides*, 69.

11. Manchester, *Syntax*, 106–135.

12. On the basis of DK <B> 28. 34–41 see, Sedley, *Parmenides and Melissus*, 119–120; Gerson, *Being and Knowing*, 107–108.

13. The primitive form of *noesis* is *nosis, eos*. The words *noos, nous*, and *noein* are most probably derived from a root meaning "to sniff" or "to smell." In Homer *noos* has several meanings, the most significant being a deeper insight itself. *Noos* penetrates behind the surface appearance to its real nature. In the Homeric poems *Noos* and *Noein* are closely related to the sense of vision—*idein* and *gignoskein*. Neither in Homer or the Homeric poems, however, does *noos* and *noein* mean propositional/discursive "reasons" or "reasoning." Nonetheless, each word denotes a thinkable as opposed to a visible disposition. With Xenophanes a different meaning emerges. God is altogether and exclusively *noon* and is different in *noema* from mortal beings. The notion that *noos* is something exceptional becomes prevalent in the generation after Xenophanes, especially with Heraclitus. In Heraclitus, *Noos* is still the noun belonging to *legein*. However, *Noos* is now what few people possess because it has to do with *alethea legein*—to say true things. Saying true things, in turn, is *logos*, and it has as its focus insight into the divine *nomos* that governs everything. By inhaling this *logos* we become *noeroi* or acquire *noos*. Again, with Heraclitus, *noos* is far removed from discursive/propositional "reason" or "reasoning." Associated by Plato with *nous* (intelligence, understanding) noesis is not a thinking of extrinsic properties but a thinking of intrinsic properties/ forms (*eide*). Any thinking via images, representations, calculations, deductions or discursive propositions is not thinking where thinking and being are numerically the same. See, von Fritz, *Nous, Noein*, 23–85.

14. Grammatically *to on* is a particle and can be used either as a noun or as an adjective with a verbal sense. More precisely, when taken as a noun *to on* means that which is, a being; taken as a verbal adjective it designates that by which a being "is" or its being. *To on* can mean Being, beings or both and the interrogation of *on e on* can be of either being-in-general (ontology) or on the ultimate ground of being (theology). Plato designates *to on* as a *metoche/methexis*; or as the Latin grammarians took it—a *participium*. As a grammatical and a philosophical term *to on* participates in being as a noun, as a verb and as a universal. It exists (*einai ti*) as thinking and being are the same.

15. Parmenides, DK, <B> frs. 2–3; 5 and 8.

Greek words identity[16] and relation[17] signify; and 3) how do these questions impact the problem of ontological monism?[18] There are three claimants to the share of being here: 1) thought; 2) time; and 3) the plurality of ordinary empirical objects. All three of these options—that thought and language are claimant to a share of being—is our focus.[19]

The most popular view among Parmenides scholars is that the goddess is a sojourner in elenchus as the self-appointed interpreter of ordinary speech. She asks the ordinary speaker whether the objects we name exist. She suggests not and takes the name "being" to demonstrate her point. Everyone assumes something exists but ordinary speakers do not have an object which fits this description. They may be familiar with the name "being" but only as an indication of the reality of the objects which they are familiar with or have experience of and thus name. When scholars refer to elenchus they indicate a type of questioning and discussion akin to a cross-examination

---

16. Informally, identity is a relation each thing bears to itself: the identity of *a* and *b* implies and is implied by *a* and *b* sharing all their properties. There are two kinds of identity. *Numerical* identity or isomorphic similarity is distinguished from *qualitative* identity or exact similarity. Things are *numerically* identical only if they are one and the same thing (i.e. have the same *intrinsic* properties in common): the Evening Star and the Morning Star are the same. Things are *qualitatively* identical if they look the same (i.e. have the same *extrinsic* properties in common): planets, stars, identical twins and Ford automobiles are quantitatively identical. Objects also differ in respect of their intrinsic and extrinsic properties. A thing's intrinsic or inherent properties never change whereas its extrinsic properties do as in Cambridge properties—a subset of extrinsic properties Cambridge change is non-genuine change. In this sense, an object's *numerical* identity is *a se* or isomorphic identity with no change possible in intrinsic properties while qualitative identity is *per se* or similar identity where change is possible in intrinsic properties via shifts in an object's extrinsic properties.

17. Relation involves special cases of properties. Since relations are indispensable to first philosophy, Platonists and Aristotelians agree on the reality of first principles given that the properties of identity, relation, *aseity* and *perseity* exist. Defenders of individual essences (like Plantinga) following Leibniz argue that the framework of possible worlds enables us to make sense of *de re* modality which identifies the modal status of an objects exemplification of an attribute. Here the *haecceity* of an object provides a complete concept of that object such that it entails for every possible world W and every property P, either the proposition that the object in question has P in W or the proposition that it fails to have P in W. Thus in relational logic the formal properties of special kinds of relations as among first principles can be examined to establish an *episteme* of first principles. Accordingly an omniscient being could infer from the individual essence of an object a complete account of that object in each possible world in which it exists.

18. In contemporary analytic/phenomenological parlance: Parmenides proposes a one-level account of thinking and being; Aristotle at the level of *nous noeseos noesis* maps a single-level model; while Plato's *demiourgos* and *nous* and Plotinus' *nous noeseos noesis* introduce first and second order paradigms: on the principle of prior simplicity Forms and/or the One obviate either a *numerical* identity or unity of thinking and being.

19. For an overview see Roecklein, *Plato versus Parmenides*, 13–36.

where the speaker's attention is called to some contradictory aspect of what he has answered in a previous question. Parmenides' goddess is the champion of this doctrine. She uses it is to reveal the contradictory nature of the opinions ordinary mortals propose.[20] Much contemporary commentary has flowed from the Eleatic elenchus concerning the identity and relation of thinking and being and the distinction between ordinary and ideal language. The ordinary speaker names an object and the goddess tests such claims by asking whether the object named exists. In her language rules, the names of various objects are names for one and the same object—"a being that exists."[21] Her claim raises the two most important questions debated by contemporary scholarship: 1) does the second fragment have a subject;[22] and 2) semantic meanings of the verb 'to be.'[23]

The fundamental question thus is: what is—is?[24] Here Parmenides is sometimes associated by some scholars with ontological monism.[25] Which "monism" Parmenides' ascribes to has been subject for debate since there have been Parmenidean commentators.[26] Plato and Aristotle are inclined to read Parmenides as a "generous monist"—a position which allows for the existence of other abstract entities rather than a "strict monist"—i.e. that only one being exists. They also associate Parmenides with thesis that what is, is one (*hen to hen*); it is not subject to generation and change; and that this 'one' belongs to first philosophy or metaphysics. Aristotle claims under a rubric inherited from Gorgias that Parmenides and Melissus represent an *arche* theory that there is a single, unchanging principle but Parmenides unlike Melissus, who held that everything is a single, i.e. continuous or indivisible and unlimited quantity or extension, he proposed that everything that is, is a substance and one in the sense that the account of the being of everything is (*pros hen*) identical.[27]

---

20. Parmenides, DK <B>, fr. 8.

21. Parmenides, DK <B>. frs. 6 and 7.

22. Burnet, *Early Greek Philosophy*, 179; Popper, *Parmenides*, 69; Hankinson, *Parmenides*, 75–76.

23. G.E.L. Owen, *Eleatic Questions*, 16; Kahn, *The Greek Verb 'To Be,'* 245–65; 260.

24. Parmenides, DK <B> fr. 8.

25. Following, Hankinson, *Parmenides*, 75–77. Semantic concerns also emerge in the *Theaetetus, Parmenides, Cratylus* and *Seventh Letter*.

26. "Monism" does not denote a unique metaphysical position but a family of resemblances ranging from strict monism (the position that only one being exists) to a "generous monism" ranging from numerical to generic substance monism,(the position that there is a single being or a single kind of being).

27. Aristotle, *Physics*, I.2.184b15–16. cf. *Metaphysics*, I.5.986b14–18; *Physics*, I.2.184a25–b12; *De Caelo*, III.1.298b14–24.

What is—is? Parmenides unfolds an argument from logical possibility which begins with an assumption that something exists. Since the shape of what-is is not divided, Parmenides proceeds by applying an Eleatic hypothetical 'for if . . . ' (*ei gar*) which ends in contradiction and the law of the excluded middle to prove that the identity of 'what is' precludes the possibility of any characteristic except just being.[28] To think of anything is to think of it as being. The essential nature of being is the inner necessity that a thing is identical with itself. Thus it cannot come to be or pass away. In nuce, the impossibility of any and all process, change or motion is established by the logical consequences of identity. As for claims of a world of difference and change echoing Parmenides, Plato later notes, is the error of positing two things that need not be identified.[29] To be and not to be are the same thing and not the same and so the articulate world is the consequence of a category mistake. Since nothing but being can be, being is all that is: an uncreated, imperishable, immobile, individual, homogeneous and continuous unit that neither was nor will be but simply is.[30]

Summary: The goddess has two stories to tell: the truth and mortal opinions. The way of opinion is paved with falsity, there is no trust along it and its description is deceitful. The way of truth is about "being" which is eternal and without beginning. In the latter context on the basis of the numerical/qualitative and *a se/per se* distinctions, a discussion of the identity and relation of thinking and being emerges.[31] Keys to validating claims 'that

---

28. Manchester, 2005, 115–117.
29. Parmenides, DK <B> fr. 28 8.51–54. cf. Plato, *Sophist*, 243d-244b.
30. Parmenides, DK <B> fr. 8.3–49. cf. Cherniss, *Characteristics of Pre-Socratic Philosophy*, 19–22.
31. Marked in the following claims:

1. Identity is: a) qualitative or b) numerical.
2. Relation: is a) per se or b) a se.
3. Thinking and Being is:
    a. Numerical and per se (Parmenides and Aristotle).
    b. Qualitative and per se (Plato and Plotinus).
4. Parmenides and Aristotle use versions of the modal argument to argue 'thinking and being are the same.
    a. They take necessary existence as a predicate reasoning that something the non-existence of which is logically impossible is greater than something the non-existence of which is logically possible.
    b. Though it may be odd to predicate the existence of something that already exists, it is logically possible and meaningful to ask of something existing whether its existence is necessary or not, and if so, to judge it more perfect.

thinking and being are the same' here entail use of arguments from logical possibility and modal necessity.³²

II. Eleatic Parsings

We begin by parsing an enigmatic fragment where the Goddess hints of an ontological identity and relation between thinking and being reducible to an ineluctable law of being.³³

> Come now and I will tell you the roads alone for seeking (that) be for thinking for you could not know non-being (for it cannot be accomplished) nor could you declare it, for the same is thinking as well as being (for it is the same to think and to be).³⁴

Parmenides' argument begins with an argument from the necessity of being:

> Necessarily (it) is . . . (and) necessarily (it) is not.

He adds:

> . . . thought is identical to its own object, what-is . . .
> . . . you will not find thinking separate from being.

Parmenides does not deny that thinking happens but since being is all that is, he denies that thinking is separate from being:³⁵

> . . . for it is the same to think and to be . . .

He proceeds next by applying the law of the excluded middle to prove that the identity of 'what is' precludes the possibility of any characteristic

---

c. Parmenides' and Aristotle's arguments are sound because *necessary* existence is a predicate.

5. Parmenides and Plotinus use versions of the modal argument to argue that the One is a unity—*idem*: on grounds that *necessary* existence is a predicate.

32. A state of affairs is logically possible, as distinct from causally possible, and necessary as distinct from contingent if it does not entail a contradiction. cf. Malcolm, 1960, 149. Malcolm, 1960 and Plantinga, *Does God Have a Nature*, 4 use logical possibility in conjunction with modal arguments to prove that God *necessarily* exists.

33. DK <B> frs. 2–3, 5, 8; 28b1.14ff. and 8 13–15 and 30–31. For a summary of the *Stand der Forschung* on different readings of these fragments see Roecklein, *Plato versus Parmenides*, 13–36.

34. DK, <B> frs. 2-3-5. Tr. Peter Manchester.

35. DK <B> fr.2.3–5. On interpretations of this fragment. cf. Roecklin, *Plato versus Parmenides*, 125–162 and Sedley, *Parmenides and Melissus*, 116–123.

save just being. To think of anything is to think of it as being and the nature of being is that a thing is (*numerically*) identical and in an *a se* relation with itself. This allows it neither to come to be nor to pass away as established by the logical consequences of sameness.[36] Since nothing but being can be, Being is all that is, in an increate, imperishable, immobile, indivisible, homogeneous and continuous unit that neither was nor will be but simple is.[37] As for all false notions of a world of difference and change, the Goddess claims the error that underlies them is derivable from the error of positing two things that need not be identified—that to be and not to be are the same thing and not the same.[38] Hence the possibility of motion and multiplicity; of a physical world at all was impugned and its advocates forced to face the logical, epistemological and metaphysical problems of identity and difference, of appearance and reality, of truth and error.

III. Modality

A popular view among Parmenides scholars is that his Goddess is a 'logician.'[39] It is also proposed he is aware of the principles of modal logic and employs them to map the identity and relation of thinking and being. Modal arguments are expressed in a variety of forms—causal, temporal, epistemic and normative in reference to necessity, possibility, contingency, cause and effect, knowledge, belief, time, action, and change. Modality refers to characteristics of entities described by modal propositions.[40] There are different

---

36. DK <B> fr. 28.8. 51–54.
37. DK <B> fr. 28. 8.3–49.
38. DK <B> fr. 28.6.8–9.

39. Taran, *Parmenides*, 37–38; Owen, *Eleatic Questions*, 16; Barnes, *Parmenides*, 162; Mourelatos, *Determinacy and Indeterminacy*, 47–49, 51, 57–58; Kahn, *The Greek verb 'To Be,'* 245–46, 250–51, 260, 700–724. But that she may be a mistress of modal logic has gone largely unnoticed. Modality works from the argument forms of necessity, possibility and impossibility. Modal logic is thus: 1) the study of the logic of the operators 'it is possible that' and 'it is necessary;' 2) its causality is derived logical possibility or with the ideas of modal logic (necessity, possibility, impossibility; 3) its coherence rests on a distinction between two types of proof: valid/sound and invalid/unsound; 4) the first (modal/sound) proof takes necessary existence as a predicate when it reasons that something the nonexistence of which is logically impossible is greater than something the nonexistence of which is logically possible; 5) while the second (predicative/unsound) argument takes existence as a predicate reasoning that something is greater if it exists than if it does not exist.

40. Eleatic and later Stoic modal logic is not a logic of modal propositions of the type "it is possible that it is day,". Rather their modal theory was about non-modalized propositions like "it is day" insofar as they are possible," necessary and so forth. cf. Bobzien, *Stoics*, 117.

classifications of modalities but the one favored by the Goddess is *alethic* modality which includes four possible ways a proposition may be true or false: necessity, contingency, possibility and impossibility. These modalities and their logical interconnectedness are characterized as follows: 1) a proposition which is true but possibly false is contingently true (e.g. that Aristotle taught Alexander); 2) one that is true and not-possibly false is necessarily true (e.g. that red things are colored); 3) one that is false but possibly true is contingently false (e.g. that there are no tigers); and 4) one that is false and not possibly true is necessarily false e.g. that $7+5=14$).[41]

It is proposed Parmenides employs arguments from necessity and possibility with focus on "necessary existence." It is necessary to assume the identity of thinking and being and that such identity is not dependent on any contingent feature of the world.[42]

If we grant this plausible assumption, the Goddess presents the argument in the following way:

1. Being is either necessary or logically impossible.

2. It is not impossible for being to exist (i.e. there is no contradiction involved in assuming being exists).

∾ ∾ ∾

Therefore: Being exists necessarily.

It appears Parmenides' argument applies only to entities that have a maximum (of properties) in this case "that (it) is. If this line of reasoning is correct it is false to claim the existence of a non-existent 'That (it) is not to be."

The Goddess tells us there are two ways of enquiry and warns Parmenides to take the first not the second way:[43]

> that (it) is and that (it) is not to be ...
> and that (it) is not and that (it) must not be.[44]

The Goddess argues next it is necessary to say and think "what is" (*to eon*) not "what is not" (*to me on*) on three grounds: 1) reliance on the things of sensation or "what not is," possesses possibility not necessity; 2) what is to

---

41. For analysis of modal argument forms in Parmenides, see Robinson, *Theaetetus*, 623–633; Hansen, *Parmenides*, 1–10.

42. Following Robinson, *Theatetus*, 1975; Palmer, *Hermeneutics*, 2009; Wedin 2014.

43. Parmenides, DK <B> fr. 2.6–8.

44. Parmenides, DK <B> fr. 2.3 and 2.5.

be (or to exist) must be across times for 3) the attributes of "what is" belong to perfection or everlasting existence, immutability, internal invariances of wholeness, uniformity and shape.[45] The Goddesses' line of reasoning here is suppose something does not exist. How then would it be possible for non-existence to exist or come into existence when there is nothing for it to come into existence from?[46] If it doesn't necessarily exist now, it couldn't possibly exist and could never come into existence:

> For what birth will you seek for it? How and
> From where did it grow?[47]

Upping the ante Parmenides claims it is impossible to think or talk about what does not exist for:

> Thinking and the thought that it is are
> the same. For not without what is, in
> which it is expressed, will you find thinking.[48]

If Parmenides' thinking of 'something' is to say there is an object of thought—a necessary existing entity—being—which has the feature of being thought and spoken about;[49] then thinking is thinking of or speaking about something that *necessarily* exists. The basic calculus of reasoning is:[50]

Every P is necessarily Q.

If we grant this plausible assumption, we can present the argument form in the following way:

a. S is thinking > S is thinking of something. *premise*

b. S is thinking of something > there is something S is thinking of   *premise*

c. S is thinking of what does not exist > there is nothing S is thinking of   *premise*

---

45. Parmenides, DK <B> fr. 6.

46. Robinson, *Theatetus*, 1975, 627–633. cf. Hansen, *Parmenides*, 7-8; Also see Wedin, *Parmenides*.

47. Parmenides, DK <B> fr. 8.

48. Parmenides, DK <B> fr. 8. Lines 34–35.

49. Plato interpreted Parmenides similarly (e) where what is at issue is "saying," or "talking about," rather than thinking (Plato, *Sophist* 237c).

50. These inferential intuitions take several forms such as necessity implies truth; truth does not imply necessity; and ideas about connections between different modal notions such as necessity of some proposition *phi* being equivalent to impossibility that not *phi*.

d. There is nothing S is thinking of > S is thinking nothing   *from (b) by contraposition*

e. S is thinking of nothing > S is not thinking   *from (a) by contraposition*

f. S is thinking of what does not exist > S is not thinking   *from (c), (d), and (e) by hypothetical syllogism*

In each case *necessary* existence is taken as a predicate with the reasoning that something the existence of which is logically impossible (not-being) is greater than something the non-existence of which is logically possible (being). Though it may be odd to predicate the existence of something that already exists, it is logically possible and meaningful to ask of something existing whether its existence is *necessary* or not, and if so, to judge which is more perfect (non-being or being). Since Parmenides does not deny that thinking happens and since being is all there is, thinking is *necessarily* inseparable from being: every P is necessarily Q. Since that which thinks is, and that what is thinks, the *numerical* identity of thinking and being and the relation of thinking and being is *a se*.

Summary: With this Eleatic argument in place, Plato, Aristotle and Plotinus offer versions of the modal argument 'that thinking and being are the same.' Each of their arguments are valid and sound because *necessary* existence is a predicate of being, the Form of the Good, *Nous* or 'thought as thought thinking itself' and the One for *necessary* existence or the conditions for necessary existence is a predicate of each. Differences arise nonetheless. While Aristotle argues thinking and being are *numerically* the same and *a se* relational; Plato and Plotinus claim a *qualitative* identity of 'thinking and being' and a *per se* relation of thinking to the Forms and the Forms to the One.

III. Unity, Plurality and Necessity

Interpretations of Plato's reading of Parmenides are again exceedingly contentious but his rejection of a radically monistic interpretation of being—that it cannot be known or thought about at all are the likely origin of Plato's reading of Parmenides.[51] The first hypothesis of the *Parmenides* is central to understanding how Plato tacks.[52] Since the theory of Forms is

---

51. Plato, *Parmenides*, 142a; *Sophist*, 244b-245e. Gerson summarizes in *Being and Knowing*, 107–112.

52. Cherniss and Guthrie claim that the subject of criticism is the first hypothesis

what is subject to criticism in hypothesis I of the *Parmenides*;[53] a critique of a radically monistic interpretation of the unity of one being and the *identity* and *relation* of thinking and being emerges.[54] Here Plato's theories of identity, predication and relational statements play a significant role in his reading of Parmenides.[55]

Plato begins by assessing what unity means in the first hypothesis. He begins by enumerating a list of the parts or attributes of being proposed by Parmenides. These include circularity, perfection, sameness, limit and being. Plato notes that an attempt at a unity of thinking and being in line with such attributes fails. In the wake of this critique Parmenides is forced to admit that parts cannot be reconciled with a partless being which encompasses the identity of thinking and being:

> Well then, said Parmenides, if there is a one, of course the one will not be many. Consequently, it cannot have any parts or be a whole. For part is part of a whole, and a whole that from which no part is missing; so whether you speak of it as a 'whole' or as 'having parts' in either case the one would be many and not-one; but it is to be one and not many. Therefore, if the one is to be, it will not be a whole or having parts.[56]

Plato's argument is straight-forward. If being is to be accorded some dignity among real things, it will have to be as a distinct nature for unity does not indicate being, and being does not indicate unity. Such a move occurs in the second hypothesis of the *Parmenides* where unity is conceded as the qualification for any object that can be referenced or talked about.

> When you use any word, you use it to stand for something. You can use it once or many times but in either case you are speaking of the thing whose name it is. However many times you utter the word, you must always mean the same thing. Now, different is a word that stands for something; so when you say it, whether once or many times, you are using it to stand for, or naming that thing whose name it is. Hence when we say the others are

and the Eleatic view of 'one Being.' Cherniss, *Parmenides*, 125–130; Guthrie, *Later Plato*, 53.

53. See, Wood, *Troubling Play*, 2; Turnball, *Parmenides*, 19; Runciman, *Epistemology*, 100–101; Ryle, *Parmenides*, 130;

54. See, Harte, *Plato*, 83; McCabe, *Unity*, 21. cf. Cornford, *Plato and Parmenides*, 112–114; Schofield, *Antinomies*, 147–148.

55. See Gonzalez, *Plato's Forms*, 31–84. esp. 51–55. Also see Vlastos, Self-Predication, 74–78; Malcolm, *Semantics and Self Predication*, 286–94; Mates, *Identity and Predication*, 211–29; and Matthen, *Relational Statements*, 90–100..

56. Plato, *Parmenides*, 137cd.

IDENTITY, RELATION, MODALITY 99

different from the one, and the one is different from others, we use the word different twice, but nevertheless we use it always to refer to just that character whose name it is.[57]

As soon as this is asserted, Parmenides' thesis is fated for oblivion. Unity does not admit plurality. Here Parmenides is lead to various incompatible conclusions that prove useful for Plato. Although Parmenides offers a list of attributes for unity including circularity, perfection, sameness with itself, limit and being, it immediately becomes clear that unity cannot lay claim to any of these attributes. Unity would have to be a "many" to accommodate his definition. Here Plato's ups the ante claiming: 1) unity can have no cause other than the nature of unity itself; and 2) nor can it one other property into itself since that would cause it to be other than itself, or many (137cd).

Plato focuses his attack by examining Parmenides' claim that the one has the properties of limit, rest, shape, no parts, sameness, equality, place and timelessness.[58] Here Parmenides is forced to admit that the "one has neither beginning nor end and is without limits." He also admits that "if the one had either a straight or a round shape, it would have parts and so be many and since it has no parts, it is neither straight nor round." (138a). He eventually concedes the one cannot be either (a) in another, or (b) in itself (138a). "It could not be anywhere in anything" (138d) and what is never in the same place or condition is not at rest or stationary (139a). Finally, when forced to address sameness, equality and timelessness, he concludes: 1) the character of unity is one thing, sameness another (139c); 2) the nature of the one is not equal to anything neither to another or itself results in the one being either (a) equal or (b) unequal either to itself or to another (140b); and 3) the one cannot have any relation to time at all, not even to the present (141de).

Plato distinguishes two kinds of necessity: a preeminent form of necessity that stands in contrast to contingency; and a notion of necessity associated with a determinism that links *ananke* (necessity) with *heimarmene* (fate). It is the former necessity that Plato (Aristotle and Plotinus) consider metaphysically significant. Being is necessary which could be no other than that which owes its existence only to itself. In the case of the Forms (Intellect and the One) this necessity is understood: 1) as self-causation; and 2) that which exists of itself. Are thinking and being necessarily the same?

Yes—but in order to maintain every P is necessarily Q—two arguments are suggested which transform Parmenides' simple *a se: to einai*

---

57. Plato, *Parmenides*, 147d.
58. Parmenides, <DK> B. fr. 8.1–51.

into a complex *per se*: *ta onta* or *ousiai*: 1) unity, which encompasses "all things," is really a "many" based on 2) the argument: that since unity can have no cause other than the nature of unity, and since the nature of unity cannot admit one other thing into itself, for that would cause it to be other than itself or many all things must be "many not one." The inference Parmenides is forced to draw is that his alleged "seamless one" is "many." Indeed, "it cannot even be one for then it would be a thing that is and has being" (142a). In the end, the first hypothesis is a false phantom and claims to the *numerical* identity and an *a se* relation of thinking and being involves contradiction and thus is false.

Summary: The key moment in Plato's reading of Parmenides resonates when the stranger from Elea expounds the two basic modes of being as motion and rest. These are two mutually exclusive modes of being which appear to completely exhaust the possibilities of what being is. If one does not wish to conceive of rest, one must conceive of motion, and vice versa. There appears to be no possibility whatsoever of open questioning. It is not the intention of the Eleatic stranger to understand being as a universal genus which differentiates itself into two aspects of Being. What Plato has in mind is in speaking about being a differentiation is implicit that suggests not only identity and relation but otherness and difference are essential to being. These aspects far from being mutually exclusive are mutually determining. Whatever is identical with itself is thereby different from anything else. Insofar as it is what it is, it is not everything else. Being and Non-Being are inextricably intertwined.

IV. Unity, Plurality and the Forms

Plato's next move is to reformulate Parmenides' claim that 'thinking and being are the same' in the context of his theory of Forms. He begins by claiming "Being" is not an object. Rather it is part of any object that is real, has existence and where one name corresponds to one property alone. A problem immediately surfaces. In the first hypothesis of the second part of the *Parmenides* (142a), and in the *Sophist* (243b-245e) Plato claims Parmenides' unity cannot encompass "being" for *to on/ousia* is complex. Moreover, whatever exists is distinct from the existence it has.[59] This applies not only to that which exists in the world of *genesis* but also to the distinction between an *arche* of *ousia* and complex *ousia* itself. If *ousia* is complex, it cannot be the source of being for all things. Complexity presupposes

---

59. Plato, *Sophist*. 245d4–6.

IDENTITY, RELATION, MODALITY   101

simplicity which is why the *arche* of all must be beyond *ousia*. Plato also argues that the *arche* of *ousia* is the *arche* of knowability (*to gignoskesthai*) itself in two tropes. Firstly, all that is knowable, even *ousia* itself and the *Ideai* require a simple *arche* beyond each which is the *Idea tou agathou*, the Form of the Good.[60] Secondly, since an *arche* of *ousia* beyond *ousia* exists, identified with the *Idea tou agathou* and the *anupotheton arche* of Republic 509ab, all things again must be "many not one."[61]

Finally, in *Theatetus* (188d-189b) Plato suggests that Parmenides' claim that 'thinking and being are the same' ultimately rests on a *per se* analogy, not an *a se* identity, between believing, seeing, and touching.[62] Just as touching what is not is touching anything, which is not touching at all, so false belief (believing what is not) does believe nothing, which does not believe at all. In the *Sophist* (236d-237e) he claims that speaking may be understood in the same way—as *per se* contact with an object. We give a name to something by pointing to it and uttering the name. If we point at nothing, we are naming nothing, and just utter empty noise. Hence, speaking of what is not is not really speaking of any-thing at all.[63]

Plato, a water-diviner pointing out the metaphysical traps of his predecessors, raises two final objections that undercut Parmenides' version of the claim that thinking and being are the same. Firstly, he asks s the identity of thinking and being *numerical* or *qualitative*; and secondly, is the relation of thinking to being of *a se* or *per se*? Behind such questions lie an attempt to construct a chain of *qualitative/per se* identity arguments grounded in his theory of Forms.

Plato proposes his *qualitative/per se* option on five grounds. First in the *Parmenides* (183e-184a) he challenges Parmenides' notion of a divisionless unity. In its place he proposes an argument from a variety of distinct natures which reconciles the divisionless and partlessness of being.[64] Secondly, he combines the knowledge argument from the *Phaedo* (79a6-7) and the meaning argument from the *Sophist* (248a6-7) to underscore that all thinking is necessarily a duality of thinking and of object of thought.[65] Since all thought

60. Plato, *Republic*. 509b6-10.

61. Plato, *Rep.* 509b6 refers to that which is *noeton* (cf. 509d4) which are the Forms, which have their *arche* in the Form of the Good.

62. Plato, *Theatetus*. 188d-189b.

63. Plato, *Sophist*. 236d-237e.

64. Hintikka suggests that Plato's main proofs for the existence of Forms are forged out of the same materials as Parmenides in that both affirm that 'one can only think of what is.' cf. Hintikka, *Parmenides*, 1980, 17.

65. This knowledge argument, outlined in the *Phaedo* (79a6-7) complemented by the meaning argument in the *Sophist* (248a6ff.) show that *to pantelos on* includes

including self-thought is constituted through a duality of act and of the object of thinking, and the object as constitutive of thought, exists prior to thought as well as in thought, thinking implies plurality not unity.[66] Thirdly, he proposes another way in which thinking shows itself to be composite is in the multiplicity that characterizes any object of thought. Using the example of the demiurgic intellect at *Timaeus* (30d1-2; 37a1-2) he shows that it thinks manifold Forms.[67] Fourthly, he notes that all thinking implies deficiency. Since it reaches toward its objects, again being cannot be absolutely simple, ultimate and unitary as Parmenides proposes.

Summary: Plato has undermined Parmenides' assertion of the *numerical* unity of thinking and being and thus the possibility of a 'strict' Eleatic *a se* monism.[68] The identity of thinking and being is *qualitative* and the relation of thinking to being is *per se*. It is this reading of Parmenides as a 'generous monist' that a bridge to Aristotle's reading of Parmenides emerges.[69]

V. A Peripatetic Way

Aristotle claims Parmenides holds a theory of formal unity: "what is" is one with respect to the account of its being.[70] But a plural theory of "what is" is in respect to perception.[71] Alexander quoting Theophrastus also argues that Parmenides supposed that: "what is", is one in account but plural in respect to perception."[72] Thus does Parmenides claim in a strong sense that what is, is one but it is also many in and for perception. Does he hold an "aspectual" view of the relation between the two phases of the Goddesses' revelation?[73] Aristotle, Theophrastus and Alexander

---

nous—a plurality. Thus soul and life reduces unity to a mental state or activity of knowledge (*episteme*) wherein *nous* identifies *per se* with the Forms and the *Idea tou agathou*.

66. At *Republic* (510a9) it is clear that the *tois gignoskomenois* of (509b6) refers a knower and that which is known (*to noeton*)—the Demiurge and the Forms.

67. Although Pepin and Archer-Hind interpret *Tim.* 37a1 *ton noeton aei te onton* as indicating the identity of the Demiurge with the Forms. Taylor thought little of attempts to turn Plato into an idealist. cf. Taylor, *Plato*, 176.

68. Following, Roecklein, 136-150.

69. For an epitome of Aristotle's reading of Plato reading Parmenides see Gerson, *Being and Knowing*, 110-112.

70. Aristotle, *Metaphysics*, I.5.986b18-19; 986b27-31..

71. Aristotle, *Metaphysics*, I.5. 986b27-34.

72. Alexander, *in Metaphysics*, 31-7-16. cf. Simplicius, *in Ph.* 25.15 = DL 9.21-22.

73. In support of Aristotle's reading of Parmenides see Owens, *Doctrine of Being*, 378-95 and Finkelberg, *Being*, 233-48.

clearly think so and their readings fit rather well a Peripatetic version of what Parmenides means by being *qua* being. Such as revision begins with Aristotle's focal theory of meaning.

At the beginning of *Metaphysics* Γ Aristotle claims that there is a science (*episteme*) which is concerned with being *qua* being.

> There is knowledge (*episteme*) that contemplates (*theorei*) being as being (*on e on*) and that which belongs to it per se (*kath auto*).[74]

Being is constituted within *episteme*, in accordance with the logic proper to being. G.E.L Owen translates this πρός εν formula as "focal meaning", and in his paraphrase, it means that all the "senses (of 'being') have one focus, one common element", or "a central sense", so that "all its senses can be explained in terms of substance and of the sense of 'being' that is appropriate to substance."[75] According to Owen, "focal meaning" is new and revolutionary in *Metaphysics Gamma*, and introduces a "new treatment of *to on* and other cognate expressions" expressed in the following two theses:[76]

1. "Focal meaning" contradicts and replaces Aristotle's earlier view in the *Organon, EE* and others that beings differ in different categories, and 'being' has various distinct senses.

2. "Focal meaning" makes it possible for Aristotle to establish a universal science of being qua being in *Meta.* Γ which contradicts and replaces his earlier view because beings differ, a universal science of being is impossible.

3. "Focal meaning" makes it possible to propose two *pros hen* notions of identity and relation: *per se* (qualitative) and *a se* (numerical).

Two theses concerning identity and relation follow:

4. While Plato proposes a *qualitative* identity of thinking and being and a *per se* relation of thought thinking being and the Forms.

5. Aristotle offers a *numerical* identity of thinking and being and an *a se* relation of thought thinking itself (*noeseos noesis*).

---

74. Aristotle, *Metaphysics*, I.1 981b29-928a1-3.

75. Owen, *Logic and Metaphysics*, 168-9,189.

76 Owen, *Logic and Metaphysics*, 163-90. The quotations are from 168-69 and 189; 1965, 69-75; *Aristotle*, 1966, 125-50.

VI. Modality: The Identity of Thinking and Being Revisited

Aristotle was well acquainted with modal logic.[77] Forms of argument that work with the ideas of modal logic include necessity, possibility and impossibility.[78] Explicitly, like Parmenides his modal expressions show a great variety: causal, temporal epistemic and normative and occur in reference to necessity, possibility, contingency, cause and effect, knowledge, belief, time, action, and change.[79] He uses a calculus of reasoning with modal syllogistic forms like: Every P is necessarily Q. He also claims that the optimal way to determine that something is possible is to show that actuality entails possibility. Here, for example, Aristotle takes necessary existence as a predicate, and reasoning that something the existence of which is logically impossible (not-being) is greater than something the non-existence of which is logically possible (being), yields the conclusion: Intellect exists necessarily. The form of his modal argument is:

1. Intellect's existence is either necessary or logically impossible.

2. It is not impossible for Intellect to exist *a se* (i.e., there is no contradiction in assuming Intellect exists).

---

77. At *De Interpretatione*, XXI.34a-37 Aristotle distinguishes modal judgments 'A is B,' 'A must be B,' and 'A may be B.' The two latter are reduced to the forms 'That A is B' is necessary,' 'That A is B is possible,' and both are coordinated with the form 'that A is B is true.' cf. *De Interpretatione*, XXI.26b-33; XXII.8a-13.. The possible must be something that involves no impossible consequence and also includes something whose contrary is not necessarily false. cf. *Prior Analytics*, XXXII.18a-20. Modal and intentional contexts thus are instances of intensional contexts. Intentional verbs that generate intensional contexts include 'think', know', 'doubt', and 'will.'

78. Modal logic is: 1) the study of the logic of the operators 'it is possible that' and 'it is necessary;' 2) its causality is derived logical possibility or with the ideas of modal logic (necessity, possibility, impossibility; 3) its coherence rests on a distinction between two types of proof: valid/sound and invalid/unsound; 4) the first (modal/sound) proof takes necessary existence as a predicate when it reasons that something the nonexistence of which is logically impossible is greater than something the nonexistence of which is logically possible; 5) while the second (predicative/unsound) argument takes existence as a predicate reasoning that something is greater if it exists than if it does not exist.

79. These inferential intuitions take several forms such as necessity implies truth; truth does not imply necessity; and ideas about connections between different modal notions such as necessity of some proposition *phi* being equivalent to impossibility that not *phi*.

Intellect exists necessarily.

On this basis, Aristotle associates *nous/ousia* with the highest form of thinking as *noesis via energeia* (*Met.* VI.1072b8). *Nous* is identical with pure activity (*energeia*) which is *noesis*. Since this pure activity of thinking is also the highest being—an *a se Nous* when it thinks itself is *numerically* identical with being.

> And thought thinks itself through participation in the object of thought, for an object of thought it becomes (by the act of) apprehension and thinking, so that they are the same: thought and the object of thought, i.e. being, is thought. And it actually functions (when it) possesses (this object).[80]

While there is a distinction between *noesis noeseos*, there is no gap between *act* and *concept*, and so no potentiality. Intellect is thought thinking itself as self-reflexive thinking or thought being thought and being thought eternally without interruption. In nuce, with nous noeseos we witness a *numerical* identity of thought and being and an *a se* relation of thought to being. A parsing of the identity of thinking and being follows: first, if the object of thinking and being is the identity of self-contemplation, then *noesis* is a kind of *numerical* self-contemplation; and secondly, if *Nous* is in a *a se* relation to itself, thinking being is an act of *noesis noeseos noesis* itself.[81]

With Aristotle a *pros hen* aseity argument begins to emerge—from the term *aseitas* derived from the prepositional phrase *ens a se*—where an Intellect/Being *ens a se* is postulated[82]—completely self-sufficient and independent *a se*—but in a *per se* relation with other beings.[83] As an *ens a se*, *Nous* is 'from itself;' not *ens ex se* 'out of itself.' It does not depend on any necessary property *a se* or contingent property *per se*. Its identity, just to itself, is *numerical* not *qualitative*, and if there are changes to this *a se*

---

80. Aristotle, *Metaphysics*, XII.9.1072b20-23

81. Analysis of essence and essential predication, with focus on the distinction between *what* an object is and *how* it is, is crucial. Indeed, a distinction between *kath hauto* or *per se* predications (*what* universals) and *kata sumbebekos* or *per accidens* predications (*how* universals). The first displays what necessary to an object; the second what is not.

82 A primary being *ens a se* is the greatest conceivable being. If a primary being *ens a se* depended upon itself, it would cause itself to exist which is a logical contradiction. Thus *per se* relations are Cambridge properties where Intellect and the One exhibit reciprocal independence *a se*. cf. Wolterstorff, *On Universals*, 263–65.

83. Aristotle, *Categories*, XII. 14a30-45; 14b11-24; Plotinus, VI.8.8.12-15, 11.32. cf. O'Meara, *Plotinus*, 68–71; Bussanich, *Plotinus' Metaphysics*, 38–65.

identity, it is a mere Cambridge change—a claim that emerges again in different forms in Plotinus, Leibniz and Plantinga[84]

Summary: The question of how knowing is identical with being is fundamental. Is the identity of thinking and being *numerical* or *qualitative*? Is the relation of thinking to being *a se* or *per se*? Aristotle affirms the *numerical* and *a se* options. *Nous* is a self-sufficient *arche/principium* of all reality; it is a mind a mind whose identity is *numerically* a unitary whole. Its existence is necessary (*a se*) and not contingent (*per se*). Within a *pros hen* context *Nous* is in an *a se* relation to itself and in a *per se* relation with other minds and beings.[85]

VII. Thinking about Forms Revisited

In these contexts, what focuses our attention is Aristotle's critique of Plato's theory of Forms and his "alleged" confusion of the particular and the universal in reified universals:[86]

> But those who speak of the Forms in one respect speak correctly in separating the Forms, if they are substances; but in another sense incorrectly, because they say the one in (*epi*) many is a Form.[87]

We also find the following:

> And to that they (the Forms) are patterns and the other things share them is to use empty words and poetical metaphors.[88]

Three questions generate Aristotle's critique: 1) are Forms universals; 2) are Forms preconditions for universal predication; and 2) are Forms the basis for an application of predicate terms at all? Three answers emerge from his critique: 3) since Plato's Forms are *ousiai*, they are separate in the way substances in his view are separate and cannot be universals; 4) since Forms are separate substances and individual universals existing on their own and not in anything else, they cannot be common to or in a plurality of things and thus cannot be universals; and 5) since Forms are merely properties considered in isolation, they are not capable of sustaining universal predication in any

---

84. Berchman, *Ultimate Presuppositions*, 329–48.
85. Following Schroeder, *Aseity*, 303–13.
86. Following Gerson, *Being and Knowing*, 107–9.
87. Aristotle, *Metaphysics*, VII.15. 1040b28–30.
88. Aristotle, *Metaphysics*, I.9. 991a20–22.

meaningful sense at all. In nuce, Aristotle's theory of substances (*ousiai*) is incommensurable with a Platonic theory of Forms (*eide; ideai*).

Next Aristotle makes a bold move that requires us to leave aside Platonic habits of thought. However difficult it may be for us to grasp what the perfect knowledge of divine intellect might be like there is in Aristotle's view no gap between thinking and being. *Nous* as *ousia* exhibits *numerical* identity and *a se* relation as *to ti ein einai* (what it is to be) whereas Plato's claims necessitate a *qualitative* identity of *ousia* and Forms and a *per se* dependence of *Nous* in relation to Forms.[89]

Après Aristotle, a *per se* demotion of Universals and Forms follows that led later Platonists and Aristotelians to consider whether a *numerical/a se* identity applies to Forms (intelligibles) and Universals (sensibles) at all. This led later Platonists to consider there was something unsatisfactory with positing Forms *a se*. Their solution was to place Forms within divine intellect. Since the existence of *Nous a se* does not depend on any contingent property *per se*; and the existence of *per se* properties depends on the *a se* existence of *Nous*; a Neo-Aristotelian-Neoplatonic "hierarchy" of forms and universals belonging to different levels of reality emerges where forms are intelligible and universals are sensible.[90] Both reformulations preserve a theory of Forms in two novel ways. First, Forms do not have to withstand judgment as a theory of universals. Secondly; Forms account for the ontological preconditions of universal predication for the application of predicate terms.[91] Perhaps here, in light of the debate on whether or not Platonic ideas are universals, Gerson is correct to argue that Aristotle's universals are not Plato's Forms[92] and

---

89. Aristotle's solution is universals do not replace Forms (Platonic Ideas are universal properties); nor are Forms hypostasized universals, as if Plato offered *ante rem* as opposed to Aristotle's post *rem* universals. Moreover, since any dependence of things on the Forms does not fit his account of causation, any such notion dependence is incoherent. This is doubly so because if the Forms are universals (in his sense), substances (in his sense), and objects that cannot be both universals and substances (in his sense)—since a universal is common and a substance individual.

90. Distinctions among mental acts, their intentional contents, the objects represented or "intended" in these mental acts, and the states (of intellect, perception, sensation, volition, and belief) which underlie them presupposes—are neither the activity of thinking Forms, nor are they bodily actions or behavioral dispositions, but a state or activity of thinking (*noesis*)—or in analytic parlance—a mental occurrence alone.

91. Since properties are a kind of universal, the ontological status of universals has been applied to properties in three ways: 1) nominalism—since only particulars exist either properties do not exist or are reducible to collections of particulars; 2) conceptualism—properties exist but are dependent on the mind; realism- properties exist independently of the mind either *in rebus*, it has real spatio-temporal instances or *ante rem*, a property can exist even if it has no real spatio-temporal instances.

92. Gerson, *Aristotle and Other Platonists*, 209–41.

Wolterstorff that Plato's Forms are not hypostasized universals—as *ante rem* universals distinct from *post rem* universals.[93]

VIII. Another Turn in the Way

Plotinus' knows his Parmenides well. The key passage is:

> And Parmenides ... identified Being and Intellect and that it was not among things perceived by the senses that he placed Being, when he said "Thinking and Being are the same." (*En.* V.1.8.15–18)[94]

He appropriates Plato's and Aristotle's formulations of the relation of being and intellect.[95] Of particular interest is his use of Aristotle's doctrine of actuality (energeia) as an eternally *a se* active intellect underlying an intermittent *per se* passive intellect in a novel way.[96] He argues that the intelligibles are not outside Intellect.[97]

> All will be at the same time one: intellect, intellection, the object of intellection. If therefore its (i.e. Intellect's) is the object of intellection, and this object is (intellect), intellect will then itself think. For it will think with intellection, which it is. So in both respects it will think itself, in so far as the intellection is itself, and in so far as the object of intellection is itself, which it thinks with intellection, which is itself.[98]

Behind this claim lies Plotinus' theory of the causality of intelligible realities as formulated in (V.4). In these chapters an issue previously formulated in (V.9.14 and IV.8.6) of knowing how all things including *Nous* derive from the One is formulated.[99] Even though One, Mind, and Soul are distinct and hierarchically arranged, they are not causally separate

---

93. Wolterstorff, *On Universals*, 263–65.

94. Plotinus also cites this passage at *Enneads.* I.4.10.6 and III.8.8.

95 For a mapping of Plotinus reading of Parmenides see Gerson, 2002, 106–12. The problem of relationality and the One falls outside of enquiry, see Filler, *Relationality*, 1–23.

96. Aristotle, *Metaphysics*, IX.6.1048a32–34; *De Anima*.III.5, 430a14–25. cf. Emilsson *Intellect*, 29–30; Tiomkin, *Causality*, 14–16.

97. Plotinus, *Ennead*, V.9.2.20–22; V.3.21.

98. Plotinus, *Ennead*.V.3.5.43–48.

99. Rutten, *La doctrine*; Lloyd, *Cause and Effect*; D'Ancona Costa, *Amphoron kai aneideon, Plotinus, Modeles*; Narbonne, *Henologie*; Tazzolio, *Causalite*; Emilsson, *Intellect*, 2007; Fronterotta, *La Critique*; Corrigan, *Divine and Human Freedom*; and Tiomtin, *Causality*.

IDENTITY, RELATION, MODALITY   109

from one another. The type of causality defining the relationship between the One and the realities that proceed from it are a necessity.[100] However, does Plotinus maintain that being is necessary: as in every P is necessarily Q? On the basis of preeminent form of necessity, being that which can be no other than what it is and which owes its existence only to itself is indeed necessary.[101] In the case of the One, necessity is understood as self-engenderment and self-causation.[102] Does he hold that thinking and being are necessarily the same? Yes—but not without some razor thin parsing of the identity and relation of Intellect to the Forms.

IX. Rethinking Nous and the Forms

Aristotle's account of self-thinking is essentially based upon on *Metaphysics* (XII.9.1074b) while Plotinus adds Plato's *Sophist* (248c-249) to claims that Intellect as a subject always thinks and where *nous, noesis*, and *to noeton* are all said to be one.[103] There was disagreement among Platonists about the relation between *Nous* and the Forms provided by a difficult passage in Plato's *Timaeus* (39e). Plotinus refers to this passage in the context of the independence of the Forms—they exist independently of the intellect that thinks them.[104] Separating himself from Aristotle that *Nous* must have itself as the object of its thinking, Plotinus identifies the divine intellect with the Forms as the thoughts, the thinking activity of *Nous* itself.[105] With this move he admits potentiality into the divine intellect claiming that divine thinking is the activity of the Forms.[106] He also claims that the divine intellect is one, as thinking itself, and many, as the multiplicity of Forms which are the objects of its thought.[107]

Plotinus revision of Aristotle's analysis of thinking results in the claim that all thinking, including self-thought involves a duality of thinking and of object of thought so that the constitution of intellect depends on the prior existence of the object of thought which makes possible the actualization

---

100. Tiomkin, *Causality*, 13–18.
101. Plotinus, *Ennead*, IV.8.
102. Plotinus, *Ennead*. VI.8.14.41–41.
103. Plotinus, *Ennead*, V.3.5.28–48.See Szlezak, *Nuslehre*, 122–35; Emilsson, *Intellect*, 148–53.
104. Plotinus. *Ennead*, III.9.13.1.1–5.
105. Plotinus, *Ennead*..V.9.5.
106. Plotinus. *Ennead*. V.9.7–8.
107. Plotinus, *Ennead*. V.9.6.

of the potential to think.[108] Consequently, when intellect thinks itself, it is single as thinking itself and double as thinking something. Since all thought is constituted through a duality of act and of the object of thinking where the object as constitutive of thought exists prior to thought as well as in thought, Aristotle's thought thinking itself cannot be what he claims it to be—absolutely simple and ultimate for all thinking implies variety, differences and contrarieties in what is thought.[109] In nuce, thinking implies deficiency, which means thinking and being can only be *qualitatively* the same and merely in a *per se* relation to *Nous* itself.[110]

Plotinus bases this parsing of *Nous* on the principle of prior simplicity where there is:

> ... something prior to all things which is simple, and this must be different from all that comes after it, being by itself, not mixed with those that come after it, and yet being able to be present in the others in a different way, being truly one, and not something else which is then one ... For what is not first is in need of what is prior to it, and what is not simple is in need of those which are simple in it so that it may be from them.[111]

This One:

> ... must be simple, if it is to be seen in others. Unless one were to say it has its existence by being with others. But then it would not be simple, nor will what is made up of many parts exist. For what is not capable of being simple will not exist, and if there is no simple, what is made up of many parts will not exist.[112]

A direct way of mapping these moves is to reflect on Plotinus' reading of the simple opposition which Plato established in the *Sophist* between a part of Otherness and the Being of each thing (258d7-e3) and Plotinus's reading of (287d7-e3) where opposition between a part of Otherness and the Forms is proposed (*En.*, II.4.16.1-3) through a re-interpretation of Aristotle's *Categories* (*En.* I.8.6.28-59).[113] Briefly, the simple opposition which Plato established in the *Sophist* between a part of otherness and the being of each thing (258d7-e3) is transformed by Plotinus into an opposition

---

108. Plotinus, *Ennead*. V.6.1-2.
109. Plotinus, *Ennead*. V.3.10.31-43.
110. Plotinus, *Ennead*. V.3.49.10.49-50.
111. Plotinus, *Ennead*. V.4.7.1.5-15.
112. Plotinus, *Ennead*. V.6.3.10-15.
113. Following O'Brien, *Plotinus on Matter and Evil*, 174-78.

into an opposition between a part of otherness and the Forms[114] through a modification of Aristotle's categories into a contrariety which establishes the "form of Non-Being."[115] To arrive at this formula, Plotinus takes issue with Aristotle's refusal in the *Categories* to allow any contrary to being.[116] Although there is no contrary to individual beings, there nonetheless can be a contrary to being as such (I.8.6.28-36.). Indeed, amending Aristotle's definition of *contraries* as:

> Things which stand furthest apart within the same genus.[117]

Plotinus says *contrariety* designates:

> things which stand "furthest apart" and which are not in the same genus.[118]

To underscore this point, Plotinus claims that even individual substances such as fire and water could be constituted as to allow contrariety.[119] And the same conclusion holds for the opposition between Being and Non-Being.[120] Whereas Plato's Eleatic Stranger dismisses Parmenides' "absolute" Non-Being as an impossible and inconceivable *contrary* to Being itself (*Sophist*, 258e6-259a1), Plotinus parses Plato's Stranger's notion of *contrary* with five *contrarieties*. First, he rescues Non-Being as a *contrary* by circumventing Aristotle's categories, and by establishing matter as the contrary. Secondly, following the argument of Plato's Stranger, he proposes that Non-Being implies Becoming or that. Being implies its *contrary*—Non-Being. Thirdly, *contrariety* establishes the "Form of Non-Being" since it is contrary to all the positive characterization of the "Form of Being. Non-being is not merely not beautiful, but ugly; not merely not good, but evil (*En.* I.8.10). Fourthly, he argues that each contrary is also a kind of unity representing different degrees of intensity and unification that point to a source of unity itself which presupposes identity and relation among contrarieties(*En.* VI.9.9). Fifthly, the series ends with a source of unity which is absolutely non-composite and the single source of the identity of everything superior to all contrarieties in power and being ending with the One—the absolute simple presupposed by *Nous* and the Forms and superior to both.

---

114. Plotinus, *Ennead*. II.4.16.1-3.
115. Plotinus, Ennead. I.8.6.28-59.
116. Aristotle, *Categories*, V.3b24-32.
117. Plotinus, *Ennead*.VI.6a17-18.
118. Plotinus, *Ennead*. I.8.6.36-41.
119. Plotinus, *Ennead*. I.8.6.49-54.
120. Plotinus, *Ennead*. I.8.6.54-59.

> For intellect is something, one of the beings, but it (the One) is not some-thing, but is prior to each, nor is it a being. For being has as it were the shape of being but it is without shape and intelligible form . . . Nor is it something, or a quality, or a quantity or intellect or soul. Nor does it move or rest. Nor is it in place or time but is itself by itself uniform (Symposium, 211b) or without form or prior to all form, prior to movement, and rest. For these have to do with being, making it many.[121]

Since the One and Intellect are always present to Soul a new mapping of Parmenides' claim that thinking and being are the same emerges in the context of rethinking claims of that the whole is in the part—holenmermism.

X. Holenmermism

Aristotle's claim that 'the whole is in the part' is based on the notion that exclusion is always posterior to inclusion.[122] Consequently, the perfection of divine *nous* thinking itself (*kai estin he noesis noeseos noesis*) includes intellection of individuals—for to be perfect is to be complete and self-sufficient and "that from which nothing is wanting.

> For thus we define the whole—that from which noting is wanting . . . what is true of each particular is true of the whole as such—the whole is that of which nothing is outside.[123]

> . . . for this is the sort of principle that constitutes the nature of each . . . all must at least come to be dissolved into their elements . . . in which all share for the good of the whole.[124]

Plotinus's version of *holenmermism* claims that every form in *Nous* contains every other Form by the interiority of its relations to other Forms. Each Form is all the other Forms and each mind is cognitively identical with each and every Form because the multiplicity of divine intellect is not spatially articulated:[125]

---

121. Plotinus, *Ennead.* VI.9.3.36–45.

122. Aristotle's claim that 'the whole is in the part' is based on the notion that exclusion is always posterior to inclusion. Consequently, the perfection of divine *nous* thinking itself (*kai estin he noesis noeseos noesis*) includes intellection of individuals: "for to be perfect is to be complete and self-sufficient and "that from which nothing is wanting." cf. Aristotle, *Physics*, III.6.207a8–15; *Metaphysics*, XII.8.1074b33–35; XII.10.1075b21–24. cf. Berti, *Intellection*, 1978, 141–63.

123. Aristotle, *Physics*, III.6.207a8–15; cf. *Metaphysics*, XII.9.1074b33–35.

124. Aristotle, *Metaphysics*, XII.10.1075a23–26.

125. Plotinus, *Enneads*, V.V.1.19–43; V.8.3.30–34; V.9.6; V.9.8.3–7.

Intellect and the intelligible substance; each individual Idea is not other than Intellect, but each is Intellect. And Intellect as a whole is all the Forms, and each individual Form is an individual intellect . . . we must assume that the real beings have their place in the thinking subject.[126]

Aristotle and Plotinus map a *holenmermism* where the individual self or mind (*ego*) is continuous with a supra-personal identity or mind (*nous*) that exists throughout reality. The view that the universe exists as a continuous whole of all of its parts with no part being fully separate, determined or determinate opens up a revision of Aristotle's reading of Plato and Parmenides. Based on the principle of prior simplicity thinking and being are *qualitatively* the same and in a *per se* relation to the One.

On the metaphysical side Plotinus proposes a description of a tightly woven universe woven not within layers of an identical (the same kind) of reality but between layers of reality in a scalar fashion. On the methodological side he offers a *qualitative* and *per se* grounds for connections and continuous strata between seemingly disconnected entities, events and first principles.[127]

XI. Focal Meaning, Pros Hen Unity and the Categories Revisited

These claims suggest the following conclusions:

1. Plato proposes a *qualitative* identity of thinking and being and a *per se* relation of thought thinking being and the Forms and:

2. Aristotle offers a *numerical* identity of thinking and being and an *a se* relation of thought thinking itself (*noeseos noesis*). In these contexts:

3. Plotinus maps a *qualitative* identity of thinking, being and Forms in *Nous* and a *per se* relation of each to the One.

Plotinus parses Aristotle's theory of focal meaning and proposes two *pros hen* notions of identity and relation: one *qualitative* and *per se* and a second *numerical* and *a se*.[128] Before we reach an understanding of this move, Ploti-

---

126. Plotinus, *Ennead*, V.9.8.1–5; 10–12.

127. The notion that 'the whole is in the part' is based upon Plotinus's doctrine that every form in *Nous* contains every other Form by the interiority of its relations to other Forms. Each Form is all the other Forms and each mind is cognitively identical with each and every Form because the multiplicity of divine intellect is not spatially articulated. cf. Plotinus, *Enneads*, V.V.1.19–43; V.8.3.30–34; V.9.6; V.9.8.3–7. cf. Schroeder, *Plotinus and Language*, 336–55; Trouillard, *Logic*, 125–38.

128. Bussanich, *Plotinus' Metaphysics*, 60.

nus deserves a hearing on the problem of the *pros hen* unity and multiplicity of One and the Many. Unity or *qualitative* identity and *per se* relation is what characterizes the intelligible world. Identity is qualitative and relation is *per se* due to the duality of subject thinking its objects. The absolute and unqualified unity between subject and object can only be reconciled in the numerical identity and *a se* relation of the One—which like Plato's Good—is above the other Forms and beyond being. In nuce, Plotinus can only affirm a *qualitative* identity given to the Forms by the Form of the Good, and a *per se* relation of Forms and *Nous* given to each by an *a se* One.

The consequences of such a formulation reinforce a *qualitative* identity of thinking and being and *per se* relations of that which is beyond thinking and being—the One. First, since Non-Being is an essential condition of the existence Being, and all Being participates in "otherness" in relation to Non-Being, there is a *per se* relation of Non-Being to Being. Secondly, since Being participates in "otherness" and is in a *per se* relation to Becoming and Non-Being, Being is *qualitatively* identical with Becoming and Non-Being.

Qualitative identity and *per se* relation also follows in respect of *Nous* and the Forms. When *Nous*, despite its unity, thinks the Forms a duality of subject and object remains. Even in the activity of contemplation, Intellect's attempts to know the One are productive but limited.[129] To know fully, *Nous* must become *numerically* one with and in an *a se* relation with Forms and the One but given the principle of prior simplicity (V.4.1.5–15) and a One which is the ultimate simple (V.6.3–4) both options are impossibilities. First, knowledge necessarily includes a distinction between knower and the known; and secondly, since *Nous* is a composite (V.4;V.6;V.4.2) of the act and the object of thinking, where the act of thinking (*noesis*) and the object that defines this act (*noeton*) make up intellect (*nous*), knowledge and being cannot be *numerically* the same. In nuce, another contrariety emerges. If intellect thinks itself, it is single as thinking itself and dual as thinking something or a duality of act and of the object of thinking. Moreover, if the object as constitutive of thought must exist prior to thought as well as in thought, then *Nous* cannot be absolutely simple and ultimate—as either a *numerical* unity or an *a se* relation.

Plotinus interprets Parmenides, Plato, and Aristotle to underscore his own doctrine of the *qualitative* identity and *per se* relation of Being,

---

129. Soul also contemplates but its contemplation is distinguished from Mind's— while Soul's thought is discursive or that in which objects are known successively, Intellect's thought is both propositional/discursive and non-propositional/non-discursive. Soul is the cause of the sense-world and represents the intelligible in the sense world. Not only does it think discursively, but it also has the lower forms of sense consciousness. Nonetheless, although distinct from Intellect, Soul reaches the realm of Mind, and with Intellect it can rise in self-transcendence to union with the One. cf. Blumenthal, *On Soul and Intellect*, 82–84.

Intellect and the Forms to the One.[130] If *Nous* is *per se* in relation to an *a se* One, and if Being is identified in terms of Intellect's thinking the Forms, then Parmenides' saying for Plotinus is an assertion about thinking, and the belonging-together of both in composite difference. That is to say, thinking and being in *Nous* and the intelligible realm of the Forms is a participation understood as *qualitative*, not as *numerical* identity; and as *per se* and not as an *a se* relation.

Summary: It is difficult here to ask whether one should view intellect as a special substance attached to each human body, as a special power (*dunamis*) which the body has, or a single substance shared by all humans. Aristotle vacillated between the first two options with Platonizing Aristotelians vacillating between the second and third. In all these disputes controversy was not only about the survival of *nous* but also about the indestructibility of *episteme/scientia*. Here Augustine proposes the simplest and most counter-intuitive Neo-Aristotelian argument of all—worthy of further study. The soul is "immutable" because it is the subject or seat of reason (*episteme/scientia*):

> The human body is mutable and reason is immutable. For all which does not exist always in the same mode is mutable, but that two and two are four exists always in the same mode . . . This sort of reasoning, then, is immutable. Therefore reason is is immutable.[131]

Thus a *Stimmung* concludes enquiry. Is the ascent of the soul necessary at all? Plotinus notes that at this stage (VI.7.36.10–14) the soul realizes that even in the goodness and beauty of the intelligible world it has not quite grasped what it is seeking (VI.7.22.22) and that it must ascend further to the One (VI.7.35.33–34). Thus is it a realization that one cannot attain *numerical* identity and *a se* relation of thinking and being that triggers desire to ascend to Forms, *Nous* or the One? Aristotle's soul, however, requires no erotic ascent. Neither deficient nor fallen immortality is attained when thinking and being are *numerically* the same; where *nous* as "separable," eternal, and in *a se* relation to itself.

Conclusion

Three outcomes emerge from this study: 1) Parmenides proposes a *numerical* identity and *a se* relation of thinking and being; 2) Plato maps a *qualitative* identity and *per se* relation of thinking and being; and 3) Aristotle

---

130. Plotinus, *Ennead*. I.4.10.
131. Augustine, *On the Immortality of the Soul*, 61.

offers a *pros hen numerical* identity and *a se* relation of thinking and being; 4) Plotinus revises to a *polla hen qualitative* identity and *per se* relation of thinking and being; with 5) modal arguments not only for the *necessary* identity and relation of thinking and being but; 6) also for the existence of abstract objects such a *Nous*, Forms and a One.

If one were to put Parmenides' statement 'that thinking and being are the same' in the context of Cusanus the problem of identity is viewed, not that of the unity of beings, but the relation of God to the world—of the infinite to the finite. Cusanus' initial formulation of the problem was as *coincidentia oppositorum*—the coincidence of opposites. But what is more provocative is his later formulation: the non-other is none other than one-other which means that the 'non-other' admits of no difference, no otherness whatsoever. Its very nature is to be non-other. God is thus formulated as non-other, as nothing other than himself and as noting other than the world. In nuce, if two things have nothing which distinguishes them from each other, they are identical, they are the same thing.[132]

Kant's and Hegel's coherentism may be helpful here. Kant proposes that a thinker is not an addition to experience but it's pre-condition. Concepts cannot be derived from strictly the 'given' of empirical sense data; rather abstract objects provide *a priori* synthetic foundations for *a posteriori* synthetic facts. Hegel argues it is impossible to determine or articulate any single Idea by itself, independently of the dialectical totality and coherentism of other Ideas. Both place identity at the center of transcendental reflection as the mediated synthesis of subject and object, of subjectivity and objectivity. The relationship between intentionality and meaning has shown itself to be a dialectical one. What happens next with identity and relation raises the question if unity under the aegis of reason (or *logos*) turns out to be dialectical as well. As Plato reminds us any turn toward *logoi* requires a move exclusively in the medium of the concept "in Ideas, through Ideas, toward Ideas.[133]

---

132. If one were also to put Parmenides' statement 'that thinking and being are the same' in the context of Leibniz, Kant, Fichte, and Hegel one would get a statement something like: using the principle of the identity of opposites, unity is simplicity, individuality and uniqueness; being is thought and all being is ultimately thought; the absolute Idea is destined to become thought and whatever being there might be outside of thought is simply not yet thought or mediated in the absolute synthesizing activity of the Idea. In nuce, the real is the rational and the rational is real with the result the principle of identity becomes Leibniz's Monad, Kant's Ich Denke or unity of apperception; Fichte's transcendental Ego; and Hegel's dialectic of Begriff und Aufhebung.

133. Plato, *Phaedo*, 99e; *Republic*, 511c.

6

Rethinking Categories

Our nature was not what it is now....
the shape of each human was completely
round with back and hands in a circle.

—PLATO, *SYMPOSIUM*, 189E

Précis

WE BEGIN WITH THE question how many meanings are implied in the simple Greek word *archai* (principles)?[1] The occasion is famous, the protagonists distinguished. Origen struggling over an 'elementary and foundation principles' in accordance with the commandment which says, 'Enlighten yourselves with the light of knowledge.'[2] Later Eusebius, Epiphanius, Pamphilius, Methodius, Rufinus, Jerome, and Justinian are suitably present to elicit their judgments on whether or not Origen gave the correct answer concerning first principles.[3] Origen wrote, his critics answered this study maps the back-

---

1. The anathemas of Justinian suggest the theological difficulties inherent in attempts to map Christian first principles. cf. Mansi, *Concilia*, IX 396–400; 524–533.

2. See, Eusebius. *Con. Marc.*, I 4 = fr. 1, 31, 32 Koe.; *Epiph. Haer.*, LXIV 4 = Migne *PG* XLI 1076–77; *Pamph. Apol. p. Or.*, = Migne, *PG* XVII 539; cf. Photius, *Bibl., cod.* CXVIII; Rufinus, *Liber de adult. lib.* Orig., = Migne, *PG* XVII 615; *Apol.*, I 3, 31, 39; II 9, 44; Jerome, *Apol.*, I 7, 21; II 11b, 18–19; 3.9; *Ep. ad. Pamm. et Ocean.*, LXXIV 9; *Ep. ad Av.*, CXXIV; For the text of Justinian's *Anath.*, see Mansi, *Concilia*, IX 396–400; 524–533.

3. The texts surveyed in this study are largely restricted to the *Periarcon, Commentary on John*, and *On Prayer*.

ground of the Alexandrian's first principles within the context of Middle Platonic and Aristotelian category theory.[4]

Origen achieves an identification of theology and ontology through use of categories. In Middle Platonic fashion he applies the Aristotelian categories to both the sensible and intelligible worlds.[5] It is proposed the *ousia* of God is different from any other *ousia* but not separated from it in that God is the sole subsistent and necessary being and the source of being to a variety of subordinate beings. He is aided in achieving this synthesis by use of the Aristotelian categories both to distinguish degrees of reality and to maintain the connection between the levels thus distinguished. Origen is also a realist rather than an anti-realist who rejects representationalist claims that mind mirrors nature and that categories thus merely "image" reality. His veridical understandings and uses of 'being' and the verb 'to be;'[6] lead to a rejection of a spectator theory of knowledge where mental states indirectly represent reality with at best the accuracy of a mirror.[7] He does not confine meaning to what is linguistically and conceptually mapped within an interiorized or self-referential mental space. Thus what is meaningful includes signs (*semata*)

---

4. The extent to which Origen was a "Platonist" remains an open question partially dependent upon whether distinctions exist between Origen, the Christian and Origen, the Neoplatonist. Those skeptical of Origen's "Platonism" include Crouzel, *La Connaissance* and *Le Dieu D'Origene*, 406–17; Dorival, *L'Apport*, 189–216; and Edwards, *Origen against Plato*. Those open to reading Origen as a "Platonist" include Ramelli, *Patristic Philosophy*, 217–63; Chase, *Porphyry*, 383–405; Heide, *Heresy*, 41–59; and Burns, *Does God Care?*.

5. Plotinus rejects this Middle Platonic use of Aristotle's categories. Plotinus' and later Neoplatonic readings of the Aristotelian categories involves reinterpretation and replacement of them with the *megista gene* of Plato's Sophist and his middle dialogues. cf. Blumenthal, *Aristotle in the Service of Platonism*, 340–64; Schroeder, *Form and Transformation*, 30–31 and *The Categories*, 115–36; Gurtler, *Origin of Genera*, 3–15.

6. Anti-realism is any view that rejects: a) that there are real objects; 2) that exist independently of our experience; 3) have properties and enter into relations independently of the concepts with which we understand them or of the language with which we describe them. Consequences of anti-realism include there are no minds and their states; no concepts and words; no properties and relations; and knowledge cannot be understood as correspondence to real objects or abstract objects such as numbers, mathematicals and universals; Forms and Intellect.

7. Skeptics must explain whether and how our thought and language correctly represent objects accurately which raises the question of the origin of the structure and order of a reality external to us. Unable to explain the origin of this ordering opt for the notion that thought and language do not transparently know objects so much as construct them, with the consequence that we as subjects are cut off from objects in an external world. The 'conflicting appearances' argument of the Skeptics has its origins with Democritus. cf. Sextus, *Pyrrhonian Outlines*, II.63; I.8–10; *Against the Professors*, VII.135–140; Theophrastus, *Senses*, 65–67 and 69–70; Galen, *Elements*, I.2.12. On problems in Hellenistic philosophy of mind see Annas, 1992.

which disclose and make present first principles, objects and properties. As a result mind as an "imitative artifice" that reproduces in a counterfeit form the appearance of things is brought into question for' thinking and being are the same'.[8] Now, "one has to know how to look and what to look for; to be able to recognize a sign (*sema*), interpret it correctly, not to be led astray by images that are misleading, ambiguous or deceitful."[9]

I. Horizons

Several parsings map enquiry. Prior to the notion of the image as 'imitative artifice' that reproduces in visual form the external appearance of real things, they were thought to be signs (*sema*) that make present what is invisible to the eye, and where the relation of subject to object was not that of a spectator looking at external images of things. The assumption is that thought and language directly map what is real and such parsings do not stumble over the ontological and epistemological gulf posited by representationalism.[10]

Three focusing mechanisms guide enquiry: Firstly, there exists a distinction between representational and realist views of thought and language. Representationalism assumes there is an ontological and epistemological gulf between the subjective and the objective and an ocular analogy between perceiving and knowing in what has been called the spectator theory of knowledge.[11] Realism assumes neither an ontological or epistemological gap between the subjective and the objective, nor a metaphorical analogy between perceiving and knowing as in a "spectator" theory of knowledge.[12] Secondly, the categories are not conceptual and linguistic "images" (*eikona*) that represent objects in the world. They are symbols or signs (*semata*) that make present the objects of the world.[13] Thirdly, a ve-

8. Berchman, 2020: 31–48.
9. Waugh and Wilkinson, 2002: 223.
10. See Waugh and Wilkinson, 2002: 221–23.

11. Traced back to an epistemological-linguistic position of an alleged Platonic analogy between perceiving and knowing in the *Theatetus*; whether these exists a correspondence between a name and a thing in the *Cratylus*; and whether language adequately represents reality in the *Seventh Letter*. cf. Rorty: 1979, 157–58; 159, n. 40.

12. On realist views of thought and language see Kennedy, 1989: 78; Detienne, 1996: 72ff.On representational views of thought and language see Rorty, 1991:157–59; McDowell, 1995: 877–893.

13. On this point, Philo stands in opposition to skeptics (*skeptikoi*) who examine different justifications for accepting one image over another and thus either do not commit themselves to the truth of the premises they rely on (Academic) or refrain from accepting various sets of beliefs as justified at all (Pyrrhonian). A major source for Pyrrhonian and Academic skepticism is Sextus Empiricus. Pyrrhonism is a global

ridical understanding of "being" (*ousia; to on*) and the verb "to be" (*einai*) underlies mappings of what the 'true' structure of reality is as opposed to others based on false appearance or opinion.[14]

II. Foundations

Origen drew upon Middle Platonic sources to map his first principles. Although much remains conjecture, Seneca in *Letters* 58 and 65 maps a Middle Platonic metaphysical model that may stand behind those used by Philo and Origen.[15] Seneca borrowing from a Platonic source reads the through a 'metaphysic of prepositions' where Plato's six modes of Being are linked to the Four Causes of Aristotle to which Plato adds a fifth.[16] The first parses Plato's six modes of 'things that are' inclusive of Being, the Demiurge, the Forms, intelligibles, physicals and matter. The second lists Aristotle's 'five' causes in the form of prepositional phrases: "that from which" (matter); "that by which" Demiurge/Logos); "that in which" (immanent Form); "that towards which" (Paradigm); and "that for the sake of which" (Final Cause). Diogenes Laertius also mentions a 'metaphysic of prepositions' ascribed to Potamon of Alexandria that Origen knew of from his reading of Philo.[17] Although it is difficult to determine the extent and depth of his use of Platonic and Middle Platonic category interpretation Origen likely knew enough: 1) to reduce the Aristotelian categories to the Platonic Absolute (*kath'hauto*) and Relative (*pros ti*);[18] 2) to claim the Aristotelian categories refer to the sensible and intelligible worlds;[19] 3) to read Aristotle in an Aca-

---

skepticism formulated by Aenesidemus. Academic skepticism is local in scope proposed by Arcesilaus and Carneades. cf. Sextus, *Pyrrhonian Outlines*, I.226; Photius, *Library*, 169b18–170a2.

14. Following Kahn's claim about Parmenides' veridical use of being developed by Plato—that the value of *einai* when used alone is not 'to exist' but 'to be so' and 'to be true.' cf. Kahn: 1966: 246; 250–51; 260. The word 'is' means one thing when it represents the existential quantifier, something else when it represents class inclusion or class membership, and something else when it represents identity. Kahn, 1966: 246; 1969: 700–724.

15. On the *Sitz im Leben* of these texts see Theiler, 1964; Dillon, 1977: 135–39.

16. Seneca, *Epistle*, 58.16–22; 65.4–8. On the *Sitz im Leben* of this text reception see Dillon, 1977: 136–39.

17. Diogenes Laertius, *Proem.* 17. Philo, *Prov.* I.23; *Cher.* 123–27.

18. Working off Plato's *Sophist*, 255c see Xenocrates, fr, 12 Heinze. Eudorus = Simplicius, *In Cat.* 174.14–16; Philo. *Dec*.30–31.

19. On Pseudo-Archytas' reading of Aristotle's categories see Szelzak, 1972: 22, 31, 31.5.

demic manner where logic is closely linked to metaphysics; and 4) to use the Aristotelian categories to map 'first principles.'[20]

Origen's readings of Aristotle are complicated.[21] Andronicus published a 'new' addition of the works of Aristotle and Theophrastus.[22] Aristotle claims the category of substance answers the question "what is"? His response is a definition: something is defined and limited. Here Plato's clam that the Good is beyond being" anchors Origen's reformulation of the category of substance.[23] The Good or God is something defined and limited but beyond being or substance.

Here, the *De Mundo* drew his attention.[24] His praise for Aristotle's admiration of the perfection of the universe, God's relation to the cosmos as its creator, providential sustainer and that indestructibility is a fitting attribute for the cosmos resonates.[25] First, Aristotle's God is different in kind from all other entities[26] He is unmoved, eternal, non-spatial, and incorporeal and causes motion by being the object of desire.[27] Secondly, God exhibits transcendent and immanent power[28] Cosmic motion is derived from its prior and ultimately from this first unmoved mover.[29] God is in heaven (*en ourano*) and as *ourano theos* he resembles the first mover of *Metaphysics* XII.9 who causes, orders, and sustains the world yet remains distinct in kind from the world it creates.[30] Thirdly, as divine substance it pervades all things

20. Following Philo. cf. Roskam, 2011: 51; Sharples, 2008: 55–73. On Eudorus see Dillon, 1977: 133–35.

21. Limone, *Origene*.

22. Krayle, *Aristotle's God*, 339–58.

23. Plato, *Republic* 509b.

24. On the authenticity of the *De Mundo* see Krayle, *Aristotle's God*, 339–58; Bos, *Aristotle*. For similarities between the theology of the Greek *Peri Kosmou* and other Middle Platonic theologies see Gersch, *Middle Platonism and Neoplatonism*, 265–80. esp. 273–77.

25. See, Bos, *God as Father*, 311–32. Also see Runia, *Philo of Alexandria*, 112–40.

26. *PK.*, VI 398a2–3. Heaven is called the 'highest place' of the divine. cf. VI 398b7–8. The term *hyperourano theos* would be a direct reminiscence of the *epekeina* of Plato, *Rep.*, VI 509bc.

27. Aristotle, *Metaphysics* XII.7.1072a26–b1.

28. God is *Ousia* at *PK.*, VI 397b20 and *dynamis* at VI 398a2–3. God has the highest and primal station in reality, *PK.*, VI 397b25. He is in heaven, VI 398a2–3; he is in the highest place, VI 398b7–8; while the things caused by God are far away, VI 397b24–28 and at the greatest distance, VI 397b30–31; VI 398a3. Also see *PK.*, VI 397b19; 397b23; 397b28; 397b8; VI 397b31; 398a1. *PK.* VIII 4,254b7ff.

29. For what unmoved means in *PK* also see Aristotle, *Physics* VIII 5,257a33–258b9; for eternal see *Physics* VIII 6,259a6–19; for non-spatial see *De Caelo* I 9,279a18–22; for incorporeal see *Physics* VIII 10,267b17–26.

30. Aristotle, *Physics* 8.4.254b7ff.

caused and caused things partake in divine substance.[31] Such telescoping of the powers and functions of *Nous*, Demiurge and World Soul serves Origen's reading of the categories well.[32]

It is difficult to say with any certainty how Antiochus' version of Aristotle's *Categories* was read by Origen.[33] The 'greatest classes' of the *Sophist* or the common properties of the *Theatetus* have little in common with them[34] The *Categories* begin with a consideration of things said without combination from those said in combination.[35] Words uncombined mean one or more of the ten categories.[36] Thus they are likely never properly predicates but subjects. The primary category is substance, the substratum presupposed by all others. Primary substances fit into Aristotle's category doctrine in the following way. If we ask what a thing is, the ultimate answer is a substance, just as if we ask what red is, the ultimate answer is a quality.

The ten categories thus are a catalogue of paronymous uses of 'exists' and the most fundamental category is substance (*ousia*). Substances are the basic or primary constituents of reality which means that all the other categories indicate dependent existents. Substance, quality and quantity are included in all lists of the categories.[37] Although the categories offer a linguistic classification of predicate terms, they also list the different ways in which things can exist.[38] Within substance Aristotle distinguishes primary substance (individual things) from secondary substances (the universal species and genera from which primary substances are included). All categories save substance are present in a subject.[39] It is in this sense that the categories indicate the fundamental classes into which all things fall and indicate the fundamental types of existing things. The reasoning that led Aristotle to claim that this list of basic predicates is the same as

31. The divine element pervades all things, *PK*, VI 397a33; and the whole world, VI 398b8. Things caused by gods are full of gods, VI 397b17–18; they draw off the divine power, VI 397b28–29; and they participate in its benefits, VI 398a1.

32. Aristotle's categories remain a *Truemmerfeld* of controversy. The best that can be done here is to map a 'likely account' of what the theory might mean in later Platonic-Aristotelian contexts.

33. On the influence of Andronicus on the interpretive tradition see Hatzimichali, 2016: 2–17; 81–100. cf. Plezia: 1946.

34. Plato, *Sophist*, 254d; *Theatetus*, 185ab.

35. Aristotle, *Categories* Ia16.

36. Aristotle, *Categories* Ib25.

37. Following how Plotinus likely read the Aristotelian categories. cf. Schroeder, *Categories*, 123–25.

38. Andronicus modified Aristotle's definition of relation and claims the *postpraedicamenta* are separate from the categories proper. cf. Dillon, *Middle Platonists*, 135.

39. Aristotle, *Categories* IIa11.

that of basic types of existents is the following: if we ask what blue is, the answer is color; and if we ask what color is, the answer is quality. In nuce, we cannot ask for a higher classification for quality than the category quality itself, an ultimate classification which is why Aristotle claims that the terms 'exists,' 'is,' and 'be' are paronymous.[40]

III. Ontology

Origen's ontology is very generous. It contains objects like angels, humans, fishes, bread and wine. It also has qualities like colors and quantities like sizes. He refers to principles as "*archai*" and to objects as "*ousiai*." Both exist in their own right but *ousiai* depend for their existence on *archai*. He refers to each in this way because all things and properties depend for their being on objects that underlie everything else and which there is nothing that underlies them as their subject. Origen's use of the categories also highlights two contrasting tendencies in his thought—hierarchism and modalism.[41]

1. hierarchism: the separation and attenuation of levels of divinity and reality.
2. modalism: the telescoping of these levels into an ultimate principle of unity.[42]

A tension between hierarchism and modalism is endemic to any degree of reality metaphysic. Thus while Origen's application of the categories accentuates separation between levels of divinity and reality their utilization also permits the telescoping of these levels into an ultimate principle of unity. Here distinctions between necessary and contingent, essential and accidental beings are resolved in that all reality is subsumed under an ultimate divine principle of unity. Although the categories function excellently to join together the various levels of reality, their use also dramatically underscores distinctions between kinds of divinity. Whether or not Origen successfully combines hierarchism and modalism remains an open question. His use of "Aristotle's" *Peri Kosmou* and Alexander's writings suggest how the tension between the two options is reconciled.

---

40. Two things are paronymous when the two names do not pick out the same thing and do not have the same definition but the one term is derived from the other.

41. For the origin of these terms see J.P. Kenney, *Proschresis*, 217–30.

42. Passmore, *One Hundred Years*, 1–32. For a critique of generative problematics, see Runia, *Philo*, 46.

The God of the *Peri Kosmou* is unmoved, eternal, non-spatial, and incorporeal and causes motion by being the object of desire.[43] Secondly, God exhibits transcendent and immanent power.[44] Cosmic motion is derived from its prior and ultimately from this first unmoved mover.[45] God is in heaven (*en ourano*) and as *ourano theos* resembles the first mover of *Metaphysics* XII.9 who causes, orders, and sustains the world yet remains distinct in kind from the world it creates.[46] Thirdly, as divine substance it pervades all things caused and caused things partake in divine substance.[47]

Alcinous and Alexander of Aphrodisias also drew Origen's attention. He accepts their postulate of three different spheres of being rather than a monistic or dualistic one.[48] God is a being and intellect by virtue of his own nature which means he is a necessary being and intellect. Subsistent by nature God is the cause of all lower beings and intellects. Therefore these beings and intellects are in varying degrees contingent and accidental. His God is *toto caelo* distinct from all other kinds of being and intellect in that it alone is subsistent and necessary. Here two conceptions of the ultimate principle are frequently found in combination: the ultimate principle is conceived of as *ousia* and *nous*.[49] God is characterized by its transcendence, essentiality, and necessity are its characteristics.[50] Only God ... "is an intelligible in its own proper nature."[51] All potential intelligibles become intelligible in act only by virtue of this first principle. This appears clear from the fact that Alexander combines the productive intellect with the first cause who is the source of all things. God is distinct from all other intellects

---

43. Aristotle, *Metaphysics*, XII.7.1072a26-b1.

44. God is *Ousia* at *PK*., VI 397b20 and *dynamis* at VI 398a2-3. God has the highest and primal station in reality, *PK*., VI 397b25. He is in heaven, VI 398a2-3; he is in the highest place, VI 398b7-8; while the things caused by God are far away, VI 397b24-28 and at the greatest distance, VI 397b30-31; VI 398a3. Also see *PK*., VI 397b19; 397b23; 397b28; 397b8; VI 397b31; 398a1. *PK*. VIII 4,254b7ff.

45. For what unmoved means in the *PK* also see Aristotle, *Physics*, VIII 5,257a33-258b9; for eternal see *Physics*, VIII 6,259a6-19; for non-spatial see *De Caelo*, I 9,279a18-22; for incorporeal see *Physics*, VIII 10,267b17-26.

46. Aristotle, *Physics* 8.4.254b7ff.

47. The divine element pervades all things, *PK*., VI 397a33; and the whole world, VI 398b8. Things caused by gods are full of gods, VI 397b17-18; they draw off the divine power, VI 397b28-29; and they participate in its benefits, VI 398a1.

48. Berchman, *Philo to Origen*, 83-86; 146-56; 190-200.

49. Schroeder, *Analogy*, 215-25 and *Potential or Material Intellect*, 115-25. Also see, Moraux, *Alexandre d'Aphrodise*; Hager, *Aristoteles*; Rist, *Tracking Alexander of Aphrodisias*.

50. A *locus classicus* is Alexander. cf. *In Met.*, 821.33 {Hayduck}.

51. Alexander, *De Anima*, II. 111.28-30.

because they are derivative of this first cause and source. Therefore they are potential, accidental and inherent by nature.[52]

Such telescoping of the powers and functions of *Nous*, Demiurge and World Soul serves Origen well. The ultimate principle is conceived of as *ousia* and *nous*. Moreover, God is a unique principle. Transcendence, essentiality, and necessity are its characteristics. Here the theological formulations of the Greek *Peri Kosmou* and Alexander reflect not only the *ourano nous* of Aristotle's *Physics* and *Metaphysics* but the God of Origen's *Peri Archon* and *Commentary on John*. Such a first principle does not transcend being and intellect rather God is different in kind from all other beings and intellects. Thus the assertion that the first principle transcends essence and intellect is rejected. In response a divinity is different in kind in being and intellect from all other beings and intellects is proposed which leads to the question of the nature of divine transcendence.

IV. Divine Transcendence

Plato's statement that the first principle is *epekeina tes ousias* is a Middle Platonic commonplace. Eudorus, Moderatus, Numenius, Hippolytus and Albinus cite the text frequently as do[53] Philo,[54] Justin,[55] Clement[56] and Origen.[57] Indeed, Origen maintains the seemingly paradoxical position that the first principle is both substance and beyond substance.[58] How does Origen tie together these notions? What sense can be given to such a combination and what was the inspiration behind his view of the first principle? Origen's formulation is not derived from Plato's statement that the Good is beyond being and intellect alone.[59] Nor is it culled from theories of physical transcendence advocated by its representative Seneca,[60] the theoretics which stressed the metaphysical immanence of God

---

52. Alexander, *De Anima*, I 89,4–18; II .112.19–20.
53. See Whittaker, *EPEKEINA*, 91–104.
54. Philo refers to God as the really existent (*to ontos' on*) cf. *Quod Deus*, 11; *Spec. Leg.*, II 176; *Op. Mun.*, 17–20; *Cher.* 49. On this issue see Berchman, *From Philo to Origen*, 27–42.
55. Justin, *Dial. c. Tryph.* IV = *MSG* 6, 484a.
56. Clement, *Strom.* VII 1.2.1–3.
57. Origen, *C. Cels.* VII.45; VI.64; VII.38; *ComJn*. XIII.26.152; XXIII.21.19–22.
58. Plato, *Rep.*, VI 509b is often interpreted in conjunction with *Parmenides* 141e as with Plotinus, *Ennead*, V 1.10 (8), 1–27. cf. Doerrie, *Les Sources de Plotin*, 229.
59. Plato, *Republic*, VI 509b.
60. Seneca *Ep.*, LXV 3–12.

characteristic of some other types of Stoicizing Middle Platonism[61] or from proposed by Celsus alone.[62] It is also parsed from Philo, Numenius, Justin, Clement[63] and Ammonius Saccas.[64]

Origen's God is: 1) a simple, perfect unity; 2) the good; 3) a being; 4) beyond being; 5) an intellect; 6) beyond intellect; 7) efficient cause; and 8) final cause. Deity is explained in terms of the manner of knowing him, the names ascribed to him, and the causality attributed to him. Although the terminology employed by Origen to define his first principle are common to the Platonisms of the age two attributes above require special comment: these are that God is being and intellect but beyond being and intellect.[65] The question is

Not only did Philo, Clement and Origen address divine transcendence.[66] Aristotle,[67] Aristotelians,[68] Neopythagorean,[69] and Middle Platonists

---

61. Plato does not bring all principles of an immanent metaphysical principle together although readings of *Timaeus* 36e-38b makes such a construct possible.

62. Celsus ap. Origen, *CCels.*, VII 45; VI 64.

63. See, Sharples, *Philo*, 55-73; Lilla, *Aristotelianism*, 228-35; Runia, *Festugiere*, 1-34; Crouzel, *Traite des Principes*, 161-86; 241-60. cf. Dorival, *L'Apport*, 189-216.

64. Eusebius mentions Ammonius Saccas among the teachers of Origen. cf. *HE* VI 19,5-14. Nemesius claims that Alexander was read in the school of Ammonius. cf. *De Nat. Hom.*, III 58; Hierocles, *ap. Photius*, 172b10; 461b25. Plotinus corroborates the testimonies of Hierocles and Nemesius. cf. Enn., IV 20.15ff. Alexander's De Anima XIV 23 was read by Plotinus while a student of Ammonius Saccas.

65. As *ousia* see *PArch.*, I 1.5-7; as *epekeina tes ousias kai nou* see *CCels.*, VIII 38. cf. VI 64-65; *as hyper ekeina ousias presbeia kai dynamei* see *ComJn.*, XIII 21.19-22; 26.152.

66. See, Ramelli, *Patristic Philosophy*, 217-63. cf. Edwards, *Origen against Plato*; Koch, *Paideia*; Andresen, *Logos und Nomos*; Lilla, *Clement*.

67. Aristotle, *Metaphysics*, XIV.4.1092a14f.

68. The author of the *Peri Kosmou* identifies God with being and power. cf. VI 397b19-20.

69. Syrian says ps.-Brontius maintained that the first principle is beyond being in virtue of its power. cf. *In Met.*, 165.5ff {Kroll}. While Alexander says the Pythagoreans claimed the first principle is beyond being, they also held it to be *ousiotai en to hen einai, hos pollakis eiretai*. cf. *In Met.*, 821.33 {Hayduck}.

were aware of it[70] while Speusippus,[71] Eudorus,[72] Moderatus,[73] Numenius,[74] and several Middle Platonists debated its significance.[75] The author of the Greek *Peri Kosmou* and Alexander of Aphrodisias also address divine transcendence.[76] Origen knew of the debate concerning the nature of divine transcendence.[77] In response to Celsus, he claims that while the first principle is being (*aitios . . . aute ousia tou einai*) the locution (*panton ekekeina*) must imply beyond being (*epekeina tes ousias*).[78] This conclusion is drawn on the basis of this passage from Celsus by Origen himself but he admits that the matter is *dystheoretos*.[79] That this was the case becomes apparent when Origen reflects on this problem and heightens the wording of divine transcendence to indicate not that God or the Logos is beyond *ousia* but beyond *ousia* in virtue of his being and power (*hyper ekeina ousias presbeia kai dynamei*).[80] In response to Celsus he claims that while the first principle is being (*aitios . . . aute ousia tou einai*) the locution (*panton ekekeina*) must imply beyond being (*epekeina tes ousias*).[81] This conclusion is drawn on

---

70. For Middle Platonic usages cf. Dillon, *Middle Platonists*. cf. Philo Judaeus, 155; Albinus, 279.
   Dodds argued that there existed in the first century C.E. Neopythagorean interpretations of the hypotheses of the Parmenides. Dodds, *Neoplatonic One*, 136ff. cf. Merlan, *Greek Philosophy*, 94.

71. *ap.* Aristotle, *Metaphysics*, XI.4.1092a14f. On the authenticity of Aristotle's account of Speusippus' position see, Merlan, *Platonism to Neoplatonism*, 1953, 94ff; Kraemer, *Der Ursprung*, 351ff. Regardless of its authenticity Aristotle's report suggests that this issue was debated in the Old Academy and Early Lyceum.

72. Eudorus *ap.* Simplicius, *In Phys.*, 181.10ff. {Diels}. cf. Theiler, *Geschichte*, 206ff.

73. Moderatus, ap. Simplicius, *In Phys.*, 230.34ff. {Diels}. Festugiere dismisses a connection between Moderatus and the Parmenides. cf. Festugiere, *La revelation*, 1954, 22. But see Kraemer, *Der Ursprung*, 1964, 251ff.

74. Numenius, fr. 25; 11 {Leemans} where the *autoagathon* is not entirely dissociated from *ousia*.

75. Calcidius preserves a Middle Platonic commonplace at *In Tim.*, 175.204.5ff. {Waszink}.

76. On Aristotle as the author of *Peri Kosmou* see Bos, *Aristotle On God's Life*. The question whether or not the first principle transcends *nous* was disputed by Aristotle and Speusippus. Aristotle. cf. fr. 1 Ross = Simplicius, *In De Caelo*, 485.19ff. {Heiberg}. Speusippus. cf. *Dox.* 303. *Rep.*, VI 509bc was considered central to the discussion. *Peri Kosmou*.VI 397b19ff., and Alexander of Aphrodisias *In Met.*, 821,33ff. {Hayduck}; *De Anima*, I 89,4–18; II 111,28–30; 112,19–20. {Bruns}

77. See Berchman, *From Philo to Origen*, 123–26.

78. Origen, *CCels.*, VII 45.

79. Origen, *CCels.*, VI.64.

80. Plato, *Republic*, 509b; Origen, *ComJn.*, XIII 21,19–22; 26,152.

81. Origen, *CCels.*, VII 45.

the basis of this passage from Celsus by Origen himself but he admits that the matter is *dystheoretos*.[82] That this was the case becomes apparent when Origen heightens the notion of divine transcendence to indicate that God is beyond *ousia* (*epekeina tes ousias*) and beyond *ousia* in virtue of his being and power (*hyper ekeina ousias presbeia kai dynamei*).[83]

Origen's knowledge of Aristotle and later Peripatetics is limited but solid.[84] He had access to an alphabetical lexicon of the works of Aristotle, refers directly to Hermippus of Smyrna, and quotes from doxographical sources.[85] It is possible that Origen like Plotinus read Alexander for is reported that he was read in the school of Ammonius Saccas.[86] Is there a solution to the problem of divine transcendence based on Peripatetic assumptions? If God is beyond 'beyond being and intellect in virtue of his being and power'[87] does it mean that deity is a being and intellect different in kind from all other beings and intellects?[88] Finally, does this formulation signal a claim that the first principle is a being and intellect *toto caelo* distinct from all other beings and intellects?[89] To answer these questions it might be helpful to examine again solutions proposed in the *Peri Kosmou*[90] and by Alexander of Aphrodisias.[91]

82. Origen, *CCels.*, VI.64.

83. Plato, *Republic*, VI 509bc; Origen, *ComJn.*, XIII 21,19–22; 26,152.

84. See Lilla, *Aristotelianism*, 228-35. Runia, *Festugiere*, 7-8; Also Dorival, *L'Apport*, 189–217; Crouzel, *La Dieu*, 406-17.

85. If Langerbeck is correct the Peripatos exercised influence on Origen through Alexander, especially in the area of first principles, through his concept of *boulesis* and his notion of *hexis*. cf. Langerbeck, *Aristotelischer und Christlicherelemente*, 146–66.

86. Origen, *HE* VI 19.5–14. Nemesius claims that Alexander was read in the school of Ammonius. cf. *De Nat. Hom.*, III 58; Hierocles, *ap. Photius*, 172b10; 461b25. Plotinus corroborates the testimonies of Hierocles and Nemesius. cf. *Ennead.*, IV 20.15ff. where we are informed Alexander's *De Anima* XIV 23 was read by Plotinus while a student of Ammonius Saccas.

87. As does ps.-Brontius. *ap.* Syrian, *In Met.*, 166.5. Clarification is also provided by Alexander, *In Met.*, 821.33. {Hayduck}.

88. Origen, *CCels.*, VIII 38; IV 14; *PArch.*, I. 1.6; cf. I. 1.5 and I. 1.7.

89. Origen, *In Lib. I Sam.*, I. 11; and *PArch.*, I 3,5.

90. The authorship and date of the Greek *De Mundo* have not been determined with certainty. According to Lorimer it was the work of an unknown author dated between 40 and 140 A.D. The former date is furnished by the occurrence of the phrase *hosper amelei* which appears in literature around the time of Plutarch. The latter date is based on its priority to the Latin version of Apuleius. On the authenticity of the *De Mundo* see Krayle, 1990: 339–58. Bos argues the *De Mundo* is an authentic work of Aristotle's. cf. Bos, *Aristotle on God's Life*.

91. To raise Alexander as a source for Origen remains a controversial one. Rist maps the reasons why. cf. Rist, *The One of Plotinus*, 75–87. For studies on Plotinus reading

Two conditions also exist for the possibility of Peripatetic influence on Origen's model of first principles:[92] 1) in *Peri Kosmou* a first principle distinct in being and intellect from the lower gods and powers is evident;[93] and 2) Alexander postulates a necessary-contingent, essential- accidental distinction between deity and reality.[94] There is evidence *Peri Kosmou* indirectly stands behind the theology of *Peri Archon*.[95] The argument for his knowledge of Alexander is stronger. Nemesius reports that Alexander was read in the school of Ammonius Saccas.[96] Origen was allegedly a member of the Saccas circle. Thus, a mapping of degrees of divinity in is warranted.[97]

V. Degrees of Divinity

Origen's theology is characterized by a triadic system of divine principles anchored by a system of derivation which corresponds to a scale of degrees of reality.[98] That Origen calls his first principle substance (*ousia*) is not unprecedented in later Platonism and Aristotelianism.[99] Here his is use of the terms *ousia, epekeina tes ousias kai nou* and *hyper ekeina ousias presbeia kai dynamis* to describe the first principle is reminiscent of the Alcinous.[100] Origen's view of God's immanent relation to the world is also based on the Stoic doctrine that all cosmic motions are produced by the Logos or Pneuma[101]

Alexander see Moraux, *Alexander*; Hager, *Aristoteles*.

92. For knowledge and use of Aristotle and later Peripatetics by the *Patres* see Karamanolis, *Early Christian Philosophers*, 460–79. cf. Runia, *Festugiere Revisited*, 7–8.

93. "Ps-Aristotle," *Peri Kosmou*, 6.397b-398b8.

94. Alexander of Aphrodisias, *In Met*. 821.33; *De Anima*, 1.89.4–18; 2.112.19–20; 2.111.28–30.

95. For similarities between the theology of the Greek *Peri Kosmou* and Latin Middle Platonic sources see Gersch, *Middle Platonism and Neoplatonism*, 1986, 265–80. esp. 273–77. Harl suggests genre parallels between the *Peri Kosmou* and *Periarchon*. cf. Harl, *Structure et Coherence*, 11–32. Also see Kuebel, *Zum Aufbau*, 31–39; Steidele, *Untersuchungen*, 236–43.

96. Nemesius, *De Nat. Hom.*, III 58.

97. See Sharples, *Philo*, 55–73. cf. Dorival, *L'Apport*, 189–216; Berchman, *From Philo to Origen*, 227–29.

98. This is spelled out by Origen in *PArch.*, I 2,2–9; 3,5–8; and summarized at *Praef*. 4; and *IV* 4,1.

99. Origen, *CCels.*, VII 38; *Exh Mart.*, XLVII 43,8.

100. Alcinous, *Did.*, 165.5–166.25.

101. See, von Arnim, *SVF*, 1903, II 410; 439; 442; 786; 418.

which acts dynamically on matter.[102] It causes motion throughout the universe due to its own directional tendencies.[103]

The basic features of the system include: 1) a first principle, which is unique, a simple unity, a substance, and ontologically self-directed as the ground of all reality; 2) a second principle which is derivative of a prior one, a unity in plurality, a substance, and cosmologically directed as the ground of all rational creatures and the demiurge of the world; and 3) a third principle which is derivative of two prior ones, a substance, and soteriologically directed as the equivalent of a guide for the saints or the helmsman-guardian of be-knighted souls.[104]

Origen argues that God is not a genus but is predicated by focal meaning of different entities within the hierarchy of being.[105] He claims God the Father is an eternal, un-generated intellect (*nous*) and an intellect at rest (*akinetos*).[106] God is also called *ousia, monas, henas, epekeina tes ousias kai nou*, and *hyper ekeina ousias presbeia kai dynamis*.[107] That God is called a One and an intellect is common in Middle Platonism.[108] Origen's second principle is called *logos, ousion hen, idea ideon*, and *demiourgos*.[109] The Logos is characterized as an eternally generated intellect (*nous*).[110] He is the impress and form of the substance and subsistence of the first One, the Father.[111] As *ousion hen* and *idea ideon* the second One is not a simple *hen* or *monas* like the first One. He is a unity in plurality who as *ousion hen* and *idea ideon* is the rational and substantial ground of all created things; the rational sustainer of the universe.[112] As the principle that contains the intelligible world in its intellect, the Logos is the pre-figuration of the sensible world who instantiates this sensible world in matter. Therefore he is

---

102. *SVF*. II. 458; II. 442.

103. *SVF*. II. 525.; II. 527. cf. Cicero, *De Nat. Deorum*, II.57–58; 2.77–78; 81; 83–84; 87.

104. This type of figure is wide-spread in Greco-Roman antiquity. See the account of the beneficent guardian-daemon in Plutarch, cf. *De Daem. Soc.*, 591d. In Origen's system this guardian figure has been promoted to the rank of a principle.

105. Like the One of Plotinus, nothing can be predicated of God the Father. cf. Wurm, *Substanz und Qualitaet*, 217–18.

106. Origen, *FragmJn* 13 (GCS 4.495.20, 24).

107. Cf. e.g., *PArch.*, I 1,6; *CCels.*, VII 45; VI 64; *ComJn.*, XIII 21,19–22; 26,152.

108. Berchman, *Philo to Origen*, 123–26.

109. Origen, *PArch.*, I 1,2; *CCels.*, 6.64; *ComJn.*, I 119.113f. cf. ap Justinian, *Ep. ad Men.* = Mansi, IX 528.489d.

110. Origen, *ComJn.*, I 24; *CCels.*, VI 64; cf. III 64; II 135; *PArch.*, I 2,30; 4,5.

111. Origen, *PArch.*, I 2,2–6.

112. Origen, *CCels.*, IV 54; *PArch.*, I 4,5; *ComJn.*, I 1,20.

also the creator (*demiourgos*) of the universe. Here Origen reduplicates the paradigmatic cosmology and concomitant prepositional causality common to Middle Platonism to explain creation.[113] Although creation has its ground of being in the Father, it has the ground of its existence in the Logos.[114] As demiurge the Logos creates the universe, gives form to matter whereby his reason principles (*logoi*) unceasingly penetrate the material substratum introducing differentiating quality to the physical world.[115]

The second principle is subordinate to a primary principle, God the Father. The cause or foundation of the second principle and creation is the first principle. It would seem to follow from this that its proper location is at the second level, that of the active, generic, demiurgic intellect—the Logos and the intelligible world. Subsequent evidence clarifies the nature of the relationship between these two levels of divinity. Origen states:

> But in regard to the Son of God . . . the image may be compared to our second illustration . . . he is the invisible image of the invisible God . . . This image preserves the unity of nature and substance common to a Father and a Son.[116]

Next, below these first two principles, is the Holy Spirit. Called *ousia*, the Holy Spirit is the first generated intellect.[117] Properly speaking the Holy Spirit does not appear to be a metaphysical principle but a soteriological principle. His function is as a helmsman, one who guides the saints towards the Father and thus ultimately to salvation.[118] Thus, with the inclusion of the Holy Spirit, Origen's noetic triad is complete.

The formal structure of Origen's theology is fairly clear. There are three divine levels corresponding to gradations of value and related in terms of substantial imitation. The use of imitation language reflects Platonic and Pythagorean explication of the dependence of lower principles on a higher one at the level of being and intelligence itself.[119] The divine world, thus, is distinguished by clear cut distinctions between higher and lower levels, upon which the latter depends. His demotion of the demiurgic intellect is in

---

113. Origen, PArch., I 2,12.
114. Origen, PArch., I 4,3.
115. Origen, CCels., IV 54 PArch., I 4,5; FragmJn.1.
116. Origen, PArch. I 2.6.
117. Origen, PArch.Praef. 4.; I 2,3; 2,10; FragmJn 1; 2.10. Epihanius, *Haer.* LXIV, 5; Justinian, *Ep. ad Men.* = Mansi IX 528.489; Jerome, *Ep. ad Av.*II = Migne XXII 1060.
118. Origen, PArch., I 3,5–8.
119. Origen, PArch., I 2,2–9.; IV 4,1.

keeping with the hierarchism of the theologies of Philo,[120] and Clement.[121] Although his inclusion of a soteriological intellect is common Christian practice there are parallel notions in Philo[122] and again Plutarch.[123] Both assume the existence of guardian daemons but neither promotes such a figure to first principle status, however.

Although these first principles are connected, there remain degrees of reality within divinity itself. Origen says:

> God the Father bestows on all the gift of existence . . . therefore they obtain first of all their existence from God the Father . . .[124]

And:

> The God the Father, who holds the universe together, is superior to every being that exists, for he imparts to each one from his own substance that which each one is; the Son being less than the Father, is superior to rational creatures (for he is second to the Father); the Holy Spirit is still less, and dwells within the saints alone.[125]

Summary: God the Father is a principle of self-intellection and the ground of being who exhibits simple unity and stability. The Logos is a primary genus and secondary intellect who exercises the function of cosmic production. He is a one in many who as the sum-total of the intelligible world demiurgically divides from the Father in the process of shaping the pre-existing forms and matter into a cosmos. The Holy Spirit is an intellect and substance equivalent to a divine helmsman or guide who soteriologically divides from the Father and the Son in the process of coming into contact with created being. Here an examination of his notion of degrees of reality is instructive.

---

120. Philo, *Abr.* 151; *Ling.*, 146; *Op Mun.*, 16–20; 24–25; *Conf.*, 172; *Cher.*, 49.
121. Clement, *Strom.*, IV 156,1–2; V 12,81; VII 7,4.
122. Philo, *Gig.*, 6–9; 16.
123. Plutarch, *De Daem. Soc.*, 591d.
124. Origen, *PArch.* I 3.8.
125. Origen, *PArch.* I 3,5 = Just. *Ep. ad Men.* = Mansi IX 524 = fr. 9. Koe. Debate rages over the authenticity of this account. cf. Jerome, *Ep. ad Av.*, II.

VI. Degrees of Reality

Origen grounds substantial function in the first level of divinity, demiurgic function in the second level, and soteriological function in the third. In doing so it reserves a unique intellectual and substantial condition for the primordial principle, God the Father. The intellective and demiurgic demotion of the Son and the limitation of the Holy Spirit to helmsman status, appear to be central elements of Origen's theology or first principles. No doubt this is in keeping with his hierarchism, since it serves to maintain the uniqueness of the Father. It also functions to reinforce the dependence of the Son and Holy Spirit on a primary principle, thereby promoting the theme of differentiation between first principles. This raises further questions about the implications of this type of theology. How is the essence and existence of the second and third principles treated in this theology? Are they real being or a copy of real being? What is their ontological valuation?

It is suggested that Origen's thought evinces a concern for the establishment of some more subtle connections between degrees of divinity and reality than Pythagorean imitationism and Platonic paradigmatism allow because he is concerned with establishing a substantial link between the divine *ousia* and the *ousia* of the world. For Origen all levels of divinity and reality are related in spite of the essential and existential differences between them. To demonstrate this he employs a doctrine which has a long history in the Middle Platonisms and Stoicisms of the imperial age—the `metaphysic of prepositions. This doctrine, along with those of the categories, extends his 'theological' paradigmatism and imitationism rather nicely.[126]

The doctrine is extant in the writings of Seneca, Varro, Philo, and Clement.[127] The basic idea is that production by higher principles of lower entities can be explained prepositionally with each preposition designating a type of cause linked to one or more first principles thereby offering a mechanism that explains causation. Origen telescopes the five causes of prepositional metaphysics into his first principles.[128] There are five causes linked to distinct prepositional formula. These are: 1) material = that from which; 2) agent = that by which; 3) immanent form = that in which; 4) paradigm = that towards which; and 5) final = that for the sake of which. He also employs a prepositional metaphysic to define how things are caused in

---

126. This term was introduced by Theiler, 1932, 16ff. Also see, Bickel, 1969, 1–20; and Gersch, 1986 v.1, 188–95.

127. Seneca, *Ep.*, LXIV 4–12; Philo, *Prov.*, I 23; *Cher.*, 125ff; and Clement, *Strom.*, II 20,110. These reports stand behind Origen's; cf. *PArch.*, III 1,1 and *De Or.*, VI 1.

128. Origen's source is likely Clement. cf. *Strom.*, II 20,110. This telescoping activity is extant in *PArch.*, *Praef.* 4; III 1,2; *De Or.*, VI 1.

nature. The prepositions used by Origen to characterize the physical world are: 1) out of; 2) from within; and 3) through.[129]

The prepositions Origen employs to express divine production is that by which (of); that from which; and that in which. This suggests that the Father functions as his formal cause, substantial cause,[130] and immanent form of the Son.[131] This can be seen directly in excerpts from the *Peri Archon* where the paradigmatism and immanentism of first principles are parsed through a 'metaphysics of prepositions:'

Then again:

> Christ Jesus, he who came to earth, was begotten of the Father before every created thing . . .

The Son was:

> . . . born indeed of him and draws his being from him . . .[132]

And:

> . . . the Father's image was reproduced in the Son . . .[133]

Finally:

> . . . to understand still more completely how the saviour is 'the image of God's substance' let us use an illustration . . . Let us suppose . . . that there existed a statue of so great a size as to fill the whole world . . . it is by some such likeness as this that the Son, in emptying himself of his equality with the Father, and showing to us a way by which we may know him, becomes an 'express image' of God's substance.[134]

Origen assumes that a prior cause or reason begets the Son and he explains this through use of the artist simile. He tells us that the relation between cause and effect can be explained by the illustration of the sculptor molding a statue. Thus, prepositionally, the Father is the agent, the

---

129. Origen, *PArch*. III 1,2 = Philoc., 21 = fr. 26 Koe.

130. When the Father functions as the 'that from which' the Son comes Origen does not mean the first principle is the material cause of the second principle. Since God is substance it appears he serves as the substance from which the Son derives. cf. *PArch.*, I 2,5.

131. Origen apparently equates form not with a primary intelligible but with substance. cf. e.g., *PArch*. I 2,5.

132. Origen, *PArch,*. I.2.2.

133. Origen, *PArch.*, I 2.6.

134. Origen, *PArch.,*. I 2,8.

substance, form and necessary cause by which, from which, and in which Son, Holy Spirit all creation come into being. He also distinguishes between necessary and contingent cause. God the Father is a necessary cause while the Son and Holy Spirit are contingent ones.

Summary: If this reading of Origen is correct, then his 'metaphysic of prepositions' has the following formal outline. God the Father is the: 1) efficient cause: 'that from which' all things derive; 2) final cause: he is 'that on behalf of which' all is produced 3) immanent form: his Wisdom is 'that in which' all things are pre-figured and pre-formed; 4) paradigm: the Logos is 'that by which' creation is accomplished; and 5) agent: depending on the degree of reality the Father (as substance) and Son (as Logos and Demiurge) are 'that according to which' things are fashioned In order to clarify the specifics further and come to a better understanding of the theoretical bases we might look at his doctrine of the categories. Here Origen ties together the loose strands of his theoretic in rethinking the Aristotelian categories.

VII. Rethinking Categories

Origen modifies earlier notions of the categories and alters their traditional interpretations.[135] Evidence of received category doctrine in Origen is diffuse but wide-ranging. He links the categories to a 'metaphysic of prepositions' in the *Peri Archon*[136] and the *De Oratione*[137] and he provides a list of the categories in his *Commentary on John*,[138] and in the *Peri Archon*.[139] His doctrine shares formal features with Philo, Clement, and of Albinus.[140]

---

135. Foundational doctrines and theories were subject to systematic reinterpretation in this period. cf. Kahn, 1976; Stead, 1977.

136. Origen, *PArch.*, Praef. 4; III 1,1.

137. Ibid. *De Or.*, VI 1.

138. In *ComJn.*, II 18,15–22 the categories which have referential efficacy to the sensible world are listed. For example when substance is defined at II 18,18 material substance is distinguished from intelligible.

139. The intelligible categories include substance at *PArch.*, Praef. 4; I 1,6; 2,2; 2,5; 1.2.7–9; 3,5; 3,8; 4,5; IV 4,1; quantity, quality, and relation at *PArch.*, Praef. 4; I 2,6; 2,13; 3,5; Space, place, motion, magnitude, and time are mentioned at I 1,5; 2,13; IV 4,1; 4,2; 4,4. These categories do not refer to the intelligible world, only to the sensible world. cf. ComJn., XXIV 18,16ff.

140. Origen's sources include Philo and Clement. cf. e.g., Philo introduces the Peripatetic and Stoic categories at *Dec.*, 30 while Clement at *Strom.*, VIII 24,1 parses each claiming reality is subsumed under a common *ousia*. See Berchman, *Categories of Being in Middle Platonism*, 1995. Although there is no direct evidence Origen read Alcinous there are similarities in their understanding and use of the categories. Alcinous claims

He uses the categories to map the identity and relationship between levels of divinity and reality. Intelligibles and sensibles are defined through the categories. Intelligible things are characterized by substance, quantity, quality, and relation. Natural things are characterized by substance, quantity, quality, relation, motion, place, time, and magnitude.[141]

Origen offers a distinct theory of the categories in respect to first principles. The basic features of the system are knowable, its functions are clear, and its implications are straightforward. The categories function to separate levels of divinity from one another and to bind degrees of reality to each other. They serve to define the hierarchical and modalistic distribution of divine substantiality throughout reality.[142] First, the category substance pertains to primary divine substance, the Father alone. The categories substance, quality, quantity, and relation pertain to secondary divine substance, the Son and Holy Spirit. All the categories pertain to secondary created substance. If these propositions are plausible, then the formal structure of Origen's category theory can be reconstructed. Origen makes distinctions on the intelligible and sensible levels between essences and accidents (between individuals and what is present in them),[143] between substances themselves (individual or primary substances), and kinds of substances—secondary substances.[144] Following Aristotle, he takes primary substances are singular things in which properties inhere and to which predicates can be attached. Secondary substances are genera or species which can be predicated of primary substance and are therefore substances in a secondary sense.[145] He seems to assume that genera and species group primary substances in various kinds of substance and that the categories are predicated of primary substances to determine the degree to which primary and secondary substances partake of divinity.[146] He also appears to know that only genera and species give us what is essential to a primary substance, for they tell what a primary substance must have in order to be that kind of reality.[147]

---

the Aristotelian categories for Plato and his primal god is characterized by substantiality (*ousiotes*). cf. *Did.*, 159.34ff; 164.28ff.

141. Berchman, *Categories of Being in Middle Platonism*.
142. Origen, for divinity *PArch.*, Praef. 4; for creation *PArch.*, III 1,1; *De Orat.*, VI 1.
143. Origen, *PArch.*, I 1.7
144. Origen, *PArch.*, I 2.7.
145. Aristotle, *Categories*, 125b.
146. Origen, *PArch.*, II 9.1.
147. Origen, PArch I 2.7; II 9.1.

Second, all of divine being shares a common *ousia*. The Son is the image or impress of the *ousia* of the Father.[148] However the *ousia* of God is radically different from all other *ousia* which for Origen means the Father is a primary substance while all other entities are secondary substance.[149] He appears to argue for this in two ways: first through the paradigmatic and prepositional language common to later Platonism and Pythagoreanism; and second through the categorical language common to later Aristotelianism. The first option explains the levels of divinity and reality in the manner of the relation of primary form to secondary forms and paradigm to copy. The second option determines the degrees of divinity and reality through the categories which are determinations of being.

For Origen there is only one primary substance—God the Father. We know this because *ousia* refers to him alone.[150] God the Father is a primary substance because he is a singular thing in which being subsists and to which other beings inhere.[151] The Son is secondary substance because he derives his from God who is a primary substance and what he is can be predicated of God.[152] Secondary substances like the Son and Holy Spirit tell us what *ousia* they are essentially while, for example, their *epinoiai* tell us what predicates are added to their *ousia*.

This is the reason why Origen's analysis of being starts from the singular thing, God the Father. He is the primary substance from which all things beginning with the Son become existent[153] Modification and qualification starts with the Son himself.[154] The Logos and Holy Spirit, thus, are characterized by the category of substance while the categories of place, relation, and quality refer to the degree to which divine substantiality inheres in the Logos and the Holy Spirit.[155]

Origen's theology treats God the Father as a necessary being who has necessary existence. In God being and essence are one, for God is the primary substance under which all that is derives being and existence.[156] In this

---

148. Origen, *PArch.*, I 2,8.

149. This is what Origen means by God's substance, cf. *PArch.*, I 2,8.

150. Origen, *PArch.*, I 2.2.7–8.

151. If one reads *In Lib. I Sam.*, I 11 together with *PArch.*, I 1,6; 2,2; 3,8.

152. This is because God's substance is the first cause of being. *PArch.*, I 3,5. cf. Arist. *Metaphysics*, VII..17.1041a10ff.

153. Origen, *PArch.*, I 2,8.

154. This assumption stands behind the emanation theory Origen proposes in *PArch.*, I 2,8–10.

155. Whenever Origen refers to the Son and Holy Spirit it is in terms of categorical reference or relation to the Father. cf. *PArch.*, Praef. 4.

156. Origen, *PArch.*, I 1,6; 2,5–8.

context the categories function to determine the extent to which divinity is transferred to the lower degrees of divinity and reality. As one moves down the degrees of reality, entities are encountered which accrue more qualifications which means that although it appears that divinity and reality share the same essence the fact is that each entity within the chain of reality evinces a distinct kind of existence. Motivated to maintain radical monotheism Origen thus stresses the distinctiveness of his first principle. We can best see evidence how Origen understands the Father by turning to his Commentary on Samuel. Here he conveys the uniqueness of the Father's nature by stressing the unity of his essence and existence. He says of God:

> . . . non est praeter te . . .
> {there is none besides you}

to mean:

> . . . nihil eorum, quae sunt, hoc ipsum,
> quod sunt, naturaliter habent . . .
> {nothing save the Father is by virtue
> of its own nature}[157]

The "Father is by virtue of his own nature." Therefore God is the only substance whose existence is given by none.[158] Deity never received any beginning of being, his existence and essence are identical—substance refers to God the Father alone.[159] The first principle is the only existent whose existence is necessary. Thus universality and necessity belong to primal deity alone.[160] All entities below the first principle exist differently than primal essence. Their essence and existence are by virtue of a being (God) prior to their own being-ness.[161] They are derivative and contingent. They derive their essence from God, their existence from God through the Logos, and their salvation from God and the Logos through the Holy Spirit.

---

157. Origen, *Hom* 1R(S) 1.11. cf. *PArch.* I 2.9.

158. Following Origen, *Hom.* 1R(S) 1.11.

159. The similarity between the formulation of this first principle and the Aristotelian is striking: "Now since we are seeking the first principles and highest causes, clearly there must be some thing to which these belong by virtue of its own nature." Aristotle, *Metaphysics*, IV.1.1003a26ff.

160. Origen, *PArch.*, I 2,2; 2,4; 2,8; cf. *HomJr.*, X 7; *ComJn.*, XX 18; *PArch.*, IV 4,1. They are and exist *kata symbebekos*, cf. *ComJn.*, II.18,75.

161. Origen, *PArch.*, I 3.5 = Just. *Ep. ad Men.*, = Mansi IX 524 = fr. 9. Koe. cf. Jerome, *Ep ad Av.*, II.

Summary: The implications of this formula are significant. Origen accentuates the unique status of the first principle by emphasizing its difference and separation from all other principles. This establishes subordination within divinity. God the Father is the only principle whose essence and existence are identical. He is independent of any other existent and the source of the existence of all other beings. He exists necessarily (*a se*) while the Son and Holy Spirit exist contingently (*per se*).

VIII. Degrees of Divinity and Reality Revisited

Origen argues for the substantial unity of the Father, Son, and Holy Spirit.[162] Nonetheless the Father *toto caelo* distinct from all other kinds of beings and intellects. There is only one entity in Origen's system that is (*ens a se*)—God the Father. All other entities below the first God, like the Son and Holy Spirit, are substances *kath'hauto* (*per se*) but in a different sense from the first principle, or *kata symbebekos* (*per accidens*) like all created beings. This formulation helps explain one puzzle in the evidential record on Origen's first principles. We are told by Justinian that:

> The God the Father who holds the universe together is superior to every being that exists, for he imparts to each one from his own substance that which each one is...[163]

And that:

> God the Father bestows on all the gift of existence ... therefore they obtain first of all their existence from God the Father which endows all with existence.[164]

It is easy to see why the second and third principles might be considered derivative, indeed contingent principles. The Father is the only eternal, non-generated, non-created principle who imparts to all other beings their existence.[165]

Origen states:[166]

---

162. Origen, *PArch*. I 2.2–8.
163. Origen, *PArch.*, I 3,5 = Just. *Ep. ad Men.*, = Mansi IX 524 = fr. 9 Koe. The same definition is preserved in Jerome, cf. *Ep. ad Av.*, II.
164. Origen, *PArch.*, I 3,8.
165. Ibid. I 2,6; 3,3; 3,5; *ComJn.*, II 10,65. cf. Jerome, *Ep. ad Av.* II = Migne XXII 1061.
166. With caution for this is Justinian speaking. Nonetheless the hierarchism of the statement appears congruent with Origen's position. cf. *PArch*. I 2,2–7.

> The God and Father who holds the universe together, is superior to every being that exists, for he imparts to each one from his own existence that which each one is; the Son being less than the Father, is superior to the rational creatures alone (for he is second to the Father); the Holy Spirit is still less, and dwells within the saints alone.[167]

As these passages make clear, the Son and Holy Spirit are subordinate to a primary principle, God the Father. It also appears that his being is identified with primary substance. If so, it follows that the proper designation for the derivative principles in this system are secondary substance. Their ground and cause is the principle who imparts existence to them, God the Father. The clear implication of this is a separation of the first principle from all other principles.

If this reconstruction is accurate, then the first principle's transcendence signifies that it is not an essence like other essences and therefore exists differently than all other entities. There is little question Origen distinguishes quite sharply between this first principle of his system from the second, the second principle from the third, and then the first principles from all created things. His system clearly reflects a theological and ontological hierarchism which attenuates a separation between types of divinity and reality. The same logic applied to the levels of divine being also are involved in characterizing the valuation of the divine principles, and this is what one might expect given the fact of the existence degrees of reality. Hence the location of principles itself becomes a complex question and this is done through the categories. This is well illustrated by Origen's terminology.

The Father is a primary substance, that is a substance beyond genus, species, differentia—a God *hyper ekeina ousias presbeia kai dynamei*.[168] The Son is a secondary substance, that is a primary genus—an *ousion hen*, an *ousia ousion* or an *idea ideon*.[169] The intelligibles are a secondary substance that is universal genera and species.[170] The sensibles are a secondary substance, specific genera and species.[171] In the case of the created intelligibles and sensibles we encounter created entities which are substances that exist by nature *kata symbebekos* (per accidens).[172] Their essence is accidental and

---

167. Origen, *PArch*. I 3.5 = Just. *Ep. Ad Men.* = Mansi 9.524 = fr. 9 Koe. The same definition is preserved in Jerome. Cf. *Ep. Ad Av.* 2

168. Origen, *PArch*. I 1,6; *CCels*., VII 38.

169. Origen, *PArch*., I 2,2; *CCels*., III 64; VI 64; *ComJn*., I 119,113f.

170. Origen, *CCels*., VI 64; *PArch*., I 4,5.

171. Origen, *CCels*., V 39; *ComJn*., I 1,24.7ff.

172. Origen, *PArch*, I 2,13; *ComJn*., II 18.

their existence is inherent.[173] Thus although Origen argues for the essential unity of the Father, Son, and Holy Spirit, it also appears he assumes an existential difference between first principles.[174] Consequently Origen's hierarchism has its proximate foundation in the theological assertion that God is an essence whose existence is totally different from all the other kinds of essences and existences. This is based on the assumption that only in God are essence and existence one which means the first principle is the only subsistent being while all others beings are inherent for they derive their essence and existence from the Father.

Summary: Origen throws into relief some of the issues previously raised in Platonic and Peripatetic thought. The results are an articulation of the distinctness between levels of divinity and a telescoping of the levels of reality into a ultimate unitary substance. These may best be explained by examining the levels of divinity and reality arranged below the first principle in his system. Universality and necessity belong to the Logos. The Logos is the creator of all things.[175] He pertains essentially to God while all rational being pertains to him. In this sense the Logos is the sustainer of all types of being.[176] Particularity and necessity belong to the Holy Spirit who is the sustainer of the "saints".[177] He pertains essentially to God the Logos and only the saved pertain to him. The Holy Spirit is the sustainer of certain types of rational being in that particularity and contingency belong to the created intelligibles and the sensibles.[178]

IX. Being Divine

Origen provides an analysis of first principles different from earlier thinkers such as Philo, Clement, Numenius and Alcinous in two ways. First, he treats the first principle as a being different in kind from all other beings; and secondly by analyzing the nature of divinity and reality in terms of the essence-existence relation, he makes necessary substance the very ground of

---

173. Origen, *PArch.*, III 1,3. This is a prelude to the argument that rational beings un-like non-rational ones have free-will. cf. *PArch.* III 1. 3–6.

174. Origen, *PArch.* I 2.2–8.

175. There was no time when he was not, cf. *PArch.* IV 4,1. He also gives existence to all things, cf. *PArch.* I 5,5.

176. Origen, *PArch.*III 1,2 where the Logos is the efficient or instrumental cause of created things.

177. Origen, *PArch.*, Praef.4.; I 2,3

178. Origen, *ComJn.*, II 10.

a hierarchical divinity-reality relation. It is perhaps on these grounds Origen categorically and prepositionally refers to God as being and intellect and beyond being and intellect, finally reaching the formula that he is beyond being and intellect in respect to his dignity and power. This compromise not only throws into relief one of the central issues in later ancient philosophical theology—transcendence. It also offers an abrasive category edge for those who toil in the garden of later Patristic and Platonic theology—hammering out what the identity and relation among first principles are or could be.

Origen assumes reality is subsumed under a common *ousia* and the categories modify or qualify the kind of reality each substance is[179] but he also argues that the substance of the Logos is the impress and image of God's substance[180] and the substance of the Holy Spirit is the copy of the substance of the Logos.[181] The Logos and Holy Spirit appear to be necessary beings whose existence is contingent, for their existence is either eternally generated in the case of the Son, or generated in the case of the Holy Spirit.[182] The ontological fault-line within Origen's degree of reality system rests on distinctions between essential being and accidental being and subsistent and inherent existence. If only the Father is essential and subsistent and all other entities are accidental and inherent; then it follows a *qualitative* identity and *per se* relation exists among first principles.

Thus only God the Father has a unity of essence and existence. The distinction between essence and existence for the Logos and Holy Spirit means a likeness or co-equality (with God the Father. They are principles whose essence and existence are not identical. The Logos and Holy Spirit are not by virtue of their own nature but by virtue of God's nature.[183] The Trinity in nuce is a triad of *pros hen* equivocals. The core of this explanation lies in Origen's acceptance of the notion of hierarchy within the divine world. What is found in Origen is a first principles based on degrees of divinity categorically indexed to an ontological hierarchy recognized within the level of real being itself. Since this hierarchical theology is explained through the categories each divine level represents a separate degree and type of being and intellection which means the higher nature of the first principle is fixed in character and so it is properly related to true being as

---

179. Origen, PArch. I 1,6; 2,2; 2,5; 2,7; 2,8; 2,9; 3,5; 3,8; cf. I 4,5; IV 4,1.

180. Ibid. PArch. Praef 4; I 2,6; 3,5. cf. Jerome, Ep. ad Av. 2 = Migne XXII 1060; Hieron. Ep., XCII= Migne XXII 762.

181. Origen, ComJn., II 10; PArch. Praef. 4; Justinian, Ep. ad Men.= fr. 9 Koe. = Migne XXII 1060.

182. Origen, PArch.,I 3,5; 2,6; ComJn., fr. 1 {Koe}.

183. The statements that claim this are numerous. cf. e.g., PArch., I 1,6; 2,2; 2,5; 2,6; 2,7; 2,8; 2,13; cf. I 3,5; 3,8.

the union of essence and existence just as the lower natures of the second and third principles are fixed in character so as they are properly related to true being as the separation of essence and existence.

While this categorical theology distinguishes between types of deity, it also functions to reinforce the central connection and similarity between first principles and the lower ranks of reality. All reality is subsumed under a common substance identified with the first principle and each degree of reality is linked to divinity because of its fundamental substantiality. In this sense Origen's degree of reality system displays a modalism that eschews any claims of radical discontinuity within the theological and ontological hierarchy.[184] Although Origen affirms the radical transcendence of the first principle the Father is nonetheless a substance who shares his substantiality with all levels of divinity and reality. There is no fundamental separation between levels of divinity and reality. Divinity exhibits the character of kinds which can admit degrees and hypostases. Each hypostasis manifests in its own way the essence-existence relation. They are separate divine entities who share being equally but who exist differently. As the necessary ground of being they are the necessary and contingent product of his substantiality, intellection, and volition.

Conclusion

Origen of Alexandria wrote no commentaries on the works of Plato, Aristotle or the Stoa let alone on the categories devoting himself largely to exegeses of Scripture. Thus a popular view among some Origen scholars is thus that he was a tangential sojourner in the rarified air of later ancient philosophy. Although there is much to support such a reading, this enquiry takes a different tack. It is proposed that the categories are not merely utterances reduced to propositions in representational terms but are signs (*semata*) that make visible—*hic et nunc*—reality. Categories map a reality that is not normally or momentarily visible. In this sense, Origen did not confine the categories to what is merely linguistic, conceptual and interiorized space, where the relation of subject to object is that of a spectator looking at reality through images. Thus he did not read categories in a random manner, nor did he juxtapose them with little regard for metaphysical coherence. Rather he understood the categories as a classification of being with grammatical, logical and ontological meaning.

Mapping the Aristotelian categories under the Platonic categories of the Absolute (*kath' hauto*) and the Relative (*pros ti*), Origen established a list of

184

ultimate classes of 'what there is' and assigned corresponding Aristotelian categories to each so that categorical distinctions map the way 'beings are' in terms of their ontological properties and qualities. He mapped ontology as a scale of beings in which the less perfect is to be understood in terms of the more perfect and ultimately in terms of their dependence on God the Father himself—as if everything is like him in the limited way it could be. Origen uses the categories to make two main points. Firstly, God is the essential and necessary being and intellect and all other entities are accidental and contingent beings and intellects. Secondly, all levels of contingent reality have their ground in a necessary principle of unity.—God the Father. Although the *ousia* of God is different from any other it is not separated from other beings—or the being of others—which results in a unity between different levels of divinity and reality. The result is a model of divine hypostatic levels where Father, Son and Holy Spirit share a common substance (*ousia*) but also where God the Father is a being different in kind from generated or created being. On Origen's theory, then, substantial forms such as God, Logos, and Holy Spirit rather than concrete objects like angels, humans, fish and bread are the basic 'abstract entities.' Everything else that is depends on these substantial forms for their being. He also proposes that their 'divine' properties are realized in objects with 'ordinary' properties as forms (*logoi*) that constitutes an object and with suitable discipline we can acquire such properties and 'become' 'like' these intellects and even engage in a kind of divine thinking. Here Origen transforms later Platonic conceptions of non-discursive thinking by treating quite differently the idea of contact with incomposites like God the Father and God the Son. Contact is not spread out but timeless and consummated in the *praxis* of contemplative prayer.

7

Transcendentals and Methodological Solipsism

> O star of evening, you bring all things homeward
> that the shining dawn dispersed.
>
> —Sappho, fr. 95

Précis

SCHROEDER NOTES THAT ARMSTRONG's metaphor of "intelligible architecture" has entered and informed the language of Plotinian metaphysics.[1] A part of the "intelligible architecture" includes use of categories to map reality. Plotinus sets forth his doctrine of the categories in (*Ennead*, VI.1-3). He attacks the Aristotelian categories on grounds that they cannot apply to both the sensible and intelligible worlds.[2] Plotinus and Hegel propose new sets of categories on grounds that the Aristotelian and Kantian categories

---

1 See Schroeder, *Plotinus*, 83.

2. An immense literature exists on Plotinus' critique of Aristotelian (and Stoic categories). See Schroeder, *Form and Transformation*, 30-31 and *Categories*, 115-19; Calouri, *Primary Being*, 85-103; Donini, *Plotino*, 17-32; Dufour, *Plotin*, 177-94; Chiaradonna, *Categories*, 12-37, *Catagorie in Plotino*, 121-36 and *Sostanza*; Zhyrkova, *Doctrine of Categories*; Collette, *Dialectique*; Haas, *Context and Strategy*, 39-53 and *Plotinus and Porphyry*, 492-526; Baltzly, *Porphyry and Plotinus*, 49-75; Gerson, *Plotinus*, 79-103; Evangeliou, *Aristotle's Categories*, 73-82 and *Ontological Basis*; Gurtler, *Origin of Genera*, 3-15; Strange, *Plotinus, Porphyry*, 955-974; Aubenque, *Plotin e Dexippe*, 7-40, *Occasion Manquee*, 365-387; Anton, *Categorical Theory*, 83-100; Szlezak, *Nuslehre*, 216-25.

are insufficient to do so.³ On the basis of the principle of prior simplicity *transcendentals* are offered in their place.⁴ Here Plotinus rethinks Plato's five *megista gene*—being, motion, rest, identity and difference.⁵ These categories are 'transcendental' in that they go beyond Aristotle's classificatory logic that the essence of a thing is determined by its genus and specific difference.⁶ Hegel rethinks them as Being, Non-Being, and Becoming.⁷ He calls them by the striking singular term—category in that they 'sublate' Kant's 'transcendental' categories.⁸

I. Horizons

What would Plotinus have to say about transcendentals?⁹ The origins of 'transcendentals' arises from Plato's five genera of being;¹⁰ Aristotle's accounts of the identity and relation between the concepts of being and 'the one' where being is said in many ways;¹¹ where he explains the proper

---

3 Plotinus' and later Neoplatonic readings of the Aristotelian categories involves reinterpretation and replacement of them with the *megista gene* of Plato's Sophist and his middle dialogues. cf. Schroeder, *The Categories*, 115–36.; Blumenthal, *Aristotle in the Service of Platonism*, 340–64; Gurtler, *Origin of Genera*, 3–15. Also see Corrigan, *Essence and Existence* and Gerson, *Aristotle and Other Platonists* on the reception of Aristotle's categories in Plotinus and the Neoplatonic tradition. Hegel's transcendentals arise out of the medieval problem of universals which began with Philip the Chanchellor's *Summa de bono* to be continued by a variety of Scholastics including Alexander of Halles, Gregory the Great, Thomas Aquinas, Duns Scotus, Suarez, and Nicholas of Cusa. See Allan and Wippel, *Medieval Philosophy*; and Aersten, *Transcendentals*.

4 For the background of this category shift see Bauloye and Rutten, *Genres e Categories*, 103–19.

5 Plato, *Sophist*, 249e–259e esp. 255e–257a; Plotinus, *Ennead*, VI.1-.3.

6. Aristotle, *Topics*, VI139a27–30.

7. With focus on the scholastic notion of Super-transcendental Being. For the background to Hegel's use of scholastic and early modern notions of transcendentals see, Vescovini, *Transcendentaux*; di Vona, *Spinoza*.

8 Hegel, *Phenomenology of Spirit*, 1977, 142–43. cf. Doyle, *Borders*, 2012.

9. Plotinus' transcendentals are the five genera of Plato's *Sophist*. Motion and Difference are associated with the descent into plurality that occurs at the phase of descent or Procession, while Being, rest, and Identity are identified with the stability acquired through ascent or Reversion. *Nous* has determinate contents and carries plurality within itself. It is the principle through which Being proceeds from itself. Plotinus uses the 'transcendental' categories to map its descent where there is loss of knowledge and in its ascent where there is an increasing richness in the content of Being. cf. Plotinus, *Enneads*, II.4.5.28–35; III.7.3.8–11); V.1.4.30–43; VI.2.7–8.

10 Plato, *Sophist*, 249e–259e esp. 255e–257b.

11 Aristotle, *Metaphysics*, IV.2.103b23–24.

meaning of 'the one' is indivisible;[12] and his focal meaning of being which reduces the homonymy of the term to insure the unity of metaphysics and its possibility as a science (*episteme*).[13]

Plotinus's and Hegel's analysis of the Aristotelian and Kantian categories are straightforward. Aristotle uses categories of classificatory logic to define the essence of what a thing is determined by the concept of genus and specific difference, and Kant treats categories as the condition for the possibility of things or objects.[14]

They claim that Aristotle's class logic of definition and Kant's 'transcendental' categories reach their limits in the realm of philosophical principles. First principles cannot be classified 'categorically.' They can only be approached by a kind of reflection which Aristotle following Plato's called *nous*.[15] Here Plotinus and Hegel tack boldly and differently. 'Transcendentals' allow a mapping of the highest kinds or essences and thus the meanings such entities might have.[16]

The bridge from Plotinus to Hegel lies through Spinoza and Kant. It is with Spinoza that Hegel finds the most fully developed "standpoint of substance" before he offered his own absolute formulation.[17] Spinoza claims thinking begin with the absolute—substance. Here substance is not yet pure thought or *Geist*, as Hegel proposes but Spinoza understands correctly—thinking begins with absolute substance, equally fundamentally and resolutely as thinking itself. Hegel argues Kant's path is even more decisive than Spinoza's. He sees Kant's idea of the original synthesis of apperception "one of the most profound principles for speculative development.[18] His claim that the pure forms of intuition, space and time and the pure concepts of understanding are transcendental in the sense that they constitute the conditions for the possibility of experience is a revolutionary move. "Ich Denke" is a formal necessity and unifying principle of apperception which constitutes the necessary precondition for any "consciousness." As such

---

12. Aristotle, *Metaphysics*, X.1052b16

13. Aristotle, *Metaphysics*, IV.2.1003a32ff.

14. Aristotle, *Topics*, VI139a27–30; Kant, *KrV*, A80/B106.

15. Aristotle, *Posterior Analytics*, II.100b5–17; For *nous* in Plato see, *Phaedo*, 99e; *Republic*, 511c.

16. Husserl's distinction between meaning and object categories is helpful here. Plotinus' and Hegel's transcendentals are categories that carry meaning. Husserl, 1913, *Ideen* SS 61–62.

17. Hegel, *Logic*, III.2.216–217.

18. Hegel, *LL* sect. 20.

"transcendental" is in the sense of providing the ground or structure of "absolute" knowledge that which transcends our experience.[19]

Summary: Hegel is dissatisfied with Kant's notions of 'transcendental' and self-knowledge. Thus he introduces the concept of *Geist* or universal mind to replace traditional concepts of soul, consciousness and *ego*. Descartes *Cogito* and Kant's transcendental *ego* are too subjective and self-referential and thus incapable of resolving or solving philosophical *aporiai*. Hegel has a rather different starting point:

> A self having knowledge purely of itself in the absolute antithesis itself . . . The beginning of philosophy presupposes or demands from consciousness that it should feel at home in this environment.[20]

II. Transcendentals

A comparison of Plotinus' and Hegel's 'transcendental' categories to the medieval notion of transcendentals is at best analogical.[21] They share little in common with Kant's notion of the 'transcendental'.[22] Plotinus uses 'transcendentals' in thought experiments to address problems such as that of evil.[23] Hegel's employs 'transcendentals' as speculative propositions that mirror the *Aufhebung* (sublation) of their immanent positing—in the senses of the word "limit" (*horos*) as both boundary and definition. Like the sayings of Heraclitus about the One, Hegel's transcendentals map the "Absolute" in its contradictory and dialectical forms.[24]

---

19. Kant, *KrV* B133.

20. Hegel, *Phenomenology*, 86.

21. The *Summa de bono* of Philip the Chancellor (ca. 1225) is considered the initial formulation of a doctrine of the transcendentals. cf. Aersten, 2012, 109–27. Plotinus and Hegel's categories are not transcendentals in the sense developed in detail in medieval Scholasticism. This medieval doctrine presupposes an Aristotelian ontology ultimately rejected by Plotinus and Hegel. Rather what is suggested is that Plotinus' five genera and Hegel categories of Being-Becoming-Non-Being are employed in a transcendental manner akin to the way transcendentals functioned in medieval philosophy.

22 For Kant, the term transcendental no longer signifies that which transcends our experience in the sense of providing its ground or structure. Here the pure forms of intuition (space and time) and the pure concepts of the understanding (such as substance and cause) are transcendental in the sense that they constitute the conditions for the possibility of experience.

23. See, O'Brien, *Plotinus*, 171–95.

24. On "limit" see, Hegel, *Science of Logic*, 122–29.

A way into Hegel's notion of 'transcendentals' is through his conception of *Geist* which refers to a general consciousness common to everyone, an "absolute" conception of humanity as one and recognition of one's identity as universal Spirit. *Geist* is universal only in that it is a name of those properties possessed by every human consciousness. It is something more and other than a Cartesian *cogito* or Kantian transcendental *ego* which carries with it notion that there is one *cogito/ego* for each person: that "I" and "I" think refer to individual persons. *Geist* does not individuate individual persons. In this sense, it is not the substantial "self" of Descartes and Locke; or Wittgenstein's and Ryle's "I" which are the confused use of a grammar of self-reference but Kant's synthetic unity of consciousness"—an abstract "I" that disassembles and analyzes its own content as an activity of self-knowing in reference to itself that motivates Hegel.[25] As a universal consciousness *Geist* is Kant's *ego* but without the claim that there is one *ego* per person. Rather it is it is the name of a single mind common to every individual; that is a concrete reality not the invention of abstraction.[26] It is being-in-itself; its existence and knowledge of its existence are one and the same.[27]

In the shadow of *Nous* and *Geist*, why do Plotinus and Hegel introduce the 'transcendentals' as new categories? First, they assume earlier Aristotelian and Kantian attempts to map being are incomplete and insufficient. Secondly, they parse Non-Being as a contrary and by establishing matter as the *contrariety*, not of being as such but of substance, a novel thought emerges. This begins with the simple opposition which Plato establishes in the *Sophist* between a part of otherness and the being of each thing (258d7-e3) transformed by Plotinus into an opposition between a part of otherness and the Forms (II.4.16.1-3). This 'move' transforms opposition into a *contrariety* (I.8.6.28-59) and establishes the "form of non-being" as a contrary to positive characterizations of substance as merely not beautiful but ugly; as not merely not good but as evil (I.8.10).[28]

Hegel claims both Aristotle's and Kant's categories fail to adequately map Being.[29] His predecessors make the mistake of treating reality as made up of discrete particulars when it is a dialectical whole. Moreover, since their categories of thought are abstractions they do not properly represent

25. Hegel, *LL*, sect. 20. cf. Findlay, *Hegel*, ch. 2.
26. Hegel, *Encyclopedia, Lesser Logic* (*LL*) sect. 34.
27. Solomon, *Hegel*, 3-17.
28. O'Brien, *Plotinus*, 171-95.

29 Hegel illustrates this in his mapping the dialectical relationship of Being, Non-Being, and Becoming. The dualism of (1) Being and (2) Non-Being is overcome by duality. That is to say, the duality of Being and Non-Being is dialectically "sublated" in (3) Becoming.

the continuum of reality. They do not, for example, indicate a thing's identity includes its relations to that which it is *not*.

In mapping a thing's identity or relation with the Peripatetic categories, for example, an object is represented "abstractly" not concretely. Consequently, things are related externally not internally. The concreteness of objects are internal not external; real not abstract.

In each of the first three chapters of the *Phenomenology* Hegel parses a "form of consciousness" that is not specifically mental but an intentionality, a knowing something in which we are watching a process or a contradiction through three states of consciousness—sense, perception and understanding—until we reach a form of consciousness that is self-reflective.[30] Leaving understanding and consciousness we enter self-consciousness to attain reason where individual consciousness is inherent absolute reality or the conscious certainty of being all reality.[31] Here Hegel claims epistemology becomes ontology of knowledge.[32] Thus Kant's insistence that the categories are merely subjective concepts of the human mind precluded Hegel's use of them as principles for an explanation of reality. The Kantian categories are not ontological principles of being, but epistemological principles of knowing.

Summary: Plotinus' five genera and Hegel's triad of categories function as transcendentals of Reason not of Understanding Plotinus and Hegel propose that only 'transcendentals' can be used to map Being. Moreover, since Plotinus' *Nous* and Hegel's *Bewusstsein* are expressions of a *We* consciousness, not an *I* consciousness. Thus *We* consciousness requires new categories, otherwise Being as a *We* continuum cannot be mapped or known at all.

III. Thought Experiments

Plato's *megista gene* and Plotinus' interpretation of them have produced commentaries from late antiquity to the present age.[33] Since it would be redundant to review these commentary traditions, focus is on how

---

30. Hegel, *Phenomenology of Spirit*, 75/B149-151.
31. Hegel, *Phenomenology of Spirit*, 131/B219; 174/B272; 175/B273..
32. See Solomon, *Hegel*, 20-24.
33. On Being and Non-Being in Plato's *Sophist* and Statesman On Plotinus reading of Plato's *Sophist* see, See Gill, *Method and Metaphysics* and *Division and Definition*. On Plotinus' reading of Plato's *megista gene* see Corrigan, *Essence and Existence*, 103-29. On Neoplatonic readings of Aristotle's categories see Gerson, *Aristotle and Other Platonists*, 76-100; Blumenthal, *Soul and Intellect*, 82-104.

Plotinus and Hegel employ 'transcendentals' to map reality through thought experiments.[34]

III.1. Mapping Reality

How do Plotinus and Hegel map reality? With Plotinus the descent from unity to multiplicity and the ascent from multiplicity to unity are not historical movements. We do not see the past, present, and future as directed toward greater and greater realization of Being itself. For Plotinus, the One is ever complete and realized. It radiates its fullness always. Thus, there is no temporal or historical dimension to the One. Time and history are of no significance for the One itself. Second, as we move from the One, we have less and less unity and more and more multiplicity. Hence, we are further and further from true being and reality. With Hegel as we get more and more concrete articulation in time and space in the course of history, we get a greater realization of *Geist* itself. Hegel views the entire cosmos and history as the Absolute coming into greater actualization and greater articulation in multiplicity in an orderly, rationally understandable way.

Where there is agreement Plotinus and Hegel bring *contrariety* and *change* into mapping reality in two different but complementary ways. The use of the contraries to designate sameness and difference not as opposites but as relatedness, allows Hegel to read Plotinus' theory as a precursor to his own notion of the dialectical unfolding of contrarieties as Being, Non-Being, Becoming. In the mapping of Being reached by Hegel, Being is thought thinking itself; and thought thinking itself as Absolute Idea dialectically thinking itself.

Each arrives at their conclusions by viewing epistemological theories as ontological claims. Both assert that ontology is limited by epistemology, but they also argue that no epistemology can avoid ontological commitments. Thus, attention has to be made to the role of philosophical critique in the determination as well as the analysis of understanding. Philosophy is not only reflection upon but also includes the structuring of our knowledge. Accordingly, philosophy is a matter of *reason* rather than merely *understanding*. Philosophizing about knowing is a self-confirming activity.

Claims—that knowing and philosophizing about knowing are self-confirming activities does not entail the fallacy that all knowledge is of *my* own creation. Rather concepts and propositions that arise from philosophizing about knowledge and being are concepts. Such concepts function as

---

34. On the thought experiment in Plotinus see A. Smith, *Porphyry' Place*. On its application see Rappe, *Self-Knowledge and Subjectivity*, 250–74.

rules or basic presuppositions or self-confirming stipulations that provide a framework for knowledge of being. It is in this sense, however differently Plotinus conceives of intellect and Hegel of consciousness, both insist that knowledge is self-confirming and that certain basic concepts of *intellect* and *reason* are contributed by the knower. Another way of viewing this is that for Plotinus and Hegel there are no concept-free representations. What *we* know is determined by the concepts and language *we* provide to describe what *we* know. The central and fundamental theoretical commitments in the organization of experience and knowledge are our *own* contribution. That is to say, if knowledge depends on the way *we* understand it, our understanding in turn depends upon the way *we* reason.

Summary: The difference between understanding (*dianoia, Verstand*), intellect (*Nous*), and reason (*Vernunft*) is that the *dianoia* and *Verstand* applies categorical concepts in an unreflective, rigid, and mechanical way, while the *Nous* and *Vernunft* apply categorical concepts in a *we*-reflecting manner that takes into consideration every possible coherent conceptualization of experience and knowledge. Understanding which is finite can only understand the finite. Thus, understanding alone is not equal to the tasks of philosophy. Only *Nous* and *Geist* are.

IV. Methodological Solipsism

How can an analysis of self-reflexivity (*sunaisthesis*) and self-consciousness (*Selbstbewusstein*) be carried out from the vantage-point of methodological solipsism? We cannot appeal to an empirical study of consciousness, to other person's experiences of themselves, or to the language we use when we communicate about ourselves, or even to myself as a person for persons have bodies. The test for methodological solipsism is an analysis of the basic concepts of the method itself. Thus Aristotle, Plotinus, Descartes, Kant and Hegel are concerned to analyze the first-person standpoint and self-consciousness which lie at its foundations. Thus according to methodological solipsism, I ask two questions: firstly, "how can I come to be self-reflective or conscious of myself; and secondly, how can I come to be self-reflective or conscious of the existence of other minds?"

Methodological solipsism is the thesis that mental states and properties can be individuated on the basis of that state or property's relations with other internal states without reference to the external world.[35]

---

35 As a research strategy methodological solipsism was introduced by Husserl (as eidetic reduction or epoche), Carnap, Putnam and Fodor. cf. Fodor, *Methodological*

It is a strategy developed to defend an internalist conception of the mental.[36] It is used to defend the possibility of the existence of other minds on perceptual grounds. It can also be used to access other minds on cognitive grounds. The fundamental difference between ancient and modern methodological solipsisms is that ancient philosophers tend toward realism which entails the extensionalist-internalist claim that a real thinking being is essential for my self-reflexivity or consciousness. Modern philosophers generally argue the contrary—that no external thinking being is essential for my mental states or properties.

Aristotle, Plotinus and Hegel employ methodological solipsism to expand the kinds of questions one might ask, and the types of appeal one can make from an *I* to a *We* philosophical standpoint.[37] They view methodological solipsism as a first-person philosophical orientation that restricts the kinds of questions one might ask and the types of appeal one can make from the *I* philosophical standpoint or from the *I* to *We* philosophical standpoint. Consequently, notions of self-identity as *We*, and their use of methodological solipsism as a philosophical rule which allows a move from an *I* to a *We*, opens up new horizons for philosophical thinking.[38]

Solipsism, 63–109. Several variants go under the rubric of methodological solipsism which is: (a) is a first-person philosophical orientation that restricts the kinds of questions one might ask and the types of appeal one can make from an I standpoint. It is the idea that when we seek to explain why sentient beings think/behave in certain ways by looking to what they think, believe, desire, hope and fear, we should identify these mental states only with events that occur inside the mind (or brain), not with external events, since events that occur in the mind/brain alone are the proximate and sufficient causal explanations for thinking/consciousness. (b) Methodological solipsism also makes possible the expansion of the first-person perspective into a collective one that includes other minds. Thus it is not a strategy that restricts the validity of certain metaphysical claims within a first person standpoint, nor is it the view that the only things that can be meaningfully said to exist are our subjective mental states. It is employed to expand the kinds of questions one might ask, and the types of appeal one can make from an *I* (self-identity) in order to arrive at a *We* (other minds) standpoint. Other types of solipsism include epistemic, emphatic, semantic, psychological, ontological, and absolute solipsism.

36 The question is whether it is possible for two people to have the same beliefs about things in an external world. Externalists argue such claims are invalid. See the twin earth thought experiment. cf. Putnam, *Ready Made World* and *Mind, Language, Reality*.

37. Solomon claims this strategy is employed by Hegel. cf. Solomon, *Hegel*, 18–36. Its use by Aristotle and Plotinus, however have received limited attention. cf. Oehler, *Subjektivitaet und Selbstbewusstsein*.

38. In pursuit of a physicalist ontology, Fodor reduced the representational character of the mental and intentionality to physical-causal relations. He analyzed particular mental event types in terms of: 1) functional states within the thinking organism, defined by causal relations among beliefs, desires etc.; and 2) reference relations to things

It is clear—"*We* think" holds a precious place in Aristotle's, Plotinus' and Hegel's methodological solipsisms. It is not only one self-evident truth among others, but the highest principle in the whole sphere of human knowledge. It is also the first principle of philosophical methodology and a criterion for philosophical truth. In egoistic solipsism, every philosophical problem is *understood* as *my* problem. The question "what is knowledge" is generally cast as "what is it for *me* to know something?" *I* determine what is justifiable for *me* to believe or know according to the evidence which *I* have. Here there can be no appeal to other persons, to common sense, to theories or models which *I* cannot justify for myself. In methodological solipsism "what is knowledge" is cast as "what is it for *us* to know something?

Summary: In their respective methodological solipsisms "what is knowledge" is cast as "what is it for *us* to know something? Accordingly, *our* knowledge can be understood and defended only in terms of the *We* of self-reflexivity or absolute consciousness. Eventually, every philosophical problem is *reasoned* as *our* problem. Now *We* determine what is justifiable for us to believe or know according to the evidence which we have.[39]

V. Mapping Methodological Solipsism

V.1. Aristotle

Aristotle uses methodological solipsism to move from a first-person I to a first-person We standpoint. A 'first person' methodological perspective is derivative of *episteme*:

> There is an *episteme* that contemplates (*theorei*) being as being (*on e on*) and that which belongs to it per se (*kath'auto*).[40]

---

outside the organism, defined by causal relations between internal states of the organism and the environment. Aristotle, Plotinus, Hegel and Husserl do not agree with Fodor's physicalist-functionalist ontology nor with either aspect of his reduction of the essence of the intentional to patterns of causal-functional relations among experiences. What they do agree upon is the use of methodological solipsism as a research strategy.

39 Fodor, following Carnap's and Putnam's earlier investigations, claims that methodological solipsism is a research strategy whereby mental activity is abstracted from its physical basis. Here the focus is upon the agent's contribution to propositional attitudes, subtracting away the contents. The result of methodological solipsism is the claim that no real being is essential for the being of consciousness. cf. Fodor, *Methodological Solipsism*, 63–109.

40. Aristotle, *Metaphysics*, 1003a21, 29, 28.

This *episteme* is a first philosophy (*prote philosophia*) that directs its contemplation to being as being treats it not in a piecemeal fashion but as a whole and treats it universally. Its goal is wisdom (*sophia*) of the first causes (*ta prota aitia*) and of the principles (*archai*).[41] In the opening paragraphs of the second chapter Aristotle refers to the ways one speaks about being. Language reveals that all-that-is is related to one nature—being (*ousia*) and has the character of *noesis* whose subject matter is a *noeton* described as an a-synthetic whole that is pre-given and constitutes itself in the noetic act as the unity of its momenta.

> For that which is capable of receiving the *noeton* and the *ousia* is *Nous*. But it is active when it possesses it.[42]

And it is this active possession of thought as thought which is *theoria*.[43] It has the character of *adiaireta* or *asuntheta*—indivisibility—and in *noesis* one grasps or touches (*thigein*) them. Human *noesis*, unlike the divine, has various *noeta* possessed in thought by thought.[44] These can be *Nous* or *noesis* itself;[45] or principles and ultimate causes;[46] or *ousia*.[47] Such thinking requires a specific human attitude or *praxis* which fulfills (*entelecheia*) the human task (*ergon anthropinon*) of an *episteme* that contemplates being as being.[48] Such thinking involves a kind of methodological solipsism.

Summary: Aristotle lies open to Wittgenstein's skeptical challenge that the meaning or referents of all words are mental entities uniquely accessible only to the language user (*semantic solipsism*); that semantic solipsism can lead to its variant (*psychological solipsism*) where first person ascriptions of psychological states have a meaning fundamentally different from that of second or third person ascriptions; and that in extreme forms semantic solipsism can lead to the view that the only things that can be meaningfully said to exist are ourselves or our own mental states (*ontological solipsism*).[49]

---

41 Aristotle, *Metaphysics*, I.1.981b29–982a3.
42. Aristotle, *Metaphysics*, XII.7.1072b22.
43. Aristotle, *Metaphysics*, XII.7.1072b24.
44. Aristotle, *Metaphysics*, XII.7.1072b22.
45. Aristotle, *Metaphysics*, XII.7.1074b35.
46. Aristotle, *Metaphysics*, I.1. 981b28ff; 982b1ff; 983a5ff..
47. Aristotle, *Metaphysics*, XII.9. 1075a2; *De Anima* III.6.430b26.
48 Aristotle, *Nicomachean Ethics*, 1177a10ff.
49. Wittgenstein, *Blue Book*, 48, 55. 67.

V.2. Plotinus

Plotinus also discusses the ways in which we know. Knowledge (*episteme*) is found in the intellect that thinks itself where there is the self-presence of knower and known and in which there is no separation between knower and known.[50] This kind of knowledge is very different from which we are familiar. It negates what characterizes what we normally know by not depending on mediating images, logical processes, deliberations, calculations, arguments and deductions. It is an awareness of the existence of another *Nous* from which we derive our concepts. It is 'thought thinking itself,'[51] which involves a methodological solipsism different in kind from Aristotle's. All thinking implies variety and differences in what is thought even at the level of *Nous*.[52] Even Intellect's thinking implies deficiency and thus methodological solipsism has a certain uncertainty. It has a yearning for a type of 'absolute solipsism' absolutely simple and complete but which is possessed only by the One.[53]

It makes no sense to ask what things are like apart from one's possible knowledge of them. Nonetheless, the ultimate challenge to methodological solipsism is skepticism: that methodological solipsism might degenerate into psychological, ontological or absolute solipsism. Traditional skepticism is a direct consequence of phenomenalism—the separation of knowledge and object. Hegel would answer that since our experience is necessarily experience of physical objects and our knowledge necessarily knowledge of mental objects, such a slide is impossible. Since *We* constitute *our* experience and knowledge there is no place for the skeptic to get a wedge in. Self-knowledge is grounded in a *Nous* that thinks itself.[54]

Summary: The skeptic may get a second chance with Plotinus in two ways:[55] First, the possibility of true knowledge can be known only if the object known is the same as the subject that knows. But even at the level of *Nous* there remains a vulnerable gap between knowledge and object. Secondly, *Nous* cannot think beyond itself to "think" the One. On both counts a possible slip into psychological or ontological solipsism could be avoided by shifting *nous* to

---

50. Plotinus, *Ennead*, V.3.5.43–46.
51. Plotinus, *Ennead*, V.3.5.46–48.
52. Plotinus, *Ennead*, V.3.10.31–43.
53. Plotinus, *Ennead*, V.3.10.49–50.
54. Plotinus, *Ennead*, V.3.5–9.
55. Plotinus, *Ennead*, V.5.2.18–20. cf. Emilsson, *Intellect*, 234–44.

the One. But this is a metaphysically impossible 'move'—even if at the dyadic level there is a kind of proto-noetic One.⁵⁶

V.3. Kant and Hegel

The skeptic gets a third chance at Kant when he asserts a gap between object as phenomenon and object as thing-in-itself. Kant could have addressed the claim that asserting things-in-themselves open up the possibility, at least in the context of methodological solipsism, that *I* can know the *Ding-an-Sich*. If Kant were consistent, if consistency is important, he could avoid slippage out of methodological solipsism by abandoning claims that synthetic *a priori* intuitions and categories are the conditions for the possibility of knowledge. But within Kant's "horizon" this is impossible. There is no way to acknowledge the possibility of a world beyond the transcendental conditions for the possibility of knowledge.

Hegel agrees. He does not deny differences in individual mental states but he suggests we can ignore them. Indeed, *Geist* is a way of thinking about the common properties of all people without denying their differences. Like the transcendental *ego*. It is the subject of all possible experiences but it is not a "thing" to which traditional categories can be applied. It is an "activity" not in the Cartesian/Lockean sense of a mind or soul "substance" lying behind consciousness. Rather *Geist* is consciousness as being-for-itself where its existence and knowledge of its existence is one and the same. As the universal in action, it knows itself as both reference-to-self and being-for-itself.⁵⁷

Nonetheless, there are profound differences between Kant's and Hegel's notions of transcendental *ego*. With Kant there is no appeal to *other* intellects, or to *other* persons which *I* cannot justify for *myself* epistemologically while Hegel appeals to a *common* intellect shared by *other* intellects, or *other* persons which *we* can justify as an epistemology of ontologically for *ourselves*. The rub is for Kant methodological solipsism is a "fact" of *my* intellect, *my* consciousness, or *my* self-consciousness while for Hegel it is a "fact" of self-consciousness. In brief, once the *I* drops out of the formulation, the possibility of individuating intellect and consciousness drops out as well. Thus at the level of *Geist* the subject-object dichotomy dissolves with the consequences that: 1) *We* sublates (*aufhebt*) *I*; 2) then consciousness moves from *I* understanding to a *We* or self-consciousness or reason; whereby 3) *I* attains a *We* knowledge of reality.

---

56. Any image even of the One is not real. It is merely an imagining of the One that takes place in *chora*. cf. Plotinus, *Enneads*, VI.8.11–15–22; I.8.14.5; 15.18.

57 Following, Solomon, *Hegel*, 12–13.

But in rejecting what Russell calls "knowledge by acquaintance" the skeptic gets a fourth chance—now at Hegel. There is a philosophical problem about claims that: a) a dialectical development of consciousness is possible; b) there is an absolute character to knowing (*Wissen*) thus; c) how can a knowing-itself verify itself to itself and for itself? Secondly, does Hegel ignore the possibility of solipsism as a factual and logical impossibility? As Sartre echoing Husserl notes if "consciousness" is translucent—it has no parts and nothing can be hidden in it. But this does not seem to be the case at all. Starting from the distinction between 'being-for-itself' (conscious beings) and being-in-itself (inert objects) consciousness requires the capacity to distinguish it-self and its object. Privacy thus appears to be the defining trait of minds. Or as Locke claims minds are distinguished from one another by the private access each has to its own contents.[58] Here the temptation to say that *Geist* is a mistake nourished on grammar resonates.[59] Or as Ryle puts it—"his quarry was (may be) the hunter."[60] Does the notion of a universal consciousness really make sense when different persons have different ideas, thoughts, feelings and indeed different minds?

Summary: Hegel might respond to the skeptic's challenge in this way. No denial of the privacy and individuality of my mind or other minds is suggested. *Geist* is not we are all one consciousness but at the level of absolute self-consciousness knowing (*Wissen*) and self-consciousness (*Bewusstein*) we are one.[61] Absolute self-consciousness also stands in sharp contrast to any first-person orientation that argues only *my* knowledge can be understood and defended as *my* privileged understanding. If grammar comes into play at all, it is only at the point that it is not clear at all that a change of notation would be of any use. *Geist* does not individuate or speak an individual ordinary language. Even its 'transcendental' grammar and syntax is nothing like that of traditional philosophical discourse. Moreover, methodological solipsism is something to be used. *We* can at any time step out of it and back into absolute solipsism any time -seeing it only as a methodological principle and a dispensable one at that.

---

58. Locke, *Essay*, II.27.9–10.

59. Geach's critique of the Cartesian *cogito* could be extended to Hegel's *Geist*. cf. Geach, *Mental Acts*, 113–17.

60. Ryle, *Concept of Mind*, 198.

61. It becomes the function of the *Phenomenology of Spirit* to discern this relationship.

Conclusion

Gadamer and Collingwood propose that interpretation is not a psychological and subjective act. It is an ontological and epistemological process that occurs in a historical tradition where understanding consists of the making of latent meanings explicit through question and answer logic.[62] In their critiques of the "class" and "transcendental" logics of Aristotle and Kant, Plotinus and Hegel propose theories of 'transcendentals' that move exclusively, however differently, through the medium of what Plato called the concept—"in Ideas, through Ideas, toward Ideas."[63]

For Descartes and Kant, the *Cogito* and *Ich Denke* hold a precious place.[64] It is not only a self-evident truth, the highest principle of knowledge and a criterion of truth but the first principle of what emerges as methodological or phenomenological solipsism. Husserl ups the ante—every philosophical proposition must be justified from a first-person standpoint:

> Anyone who seriously intends to become a philosopher must "once in his life" withdraw into himself and attempt within himself, to overthrow and build anew all the sciences that up to then, he has been accepting. Philosophy—wisdom is the philosopher's quite personal affair. It must arise as his wisdom, as his self acquired knowledge tending toward universality, a knowledge for which he can answer from the beginning, and at each step, by virtue of his own absolute insights . . . All the various insights proceed, as they must, according to guiding principles that are immanent or "innate," in the pure *ego*.[65]

The privileged status of "I" is suspect for Aristotle, Plotinus and Hegel, however. Methodological solipsism can only be defended, if it can be at all, as the first-person *plural* not as a strategy that restricts the validity of certain metaphysical claims within a first person standpoint but as a strategy that makes possible the expansion of the first-person perspective into a collective one. As the "I" drops out of the formulation, the possibility of a mere individuating "self-reflexivity" and "consciousness" drops out also. Moving from *my* thoughts or mental states to *our* thoughts and mental states the psychological and ontological "I" no longer functions as a first principle, axiom, or premise. But as a methodological rule where philosophical problems are reasoned as *our* problem and where philosophical problems are

---

62 Gadamer, *Truth and Method*, 369–70; 373–79. Collingwood, *Essay*, 27–37.
63. Plato, *Republic*, 511c.
64 Descartes, *Meditations*, II-III; Kant *Kr*VB134.
65 Husserl, *Cartesian Meditations*, 2–3.

justified from a first-person standpoint *ourselves*. This attempt to move from *I* to a *We* self-reflexivity or consciousness is perhaps the most fundamental and seductive theme in Hegel's notion of reconciliation (*Versoehnung*). If the task of philosophy is to show how differences, oppositions, ruptures, contrarieties, and contradictions can and must be rectified in the self-identical and self-differentiating totality of *Nous* and *Geist*, then this *aufgehoben* is helpful in addressing our next problem.

8

In and Between Mind and Consciousness

> For my part, whenever I enter most intimately into what I call myself, I always stumble upon some particular perception or other . . . I can never catch myself at any time without perception . . . The mind is a kind of theatre, where several perceptions successively make their appearance to pass, re-pass, glide away and mingle in an infinite varieties of postures and situations. There is properly no simplicity in it at any one time, nor identity in different, whatever natural propensity we may have to imagine that simplicity and identity.
>
> —Hume, *A Treatise of Human Nature*

Précis

THE VERY WHISPER OF "consciousness" has a Cartesian ring to it. Although there are notions of a unified internal subject with thought, language and agency there is no word in Ancient Greek that corresponds to "consciousness" or its concepts and concerns for what we now think of as consciousness characteristic of the modern subjective and reflective self.[1] Does the Latin term *conscientia* adequately translate the Greek terms *nous, sunaisthesis, katanoesis* and/or *parakolouthesis* and their cognates, let alone modern notions of "consciousness," "connaissance," "coscienza" or "Bewusstsein" at

---

1. This includes roughly translating *parakolouthein* as consciousness, *katanoesis* as "I" self-consciousness and *sunaisthesis* as "We" self-consciousness. For a survey of modern and contemporary approaches to what consciousness is see Wilkes, *Losing Consciousness*, Yishi, *Is Consciousness Important?*

all?[2] When does 'consciousness' enter the philosophical lexicon as a technical term? Is it with Augustine or Descartes?[3] Is "consciousness" a "given"[4] in Aristotle[5] and Plotinus?[6] Additional questions include the dependence of time on consciousness[7] and the nature of time-consciousness.[8]

I. Horizons

All of these points shall not be addressed here. To do so would require an examination of mind, soul and consciousness in Aristotle and Plotinus from the precipice of studies ranging from O'Daly, Emilsson and Manchester to Hutchinson, Calouri and Remes—a task too grand in so brief the space allotted. Another tack is suggested: an investigation into the logical structures of mind and consciousness.[9] Focus here is on the basic strategic moves by which philosophers in the history of philosophy have attempted to understand the gap between mind and consciousness, i.e. the ontological and epistemological discontinuity between these two mental states. Descartes, Spinoza and Leibniz exacerbates the problem by undermining Aristotle's numerical and Plotinus' qualitative isomorphism between mind and reality while Locke and Hume further undermine such claims by asserting knowledge is the perception of the agreement or disagreement of our ideas.[10]

   2. See H.M. Robinson, *Objections*.
   3. O'Daly, *Plotinus*, 159-69; Sorabji, *Intentional Objects*, 105-14. 2001; Burnyeat, *Idealism*, 3-40.
   4. Although consciousness is considered a 'given' by many scholars introspection and the phenomena of mental states in Aristotle and Plotinus remain problematic. Stern-Gillet is helpful in noting incommensurability between Plotinus and Augustine on consciousness and introspection: that while each share a theory of "consciousness" only Augustine holds a theory of introspection. cf. Stern-Gillet, *Consciousness*, 1-33 and *Plotinus*, 19-27. Stern's study gives rise to another question. Is introspection a necessary/sufficient condition for consciousness? If so, since Plotinus does not have a theory of introspection does it not follow he also lacks a theory of consciousness? Claims about parsing 'phenomena of consciousness' in Aristotle and Plotinus are another tenuous concern: a central presupposition of phenomenalism is that we understand our relation to the world through sensation and that justified belief in the world rests ultimately on non-inferentially justified beliefs about our sensations—commitments neither Aristotle nor Plotinus hold. cf. Gerson, *Introspection*, 153-73.
   5. See Casten, *Aristotle*, 751-815.
   6. See Blumenthal, *Nous and Soul*, 203-19; Gurtler, *Self and Consciousness*, 113-30; Gerson, *Aristotle and Other Platonists*, 131-72.
   7. Sorabji *Time Creation, Continuum*, 89-97 and Manchester, *Syntax*, 55-105.
   8. Manchester, *Syntax*, 55-105. cf. Calouri, *Plotinus*, 75-103.
   9. Brinkmann, *Objectivity*, 7-9.
   10. Brinkmann, *Objectivity*, 72.

We continue with the observation that Aristotle's reinterpretation of the Platonic Forms and Plotinus' rehabilitation of them allows him to claim an isomorphism between indwelling and intelligible forms which yields a structural parallelism between thinking and being, *nous* and *to on*. The notion of a separate entity in which self-conscious "processes" occur is owed to Descartes; of conscious "processes" to Locke and Hume; and degrees of consciousness, and explicit distinctions between primary/secondary properties, perception/awareness and apperception/self-awareness, to Berkeley, Leibniz, and Kant. In each case "consciousness" best fits into the accuracy of the mind as 'mirror' and questions of the reliability of 'consciousness' to provide accurate reflection on its own representations becomes of paramount importance.[11] The problem is if mind's images no longer point to an archetype "outside" of my mind; then the possibility that thought and language may be transparent to the world is torn asunder.[12] Kant's transcendental turn with having concepts determine reality *a priori* is the result of such a fundamental error. Here we encounter a "return" to Aristotle and Plotinus with the caveat that an isomorphism must obtain between specific objective features of reality and specific structures of the mind for knowledge to be possible at all—otherwise a coherent experience of the world would be impossible.[13]

Après Descartes, Locke, Leibniz and Hume it has also become a commonplace to speak of mental states as internal to a mind and physical states as external to a body. Since Hume, it has also been assumed that causal questions are largely empirical and mental causality is a matter that psychologists or neurophysiologists settle. The view that behavior is fundamental in understanding mental phenomena drives current research. Accordingly, scientific (psychological, methodological) behaviorism and philosophical (logical, analytical) behaviorism dominate discussions of what consciousness is and how brain and behavior account for mental phenomena. Carnap, Hempel and Ayer propose mental expressions have the same meaning as behavioral and bodily processes and dispositions are reducible via behaviorist analysis to psychology or physics and that all mental statements are expressible in a strictly extensional language. Ryle rejects Cartesian dualist and physicalist monist claims that mental statements describe or report non-physical or physical facts. Rather they rationalize or license inferences about behavior. To suppose otherwise is to make a category mistake. Wittgenstein adds to the mix by claiming that semantic statements cannot be

---

11. On consciousness in Descartes, see Judovich, *Subjectivity and Representation*.
12. Dillon, *Aisthesis noete*, 247–62.
13. Rorty, *Mirror of Nature*, 12; Hedley, 11–12.

private, introspectively accessible inner states but inter-subjectively observable behavior within a larger language game.[14]

Indeed, claims that bodies have physical properties and minds mental states and/or that behavior causes mental phenomena have become so much a 'given' a question arises—how do we escape reading modern notions of "consciousness" (*conscientia*) back into Platonic and Aristotelian notions of mind (*nous*), "self-reflexivity" (*sunaisthesis*) and their cognates?[15]

II. Mapping Mental Causality

Questions of how a purely immaterial creator could have produced matter plagued Porphyry and Gregory.[16] What causes their worry is a shared thesis about causation—a cause has to be somewhat like its effect. Gregory's solution is anticipation of theories of primary and secondary properties—that material objects are made up of properties or qualities like color and extension and thus are not material things.[17] A related problem is mental causation and it emerges in two forms: first, how can immaterial mental substance interact with a physical substance; and secondly, how can mental properties be causally relevant to bodies and cause what it does *qua* physical? Here Aristotle defines the problem succinctly:

> If there were no final cause, there would be no reason in things (*oud' an eie nous en tois ousin*). because the man who has intellect (*nous*) always acts for the sake *of* something.[18]

The claim Aristotle defends is an isomorphism between intelligible form and the structure of reality such that the world can itself be said to contain reason and that mind can cause other minds because—cause is like its effects.[19] Next he adds intentionality as a complement to final causality. The foundations of his theory of intentionality begins in where thought thinks itself through participation (*metalepsin*) in the object of thought:

---

14. Philosophical behaviorism underwent criticism by Chisholm, Taylor and Putnam and survives in modified forms as functionalism.

15. Berti offers a corrective survey of interpretations of Aristotle on *nous*. Berti, *Intellection*, 141–63.

16. Porphyry, ap. Proclus *in Tim.* (Diehl) 1.395–96; Gregory, *in Hex. PG* 44, col. 69bc.

17. Sorabji, *Time, Creation, Continuum*, 290–94.

18. Aristotle, *Metaphysics*, II.2. 994b14–17.

19. Brinkmann, *Objectivity*, 71.

> And thought thinks itself through participation (*metalepsin*) in the object of thought for an object of thought becomes (by the act of apprehension and thinking, so that the same: thought and object of thought, i.e. being is thought. And it actually functions when it possesses (this object). *Metaphysics* (XII.7.1072b20–23)[20]

Aristotle then explains why all forms of cognition are intentional:

> ... knowledge and perception and opinion and understanding have always something else as their object ... for to be an act of thinking and to be an object of thought are not the same thing ... in some cases knowledge is the object ... thought and the object of thought are not different in the case of things that do not have matter, divine thought and its object will be the same, i.e. the thinking will be one with the object of its thought.

Since all forms of cognition are 'intentionally' "of something else" (*h'allou*) and only incidentally of themselves:

> Therefore it must be of itself (*auton ara noei*) that the divine thought thinks (since it is the most excellent of things) and its thinking is a thinking on thinking.[21]

We pursue enquiry with a turn to the 'transference' theory of causality: that intentionality, identity and relation provide the needed link between thinking and being. As we have seen, Aristotle and Plotinus hold to such a notion in reference to Parmenides' claims of a causal nexus between thinking and being. Linked to this is a commitment to a version of property dualism where thoughts are instances of mental properties that are not reducible to physical properties and reductionism the view that whatever causal efficacy the mental has is due to the existence of minds and not bodies alone. Two arguments for the irreducibility of mental properties are proposed. The first is the argument from divisibility—minds do not have material properties. The second is the argument from conceivability—it is not conceivable that mental properties such as intentionality are caused only by bodies.

Aristotle claims humans are animals that can contemplate things in isolation and that reality has an intelligibility that can be known and spoken about.[22] As soon as this is asserted reality has a "logical" structure and that mind (*nous*) has the capacity to know that structure it follows that in mapping reality minds become a part of the intelligibility of the

---

20. Aristotle, *Metaphysics*, XII.7.1072b20–23.
21. Aristotle, *Metaphysics* XII.9.1072b34–35.
22. Cleary, *Powers*, 19–64.

cosmos itself.[23] We follow up with Plotinus' claim that the world soul and world-intellect are not merely 'out there' we also find them within ourselves.[24] That thought and language (*logos*) are not only an expression of the intelligibility of reality but mind's instrument capable of knowing and expressing the structure of reality—akin to the "Pythagorean" conviction that the structure of mathematics and the world are the same—is a monumental one. Here Aristotle and Plotinus talk about intellect and its activities as somehow different from soul and its activities.[25] They propose a separable intellect without which there would be no cognition; and 2) a self-reflexive cognition (*noesis*) requiring incorporeality.[26] Plotinus goes so far as to divide soul into two parts descended and undecended with soul's rationality exhibiting two powers—one which is rational and reflective and another which is temporal and erring.[27]

That Aristotle and Plotinus attribute final causality to intelligibility itself (i.e. divine *nous*) is a key to unlocking differences between theories of mind and consciousness. Intellect's 'thinking on thinking' (*noesis noeseos*) is the pure act of thinking itself where the object of thinking is the *concept* of self-contemplation and *noesis* is the *act* of self-contemplation.[28] Its act and object are different in form but the same in content.[29] An even thicker content of self-contemplation emerges with Alexander's, Alcinous' and Plotinus' readings of *noesis noeseos*.[30] Although Plotinus' *nous*, and the self-reflective structure of *noesis noeseos*, harbors a formal distinction between the concept and act of self-contemplation 'thought thinking itself' does not presuppose phenomenal consciousness because its causal role and intentional context consists in its being thought eternally without interruption.[31] *Nous* is a principle that contains the intelligible Forms of all things

---

23. De Koninck, *La Noesis*, 215–18.

24. Sorabji, *Time, Creation, Continuum*, 138–39.

25. Blumenthal, Plotinus' *Psychology*, 1971, 109–11; Gerson, *Plotinus*, 1994, 254–57; Hager, *Aristotelesinterpretationen*, 174–87.

26. See Blumenthal, *Soul and Intellect*, 82–104; Gerson, *God and Greek Philosophy*, 186 and 191–201; *Aristotle and Other Platonists*, 131–72; 196–200; Wagner, *Veridical Causation*, 51–72.

27. With Plotinus' reading Aristotle via Alexander's *De Anima*, 13.9–24. cf. Blumenthal, *Soul and Intellect*, 82–104, esp. 96–97.

28. See Brinkmann in Nyvlt, *Aristotle and Plotinus*, x–xii; Dillon, *Handbook*, 102–10; Schroeder, *Analogy*, 215–25.

29. Aristotle, *Metaphysics*, XII.9.

30. Alcinous, *Ep*. 10.2–5; Alexander, *De Anima*, 80–92; *De Intellectu*, 106.19–108.7.

31. Plotinus, *Enneads*, V.4.2; V.6.1–2.

and its *noesis* is a self-reflexivity, a self-contemplation, a self-knowledge not consciousness or self-consciousness.[32]

III. Parsing Mental Causality

Many features of the contemporary debate on mental causation are present in Aristotle and Plotinus.[33] Both hold to a strong version of property dualism, one insisting that mental properties are *sui generis*—that they are reducible to *Nous* if not the One. A mental substance causes mental events as mental properties. Here a divine Intellect is postulated in order to causally explain how and what we are as noetic-rational structures. Finally, both employ versions of the infinite regress argument to demonstrate the feasibility of mental causality.[34]

Aristotle's notion of the relationship between *dunamis* and *energeia* underlies his theory of causality. The absolute simplicity and priority of *Nous* as presented in *Metaphysics* XII.7 and 9 and *De Anima* III.4–5 insures that divine *nous* while it possesses knowledge of itself and the world also has as final cause an intelligible content the unmoved movers and all subsequent sentient beings.[35] Plotinus underscores in *Ennead* V.4, V.6 and V.4.2 Intellect's causal status by claiming a unity composed by intellect and its object. *Nous* is composite in two ways: it is a compound of act and the object of thinking where the act of thinking (*noesis*) and the object of this act (*noeton*) constitute intellect; thus the object (*noeton*) is multiple.[36]

Although mind, the self and self-knowledge are notoriously obscure terms to define it is clear on the basis of the principle of prior simplicity that sentience has its origins in *Nous*. The immaterial substance imitated by

---

32. *Nous, noesis, sunaisthesis* and their cognates are best translated as self-reflexivity not as "consciousness." Casten notes "consciousness" claims in Aristotle become problematic. Casten, *Aristotle*, 751–815. Blumenthal, Gurtler and Gerson appear to concur in the case of Plotinus. Blumenthal, *Nous and Soul*, 203–19; Gurtler, *Plotinus: Self and Consciousness*, 113–30; Gerson, *Aristotle and Other Platonists*, 131–72; Also see references to consciousness in Emilsson, *Intellect* and *Sense-Perception*.

33. On Aristotle see Casten, *Aristotle on Consciousness*, 751–815. On Plotinus see Schroeder, *Categories*, 115–36.

34. The infinite regress argument shows that a thesis is defective because it generates an infinite series when either (form A) no such series exists or if (form B) were to exist the thesis would lack the role of justification that it is or supposed to play. Mental causality is justified on the argument form whenever individuals x and y share a property F there exists a third individual z which paradigmatically has F to which x and z are related as copies, by participation, by cause and effect.

35. Aristotle, *Metaphysics*, II.2. 994b14–15.

36. On Plotinus' *nous* as composite see O'Meara, *Plotinus*, 49–53.

the heavens is described by Aristotle as an intellect that thinks as 'thought thinking itself.'[37] Alexander proposes our potential to think is brought into activity by an active intellect identified with Aristotle's divine intellect.[38] Here Plotinus in a series of thought experiment proposes that the One is perceived by Intellect as an intelligible entity (*noeton*), that the One has a kind of perception of itself, that it has a thinking activity of itself which differs from *Nous*. Reflecting on Plato's Demiurge who fashions the world after models provided by the Forms and relation between this intellect and the Form of the Good, Plotinus argues for the existence of a divine mind that is separate from the universe and constitutes a unity with the Forms as the cause of my mind and other minds all which leads back to the Platonic thesis of the unity of intellect with its objects the Forms and a Peripatetic *Nous* who is self-knowledge thinking itself in an absolute activity of form—but with no need of Forms at all.[39]

Cognitive terms have emerged among modern scholars to denote mental states and activities such as *nous, noesis, katanoesis, sunaisthesis, parakolouthesis* and *antilepsis*—anchored in the term "consciousness" and its cognates. Both cover a wide range of mental phenomena—ranging from creature to state consciousness which includes particular mental states and properties and mental states which encompass notions of intentionality and meaning.[40] This 'move' signals a shift of some significance that carries with it a series of modern not ancient epistemic assumptions. Arguments of a far more rational, empirical and of idealistic sort have challenged the causal status of mental sentience. According to these arguments, consciousness and self-consciousness are a psychological after-effect requiring no mental causation whatsoever.[41]

Three questions focus on describing the features of "consciousness". The first is the descriptive question: what is the cause of "consciousness;" the second is the explanatory question: how does consciousness exist; and the third is the functional question: why does "consciousness" exist? Two methods allow answers to these questions: the first is phenomenological; and the

---

37. Aristotle, *Metaphysics*, XII.9. 1074b34–35.

38. Alexander, *De Anima*, III.5.

39. Plotinus, *Ennead*, V.9.3.3–8. cf. Plato, *Timaeus*, 28a-29b and *Republic*, 509b.

40. The following outline follows Ventureyra, *Consciousness*, 1–36; Van Gulick, *Consciousness*. cf. Berchman, *Of Clocks, Clouds and Sparrows*, 261–71.

41. For a critique of Cartesian and post-Cartesian epistemological readings of Plotinus see Gurtler, *Self and Consciousness*, 113–30; Stern-Gillet, *Consciousness*, 1–33 and *Plotinus*, 19–27; Chiaradonna, *Cognitive Powers*, 191–207.

second is the analytical where the phenomenal structure of "consciousness" and its *qualia* or qualitative character is assessed.[42]

Beginning with Descartes, "consciousness" constitutes a multitude of qualitative states or *qualia* that are considered: private features of my experience alone; and are referred to as 'phenomenal properties or states' of "consciousness." Kant claims phenomenal "consciousness" encompasses the spatial, temporal and conceptual organization of our experience of the world as agents. Here "consciousness is not treated as a substantive entity but the abstract reification of whatever properties exhibited by mind and its mental states. How much this commits one to the ontological status of "consciousness" depends on how much one is a realist or nominalist about universals.

Subjectivity is also equated with what is now called the "phenomenal aspects of consciousness." Beginning with Locke claims arise that "consciousness" requires special private forms of knowing or self-knowledge. Here any adequate answer to 'the what' question addresses the epistemic character of "consciousness." Here the fundamental perspective is that of the conscious self or self-perspectuality. Descartes, Locke and Hume claim conscious experiences do not exist as isolated mental atoms but as modes or states of a conscious self or subject.[43] Kant argues the "Ich Denke" accompanies each of these states and properties.[44] The modern self thus is taken from a perspectival point of view from which the world of objects presents itself to "consciousness." Moreover, the intentional coherence of experience relies upon the interdependence between the self and the world. The self is perspective from which objects are known and the world as the integrated structure of objects and events define the nature and location of the self as a unity of "consciousness."[45]

IV. Inventing Consciousness

Hutchinson's, Remes', and Caluori's readings of Plotinus on consciousness are at the cutting edge of scholarship and serve as something of a snapshot of

---

42. There is possible overlap between Aristotle, Plotinus assessing mind-intellect and Kant's, Hegel's and Husserl's mappings of consciousness. The noetic structure of thought and the phenomenal structure of experience are intentional, representational and involves sensory data and representations inclusive of time, space, cause, body, self and the world.

43. Descartes, *Meditations*, 1644; Locke, *Essay*, 1684; Hume, *Enquiry*, 1739.

44. Kant, *KrV*. 1767.

45. This Kantian notion is extensively mapped by Husserl in *Ideen* and *Cartesian Meditations*. cf. Kern, *Husserl und Kant*, 1964.

where such research currently is.[46] Each propose at least three levels of consciousness: the soul-trace (bodily sense and sensibility), the lower soul (perception and apprehension), and the higher soul (thinking and intellection).[47] It is proposed that their epistemological readings of Plotinus while sound are incommensurate with use of the term "consciousness" and its Cartesian and post-Cartesian introspective mind and mental states connotations.[48]

Hutchinson claims 'phenomenology of consciousness' is a suitable term that covers what the activities of mind are in Plotinus. He argues that although Plotinus does not use any single term such as "consciousness" to refer to mind and mental states, he does use a number of terms as analogies for consciousness—including *antilepsis* as sense-sensibility as second order awareness; and *sunaisthesis* and *parakolouthesis* as intellect-intellection or first order awareness.[49] Here he parses two layers of soul-consciousness: 1) soul-trace where perceptual and emotional affections occur;[50] and 2) self-awareness or self-reflexivity (*sunaisthesis*).[51]

Hutchinson also adds apprehension (*antilepsis*) to Schwyzer's list of Plotinus' properties of "consciousness." He distinguishes, but does not separate, "consciousness" (*parakolouthesis*) from "self-consciousness" (*sunaisthesis*).[52] Plotinus' self is thus the seat of consciousness. It is both a *We* that finds its home in the intelligible world and an *I* which resides in the sensible world.[53] The self as lower soul is the seat of discursive reasoning (*dianoia*) and becomes aware of sensibles and intelligibles by means of the image-making faculty (*phantasia*). The self as higher soul is intellect as self-consciousness.[54]

Remes distinguishes as many of five senses of the self in Plotinus:[55] the embodied self; the self as a process in time; the discursive self; the noetic self; and a self capable of identifying with all senses of consciousness.[56] Since

46. Hutchinson, *Plotinus*; Remes, *Plotinus*; Calouri, *Plotinus*.

47. Hutchinson, *Plotinus*, 7–10.

48. Gurtler, *Self and Consciousness*, 113–30; Chiaradonna, *Cognitive Powers*, 191–207. Also see Emilsson on consciousness in *Sense Perception*; *Intellect*.

49. Hutchinson, *Plotinus*, 7–10; cf. Schwyzer, 341–47.

50. Hutchinson, *Plotinus*, 11. cf. Emilsson, *Sense-Perception*, 83.

51. Emilsson, *Sense-Perception*, 49–63. esp. 56–57.

52. Hutchinson, *Plotinus*, 41. Here Plotinus' consciousness is read partially in the Stoic context of *sunesis*—that the world contains genuinely continuous phenomena and all minds have consciousness of such phenomena.

53. Hutchinson, *Plotinus*, 119–21.

54. Hutchinson, *Plotinus*, 72–73.

55. Remes, *Plotinus*, 10 and 240.

56. Remes, *Plotinus*, 240.

the sensible world contains the entire contents of the intelligible world, the self and self-identity is polyvalent and multi-dimensional. The immaterial, undecended soul or pure intellect is the rational or reflective self.[57] Although the composite self involves a body and is in flux as a mere quasi-substance, it nonetheless remains the same because the soul it belongs to is one in continuity and a unity that consists of parts.[58] These two notions of the self, one descended and the other un-descended, lead to tensions and possible rupture—or what Hegel called the "bad infinite" (*das schlechte Unendliche*). Remes' Plotinus reconciles our different selves in an all-encompassing, self-differentiating ethical affirmation—or what Hegel called "reconciliation" (*Versoehnung*). Remes proposes that the embodied self is a process in time which allows us to speak of soul's self-improvement.[59] Primary among these is a process self lacks completion. For completion soul must turn from its embodied to its immaterial self—the rational, reflective, pure rational soul, pure rational subject or the undecended soul which is one's pure intellect—which are capable of self-awareness (*sunaisthesis*) which makes them into individual selves.[60] In this sense, the soul's rationality has two complementary parts: a *nous* which thinks *Ideai* and its temporal counterpart *dianoia* which thinks *logoi*.[61] Both are capable of self-awareness (*sunaisthesis*) identified with the self's self-identity as I and We.[62]

Calouri's work takes a different tack. He argues that Plotinus has views on soul and intellect that differ from Aristotle's and Alexander's. While Aristotle thinks that the functions of living beings are not functions of the soul but functions that living beings possess in virtue of having a soul, Plotinus claims they belong to the soul.[63] This is because soul possesses functions that are independent of body: hence his dual (external and internal) aspect theory of soul's activities based on the fact that *psuche* is a separate *ousia* from *nous* with each contemplating the Forms differently[64] The internal activity of soul consists in the exercise of three essential functions: an intelligible contemplation of *Nous* and the Forms; a thinking about the ordering of the sensible

---

57. Remes, *Plotinus*, 11, 157, 111.
58. Remes, *Plotinus*, 34–39. cf. Plotinus, *Ennead*, III.7.11.
59. Remes, *Plotinus*, 56.
60. Remes, *Plotinus*, 126.
61. Remes, *Plotinus*, 157.
62. Remes, *Plotinus*, 126.
63. Caluori, *Plotinus*, 75–93.
64. Caluori, *Plotinus*, 76–81.

world; and the organizing the life of its soul-self. Here the soul's external activity is dependent on its internal activity.[65]

Caluori's 'consciousness' claims turn on Plotinus' reading of the *Timaeus*.[66] Here distinctions are drawn between Intellects' non-propositional contemplation of the Forms and soul's discursive reasoning (*logismos*) which is a propositional process in time. His investigation focuses on time-consciousness and the role discursive reasoning plays in the soul's divided activity (*meriste energeia*) in the creation and organization of the sensible world. Since souls are necessary for endowing corporeal entities with reason, Caluori focuses on the cognitive functions of soul as it ascends and descends through reality in two ways: internally to the soul itself; and externally in its procession and return through the intelligible and sensible worlds.[67]

Summary: Any 'consciousness thesis' is fragile unless it is extended beyond its Cartesian and post-Cartesian implications. A mapping of the emanation of Hypostases, followed by studies on *Nous*, the Indefinite Dyad, thought thinking itself, self-reflexivity, self-knowledge, self-identity and other 'abstract objects' may help clarify such a thesis. Here arguments are proposed that the source of mental causation lies in a "downward causation" from abstract entities including Intellect and Forms and possibly the One.

V. Parsing Mental Agency

While mental causation seems obvious enough, explanations of how it is possible is far from so. A re-examination of the debate concerning the emergence of *Nous* from the One guides enquiry. The 'transference' theory of causality plays a central role in whether or not the One exhibits mental properties. Here the claim is that identity provides the needed link between thinking, being and the One.

Plotinus postulates a kind of knowledge, self-knowledge and self-identity quite different from those emerging in the Cartesian and post-Cartesian traditions. He claims that sentience has its origins in a hypostatic emanation from the One. An early work (VI.9) gives a clearer picture of what Plotinus means.[68] Degrees of unity give rise to degrees of being. Each hypostasis

---

65. Caluori, *Plotinus*, 91. cf. Plotinus, *Ennead*, IV.3.10.31–39. Unlike with Aristotle, the soul's external activity is not essential to it.

66. Caluori, *Plotinus*, 86–91.

67. Caluori follows Emilsson, *Intellect*, 176–98.

68. Corrigan, *Essence and Existence*, 109–10.

has the "one" as *sumbebekos pos* as an attribute of its being rather than its essence.[69] His key point is since being and unity are different, and being requires unity and makes it what it is as the cause of its existence, "it is by the one that that all beings are beings . . . .bound together by the One."[70] In this sense, mental causality is present in a thing's organization and can be traced from Nature to Soul, Intellect and to the One itself.

Plotinus claims that the lower realities are within their principle (V.2.2.13); that the last and lowest things are in the last of those before them; and these are in those prior to them, and one thing is in another up to the first, which is the principle (V.5.9.5–7).[71] Each of the hypostases has an internal and external activity with the latter following the former. Internal activity is self-contained while external activity results in a product that is other than itself. Thus while the One is above and prior to *nous* (VI.9.6.50–55), and does not turn upon itself in a self-reflexive moment (VI.1.6.15–19), but remains *kata ten noesin* (VI.9.6.50–55; V.6.6.8–11), *noesis* is not the thinking subject but the cause of thinking activity. In nuce, the One's *noesis* transcends the *noesis* of *nous*.[72] Indeed, in (V.4.2) the One's *noesis* is perceived as an object of thought (*noeton*). But an ambiguity remains of the transition of the One to the complete development of *nous*.[73]

While the internal activity of the One is directed toward itself, its external activity or overflowing causes two intellects to emerge: one is a potential *nous* or that which is other than itself and the other an actualized *nous* in sameness with itself. With the emergence of a potential and actual *nous* two kinds of plurality arise: one a duality of subject and object of thought; and the other a plurality within objects thought. Plotinus thus maintains that intelligible objects are not without *nous* as subject for intelligible objects are within *nous* as thinking subject:[74]

> Thinking which sees the intelligible and turns toward it and is, in a way, being perfected by it, is itself indefinite like seeing, but is defined by the intelligible. This is why it is said: from the

---

69. Plotinus, *Ennead*, VI.9.1.27–28 and 30–34.

70. Plotinus, *Ennead*, VI.9.2.19–20.

71. Focus of enquiry here involves mapping of the different kinds of self-knowledge and subjectivity beginning with *nous noeseos* in Aristotle and continuing with Plotinus' concepts ranging from *katanoesis* and *sunaisthesis* to *parakolouthesis*.

72. Corrigan, *Plotinus. Ennead*, 5.4.7.2, 205.

73. Nyvlt, *Aristotle and Plotinus*, 146–47.

74. Plotinus, *Ennead*, V.4.2.10–12.

Indefinite Dyad and the One derive the Forms and numbers: that is Intellect.[75]

This level of 'seeing' constitutes a kind of self-reflexivity or a *noesis* called *katanoesis* that differs in kind from *nous*. In this higher or proto-intellection *nous* is fully aware of the intelligibles and the One.[76] The content of *nous* is not simple but many. It manifests composition; sees many things in a duality of thinking subject and intelligible object.

Much of what Plotinus proposes goes back to Aristotle who argues that thought entails the thinking subject and the apprehended object and this combination is a single active moment in which the potential intellect and the object apprehended by it are actually united. The salient point is self sees the object of thought as part of itself by the object and form of the object—an activity which *nous* apprehends immediately.[77] Aristotle's insight influenced Plotinus on rethinking the role of the Indefinite in the emergence of *Nous* from the One[78] A duality and plurality of the self emerges here which triggers a *We* and an *I* thinking—both of which are fully formed and actualized visions of the One from the precipice of *nous*[79] for it possesses a contemplative force within itself as activity:

> We are the activity of *nous* so that when that is active we are active.[80]

Aristotle's concept of intelligible matter is also borrowed by Plotinus who defines it within the context of geometrical figures as the genus of a definition as a circle is a plane figure.[81] It is in this sense that intelligible matter covers the rational basis for the emergence of species and individuals[82] characterized by otherness (*heterotes*), movement (*kinesis*) and what is indefinite (*aoristos*).[83] Thus intelligible matter is neither a simple substance like the One or a composite one such as *nous*. Its thinking activity marks

---

75. Plotinus, *Ennead*, V.4.2.7–10.
76. Plotinus, *Ennead*, VI.9.6.50–55.
77. Aristotle, *Physics*, III.3; *De Anima*, II.5; III.3–8.
78. See Corrigan, *Essence and Existence*, 278–81; Nyvlt, *Aristotle and Plotinus*, 147–54.
79. Emilsson, *Intellect*, 2007, 69–123.
80. Plotinus, *Ennead*, I.4.9.29–30.
81. Aristotle, *Metaphysics*, VIII.6. 1045a36.
82. Alexander later aligns Aristotle's doctrine with his doctrine of extension. cf. Alexander, 510.3 (Hayduck).
83. Plotinus, *Ennead*, II.4.5.32–35 and 29–37. Cf. VI.1.5.7–8.

the limits of its nature.⁸⁴ Nonetheless it is the condition for the possibility of plurality in Intellect. The One's generation of *Nous* includes both the indefinite and definite aspects of a single eternal movement of the One's unity into the multiplicity of intelligible life.⁸⁵

Summary: Potential *nous* is characterized by a *noesis* that:⁸⁶ 1) inchoately splinters its representations of the One from its productive power; 2) receives the One's *dunamis* and unable to contain it; 3) disperses it. It is at this moment that a degree of self-knowledge and subjectivity are introduced into inchoate *nous*.⁸⁷

VI. Inchoate Nous

Hypostatic emanation and mental agency in Plotinus involves addressing the 'sticky' problem of the Indefinite Dyad or inchoate *nous*. We begin by sketching a controversy that rages over whether or not the One returns to itself and how does the One generate *Nous*?⁸⁸ The crucial text is (VI.1.7.5–6) where Hadot concludes that subject of *epistrophe* is the kata-noetic One while Henry, Schwyzer, Rist, O'Daly, Igal, Lloyd, Atkinson, Schroeder and Corrigan assert it is not Plotinus' hyper-noetic One but *nous* in its declensions that turns to itself.⁸⁹ Behind this debate lies a series of provocative thought experiments wherein Plotinus offers two options. First, the One is an intelligible entity (*noeton*) that has a kind of perception of itself and a thinking activity of itself that differs from *nous*.⁹⁰ As an intelligible object it is a thinking subject that thinks itself. Thus it does not require an intelligible object external to itself to trigger its own noetic activity. Secondly, unlike the supreme principles of Aristotle and Alcinous which think themselves, the One is beyond thought and being. Moreover, because of its unity and simplicity it is incapable of the potentiality and duality implicit in it thinking itself.⁹¹

---

84. Plotinus, *Ennead*, VI.2.8.22–24.
85. See Nyvlt, *Aristotle and Plotinus*, 152.
86. Plotinus, *Ennead*, V.5.9.5–11.
87. For the genesis of *nous* from the One see Emilsson, *Intellect*, 69–123.
88. Corrigan, *Ennead*, 5.4.7.2, 195.
89. Corrigan, *Ennead*, 5.4.7.2, 196.
90. Plotinus, *Enneads*, V.4.2.15–19; V.1.7.5–6; V.6.2.
91. Which one is the 'real' One is open question. On the basis of logical possibility both options remain in play. On the basis of the developmental model of Plotinus' thought a kata-noetic One is replaced by an apo-noetic One.

All such parsing has generated a whirlwind of controversy concerning inchoate *Nous* that can be distilled into three questions:[92] 1) are the One and Intellect distinguishable prior to the first stage of *emanation*;[93] 2) is an unformed, undefined, and inchoate *nous* distinct from the One at the initial stage of its two stage genesis;[94] and 3) does *Nous*' self-knowledge and self-identity emerge with the Indefinite Dyad or later?[95]

When Plotinus applies the term *sunaisthesis* to *nous* at (VI.7.16.19) dilemma emerges.[96] Does (V.1.7.5-6 and 11-13) introduce a level of self-awareness within the One or a limited *sunaisthesis* to *Nous*? Schwyzer attributes *oion sunaisthesis* to the One by comparing it with (V.4.2.18).[97] Hadot agrees—the One's reversion and self-vision is self-referential.[98] Igal and Atkinson argue *oion sunaisthesis* refers to inchoate *nous*.[99] Thus *nous* possesses *sunaisthesis*. But Schroeder and Gerson note the notion of the One possessing *sunaisthesis* would be contradictory for the One in itself cannot be a duality. Nor can the One (corresponding to the centre of the analogy of the circle) as indivisible, produce *nous* (answering to the circle)" which is divisible?[100]

The controversy around (VI.1.7) focuses on how potential and actual *nous* are generated from the One and once generated the different mental properties each has in relation to the One. Although on opposite sides Hadot and Atkinson highlight the dilemma: is the subject of reversion (*epistrophe*) One or Intellect?[101] If the subject is the One then its self-vision would be *nous* internal to itself.[102] O'Daly concurs and proposes

---

92. The ground zero of controversy are *Enneads*, V.1.7.5-6.1-26; V.4.2. For a summary of the controversy see Nyvlt, *Aristotle and Plotinus*, 133-47.

93. See Henry, *Comparaison*, 387. cf. Plotinus, *Ennead*, V.4.2.25-26; 37.

94. See Schwyzer, *Bewusst und Unbewusst*, 159-60; 375 and 379; Corrigan, *Enneads* 5.4.7.2, 195-196; Schroeder, *Conversion*, 191.

95. See Nyvlt, *Aristotle and Plotinus*, 144-45.

96. See Bussanich, *The One*, 49.

97. Schwyzer, *Bewusst und Unbewusst*, 343-90.

98. P. Hadot, *Review*, 19.

99. Igal, *La Genesis*, 152; Atkinson, *Plotinus*, 168.

100. The exact reference of *touto* is the inchoate *nous* not the One. Inchoate intellect which is neither a circle nor divisible only becomes formed or actualized once it has turned back to "look" at the One. Rist, Plotinus, 45-46; Schroeder, *Conversion*, 191.

101. P. Hadot, *Review*, 95; Atkinson, *Plotinus*, 157.

102. Igal argues the demonstrative *aute* ensures that *horasis* attaches itself to the subject of the verb *heora*. Atkinson proposes that sight belongs to *nous* in two forms corresponding to its two momenta as inchoate and formed. Atkinson and Bussanich suggest *heora* refers to the sight of potential *nous* while *horasis* refers to the *ophsis* of actualized *nous*. cf. Igal, *La Genesis*, 135; Atkinson, *Plotinus*, 157-58; Bussanich, The

that the created is an intelligence caused by a conversion of *nous* to the One.[103] Atkinson and Schroeder up the ante—inchoate *nous* is the subject of the sentence and suggests it is potential *nous* that returns to the One.[104] Inchoate *nous* is a phase or proto-ontological aspect of actualized *nous*. Bussanich demurs noting that "Plotinus oscillates back and forth between the two aspects of Intellect or is unclear as to which he is referring to."[105] His point is well taken. Perhaps Plotinus' ambiguity is due to the nature of a thought experiment in the logical possibility of *nous*. In another thought experiment on the possibility of motion in the One (VI.8.16.12–13 and VI.9.7.17–18) he proposes that although *epistrophe* occurs in the One, this does not imply that the One is in motion.[106]

However, the One possesses self-vision and other mental states that require motion and are also quasi, pre, or hyper noetic.[107] Plotinus notes there is:

> . . . evidence of something like Intellect in the One which is not Intellect: for it is one . . . For something like what is in Intellect, in many ways greater is in the One.[108]

So what is this "something like *nous* in the One which is not *nous*"; what is this greater *nous* in the One; and what does the One see in its seeing *nous*; is *nous* an intrinsic property of the One; and is there any strict duality between the One and Intellect?[109]

Igal and Atkinson propose the fully formed and actualized vision of the One is *nous* because intelligence is a property of the One.[110] All this sets up horizons for a reading of lines (V.1.7.11–13). Depending on how lines 5–6 are interpreted it could be argued that lines 11–13 introduce a level of intelligence within the One or a limited self-reflexivity to *nous*. Schwyzer proposes that *oion sunaisthesis* refers to the One comparing it to a line in

---

One, 40.

103. See O'Daly, *Plotinus*, 72 against Hadot's reading of 6.17–19. cf. P. Hadot, *Review*, 95.

104. Atkinson, *Plotinus*, 158; Schroeder, *Conversion*, 187.

105. Bussanich, *The One*, 40.

106. Bussanich, *The One*, 41–42.

107. Plotinus, *Enneads*, VI.8.16.19–21.

108. Plotinus, *Ennead*, VI.8.16.21–22, 32–34.

109. See Igal, *La Genesis*, 132.

110. In this view *Nous* and the One share mental properties. Moreover, although there is an *in rebus* metaphysical distinction between Intellect and the One, there is no absolute *ante rem* distinction between their mental states.

Igal, *La Genesis*, 132; Atkinson, *Plotinus*, 157.

(V.4.2.18).[111] Hadot claims that the One's reversion and self-vision in lines 5–6 that the One is the subject in lines 12–14.[112] Although neither of these passages notes *sunaisthesis* or inchoate *nous*, Igal and Atkinson take a hard intellectualist view to claim that *oion sunaisthesis* refers to inchoate *nous*[113]— a reading backed up by Lloyd's insight that *nous* possesses *sunaisthesis* in this and other texts in the *Enneads* (VI.7.19.19–20, VI.7.16.19) where the latter passage specifies a *nous* self-reflexivity actualized.[114] Rist demurs—to make the One subject of (11–13) leads to a contradiction—duality within the One.[115] Schroeder approaches this problem in light of Plotinus' geometrical analogy in (7–9). The exact reference of *touto* is inchoate *nous* rather than the circle (the One) which is indivisible. Noting that potential *nous* differs from actual *nous*—inchoate *nous* is neither a circle, nor divisible until it turns to look at the One where it is formed as actualized *nous*.[116]

A key text that justifies Rist's and Schroeder's reading of (VI.1.7.6–9) is (VI.7.16.10–16) where line 10–11 accounts for the vision *nous* has of the One and lines 11–13 for the ability of *nous* to perceive its power to produce substantial reality. As Schroeder notes once it is established that the conversion in lines 5–6 is of *nous* rather than the One toward the One lines 11–13 do not signify the One's self-reflexivity (*sunaisthesis*) which would signify duality and complexity.[117] Moreover, the One is not aware of its own *dunamis* (V.3.15.32–35; V.8.10.1; V.1.7.9).[118] Nor does it need an external principle to generate *nous* (V.4.2.26–29).[119] For Plotinus there is a distinction between the act of a substance and the act from a substance. Hence the One contains its own internal power in the production of inchoate *nous* which proceeds from the One as a secondary act. Thus, it is *nous* that possesses *oion sunaisthesis* of the One's productive power (V.3.7.3–4; VI.8.18.16).[120]

First, the One is separate from inchoate *Nous* or the Indefinite Dyad. This hyper-noetic *Nous* does not think. It is characterized by intellection

---

111. Schwyzer, *Bewusst und Unbewusst*, 375 and 389.
112. P. Hadot, *Review*, 95.
113. Igal, *La Genesis*, 152; Atkinson, *Plotinus*, 168.
114. Lloyd, *Non-Discursive Thought*, 161.
115. Rist, *Plotinus*, 45–46.
116. Schroeder, *Conversion*, 189.
117. Schroeder, *Conversion*, 191.
118. Following Nyvlt, *Aristotle and Plotinus*, 2012, 143; cf. Henry, *Comparison*, 387.
119. Schroeder, *Synousia*, 682–693.
120. Rist, *Plotinus*, 1976, 46–47 and Bussanich, *Metaphysics of the One*, 50 argue that One's productive power simply causes Intellect's substance—no more.

and non-intellection.¹²¹ As loving-intellect (*nous eron*) or inebriated intellect (*nous methustheis*) it sees the Good not as its object but is a seeing that has no object.¹²² It is unclear whether the inchoate *nous* and *nous* in love are the same but Plotinus' language links the two aspects.¹²³ When inchoate *Nous* returns to the One as loving intellect it rediscovers the potential to know even if the there is no object of vision. When inchoate *Nous* reverts to itself, and sees the One what it sees is an image of the One as intelligible matter.¹²⁴ Secondly, inchoate *Nous* is distinct from the One at the initial stage of its two stage genesis. Initially, inchoate *Nous* is an outflow of the eternal activity of the One. Once it turns back to the One as its knowing principle it becomes its own internal activity as formed *Nous*. Here the One limits, defines and actualizes *Nous* as it becomes the object of Intellect's intellection.¹²⁵ At this stage, Intellect becomes a separate hypostasis and its self-thinking becomes identical with its being.¹²⁶ At this point Intellect is no longer an inchoate *nous* but a mind fully formed.¹²⁷ Thirdly, self-knowledge and self-identity have two moments: one of potentiality; the other of actuality.¹²⁸

With the generation of the Indefinite Dyad or intelligible matter a potential subjectivity emerges in two stages. The intelligible substrate creates the conditions for the generation of inchoate *nous* and the intelligibles within intellect. Inchoate nous is not yet formed and is indefinite and potential in nature. It also shares traits of ambiguity and otherness with a mental state higher imagination (*phantasia*). What the One "sees" in a self-revision from an initial generation of inchoate *nous* is a pre-noetic vision of itself. At this stage a transition from potential to actual *nous* occurs characterized as noesis.¹²⁹ The inchoate *nous* gazes at the entities from the One's productive

---

121. Plotinus, VI.7.35.30. For a close reading of this passage see Bussanich, *Metaphysics of the One*.

122. Plotinus, *Ennead*, VI.7.36.20.

123. O'Daly, *Plotinus*, 166.

124. Lloyd argues Aristotle's theory that *nous* becomes aware of *ousia* via *phantasia* comes into play. The object of inchoate intellect's vision is the image of the One. cf. Lloyd, *Non-Propositional Thought*, 163. Bussanich, *Metaphysics of the One*, 231–33.

125. Plotinus, *Ennead*, V.4.2.27–30.

126. Plotinus reading of Plato's *Parmenides*, 156b6–159b7 is a key to interpreting the text.

127. Schroeder defends his interpretation of V.1.7.6–9 with a parallel text VI.7.16.10–16. cf. Schroeder, *Conversion*, 189.

128. Plotinus, *Enneads*, VI.7.19–20 and VI.7.35.1–2.

129. Plotinus, *Ennead*, V.5.9.10–11. cf. Theiler, *EPEKEINA*, 295.

power;[130] the potential *nous* receives the One's *dunamis* and unable to contain it, disperses it to an emerging *Nous* in activity.[131]

VII. Nous Emerging

At the core of Aristotle's and Plotinus' notions of mental causation is what Davidson calls, in the context of anomalous monism, the *anomalism* of the mental—that there are no strict psycho-physical laws on the basis of which mental events can be predicated and explained. Application conditions for mental predicates feature a rationality constraint absent from the application conditions for physical predicates. Mental events thus are not reducible to psycho-physical laws.[132] The problem remains whether nomological sufficiency is causal reference. Aristotle and Plotinus think so.[133]

Aristotle's claim that *Nous* becomes self-reflexive when it thinks what it is thinking surfaces in *Metaphysics* XII.7.1072b20–23 and in *Metaphysics* XII.9.1074b34–35, where all forms of cognition are 'intentionally' "of something else" (*h'allou*) and only incidentally of themselves. Mental causality thus initially means that thought thinks itself through participation in the object of thought; *Nous* self-reflexivity is mapped further in *De Anima* III.2.425b26–27, he says that the object and the thinking of it are one in *energeia* but different in *to einai* and in *De Anima* III.5.430a10–25, he claims that *nous poietikos* makes all things.[134] Aristotle also tells us that thought actually creates the truths it understands, just as light may be said to make the colors which we see by its aid. Finally, *Nous* is separable from matter, impassive, and unmixed. It is an activity which receives universals without embodying them in matter thereby acquiring *episteme*.[135]

---

130. Bussanich, *Metaphysics of the One*, 48.

131. Controversy remains over readings of *schizomene* as a middle or passive declension. Armstrong, Atkinson and Bussanich, *Metaphysics of the One*, 48 read a middle declension while P. Hadot, *Etre, Vie, Pensee*, 95 reads a passive one. For the One as *dunamis* see, Bussanich, *Metaphysics of the One*, commentary on III.8.10.1ff.

132. Davidson, *Mental Events*, 207–25; *Thinking Causes*, 3–17.

133. Fodor, *Making Mind*, 59–79.

134. A key absolute presupposition in play here is that actuality precedes potentiality and the true cause of anything is the actual agent not its effects. This 'transmission theory of causality' implies that every cause transmits its power to another object: as in: (T) c causes x to be F inasmuch as c is itself F. See A.C. Lloyd, *Cause is Greater than Effect*, 145–57; Dancy, *Two Studies*, 85–86.

135. Aristotle, *Metaphysics*, I.I. 981b29–982a1–3.

A thicker theory of *nous* awareness appears in Plotinus. Two powers of intellect are mapped with allusions to Plato's sun simile in the *Republic*.[136] Although Plato's "light" is not part of the intelligible realm, Plotinus incorporates it into this level of reality by parsing the relationship between Intellect and the Good with a modification of Good, light, Intellect and the Forms. Just as Plato states the eye can see both things seen and the light that shines on them, Plotinus proposes that *Nous* apprehends both the Forms and the light that makes them intelligible. According, he develops a doctrine of the two powers of Intellect, each of which contemplates one of these objects: *noein* and a so-called hyper-noetic intellect. The hyper-noetic faculty looks at what is superior to it. In its activity there is a distinction between two logical movements. In the first movement (*proteron*): it only saw (*eora monon*). In the second movement (*husteron*): there are two simultaneous results (*kai . . . kai*) of vision (*horon*). The first is a unification of the object of vision (*hen esti*); and the second in allusion to the first faculty is an acquired intellect (*noun esche*). The noetic faculty contemplates the Forms and the hyper-noetic faculty contemplates light. Neither contemplates the One directly but light is the closest thing to the One that *Nous* can contemplate by turning itself and becoming one with light.[137]

Different interpretations concerning the identity and relation between intellect, hyper-noetic intellect and their properties are proposed: 1) Hadot's claim is that the hyper-noetic intelligence = pre-noetic intelligence = a loving irrational intellect as real aspects of *Nous* to which they are assimilated;[138] 2) O' Daly's that the hyper-noetic intelligence = pre-noetic intelligence where the procession and return of intellect are temporal metaphors for the moment in which Intellect's originative vision of its first principle is made conscious to itself in an instant of unmediated pre-consciousness;[139] 3) Bussanich's that the hyper-noetic intelligence is not pre-noetic intelligence but one different in kind; and 4) Gerson's that a pre-noetic intellect is a likely fiction introduced to test a logically possible mental causality relationship between One and *Nous*.[140]

Focus on his property language is instructive. Properties are identical if they necessarily have the same instances or form and their qualitative constituents are identical. The properties an entity has divide into two disjoint classes: those that are essential to an entity and those that are accidental to it.

136. Plotinus, *Enneads*, VI.7.35.19–30. . VI.7.16.26; 16.22–25; 36.3–6; 37.23–24.
137. Plotinus, *Ennead*, VI.7.35.19–30.
138. P Hadot, *Review*, 459–65 and *L'union de l'âme*, 624–76.
139. O'Daly, *Plotinus*, 159–69.
140. Gerson, *Plotinus*, 39, 192; Schroeder, *Conversion*, 187.

A property is essential an entity if, necessarily, the entity cannot exist without it. A property is accidental is it is possible for the entity to exist without being an instance of the property. Being a number is an essential property of nine; being the number of planets is an accidental property of nine. Plotinus appears to propose that mental states and properties are intrinsic and essential to beings with minds but extrinsic and accidental to those beyond being and intellect. Thus when he tests if the One is hyper-noetic or pre-noetic he concludes the One's acquisition of either property is a fiction—a Cambridge (or non-genuine, extrinsic) change. In nuce, the One acquiring hyper or pre-noetic properties is not a sufficient condition for it to genuinely change its 'beyond being and intelligence' status.

Why this is so is explained by Plotinus in an early treatise (V.4.2) where the One is perceived as an intelligible entity (*noeton*) that has a kind of perception of itself but also has a thinking activity of itself different from *Nous* (V.4.2.15–19). This theme appears in two other earlier treatises as well. In (V.6.2) he argues that the One is elevated to an intelligible object but it does not think for as a thinking subject of itself, it does not require an external object to itself to stimulate its 'noetic' activity.[141] Plotinus provides three additional texts for sorting all this out.[142] In (VI.1.6) the procession of *nous* from the One is discussed; in (V.1.7) the return of *nous* to the One is mentioned; and in (V.7.1.5–6) the procession and return of *nous* as image and product of the One is outlined.[143] The procession, return and image-product motifs rests on the basis of the principle of prior simplicity and the notion that each hypostasis posterior to the One attempts to approximate the One but fails to do so due to its predetermined limitation. Two questions emerge from this procession-return-image model. The first is whether the subject of return (*epistrophe*) and seeing (*heora*) refers to *nous* or the One.[144] The second is what kind of sentience has One and Intellect? The Hadot, Igal-Schroeder-Atkinson, and Hunt theses offer three possible answers to two questions.

---

141. Following Corrigan, *Enneads* V.4.2, 195.

142. See a reconstruction in Nyvlt, *Aristotle and Plotinus*, 131–64.

143. For a full discussion of *gennomenon* and *genomenon* see Bussanich, Metaphysics of the One, 1988, 36 and Nyvlt, *Aristotle and Plotinus*, 2012, 133.

144. Armstrong's translation assumes the subject to be *nous*: Upon its return (*epistrophe*) to the One, *nous* sees (*heora*) the One and this seeing is Intellect."

Question One:

(V.1.7.5–6) is among the most controversial passages in the *Enneads* and is related to the generation of *Nous*. Hadot argues on the basis of (V.1.8) that the One is the subject of return and seeing. This is so because; 1) in order to revert to the One *nous* would have to already be engendered but this is not possible because there is nothing in the passage that suggests the generation of *nous*;[145] 2) if anything comes into being after the One it does so only when the One turns toward itself, sees itself (VI.1.6.16–19) and remains identical (*auto*) with itself (V.4.2.19); and 3) on the basis of the principle that generation is followed by conversion, *nous* cannot be generated from the One unless the One is turned toward itself. Once the One is turned toward and sees itself *nous* is generated and turns back toward to the One in two movements: a first *nous is* generated inchoate, incoherent, unfinished, requiring form from the One; and a second *nous* turning backward and seeing the One becomes *aware* of itself, and a desire for reversion to the One.[146] Igal, Schroeder and Atkinson claim the One as the subject of 'seeing' itself violates two basic principles: 1) the principle of prior simplicity and the absolute unity of the One; and 2) the principle that hypostases are independent and autonomous from the other violates claims that *nous* would be internal to the One as the self-vision of the One.[147]

Question Two:

Hadot proposes One generates Intellect either: 1) by turning to itself—the One sees itself;[148] or 2) by turning to the One—*nous* sees itself as an image of the One.[149] Two consequences follow: once the One turns on itself, sees itself, it becomes sentient and *aware* of itself; if the One does not turn upon itself, see itself, it is *not aware* of itself and thus not sentient.[150] Igal, Schroeder and Atkinson propose Plotinus uses two terms for seeing: *heora* and *horasis*: 1) that *heora* refers to the seeing of an inchoate, unformed potential *nous*—an *atupotos ophsis*—and when it sees what it sees it is not

---

145. P. Hadot, *Etre, Vie, Pensee*, 1960, 95.

146. P. Hadot, *Etre, Vie, Pensee*, 1960, 92–95. cf. Hadot, I.321.fn. 4.

147. Schroeder, *Conversion*, 1986, 187.

148. See P. Hadot, *Revue of Harder*, 158–59, and *Porphyre et Victorinus*; Graeser, *Der Ursprung*, 133–34; Beierwaltes, *Ewigkeit und Zeit*, 14–15; and *Denken des Einen*, 45, 52–53.

149. See Rist, *Plotinus*, 1967, 267 fn. 44; Corrigan, *Enneads* 5.4.7.2, 1986, 196–98; Schroeder, *Conversion*, 1986, 187; Lloyd, *Plotinus on Genesis*, 160.

150 See Atkinson, 157–60; Bussanich, *Metaphysics of the One*, 38.

a "vision" of the One in itself but of its potentiality; and 2) that *horasis* is the full actualization of *ophsis*[151] or the vision of an actualized *nous*, who upon 'seeing' the One desires a return to the One, and upon its reversion becomes an image of the One (7.1–4).[152]

Plotinus uses thought experiments (*enhorasis*) to test the coherency of his proposals by invoking an introspective stance in a dialogue with his interlocutors.[153] In (V.1.7.5–6) describes the One as the sun and *nous* as its light;[154] and *nous* is called an image of the One, just as soul is an image of *Nous*.[155] On the basis of these passages, Hunt argues if the One contemplates at all it has no unmediated knowledge.[156] Knowledge is achieved through the *representation* that the One has of other beings. Thus would Plotinus' One "think" like Aristotle's *Nous* thinks in *Metaphysics* XII.9 where thought thinking itself is: 1) always and continuously enacted through self-contemplative activity; and 2) where there is always a formal difference between the act of thinking and its object this is a difference that does not amount to a subject-object distinction as long as the object, the subject and the objects thought by a subject exist self-sufficiently? The brief answer is no. The One's "objects of thought" are known through Intellect's representational interpretation.[157] There are two different representations of One in Intellect—one is

151. Igal, *La Genesis*, 129–57; Schroeder, *Conversion*, 190.

152. Atkinson, *Plotinus*, 18–19 fn.5.

153. Igal argues there is an *aporia* in play that links (7.5.5–6) with (6.18–19). Thus "*pos oun*" is not so much a request to reveal information but an "answer" within an aporetic thought experiment. Several questions emerge from this thought experiment: 1) is the subject of reversion (*epistrophe*) in (6.18–19) the One or Intellect; 2) is *auto* reflexive in reference to *nous* and the One; 3) are the *epistrophe* and *sunaisthesis* of *nous* and the One identical with each other; 4) if *nous* is internal to the One (much in the same way that Alexander's intelligibles are internal to Intellect)—is this a contradiction of the doctrine that hypostases are distinct and separate from their cause and thus external to the One (V.3.9–10); 5) does the word *oion* in the phrase regarding the self-vision of the One (VI.8.16.19–21) (*oion . . . blepein*) refer to the internal activity of the One without any reference to *nous* or its generation; 6) is the vision of inchoate *nous* of the One in (7.5.6) the subject of the sentence with the change of subject as an interruption of an interlocutor; and 7) and if so how can the One generate Intellect at all? cf. Igal, *La Genesis*, 1971, 135; Atkinson, *Plotinus*, 157–59; Nyvlt, *Aristotle and Plotinus*, 134–40.

154. Plotinus, *Enneads*, I.7.1.24–28; cf. V.3.12.40.

155. Plotinus, *Ennead*, VI.4.6–8.

156. Hunt, *Contemplation*, 76.

157. Representations can be known in two ways: 1) *qua* object. Leonardo's picture of the Last Supper; and 2) an object represented by a representation as it is known *through* the representation—triangle (-ness) is known through its representation in sand. A third possibility is non-representational where an object is known unmediated by any representation. According to Hunt every instance of (1) and (3) in Plotinus is in fact (2). cf. Hunt, *Contemplation*, 91–99.

through the Forms and the other is via light. Neither as Cambridge properties, however, are essential to the One.

VIII. Thought Thinking Itself

Aristotle and Plotinus propose a *nous* that models mind or intellect as the causal ground of reality. *Nous* has no determinate character of its own and understanding has no structure of its own. It is simply a capacity (*dunamis*) for apprehending identity and interconnection. Aristotle notes: "what I call *nous*—that with which the soul thinks and understands—is not actual thinking until it thinks."[158] Such claims exclude any doctrine which credits the understanding with either furniture of its own such as "innate ideas," or a fixed structure of its own. Outside of a few passages referencing *Nous* in Metaphysics and *nous poietikos* in De Anima, Aristotle's notion of self-knowledge, self-awareness and subjectivity are rather thin. Aristotle claims there is no duality or potentiality in thought thinking itself (*nous noeseos*) and Mind is *numerically* identical and in an *a se* relation to itself.[159] Since *noesis* consists in thinking eternally and without interruption there is no mental transition into or out of potentiality and dualism ever for however different act and concept are in *form* they are the same in *content*. The object of thinking is the *concept* of self-contemplation; and thought thinking itself is the *act* of self-contemplation and no thought becomes an abstraction opposed to another that limits it.[160]

Alcinous offers a Middle platonic theory of *nous* in which he harmonizes Plato and Aristotle into a single doctrine of a potential and actual *nous* or of an Intellect superior to the cosmic *nous* and Forms within Mind itself. Alexander develops both doctrines introducing formal and efficient causality into an actual *nous* who governs the world and who causally influences a potential and material Intellect. This first *Nous* supplies Plotinus with the tools to argue not only for a principle that is its superior but to formulate a *Nous* principle of his own.[161] Here Sextus Empiricus raises a dilemma about the intellect being able to apprehend itself that grasps Plotinus' attention. Crystal argues that the significance of Sextus is that he sets out a framework within which cognitive activity must apprehend itself qua part or qua whole which according to him are impossible. He suggests that Plotinus improves upon Aristotle and can explain how *nous*

---

158. Aristotle, *Metaphysics*, XII.9.1074b 34–35.
159. Berchman, *Hunting*, 31–48.
160. Brinkman in Nyvlt, *Aristotle and Plotinus*, x–xi.
161. See Nyvlt, *Aristotle and Plotinus*, 187–214.

thinks qua whole by asserting that self-intellection involves the thinker active in generating the content of its own intellect—which means that *nous* constitutes itself in its self-awareness and self-intellection.[162]

It might be that Aristotle and Plotinus would agree but underscore a vital point that without a separable intellect there would be no self-cognition. The reason is that cognition is not only self-reflexive but requires incorporeality.[163] It is difficult to say here whether either view *nous* as a special substance attached to each human body, as a special power (*dunamis*) which the body has or a single substance which was shared by humans. Aristotle vacillated between the first two options with later Platonists and Aristotelians vacillated between the second and third. Augustine proposes the simplest solution of all. The soul is immortal because it is the subject or seat of reason (*episteme*) which is eternal:

> The human body is mutable and reason is immutable. For all which does not exist always in the same mode is mutable, but that two and two are four exists always in the same mode ... This sort of reasoning, then, is immutable. Therefore reason is is immutable.[164]

In all these disputes controversy was not about the survival of *nous* but about the indestructibility of *episteme* based on a *nous* identity distinct from an *ego* identity.

Plotinus builds upon Aristotle's thought-experiment. He endorses Aristotle's identification of intellect, intellection and intelligible object.[165] He also states that the intellect in thinking itself has self-awareness (*parakolouthein*).[166] He departs from Aristotle's notion of 'thinking on thinking' (*nous noseos*) which now involves a duality of intellect thinking its objects[167]—the world of Forms[168] which are beings that think.[169]

This is the kind of thinking that the human intellect may do when the soul is free from interference from the sensible world and reasoning about

---

162. Crystal, *Self-Intellection*, 264–86.
163. Gerson, *Aristotle and Other Platonists*, 139.
164. Augustine, *On the Immortality of the Soul*, 61.
165. Plotinus, *Ennead*, V.3.5.
166. Plotinus, *Enneads*, II.9.1.34–47; III.9.9.13–25.
167. See Emilsson, *Intellect*, 2007, 110–13.
168. Plotinus, *Ennead*, V.3.13.12–14.
169. Plotinus' starting point is Plato's *Sophist* (248e-249a). For his identification of Intellect with the Forms cf. *Ennead*. V.1.4.26–29; and individual Forms with individual intellects cf. *Ennead*.V.9.8.3–7.

it.[170] Once this is done the human intellect does as Intellect does. It thinks and is thought. Indeed, by raising oneself to the level of *Nous—ego identity* attains *nous* identity. Here Plotinus makes a significant move. He gives new meaning to the Delphic motto—"know thyself"—by transforming what *I* and *We* self are in the context of what a return to the One means.

Summary: Perhaps the best means for understanding Plotinus here is via his double *energeia* theory.[171] Sense perception finds its end in imagination which elevates sensible objects into a unified intelligible object. *Phantasia* has a power to unify the sensible impressions which are retained by memory thereby triggering an apprehensive power (*antilepsis*) which arises when imagination seizes its sensible or intelligible objects. As a consequence self-knowledge (*parakolouthein*) emerges.[172] However, whenever, one is not directing attention to an activity one is engaged in—this is the difference between *parakolouthesis* and *sunaisthesis*—which opens questions of the nature of self-reflexivity and self-identity.[173]

IX. Self-Reflexivity (*Sunaisthesis*)

Two key and inter-connected notions self-knowledge and difference drive readings of self-reflexivity (*sunaisthesis*) in Plotinus. This framework also provides an explanation of the structure of the self employing a model where each ontological level simultaneously involves a distinct mode of knowledge. True knowledge takes place in *nous*, and this is self-knowledge, since in the second hypostasis knowing is a movement toward self-identity. Since it warrants procession, the notion of difference is also fundamental for self-knowledge to occur at the level of the generation of Intellect. Here self-knowledge involves a duality composed by *nous* and *noeton* which are qualitatively identical. At the level of *psuche* there is a greater difference between subject and object and this distance reaches its maximum degree at the level of the sensible world structured as a composite of matter and *logos*.

Plotinus is a property dualist who sees properties as universals that exist independently of the mind and when mapping mental properties he offers versions of both *in rebus* realism: a property exists only if it has instances; and *ante rem* realism: a property can exist even if it has no instances. Here Plotinus uses arguments from logical and causal possibility.

170. See Plotinus, *Ennead* V.3.27–29; IV.3.30.11–16.
171. See Emilsson, *Intellect*, 22–68.
172. Plotinus, *Ennead* IV.4.13.3–17.
173. See Gurtler, *Ennead* V.4.30–45 and IV.5, 144.

Principal among these is that although each hypostasis is metaphysically distinct and separate from the other it is logically possible that *Nous* and the hyper-noetic One exhibit mental properties.[174]

Plotinus also conceives of reality as a productive process. Each level of reality generates that which comes next to it—One, Mind, Soul, and Nature. Soul is amphibious and intermediate between the intelligible and sensible worlds. It also has two "parts" or functions. The higher soul is inclined toward *Nous* while the lower part of soul is Nature which gives life, order and shape to the sensible world.[175] There are two key notions in this explanation of reality: contemplation (*theoria*) and double activity (*energeia*).[176] Contemplation is paradigmatically a property of *Nous* as its primary activity.[177] Self-reflexivity (*sunaisthesis*) is an activity of *noesis* and is contrasted with *aisthesis*. It is ascribed: 1) to the universe as the cognitive equivalent of *sumpatheia*; 2) to Nature; and 3) even obliquely to the One.[178]

If the cognitive activities of Nature and the One are conceived as a sort of apperception, a proto-noetic form of self-reflexivity, then their "cognitive" activity is not directed is not directed toward anything beyond itself. The One has a hyper-noetic awareness of itself and Nature an infraawareness of itself. The One is awake while Nature sleeps.[179] In this sense, Nature's contemplation in the context of double *energeia* is weaker than that of the higher soul and the higher soul weaker than that of *Nous*[180]— where self-reflexivity (*sunaisthesis*) is a perception of something that is many (*polla tinos aisthesis*):

> *sunaisthesis* is the immediate perception of an inner content, an unfolded self-reflexivity, one with its object not external to it. it is an awareness of a unity of a whole with itself, or a plurality in unity. Hence it is in the proper sense the cognitive activity of *Nous*, because in Intellect there is a unity that is at the same time multiplicity, although there are no real divisions.

---

174. Although it remains an open question whether it is an *ante re* property realism or an *in rebus* realism in play when Plotinus proposes One and Intellect have mental properties, neither proposal involves a contradiction. It remains, however, that mental properties ascribed to the One in a thought experiment are a Cambridge change.
175. Plotinus, *Ennead* IV.8.8.13–16.
176. Plotinus, *Enneads* III.8.1.1–10 and III.8.7.1–3.
177. Plotinus, *Ennead* III.8.8.
178. Plotinus, *Enneads* III.9.7.1–6; V.3.13.6–8; V.4.2.16–20.
179. Plotinus, *Ennead* VI.8.16.32–35.
180. Plotinus, *Ennead* III.8.5.21–25.

Nous is *hen-polla*. In soul sunaisthesis is weaker because soul is *hen-kai-polla*.[181]

If Plotinus distinguishes three levels of mental activity and maps three levels of self-identity: the soul-trace (bodily sense and sensibility), the lower soul (perception and apprehension), and the higher soul (thinking and intellection),[182] then each is a discrete stage in the actualization of the self moves along the following levels. *Antilepsis* emerges as bodily sense-sensibility as first order awareness; *parakolouthesis* occurs as perception-apprehension at both sensible and intelligible levels of soul-intellect cognition as second-order awareness; and *sunaisthesis* activates as thinking-intellection at the level of *nous* as first order awareness.[183]

X. Self-Knowledge and Self-Identity

Mental causality for Aristotle and Plotinus is now an established "fact." Causal transactions involving mental states begin with *Nous* and involve such mental properties as intentionality (or in analytic parlance propositional attitudes) that are not reducible to physical properties. With the "horizons" of mental causality in place enquiry concludes with a mapping of the self, the problem of solipsism and its dependence on abstract objects including Aristotle's *Nous*, and with Plotinus, Intellect's content the Forms.

The problem of self-knowledge and self-identity focuses on how unified the self really is. Am *I* a singular self, a *We* self, how are they related to each other and when do *I* become a *We* self-reflexive self? Enquiry begins with Aristotle's the claim that what is called mind is not an actual thing until it thinks and that it excludes notions that credit it with either furniture of its own such as Descartes' theory of "innate ideas" or a specific structure of its own such as Kant's "intuitions of the understanding." *Nous* has no structure; it develops a structure for itself in thinking itself. Moreover, mind is only real in the actual process of understanding its objects and in this sense the understanding and the things it understands are one, a unity, and identity. Finally, "thought" in its activity creates the truths it understands—just as light may be said to make colors which we see by its aid.[184]

---

181. Plotinus, *Ennead*, V.3.13.21–22.

182. Again see Hutchinson, *Plotinus*, 7–10. cf. Schwyzer, *Bewusst und Unbewusst*, 341–47.

183. Plotinus, *Ennead*, V.3.13.12–14. cf. Schroeder, *Synousia*, 677–699.

184. Aristotle, *Metaphysics* XII.7.1072b20–23; XII.9.1074b34–35; and *De Anima* III.2.425b26–27; III.5.430a10–25.

Thinking has three foci: the first is epistemological—which encompasses levels of self-identity through—sense-perception (*aisthesis*) and knowledge (*noesis*); the second is ontological—which involves a seeing, a touching and an illumination of the subject by thinking itself as Aristotle's Intellect thinks itself and Plotinus' itself and the Forms. Aristotle's account of self-thinking is essentially based upon on *Metaphysics* (XII.9.1074b) while Plotinus adds Plato's *Sophist* (248c-249) to claims that Intellect as a subject always thinks and where *nous, noesis,* and *to noeton* are all said to be one.[185] The third is to propose that Plato, Aristotle and Plotinus offer a nuanced version of dualism—property dualism. Each rejects Cartesian substance dualism and proposes that our minds have a purely immaterial foundation. Thus they deny that mental properties can be reduced to physical properties and accept *qualia* as reducible to mental properties.[186]

Plotinus' concern is how to include the thinking subject in Intellect's thought as self-thought.[187] Of note: with life and thought integral to it, and because the object of thought is not potential since it is the same as the act of though, there is no remainder to the thinker that is not actual in thought.[188] Clarifying what all this means is difficult. Emilsson argues the identity and relation of cognition to its objects may be clarified further by examining Plotinus who proposes a type of cognition that is identical with its object in three modes: a subject-side which knows the intelligibles (ego/identity); an object-side which constitutes what is known (ego/nous identity); and a self that apprehends itself as a thinking subject (nous/identity) 'by some sort of addition from itself' (*prosthesai par' hautou*).[189] Plotinus continues:

> ... it at the same time adds what it sees. If the things contemplated are in the contemplation, if what are in it are impressions of them, then it does not have them themselves, it does not see them as a result of dividing itself, but it was contemplator and possessor before it divided itself.[190]

Emilsson's point is two kinds of otherness are in play. One is the otherness of subject and object; the other the otherness within the subject; and

---

185. Plotinus, *Ennead*, V.3.5.28-48. See Szlezak, *Nuslehre*, 122-35; Emilsson, *Intellect*, 148-53.

186. In this sense they differ from contemporary versions of property dualism which rejects substance dualism but agree with physicalists that minds have a purely physical foundation and that *qualia* are irreducible mental properties.

187. Emilsson, *Intellect*, 146-47.

188. Plotinus, *Ennead*, V.3.5.33-41.

189. Emilsson, *Intellect*, 144-45.

190. Aristotle, *De Anima*, III.5.430a.20-25; Plotinus, *Ennead*, V.3.5.17-21.

both coincide in mind's self-thinking when *nous* thinks its contents the Forms. He argues that the duality of subject and object and the multiplicity of intelligibles in *Nous* are brought together by Plotinus through first-person *I am F* statements. When Mind asserts its identity its thoughts have the form '*I am F*'—where F holds the place of any of *Nous*'s content.[191] Four outcomes emerge here: Firstly, although subject and object are distinct, they remain intertwined.[192] Secondly, when *Nous* 'thinks itself' in *I am F* statements whatever plurality that exists within *nous* is sublimated in a 'shift' from a *polla hen* to a *pros hen* notion of identity. Thirdly, by thinking itself in *I am F* statements *Nous* thinks itself *per se* relationally with its objects of thought thereby overcoming the duality of subject and object and the multiplicity of intelligibles within itself. Fourthly, in *I am F* statements the otherness within *Nous* is overcome in a *qualitative* identity of subject and object.[193]

Before this first-person *I* am *F* case can be mapped out we must understand what it does not imply.[194] Descartes, Hume, Kant, Wittgenstein, and Ryle parse "the first-person case" from the precipice of the ego-centric predicament and the possibility of solipsism. Descartes' *cogito*, Hume's bundle of perceptions Kant's transcendental *ego* and Wittgenstein's and Ryle's semantic *I* rest on claims that although `I think' accompanies all my ideas, perceptions and apperceptions in the end I am only aware of my own thinking.[195] Knowing that I have a mind is a matter of knowing it as it knows itself—which is shorthand for I can never say why I should not be a solipsist.[196]

Descartes' first certitude is his existence as mind but his introspective conception of the content of mental states ends with two problems: what *antirealist-internalist* basis may a person have for the claim that other persons

---

191. Emilsson, *Intellect*, 32.

192. Emilsson, *Intellect*, 188.

193. Emilsson spends the bulk of analysis on Mind's first-person singular statements. *Intellect*, 117–19. cf. On Plotinus' use of and language also see, Schroeder, *Plotinus and Language*, 336–52.

194. Emilsson argues *I am F* self-knowledge at the level of *Nous* does not necessarily suggest a proto-Cartesian reading of Plotinus' *Nous*. For a critique of the first-person I am F statements in Emilson along this line see Stern-Gillet, *Emilsson Review*, 2008, NDPR 03.14.

195. Descartes, *Meditations*, I-II; Hume, *Treatise*, I.V.IV; Kant, *KrV*, B131; Wittgenstein, *Tractatus*, 5.6; Ryle, *Concept of Mind*, 17.

196. As Wittgenstein notes solipsism thus is a position that must be explained away, defended or disputed. This is because appeals to rational, empirical or a transcendental "consciousness" is always an examination of "self-consciousness." *I* cannot even appeal to myself as a person, for persons have bodies, and the existence of my body or of any connection between body and my mind is problematic and must be held in philosophical suspension. *I* can only ask "How can *I* come to be conscious of *myself*?" cf. Wittgenstein, *Tractatus*, 5.6.1; *The Blue Book*, 48, 55, 67.

are similarly self-reflexive and have minds?[197] Being aware of my internal mental states *I* know that *I* have a mind but the mental states of others are not so obvious—which is an answer grounded in a form of epistemological solipsism based on the priority of an *I* or (*ego*) access to mental states—where *I* stand in isolation from the world as a result of the epistemic priority possessed by first-person access to mental states. Whereas others have experiences, only *I* really have them—they are *my* own alone. Wittgenstein ups the ante and proposes it might well be that the metaphysical subject is not the human body with which biology deals, or soul or self with which psychology deals, but an *I* which is in the end a grammatical subject where— "the limits of my language mean the limits of my world;" where 'the subject does not belong to the world but is the boundary of the world (not a part of it)"; where "we cannot therefore say what we cannot think"; and where "the boundary of language (the language that *I* alone understand) is the boundary of my world."[198] Ryle's *I* is reduced to a disposition to behave and mental language a category or semantic mistake.[199] With such presuppositions in place, the solipsist argues that *my* mind is not one mind among others, and *I* am not one person among others. But every proposition depends upon *my* mind for justification which means my mind (and the existence of other minds) remains a philosophical problem.

Aristotle and Plotinus do not accept solipsism as a metaphysical or epistemological option. It is something to overcome and as a problem dissolve. They propose it is possible for *I* to be a person, to know myself and other minds, but this occurs only in a supra-personal sense within the activity of *Nous*. *We* gain an inter-subjective perspective when *I* attain a perspective that amounts to the disappearance of *I* acknowledging only myself. Eschewing use of "first-person" language to describe "I think," Aristotle and Plotinus propose a universal—"We think." At this level of thinking, there is no longer merely a personal *ego* thinking itself.[200] There is an interpersonal *ego* thinking abstract entities such as Platonic Forms and Aristotelian Universals.[201]

197. Descartes, *Meditations*, I.

198. Wittgenstein, *Tractatus*, 5.6; 5.61; 5.62; 5.632–33.

199. Ryle, *Concept of Mind*, 65.

200. See Hutchinson, *Plotinus*, Remes, *Plotinus* and Calouri, *Plotinus* on "consciousness" in Plotinus. For a critique see Stern-Gillet, *Consciousness and Introspection*, 1–33; Gurtler, *Self and Consciousness*, 113–30.

201. Plato claims Forms are the only abstract and real entities, instantiated or participated in by spatio-temporal objects in a world of appearance or empirical phenomena. Aristotle denies the independent existence of Forms but form remains as secondary substances that inhere in primary substances or spatiotemporal particulars as genuine

Aristotle and Plotinus practice methodological solipsism to overcome epistemological and ontological solipsism. In methodological solipsism, every philosophical problem is *understood* as *my* problem. The question "what is knowledge" is cast as "what is it for *me* to know something?" *I* determine what is justifiable for *me* to believe or know according to the evidence which *I* have. Here there can be no appeal to other persons, to common sense, to theories or models which *I* cannot justify for myself. Accordingly, inter-subjectivity can be defended only by looking to what I think about that exists outside my internal mental states. Thus appeals are made to abstract entities.

Summary: Aristotle and Plotinus reject traditional *egoistic* concepts of self-reference. If we wish to talk as the methodological solipsist supposes we must, it cannot be through this traditionally misleading use of the personal "I." The subject is not merely a person, or an individual *ego*. The subject is also a general or universal self. Here every intellect is indistinguishable from every other. If this interpretation is valid, *We* consciousness is a theory just as any *I* consciousness of perception, understanding, intellect, and reason are theories. The difference is *We* consciousness is an examination of 'thinking on thinking.' Self-identity and subjectivity in relation to abstract objects is crucial to extending this last argument.[202]

XI. Abstract Objects

A pre-analytic distinction between intuitions and concepts at least as old as Parmenides' allusion to the ways of truth and opinion and to Plato's aviary image in the *Theaetetus* of birds "in the soul" (*en te psuche*)—that there is a distinction between functions of thought.[203] Sensory perception is the source of contingent truths, concepts as the source of necessary truths, where differences in certainty correspond to differences in the objects known. Indeed if Parmenides' and Plato's primary distinction is not between two kinds of entities in "inner" space or two sorts of inner representations, but between

---

existents. This dispute persisted among medieval realists and nominalists who debated whether abstract objects may be referred to by the same name without participating in an abstract 'form.' Modern rationalists and empiricists extended the debate on grounds by arguing that since all ideas are particular, no adequate concept of an abstract object is possible. When we think, we think about particular ideas which are delegated by mind to represent an entire class of resemblant particulars.

202. *Noesis* is a term that closely resembles Plato's notion of intuition. cf. Cornford, *Mathematics and Dialectic*, 37–52, 173–90; Hedley, 2016, 127.

203. Parmenides, DK, <B> frs. 2–3; 5; Plato, *Theaetetus*, 197de.

nous and kinds of objects external to my thinking, we may have a bridge to Aristotle and Plotinus on the meaning of 'abstract objects.'[204]

The status of abstract objects such as Forms and mathematicals was not only a matter of deep concern in the Academy. It remains so in contemporary philosophy of mathematics for stated simply—we cannot do science without numbers.[205] Aristotle and Plotinus claim that abstract objects such as Intellect, first principles, causes, Forms, the One and numbers exist. Later Leibniz, Frege and Putnam propose possible worlds, sets, relations and properties exist. The *a priori* and *a posteriori* and *a se/per se* distinctions grounds the existence of abstract objects.[206] Modal logic or arguments from necessity, possibility and impossibility also support the existence of abstract entities.[207] Taking *necessary* existence as a predicate and that something the existence of which is logically impossible (not-being) is greater than something the nonexistence of which is logically possible (being), it follows *necessary* existence is a predicate not only of Nous, the Forms and the One but other abstract objects such as numbers, sets and universals exist as well.

Two possible approaches to ontology are useful in setting up arguments for abstract entities. An inventory approach to ontology maps the different kinds of things in reality; a fundamental approach to ontology establishes

---

204. Following Cleary, "Nous as the Ground of Aristotle's Metaphysics;" *Aristotle and Mathematics*, 143–98.

205. The status of abstract entities, such as mathematical objects, was at the center of debate in antiquity. cf. Findlay, *Doctrines*, 57–58; Cleary, *Aristotle and Mathematics*, 424–94. Abstract objects have their contemporary origins in the distinction between abstract and concrete objects where numbers, sets, relations and properties are viewed as both abstract (a priori) and real.cf. Frege, *Foundations of Arithmetic*.

206. Both distinctions have been under stress since Quine's and Davidson's dissolution of the distinction between the a priori questions of meaning and a posteriori questions of fact and the analytic-synthetic distinction (given-versus-interpreted and necessary-versus-contingent) based on Kant's distinction between the receptivity of sense and the a priori concepts given by spontaneity. For a critique of Davidson's holism see Dummett, *Mind and Language*, 97–138 (esp. 117 and 137); 1973, Frege, *Foundations of Arithmetic*, 559. For a critique of Quine see Putnam, *Mind, Language, Reality*, 1975, 153–91

207. Modal logic is: 1) the study of the logic of the operators 'it is possible that' and 'it is necessary;' 2) its causality is derived logical possibility or with the ideas of modal logic (necessity, possibility, impossibility); 3) its coherence rests on a distinction between two types of proof: valid/sound and invalid/unsound; 4) the first (modal/sound) proof takes necessary existence as a predicate when it reasons that something the nonexistence of which is logically impossible is greater than something the nonexistence of which is logically possible; 5) while the second (predicative/unsound) argument takes existence as a predicate reasoning that something is greater if it exists than if it does not exist. On the use of modal logic and defense of abstract objects see Gould, *Abstract Objects*, 255–74; Plantinga, *Does God Have a Nature?* 5.

what is foundational or primary in reality.[208] In first principles ontologies the existence of what are fundamental and primary in reality precede ontologies that sort out the different kinds of things there are.[209] Several questions follow from these approaches: 1) is it plausible to consider such entities as really instantiated (or real) at all; 2) what is the ground or source of such necessary and independent objects;[210] 3) if abstract objects exist but it remains unexplained *why* they do an *aporia* emerges: the first is, if abstract entities do not derive foundationally from some ground or source, but nonetheless "exist"—a realist 'first philosophy' is incoherent.[211]

With the collapse of the verifiability argument a variety of proofs have emerged in support of the existence of abstract entities.[212] These include: 1) the indispensability argument, which shows that since we cannot do empirical science without numbers, the claim that metaphysically good reasons exist to affirm the existence of non-physical entities also merits attention;[213] 2) the

---

208. Moravcsik, *Plato and Platonism*; Lowe, *Four Category Ontology* and *More Kinds of Being*.

209. O'Meara *Plotinus*, 66–81.

210. O'Meara, *Plotinus*, 132–34.

211. Craig, *Abstract Objects*, 305–18.

212. Schlicht, *Positivism and Realism*, 16–20. The verifiability principle asserts that the meaning of a proposition its method of verification. It is a simple principle which draws a sharp distinction between cognitive and non-cognitive expressions. The former being factual, are either true or false; they set out to give us information about the world, and if they are true, they do so. The latter, being non-factual, are neither true nor false. The function of the verification principle is to demarcate sentences that are statements of fact from non-sensical or "pseudo-sentences." Verifiability is a claim about what meaningfulness is: a sentence is meaningful if there is a method for verifying it; if a sentence has no such method, it is meaningless. With the verifiability principle, logical positivists hoped to strip metaphysical language of its pretensions of factuality. In nuce, metaphysical and ethical sentences are not cognitively meaningful—therefore they are not factual only "emotive". Thus whether there is a reality external to the mind as realists claim (Aristotle/Plotinus) or whether all reality is made up of "ideas" (Kant/Hegel) or "appearances" (Berkeley) as idealists claim is a "meaningless or pseudo-problem."

213. Field, *Realism, Mathematics, Modality*, 14–20. The indispensability argument establishes the truth of a claim based on the inferential indispensability of the claim. Descartes claims something is conceivable if it is logically possible (*Meditations* VI). Hume proposes that if it is causally possible, whatever is conceivable is possible. Another version of the conceivability argument is Leibniz's law. On the basis of these arguments God and mind are logically possible: 1) such claims involve no contradiction; and 2) entities are identical only if they share all properties in common. Since abstract objects do not share the same properties as physical entities no contradiction surfaces. The Quine-Putnam indispensability argument has attracted a great deal of contemporary attention, in part because many see it as the best argument for mathematical realism (or platonism). Thus anti-realists about mathematical entities (or nominalists) need to identify where the Quine-Putnam argument goes wrong. Many platonists, on

ontological commitment argument that a theory could be reduced to a series of ontological commitments in a variety of ways; so that a single theory can admit of a plurality of ontological interpretations without favoring one over others;[214] 3) the conceivability argument, which proposes that something is

---

the other hand, rely very heavily on this argument to justify their belief in mathematical entities. The argument places nominalists who wish to be realist about other theoretical entities of science (quarks, electrons, black holes and such) in a particularly difficult position. For typically they accept something quite like the Quine-Putnam argument as justification for realism about quarks and black holes. This is what Quine calls holding a "double standard" with regard to ontology. The indispensability argument also offers a good argument for metaphysical realism for it places physicalists, who are realists about the existence of the theoretical entities of physics, to consider the existence of the theoretical entities of metaphysics (Ideas, first causes and principles, minds, God and such) as real. To consider the Quine-Putnam argument as justification for realism about quarks and electrons but not about Ideas and first causes, would involve another "double standard" with regard to ontology.

The indispensability argument is stated in the following explicit forms:

I. Mathematics

(P1) We ought to have ontological commitment to all and only the abstract entities that are indispensable to our best scientific theories.

(P2) Mathematical entities are indispensable to our best scientific theories.

(C) We ought to have ontological commitment to (abstract) mathematical entities.

And:

II. Metaphysics

(P3) We ought to have an ontological commitment to all and only the abstract entities that are indispensable to our best metaphysical theories.

(P4) Ideas, first causes and principles, Mind and God are entities indispensible to our best metaphysical theories.

(C) We ought to have ontological commitment to abstract entities such as Ideas, first causes and principles, God and Mind.

214. Quine, *Logical Point of View*, 13–19. The ontological commitment argument has generated contemporary controversy because it offers a good argument not only for ontological pluralism and ontological relativity but for Aristotelian and Neoplatonic ontologies. Whatever ontology a given theory or language commits to, are the sorts of existences that the theory commits itself to. Ontological commitments are commitments to the existence of certain sorts of entities. When we talk about either individual things or kinds of things, we commit ourselves to the existence of the things we talk about. Commitment to kinds of things is a bit more complicated. It involves an existential quantifier or a commitment to the existence of the things it quantifies over. In order to show that a theory assumes a given object, or objects of a given class, we must show that the theory would be true if that object existed, or would be true if that class of objects is not empty. Provided there is no way in the theory of eliminating the existence of such entities, on either of these grounds such entities exist. This is why a single theory or form of discourse can admit of a plurality of ontological interpretations without there being any evidential way of favoring one over others. The ontological commitment argument to Aristotelian/Neoplatonic ontologies can be stated in the following

conceivable if it does not involve a contradiction,[215] 4) the aporetic question explicit form:

- (P1) We commit ourselves to an Aristotelian/Neoplatonic theory of a class of abstract ontological entities inclusive of 'first causes and principles inclusive of Ideas, Nous, and the One.'
- (P2) According to the ontologies fulfilling the theory there is no way of eliminating the existence or class of such abstract entities
- (C) The ontological commitment to this theory is true because this class of abstract entities exists and as a class of objects it is not empty.

215. Conceivability = logical possibility. On the basis of the conceivability argument Frege, Wittgenstein, Collingwood, Brentano, Husserl, and Gadamer offer six necessary and sufficient conditions for sustaining the possibility of not only 'foundational' philosophy' but a Platonic-Aristotelian 'first philosophy' as well. Bracketing physicalist-reductionist claims about what 'exists', Frege, Wittgenstein, Collingwood, Brentano, Husserl, and Gadamer propose that, on the basis of different versions of the 'conceivability argument' or Leibniz's law (A and B are identical to each other only if they have all properties in common) a distinction between the content of thought and language and the neurological-psychological processes of thinking and speaking can be made. The content of thought and language, as distinct from their processes, are inclusive of sense, meaning or reference. Thus, if Frege's 'logical model' is sound, then an intensional-abstract entity of sense and reference can be mapped; if Wittgenstein's 'language thesis functions', then there are meaningful languages that can logically either 'picture' or 'game' what reality is; if Husserl's 'intentionality thesis' holds, then there is a difference between mental and physical states, and if Gadamer's 'hermeneutic thesis' holds, then 'first philosophy' can be assessed in these 'foundationalist' contexts.

The first proposal emerges in Frege's *The Foundations of Arithmetic* as the Extensional-Intensional thesis: intensional concepts involve the existence of non-physical entities such as numbers and meanings. The second arises from Wittgenstein's *Philosophical Investigations* as the Life-Form (*Lebensform*) thesis: that forms of (thought and) language or 'logical space' are or 'model' ' a priori principles' or logical structures which are characterized within different systems as 'synthetic a posteriori' regulative principles. Consequently, there are no 'private languages' based on sense data alone, rather language is a 'public' game grounded in a complex of inter-related 'family resemblances.' Moreover, any particular structure of mind and language is compulsory and the 'synthetic a priori' truths which express that 'logical space' or structure are relevant and applicable within the scope of their 'synthetic a posteriori' conditions—or their *Lebensformen*. The third derives from the *Tractatus* as the Language (*Sprache*) thesis: that the limits of language (*die Grenze der Sprache*) can be mapped; and that there are boundaries between what can be said or spoken—the 'sayable'—and what can only be shown—the 'displayed.' The fourth possibility emerges in Collingwood's *An Essay on Metaphysics* as the Presuppositional thesis: that 'ultimate presuppositions' are the necessary, non-tautologous, and propositionally unverifiable foundations of thought and language. With the analytic/synthetic distinction, for example, Collingwood challenges the positivistic equation of the "necessary" with the "tautologous" as too shallow. This point is not countered by turning the distinction, as G.E. Moore does, into a conundrum—there are only two kinds of necessity—one which can plausibly be equated with tautology; the other which cannot. Nor is it met by Quine: that the distinction between the necessary (analytic) and the contingent (synthetic) is never applicable, except contingently—which collapses or reduces the analytic-synthetic

and answer logic of ultimate presuppositions,[216] which establishes foundations for a realist language of metaphysics,[217] and 5) the eclipse of the hypothetical-deductive model of rationality with its notion of correspondence rules based on a distinction between theoretical terms ('entities" or "forces" and observational terms ("observed happenings").[218]

Summary: Abstract entities are: 1) independent of any other existent; and 2) are the source of the existence of all other entities. Moreover, if abstract entities such as numbers, possible worlds, sets, relations and properties exist it follows that they also: 3) exist necessarily; 4) do not depend on *a se* Forms, 'first principles and causes,' *Nous* or the One for their existence; and 5) are uncreated and independent. Hence the problem: if realists reject (3) they are faced with the landscape of Quine's nominalism. If they reject (4) the problem of ultimacy emerges—there is no ultimate principle. The denial of (5) raises the problem of dependency—how can eternal, uncreated abstract objects be said to depend on anything; and 6) the problem of dependency raises the question of hierarchy—what is the relation of abstract entities to each other?[219]

---

distinction altogether into a propositional-discursive synthesis. The question at issue is: on what conditions does the analytic-synthetic distinction remain applicable? In what contingencies are we obliged to admit the applicability of necessary relationships that cannot be verified—contingently (or a posteriori synthetically)? The fifth possibility emerges from Brentano's *Psychologie vom empirischen Standpunkt* and Husserl's *Ideen* as the immanence and/or non-immanence intentionality thesis: that there is no pure consciousness, that consciousness is known only insomuch as it is *consciousness of* objects which includes (transcendent existent and non-existent) intended objects (as initially proposed in Twardowski's and Meinong's *Gegenstandstheorie* of mind and meaning). The sixth surfaces in *Truth and Method* where Gadamer seeks to avoid the 'reductionism' and 'relativism' inherent in formalistic, scientific and deconstructive approaches to mind, language and reference. Here, in response to the logical positivist claim that the methodology of the natural sciences could be imported into the human sciences, he applies the principles of a hermeneutics of intentionality to texts, proposing that hermeneutics must be contrasted with causal explanations based on mechanical causal laws—or hermeneutical intentionality/causality is different in kind from physical/mechanical causality.

216. Collingwood, *Essay*.

217. Berchman, *Commentary*, 175–90.

218. Suppe, *Structure*, 17. It is on this model that distinctions are made between scientific knowledge and the unobservable objects of metaphysical and religious belief. Because unobservable entities are beyond empirical observation or falsification they are judged non-cognitive, unintelligible, and non-sensical. cf. Berchman, *Rationality and Ritual*, 2002, 229–32; Addey, *Divination and Theurgy*, 2014, 183–89.

219. See, Hedley, *Iconic Imagination*, 133.

Conclusion

We begin this enquiry with the observation the very whisper of "consciousness" has a Cartesian ring to it.[220] We suggested although there are notions of a unified internal subject with thought, language and agency there is no word in Ancient Greek that corresponds to "consciousness" or concepts and concerns for what we now think of as consciousness characteristic of the modern reflective self. We asked how we escape reading Cartesian "consciousness" (*conscientia*) into Platonic and Aristotelian notions of *nous noeseos*, *sunaisthesis* and their cognates. If there are not two distinct substance realms in play as Descartes claims—the mental and the physical—we are left with Casten's, Gurtler's and Gerson's claims that *nous*, *noesis*, *sunaisthesis* and their cognates are best translated as mind, intellect and self-reflexivity and not as "consciousness."[221] We concluded with the claim that the self is itself an abstract entity and that self-knowledge and self-identity depend upon the existence of *necessary, a se,* and *numerically identical* abstract entities or hypostatized universals.

The in and between of mind and consciousness appears rather differently than Descartes and most post-Cartesians would had supposed. How did these rather dusty little questions about self-knowledge and self-identity ever get mixed up with questions of universals with the consequences that the mental-physical distinction is parasitic on universal-particular distinction and not the other way around? At this point we might want to say that we have dissolved the self-knowledge and self-identity problem. All that we need to find this problem more unintelligible is to become nominalists and refuse to hypostatize individual properties. We shall not be fooled by claims that there are phenomenal entities called pains—which because they are phenomenal they cannot be physical—enough is enough—pains are really real!

As fast as dissolutions of philosophical problems go, this one has its points. But has anything been resolved by arriving at this diagnosis? It appears not. Isn't there some connection between our ability to have knowledge and having minds? And is this accounted for by my mind having intentional properties but other minds possessing them as well? Or has something been left when we treat the mind as simply an assemblage of phenomenal and intentional states? Wittgenstein's comment there is nothing odder than a special ontological genus called the mental resonates here: the notion whatever we think of from a 'language-game' has no more ontological significance than unicorns exist because I think it so. But it is

---

220. See Gurtler, *Self and Consciousness*, 113–30.
221. See Casten, *Aristotle*, 751–815; Gurtler, *Self and Consciousness*, 113–30; Gerson, *Aristotle and Other Platonists*, 131–72.

exactly the touch, sight, and smell of hypostatized universals or 'abstract entities' like Mind, Forms and the One that motivates further enquiry with results that might surprise a Ryle.

Après Aristotle and Plotinus, it also surprisingly turns out that the universal-particular distinction is the only metaphysical distinction we have got, the only one which moves anything at all outside of space, time and the continuum. Moreover, the only way to associate self-knowledge and subjectivity with abstract objects is to identify both with what is real; the only way to identify self-knowledge and subjectivity with what is real is to identify each with the immaterial; and the only way to do this is to hypostatize universals, to think of them as particulars rather than abstractions from particulars giving them a non-spatio-temporal habitation. Whereas Aristotle, Origen and Plotinus took only the universal-grasping part of Descartes extended substance as separately existing, contemporary dualists like Searle take only the event-like blooming, buzzing collection of raw "feels" of phenomena as "separately existing." In the end, mind and its intentionalities may indeed be a subspecies of the functional; and the functional as a sort of 'abstract' property whose attribution depends upon knowledge of context—or how we rub-up against and talk with hypostatized universals. Ultimately, Wittgenstein may have got it partly right—that making sense of it all is not only about familiarity with language-games—and as Gadamer and Collingwood note—is a reliving the history of one we find ourselves currently playing in.

9

Touching Self-Identity and Subjectivity

"Know thyself," if it knows not either what "know" means or what "thyself" means . . . but . . . if it knows both, then it knows also itself.

—AUGUSTINE, *SELF KNOWLEDGE AND THE THREEFOLD NATURE OF THE MIND*, 9.

Précis

SELF-IDENTITY AND SUBJECTIVITY REMAINS a notoriously elusive topic that involves not a single problem but rather a set of loosely connected questions. The first emerges from Aristotle's and Plotinus' appeal to first principles to account for and explain thought and contemplation. The second arises from claims this active intellect is the immortal (*athanatizein*) part of the self capable of 'touching' and 'seeing' *Nous*.[1] This active intellect resides both in us, and separately from us, it has no memory and makes all things.[2] Aristotle makes little additional comment on this 'agent' intellect but later commentators make a great deal of it. Alexander of Aphrodisias claims it is not only divine,[3] but it can become one with this agent intellect.[4] Plotinus also claims we can attain identity with this *nous* in self-

---

1. Aristotle, *Nicomachean Ethics*, X.7.1178a2; IX.4.1166a16–17 and a22–23; IX.8 1168b28–35; 1169a2; *Protrepticus* fr. 6 (Walzer).

2. Aristotle, *De Anima*, III.5.430a10–22. Aristotle bases this claim on his teaching in *Metaphysics*, IX.8.1049b24–29.

3. Alexander, *De Anima*, CAG 80, 16–92.11.

4. Alexander, *De Anima*, CAG 89, 21–22. See Schroeder, *Analogy*, 215–225; Sorabji, *Transformation*, 181–98.

thought.[5] Here there are two stages of intellectual ascent: the first is up to the intelligible world; and the second up to its highest point, the One.[6] At the level of *Nous*, mind necessarily knows itself when it takes an introspective or subjective stance towards itself.[7]

I. Horizons

A.C. Lloyd has shown that Plotinus' question of what is left over in a perceptible substance when all its properties (*poietes; idiotes*) are stripped away, led later Platonists such as Porphyry, Proclus and Simplicius to treat the individual as a bundle of qualities, unique in that the same combination could not occur in another individual.[8] Anticipating Berkeley's idealism, Sorabji notes the striking aspect of this bundle theory is that Gregory and Philoponus turn material properties or qualities into immaterial ones as a bundle thoughts or concepts and thereby suggests that body and matter consist of nothing but qualities thought of as thoughts or concepts in such a way the body would be dissolved. While he notes that the Greek terms (*ennoiai, noemata* and *logoi*) may mean no more than things thought of they nonetheless signify thoughts or concepts otherwise Gregory would have not "solved" the causal problem he started with.[9]

Burnyeat and Edwards note that while Gregory's theories anticipate Berkeley's *percipio* they overlap with other bundle theories of the self in several ways.[10] These include Descartes' *cogito*, Locke's self as consciousness, and Hume's self as a bundle of perceptions with the most significant claim being we can only perceive our own ideas. Here, Cartesian theories of self and subjectivity turn on the *cogito* as a privileged source of knowledge where the subject (mind or ego) is a substance that endures as something self-identical. Berkeley holds that ideas (and properties) are eternally in

---

5. Plotinus, *Ennead*, V.3.521–48.
6. Plotinus, *Ennead*, I.3.1.13–18; V.3.4.28; VI.7.34.31; VI.9.3.22–23; V.5.8.3–7.
7. Augustinian antecedents are likely here. Not concerned with epistemology in the modern sense nonetheless Augustine's decision to go into himself to find truth is a radical one: "Since it is clear you exist, and this would not be clear to you unless you lived, it is also clear that you are alive. So you understand that these two points are absolutely true . . . Furthermore, it is very certain that he who understands both is and lives." Augustine, *On Free Choice and Will*, 40.
8. Plotinus, *Enneads*, VI.3.8.12–19 and II.34–37. cf. Lloyd, *Form and Universal*, 67–68.
9. Sorabji, *Time, Space, Continuum*, 290–91.
10. Burnyeat, *Idealism*, 3–40; Edwards, *Bouquet*, 569–580. cf. Sorabji, *Time, Space, Continuum*, 293.

God's mind and made perceptible to the self upon the world's creation. The self becomes with Hume a bundle of perceptions and properties, with Kant an apperceptual I, and with Husserl an absolute individuator, a source of intentionalities with a history in its own right. Ryle calls such subjectivity a category mistake[11] which ends in Wittgenstein's ironically semantic and thoroughly solipsistic I.[12] Recently, exponents of behaviorist, functionalist and causal theories of mind currently argue that the content of mental states cannot be defined purely introspectively but rather must be specified on the basis of the physical or causal role of mental states.

Aristotle and Plotinus are largely innocent of such modern notions. It is inconceivable that there are purely self-conscious mental states, that these mental states are distinct from perceptions or that perceptions are equivalent to sensations, or that idea covers both sense-data and concepts, or for that matter that the mind is separate from the body. Once all this is admitted, the Aristotle's and Plotinus' distinction between intellect-as-grasp-of-universals, and the living body which perceives sensation and motion, is lost. In its place a new distinction emerges—that between consciousness and non-consciousness wherein consciousness or thinking covers both sense and intellect. From here it is a short step to the Cartesian distinction between an event in non-extended and extended substance, and the claims of empiricists that the real world must be psychological, of idealists that the real world must be mental, and of phenomenologists that intentionality is sufficient to unite the *ego cogito cogitatum*—an *ego* and its intended objects.

Four claims provide context for Aristotle's and Plotinus' "innocence." First, Locke, Berkeley and Hume propose that the simplest element of knowledge is inner representations or impressions and that the mind is like a wax tablet or *tabula rasa* upon which objects make impressions. Consequently, the mind is made to think by some impression upon it, or some impulse given to it by contiguous bodies. In a quasi-mechanical way our immaterial tablets or minds are dented by the material world. These representations help us know what we are entitled to believe. However, the imprinting is of less interest than the observation of the imprint—which is the activity of perception-as-knowing. Aristotle and Plotinus are largely innocent of modern notions of inner representations or impressions and thus avoid the empiricist confusion between a mechanistic account of the operations of the mind and a grounding of the self in a theory of perception.

---

11. A category mistake is one in the logic of mental statements and concepts which lead to the metaphysical theory that the self and subjectivity is composed of two separate and distinct (though somehow related) entities). cf. Ryle, *Concept of Mind*, 19.

12. Language is the boundary of my world—a solipsism worthy of Pyrrho. cf. L. Wittgenstein *Tractatus*, 5.6; 5.61; 562; 5.6.32–33; *Blue Book*, 55.

Secondly, Aristotle and Plotinus do not hold that perceptions are equivalent to sensations, or that "ideas" cover both sense-data and concepts. Once this is admitted Aristotle's and Plotinus' distinction between intellect-as-grasp-of-universals and the living body which perceives sensation and motion is lost. This confusion is what T.H. Green calls:

> The fundamental confusion, on which all empirical psychology rests, between two essentially distinct questions—one metaphysical, what is the simplest element of knowledge? The other physiological, what are the conditions in the individual human organism in virtue of which it becomes a vehicle of knowledge?[13]

Thirdly, knowledge is not the possession of accurate representations of an object but rather *nous* becoming qualitatively or numerically identical with its objects of thought. Here *Nous* is both mirror and eye in one. The retinal image itself is the intellect which becomes all things.[14] Thus, the key issue is not whether Aristotle and Plotinus lacked a concept of mind, or even of a mind separable from the body.[15] Rather the issue is why there is no way or need for Aristotle and Plotinus—as there was for Descartes, Berkeley, Locke, Hume, Kant and Husserl—to divide "mental states" or "mental events" from "nousing" an "external world."

Fourthly, Aristotle and Plotinus do not have to worry about an eye, or for that matter an ear, tongue, finger, or nose of the mind. Knowledge is the identity of the mind with the object known. However, Locke and Hume do not have this possibility available. Since impressions were representations, they needed a faculty which is aware of representations. Moreover, they needed a faculty that judged representations rather than had them. The rub is they could not postulate such a "nousing" faculty in the quasi-machine they hoped to describe. To do so would be to introduce a ghost in the machine. But there an obvious tension between thought and matter in the cerebral tablet persists nonetheless. Green reflecting on Locke's "ideas of reflection" says:

> Locke disguises the difficulty from himself and his reader by constantly shifting both the receptive subject and the impressive matter. We find the "tablet" perpetually receding. First it is the "outward part" or bodily organ. Then it is the brain . . . Then it is

---

13. Green, *Collected Works*, 19.

14. This is a rather different metaphor than Descartes' where the *Cogito* inspects images modeled on retinal images, see Rorty, *Mirror of Nature*, 45.

15. Rorty, *Mirror of Nature*, 47.

the perceptive mind, which takes an impression of the sensation or has an idea of it. Finally, it is the reflective mind . . .[16]

If knowledge-of is construed as "having in mind" and mind is a tablet, then Locke is thinking in physiological terms. If knowledge-of is construed as a "reflective mind" and mind is an activity, then Locke is thinking in psychological terms. As Kant puts it Locke exhibits the basic error of empiricism which is confusion between a "successions of apprehensions within an apprehension of succession." That is to say, we have a succession of flowers and redness, and yet we synthesize these into the judgment—"flowers are red." Locke cannot explain how this happens because he models knowing on seeing representations which become, somehow, "ideas." What Kant claims is significant—only thought relates. An object of which several predicates are judged true is always a result of a "mental" synthesis undertaken by a "mind."[17]

We return to the theory of the self as a bundle of properties or qualities. Problems about *qualia* or the phenomenal aspects of mental states (in analytic parlance) come into play here.[18] It seems hard to deny that mental states, even sensations, have a characteristic phenomenal feeling (i.e. *qualia*) when we experience them. When freshly brewed coffee is smelled, when my fingers run over sandpaper or when red is seen, mind is the subject of mental states with distinctive phenomenal characteristics. When mind touches or sees abstract objects it is the subject of mental states with distinctive cognitive characteristics. The *qualia* problem permits the introduction of property dualism which is a mixture of mentalism and dualism. If Plotinus and Aristotle propose a kind of property dualism, they reject substance dualism, deny mental properties are reducible to physical properties and that minds have a physical foundation. This puts them, as property dualists, in a position to accept mind as both a substance (*ousia*) and a as a bundle of properties or qualities—and to accept *qualia* as irreducible mental properties. Here the

---

16. Green, *Collected Works*, 11.

17. See, Green, *Collected Works*, 52–91. Kant goes on to argue that the mind constitutes knowledge of phenomena, not things-in-themselves. From here it is a short step to the Cartesian distinction between an event in non-extended and extended substance, claims of empiricists that reality is perception, claims of idealists that reality is apperception, and claims by phenomenologists that intentionality is sufficient to unite the *ego cogito cogitatum* with its intended objects.

18. *Qualia* are properties of mental states or events associated with sensations and perceptions which determine "what it is like" to have them. The felt difference between pains and itches resides in differences in their qualitative character or *qualia*. Qualia include such properties as "phenomenal redness" and "phenomenal redness" which are properties of sense-data, phenomenal objects or portions of a visual field. cf. Chalmers, *Conscious Mind*; Johnson, *Epiphenomenal Qualia*, 127–36.

individual as a unique bundle of qualities, distinct from other 'bundles of properties,' would create its own self-identity and subjectivities.

II. Mind-as Intellect and Mind-as-Consciousness

A pre-analytic distinction between intuitions and concepts is as old as Parmenides, Plato, Aristotle, and Plotinus. This is associated with the mind-as-intellect model. Sensory intuitions are identified with contingent truths, and concepts with necessary truths. The distinction is not between two kinds of entities, inner and outer. Rather intuitions and concepts correspond to differences in objects as known. Thus distinct faculties or powers of mind grasp different objects—from nappies to numbers—differently. The pre-analytic distinction between intuitions and concepts thus are not for Plato, Aristotle and Plotinus, as Descartes, Locke, and Kant argue between kinds of "inner representations," *a posteriori* "ideas, or the *a priori* "conditions" for ideas in "inner space." This reflects an epistemological effort by Plato, Aristotle and Plotinus to treat 'knowledge-of' as grounding 'knowledge that.' The result is a 'concept' is 'knowledge-of' and an 'intuition' is 'knowledge that.'

The 'mind-as-intellect' model might strike moderns as hopelessly quaint, while Descartes 'and Locke's mind-as-consciousness model could impress them as hopelessly familiar. Between the quaint and familiar arises a series of philosophical problems that need to be addressed. The key issue is not whether Aristotle and Plotinus lacked a concept of mind, or even of a mind separable from the body.[19] Rather the issue is why there was no way or need for Aristotle and Plotinus, as there was for Descartes, Berkeley, Locke, Hume, Kant, and Husserl, to divide "mental states" from events in an "external world."

Descartes used thought or consciousness to cover all forms of doubting, understanding, willing, refusing, imagining, dreaming, and feeling.[20] An idea for Descartes is whatsoever object of understanding that is thought. Hume puts it more bluntly—"everything that appears to the mind is nothing but a perception."[21] Once Descartes defined thinking so inclusively, it was a short step to Locke's, Berkeley's, Hume's, Kant's, and Husserl's uses of "idea" in a way which has no equivalent in Aristotle or Plotinus.[22] This modern "turn" highlights two further distinctions. First, from the precipice of Aristotle and Plotinus, the modern mind is a thoroughly subjective entity.

---

19. Rorty, *Mirror of Nature*, 47.
20. Descartes, *Meditation*, II.
21. Hume, *Treatise*, I.4.2.
22. See, A. Kenny, *Descartes*, 226.

Secondly, once mind is no longer synonymous with intellect (*nous*), then something other than intellect's grasp of universals, must serve as the mark of the mind. The mark of the mind now becomes the self-reflexivity of "consciousness" and "self-consciousness." The crucial point here is that there is no equivalent in Aristotle or Plotinus for "consciousness" (*Bewusstsein*) or "self-consciousness (*Selbstbewusstsein*)."

This raises another difference between the mind-as-intellect and the mind-as-consciousness models. This is the conflicting notions of indubitability associated with each. For Descartes, the clear and distinct ideas of self-consciousness alone are indubitable. Doubt, however, is possible about everything physical. Here the crucial point is that indubitability is solely a criterion of rational self-consciousness. From Descartes a distinction is made between a special metaphysical ground for certainty about our inner states and various epistemological reasons which grounds certainties about anything else. Once the Cartesian metaphysical ground for certainty dissolves under the gaze of Hume, a mind-as-sensation theory emerges. This theory cancels out Descartes' certainty that we have clear and distinct perceptions of substance, thought, and motion, Locke's certainty concerning substance, and Berkeley's certainty concerning the existence of God. Hume's only certainty was that his own sensations of pain, pleasure, or "blue" signify something "real." Here indubitability is solely a criterion of the evidence of "an" empirical consciousness of sensations. If mind is intellect not perception, Aristotle and Plotinus argue, only what has eternity cannot be doubted. Now eternity is known with certainty solely through *noein*—which encompasses the activities of *nous*. Specifically, reason-as-grasp-of-universals alone are indubitable. Doubt is possible, however, about everything particular.

IV. A Turn in the Way

Self-identity and subjectivity are closely tied to two notions: 1) identity theory—that my mental states are the same as and ultimately reducible to those of divine *nous*; and 2) that minds are immaterial thinking substances with mental properties. Arguments in support of these claims are the conceivability and intentionality arguments. The first argument rests on the claim: if we can conceivably find at least one property of minds that We share as intellects we are entitled to draw the conclusion that our minds are one and the same thing.[23] The second proposes that if intentionality is a property of

---

23. This is a weaker version of Leibniz's Law that A and B are identical with each other if they share *all* properties in common.

mental states to represent something else, and only minds share this property, we are entitled to claim that all intellects are potentially identical.

In standard form this argument appears as follows:

1. I can conceive that my mental states are the same as those of a divine intellect.
2. I cannot conceive that I exist without mental states and properties.
3. If my mind has at least one identical property, i.e. intentionality, with a divine intellect, then my mind is identical with this intellect.
4. If my mental states and properties are ultimately reducible to those of a divine intellect, then my mind, its states and properties are identical with this intellect.

∽ ∽ ∽

Therefore: my mind is identical with divine intellect.

At first glance all premises of this argument appear to be logically possible and make a case for the identity and conceivability arguments. However, there are reservations about premise 1: Can I really conceive of an identity of our mental states? The second problem is that the concept of conceivability is not sufficient to justify the conclusion that minds are identical to one another.

Thus the argument demonstrates we must be careful when applying the law A and B are identical with each other if they share identical properties to properties that are the result of my beliefs. There is a crucial difference between the sentences "the car in the yard is red" and "I believe the car in the yard is red." The latter sentence can be true even if the car in the yard is yellow. In brief, conceiving A and B as the same does not warrant the conclusion that A and B are identical. Conceived identities might be caused by the fact we describe A and B similarly and that these similar descriptions cause us to have different beliefs about A and B. All this Ryle on a category mistake might be a bit much but it is cautionary to note our ability to conceive that we are commensurate with a divine mind might merely reflect that we describe all minds similarly. Thus the observation that we can conceive of the relationship between minds as identical is not strong enough to establish that minds are ontologically dependent entities.

IV.1. Arguments for Identity and Conceivability

We now shall see how a defense self-identity and subjectivity on the basis of identity theory and the conceivability argument emerges. It might be helpful here to refer to questions mapped earlier. These include the identity and relation of thinking and being; mind's intentionalities; and thinking 'abstract objects.'

Plato takes a decidedly 'linguistic" turn toward clarifying the identity and relation of thinking and being by focusing on the central problem of false statements made regarding the nature of being. This strategy allows Plato to suggest that identity is associated with being and thinking, not with non-being and perceiving. This course of analysis allows for whatever identity 'is' must correspond to 'what is out there.' Here Plato turns to the problem of the relation of thought and language to the world 'out there' with focus on the contrast between 'non-being' and being.

In the *Sophist* the case of 'non-being' confusion rests on a misunderstanding of the particle "not" in "not-being." Because of this misunderstanding, one tends to think what is not, or non-being is nothing what-so-ever and hence not something that could be said in a statement. Moreover, there is also confusion about what a statement is. Thus, one fails to realize the truth or falsehood of a statement is a matter of what gets said, or predicated of a subject. Here what gets said by the false statement is something that "is not." It is linguistically something quite real but it is something that is not true in the case of the particular subject in question—being. Plato is keen to show that false statements, such as "is not" are merely linguistic confusions, and that it is the task of the philosopher to find a coherent way of thinking about them such that, thought of in this way, they no longer pose an epistemological or ontological problem.

This "linguistic solution" prompts Plato to pursue not only a "proper" understanding of being, which includes the attempt to refute Parmenides, to show there is something that "is not."[24] He defines being as whatever is in motion and whatever is at rest because these two classes exhaust whatever there is.[25] However, there remains the problem of what being is.[26] Though it is true that whatever is, is in motion or rest, being itself is neither in motion nor at rest. To be neither is what it is "to be." But if it being is neither in motion or rest, the argument could be made being does not seem "to be" a "being."[27] His solution is to say that the being we attribute to things is of two kinds. Some of

---

24. Plato, *Sophist*, 243c-2–5; 250e5ff.
25. Plato, *Sophist*, 242c5–6.
26. Plato, *Sophist*, 249d6ff.
27. Plato, *Sophist*, 250c1-d5.

the things we say something is, it is by itself; other things we say something is, it is with reference to something else.[28] Once we understand that *ousia* takes these two forms, we understand how it is possible that we can tell a thing not only by its specific name, but by many names.

But what is more, Plato sees how the solution to the problem of being sheds light on the problem concerning non-being or not-being. *Ousia* lies in the nature of being that whatever "is." It also lies in the nature of being the many things that it "is not," specifically in reference to whatever it "is" to something else. Now this does not suggest the controversial claim that Plato distinguishes, following the analytic "praxis," two uses of "is"—the "is" of identity and the ordinary copulative, or predicative "is."[29] Rather it suggests that Plato recognizes just one being, which involves saying that not being "is," is "not-being." It also involves that when saying something "is," is to say "is" is different from something else. The linguistic point being that both meanings of "is" are one and the same thing. This insight leads Plato beyond *logos* to an ontological study of the being, and non-being, which ends in yet another set of *aporiai*—that being is a going "beyond" the "being" and "non-being" of language and experience, to the being of the Forms, or *Ideai*. Truth is not merely a *logos*-conformity with *ousiai* and *Ideai*. It is a *logos* and *nous*-conformity with real objects, or *ousiai*, which are the *Ideai*.

What are striking about the *Sophist* is how Plato sketches out the *aporiai* of being, which includes non-being, and then how he attempts an onto-logical resolution of these *aporiai*. Here Plato anticipates Aristotle, who shall also argue that to say something about *ousia* is not the same thing as knowing what *ousia* is.

Aristotle gives two answers to the question of being. First, "to be" anything means "to be something that can be stated in language (or *logos*. Second, "to be" anything in the world of natural processes means "to be something that comes into being and passes away." In this sense, any *ousia* is the result of process or *kinesis*. It is any outcome of a process, the full activity (*energeia*) of powers (*dunameis*).When Aristotle enlarges his analysis to the unchanging stars, and Intellect he modifies the meaning of his concepts. Here ousia is generalized as activity (*energeia*). In nuce, "to be" involves in talking *logos*, in natural processes, *kinesis*, and in pure activity, *energeia*.

Two sets of distinctions emerge: one set appropriate to understanding any *ousia* as a subject of discourse that can be made the subject of a proposition; the other set appropriate to understanding any *ousia* as the outcome of a process (*kineseis*), as the operation of powers (*dunameis*),

---

28. Plato, *Sophist*, 255c12–255d5.
29. Following, D. Bostock, *Plato*, 89–119.

and ultimately as pure activity (*energeia*). Here *ousia* is defined as that which undergoes change in change and in the most fundamental kind of change of all—*genesis kai phthora*—generation and corruption, a new *ousia* is present at the end that was not there at all in the beginning. Motion and change displays a pattern of novelty that emerges in process. Furthermore, what a thing can be said to be, is its form—but what is "essential to" (*kath'auto*) and "what is incidental to" (*kata sumbebekos*) being that kind of thing, cannot be determined by *logos* alone. The *ousia* expressed in statement leads beyond itself to the ousia encountered in its natural operations. Consequently, starting with what things are said to be—*ta legomena*, we are led to things themselves—*ta onta*.

Aristotle argues that all existence is determinate and individual. Thus, existence forms a 'many' of things and processes, *ousiai* and *kinesis*, and "to be" means "to be some-thing," an *ousia*. In Metaphysics Z (3.1029a27–28) he ups the ante, and asks in what sense can other types of being be said to be *ousia*? "His answer is that to be separate (*to choriston*) and individual (*to tode ti*) belongs above all to any *ousia*. This inquiry leads Aristotle to an *episteme* that investigates being as being and first causes. Any *ousia* who knows these objects knows necessary truths.[30] Thus, knowledge (*episteme*) is chiefly concerned with what is primary, that upon which all beings depend and upon which they are derived. If *ousia* is this primary nature, then the philosopher must grasp the *archai* and *aitiai* of such primary *ousiai*.

This judgment entails a study of the factors involved in every case of what can "be said to be." In Book Zeta of the *Metaphysics* this includes a number of ultimate distinctions such as unity, opposites, plurality, sameness, otherness, similarity, dissimilarity, equality, inequality, identity, and difference, the axioms of mathematics, and analytics or logic. In the *Categories* the many senses of the term "being" are also studied. The point Aristotle makes is *ousia* is articulated through *logos*—in definition, in knowledge, in space, and in time. What *logos* grasps and states really is—it is *ousia*. Thus *logos* displays the character possessed by *ousia*. Consequently, "what is being" (*ti to on*)? is the same as the question, "what is *ousia*" (*tis he ousia*)?[31] Here again *ousia* has four main senses—as essence (*to ti en einai*), the universal (*to katholou*), the genus, (*to genos*), and the subject (*to hupokeimenon*). What does Aristotle mean when he says *logos* can state what things are, but things are not *logos*, things are *ousia*?

Keen to avoid the mistakes of the "Platonists," he claims that the formulations of *logos* are not "what is:" they are not beings (*ousiai*). Nor are they

---

30. Aristotle, *Metaphysics*, VII.3.1003a21–32.
31. Aristotle, *Metaphysics*, VII.3.1028b2–4.

separate and individual. Thus the Platonic confusion of hypostatizing Forms, objects of mathematics, universals, genera, and other such *logos* formulations is simply a category mistake. Words (*logoi*) are not beings, *ousiai*. Nor are they concrete particulars. Words are merely predicates common to many things. Only the "essence" or "being" of a thing can be said to be that thing (*to ti en einai*). The *ousia* of an individual thing is peculiar to it and belongs to nothing else. What things are cannot be reduced to words.[32]

Plotinus argues the need to go beyond divine intellect for the ultimate cause and ground of being. With this he separates himself from Platonists and Aristotelians who claim that the unity of divine *nous* and being is absolutely simple and therefore ultimate. Conceivability arguments that Mind is composite has two forms: 1) it is a compound of the act and of the object of thinking; and 2) the act of thinking (*noesis*) and the object that defines this act (*noeton*) make up intellect (*nous*).[33]

Plotinus develops a conceivability argument when he asks what 'presence' might mean when spoken of in respect to immaterial being. He proposes that we must think of immaterial being, not in terms of categories that apply to bodies, but those relevant to its particular nature. In contrast to material being or what approximates 'becoming and not-being' which are subject to motion, change and division, he maps the properties of intelligible being which are:

> . . . eternally unchanging being is neither generated or destroyed, having no location or place or base, not coming from somewhere or going somewhere, but staying in itself . . .[34]

Immaterial being is unchangingness with the properties of independence from any particular place or body in which it exists and a perfection of existence that excludes its 'going away from itself' to be in another. The perfection of its existence is a kind of total 'presence' of each to each other.[35] Plotinus explores an identity argument that justifies his claims. He explores the word 'in' to argue immaterial being is 'in' nothing and requires no body

---

32. Aristotle attempts to clarify what he means here in the *Categories* where he makes the distinction between primary and secondary *ousia*. *Ousia* as subject matter, "primary *ousia*," exhibits something that cannot be expressed in words but only denoted by pointing: "this here man." This is its material (*hule*), that which makes it a *tode ti*. *Ousia* that designates a predicate is "secondary *ousia*." It exhibits what can be expressed in words about an *ousia*: "this is a table." Aristotle, *Categories*, V.2a11–16.

33. Plotinus, *Enneads* V.4.2 and V.6.

34. Plotinus, *Ennead*, VI.5.2.6–22.

35. Plotinus, *Ennead*, VI.5.3.1–8. See O'Meara, *Plotinus*, 24–27.

for its existence. If the relation of dependence is one of cause and effect, this is how immaterial being should be thought:

> If then real (intelligible) being is this, unchanging, not departing from itself, subject to no process of becoming, not being said to be in place, it must always be as it is and with itself, not departing from itself, nor a part of it being here and another part there, nothing issuing from it—for then it would already be in another and in another, and in general in something, and by itself and free from being affected, for it would be affected if it were in another, but to be unaffected it must not be in another.[36]

Summary: Whether Plotinus' solution to the problem of 'presence' of the immaterial in the material is valid relies on the extent to which one: 1) already accepts the claim that there exists another type of reality, immaterial being, which can be thought of and which when thinking I am identical with; and 2) that the relation of an ontological dependence of material on immaterial being. Such requires one to think of causal relations, not as material properties in contact with and acting on bodies but as immaterial properties in contact with and acting on minds. Plotinus does say that the One has an activity (*energeia*) which produces lower levels of reality. This activity does not involve change and when lower levels of reality produce things in turn, it is by means of a static and changeless contemplation or causal thinking.[37] It is difficult to ascertain how early examples of changeless causation appear.[38] Aristotle's analysis of being and intellect provides a field of such concepts that are useful. Is it logically possible that in thinking about being the self shares in mental properties common to *Nous* and other 'abstract objects?'

IV.2. Thinking and Being

Thinking according to Aristotle involves the generative act of being in intellect. The Knowledge is of and about things that are, *ta onta*. However, what *ta onta* are, what *nous* grasps in knowing their *ti esti*, "what," *to eidos* "form," and *ousia* "being" or "essence" is to know their knowable rather than sayable aspect. This suggested by the fact that these kinds of thinking are compared

---

36. Plotinus, *Ennead*, VI.5.3.1–8.
37. Plotinus, *Ennead*, III.8.3–5.
38. See Sorabji, *Time, Space, Continuum*, 305–12.

with touching.³⁹ This kind of thinking is about subjects that are incomposite (*asuntheta and adiaireta*).⁴⁰ It is a thinking which states what their essences are by defining these incomposite subjects are. Hence the reference to 'what it is' (*ti esti*) and what it is in respect of being (*ti esti kata to ti en einai*).⁴¹

Aristotle views definitions as being statements of identity such as the relation of thinking and being are the same. This means they do not require us to predicate one thing of another but referring to the same thing twice. When referencing a non-composite subject he says the subject is identical with its being or essence.⁴² And in this type of thinking you cannot be mistaken but can only touch or not touch (*thigein, thinganein*). Failure means you are not in error. You have not made contact with it.⁴³ Sorabji suggests contact language is more useful here because there are degrees of clarity in seeing while contact is an either/or affair.⁴⁴ Aristotle appears to claim that true knowledge and their justifications are a privileged relation of mind to being, of *nous* to *ousia*. If this is so, then the identity and relation of thinking and being lies in *nous* touching the contents of *Nous* as *ousia*.⁴⁵

Plotinus argues similarly. First, on the basis of prior simplicity he claims that the various compounds found in reality are organized unified structures. And while soul constitutes and unifies the world *Nous* and One are its prior sources of unity, with the One being both absolutely non-composite and the single source of the unity of everything. Secondly, *nous's energeia* is *ousia* and as an act that comes from the One, thinking is a self-dependent power (*dunamis*) that accompanies and gives to being (*ousia*) existence:⁴⁶

> It generates and its active actuality is *ousia*, and also in being it is there with it, and the thought and this *ousia* are not different things.⁴⁷

This claim is also seen in Plotinus' definition of being. He uses the infinitive of the verb "to be" (*to on*) with the neuter article (*to einai*) to refer "the being" which may be attributed to anything, intellect, soul, matter, or even the One. He also employs with the neuter participial form of

---

39. Aristotle, *Metaphysics*, IX.10.1051b24–25; XII.7.1072b21.
40. Aristotle, *Metaphysics*, IX.10.1051b17; *De Anima*, III.6.430a26.
41. Aristotle, *Metaphysics*, IX.10.1051b26; De Anima, III.6. 430b28.
42. Aristotle, *Metaphysics*, VII.11.1037a33-b7.
43. Aristotle, *Metaphysics*, IX.10.1051b24–33.
44. Sorabji, *Mind, Meaning, Continuum*, 141–42.
45. Aristotle, *Metaphysics*, IX.9. 1051a25–32.
46. Aristotle, *Metaphysics*, VI.7.40.10–24.
47. Plotinus, *Ennead*, II.8.2.13–15.

the verb "to be," *to on* and the plural (*ta onta*) to refer to intelligible being and the real beings that form Intellect's content as well as the five genera of Plato's *Sophist* (being, motion, rest, sameness, and otherness). He adapts the term substance, or entity, or essence (*ousia*), which is "what is" (*ho esti*) to indicate "stuff," individual substance, and that in the substance that makes it real. Generally, *ousia* and *to on* are coterminous, although on occasion *ousia* means something more than *to on*—as when number is called the "very *ousia* of being" (*En.*, VI.6.9.27). *To einai, to on,* and *ousia* are often applied in general ways, like the terms hupostasis and *huparxis* often denote the same basic reality or existence of anything (cf. e.g., *En.*, VI.6.5.16–25 and III.7.3.49–50) .

Plotinus also comes close to a distinction between essence and existence when he proposes that the One has neither his being (*to einai*) nor his being what he is (*to hopoios estin einai*) from another (*En.*, VI.8.17.24–25). However, he steps back from this in that the One is also the cause of existence for everything else, whereas all other beings are both self-existents and determinate substances like *nous* and *psuche*, or derivative qualities and quantities in matter" (*En.*, VI.8.21.30–33).[48] But in the end all human knowledge is the work of Intellect. Once I know Being and the Forms I come to know myself reflectively as a *We* not an *I*.[49]

Nonetheless, Plotinus claims that all thinking involves a duality of thinking and object of thought. This is because mind depends on the prior existence of its object of thought in order to make possible the actualization of the potential to think. Thus when intellect thinks itself, it is both an individual mind thinking itself and a duality of thinking something. All thought including self-thought is constituted through a duality of act and the object of thinking.[50] This why Plotinus prefers the seeing to the contact metaphor—there are degrees of clarity in seeing that corresponds to a duality of thinking and object of thought.

---

48. Following, Corrigan, *Essence and Existence*, 106–7.
49. Plotinus, *Ennead*, V.5.2.15–20.
50. Plotinus, *Ennead*, V.6.1–2. cf. O'Meara, *Plotinus*, 49–51.

V. Thinking Abstract Objects

For thinking, Aristotle offers a cognitive model of the actualization of knowledge.[51] Knowledge (episteme) is achieved by thinking abstract objects wherein *noesis* and *noeton* become identical:[52]

> And *Nous* thinks on itself to the extent that it participates in the object of thought (*noeton*). It becomes the *noeton* when it touches and intuitively apprehends its objects so that *noesis* and the *noeton* are the same.[53]

This doctrine of *noesis* is also found in *Posterior Analytics* (II.19. 100b10-7) where *noesis* guarantees the emergence of *episteme* and the condition for the emergence of universals whereby the one and its species are grasped by *noesis*.[54] Such participation and touching is characterized as an active possession of the thought as thought:

> For that which is capable of receiving the *noeton* and the *ousia* is *Nous*. But it is active when it possesses it.[55]

The crucial difference between divine and human *noesis* and *theoria* is that *Nous* grasps the *asuntheta* actually while the human mind, in potential thinking is concerned with synthetic things only. But in the few occasion's humans enjoy actual *noesis*, the *nous poietikos* actually touches (*thigein*) the *asuntheta*. It is in this noetic activity (*energeia*) that subject-object dichotomy and complexity is resolved in subject-object simplicity and unity. This only occurs when *Nous* and *nous poietikos* touch the *noeta* which are *asuntheta*. When this occurs there is no gap between knower, knowledge, and object of knowledge. This is Aristotle's meaning of the activity (*energeia*) of *Nous* and *nous poietikos*.

Plotinus counters. He argues that thinking involves movement and sight.[56] He claims it is desire that generated thinking and produced it within

---

51. *Noesis* is a term that closely resembles Plato's notion of intuition. See Cornford, *Mathematics and Dialectic*, 37-52, 173-90; Cleary, *Aristotle's Criticism of Plato's First Principles*, 70-97. cf. M. Nyvlt, *Aristotle and Plotinus*, 60.

52. See Cleary, *Aristotle and Mathematics*, 143-98; 268-344.

53. Aristotle, *Metaphysics*, XII.9. 1072b22.

54. See Aristotle, *Posterior Analytics*, II.19; cf. *Metaphysics*, V.2.1014b6 and XIII.8.1084b14

55. Aristotle, *Metaphysics*, XII.9.1072b22.

56. Aristotle correlates movement as otherness within matter. cf. *Gen & Corrup.* I.3.319a; and movement with matter. cf. *De Caelo*, II.12.239a9. Plotinus proposes the possibility of movement within *Nous* given the subject-object distinction which is resolved in the unity and simplicity of the One.

itself—"just as seeing is the desire of sight."[57] On the basis of this spectator analogy, Plotinus in a very difficult passage reassesses Aristotle's claim that thinking *Nous* is a touching:

> Therefore the thinker must apprehend one thing different from another and the object of thought in being thought must Contain variety; or there will not be a thought of it (*noesis*) But only a touching and a sort of contact (*thixis . . . epaphe*) without speech or thought, pre-thinking (*pronoousa*) because Intellect has not yet come into being, and that which Touches (*thinganon*) do not think (*ou noountos*). But the thinker must not itself remain simple, especially in so far as it thinks itself: for it will duplicate itself, even if it gives an understanding which is silent.[58]

Sight, touch, and illumination are 'intentionalities' and 'meanings' by which we access abstract objects. They are also necessary for 'thinking' such entities.[59] Given that touch, sight and illumination denote meaning is knowledge a touching and seeing that consummates in simple contemplation or is knowledge a seeing that ends in a contemplative multiplicity? If knowledge involves multiplicity, does this deficiency necessitate, as Plotinus argues, an ascent from *Nous* to a prior principle—the One? Which 'meanings', touch or sight, model the highest type of knowledge? Is it Aristotle's *nous* touching *Nous*; or Plotinus' *nous* touching the Forms and being illuminated by the One?

These are exceedingly difficult questions to answer. Aristotle identifies *Nous* with a simple *aitia* and *arche* is content with the primacy of tactile meaning. In the simplicity, called touch Intellect acquires completeness. *Nous*'s non-material touching of *asuntheta* is *pros hen*—simple and unitary. *Nous* is identical with what it knows—being and thought are numerically the same. Plotinus identifies *Nous* with knowing a complexity of *eide* and is content with the primacy of spectator meaning. In the complexity called sight Intellect acquires completeness. *Nous*'s non-material vision of *asuntheta* is *polla hen* and complex. *Nous* is not identical with what it knows.—being and thought are qualitatively the same.

---

57. Plotinus, *Ennead*, V.3.10.31–43.
58. Plotinus, *Ennead*, V.3.10.42–45.
59. Beierwaltes, *Metaphysik des Lichtes*, 334–62.

V.1. Movement, Sight and Touch

Intellect and knowledge are characterized by Aristotle's notions of touch and Plotinus' of seeing.

The background to Aristotle's notion of touch goes back to his reading of Parmenides:

> It appears that Parmenides conceived of the Unity as one in definition, but Melissus as materially one. Hence the former says that it is finite, and the latter that it is infinite . . . but Xenophanes, the first exponent of the Unity (for Parmenides is said to have been his disciple) gave no definite teaching, nor does he seem to have touched (*thigein*) either of these conceptions of Unity.[60]

Subsequently, Aristotle ups the ante by claiming that touch is not only unity as one in materially one, but also unity as noetically one. Here his metaphor suggests concrete touch of *aitia* and *archai*. In touching first causes and principles you cannot be mistaken. Thus, touch is always an either/or. A tactile intellect either knows or does not know its causes and principles. This is because in the activity of touch-thinking, *noesis* is an activity (*energeia*) which results in contemplation, *theoria* rather than movement or a process (*kinesis*).

Plotinus' metaphor of seeing suggests there are degrees of clarity in accessing the Forms and the One. Consequently, a spectator *Nous* and *noesis*, unlike a tactile one, is open to epistemic ambiguity. It sees through a glass darkly. In the activity of spectator-thinking, *noesis* is a process (*kinesis*), what Plotinus calls an "unrolling itself, a search." This is why thinking is seen as a deficiency by Plotinus, and one must, on the basis of the principle of prior simplicity, go beyond intellect thinking itself, to a One, which is absolutely simple, because it is beyond intellect and being. In brief, Plotinus recourse to the One would not have convinced Aristotle or his followers. They would likely suggest that Plotinus holds to the duality of thinker and objects of thought because he has another, more primitive metaphysical motive—defense of the doctrine of Forms, and the principle of prior simplicity. This motive is revealed in Plotinus' claim that since Forms are a multiplicity, thinking implies variety, and differences in thought and language.[61]

Plotinus states:

> What thinks must therefore take different things, and what is thought, as being thought, must be varied, or there will not be

---

60. Aristotle, *Metaphysics*, I.V.986b19–21.
61. Plotinus, *Ennead*,. V.5.7.16–21. cf. Schroeder, *Plotinus and Language*, 341–43.

thought of it, but a touching and so to speak an ineffable and unintelligible contact.[62]

Plotinus' point is that whenever we think we have the multiplicity of thinker and object thought; and whenever we speak in propositions we have as spectators a multiplicity of subjects, verbs, and predicates that map being. It is difficult to say whether it was Plotinus' view that all knowledge is essentially a kind a seeing which echoes the theory that mathematical and logical objects (abstract objects) have to have seen objects just as sight has to have something to see or that the way abstract objects are known is analogous to the way that existing objects are seen.

V.2. Illumination and Touch

The analogy between seeing and understanding is a deeply embedded Platonic metaphor—the intelligible light of the Forms is the analogue of the light which renders material things visible. Intelligible light emanates from the supreme Form, the Good, to illuminate inferior forms thus rendering them intelligible; and the mind that understands them like the sun makes other things visible by illuminating them. Moreover, since the Forms are within the divine mind, and the divine light which renders them intelligible is a divine illumination within the human mind, illumination is mapped in a variety of ways—as the mind's participation in *Nous*, as the One's interior presence to mind, or as *nous* dwelling in the human soul and teaching it from within.

This explains why Plotinus is fond of the ocular metaphor of reflection as incorporeal illumination.[63] Light and the presence of light to the object it illuminates are inseparable, which is why reflection is an obvious instance of illumination. Consequently, as Schroeder notes, Plotinus argues against Aristotle (and Alexander of Aphrodisias), claiming light is an activity that proceeds from a luminous source, rather than an effect that arises both from the source of illumination and the illuminated object.[64] Finally, light is also the consciousness that *Nous* has of the One. If Intellect abstracts (*aphesei*) the objects of its vision, which are the Forms, it sees the light by which it saw them—the One. Now tied as Plotinus was to the ocular metaphors of light, illumination, look (*enhorasthai*), and the noetic multiplicity suggested by these optical metaphors, it becomes clear why he could not

---

62. Plotinus, *Ennead*, V.3.10.42–44.
63. Plotinus, *Ennead*, I.4.10.14; V.8.4.42–43.
64. Schroeder, *Conversion*, 341–43.

concur with any non-spectator theory of *noesis*—especially the one held by Aristotle in his touching metaphor of noesis.

The crucial question that emerges now is how does Aristotle connect thinking (*noesis*) with *ousia* as an *entelecheia*? Aristotle begins by claiming that knowledge of universals is non-discursive and it is compared with touching.[65] In this kind of thinking we do not predicate anything of anything (*ti kata tinos*),[66] nor is there any assertion (*kataphasis*).[67] The objects of such knowledge are incomposite (*asuntheta; adiaireta*)[68] in that they do not involve matter and form. If one can offer definitions of such in composite objects, then one can state what their beings are. Hence the reference to what is (*ti esti*),[69] and to what it is in respect of being (*ti esti kata to ti en einai*).[70] Here definitions are seen as statements of *identity*. Such statements are always about an object which is not a composite for it is here that an object is identical with its being.[71]

Note how Aristotle carefully switches from seeing to touching when discussing *noesis* rather than *aisthesis*. In this kind of thinking you cannot be mistaken. Only touch or contact is true or false—an either/or. Moreover, only touch suggests unity of contact. Thus, in the case of *asuntheta*, when thinking is identical with the object of thought in a non-propositional way, *Nous* grasps truth. This idea is amplified by Aristotle when he claims that the activity of thinking is identical with the actively working object of thought, as touch (*thigein; thinganein*).

> Truth and falsity are as follows: contact (*thigein*) and assertion (*phanai*) are truth (for assertion is not the same as affirmation), and ignorance is non-contact (*me thigganein*). I say ignorance, because it is impossible to be deceived with respect to what a thing is, except accidentally (*e kata sumbebekos*); and the same applies to in composite substances (*tas me suntheta ousia*), for it is impossible to be deceived about them. And they all exist actually (*energeia*), not potentially (*ou dunamei*); but as it is Being itself is not generated nor destroyed (*ou gignetai oude phtheiretai*) ... With respect, then, to all things which are essences and actual (*einai ti kai energeia*, there is no question of being mistaken,

65. Aristotle, *Metaphysics* IX.8.1051b24–25; 1072b21.
66. Aristotle, *De Anima*, III.6, 430b28.
67. Aristotle, *Metaphysics*, IX.8. 1051b24.
68. Aristotle, *Metaphysics*, IX.8.1051b17; *De Anima*, 430a26.
69. Aristotle, *Metaphysics*, IX.8.1051b26; b32.
70. Aristotle, *De Anima*, III..5.430b28.
71. That Aristotle thinks of statements, which give the being of something, has been argued by Owen, *Snares of Ontology*, 125–50, esp. 136–39.

but only of thinking Or not thinking (*all'e noein e me*) them . . .
Truth means to think these objects (*to noein tauta*), and there is
no falsity or deception, but only ignorance . . .[72]

Aristotle's point seems to be that while there are degrees of clarity in seeing, the form of the object and its defining characteristics, no such abstraction characterizes touching. Hence, when we think of something, its intelligible form is in the soul, which means that thinking activity of the soul receives the form, and is the place of the forms. The most common way for an intelligible form to be in the soul is to be embodied as a mental image, but again the metaphor of touch informs what the nature of knowing an intelligible form embodied as a mental image is like. In these special cases of touching, a human thinker is nothing but an intellect, and identical with the object of its thought. Like God, the human intellect thinks itself. Here there is the activity of self-thinking, for in thinking of the objects, the human intellect thinks.

Summary: The difference between divine and human thought is that God's thought does not entail images *tout court* for images depend on physiological organs. At *De Anima* III.5, in the activity of touch-thinking, or "nousing," Aristotle postulates a second intellect which thinks incessantly and forever. It can reside both in us and separately from us, and it involves no memory. When a human thinks using the "active-intellect" he thinks as an activity (*energeia*) rather than as a process (*kinesis*). Such thinking constitutes the happiest and most pleasant possible life because it involves contemplation (*theoria*) of the Unmoved Mover.

V. 3. Touching and Seeing

God as *Nous*, as formal and final cause, transcends the world as its end and it is in the world as its intelligible order. Where is *nous* actualized; where does it think itself—in things, in a separate existence? His answer is in human *nous*, in the human intellect. Consequently, the only "reason" for the existence of the world, the only fact that makes it more than a mere occurrence, and renders it intelligible, the only fact the justifies nature to man, is that the world exists to make being and life possible, and at its fullest, to make possible the best life, which for Aristotle is the noetic life, a life devoted to *Nous*. Thus, Aristotle's Unmoved Mover can only be known by touch. What is touched is not the "creator," "beginner," or "initiator" of

---

72. Aristotle, *Metaphysics*, IX.9. 1051b25–1052a2.

motion in any temporal sense of "first." What is known is an *arche*, a principle of intelligibility, and a "reason why." This means the Unmoved Mover renders natural processes intelligible through touch. Consequently, it is a logical explanation, not a physical cause, natural law, or a force. It does not make things occur, any more than a natural law "makes" anything happen. However, it does make things known—again by touch.

In this sense, the *arche* of motion is its final cause or reason why, the factor expressing what it is directed toward, and the fullest expression of what it can do. Since for Aristotle, what a thing can do is identical with what it fundamentally is—its entelechy is its intelligible structure—the final and formal cause of a process is identical. It follows from this that the Unmoved Mover is both the final and the formal cause of motion that is known through tactile contact. Since final and formal causes are alike, in that in both no infinite regress is possible, or else they would not be *archai* and hence not genuine beginnings of understanding, there has to be a non-temporal, circular motion that is a "first efficient cause." This is the eternal circular motion of the outermost heavenly sphere. It is the trigger of cosmic motion. Here there is no action at a distance—between an Unmoved Mover and motion. Rather there is direct physical contact between what is acting and what is being acted upon when eternal motion triggers motion in time.

In nuce, the Unmoved Mover is not the "creator" of anything for the world is eternal, and motion and time are eternal. It is not the "sustainer" of the world, it exercises no providence, it has no will, and it has no purpose. It knows itself, it is intelligent, but not as humans have the power of intelligence, and it thinks, but again not as human are said to think most of the time. It can be called *Nous* only in the sense in which Spinoza's *substantia* can be said to be intellect. As *Nous* then, the Unmoved Mover, is the intelligible structure, order, and principle of intelligibility in the universe. Moreover, it is known by noetic contact alone. Thus, Aristotle argues that the perfected functioning of the highest activity in the world is the only justification, the only "reason why" for the world's existence. Now if God is pure and perfect activity, then God must be pure *nous* as well for the perfect functioning of intellect offers the direct intellectual vision of "why."

Nous, therefore, exerts its power by making the cosmos self-transparent. The *nous poietikos* 'by virtue of which all things become' is likened to:

A positive state of light . . .[73]

And the activity of light is:

---

73. Aristotle, *De Anima*, III.5.430a15–16.

An actuality which is present.[74]

For Aristotle there is no distinction within *noesis noeseos*, there is no gap between *act* and *concept*, and thus there is no potentiality within *Nous*, nor is there a conceptual distinction between the act of thinking and its object. *Nous* is a first principle that does not contain dualism within itself. Moreover, it is intelligible since it is not beyond being and intellect. Finally, its *noesis* is not an empty thinking about nothing. The concept of divine *noesis* consists in its being thought, as being thought eternally without interruption, and there is no transition into or out of potentiality ever. This means that Mind or Intellect is always and continuously enacted, and realized through the activity of self-contemplation. In nuce, there is no need to leave *Nous* behind in an ascent to something prior, the One.[75]

Summary: Self-knowledge and self-identity involves thinking abstract objects. But several questions remain—what does thinking intelligibles and universals mean? Does thinking in some sense constitute intelligibles and universals?[76] Does the mind-stuff that out of which abstract entities are made make any more sense as that out of which universals are made? We have no idea of what mind is save that it is made of whatever abstract objects and universals are made of.[77] Plotinus agrees with Aristotle that a 'real' relation of thinking to the intelligible object of thought occurs at the level of *Nous* and that truth is attained in the knowledge to which *nous* knows *Nous*.[78]

XI. Objects Abstract and Divine

Aristotle and Plotinus do not have grave misgivings thinking about *Nous*, the One or mathematicals as "abstract" objects.[79] These entities are what we

74. Aristotle, *De Anima*, II.7. 418b9

75. R. Norman, *Aristotle's Philosopher God*, 63-65.

76. Emilsson, *Sense-Perception*, 217-49.

77. Is the battle between realists and anti-realists empty after all? In constructing a Lockean idea or Platonic Form we go through the same process—a single property from something is lifted from the property of being red, painful, or good—and then treated as if it were a subject of predication with causal efficacy.

78. There is also little to suggest he subscribes to Descartes', Locke's, and Berkeley's notions of internal mental states—both of which entail antirealist ontological and epistemological assumptions. Emilsson comes to the same conclusion on similar grounds. Emilsson, *Sense-Perception*, 217-34.

79. On abstract objects in Aristotle see Cleary, *Aristotle and Mathematics*, 143-98; 268-344; 424-94.

touch and see in the activity of *nous noesis noeseos*.[80] Aristotle claims the very possibility of 'first philosophy' depends on whether the soul is separable from a material body. This depends on a special activity of *nous* that grasps the self-identical essences which are the objects of first philosophy thereby making it possible. This 'divine' mode of cognition, involving the complete identity of knower and known, is a higher-level noetic activity distinct from a lower-level activity common to all kinds of thinking and perception. Here we find exemplified the identity of *nous* with its abstract objects of thought independent of matter as pure actualities.[81] How do we know that 'abstract objects' exist? A brief excursion into universals, aseity and a modal version of the ontological proof may provide an answer.

Aristotle claims universals to be 'real' for without universals experience would be incoherent. If Wolterstorff's[82] claims are added to Gerson's the following thesis emerges: 1) Forms are not hypostasized universals (even if *ante rem* universals are distinct from *post rem* universals); and 2) Aristotle's universals are not Plato's Forms;[83] arguments emerge where Malcolm[84] and Plantinga[85] read versions of Anselm's own use of Aristotle

80. Aristotle, *Metaphysics*, XII.9. 1074b34-35; Plotinus, *Enneads*, V.6.1-2V.3.49 .1-6; V.3.5.43-48.

81. Cleary mapped the contours of this cognition kind in an unpublished lecture "Nous as the Ground of Aristotle's Metaphysics" (1993) *SAGPNL* 164 at the APA/Eastern Division in Atlanta in December 1993.

82. Wolterstorff, *On Universals*, 1970, 263-65.

83. Gerson, *Aristotle and Other Platonists*, 209-41.

84. Malcolm, *Anselm's Ontological Arguments*, 143-51. Malcolm claims any statement with that x necessarily exists once translated into its hypothetical equivalent ends in a contradiction: firstly, if x necessarily exists, to suggest it does not exist is contradictory or incompatible with the original assertion that x necessarily exists; secondly, a lack of symmetry exists between the statement "a triangle has three angles" and "god necessarily exists." The former statement may be translated into a meaningful conditional form if a triangle exists, then it has three angles while the latter cannot; and thirdly, the statement x necessarily exists (or is a necessary being) is not equivalent to the hypothetical if x exists then it necessarily exists—no existential proposition can be necessary. There are many different conceptions of what a necessary x might be. It depends: 1) on the different language games in which they perform their duties; and/or 2) what is logically necessary is that if x exists, then it exists.

85. Plantinga, *Does God Have a Nature?* The argument runs:1) existence is a predicate; 2) whether existence is better than non-existence; on the basis that such an argument is sound; 3) because *necessary* existence is a predicate; and 4) if *necessary* existence is that than which nothing greater can be conceived, or an unlimited being then; 5) by its very conception its existence or non-existence cannot be caused or simply happen because it would be dependent or contingent upon something outside itself and thus a limited being which means; 6) if it does not exist, its existence would be logically impossible; and if it does exist its nonexistence would be logically impossible. It either exists or does not exist.

to justify the existence of *a se* and *necessary* abstract entities.[86] Plantinga's modal argument takes the form:[87]

1. God's existence is either necessary or logically impossible.
2. It is not impossible for God to exist (i.e., there is no contradiction in assuming that God exists).

Therefore: God exists necessarily *a se*.
A second version unfolds:

1. First principles, first causes, Nous or the One's existence is either necessary or logically impossible.
2. It is not impossible for them to exist *a se* (there is no contradiction in assuming that first principles, first causes, *Nous* or the One exists).

Therefore, they exist necessarily *a se*.[88]
To this argument Aristotle, Origen and Plotinus might add:

3. The existence of abstract entities *per se* (Forms etc.) is either necessary or logically impossible without the existence of abstract entities *a se*.
4. It is not impossible for Forms etc. to exist *per se* without the necessary existence of abstract entities *a se*.

Therefore, *Nous*, God and the One exist necessarily and numerically— *a se*.

Conclusion

Self-knowledge and subjectivity is about a self who not only enquires about abstract objects and universals but about soul and body; who wonders how

86. Anselm, *Proslogion*, 3. cf. Malcolm, *Anselm's Ontological Arguments*, 143–51.

87. Plantinga, *Does God Have a Nature?* 5; cf. Hedley, *Iconic Imagination*, 132–34.

88. Plantinga contra Malcolm asserts the necessity of x remaining in existence (if x exists) or out of it (if x doesn't exist) is nothing that bears on the contingency or necessity of x's existence or nonexistence—but only on the *necessity* of x's existence or nonexistence. Thus it is possible and meaningful to ask whether its existence is necessary or logically possible. A twofold conclusion follows: 1) either x does not exist or it necessarily exists; 2) the only reason x could not necessarily exist would be if the concept of x were self-contradictory or logically absurd; 3) since we cannot say its existence is impossible, its existence is necessary; 4) however empirically impossible, nothing prevents the possible truth of an idea so long as it is logically consistent, i.e. free from self-contradiction or logically possible; thus it is logically possible green men might inhabit the far side of the moon; but it is not logically possible that a square circle might exist—which is self-contradictory.

soul derives whatever structure and value it has from substance and memory theories of the self; and that whatever subjectivity is, it is experienced through space, time and the continuum. Add to this *Nous* (or possibly a One that has "itself" as an object of its thinking or proto-thinking)—a question emerges: Why should we take abstract entities and hypostatized universals seriously at all? Aristotle and Plotinus propose that a 'transcendent' subjectivity is possible but such is dependent upon *Nous* (or the One) triggering awareness of a transcendent self beyond an empirical self. By seeing, touching, and participating with *Nous* (or the One) the 'intentionality' of other minds and languages are grasped—not as generalizations derived from experience (psychologism), not as subjective mental states with psychological properties (intuitionism); not as manipulation of linguistic symbols, signs or a language game (formalism) but as abstract objects or conceptually independent intelligible objects (realism).[89]

---

89. Enquiry shall focus next upon a bricolage of passages in *Metaphysics* XII, IX VIII, *De Anima* III.2, III.5, *Posterior Analytics*, II.9 and *Ennead* V. The historical context of the problem of other minds likely involves disagreements with Sceptics on the possibility of knowing other minds at all.

10

Other Minds

If circumstances lead me, I will find
where truth is hid, though it were hid indeed
within the centre.

—Shakespeare, *Hamlet*

Précis

THIS ENQUIRY IS AGAIN parsed from two similes in the *Theaetetus* where mind is an aviary and each new piece of knowledge is a wild bird caught and caged.[1] The aviary is the mind, knowledge is the birds, and when we think we hold a bird in our hands.[2] Three metaphors are transposed from

---

1. Plato, *Theaetetus*, 197de: Now consider whether knowledge is a thing you can possess in that way without having it about you, like a man who has caught some wild birds ... we might say his "has" them all the time inasmuch as he possesses them ... but in another sense he "has" none of them though he has got control of them, now that he has made them captive in an enclosure of his own; he can take holds of them whenever he likes by catching any bird he chooses, and let them go again and it is open to do that as often as he pleases.

2. Plato, *Theatetus*, 199ab: Thus think of an aviary in which birds are kept. I may be said to possess the birds as long as they are in the aviary but I may have and hold the birds more closely if I have them in hand. If we have caught the wrong bird we make a false judgment. When in hunting for some one kind of knowledge, as the various kinds fly about ... so in one example he thought eleven was twelve, because he caught the knowledge of twelve, which was within him, instead of that of eleven, caught a ringdove instead of a pigeon.

Thus think of an aviary in which birds are kept. I may be said to possess the birds as long as they are in the aviary but I may have and hold the birds more closely if I have

these similes:[3] "Orioles" stand for individual minds; "owls" for other minds and abstract entities; and aviaries for holenmermism—"the whole of reality is continuous in its parts." Aristotle[4] and Plotinus[5] claim orioles—indeed even the most solipsistic of orioles—know owls to some considerable degree if for no other reason than: orioles and owls share marks of the mental;[6] and fly about in "aviaries" where the whole is in the part (*holenmermism*) and the world contains genuinely continuous phenomena together (*synechism*)—an inversion of the ego-centric view that orioles and owls know only themselves and live in their own singular aviary ways.[7]

---

them in hand. If we have caught the wrong bird we make a false judgment.

3. To transpose: in mathematics—to transfer a term with a changed sign from one side of an algebraic equation to the other so as not to destroy the equality of the members; in music—to move a chord, melody, composition upward or downward in pitch while retaining its internal interval structure—as said of players or instruments. cf. *OED*.

4. Aristotle's claim that 'the whole is in the part' is based on the notion that exclusion is always posterior to inclusion. Consequently, the perfection of divine *nous* thinking itself (*kai estin he noesis noeseos noesis*) includes intellection of individuals: "for to be perfect is to be complete and self-sufficient and "that from which nothing is wanting." cf. Aristotle, *Physics*, III.6.207a8–15; *Metaphysics*, XII.8.1074b33–35; XII.10.1075b21–24. cf. Berti, *Intellection*, 141–63.

5. The notion that 'the whole is in the part' is based upon Plotinus's doctrine that every form in *Nous* contains every other Form by the interiority of its relations to other Forms. Each Form is all the other Forms and each mind is cognitively identical with each and every Form because the multiplicity of divine intellect is not spatially articulated. cf. Plotinus, *Enneads*, V.V.1.19–43; V.8.3.30–34; V.9.6; V.9.8.3–7. cf. Schroeder, *Plotinus and Language*, 336–55; Trouillard, *Logic*, 125–38. The notion that 'the whole is in the part' is based upon Plotinus's doctrine that every form in *Nous* contains every other Form by the interiority of its relations to other Forms. Each Form is all the other Forms and each mind is cognitively identical with each and every Form because the multiplicity of divine intellect is not spatially articulated. cf. Plotinus, *Enneads*, V.V.1.19–43; V.8.3.30–34; V.9.6; V.9.8.3–7.

6. Following Feigl, the marks of mental include (but are not exhaustive of): 1) non-spatiality (having a non-spatial space or element); 2) an ability to exist separately from bodies; 3) an inability to be identified with any object "in the world; 4) an ability to know itself incorrigibly ("privileged access"); 5) an ability to grasp universals; 6) an ability to sustain relations ("intentionality"); 7)an ability to use language; 8) an ability to act freely; and 9) an ability to form part of a social group. See, Feigl, *Mental and Physical*.

7. Popper contrasts "clouds"—his metaphor for indeterministic systems, with "clocks", meaning deterministic ones. Siding with indeterminism, he comments—"Peirce was right in holding that all clocks are clouds to some considerable degree—even the most precise of clocks. This, I think, is the most important inversion of the mistaken determinist view that all clouds are clocks." cf. Popper, *Clouds and Clocks*, 215.

I. Horizons

Logical positivists have long argued the task of philosophy is a critique of language and the clarification of propositions.[8] Here Wittgenstein notes that in the end, when all has been said and done, the correct method in philosophy should be to say nothing.[9] Carnap and Ayer will amend this caveat to what can only rightly be said—which are the propositions of natural science alone. As for anyone who wants to say something 'metaphysical,' it should be demonstrated to them that they have failed to give meaning to certain signs in their propositions. Scholars of the *Theatetus* anchored in logical atomism agree and argue that objects can only be named not known and that mistaken metaphysical theories arise from failed semantic idioms or category mistakes.[10] The world is said to be a totality of facts which themselves consist in their existence to a reduction of 'atomic facts' composed of simple objects, each of which can be named.[11] Names are then combined in ways that express elementary propositions but each elementary proposition is logically independent of its fellows. Each depicts a possible state of affairs which constitutes its sense. Compound propositions are formed out of these elementary atomic facts. The whole of these parts constitute objects of knowledge. Since any object named is a complex of composed parts, because we cannot speak a coherent sentence about an indivisible object, we must combine words or make a compound proposition in order to truly say something; all knowledge statements begin with its nameable parts.[12]

Ryle claims Plato advances five premises in the *Theatetus* that offer a critique of language and a clarification of propositions: 1) objects known must be of a complex composed of parts; 2) indivisible objects are not knowable; 3) coherent sentences cannot be spoken of about an indivisible object; 4) all complexes reduce to elements as names that cannot be taken as objects of knowledge; and 5) simple objects of perception cannot be objects of knowledge. They can only be named.[13] Ryle's insistence that we must make a proposition in order to truly say something and that we must combine words to speak at all leads him to claim further that: no atomic expression like '7' or '12' or Theatetus is something that can be known, it is only something

---

8. Wittgenstein, *Tractatus*, 4.003.

9. Wittgenstein, *Tractatus*, 6.5.3; 6.54; 7.

10. Ryle, *Concept of Mind*, (3).

11. Wittgenstein, *Tractatus*, 3.221.

12. Following Ayer's apt description see Ayer, *Philosophy in the Twentieth Century*, 111–12.

13. Ryle, "Logical Atomism in the *Theatetus*," 31.

that can be named; an 'atomic' expression '7' or '12' or Theatetus "could not tell a truth or falsehood; nor could it tell what someone believes or guesses rightly or wrongly; or tell what someone has taught or discovered; or tell what someone has forgotten; or tell what someone may be ignorant of; or tell what he might know."[14] Only a compound proposition comprised of 'atomic facts' like 7+5=12 can be known and can tell a truth.[15] If a series of signs fails to express an elementary proposition or a compound proposition and does not serve to affirm or deny a mathematical equation, then it does not express any proposition at all. In short, it is non-sensical.

On this basis, Wittgenstein argues most propositions found in philosophical works are not merely false but non-sensical.[16] Here he employs the term 'metaphysical' to characterize the peccant utterances of ethical, religious and aesthetic discourse with the goal to set the limits to what cannot be thought and to signify what cannot be said by presenting clearly what can be said made famous in the Ogden rendering: "whereof one cannot speak, therefore one must be silent."[17]

All this Wittgenstein and Ryle might be a bit much—but did not Plato's Socrates bring Parmenides' entire argument down to just such a critique—to say nothing except what can be said and known;[18] and was not Protagoras silenced because he cannot utter a coherent statement?[19] This is not the case at all.[20] It is not Socrates' view that knowledge can be rescued or needs to be rescued by supporting the whole-of-parts theory of knowledge.[21] In the *Parmenides*, after it has been proved that unity and being are the original co-equal characters of any object that we can refer to without the help of a hypothesis, the "whole" and "part" is the first characteristics of an object to be proved. The whole (universal) exists as a container, and as demonstrated in the second hypothesis, while the parts (particulars) it contains are infinite in number the whole (universal) also exists as that which is contained as the place of parts (particulars). Here the whole does not have infinite parts but extremities. As the whole *qua* whole existing in space and time it also has

14. Ryle, "Logical Atomism in the *Theatetus*," 24.
15. Ryle, "Letters and Syllables in Plato," 431–51; cf. Wittgenstein, *Tractatus*, 4.00031.
16. Wittgenstein, *Tractatus*, 6.53.
17. Wittgenstein, *Tractatus*, 7.
18. Plato, *Parmenides*, 142a.
19. Plato, *Parmenides*, 183b.
20. See the excellent analysis of Roecklein, *Plato versus Parmenides*, 177–81.
21. As argued by Fine, "Logos and Knowledge in the *Theatetus*", 384; Annas, "Knowledge and Language: The *Theatetus* and *Cratylus*" 111; and Burnyeat, *Plato's Theatetus*, 143.

parts that come into being and pass away. It is principally for this reason it is logically impossible for bodies to be objects of knowledge. Their infinite parts limit what can be known or knowable about them.

What thought thinks is always a universal—a "whole" or a "form." The difficulty as Simplicius notes, is not the reality of the form but the possibility that its "presence" is just a thought in our minds—a way of looking at things—where a "whole" is treated simply as a point of view from which mind contrives to look at a plurality of things with a single glance.[22] Nor is it Wittgenstein's or Ryle's claims that utterances are reducible to elementary propositions and what they express and imply are knowable but only if expressed in complex propositional terms that resonates either.[23] Rather as Socrates insists: firstly, "elements" or parts of wholes are not objects of knowledge—wholes are; and secondly, although we must speak of whole and parts in order to speak coherently at all—words and statements themselves are not real objects but rather images of objects and thus not objects of knowledge. Parmenides, for example, could not so much as utter a coherent statement or any sound at all unless he admitted his "one" has "being" added to it. He even confesses one must allow that his "one" has "existence" and that objects of speech are themselves wholes of parts or perishable bodies and with this an Eleatic edifice crumbles:

> What I mean is this. When you use any word, you use it to stand for something. You can use it once or many times but in either case you are speaking of the thing whose name it is. However many times you utter the same word, you must always mean the same thing." (147d). "But Parmenides, the best I can make of the matter is this- that these forms are as it were patterns fixed in the nature of things. The other things are made in their image and are likenesses, and this participation they come to have in the forms is nothing but their being made in their image." (132d).

Whenever Socrates talks about the Dream Theory and its unknowable complex objects, he insists: 1) bodies cannot be objects of knowledge.[24] The alphabet, numbers and musical scales are examples of why this

---

22. Diogenes Laertius, II.35. Simplicius, Arist. *In Cat.* 8b25. Objecting to negative predication with the Eleatics, conceptualists like Menedemus of the "school of Eretria" denies that universals exist at all except *in intellectu*. Qualities are mere thoughts or notions (*philia ennoiai*).

23. In the third, sixth, and seventh hypotheses of the *Parmenides* Plato extends his Eleatic critique beyond Parmenides to the atomisms of Empedocles, Anaxagoras and by implication Democritus. Wittgenstein's 'atomic facts' resemble Democritus' atoms which in turn are miniature versions of Parmenides' ungenerated unity.

24. Plato, *Theatetus*, 206b.

is so;[25] 2) it is non-sensical because language is not the object to be known; 3) parts of wholes cannot be not objects of knowledge; 4) that which has parts has infinite parts; 5) what is divisible is infinitely divisible because there is in itself no such thing as an irreducible divisible part.[26] An object which has one part cannot avoid having all the parts including the parts of being a "whole," having extremities and coming into being and passing away; and 6) it does not follow from the fact that we cannot speak a coherent utterance without individual parts of a whole that thought must be made up of single, divisible units. On the other hand, wholes like the number 6 are an indivisible form. It can be named, known and tell a truth.[27] Other forms might even tell something a person might know, or guess, or believe, or might be taught, or discovered, or forgotten, or be ignorant of such as the possibility of other minds.[28]

When Plato introduces the number 6 as a form and treats it as a whole of parts, he introduces the issue of the aviary and the "missing 7+5 bird."

Entrance into Plato's aviary of wild birds must be nuanced and subtle. Here Wittgenstein is instructive:

> My sentences are illuminating in the following way: to understand them you must recognize them, once you have climbed through them, on them, over them—as senseless. (You must, so to speak, throw away the ladder after you have climbed upon it). You must climb out through my sentences, then you will see the world aright.[29]

Russell's and Ayer's logical atomism was reduced by Wittgenstein until the full power of aporetic logic could be unleashed upon language. This idea is analogous to what in logic can be achieved following Frege and Russell only outside of ordinary language (or beneath it). Think of minimalism in music or architecture. What is hidden by the melodic or aesthetic structures minds enjoy gives way to syntactical formula and symbols much in the way of touching or viewing a symphony by Schoenberg, Paert or Glass achieves. Aristotle and Plotinus anticipated how much can be gained by such an approach.[30] What you have are forms of tactile and visual language which access an ideal language of 'thought thinking itself.'[31]

25. Plato, *Theatetus*, 205a.
26. Plato, *Theatetus*, 207c.
27. Plato, *Theatetus*, 204c.
28. Plato, *Theatetus*, 202ab
29. Wittgenstein, *Tractatus*, 6.5.4.
30. Schroeder, "Categories and Plotinian Aesthetics," 130.
31. The central texts referencing *noesis noeseos noesis* in Aristotle are *Metaphysics*,

II. Foundations

In the *Theatetus* Plato presents the mind and its constituents as an aviary of birds that leap into flight when our mind attempts to grasp them.[32] His key points are that: firstly, the birds represent functions of thought rather than memories of Forms and that false judgment resides not in our perceptions or thoughts but in the fitting together of perception and thought.[33] The challenge the aviary illustrates is—what if we ask what the sum of seven and five is? They could be added incorrectly: that seven and five = eleven not twelve. If so, one has and does not have knowledge of twelve at the same time which means the principle that one cannot know and not know the same thing is invalidated. Secondly, that there are certain kinds of knowledge that require some application before knowledge itself becomes active.[34] Thus there is a kind of knowledge we may 'have' but not 'possess.' Socrates' example is until we apply our knowledge of mathematics even if we know the number twelve, we do not "possess" the knowledge that seven plus five equals twelve.[35] Thirdly Plato also proposes there are ignorance and pieces of knowledge in the aviary. Thus he is keen to distinguish possession of knowledge from having knowledge. Here someone who has caught and caged wild birds possesses them all but may not have any in hand—although he can put his hand on them.[36] Thus to have knowledge (*episteme*) true judgment must be accompanied by discourse (*logos*).[37] Moreover, since a distinction exists between simple apprehension and apprehension attended by discourse, knowledge (*episteme*) is denied to simple apprehension. Beliefs turned into knowledge are secured (*aitias logismo*) by providing foundations for them.[38]

Aristotle follows up on Plato's argument' one has to have 'justified true belief' that 7+5=12 or it remains unknowable. Here he suggests that there is probably *something* to the notion that *nous* is separable even though nothing

---

XII.9 1074b34–35; *De Anima* III.5.430a15–20; and in Plotinus, *Ennead*, I.6.8.21–27; V.3.5.43–48.

32. Plato, *Theatetus*, 199ab. On uses of this simile with claims of the identity and relation of thinking and being see Berchman, "Of Hunting Doves and Pigeons," 31–48.

33. Plato, *Theatetus*, 195e; 197de.

34. Plato, *Theatetus*, 199a.

35. Plato, *Theatetus*, 198d. cf. Burnyeat, *Theatetus*, 112; Roecklein, *Plato versus Parmenides*, 176–77.

36. Each new piece of knowledge is caught and caged but actual knowledge is putting our hands on the bird we "know" when taking it out of the cage. But we may put our hands on the wrong bird instead of the one we want thereby having false knowledge and judgment. Cf. Plato, *Theatetus*, 197de and 199ab.

37. Plato, *Theatetus*, 201d–202c.

38. Plato, *Theatetus*, 201d–210d.

else about the soul is and it is upon this claim that we have 'justified true belief' in the existence of other minds. First, because as a kind of power (*dunamei pos*) it can think itself; secondly, because it thinks all things it is unmixed (*apathes*); thirdly because though it is nothing at all until it thinks, it is the power (*dunamis*) of becoming all objects of thought (*noeta*) when it thinks;[39] and fourthly, since an *episteme* of universal concepts or truths as *theoria* is available to *nous*, knowledge (*episteme*) provides answers to what my mind and other minds may be.[40] Plotinus ups the ante to propose that the internalization of the intelligible includes the recognition by my mind of other minds and the intelligible reality discovered within me; it is not merely of or about me; but intentionally of other minds and divine *Nous* as well.[41] Significantly, both concur that while universals exist only in the mind, they have some foundation in the extra-mental natures of individuals of the *same class* that exhibit intellect as *Nous* and Forms do; and intelligibility as 'abstract objects' such as mathematicals, meanings, and values do.

Since mind is a whole that has no parts, it is knowable. Aristotle's and Plotinus' arguments for other minds take the logical form of a *modus ponens* argument.

1. If we have *nous*, then *episteme* plays an important role in justifying our beliefs in other minds.

2. We have *nous*.

༄ ༄ ༄

Therefore, *episteme* plays an important role in justifying our belief in other minds.

The existence of other minds are tied to two additional notions: 1) identity theory—that mental states are the same and ultimately are reducible to those of divine *nous*; and 2) that minds are immaterial thinking substances with mental properties. Arguments in support of these claims

---

39. Aristotle, *De Anima*, III.4.429b5–9; 429°18–20. III.5.3.

40. Aristotle claims it is not with the body that *nous* is to be contrasted but with particularity. If the activity of *episteme* (thinking) is a *theorein* (theorizing) that contemplates ultimate causes and first principles, then *nous* must join *episteme* (thought) in *theoria* (contemplation), for it is *nous* that apprehends the causal structure of reality that *episteme* contemplates. Moreover, its subject-matter is a *noeton* or a-synthetic whole (*asuntheta*) which manifests or constitutes itself in *noesis* (thinking) as the unity of its *noeseos* (on thinking). cf. Aristotle, *Metaphysics*, XII.9.1076b34–35; *Metaphysics*, XII.7. 1072b22.

41. Plotinus, *Ennead*, IV.7.10.

are the conceivability and intentionality arguments. The first argument rests on the claim: if we can conceivably find at least one property of minds shared by all minds we are entitled to draw the conclusion that other minds exist.[42] The second proposes that if intentionality is a property of mental states to represent something else, and only minds share this property, we are entitled to claim other minds exist.[43]

Plato and Aristotle are of assistance here. Again Plato is keen to distinguish possession of knowledge from having knowledge. He uses the simile of the mind as an aviary.[44] Each new piece of knowledge is caught and caged. Actual knowledge is putting our hands on the bird we want when taking it out of the cage. However, we may put our hands on the wrong bird instead of the one we want thereby acquiring false knowledge and judgement.[45] The only way to arrive at justified true belief and knowledge is by appeal to arguments from justified belief or mathematical proof.[46] Aristotle tacks on the basis of Plato's lead. He fashions an epistemic regress argument where a set of beliefs is justified if it occurs in an evidential chain including at least two links: a supporting link (e.g. the evidence) and the supported link (e.g. the justified belief). Only chains anchored in foundational beliefs do not derive their justification from other beliefs. On this basis he claims a belief in other minds is justified. More precisely, if we have any justified beliefs, we have some foundational, non-inferentially justified beliefs.[47] The epistemic regress argument is central to Aristotle's claim of the existence of other minds. The error implied in a denial of other minds lies in chains that are circular, endless or ending in unjustified

---

42. This is a weaker version of Leibniz's Law that A and B are identical with each other if they share *all* properties in common.

43. In standard form this argument appears as follows:

1. I can conceive of mental properties shared by all minds.

2. I cannot conceive that minds exist without mental states and properties.

3. If minds share at least one mental property, i.e. intentionality, then other minds exist.

4. If mental states and properties are ultimately reducible to a divine intellect, then all minds and mental states and properties are reducible with the mental states and properties of this divine intellect.

Therefore: the states and properties of my mind and other minds exist because they are reducible and identical with those of a divine intellect.

44. Plato, *Theatetus*, 201d-202c.
45. Plato, *Theatetus*, 201d-210d.
46. Plato, *Meno*, 82b-85b.
47. Aristotle, *Posterior Analytics*, II.19.99b15–100b19.

beliefs or the term is put mind into the wrong onto-logical-semantic category thereby committing a category mistake.[48]

III. Ego-Identity and Nous-Identity

When Aristotle and Plotinus propose that it is possible to know other minds they do not argue that *my* mind is not a mind among other minds; or that *I* am not one person among others, or that knowledge of other minds depends upon *my* mind for justification. The "fact" of *my* intellect, *my* consciousness, or *my* self-consciousness is not simply a subjective mental state, *my* brain activity, or *my* response to external empirical events suggestive of a subjective reception of brute facts *tout court*—but something rather different. There is no longer only a personal *ego* thinking only internal mental states; but there is an interpersonal *nous* thinking other minds—which amounts to the disappearance of a *me* and the acquisition of a *we* knowing. *Ego* (*I*) concepts of self-reference are abandoned and the subject becomes a *nous* (*We*) self where the potential to think is brought to activity by receiving forms and concepts.

Here Aristotle and Plotinus are keen to stress that when *I* raise myself to *Nous* and intellection, *I* in no sense lose my identity. *I* merely think as *Nous* does, thus becoming like *Nous*—a *totum simul*. In an attempt to clarify what self-identity as *ego* and *nous* identity means, Aristotle claims in *Metaphysics* XII.7.1072b18–23 that thought thinks itself through 'participation' in the object of thought: And thought thinking itself deals with that which is best in itself; and that which is thinking in the fullest sense with that which is best in the fullest sense. And thought thinks itself because it shares the nature of the object of thought; for it becomes an object of thought in coming into contact/touch with and thinking its objects, so that thought and object of thought are the same. But it is active when it possesses this object. Therefore the possession rather than the receptivity is the divine element which thought seems to contain, and the act of contemplation is what is most pleasant and best.[49]

---

48. See Aristotle concerning the attribute 'snub' and 'concave' in *Metaphysics*, VII1030b14–1031a14.5. esp. 1030b28–37. Interest in category mistakes in the 1930's and 1940's was initially fueled by Aristotle's notion that category mistakes reveal some deep facts about ontological and semantic categories. Following Husserl, Ryle claimed that distinguishing between categories is the primary task of metaphysics. cf. Ryle, *Categories*, 189–206. On category mistakes see Ryle, *Concept of Mind*, (3).

49. Aristotle, *Metaphysics* XII.7.1072b18–23.

At *Metaphysics* XII.9.107b34–35, we are told all forms of cognition are 'intentionally' "of something else" (*h'allou*) and only incidentally of themselves:

> Therefore it must be of itself (*auton ara noei*) that the divine thought thinks (since it is the most excellent of things) and its thinking is a thinking on thinking.[50]

In *De Anima* III.2.425b26–27, he says that the object and the thinking of it are one in *energeia* but different in *to einai*:

> The activity of the sensible object and that of the percipient sense is one and the same activity and yet the distinction between their being remains. Take as illustration actual sound and actual hearing.[51]

Aristotle also claims, in a few broken lines (*De Anima* III.5.430a14–25) that *nous poietikos* makes all things:

> Mind ... is what it is by virtue of becoming all things, while there is another which is what it is by virtue of making all things: this is sort of a positive state like light; for in a sense light makes potential colors into actual colors. Mind in this sense is separable, impassible, unmixed, since it is in its essential nature activity (for always the active is superior to the passive, the originating force to the matter which it forms. Actual knowledge is identical with its object: in the individual, potential knowledge is in time but in the universe as a whole it is not prior even in time. Mind is not at one time knowing and another time not. When mind is set free from its present conditions it appears just as it is and nothing more: this alone is eternal and immortal ... while mind in this sense is impassible; mind as passive is destructible and without it nothing thinks.[52]

In nuce, thought actually creates the truths it understands, just as light may be said to make the colors which we see by its aid. This *nous poietikos*, he cryptically adds, is separable from matter, impassive, unmixed, and essentially in its nature an activity which receives universals without embodying them in matter, thereby acquiring *episteme*. A point stressed is not the

---

50. Aristotle, *Metaphysics* XII.9.1072b34–35.
51. Aristotle, *De Anima* III.2.425b26–27.
52. Aristotle, *De Anima*, III.5.430a14–25.

survival of *nous* but about the indestructibility of *episteme* based on a *nous* identity distinct from an *ego* identity:[53]

Plotinus builds upon Aristotle's thought-experiment. *Nous* is a thinking of abstract objects which are its own contents. *Nous* is a hypostasis composed of Forms, or at least every species in the world as well as all moral and mathematical forms.[54] Here the Forms are not merely self-subsistent universals but beings which think. This follows from Plotinus' identification of Intellect with the Forms:

> Intellect is all things (*hode nous panta*) . . . and the whole is universal intellect and being, Intellect making being exist in thinking it, and being giving Intellect thinking and existence by being thought . . . but this one is two things: Intellect and being and thinking and thought; Intellect as thinking and being as thought.[55]

And with identification of individual Forms and individual intellects:

> Intellect and the intelligible substance; each individual Idea is not other than Intellect, but each is Intellect. And Intellect as a whole is all the Forms, and each individual Form is an individual intellect . . . we must assume that the real beings have their place in the thinking subject . . .[56]

And:

> This is the kind of thinking that the human intellect may do when the soul is free from interference from the sensible world and reasoning about it. Plotinus puts it aptly: human intellect (*nous*) is a substance or being (*ousia*) that accesses Intellect (*Nous*) by turning toward it.[57]

---

53. It is difficult to say whether one should view *nous* as a special substance attached to each human body, as a special power (*dunamis*) which the body has or a single substance which was shared by humans. Aristotle vacillated between the first two options with later Platonists and Aristotelians vacillated between the second and third. Augustine proposes the simplest and most controversial solution of all. The soul is immortal because it is the subject or seat of reason (*episteme*) which is eternal: "The human body is mutable and reason is immutable. For all which does not exist always in the same mode is mutable, but that two and two are four exists always in the same mode . . . This sort of reasoning, then, is immutable. Therefore reason is immutable." cf. Augustine, *On the Immortality of the Soul*, 61.

54. Plotinus' starting point is Plato's *Sophist*, 248e-249a.

55. Plotinus, *Ennead*, V.1.4.26-32.

56. Plotinus, *Ennead*, V.9.8.1-7.

57. Plotinus, *Ennead*, V.3.30.27-45.

For:

> ... contemplation must be the same as the contemplated, and Intellect the same as the intelligible; for if not the same, there will be no truth; for who is trying to possess realities will possess an impression different from the realities, and this is not truth. For truth ought not to be the truth of something else but to be what it says. In this way, Intellect and the intelligible are one, and this is reality and the first reality, and also the first Intellect which possess the real beings, or rather is the same as the real beings ... for the intellection will in a way encompass the intelligible or be the same as the intelligible ... All together are one, Intellect, intellection, the intelligible. If therefore Intellect's intellection is the intelligible, and the intelligible is itself, (then) it will itself think itself. ... And in a turning way from any distractions arising from lower levels of reality ... The intellectual act is without parts ... the verbal expression unfolds its contents and brings it out of the intellectual act into the image making power, and so shows the intellectual act as if in a mirror, and this is how there is apprehension and persistence and memory of it. The intellectual act is one thing and the apprehension of it another, and we are always intellectively active but do not always apprehend our activity; and this is because that which receives it does not only receive acts of intelligence but ... perceptions.[58]

Plotinus makes a significant move here. Corresponding to the state of the knower's identity with the known by raising ourselves to *Nous* we in no sense lose self-identity but heighten it.[59] By raising *I* to the level of *We nous*-identity sublates *ego*-identity and obtains not only attentiveness (*parakolouthein*) but self-awareness (*katanoesis*) and self-reflexivity (*sunaisthesis*).

> Often I have woken up out of the body to myself and have entered into myself, going out from all other things; I have seen a beauty wonderfully great and felt assurance that then most of all I belonged to the better part; I have actually lived the best life and come to identify with the divine ... setting myself all the rest of that which is in the intelligible.[60]

Aristotle and Plotinus claim that *my* mind (*nous*) is related to other minds because it is dependent on a supra-personal mind (*Nous*) which causes my mind and other minds.

---

58. Plotinus, *Ennead*, V.3.30.11–16.
59. See, Blumenthal, *Soul and Intellect*, 82–104.
60. Plotinus, *Ennead*, IV.8.1.1–7.

IV. The Problem of Other Minds

Plato's arguments for knowledge of wholes not complex objects with its unknowable elements, justified true belief and Aristotle's infinite regress argument constitute the basis for the possibility of other minds. The problem of other minds begins by assuming that everyone knows how to divide the world into the mental (inner) and the physical (outer). Plato suggests an epistemic distinction between two kinds of mental states outer and inner:

> So if the real is the object of knowledge, then the object of belief must be something other than the real.[61]

Aristotle—a water-diviner pointing out the metaphysical traps of his predecessors—suggests that there is probably *something* to the notion that *nous* is separable even though nothing else about the soul is and it is upon this claim that we have justified true belief in the existence of other minds. First, because as a kind of power (*dunamei pos*) it can think itself; secondly, because it thinks all things it is unmixed (*apathes*); thirdly because though it is nothing at all until it thinks, it is the power (*dunamis*) of becoming all objects of thought (*noeta*) when it thinks;[62] and fourthly, since an *episteme* of universal concepts or truths as *theoria* is available to *nous*, knowledge (*episteme*) provides answers to what my mind and other minds may be.[63] Plotinus ups the ante to propose that the internalization of the intelligible includes the recognition by my mind of other minds and the intelligible reality discovered within me; it is not merely of or about me; but intentionally of other minds and divine *Nous* as well.[64] Significantly, both concur that while universals exist only in the mind, they have some foundation in the extra-mental natures of individuals of the *same class* that exhibit intellect as *Nous* and Forms do; and intelligibility as 'abstract objects' such as mathematicals, meanings, and values do.

Descartes turns on Plato's epistemic distinction into a metaphysical one. His first certitude is his existence as mind but his introspective

---

61. Plato, *Republic*, 478b.

62. Aristotle, *De Anima*, III.4.429b5-9; 429°18-20. III.5.3.

63. Aristotle claims it is not with the body that *nous* is to be contrasted but with particularity. If the activity of *episteme* (thinking) is a *theorein* (theorizing) that contemplates ultimate causes and first principles, then *nous* must join *episteme* (thought) in *theoria* (contemplation), for it is *nous* that apprehends the causal structure of reality that *episteme* contemplates. Moreover, its subject-matter is a *noeton* or a-synthetic whole (*asuntheta*) which manifests or constitutes itself in *noesis* (thinking) as the unity of its *noeseos* (on thinking). cf. Aristotle, *Metaphysics*, XII.9.1076b34-35; *Metaphysics*, XII.7. 1072b22.

64. Plotinus, *Ennead*, IV.7.10.

conception of its content ends with two problems: what basis may a person have for the belief that other persons are similarly self-reflexive and thus have minds?[65] Aristotle and Plotinus tack differently. Minds and bodies are as distinct as invisible parallelness is from visible mountain ridges. But minds are something else. The "fact" of *my* intellect, *my* consciousness, or *my* self-consciousness is not simply a subjective mental state, *my* brain activity, or *my* response to external empirical events.[66] Indeed, my mind (*nous*), self-reflexivity (*sunaisthesis*), awareness (*parakolouthein*) and self-awareness (katanoesis) are dependent upon a *Nous* identity. That contains 'other minds.'[67] Moreover, Aristotle and Plotinus are keen to parse the many reasons which support the existence of my mind and other minds. Firstly, Mind/Intellect is *something* as different from bodies in that they share common properties that bodies do not; and secondly 'thought thinking on itself' has no determinate character of its own, and its understanding has no structure of its own.[68] It is simply a capacity (*dunamis*) for apprehending identity and interconnection. Aristotle states:

> "what I call *nous*—is that with which the soul thinks and understands—is not actual thinking until it thinks."[69]

Such claims exclude any doctrine which credits the understanding with either 'inner' furniture of its own such as "innate ideas," or even a specific 'outer' structure of reality. Indeed, if the results of our thinking arose partly from the structure of reality and partly from inherent laws of the structure

---

65. Realism is the view that: 1) there are real objects that exist independently of our knowledge or experience of them; 2) that these mental and physical objects have properties and enter into relations independently of the concepts with which we understand them, or 3) the language with which we describe them. Anti-realism is any view that rejects any one of these tenets and includes all claims to representationalism, transcendental deduction, and phenomenology. If we were to frame a question to capture the realist and anti-realist position it would be: Is the truth or falsity of the statement x exists independent of mind (human/divine)?

66. No appeals to *other* intellects or to *other* persons on the grounds of radical subjectivity alone; or on that which *I* cannot justify for *myself* ontologically and epistemologically can possible be made. Rather an appeal is made to the existence of a *common* intellect shared by *other* intellects.

67. The *nous*-analogical argument proposed by Aristotle and Plotinus complements Wittgenstein's public language argument on externalist grounds: 1) that any inner process that other minds exist or not stand in need of external criteria; and 2) first person singular mental states are different from first person plural ones.

68. Aristotle, *Metaphysics*, XII.9.1074b34–35. Foundational studies on 'thinking on thinking' (*he noesis noeseos noesis*) in Aristotle include De Koninck, *La Noesis*, 215–18; *Aristotle on God*, 474–515; Beierwaltes, *Metaphysik des Lichtes*, 334–62.

69. Aristotle, *Metaphysics*, XII. 9.107b34–35.

of mind, our thoughts could not reproduce universals and their connections as they really are, but would distort them, as the shapes of things are distorted when seen through a lens.[70] Whereas Aristotle and Plotinus had not to worry about an Eye of the Mind, claiming knowledge to be either a numerical or qualitative identity of the mind with objects known, après Descartes and Locke such an option was no longer available—ideas and impressions are mere inner representations which makes Humean skepticism and Kantian transcendentalism possible.[71]

Arguments for other minds take the logical form of a *modus ponens* argument.

1. If we have *nous*, then *episteme* plays an important role in justifying our beliefs in other minds.
2. We have *nous*.

Therefore, *episteme* plays an important role in justifying our belief in other minds.

Upon initial reflection all premises of this argument appear to be true and the argument form seems to make a necessary case for other minds.[72]

---

70. Aristotle often talks as if knowledge (*episteme*) is knowledge of the general or universal and as if knowing something is knowing its form or essence, (*Metaphysics* IV.1. 1003a 13–14). And while he is inclined to think that the form is the principle of substance, and that it is individual, he also does not want to say there is no knowledge of that which is strictly speaking real or universal, i.e. the form. His solution is to say that knowledge is knowledge of the particular entity and only potentially knowledge of the general or universal entity (*Nic. Ethics*, I.3). Here Aristotle is keen to emphasize that the study of being qua being focuses on the most general and necessary characteristics that entities must have to count as a being, an entity. Examples of entity criteria are enumerated by the categories: everything must be either an individual thing, or a relation, or a state of affairs, or a set. Here 'entity' in its broadest sense denotes anything real and more specific questions address the existence and nature of individuals or particulars (e.g. minds, numbers, forms) or properties (e.g. meanings) or relations (e.g. is there a causal relation that is necessary or a conjunction between events)? Questions which follow include: do entities have essential or accidental properties; are properties and relations particular or universal; is existence itself a property; should we countenance objects having no existence; is there a relationship between an entity and its properties and between that relation and the entities it relates; and must every entity be logically self-consistent?

71. See, Rorty, *Mirror of Nature*, 143.

72. Plato thought that a mathematical proof once discovered stood as an example of a necessary truth that could not later be revised. Aristotle proposed that a logical proof offers a similar example.

Reservations can be raised about the argument, however. Such an *a priori* justification rests on the distinction between analytic and synthetic truths and that analytically true statements are true only by virtue of the meaning of the words involved. Such grounds are not enough for this other minds argument to succeed. One could equally argue that I could exist with a different mind or no mind at all—that I am a brain with physical states and properties not a mind with mental states and properties. So to draw the necessary correspondence between my mind and other minds, sense has to be made on the basis of the prior simplicity principle that my mind and other minds cannot exist without a grounding or primal intellect.

The existence of other minds are tied to two additional notions: 1) identity theory—that mental states are the same and ultimately are reducible to those of divine *nous*; and 2) that minds are immaterial thinking substances with mental properties. Arguments in support of these claims are the conceivability and intentionality arguments. The first argument rests on the claim: if we can conceivably find at least one property of minds shared by all minds we are entitled to draw the conclusion that other minds exist.[73] The second proposes that if intentionality is a property of mental states to represent something else, and only minds share this property, we are entitled to claim other minds exist.[74]

In standard form this argument appears as follows:

1. I can conceive of mental properties shared by all minds.

2. I cannot conceive that minds exist without mental states and properties.

3. If minds share at least one mental property, i.e. intentionality, then other minds exist.

4. If mental states and properties are ultimately reducible to a divine intellect, then all minds and mental states and properties are reducible with the mental states and properties of this divine intellect.

∽ ∽ ∽

Therefore: the states and properties of my mind and other minds exist because they are reducible and identical with those of a divine intellect.

At first glance all premises of this argument appear to be logically possible and the identity and conceivability argument claims seem to make a case

---

73. This is a weaker version of Leibniz's Law that A and B are identical with each other if they share *all* properties in common.

74.

for other minds. Two problems arise, however. The first are reservations about premises 1, 2, 3 and the conclusion are warranted. Are mental properties shared by all minds; is it really conceivable that minds cannot exist without mental properties; does a sharing of mental properties infer other minds exist; and are we justified in concluding that human mental states and properties are reducible to those of divine *nous*? The second problem is when added to a necessary *modus ponens* argument, are the identity and conceivability arguments, sufficient to justify the existence of other minds?[75]

Plato and Aristotle are of assistance here. Plato is keen to distinguish possession of knowledge from having knowledge. He also uses the simile of the mind as an aviary.[76] Each new piece of knowledge is caught and caged. Actual knowledge is putting our hands on the bird we want when taking it out of the cage. However, we may put our hands on the wrong bird instead of the one we want thereby acquiring false knowledge and judgement.[77] The only way to arrive at justified true belief and knowledge is by appeal to arguments from justified belief or mathematical proof.[78] Aristotle fashions the epistemic regress argument where a set of beliefs is justified if it occurs in an evidential chain including at least two links: a supporting link (e.g. the evidence) and the supported link (e.g. the justified belief). Only chains anchored in foundational beliefs do not derive their justification from other beliefs. On this basis he claims a belief in other minds is justified. More precisely, if we have any justified beliefs, we have some foundational, non-inferentially justified beliefs.[79] The error implied in a denial of other minds lies in chains that are circular, endless or ending in unjustified beliefs or put the term mind into the wrong onto-logical-semantic category and thereby

---

75. We must be careful when applying the law A and B are identical with each other if they share identical properties to properties that are the result of my beliefs. There is a crucial difference between the sentences "the car in the yard is red" and "I believe the car in the yard is red." The latter sentence can be true even if the car in the yard is yellow. In brief, conceiving A and B as the same does not warrant the conclusion that A and B are identical. Conceived identities might be caused by the fact we describe A and B similarly and that these similar descriptions cause us to have different beliefs about A and B. All this Ryle on a category mistake might be a bit much but it is cautionary to note our ability to conceive that we are commensurate with a divine mind might merely reflect that we describe all minds similarly. Thus the observation that we can conceive of the relationship between minds as identical is not strong enough to establish that minds are ontologically dependent entities.

76. Plato, *Theatetus*, 201d-202c.

77. Plato, *Theatetus*, 201d-210d.

78. Plato, *Meno*, 82b-85b.

79. Aristotle, *Posterior Analytics*, II.19.99b15–100b19.

committing a category mistake.[80] Since category mistakes are a key to delineating ontological categories, here the term mind is mistakenly understood as a specific mind rather than a whole group of minds.[81]

The problem of other minds begins by assuming that everyone knows how to divide the world into the mental (inner) and the physical (outer). Plato—a water-diviner pointing out the metaphysical traps of his predecessors—suggests an epistemological distinction between two kinds of mental states outer and inner:

> So if the real is the object of knowledge then the object of belief must be something other than the real.[82]

The problem of other minds is compounded by given certain assumptions about how language works. Aristotle and Plotinus are committed to the view that mental discourse serves to designate items that carry metaphysical and epistemological meaning. They also claim that such meaning is not the result of "occult" causes or privileged access to my stream of mental events but to a first cause of all mental activity—*Nous*.[83]

Descartes turns Plato's and Aristotle's realist distinction into a substance dualism and if not an anti-realist one.[84] His first certitude is his existence as mind but his introspective conception of its content ends with two problems: what basis may a person have for the belief that other persons are similarly self-reflexive and thus have minds? Aristotle and Plotinus tack differently. Minds and bodies are as distinct as invisible parallelness is from visible mountain ridges. But minds are something else. The "fact" of *my* intellect, *my* consciousness, or *my* self-consciousness is not simply a subjective mental

---

80. See Aristotle concerning the attribute 'snub' and 'concave' in *Metaphysics*, VII1030b14–1031a14.5. esp. 1030b28–37.

81. Interest in category mistakes was fueled by Aristotle's notion that such mistakes reveal facts about ontological and semantic claims. Following Aristotle and Husserl, Ryle claimed that distinguishing between categories is the primary task of metaphysics. cf. Ryle, *Categories*, 189–206.

82. Plato, *Republic*, 478b.

83. On a critique of such intellectualist claims see Ryle, *Knowing How and That*, 17.

84. Realism is the view that: 1) there are real objects that exist independently of our knowledge or experience of them; 2) that these mental and physical objects have properties and enter into relations independently of the concepts with which we understand them, or 3) the language with which we describe them. Anti-realism is any view that rejects any one of these tenets and includes all claims to representationalism, transcendental deduction, and phenomenology. If we were to frame a question to capture the realist and anti-realist position it would be: Is the truth or falsity of the statement x exists independent of mind (human/divine)?

state, *my* brain activity, or *my* response to external empirical events.[85] Indeed, my mind (*nous*), self-reflexivity (*sunaisthesis*), awareness (*parakolouthein*) and self-awareness (*katanoesis*) are dependent upon a *Nous* identity. That contains 'other minds'.[86] Moreover, Aristotle and Plotinus are keen to parse the many reasons which support the existence of my mind and other minds. Firstly, Mind/Intellect is *something* as different from bodies in that they share common properties that bodies do not; and secondly 'thought thinking on itself' has no determinate character of its own, and its understanding has no structure of its own.[87] It is simply a capacity (*dunamis*) for apprehending identity and interconnection. Aristotle states:

"what I call *nous*—is that with which the soul thinks and understands—is not actual thinking until it thinks."[88]

Such knowledge-as-identity claims exclude any doctrine which credits the understanding with either 'inner' furniture of its own such as "innate ideas," or even a specific 'outer' structure of reality. Indeed, if the results of our thinking arose partly from the structure of reality and partly from inherent laws of the structure of mind, our thoughts could not reproduce universals and their connections as they really are, but would distort them, as the shapes of things are distorted when seen through a lens.[89] Whereas

---

85. No appeals to *other* intellects or to *other* persons on the grounds of radical subjectivity alone; or on that which *I* cannot justify for *myself* ontologically and epistemologically can possible be made. Rather an appeal is made to the existence of a *common* intellect shared by *other* intellects.

86. The *nous*-analogical argument proposed by Aristotle and Plotinus complements Wittgenstein's public language argument on externalist grounds: 1) that any inner process that other minds exist or not stand in need of external criteria; and 2) first person singular mental states are different from first person plural ones.

87. Aristotle, *Metaphysics*, XII.9.1074b34-35. Foundational studies on 'thinking on thinking' (*he noesis noeseos noesis*) in Aristotle include De Koninck, *La Noesis*, 215-18; *Aristotle on God*, 474-515; Beierwaltes, *Metaphysik des Lichtes*, 334-62.

88. Aristotle, *Metaphysics*, XII. 9.107b34-35.

89. Aristotle often talks as if knowledge (*episteme*) is knowledge of the general or universal and as if knowing something is knowing its form or essence, (*Metaphysics* IV.1. 1003a 13-14). And while he is inclined to think that the form is the principle of substance, and that it is individual, he also does not want to say there is no knowledge of that which is strictly speaking real or universal, i.e. the form. His solution is to say that knowledge is knowledge of the particular entity and only potentially knowledge of the general or universal entity (*Nic. Ethics*, I.3). Here Aristotle is keen to emphasize that the study of being qua being focuses on the most general and necessary characteristics that entities must have to count as a being, an entity. Examples of entity criteria are enumerated by the categories: everything must be either an individual thing, or a relation, or a state of affairs, or a set. Here 'entity' in its broadest sense denotes anything real and more specific questions address the existence and nature of individuals or particulars (e.g. minds, numbers, forms) or properties (e.g. meanings) or relations (e.g. is there a

Aristotle and Plotinus had not to worry about an Eye of the Mind, claiming knowledge to be either a numerical or qualitative identity of the mind with objects known, après Descartes and Locke such an option was no longer available—ideas and impressions are mere inner representations which makes Humean skepticism and Kantian transcendentalism possible concerning knowledge as identity with objects.[90]

V. Knowledge as Identity with Objects

A clearer notion of what knowledge-as-identity means requires a definition of what impressions are and the role they play in thinking other minds. Here the Stoic notion of cognitive impressions may be of help. The early Stoics did not think of impressions as pictures or images of the world which can be looked at introspectively. They proposed that mental states are highly complex physical states. They also assumed that the distinctive feature of cognitive impressions is their causal feature. When we see and grasp objects of thought, we apprehend objects in the world *directly*—not pictures or images of them.[91]

In the case of knowledge as identity with its objects, Chrysippus claims[92] the criterion of truth is the 'cognitive impression' (*phantasia kataleptike*)—an impression that firmly grasps its object.[93] Zeno defines this as an impression which:

> ... arises from that which is stamped and impressed in accordance with the very thing; and of such a kind as could not arise from that which is not.[94]

Since assent is cognition or a grasp (*katalepsis*) of some individual fact. Knowledge requires cognition which is secure, firm and unchangeable by

---

causal relation that is necessary or a conjunction between events)? Questions which follow include: do entities have essential or accidental properties; are properties and relations particular or universal; is existence itself a property; should we countenance objects having no existence; is there a relationship between an entity and its properties and between that relation and the entities it relates; and must every entity be logically self-consistent?

90. See, Rorty, *Mirror of Nature*, 143.

91. On Stoic theories of cognitive impressions, see Frede, *Stoic Notion of lekton*, 151–76.

92. Bobzien, *Chrysippus*, 217–38.

93. Cavini, *Chrysippus*.

94. Sextus Empiricus, 40e.

reason.⁹⁵ A Stoic theory of coherentism provides context for such claims. Knowledge requires cognition which can be worked into a coherent whole with other such cognitions.⁹⁶ Weak and changeable is called an 'incognitive impression' or an impression that does not firmly grasp its object.⁹⁷ Thus since 'justified true belief' is necessary for knowledge, coherentists picture knowledge as having the structure of a raft where justified true beliefs, like the planks that make up a raft, mutually support one another. Truth is identified with verifiability which is holistic, i.e. part of an entire system of beliefs that is consistent. Assent to indubitable 'perceptions', sometimes although not always, consists in having impressions with 'meaning.' Thus it is the coherence of a belief with other beliefs that matters. All beliefs representing knowledge are justified in virtue of their coherence with other beliefs. Aristotle and Plotinus add the image of knowledge as a pyramid where assent to incorrigible impressions are based on their veridical sources and causes—such as *Nous*, Forms, and the One. Here one moves from weak assent (*doxa*) to knowledge (*episteme*) veridically—or from aesthetic to noetic impressions with each conveying different degrees of meaning.⁹⁸

Stoic philosophy of language provides another context that sets up self-awareness and self-reflexivity. *Lekton* denotes the 'meaning' of an utterance.⁹⁹ *Lekta* are what language signify and constitute the content of our mental states. They are also incorporeal which means for Stoics they do not really exist but subsist and so cannot act or be acted upon. They are what we assent to and endeavor toward for, using the raft analogy, they "cohere" with other justified true beliefs (presentations) given to rational animals.¹⁰⁰ Aristotle and Plotinus up the ante. Seeing or touching a sensible table exhibits a meaning different in kind from seeing or touching an abstract entity such as *Nous*. Thus a kind of thinking and language exists that exhibits an identity with its objects and which holds indubitable meaning.

---

95. Sextus Empiricus, 41c.

96. Arius Didymus, 41h.

97. Sextus Empiricus, 41e.

98. For the Stoics *doxa* (or weak assent) and *episteme* (knowledge) are incompatible. cf. Sextus Empiricus 41d.

99. Diogenes Laertius, 40a.

100. Stoics acknowledge *lekta* for predicates as well as for sentences (including questions, oaths and imperatives: *axiomata* or propositions are *lekta* that can be assented to and may be true or false; and since they are tensed, their truth values change. Here the Stoic theory of reference suggests singular propositions are acknowledged although they perish when the referent ceases to exist. On the *lekton* see, cf. Frede, *Stoic Notion of lekton*, 109–28.

All this presupposes that a class of rational impressions exists which by their very nature cannot be false; and that mind (of the *sophos* at least) can discriminate between true and opinable sense impressions. Chrysippus holds that cognitive impressions generally, and rational impressions specifically, are true because they are characterized by clarity and distinctness. Thus what the wise man sees and grasps, clearly and distinctively, are real objects in themselves not pictures or images of them for: "imprint" denotes "alterations" or "modifications" and the distinctive feature of cognitive impressions is clarity.[101]

Summary: That all cases of cognition are either of knowledge or opinion has one consequence that hardly seems to have been noticed but which is highly relevant to our topic. Aristotle and Plotinus are keen to make the point that the cause of our 'cognitive impressions' matter. If the cause of the impression is clear and distinct; the impression is clear and distinct. Thus playing off the matter-form and body-mind distinctions they claim that of sensible objects we have facts or opinions; and of intelligible objects we have knowledge or truth.

VI. Truth, Certainty and Justified True Belief

A discussion of cognition raises questions of truth and certainty. Here the skepticisms of Pyrrho and neo-Pyrrhonism provide context.[102] There are two types of skepticism: Pyrrhonian—we never can be certain; so how can we ever know; and Cartesian—since we cannot be certain about anything except the content of our own minds, how can we justify an inference to belief about anything else? Aristotle and Plotinus are aware of such arguments concerning and limits of knowledge but claim they are not obliged to accept them on grounds that the possibility of not only true knowledge but 'justifiable true belief' is possible if the object known is the same or identical with the subject that knows:

Plato's simile of the mind as an aviary suggests what 'true justified belief' might imply.[103] The birds in the aviary represent *functions* of thought and the *use* of knowledge. Error is said to be wrong use of knowledge of

---

101. Sextus Empiricus, *M.* VII.229–230; VIII. 400; *PH* II.70; Diogenes Laertius, VII.50. cf. Schenkeveldt, *Kinds of Speech*, 291–351.

102. On Pyrrhonic Skepticism and its modes see Sextus Empiricus, *Outlines of Pyrrhonism*, and XIII-XIV.

103. On complexities associated with the aviary analogy see, Taylor, *Plato's Timaeus*, 339–44; Roecklin, *Plato versus Parmenides*, 174–77.

which we already have in possession—rather than a recorded memories of forms:

> Now consider whether knowledge is a thing you can possess
> In that way without having it about you, like a man who has
> Caught some wild birds . . . we might say his "has" them all the
> Time inasmuch as he possesses them . . . but in another sense he "has"
> None of them though he has got control of them, now that he
> Has made them captive in an enclosure of his own; he can take
> Hold of them whenever he likes by catching any bird he chooses,
> And let them go again, and it is open to do that as often as he pleases.[104]

Having drawn a distinction between possessing knowledge and having it, Theatetus argues it is impossible not to possess what one does possess—but it is possible to get false judgements about knowledge-content.[105] The point being that even though certain kinds of knowledge by its nature require some application before the knowledge becomes active, we still have a 'justified true belief' in the power (*dunamis*) to possess knowledge before it is actualized

It is so much a part of thinking "philosophically" to be impressed with the special character and power of 'justified true belief 'claims that it is difficult to shake off the notion that there are truths which are necessary simply because of their causes. The grip is so ineluctable that Aristotle offers a defense of 'justified true belief' on the basis of a two-tier version of the epistemic regress argument:[106]

I.

1. It would be a non-inferential (or foundational) justification;

2. It would be characterized by feasibility;

3. It would exhibit a two-tier structure as described by epistemic foundationalism;

4. It would be justified by a supporting links or foundational beliefs that are truth-conductive (i.e. it tends to produce true justified beliefs).

---

104. Plato, *Theaetetus*, 197de.
105. Plato, *Theaetetus* 199a.
106. Aristotle argues that the grounds for truth and certainty rest on 'justified true belief' based on the epistemic regress argument. cf. Aristotle, *Posterior Analytics*, II.19.1001b6–18; *Metaphysics*, XII.9.1074b34–35; XII.71072b18–23. cf. Plotinus, *Ennead*, V.5.1; V.5.2.18–20.

II.

1. If one has any justified belief (i.e. mind);
2. It must occur in an evidential chain characterized by feasibility including two links:
   a. Empirical evidence (sentience) and
   b. Logical evidence (i.e. infinite regress argument.);
3. And other supporting links or justified beliefs (i.e. truth/falsity contrast, prior simplicity, priority of the mental to the physical, divine simplicity, principle of insufficient reason etc.).

Aristotle's and Plotinus' proof for the existence of other minds also rests on the truth-falsity distinction.

Aristotle holds that:

> Truth and falsity are as follows: contact (*thigein*) and assertion (*phanai*) are truth (for assertion is not the same as affirmation), and ignorance is non-contact (*me thigganein*). I say ignorance, because it is impossible to be deceived with respect to what a thing is, except accidentally (*e kata sumbebekos*); and the same applies to in composite substances (*tas me* suntheta *ousia*), for it is impossible to be deceived about them. And they all exist actually (*energeia*), not potentially (*ou dunamei*); but as it is being itself is not generated nor destroyed (*ou gignetai oude phtheiretai*) . . . With respect, then, to all things which are essences and actual (*einai ti kai energeia*, there is no question of being mistaken, but only of thinking or not thinking (*all'e noein e me*) them . . . Truth means to think these objects (*to noein tauta*), and there is no falsity or deception, but only ignorance (if one does not think these objects) . . .[107]

Plotinus accepts the arguments of the Sceptics as valid but proposes that the possibility of truth depends on a divine intellect whose object of thought is itself:[108]

> And then again, it (Intellect) will need no demonstration and no confirmation that this is so, for itself is so and itself is manifest (*enarges*) to itself . . . So that in Intellect there is also the real truth which does not agree with something else, and says nothing other than itself, but it is what it says and it says what it is.[109]

---

107. Aristotle, *Metaphysics*, IX.9.1051b25–1052a2.
108. Plotinus, *Enneads* V.5.1; V.5.2.18–20.
109. Plotinus, *Ennead*, V.5.2.18–20. cf. Emilsson, *Intellect*, 234–37.

On the basis of this argument he goes on to propose the existence of other minds:

> Intellect and the intelligible substance; each individual Idea is not other than Intellect, but each is Intellect. And Intellect as a whole is all the Forms, and each individual Form is an individual intellect ... we must assume that the real beings have their place in the thinking subject.[110]

Summary: Aristotle argues that grounds for truth, certainty and any 'justified true belief' involve chains that are: 1) anchored in foundational beliefs (not in chains that are circular, endless, ending in unjustified beliefs, or anchored in foundational beliefs that do not derive their justification from other beliefs); and 2) foundational beliefs that can be feasibly justified non-inferentially (i.e. without deriving justification from other beliefs) grounded in a divine intellect whose object of thought is thought thinking itself. Plotinus proposes that truth and certainty depends on a divine intellect whose object of thought is thought thinking on itself which guarantees a self-knowledge which raises the soul to the qualitative unity of thought and being in *Nous*. The knowledge which no sceptic can undermine is the one we have when soul knows itself in the divine mind.[111] Such certitude also points toward the existence of other minds.

VII. Thinking Other Minds

We cannot enter the bone-chilling waters of 'thinking other minds' again without reference to two concepts: 'to perceive at the same time,' or 'to be aware of oneself' (*sunaisthanomai*);[112] and 2) 'self-reflexivity' (*sunaisthesis*).[113] Après studies by Hadot and Beierwaltes, a *Truemmerfeld* of problems concerning the relationship between *sunaisthesis*, *Nous* and the One emerges that cannot be adequately addressed here.[114] However, a reconsideration of sight,

---

110. Plotinus, *Ennead*, V.9.8.1–5; 10–12.

111. Plotinus, *Ennead*, V.3. cf. O'Meara, Plotinus, 18–20; Courcelle, *Connais-toi*, v. 1, 14–15.

112. Aristotle, *HAn.* 534b18; *Nic. Eth.* 1170b4; cf. Alexander Aph. *Sent.* 36.12; Plotinus, *Enneads*, IV.4.24; VI.4.6.

113. Plotinus, *Ennead*. III.8.4

114. P. Hadot, *Review*, 92–95. Hadot's thesis is that Plotinus would lack precision if he were to assert the subject of *epistrophe* to *nous* rather than to the One—for *nous* is an image and product of the One and *nous* does not turn toward the One until after (metaphysically posterior) it is generated in order to become actualized for self-identity

illumination, touch, and participation while thinking other minds clarifies what intensional self-reflexivity entails.

As we have seen Aristotle and Plotinus claim that sight, illumination, touch and participation in *Nous* (or the One) triggers self-awareness and self-reflexivity and without such self-awareness or self-reflexivity thinking other minds would be impossible. Such sight, illumination, touch and participation are not to be taken as metaphor or simile. Rather they are real 'abstract entities' or 'noetic meanings' akin to what Descartes later calls 'clear and distinct ideas'. They are mental states we cannot help but giving assent to as *episteme* because they meet an indubitable criterion of truth—certainty.

VII. 1. Touching

Aristotle is keen to parse 'touch' (contact) to signify a unitary knowledge that guarantees the certainty and truth of what we think:

> But (a) truth or falsity is as follows—contact and assertion are truth (assertion is not the same as affirmation) and ignorance is non-contact.[115]

Aristotle claims further that in touching truth a thinker is identical with the object of its thought and thus a knower of truth:[116]

> Truth and falsity are as follows: contact (*thigein*) and assertion (*phanai*) are truth (for assertion is not the same as affirmation), and ignorance is non-contact (*me thigganein*). I say ignorance, because it is impossible to be deceived with respect to what a thing is, except accidentally (*e katasumbebekos*); and the same applies to in composite substances (*tas mesuntheta ousia*), for it is impossible to be deceived about them. And they all exist actually (*energeia*), not potentially (*ou dunamei*); but as it is Being itself is not generated nor destroyed (*ou gignetai oude phtheiretai*) ... With respect, then, to all things which are essences and

---

involves not only the sticky problem of: 1) what is the subject of *epistrophe* (procession) and *prohodos* (return); but 2) the nature of an inchoate/unfinished and a conscious nous. Beierwaltes, *Lichtes des Metaphysik*, 334–62.

115. Aristotle, *Meta*physics, IX.8.1051b24–25; 1072b21.

116. Aristotle, *Meta*physics, I.V.986b19–21. Either as a unity of definition or as materially one:

It appears that Parmenides conceived of the Unity as one in definition, but Melissus as materially one. Hence the former says that it is finite, and the latter that it is infinite ... but Xenophanes, the first exponent of the Unity (for Parmenides is said to have been his disciple) gave no definite teaching, nor does he seem to have touched (*thigein*) either of these conceptions of Unity.

actual (*einai tikai energeia*), there is no question of being mistaken, but only of thinking or not thinking (*all'e noein e me*) them ... truth means to think these objects (*to noein tauta*), and there is no falsity or deception ...¹¹⁷

Aristotle proposes that touch always involves an either/or. A tactile intellect either knows or does not know. This is because in the activity of touch-thinking, *noesis* is an activity (*energeia*) which results in contemplation, *theoria* rather than movement or a process (*kinesis*). In touch-thinking we do not predicate anything of anything (*ti kata tinos*),¹¹⁸ nor is there any assertion (*kataphasis*),¹¹⁹ and the objects of such knowledge are incomposite (*asuntheta; adiaireta*);¹²⁰ in that they do not involve matter and form, and in this kind of thinking you cannot be mistaken.¹²¹

Plotinus also associates thinking and touching but with a caveat. The thinker never remains identical with the object of its thought:

> Therefore the thinker must apprehend one thing different from another and the object of thought in being thought must contain variety; or there will not be a thought of it (*noesis*) but only a touching and a sort of contact (*thixis ... epaphe*) without speech or thought, pre-thinking (*pronoousa*) because Intellect has not yet come into being, and that which touches (*thinganon*) does not think (*ou noountos*). But the thinker must not itself remain simple, especially in so far as it thinks itself: for it will duplicate itself, even if it gives an understanding which is silent.¹²²

Plotinus holds that the possibility of true and certain knowledge is grasped only if the object known is identical (qualitatively not numerically)

---

117. Aristotle, *Metaphysics*, IX.10.1051b25–1052a2.
118. Aristotle, *De Anima*, III.6,430b28.
119. Aristotle, *Metaphysics*, IX.8. 1051b24.
120. Aristotle, *Metaphysics*, IX.8.1051b17; *De Anima*, 430a26.
121. Aristotle, *Metaphysics*, IX.10.1051b25–1052a2. Truth and falsity are as follows: contact (*thigein*) and assertion (*phanai*) are truth (for assertion is not the same as affirmation), and ignorance is non-contact (*me thigganein*). I say ignorance, because it is impossible to be deceived with respect to what a thing is, except accidentally (*e katasumbebekos*); and the same applies to in composite substances (*tas mesuntheta ousia*), for it is impossible to be deceived about them. And they all exist actually (*energeia*), not potentially (*ou dunamei*); but as it is Being itself is not generated nor destroyed (*ou gignetai oude phtheiretai*) ... With respect, then, to all things which are essences and actual (*einai tikai energeia*), there is no question of being mistaken, but only of thinking or not thinking (*all'e noein e me*) them ... Truth means to think these objects (*to noein tauta*), and there is no falsity or deception ..."
122. Plotinus, *Ennead*, V.3.10.42–48.

with the subject that knows it—or a divine *nous* whose object of thought is itself.[123] In this self-presence of knower and known—there is no spatial distance, no mediating image or representation;[124] no separation between knower and known that intervenes so as to turn self-knowledge into an unreliable, unverifiable knowledge of something else:[125] These conclusions require a good deal more explanation than can be provided here. But now that we know what 'touching' truth means, let us see what it means to become one with divine Intellect and thus with other minds as well via participation and identity.

VII.2. Illumination

The analogy between seeing and illumination is a deeply embedded Platonic one—the intelligible light of the Forms is the analogue of the light which renders material things visible. Intelligible light emanates from the supreme Form, the Good, to illuminate inferior forms thus rendering them intelligible; and the mind that understands them like the sun makes other things visible by illuminating them.[126] Aristotle is keen to associate mind with light and illumination at the level of perception. But he also claims that active intellect (*nous poietikos*) makes all things into actual colors—just as the presence of light to an object of thought it illuminates it.[127]

> Mind in the passive sense (*nous pathetikos*) is such because it becomes all things but mind in the active sense (*nous poietikos*) has another aspect in that it makes all things. This is a kind of positive state like light; for in a sense light makes potential into actual colors.[128]

And:

---

123. Plotinus, *Ennead*, V.5.2.18–20.

124. Plotinus, *Ennead*, V.5.2.18–20.

125. Plotinus, *Ennead*, V.3.10.42–48. Therefore the thinker must apprehend one thing different from another and the object of thought in being thought must contain variety; or there will not be a thought of it (*noesis*) but only a touching and a sort of contact (*thixis . . . epaphe*) without speech or thought, a pre-thinking (*pronoousa*) because Intellect has not yet come into being, and that which touches (*thinganon*) does not think (*ou noountos*). But the thinker must not itself remain simple, especially in so far as it thinks itself: for it will duplicate itself, even if it gives an understanding which is silent. cf. Plotinus, V.3.5–9; V.3.43–48.

126. Plato, *Republic*, 509b.

127. Schroeder, *Plotinus and Language*, 341–43.

128 Aristotle, *De Anima*, III.5.430a15–17.

> Actual knowledge is identical with its object... when isolated it is its true self and nothing more and this alone is immortal and everlasting... and without this nothing thinks.[129]

Alexander reads these passages as the juxtaposition of the subject of reflection and the reflective surface of the mind with self-reflection a joint effect produced by both.[130]

Light and illumination also provide a 'meaning mechanism' and thus a bridge from Aristotle to Plato. Here Plotinus criticizes Aristotle's and Alexander's analysis of light as a mere extrinsic commonplace noting that light is an activity (*energeia*) that proceeds from a luminous source, not the effect that arises from the source of illumination and the illuminated object.[131]

Reflection as an instance of illumination is a master metaphor in Plotinus.[132] For light to be—is for it to be present—as pure intrinsic presence.[133] Behind these claims stands a long tradition of *Lichtmetaphysik* wherein images of the Good as the source of light and intelligibility are employed to parse: 1) the derivation of *Nous* from the One; 2) the One's interior presence to mind; 3) the mind's participation in *Nous*; and 4) *nous* dwelling in the human soul and teaching it from within noetic illumination.[134] Key claims also include light and its source is *qua* luminous:[135] that the light we see with our own eyes is incorporeal even if its source is corporeal;[136] that since *Nous* flows from the One like a light from the sun;[137] its procession from the One is a shining out or an irradiation (*perilampsis, epilampsis*).[138] And since the generation of the intelligible world is an act of vision, reflection itself is illumination.[139]

Plotinus' claim 'reflection is illumination' results in a refinement of Aristotle's 'focal' theory of meaning. Intellect's intentionality, identity and

---

129. Aristotle, *De Anima*, III.5.430a20–25.

130. Alexander, *De Anima*, 42.19–43 (Bruns).

131. Plotinus' use of Plato's "light" sources and metaphors are many see Beierwaltes, *Metaphysik des Lichtes*, 334–62.

132. Rappe, *Non-Discursive Thinking*, 169–70; Schroeder, *Plotinus and Interior Space*, 25–28.

133. The *locus classicus* is Plotinus, *Ennead*, IV.5.7.35–49. For commentary see Gurtler, *Ennead IV.4.30–45 & IV.5*, 230–70.

134. Corrigan, *Essence and Existence*, 118–20.

135. Plotinus, *Ennead*.V.1.7.1–6.

136 Plotinus, *Ennead*, IV.5.7.41–42.

137. Plotinus, *Ennead*, V.3.12.40.44.

138. Plotinus, *Ennead*, V.1.6.26–29.

139. Plotinus, *Enneads*, IV.5.7.41–41. cf. V,I.4.10.14; V.8.4.42–43.

relation to the One are of pure light and the actualization of light. And once Mind abstracts (*aphesei*) the objects of its vision (or the Forms) it sees the One—*pros hen* not *panta hen*. Here light not only illuminates 'focal' objects of awareness such as Forms and other minds. It also illuminates the cause of a 'focal' meaning of awareness itself—the One.[140]

VII.3. Participation and Identity

Participation, identity, touch and sight are also 'mental marks' that *nous* has of *Nous* and other minds as well. Aristotle claims when inner mental processes meet external criteria, thought and the object of thought are the same.

> And *Nous* thinks on itself to the extent that it participates or partakes (*kata metaplesin*) in the object of thought (*noeton*). It becomes the *noeton* when it touches and intuitively apprehends its objects so that thought and the object of thought are the same (*hoste tauton nous kai noeton*).[141]

Moreover, such participation and touching is an active possession of thought as thought:

> For that which is capable of receiving the *noeton* and the *ousia* is *Nous*. But it is active when it possesses it (*energei de echon*). Hence it is actuality rather than potentiality that is held to be the divine possession of rational thought (*ho nous theion echein*) and its active contemplation (*theoria*) is that which is most pleasant and best.[142]

It is in this sense that:

> ... *Nous* thinks itself (*auton ara noei*) ... and its thinking is thinking on thinking (*he noesis noeseos noesis*).[143]

The crucial difference between divine and human *noesis* and *theoria* is that God grasps the *asuntheta* actually while the human mind, in potential thinking is concerned with synthetic things only. But in the few occasion's humans enjoy actual *noesis*, the *nous poietikos* touches (*thigein*) the *asuntheta*. It is in such noetic activity (*energeia*) that subject-object dichotomy and its complexity are resolved into a subject-object simplicity

---

140. Plotinus, *Ennead*, V.5.7.16–21.
141. Aristotle, *Metaphysics*, XII.7.1072b22–23.
142. Aristotle, *Metaphysics*, XII.7.1072b23–25.
143. Aristotle, *Metaphysics*, XII.9.1074b34–35

and unity. And when this occurs there is no longer a gap between knower, knowledge, and object of knowledge.

In the activity of thinking an active intellect emerges which thinks incessantly and forever. It resides both in us and separately from us, it involves no memory, and when the "active-intellect" thinks, its activity (*energeia*) makes things—rather than becomes all things as mere process (*kinesis*)—and is identical with its object.

> Actual knowledge is identical with its object . . . when isolated it is its true self and nothing more and this alone is immortal and everlasting . . . and without this nothing thinks.[144]

But how on the basis of such claims does one infer the existence of other minds? Aristotle's answer is since all forms of intellection (*noesis*) are 'intentionally' "of something else" (*h'allou*), and only incidentally of themselves, whenever we think Intellect, we think other minds as well. That is to say, the activity of thinking (seeing and touching) *Nous* points to the existence of other minds.

Plotinus offers a similar but more nuanced answer:

> . . . Intellect is all things (*hode nous panta*) . . . and the whole is universal intellect and being, Intellect making being exist in thinking it, and being giving Intellect thinking and existence by being thought . . . but this one is two things: Intellect and being and thinking and thought; Intellect as thinking and being as thought.[145]

> . . . contemplation must be the same as the contemplated, and Intellect the same as the intelligible; for if not the same, there will be no truth; for who is trying to possess realities will possess an impression different from the realities, and this is not truth. For truth ought not to be the truth of something else but to be what it says. In this way, Intellect and the intelligible are one, and this is reality and the first reality, and also the first Intellect which possess the real beings, or rather is the same as the real beings . . . for the intellection will in a way encompass the intelligible or be the same as the intelligible . . . All together are one, Intellect, intellection, the intelligible. If therefore Intellect's intellection is the intelligible, and the intelligible is itself, it will itself think itself.[146]

---

144. Aristotle, *De Anima*, III.5.430a20–25.
145. Plotinus, *Ennead*, V.1.4.20; 25–32.
146. Plotinus, *Ennead*, V.3.27–45.

Conclusion

This enquiry began with a request to reflect upon two similes in the *Theaetetus* where mind is an aviary and each new piece of knowledge is a wild bird caught and caged.[147] The aviary is the mind, knowledge is the birds, and when we think we hold a bird in our hands.[148] Three metaphors were transposed from these similes: "Orioles" stand for individual minds; "owls" for other minds and abstract entities; and aviaries for holenmermism—"the whole of reality is continuous in its parts." It was proposed that Aristotle and Plotinus claim orioles—indeed even the most solipsistic of orioles—know owls to some considerable degree if for no other reason than: orioles and owls share marks of the mental; and fly about in "aviaries" where the whole is in the part (*holenmermism*) and the world contains genuinely continuous phenomena together (*synechism*)—an inversion of the ego-centric view that orioles and owls know only themselves and live in their own singular aviary ways.

Aristotle and Plotinus justify such claims as true belief by proposing a *holenmermism* where the individual self or mind (*ego*) is continuous with a supra-personal identity or mind (*nous*). Plotinus also incorporates the Stoic notion of *synechism*—the view that the universe exists as a continuous whole of all of its parts with no part being fully separate, determined or determinate. Thus on the metaphysical side each proposes a hypothetical description of a tightly woven universe woven not within layers of an identical (the same kind) of reality but between layers of reality in a scalar fashion. On the methodological side each looks for connections and continuous strata between seemingly disconnected entities or events.[149]

Aristotle's claims of holenmermism—that 'the whole is in the part'—are based on the notion that exclusion is always posterior to inclusion. Consequently, the perfection of divine *nous* thinking itself (*kai estin he noesis noeseos noesis*) includes an intellection of all individuals including other minds—for to be perfect is to be complete and self-sufficient and "that from which nothing is wanting"—even the possibility of other minds.

---

147. Plato, *Theaetetus*, 197de.

148. Plato, *Theatetus*, 199ab.

149. Peirce variously described it as "unbrokenness" (*CP* 1.163), "fluidity, the merging of part into part," (*CP* 1.164), where "all is fluid and every point directly partakes the being of every other." (*CP* 5.402n2) The mathematical conception of continuity included the notion of infinite divisibility, which Peirce called Kanticity, after Kant, and the notion of an infinite series of points approaching a limit, called Aristotelicity. (*CP* 6.166) A third notion, derived from Cantor, characterized continuity as perfect concatenation. (*CP* 6.164).

> "For thus we define the whole—that from which noting is wanting . . . what is true of each particular is true of the whole as such—the whole is that of which nothing is outside.[150]
>
> . . . for this is the sort of principle that constitutes the nature of each . . . all must at least come to be dissolved into their elements . . . in which all share for the good of the whole.[151]

Plotinus' *holenmermism* and *synechism* rest on the claim that every form in *Nous* contains every other Form by the interiority of its relations to other Forms. Each Form is in all other Forms and each mind is cognitively identical with every Form and other minds because the multiplicity of *nous* is not spatially articulated—thus the possibility of other minds.[152]

> Intellect and the intelligible substance; each individual Idea is not other than Intellect, but each is Intellect. And Intellect as a whole is all the Forms, and each individual Form is an individual intellect . . . we must assume real beings have their place in the thinking subject.[153]

When both are brought together Aristotle and Plotinus reach a precipice from which 'the problem of other minds' is a faux problem, a category mistake "dissolved."

---

150. Aristotle, *Physics*, III.6.207a8–15; cf. *Metaphysics*, XII.9.1074b33–35.
151. Aristotle, *Metaphysics*, XII.10.1075a23–26.
152. Plotinus, *Enneads*, V.V.1.19–43; V.8.3.30–34; V.9.6; V.9.8.3–7.
153. Plotinus, *Ennead*, V.9.8.1–5; 10–12.

11

A Beautiful Mind

> In the aesthetic mode of contemplation we have found two inseparable constituent parts—the knowledge of the object, not as individual thing but as Platonic idea, and the self-consciousness of the knowing person . . . as pure will-less subject of knowledge.
>
> —SCHOPENHAUER, *THE WORLD AS WILL AND IDEA*

Précis

THIS ENQUIRY AIMS AT retracing two conceptual moments of a history of the self within the "horizon" of aesthetics. The first moment concerns the making of a beautiful mind with focus on Plotinus' faculties of imagination and judgment in respect of seeing things together in respect of the One. The second addresses a key problem that emerges out of 'thinking on thinking'—the nature of aesthetic thinking, judgment, and imagination.[1] Bringing the two moments together 'thought thinking itself' is creatively self-reflexive. Aware of existence of a separable intellect without which there would be no cognition, he also stresses aesthetic cognition is self-reflexive, creative and thus the thinker is aware of the presence of form in matter.[2] As such his aesthetics should be viewed as something far more profound than a mere defense of the transient value of the plastic arts. Since the principle of beauty is *Nous*, it is the image-making power that

---

1. See Beierwaltes, *Theorie des Schoenen*, 3–26; Schroeder, *Categories*, 115–36; Anton, *Artist*, 100; *Beauty*, 234.

2. Emilsson, *Intellect*, 217–49; Blumenthal, *Soul and Intellect*, 82–104; Gerson, *Aristotle and Other Platonists*, 139–40; Lavecchia, *La Luce*, 445–56.

links sense perception to noetic thought and the active intellect (*nous poietikos*) which in turn leads to claims that the imagination is the basis of artistic creativity.³ As an expression of intelligible form in matter, as a visible expression of ideal beauty, art has metaphysical value that carries with it purificatory possibilities for the soul.⁴ He asserts that images (*eikasia*) of the Form of beauty (*idea tou kallou*) exist in the human soul.⁵ He argues that the imagination is the mental faculty through which the soul gains initial awareness of beautiful images; and that such aesthetic awareness leads eventually to knowledge of other forms (*eide*) of beauty, if not of the Form of Beauty itself (*idea tou kallou*) in sensible and intelligible things (*algamata*).⁶ Out of all this a later Platonic aesthetics of the self emerges where the arts become a vehicle for the soul to ontogenetically reverse a situation of misfortune—her descent into corporeality.

I. To See Things Together in Respect of the One

It is a remarkable coincidence that the philosophical writings of both Plato and Plotinus take off with an analysis of beauty. The *Symposium*, *Republic*, and *Phaedrus* are far from being the earliest of Plato's dialogues, but they are the first dialogues where we encounter a full-blown theory of Ideas, the overwhelming presence of beauty at all levels of existence, and the coupling of Beauty with the Good. Beauty was a topic Plotinus also thought important enough to examine in two treatises. *On Sensible Beauty* (*Ennead* I.6.1) is the earliest of his philosophical writings. The second treatise, *On Intelligible Beauty* (*Ennead* V.8 (31), is the second section of the *Grossschrift* comprising III.8 (30), V.5 (32), and II.9 (33).⁷

We start with *Republic* 508a-509b. It is in this section of the dialogue that Plato formally expounds that the method of dialectic, has as its goal the cognition of the Idea of the Good. He conceived this idea as the source of all being and knowledge, as an *anupothetos arche* in which supreme reality and value coincide. Now recall *Phaedrus* 265d. The *methodos* here is directed at something less remarkable than the dialectical procedure of the *Republic*. There is no attempt to derive all truths of philosophy from a single first principle. What is contemplated is a piecemeal approach to knowledge, which consists in a mapping out of one field after another by a classification per

---

3. Dillon, *Transcendental Imagination*, 55–64.
4. Plotinus, *Ennead*, V.8.1; III.6.5.22–29.
5. Plotinus, *Ennead*, I.6.2. cf. Hendrix, *Artistic Imagination*, 31.
6. Plotinus, *Ennead*, I.6.5.
7. Hendrix, *Symposium*.

genera et species, which will have the effect of discriminating and relating these concepts or classifications to the actual structure of reality.

Plato formulated the task of philosophy as:

> ... that in which we bring a dispersed plurality under a single form or one, seeing it all together.[8]

Plato meant this procedure to include both the bringing of particulars under a Form or kind and the subsumption of a narrower Form under a wider one.[9] He likely also took "the scattered particulars" (*ta pollache diesparmena*), mentioned in the *Phaedrus* 265d, and connected this sentence with an earlier passage at *Phaedrus* 249b, to suggest how knowledge (a narrower form) is subsumed under a wider one (real being).

> For a human being must understand a general conception formed by collecting into a unity by means of reason the many perceptions of the senses; and this is a recollection of those things which our soul once beheld, when it journeyed with God and lifting its vision above the things which we now say exist rose up into real being.[10]

The connection between these two blocks of argument has often been obscured, and misunderstood, in contemporary studies of Plato's text. The connection is nonetheless essential to the structure of Plato's dialogue, and is no less essential to the use that was made of Plato's *methodos* by Plotinus.

Plotinus was well aware of Plato's procedure. He used it to define and explain how the experience of beauty leads to an awareness of the One. This conjunction of ideas is not at all foolish or eccentric Indeed, Plotinus is open to the possibility that "to see things together in respect of the one" is "to see things together in respect of the One." Therefore, he attempted to elicit the universal Form (*eidos*) of Beauty from the manifold appearances of beautiful things, and he then assessed the effect of the Idea of Beauty upon human judgment and imagination, because for Plotinus such an analysis explained how the soul aesthetically experiences the One.[11]

Plotinus' conception of beauty, like his conception of the Ideas and the One, had empirical as well as metaphysical and traditional roots. That the experience of beauty in judgment and imagination is perceptive (or aesthetic), and not merely cognitive (or rational), is strongly suggested by the vividness of some of his accounts, notably in treatise V.8 *On Intelligible*

---

8. Plato, *Phaedrus* 265d.
9. For a discussion of this phrase, see Hackforth, *Plato's Phaedrus*, 132. n. 4.
10. Plato, *Phaedrus*, 249b
11. Plotinus, *Ennead.*, I.6.9.30–44.

Beauty. This is also confirmed by his exhortations to his readers to attain this experience for themselves.[12] It is precisely this 'aesthetic turn' that links Plotinus to Kant and his heirs.

In this situation we must ask what it is that constitutes beauty and the experience of beauty. Briefly, seeing things together in respect of the One, led Plotinus to propose a novel interpretation of the experience of beauty. The consequences are that the Platonic relation between nature and art, *mimesis*, was reformulated by Plotinus in terms of *krisis* and *phantasia*. As we shall see the point of reconceptualization lies in Plotinus' subtle assessment of the experience of beauty. This reformulation is not as commonplace as it may appear. Plotinus utilized Aristotelian theory to explain how the soul imagines and judges beauty, and images the One. As such he suggested that the soul judge's beauty in a co-ordinate ordered series of entities extending from the intelligible to the sensible world. Significantly, he also proposed that degrees of beauty correspond to the degree to which beauty and the images of beauty is imagined, judged, and experienced by the soul. Finally, in taking such an approach to beauty Plotinus avoided a purely generic (or paradigmatic) theory of mimesis, and thus obviated the possible harmful consequences that Stoics and Gnostics detected in Plato's theory of beauty.

Summary: The relationship between nature and art that had dominated Platonic theory on beauty for centuries fills itself with new meaning in Plotinus. Beauty looks to nature and the Ideas in order to produce it anew. The soul provides the exemplary state for beauty to find expression. And yet even though the soul finds its own path to the experience of beauty, beauty does come to resemble nature and the realm of Ideas. This is precisely because it is a "speechless image of the One." There is something regular and binding about the self-contained picture of beauty that grows out from within the one to the One.

II. Mind, Soul and the Active Intellect

Goodness and beauty are known to the higher soul but not initially to the lower soul. Only souls motivated by intellect and illuminated by beauty know goodness.[13] These souls are exceptional and aware of their undecended selves. The higher soul always remains united with intelligible being; the lower soul is unaware of this link. Involved in the sensible world, in the tumult of the body, she is not self-aware of what her undecended soul

---

12. Plotinus, *Ennead*, V.8.39–43.
13. Plotinus, *Ennead*, IV.7.10.

beholds.[14] Busied with carnal desires she knows nothing of her divine link. What of these souls, unconscious of their undecended selves, and ignorant of the eternal verities? For:

> living under a crust of evil . . . filled with injustice and desires, torn by internal strife, full of the fears of its own cowardice and the jealousy of its meanness, busied in its thoughts about the perishable and the low, the friend of vile pleasure, it lives a life of submission to bodily desires.[15]

There is a way out of this situation of misfortune. Through apprehension of aesthetic symbols the soul becomes aware of the forms and begins her tenuous ascent from unconsciousness to consciousness.[16] Visible beauty points to soul to intelligible beauty.[17] In this sense art functions to make the soul aware of her divine source. Once conscious this soul becomes aware of her eternal, intelligible link to the divine. Through the aesthetic imagination the soul unites her disparate self and begins her ascent to the eternal verities and, perhaps, eventual union with the divine.[18] Consequently, art is therapeutic. It assists in the transfiguration of the soul from unconsciousness to consciousness, from an awareness of its sensibility to knowledge of its intelligibility.

Schwyzer notes the psychological shift as from" unconsciousness to consciousness," from misfortune to fortune, involves the use of the imagination, the active intellect, and at times, the plastic arts.[19] Art, thus, commits the soul to an upward passage, to an ascent from the lower to the highest divine beauty. Consequently, the various *artes* are accorded a valued place in Plotinus' system. Logic, observation, and piety all reinforced this position. For Plotinus there was something grotesquely impious in the idea that the sense-world was devoid of the forms or that physical objects, even objects of art, could not awaken in the soul images of the eternal verities.

Plotinus' soul has two dimensions.[20] The undecended soul is one of the *theia* and is characterized by *nous*.[21] Its undecended world is the unchanging, intelligible, eternal while its descended world is the changing, sensible,

14. Plotinus, *Ennead*, V.1.2; 4.1.8.
15. Plotinus, *Ennead*, I.6.5.
16. Plotinus, *Ennead*, V.8.1.
17. Plotinus, *Ennead*, I.6.3.
18. Plotinus, *Ennead*, I.6.5.
19. Schwyzer, *Bewusst und Unbewusst*, 343–68.
20. Plotinus, *Ennead*, V.1.10.12.
21. The undecended soul is one of the *theia* and associated with *nous*. cf. V.1.7.49; IV.7.1.

transient.[22] While undecended the soul revels in the realm of the forms and, hence, contemplates reality directly; the embodied the soul is consigned to the realm of the senses and hence a symbolic, indeed imaginative and sensible perception of its higher noetic source and reality.[23] Plotinus inherits his understanding of the motive for the soul's descent from Plato.[24] He assumes Plato blamed the soul for its descent and thought the master saw descent as necessary for the completion of the universe.[25] Plotinus argues the soul enters matter spontaneously.[26] Thus her descent is instinctive or biological with soul thus culpable for her descent.[27] Here audacity (*tolma*) triggers soul's fall.[28] Latter attempts reconcile notions of voluntary and involuntary descent.[29] The soul's descent is caused by illumination of what is below it. Yet even in this case a part of the soul remains in the intelligible realm united to the divine intellect. Plotinus maintains that:

> ... even our soul has not sunk entirely but there is always something of it in the intelligible realm (*kosmos noetos*).[30]

For:

> The soul has never entirely withdrawn but there is something of it that has not come down.[31]

Therefore:

> The souls of men have entered the visible realm in a leap downward from the supreme; yet even they are not cut off from their origin, from the divine intellect. It is not that they have come bringing the intellective principle down in their fall; it is that

---

22. The embodied soul is individual and an *eidolon*. cf. Plotinus, *Ennead*, IV.3.27.8–11.

23. Undecended and descended soul is called *nous*. cf. Plotinus, *Ennead*, I.1.8.1; V.1.10.12; III.2.14.

24. Plato, *Phaedrus*, 248a-249d; *Timaeus*, 42ab.

25. On this aspect of Plotinus' psychology see Blumenthal, *Plotinus' Psychology*, 1971, 8–19; O'Daly, *Plotinus*, 20–51.

26. Plotinus, *Ennead*, IV.8.1. In the middle treatises descent is seen as both voluntary and involuntary with the view of a double sin in descent. IV.8.5.

27. Plotinus, *Ennead*, IV.3.13.

28. Plotinus, *Ennead*, IV.3.12.

29. Plotinus, *Ennead*, I.1.12.

30. Plotinus, *Ennead*, IV.8.8.

31. Plotinus, *Ennead*, IV.1.12.

though they have descended even to earth, yet their higher part holds forever above the heavens.[32]

The higher soul is undecended and in continual contact with the divine:

> ... let a man purify himself and observe: he will not doubt his immortality when he sees himself thus entered into the pure, the intellectual. For what he sees (looking on himself) is an intellectual principle looking on nothing of sense, nothing of this mortality, but by its own eternity having intellection (*noesis*) of the eternal. He will see all things in this. Intellectual substance (*ousia*) himself having become an intellectual cosmos (*kosmos noetos*) and full of light, illuminated by the light streaming from the Good which radiates truth upon all that stands within the realm of the divine. Thus he will always feel the beauty of that word: "farewell I am to you an immortal God", for he has ascended to the supreme and is all one strain to enter into likeness (*homiotes*) with it.[33]

Philoponus claims Plotinus' theory by noting his use of the Aristotelian doctrine of the active intellect. He is not far off the mark in seeing a connection between Aristotle, Alexander and Plotinus who distinguish an active soul engaged in intellection and a potential soul not always perceptive because of the tumult of the body.[34] Philoponus notes that for Aristotle and Alexander the active intellect is always in the soul while for Plotinus *nous poietikos* comes from above as divine giving (*didomi*).[35] Plotinus notes this giving of Intellect to soul is an auto-noetic, perhaps even an auto-volitional act[36] that stands apart from natural sympathy (*sympatheia*) which is a necessary natural law (*physikai ananke*).[37] Thus the descent and ascent of the soul is not determined but has a voluntary aspect. Just as souls were seduced by their own images reflected in the sensible world and rushed into them from above, through contemplation they rediscover their higher selves in the intelligible world.

---

32. Plotinus, *Ennead*, V.3.9.

33. Plotinus, *Ennead*, IV.7.10.

34. Philoponus, *De Intellectu*, 45.39; 47.96. A criticism is presented in *Ps-De Intellectu*, 535.8–13; 19–21; 528.25–31. cf. Blumenthal, *Aristotle and Neoplatonism*, 315–35.

35. Aristotle, *De Anima*, II.3; Alexander, *De Anima Liber*, 88–89; *De Intellectu*, 106 (Bruns).

36. Plotinus, *Enneads*, IV.4.32.4–9; IV.5.2.29; II.3.9.34–39.

37. Plotinus, *Ennead*, IV.4.33.42–45l II.3.9.34–39.

> ... even then they are not cut off from their own principle and intellect; though they have reached to the earth, their heads remain firmly fixed above the heavens.[38]

The higher soul always remains united with intelligible being while the lower soul remains unconscious of this link. Involved in the sensible world, in the tumult of the body, she is unconscious of what the upper part beholds.[39]

> ... living under a crust of evil ... filled with injustice and desires, torn by internal strife, full of the fears of its own cowardice and the jealousy of its meanness, busied in its thoughts about the perishable and the low, the friend of vile pleasure, it lives a life of submission to bodily desires.[40]

God's love and light provide directional markers for the descended soul to ascend and turn towards its undecended self. Through divine giving (*didomi*) the lower soul comes to perception (*aisthesis*) of what the higher soul beholds. The descended soul becomes perceptively aware (*antilepsis*) of the Forms when the active intellect transmits and communicates images of the forms to the imagination (*phantasia*).[41] Visible beauty points to soul to intelligible beauty.[42] In this sense *aisthesis* make the soul aware of her divine source. Once a soul becomes aware of her eternal and intelligible link to the divine, knowledge of goodness and beauty follow and they become aware of conscious of their undecended selves.[43]

There is a way out of this situation of misfortune. Through apprehension of aesthetic symbols the soul becomes aware of the forms and begins her tenuous ascent from unconsciousness to consciousness.[44] Through the aesthetic imagination the soul unites her disparate self and begins her ascent to the eternal verities and, perhaps, eventual union with the divine. This leads to claims that art is therapeutic; that it assists in the self's move from unconsciousness to consciousness; from an awareness of its sensibility to knowledge of its intelligibility.[45] The soul's shift from "unconsciousness

---

38. Plotinus, *Ennead*, IV.3.12. cf. Homer, *Iliad*, IV.443; Plato, *Phaedrus*, 248a.
39. Plotinus, *Ennead*, V.1.2; IV.1.8.
40. Plotinus, *Ennead*, I.6.5.
41. Plotinus, *Ennead*, IV.8.4.28–31.
42. Plotinus, *Ennead*, I.6.3.
43. Plotinus, *Ennead*, IV.7.10.
44. Plotinus, *Ennead*, V.8.1.
45. Plotinus, *Ennead*, I.6.5.

to consciousness" from misfortune to fortune involves the use of the imagination, the active intellect, and divine grace.

Art also aids the soul's upward an ascent to divine beauty. Thus the arts have a valued place in Plotinus' system. There was something grotesquely impious in the idea that the sense-world was devoid of the forms or that physical objects, even objects of art, could not awaken in the soul images of the eternal verities. Nonetheless, goodness and beauty are known to the higher soul but not the lower soul. For only souls motivated by intellect and illuminated by beauty know goodness.[46] They always remains united with intelligible being. The lower soul is unconscious of this link. Involved in the sensible world, in the tumult of the body, she is unconscious of what the upper part beholds.[47] Busied with carnal desires she knows nothing of her divine link.

> living under a crust of evil . . . filled with injustice and desires, torn by internal strife, full of the fears of its own cowardice and the jealousy of its meanness, busied in its thoughts about the perishable and the low, the friend of vile pleasure, it lives a life of submission to bodily desires.[48]

The soul's descent into matter results in the unconscious splitting of the self. Her fall from the intelligible world also signals her separation from true reality and her embodiment in symbolic reality. This leap into matter is a function of a situation of misfortune. Although no clear doctrine of the vehicle of the soul (*pneuma-ochêma*) emerges from Plotinus' writings he was probably aware of it.[49] He appears to subscribe to belief in such a vehicle based on his theory of *pneuma*.[50] As the soul descends gradations of envelops of matter attach themselves to a primary body. Consequently, the soul must be purified from these envelopes to rise to its higher self and cleansed she lives peacefully with her purified *pneuma*. Plotinus says that when the soul leaves the noetic realm it goes:

> . . . first into heaven and receives there a body through which it continues into more earthly bodies.[51]

---

46. Plotinus, *Ennead*, IV.7.10.

47. Plotinus, *Ennead*, V.1.2; 4.1.8.

48. Plotinus, *Ennead*, I.6.5.

49. The doctrine was initially mapped by the second century CE. cf. Dillon, *Middle Platonists*, 371–72.

50. On *pneuma* and Plotinus see, Verbeke, *L'Evolution*, 352–63; A. Smith, *Porphyry's Place*, 152–55.

51. Plotinus, *Ennead*, IV.3.15.

There is a way out of this situation of misfortune. The arts are not only therapeutic they offer a way to salvation.[52] Through apprehension of art and aesthetic symbols the soul becomes aware of the forms and begins her tenuous ascent from unconsciousness to consciousness.[53] Visible beauty points to soul to intelligible beauty.[54] In this sense art functions to make the soul aware of her divine source. Once conscious this soul becomes aware of her eternal, intelligible link to the divine. Through the aesthetic imagination the soul unites her disparate self and begins her ascent to the eternal verities and, perhaps, eventual union with the divine.[55]

Summary: Art assists the soul to leave a sensible world of terrestrial pollution and gain an intelligible world and celestial bliss. The imagination, the active intellect, and the arts are intimately linked to the reversal of psychological and ontological misfortune. Indeed, for Plotinus the arts present to the soul one of the greatest blessings a later Roman could obtain full possession of the self, awareness of the forms, and ascent to the divine. Here a shift from "unconsciousness to consciousness", from misfortune to fortune, involves the use of the imagination, the active intellect, and at times, the plastic arts. Art, thus, commits the soul to an upward passage, to an ascent from the lower to the highest divine beauty. Consequently, the various *artes* have ontological if not an onto-genetic status in Plotinus' metaphysics. Logic, observation, and piety all reinforced this position. For Plotinus there was something impious in the idea that the sense-world was devoid of the forms or that physical objects, even objects of art, could not awaken in the soul images of the eternal verities.

III. Beauty

Plotinus' "philosophical imagination is complex, organic, many sided, at once anthropocentric, theocentric and thus polycentric."[56] A basic question now may be asked which may help explain Plotinus' bold initiative: how and why did judgment and imagination come to play such an important

---

52. Porphyry in *Vita Plotini* X reports that Plotinus encountered a god at the temple of Isis in Rome which spurred later Platonists to differentiate upon kinds of visual encounter between higher and lower gods and daemons with subsequent therapeutic and soteriological consequences.
53. Plotinus, *Ennead*, V.8.1.
54. Plotinus, *Ennead*, I.6.3.
55. Plotinus, *Ennead*, I.6.5.
56. Anton, *Artist*, 100.

role in his analysis of beauty? In the preliminaries to his analysis of beauty in *Ennead* I.6.(1).1–6, Plotinus includes not only perceptual beauty, which is the beauty of nature and art that we see and hear, but also non-perceptual beauty, which are tied to the virtues and intellect. This opening is followed by a series of provocative questions:

> Very well then, what is it which makes us imagine (*phantazesthai*) that bodies are beautiful and attracts our hearing to sounds because of their beauty. And how are things which depend on soul beautiful ... What is this principle, then, which is present in bodies? We ought to consider this first. What is it that attracts the gaze of those who look at something, and turns and draws them to it and makes them enjoy the sight? If we find this perhaps we can use it as a stepping-stone and get a sight of the rest.[57]

Now the sheer range and detail of Plato's theory of beauty are overwhelming and cannot be examined here. What can be focused upon is Plotinus' interpretation of Plato's theory of beauty. Plotinus praises Plato because he treats beauty as a complex psychological reaction.[58] But he also tacitly corrects him: first, when he argues that beauty is not limited to sensible particulars alone but beauty is also in those particulars' intelligible archetypes; and secondly, when he reflects on the experience of beauty in the activities of judgment and imagination.

What is distinctive in Plotinus is that he takes the experience of beauty and extends it far beyond what Plato originally proposed. First, he claims that imagination and judgment are key players in the complex psychological reaction to beauty.[59] Secondly, he attributes an onto-genetic capacity to beauty. Once the soul experiences beauty, she brings higher (sensible and intelligible) worlds into existence.

Plotinus begins the discussion of such possibilities by proposing:

> So then the beautiful body comes into being by sharing in a formative power which comes from the divine forms.[60]

Next, he associates the beautiful body, which shares a power that comes from the intelligible world, with the power of judgment:

> The power ordained for the purpose recognizes this, and there is nothing more effective for judging its own subject-matter, when

---

57. Plotinus, *Ennead*, I.6.1.7–20.
58. Plato, *Symposium* 210ac; *Hippias major* 297e-298b.
59. Plotinus, *Ennead*, I.6.1.7–20.
60. Plotinus, *Ennead*, I.6.2.28–29.

> the rest of the soul judges along with it; or perhaps the rest of the soul too pronounces the judgement by fitting the beautiful body to the form in itself and using this for judging beauty as we use a ruler for judging straightness.[61]

In brief, the soul, the founding principle of the whole aesthetic enterprise, is not a phenomenal entity to be added to the objects it sees and hears. Rather it brings beautiful objects to presence and so moves in a different sphere altogether. That is to say, the soul is not only a phenomenon in the world. She brings a transcendent viewpoint to the things of the world in the very act of judging objects beautiful:

> But how does the bodily agree with that which is before body? How does the architect declare the house outside beautiful by fitting it to the form of house within him? . . . When sense perception . . . sees the form in bodies binding and mastering the nature opposed to it, which is shapeless . . . (the soul) brings it back and takes it in, now without parts, to the soul's interior and presents it to that which is within as something in tune with it and fitting it and dear to it . . . And the simple power of color comes about by shape and the mastery of the darkness in matter by the presence of light which is incorporeal and formative power and form . . . the melodies in sounds too, the imperceptible ones which make the perceptible ones, make the soul conscious of beauty in the same way.[62]

Summary: It is important to note that Plotinus proposes a division between two kinds of judgment. One is perceptive (or aesthetic); another cognitive (or rational). Although this is novel itself, the true originality of his position lies in the notion of interplay between judgment and imagination in the perception of beauty. He appears to argue that the only context within which perceptive judgment is properly meaningful is when the soul grasps the unified totality of the intelligible world with the assistance of imagination.[63] Perceptive judgment, and the imaginative insight that accompanies it, makes the soul conscious of beauty. Such consciousness is born of a free association within the soul of these two powers. Once the soul focuses upon a sight or sound she judges and imagines them as beautiful, thereby making them and herself beautiful.

61. Plotinus, *Ennead*, I.6.3.1–5.
62. Plotinus, *Ennead*, I.6.3.5–30.
63. Plotinus, *Ennead*, IV.3.29–31.

IV. Judgment and Imagination

Free play between judgment and imagination has significant consequences. The beautiful object offers a reconciliation of the sensible and intelligible worlds, even of sensibility and concepts. This means the beautiful object grasped through the activity of judgment and imagination is an instantiation of the whole realm of the Ideas. Indeed, a beautiful sight or sound is a symbolic trace of the One:

> ... when it sees something akin to it or a trace of its kindred reality, it is delighted and thrilled and returns to itself and remembers itself and its possessions.[64]

Plotinus suggests the experience of beauty not only constitutes a primary realm of human experience, but that the judgment itself is a non-cognitive one. The first proposition emerges when he argues that becoming beautiful enables one to approach the source of all beauty, the One.[65] He tells us that the pursuit of beauty is the pursuit of true being, and its source, the One or the Good.[66] The second suggestion appears when he proposes the artist creates beauty with a serene lack of consciousness. The artist is unable to articulate the rules of his own creation because he works at the behest of higher and deeper forces beyond and within himself.[67] That is to say, the experience of beauty fundamentally surpasses merely cognitive "horizons" of meaning.

This leads Plotinus to the position that the experience of beauty is not confined to empirical subjectivity alone. The beautiful object rests on the presence of forms, which awaken in the soul an awareness of the source of all beauty, the One. Hence, when we become conscious of beauty there is no longer any distinction for us between the sensible and the intelligible, intuition and concept, the particular and the universal. Indeed, the experience of beauty brings into reality an imaginative reconciliation of the sensible and the intelligible. The soul acquires a point of view upon the world which a divine understanding would have.[68]

How does this point of view come about? The rational and perceptive souls each have their own imaginative power. It is through the free interplay between perceptive judgment and imagination that the soul represents

---

64. Plotinus, *Ennead*, I.6.2.9–12.
65. Plotinus, *Ennead*, I.6.9.7–12.
66. Plotinus, *Ennead*, I.6.7.
67. Plotinus, *Ennead*, I.6.9.
68. Plotinus, *Ennead*, I.6.2.1–12.

beauty to consciousness "as though in a mirror."[69] Briefly, aisthesis is nothing more than the lower soul becoming conscious of what the higher soul eternally beholds. Phantasia is nothing more than the presentation to the lower soul of an antilepsis, or sensuous perception, which permits her to identify her empirical self with her pure, true self that transcends the sensible. As a result of the experience of beauty the soul gains the capacity to establish unforeseen imaginative relations with the world of Ideas, and perhaps, even the One itself.[70]

Pursuing Plotinus' insights further, it appears that he proposes that the judgment of beauty is not based solely on determinate forms and concepts (or rules). For example, when the soul perceives a beautiful object, she associates matter with form. However, association is not regulated by a concept for the interplay of judgment and imagination is quite free in that it obeys no prescribed cognitive rule. Indeed, it is impossible to "argue" about beauty as if it were a cognitive judgment. The reason for this is that even Primary Beauty itself is formless.[71]

Two insights emerge here worth noting. First, experience of the beautiful is in little way cognitive, but it, nonetheless, has about it the form and structure of the rational. Plotinus describes aesthetic judgment as a kind of free-wheeling of the soul's judgmental and imaginative faculties. Aesthetic judgment is an undecidable half-way house between the uniform laws of cognition and utter indeterminacy. Secondly, what we have here is a fusion of judgment, imagination, and teleology.

Plotinus proposes the consoling thought of a world that is not after all indifferent to us, which has a regard for our mental capacities. Experience of the beautiful unites us with intellect, the ideas, and the One, but at an affective, intuitive level.[72] What brings souls together is knowledge, but perhaps more importantly, an ineffable reciprocity with beauty which is dispersed everywhere.[73] Significantly, Plotinus seems to suggest that the soul is at least partially modeled on a self-referential conception of beauty. If the soul is to flourish she has to extend her colonizing sway over things beautiful and stamp them with her indelible presence.[74] Indeed, when the soul finds herself in judgment of beauty, she exercises a curious form of inter-subjectivity, onto-genetically establishing within herself a link to

69. Plotinus, *Ennead*, I.6.2.1–12.
70. Plotinus, *Ennead* I.6.2.1–12.
71. Plotinus, *Ennead*, VI.7.33.37–38.
72. Plotinus, *Ennead*, I.6.2.28–29.
73. Plotinus, *Ennead*, VI.7.3.9–10.
74. Plotinus, *Ennead*, I.6.6.27–33.

the beautiful community of Ideas, and perhaps even through the Ideas a bridge to the One.[75]

For Plotinus then, some of the pleasure of the beautiful arises from a quick sense of the world's teleological conformity to our capacities.[76] In the experience of beauty, judgment and imagination create a purposive synthesis between soul and reality. A soul is home in the world because the world is designed to suit her aesthetic capacities.[77] Whether this is actually true or not—Plotinus cannot say. Since we know nothing of what the One is in itself. That the soul's experience of beauty fits reality must remain a hypothesis but it is the kind of heuristic fiction which permits us a sense of purposiveness, centeredness, and significance beyond all theoretical demonstration.[78]

This is so because Plotinus had an acute sense of crisis in the multiplicity of reality and the chain of intermediaries that reached from soul to the One.[79] Beauty and the experience of beauty functioned to erase the distinctions between the layers of the soul, and brought the ontologically distant, aesthetically present. It is, perhaps, accurate to say that for Plotinus beauty brings that which is transcendent and intelligibly distant, immanent and sensibly present. It may even be that the experience of beauty is about the joining of heaven and earth in the human soul herself.[80]

V. Mimesis, Symmetry and the One

When we turn to the account of beauty in (*Ennead* I.6) the One's unfolding power in the universe is striking. As remarkable is the role the artist plays in this activity. The artist imitates, not the sensible particular but intelligible Form. As a result, the soul is unified in the experience of beauty to inhabit two spheres simultaneously where everything beautiful in the "One" is beautiful in the other.[81] And because Form is formless, it is recognized that beauty cannot be reduced to any set of generic attributes.[82] Indeed, the ungeneric character of beauty carries with it unpredictability.[83] The same face may at

---

75. Plotinus, *Ennead*, I.6.2.1–17.
76. Plotinus, *Ennead*, I.6.6.13–18; 27–33.
77. Plotinus, *Ennead*, I.6.9.7–12.
78. Plotinus, *Ennead*, I.6.2.9–12.
79. This was brought about by the Gnostic threat. cf. Plotinus, *Enneads*, II.8; V.8; V.5; II.9.
80. Plotinus, *Ennead*, VI.7.3.9–10; I.6.6.13–33.
81. Plotinus, *Ennead*, I.6.2.28–29; I.6.3.1–5.
82. Schroeder, *Categories*, 129.
83. Plotinus, *Ennead*, I.6.1.37–40.

times be beautiful, at other times ugly. The beauty of countenance is not in its symmetry but in the light that illuminates the symmetry.[84]

With Plotinus' reformulation *mimesis* fills and indeed fulfills itself with new meaning. Beauty no longer looks to the Ideas alone to make it anew. The Ideas no longer provide the only exemplary model for beauty to follow. The beautiful soul offers her own judgmental, imaginative, even exemplary model for beauty—the One.[85] Thus:

> Beauty is that which irradiates symmetry rather than asymmetry itself and is that which truly calls out our love.[86]

Plotinus' universe is dynamic where sensible beauty is not a fixed entity but an open one. The reason for this is that being (*to on*) is not one, but a variegated one (*ti poikilon*).[87] There are many ways of grasping beauty all relative to an entity's metaphysical place in reality. In (*Ennead* I.6.1) Plotinus explains how sensible beauty is encountered and experienced from the "perspective" of the embodied, sensible soul.[88] Now from one point of view you might think that this was a fairly innocuous addition to Plato's argument, hardly more, really, than an explication of a series of ideas that Plato already put forward. But this simple step, within the framework of the *Enneads*, is not at all as simple as it might seem at first blush. Plotinus' soul does not derive its existence from itself. Rather soul, like Intellect, derives her existence from the One.

> The One is all things and not a single one of them: it is the principle of all things, not all things, but all things have that other kind of transcendent existence; for in a way they do occur in the One; or rather they are not there yet, but they will be. How then do all things come from the One which is simple and has in it no diverse variety or any sort of doubleness? It is because there is nothing in it that things come from it: in order that being may exist, the One is not being but the generator of being.[89]

To quote only one sample passage from a much latter treatise, entitled by Porphyry as *On the Knowing Hypostases*, Plotinus also writes:

---

84. Plotinus, *Ennead*, VI.7.22.22-29.

85. Plotinus, *Ennead*, I.6.6.13-18; I.6.9.40-45.

86. Plotinus, *Ennead*, VI.7.22.24-26. On this passage see Anton, *Symmetry*, 234; Beierwaltes, *Theorie des Schoenen*, 12; Schroeder, *Categories*, 130.

87. Plotinus, *Ennead*, VI.2.2.2-3.

88. For the perspectives from the vantage point of intelligible beauty see Plotinus, *Ennead*, V.8.3.1; and from the perspective of the One see Plotinus, *Ennead*, VI.7.(38).

89. Plotinus, *Ennead*, V.2.1.1-7.

> How is it that the One is the principle of all things? It is because it perceives them, having made each of them to be one (*hen hekaston auton poiesasa einai*)? It is also that it has brought them into existence (*hupestesen auta*).[90]

The One perceives and brings all things, including souls into existence, because:

> What comes to be, turned back upon the One, and was filled, and came to be by looking at the One. And this is intellect.[91]

Plotinus continues:

> Its standing toward the One made being. Its gazing towards the One made Intellect.[92]

He explains:

> Since it stood towards the One in order to see the One, it becomes at once Intellect and being.[93]

We are then told that the same is true of the production of soul from Intellect:[94]

> This activity from the substance of Intellect—this belongs to soul.[95]

> The soul, therefore, looking back to Intellect, the Intellect from which it came to be is filled.[96]

VI. Turning Back toward the One

The citations just quoted are dangled like pearls on a string. So much so that they hardly bear the weight of commentary heaped upon them by modern readers of Plotinus. Concern here is with two features of his description: first, Plotinus' use of Platonic 'spectator imagery' such as "looking, "gaze" sight," to characterize the soul's ascent to Intellect and the One. Secondly, the use of

---

90. Plotinus, *Ennead*, V.3.15.27–29.
91. Plotinus, *Ennead*, V.2. 1.7–9.
92. Plotinus, *Ennead*, V.2 1.9.
93. Plotinus, *Ennead*, V.2 (11) 1.12–13.
94. Plotinus, *Ennead*, V.2 (11) 1.14.
95. Plotinus, *Ennead*, V.2 (11) 1.16.
96. Plotinus, *Ennead*, V.2 (11) 1.19–20.

Aristotelian terms such as "power" and "activity" to describe the ability of the soul to grasp Intellect and the One. With both in mind, let me ask one very simple question. How does soul turn back to the One? The answer to this question lies in the soul's ability to judge beautiful objects, and imagine their relationship to the Idea of Beauty, and the One. The soul is only fulfilled when she looks upon beautiful things, and when she looks back, of herself, towards the Intellect from which she has sprung, she visualizes the form of Beauty itself, which itself is a "speechless image of the One."

At this point Plotinus can say that the soul aesthetically exists of herself, for without turning upon herself in the experience of the beautiful, and hence back to the Idea of Beauty, and the One, the soul would not be soul, since it would not be fulfilled by beauty. Indeed, if the soul were not fulfilled by looking inward, and hence backward, what would she be? She would have neither existence nor being. There are thus two 'moments' in the aesthetics of the soul: an awareness of beauty and a turning back on reflection of beauty to the soul's source in Intellect and the One. It is because of this duality that Plotinus can claim both that the soul exists when she experiences beauty, and that when she experiences beauty, she "sees things together in respect of the One," as a "speechless image of the One."

Aristotle said—and when do we encounter a truth in Plotinus that is not already found in Aristotle?—that a proper work is one where there is neither too little nor too much, nothing in excess and nothing missing.[97] There is a simple but difficult measure for beauty, which in Plotinus the soul now provides in a speechless image of beauty. To be "speechless" does not mean that beauty has nothing to say. On the contrary, the speechlessness of beauty is really a kind of speech. It is a rich, colorful, and resplendent language whose light brightly, clearly and fluently, shines out from the One which is the:

> ... spring and origin of beauty. (I.6.9.44)[98]

If we were to ask Plotinus to account for beauty—that "speechlessness" which addresses us so forcefully with its unique mute eloquence—his answer might be—such speechlessness is really a kind of speech for:

> ... no eye ever saw the sun without becoming sun-like, nor can a soul see beauty without becoming beautiful.[99]

---

97. Aristotle, *Nic. Ethics*, 1106b9.
98. Plotinus, *Ennead.*, I.6.9.40–45. cf. Plato, *Phaedrus*, 245c9.
99. Plotinus, *Ennead*, I.6.9.30–33. cf. Plato, *Rep.*, VI 508b3; 509a1.

In the first half of the third century, we find ourselves caught up in an unfolding crisis still incomplete. In a way, Plotinus had a heady impulse to "aestheticize" reality. I say "heady" because as a "systematic" yet "revolutionary" philosopher he fractured the foundations of earlier Platonic "aesthetics."[100] The results were a new late-classical aestheticism. Bit by bit, the static framework of the noetic world on which Platonic metaphysics rested was dismantled. The ineffaceable character of forms and gods, which earlier Platonists saw as the ultimate justification of a mimesis between the intelligible and sensible worlds, between intelligibility and sensibility has been dissolved in the experience of beauty. Plotinus views such experiential mimesis as imagining form. This usually occurs when we are confronted by the mute, yet profoundly familiar Pythagorean harmonies of form in color and sound. Later beauty is present in things whenever it succeeds in representing to the soul a configuration, an order of unity in tension, perhaps a world of its own experience of the One in miniature.

Summary: Art no longer belongs to the sensible world alone. An individual may become ecstatic or expansive upon entering a holy place or viewing a statue of a god.[101]

The aesthetic functions to erase the distinctions between the layers of the soul and to bring the ontologically distant epistemologically present. *Aisthesis* is nothing more than the lower soul becoming conscious of what the higher soul eternally beholds. *Phantasia* is nothing more than the presentation to the lower soul of an *antilepsis* which permits her to identify her empirical self with her pure, true self that transcends the sensible. All this is possible because sense-perception (*aisthesis*) and imagination (*phantasia*) with the aid of the active-intellect (*nous poietikos*) grasp forms of beauty reifying them to *sunaisthetically*.

VII. Reification

An instance of what Heidegger calls 'Verdinglichung' or reification is to associate 'ideas' with 'objects.' Ideas as objects of intellection in a divine mind fused with the image of *nous* as thought thinking itself and as creative self-awareness leads to an 'aesthetic turn' worthy of attention. What is implied in the simple Greek word *lagon*, hip? The occasion is famous, the figure celebrated. Hecate's hip pours forth a divine oracle—Porphyry and later Proclus are suitably present and ready to give the correct interpretation:

---

100. On these terms see Rorty, *Mirror of Nature*, 365–72.
101. On this belief in general in late antiquity see, Heliodorus, *Aeth.*, 2.11.

> ... About the cavity of the right hip is poured forth in abundance the plenteous liquid of the primordially generated soul who entirely ensouls the light, the fire, the ether of the worlds. In Hecate's left hip exists the source of virtue which remains wholly within and does not give away its virginity.[102]

If it is possible to imagine such hips you have entered an aesthetic turn worthy of mention. By (*lagon*) Porphyry and Proclus mean that Hecate's flanks symbolize cosmic order and virtue. One hip contains the signs (*symbola*) of the natural order and the other the source of the sublunary virtues (*aretai*) which the goddess dominates. To appreciate the boldness of this later Platonic proposition we need only to contrast it with the earlier Platonic one.[103] For early Platonists a statue of Hecate visibly imitates transient becoming and as *aisthesis* it yields an opinable reflection of the transient, physical arrangement of statuesque particulars—hardly a form or *symbola* of the gods. These hips are mere icons of cosmic order and virtue.[104] For later Platonists a statue of Hecate visibly embodies intelligible being. Her hips formally symbolize universals¾the right cosmic order and the left the source of virtue. Perception (*aisthesis*) provides entrance into an imaginative apparition of the fixed, noetic order of the intelligibles, even of the divine forms themselves.

Hecate possesses hips worthy to be remembered. What makes them so memorable are claims that *aisthesis* deals only with particulars and *noesis* with universals are called into question. If Hecate's hips had captivated Porphyry and Proclus merely in the manner they would have pleased Plato, we would not be reflecting on her statuesque anatomy in the manner of the two Romes, the old one on the Tiber and the new one on the Bosporus—but solely in the manner of classical Athens where Plato taught that although *aisthesis* and *noesis* were epistemically complementary, they remain exclusive notions.[105]

Plotinus' advocacy of aesthetics is based on something far more profound than a defense of the metaphysical value of the plastic arts

---

102. Porphyry, *Phil Orac.*, 1.152.7; Proclus, *Remp.*, 2.201.10ff.

103. Plato, *Laws* X.888e; *Phaedrus*, 249c; *Ep.* VII.341c. Also see *Symposium*. 210e. However this figure is not the craftsman of the plastic arts who is an imitative artist, cf. *Gorgias*,450c. For Plato on art see, Friedlaender, *Platon*, 59–84; Oates, *Plato*, 28; 48–62.

104. For Plato the arts are a mere imitation of nature which is but an imitation of being. Friedlaender, 1964, 60ff. Plato, consequently, places the imitative artist in class vi of viii classes among knowers of the ideas, cf. *Rep.* VII..522b; and the plastic arts among the lowest of the imitative arts, cf. *Rep.* III.401ab.

105. For Plato on the mantic arts, see Dodds, *Greeks and the Irrational*, 207–35.

themselves.[106] He claims that art is a visible expression of ideal beauty.[107] He asserts that the ideas of beauty exist in the human soul.[108] He argues that the imagination is the mental faculty through which the soul gains initial awareness of ideal beauty; and that such aesthetic awareness leads eventually to knowledge of the ideas of beauty, if not the beautiful itself, in sensible beautiful things.[109] Even though the higher soul remains in the intelligible world the lower soul is unconscious of this fact.[110] For the origin of all symbolic activity, including artistic activity emerges from the fact of the soul's descent and its ignorance of its undecended state.[111] The arts thus become a means for the soul to reverse a situation of misfortune¾her descent into corporeality. Through the arts and the aesthetic imagination the soul regains her awareness of her intelligible origins and, consequently, begins her ascent from sensibility to intelligibility.

Summary: Plotinus as "Platonist" maintained the priority and superiority of intellection over perception as laying the foundations for physics, and subsequently for psychology and epistemology.[112] Plotinus' as "neo-Platonist" claims that the mind perceptively imagines being erases a divided line which linked perception with particulars and intellection with universals. Moreover, his notion that a sensible thing instantiates being marks an inversion of an older Platonic paradigm which claims sense objects imitate being. Such reification of perception and imagination forms the basis for an 'aesthetic turn' where: 1) the intelligible world is instantiated in sensible objects such as statuary, temples and statues; and 2) through perception one imaginatively gains entrance to the intelligible world and attains salvation.

---

106. Plotinus, *Ennead*, III.6.5.22-29.
107. Plotinus, *Ennead*, V.8.1.
108. Plotinus, *Ennead*, I.6.2
109. Plotinus, *Ennead*, I.6.5.
110. Plotinus, *Ennead*, V.1.12.

111. Plotinus, *Ennead*, 4.3.15. From his use of the term *ocheisthai* we can, with caution, suggest that Plotinus was familiar with the term *ochema*. cf. A. Smith, *Porphyry's Place*, 153. However, a comprehensive elaboration of this doctrine comes after Plotinus. cf. Dodds, *Proclus*, 313-21. On the theory of the undecended soul in Plotinus, cf. Rist, *Plotinus*, 410-22; Steel, *The Changing Self*, 34-38. The important passages from Plotinus are in *Enneads* IV.3.12; V.1.2; VI.4.14.

112. On Plotinus' psychology and epistemology there are many works. cf. Blumenthal, *Plotinus' Psychology*, 8-66; 67-133; cf. Rist, *Plotinus*, 410-22.

VIII. Imagination and Memory

Plotinus accepted Aristotle's view that knowledge is a function of a series of psychological faculties. He condones Aristotle's view of the imagination plays a decisive role in his aesthetics.[113] Among the most important of the Aristotelian elements in Plotinus' system here is the notion that an actively thinking mind is identical (qualitatively) and in a *per se* relation with its objects. He also accepted Aristotle's view that sense-perception involved the reception of the forms of sense-objects without their matter.[114] As Alexander insisted the absolute certainty of knowledge springs from the fact that it has its origins in perception.[115] This is the complement of Plotinus observation that the physical world is a self-contained, cogent, and certain instantiation of the noetic world.[116] This is possible because the soul is self-moving. Always in movement she is in contact with those intelligible faculties active within her even though she is unconscious of them. The lower soul becomes conscious of her higher self when the active intellect transmits to the imagination an image of the forms. This occurs when the soul views an art form. This triggers memory of the intelligibles for the soul sees the form of beauty in the work of art.

There are two faculties of imagination. One arises in regions of the soul concerned with the body. Another emerges from the part of the soul concerned with the intellect.64 Plotinus says that the secondary act of imagination which is opinion in the soul is caused by disturbance and shock. Thus it is the product of the lower part of the organism. Its images are a faint opinion and unexamined mental picture.[117] However, it is not secondary but primary imagination that is important in Plotinian aesthetics. The primary imagination has images of the forms passed on to it by the active intellect and the higher soul.[118] Mind deploys its thoughts and shows it to the imaginative faculty as though in a mirror. This presentation of thought to the imagination makes us aware of the intellection (*noesis*) which is always in progress. The imagination apprehends it and the persistence of the image is memory.

---

113. Blumenthal, *Plotinus' Psychology*, 8–44. For a more Platonic reading of Plotinus' psychology see Armstrong, *Plotinus*, 393–413; Merlan, *From Platonism to Neoplatonism*, 8–10.

114. Blumenthal, *Plotinus' Psychology*, 137–38.

115. Alexander, *De Anima Liber*, 85; 89.21-22 (Wallis); *De Intellectu*, 112.2-4 (Bruns).

116. Plotinus, *Ennead*, I.6.2–3.

117. Plotinus, *Ennead*, III.6.4.14–23.

118. Plotinus, *Ennead*, IV.3.30.1–5.

The imagination (*phantasia*) receives the products of thought (*logoi*) and perception (*aisthesis*).[119] These products are, then, passed on to the reasoning faculty for processing.[120] Imagination is, accordingly, based on something far more profound than an awareness of physical conditions. It carries a meaning close to the idea of consciousness.[121] This means that the imagination is a power of perceptive awareness that transcends sensation. Significantly, it refers to that mental faculty which provides knowledge of the intelligibles above and within the soul.[122] This assures for Plotinus the possibility of memory (*anamneses*)—the becoming receptive on the part of the lower soul what the higher soul eternally beholds[123]—for image collecting is the basis of memory.[124]

Plotinus believed in reincarnation and assumed the form in which the soul is reincarnated depends on memory of its previous life and the extent to which it conforms to the characteristics of past lives in a present life. Memory is also the way a soul preserves its character between reincarnations. Memory thus makes the soul what it is and controls its descent.[125] A significant parsing of these claims surfaces when Plotinus assumes that souls move from an unconscious to a conscious understanding of the intelligibles.[126] This transition is effected through memory.[127] The imagination fired by its perception of a statue of a god remembers the form of the god and moves from an unconscious to a conscious awareness of the divine.[128] In a paradigmatic move art now plays an important role in the way awareness of the higher soul and the intelligibles is grasped by the lower soul.[129]

IX. An Aesthetic Emerging

Accepting the Aristotelian postulate that sense-perception involves the reception of the forms of sense-objects without their matter, images of the forms are transmitted to the imagination through sense objects:

119. Plotinus, *Ennead*, IV.3.30.5ff.
120. Plotinus, *Ennead*, V.3.2.7–9.
121. On the imagination see Schwyzer, *Bewusst und Unbewusst*, 343–90.
122. Plotinus, *Ennead*, I.4.9.25ff.
123. Plotinus, *Ennead*, IV.8.4.28–31.
124. Plotinus, *Ennead*, IV.3.29.22–24.
125. Plotinus, *Enneads*, IV.3.8.5–9; III.4.2.11.
126. Schwyzer, *Bewusst und Unbewusst*, 72–75.
127. Blumenthal, *Plotinus' Psychology*, 94–99.
128. Plotinus, *Ennead*, I.6.3.
129. Plotinus, *Ennead*, V.8.1.

> ... On what principle does the architect when he finds the house standing before him correspond with his inner ideal of a house and pronounce it beautiful? Is it not that the house before him, the stones apart, is the inner idea stamped on the mass of exterior matter, the indivisible exhibited in diversity? We call something beautiful when we see something imprinted on it that we recognize as our own, by virtue of our continuity with the Ideal world, and the immanence of that world in the object where we recognize beauty.[130]

Art objects also move the soul to imagine the form of beauty.[131] Plotinus describes an intelligible world in unity with the sensible world. The capacity to grasp this synthesis leads the mind to an understanding of beauty. Next, he examines the imagination and shows how it aids the soul in its ascent from sensible to intelligible knowledge. Finally, he illustrates how the craftsman and his *artes* concretely instantiate in visible forms the intelligible world's truth and beauty in three tropes:

First, Plotinus describes an intelligible world whereby each member remains itself, in distinction from all others, yet simultaneously all members form a single unity. He asks us to imagine a transparent globe or sphere containing all the things of the universe. Then he asks us to correct it by imagining another sphere stripped of all magnitude and spatial differences. Next we are urged to make a synthesis wherein each is all, one undivided divine power of many facets and each sharing one existence and remaining distinct from all others which is an example of the beautiful.[132] Secondly, Plotinus strains to lead our minds to the higher world of the forms and argues that sensual images lead us on our ascent. To correct the conclusions we might draw from the first-level image, he asks us not to abandon imagery entirely but to imagine another sphere, one whose properties run counter to the first. Thirdly, the deficiencies of image-thinking are eventually corrected by bringing the sense-image to a second stage and then urging our metaphysical imaginations to leap beyond this stage as well, to the desired insight into the intelligible realm. Central to this process of ascent is not of abandoning or turning away from the sensible world but of using imagery and the faculty of imagination to the point of strain and shatter. At the moment of shatter, intelligible insight occurs. He illustrates this in his comparison of hieroglyphics and art. Both

---

130. Plotinus, *Ennead*, I.6.3.

131. Awaiting the *Belles Letters* commentaries on Plotinus for early but still helpful studies this treatise see Brehier, *Plotin*, 17–24; Puech, *Plotin e Gnostics*, 161–90.

132. Plotinus, *Ennead*, V.8.9.

suggest non-discursive images of the intelligible world—the ideas are not propositional truths but reified beings (*onta*).[133]

In a stunning move 'Ideas' are envisaged as *algamata*, each bodying forth in a species of translucence the inner wealth of the intelligible and sensible world's truth and beauty. Two additional *algamata* also come into play: one is the artist; the other is the artist's creation. A self who has seen beauty reified will become a beautiful self—for even in this sensible, corporeal world, any concrete embodiment, in and through which others catch the glimmerings of the transcendent splendor of the forms—is beautiful.[134] All this comes together in Plotinus' rich notion of the *demiourgos*.

The craftsman's task is, first, to imagine the ideal specification to which reality conforms, and then—so far as the nature of matter permits—to arrange it in conformity with its ideal specification. A sculpture, for example, represents the creative ideas contained in the soul of the artist. With the assistance of the imagination the artist in an inward vision grasps the forms intuitively. Next the craftsman projects the intelligible beauty of the forms outwards, giving them visible form. This understanding emerges from his interpretation of Phidias' statue of Zeus. Plotinus states that:

> ... it goes back to the ideas from which nature itself derives and adds where nature is lacking.[135]

The craftsman's works instantiate the form of beauty. It also reflects the beauty of deity itself. Plotinus is toying with a sweeping hypothesis. Although the theme is strongly reminiscent of the Platonic Socrates, that Silenus figure which, once opened, was seen to contain the images of the gods within him, the Plotinian Phidias and that Zeus figure are strikingly distinct. Plato often returned to that mysterious, youthful experience, to that encounter with the beloved which is simultaneously an encounter with a transcendent world of value that stretches beyond the concrete person involved in the encounter.[136] Plotinus reflects and expands upon this encounter and includes within the *algamata* that permits encounter with the intelligible world through imagination, the active intellect, and the plastic arts. The forms are communicated to the soul by the active intellect through the image making faculty of the soul in reflection on the work of art.

---

133. Plotinus, *Ennead*, VI.4.5.

134. Plotinus, *Ennead*, V.8.1117–19. cf. IV.4.6.42–44.

135. Plotinus, *Ennead*, V.8.1.

136. Plato develops this theme in the *Laws* where household shrines, the aged, and the stars are concrete examples of the divine. cf. *Laws*, 930e–931a; 899b; 966e–968a.

Sculpture functions to awaken in other souls an imaginative awareness of the ideas from which all else derives. Such awareness leads to psychological enlightenment for the soul is the immovable place or subject for the immutable truth of the higher world.[137]

> ... What do you feel in the beauty of souls? When you see that you yourself are beautiful within, what do you feel? What is this Dionysian exaltation that thrills through your being, this straining upwards of all your soul, this longing to break away from the body and live sunken within the true self? These are no other than the emotion of souls under the spell of love ... All these noble qualities are to be reverenced and loved but what entitles them to be called beautiful? ... Anyone that sees them must admit that they have reality of being, and is not real being, really beautiful?[138]

Plotinus' understanding of beauty confirms a new Roman rhythm. His terminology¾imagination (*phantasia*), exaltation (*ekstasis*), love (*eros*), and emotion (*pathos*)¾ affirms that the intelligible world and its divine source can be grasped not only noetically but aesthetically. In a remarkable reversal of an older aesthetic pattern divine apperception involves patheia not apatheia. Here another *via sacra* opens up which involves a non-discursive, indeed an imaginative and erotic ascent to the divine.[139] The consequence of these assumptions propels Plotinus to propose, at least for Platonism, a novel aesthetic axiology. Psychological and ontological schizophrenia are overcome aesthetically. The soul's unawareness of her higher self is reversed and her situation of misfortune overturned through imaginative, indeed, artistic perception.

Summary: The aesthetic self has ambitions that are soberly ecstatic, uniquely autonomous and remarkably self-constrained. This self is no ordinary subject nor is it not a singular self. Its 'horizons' imply an 'aesthetic pretence—a power (*dunamis*) to create a 'beautiful mind' whose *telos* is ecstatic union with the One—to become another 'one' in miniature. Behind all this, as Plotinus claims all along, is *aisthesis* belongs to both the sensible and intelligible worlds—something hinted before but never argued. Through art the ontological distance between being and becoming is overcome in an epistemological and psychological act of imaginative

---

137. Plotinus, *Ennead*, IV.7.

138. Plotinus, *Ennead*, I.6.5.

139. This might be a development Plato introduces in the *Phaedrus* 250d. On techniques of contemplation in Plotinus see Schroeder, *Avocatio*, 2012, 147–60.

identification. Thus in turning to a statue or temple the imagination sees not merely a physical object but perceives an image of the forms. This, eventually, leads to an awareness of the eternal value of nature, the human soul, and the divine like nature of both.

Conclusion

In the first half of the third century, we find ourselves caught up in an unfolding drama still incomplete. A leading theme of this whole story is Plotinus' extraordinary concept of the self as aesthetic subjectivity. In the end it is about the joining of heaven and earth in self-reflexivity (*sunaisthesis*) where the dangerously long distance between being and becoming, consciousness and unconsciousness, is overcome through the aesthetic self that heals its disparate self. Here it would be an understatement to say Plotinus had a heady impulse to "aestheticize" reality. I say "heady" because as a "systematic" yet "revolutionary" philosopher he fractured the foundations of earlier Platonic "aesthetics." The results were a new later ancient aestheticism where bit by bit, the static framework of the noetic world on which Platonic metaphysics rested was dismantled. The ineffaceable character of forms and gods, which earlier Platonists saw as the ultimate justification of a *mimesis* between the intelligible and sensible worlds, between intelligibility and sensibility is dissolved in the experience of beauty—a *mimesis* as imagining form.

As a result a new self-reflective aesthetics beckons and where art serves to heal the disparate self. It brings that which is so noetically distant, sensibly present. It is about the joining of heaven and earth in the human soul. Thus the dangerously long distance between being and becoming consciousness and unconsciousness is overcome through an aesthetic that stresses the possibility of a beautiful mind wherein the self becomes aware of its intelligible beauty thereby triggering a journey to divine beauty itself where once confronted by the mute, yet profoundly familiar Pythagorean harmonies of form in color and sound, a self is transformed. Beauty is now present in things whenever they succeed in presenting a reified configuration, an order of unity in tension, a harmony of tones. Indeed, if *aisthesis* is nothing more than the lower soul becoming conscious of what the higher soul eternally beholds, *phantasia* the presentation to the lower soul of an *antilepsis* which permits her to identify her empirical self with her pure true transcendent self, then art brings that which is so noetically distant, sensibly present.

And lest we forget, Plotinus proposes that the arts are therapeutic. They assist in the transfiguration of the soul from unconsciousness to consciousness, from an awareness of its sensibility to knowledge of its intelligibility. It erases the distinctions between the layers of the soul, to bring the ontologically distant epistemologically present. It is here the vehicle of the soul is important for its imaginative function.[140] Since the vehicle is an intermediary between bodily sensations and intellection, sense impressions are impressed upon the vehicle and then processed by the soul which allows for a reification of particulars into universals.[141] If particulars are reified into universals the self contains within itself an ability to gain salvation. It has not only the ability to save itself through contemplation (*theoria*) it also has texts, temples and its own imaginative perception of the inner beauty of statues and mosaics to lead it to an ascent to the Forms, Intellect and the One.[142]

Postscript/ Plato's Aesthetic Philosophy: In Light of the Good

If we take seriously the intimate relation of *noûs* and *nooumena* with the inexhaustible generativity/beauty and dynamism of the Good, Plato's philosophy manifests no discontinuity with regard to Plotinus' characterization of noetic reality and selves as "aesthetic" realities. This is a perspective which has not yet consequently been considered and explicated in the literature concerning Plato, notwithstanding the fact that it presupposes only an unprejudicial comprehension of some key-passages in Plato's work. Thematizing the transcendence of the Good through the analogy between the Good and the sun, in *Politeia* 509a6–7 Plato characterizes the beauty of the Good as transcendent also with respect to *epistêmê* and *alêtheia*. This means that for Plato beauty in itself transcends and at the same time constitutes the manifestation of being (*alêtheia* and *on* are "synonyms" in 508d5), that is also the *noûs* and the *nooumena*, to which Plato points in 508c1. As a consequence: 1) beauty in itself can be interpreted as the generativity of the Good beyond all forms of being; 2) intelligible reality can be therefore intended as primarily dynamic/generative/creative as well as aesthetic reality, whereas aesthetics is here intimately connected with the inexhaustible generativity of the Good as well as with its "perceptibility" in all dimensions of being; 3) if we consider *noûs* as the archetypical form of self and selfness, Plato's eminently agathological philosophy can be intended as the first philosophy of an "aesthetic self." According to the aforesaid premises,

---

140. Aristotle, *De Gen. An.* 744a1–5.

141. Plotinus, *Ennead*, IV.3.15. On the terms *ocheisthai* and *ochema* in Plotinus see, A. Smith, *Porphyry's Place*, 153; Dodds, *Proclus*, 313–21.

142. Plotinus, *Ennead*, IV.4.44.

Plato's critique of *mimêsis* and art in *Politeia* X cannot be interpreted as prejudicial hostility, but as due to the high claims Plato connects with aesthetics: since beauty in itself can be perceived as the generativity/creativity of the Good transcending every form of being, truly legitimated forms of imitation and art can be considered in Plato's horizon only those which are capable of being generated through a direct experience of the Good. That is why Plato uses images connected with arts when he describes the generation and shaping of universe as well as of the shaping of a good community (he would not do it if he would be an enemy of art!)[143]

Salvatore Lavecchia

---

143. In Lavecchia, *La Luce*, 445–56.

12

Aesthetics Emerging

...dichterish wohnet der Mensch.

—HEIDEGGER, *VORTRAEGE UND AUFSAETZE*

Précis

BAUMGARTEN INTRODUCED AESTHETICS AS 'the science of sensible knowledge.'[1] He combined the terms *episteme* and *aisthesis* conjunctively as a *cognitio sensitivia* [a science of sensuous knowledge].[2] Ever since Baumgarten, aesthetics has oscillated between theory of knowledge and theory of art - with ambiguous results. Our question: is it possible to approach *episteme* and *aisthesis* in any form other than epistemology [Descartes' conjunction of *episteme* and *logos*]; and *episteme*, *aisthesis*, and *aisthanomia*

---

1. Baumgarten, *Aesthetica*, Section 1.
2. Baumgarten proposes a system of aesthetics where the beautiful is apprehended by a 'sensuous knowledge' governed by taste and judgment. Three epistemic models allow for aesthetic play: the first is tied to a Cartesian *cogito*, which carries out aesthetic enquiry on the basis of its own subjectivity; the second to a Pascalian sensualist theory of taste and judgment located in the one's heart or feelings; and thirdly, *homo aestheticus* is a Leibnizian monad that communicates with other 'windowless' monads through a *sensus communis* capable of parsing the criteria of the beautiful intersubjectivity as an object of subjective taste. Montesquieu in his *Essai sur la gout* [*An Essay on Taste*, 1715] exemplifies what is meant. He states: "It is the various pleasures of our soul which shape the objects of taste, such as the beautiful ... The Ancients had not properly unraveled this. They saw as positive qualities those which are relative to our soul ... The sources of the Beautiful, the Good, of the Pleasant are thus in ourselves; and to look for the reason is to look for the cause of pleasures of our soul" - which because of our shared *communis sensus* corresponds to an objective reality.

apart from science of aesthetics or philosophy of art [Baumgarten's combining *episteme* and *aisthesis*] as epistemology of aesthetics?[3] This study suggests there is. Although epistemology of aesthetics has its modern origins in Baumgarten and Kant, it begins with attempts by Plato and Plotinus to define beauty[4] followed by Aristotle's insistence on epistemic fit: that epistemology addresses both general and particular knowledge claims.[5]

This study examines the roles judgment, imagination, and taste has in the apprehension of beauty. It also casts light on how Plotinus and Kant use aesthetic judgment, imagination, [and taste] to reconcile several ontological and epistemological dualisms inherited from Platonic thought. Inherent in this uneasiness with dualisms is an awareness of the limitations of thinking and language to formulate an adequate mapping of reality or being. Failure to formulate in language the relation between language and being results in a turn to aesthetics—not as a language of propositional and discursive sayings but of non-propositional and non-discursive images and silences. Since the philosophical, historical and philological studies on *phantasia* in Aristotle and Plotinus[6] and *Einbildungskraft* in Kant are immense and far reaching, we turn our attention to an aesthetic emerging.[7]

I. Horizons

It is a remarkable coincidence that the philosophical writings of both Plato and Plotinus take off with an analysis of beauty.[8] The *Symposium*,

---

3. Baumgarten, *Aesthetica*, Sec. I, 1.This notion is a novel one since previously knowledge begins when we have ceased to be influenced by sensible particulars and have grasped universals. It was not asked that I verify my aesthetic expectations as somehow universal nor was it thought that my particular experience of beauty was somehow a case for mapping a universal response to beauty – that in the particularity of my sensuous experience we somehow relate to a universal one. Minimally, the sensible in all its particularities only enters the scene as a case of a universal law of nature.

4. Plato, *Phaedrus*, 265d and 249b; *Symposium*, 201d-212c; *Republic*, 508a-509b; Plotinus, *Enneads*, I.6 and V.8.

5. Aristotle, *Nic. Eth.* I.3.

6. On *phantasia*, see Nyvlt, *Aristotle and Plotinus*, 165-186.

7. On *Einbildungskraft* see Cassirer, *Commentary*.

8. To study Plotinus on beauty is to risk telling in one's own words a story that has often been excellently told before. In vivid works, de Keyser and Rist brought Plotinus' theory of beauty to the attention of the historians of philosophy. cf. de Keyser, *La Signification*; Rist, *Plotinus*. The patient work of Anton, Armstrong, Horn, Moreau, O'Meara and Rich have increased and clarified the substantial dossier of Plotinus' philosophy of art in studies ranging from a critique of the theory of symmetry to the relation between beauty and the Good. cf. Anton, *Plotinus' Refutation of Beauty*, 233-237; and *Plotinus' Conception of the Functions of the Artist*, 91-101; Armstrong, *Beauty and the Discovery*

Republic, and *Phaedrus* are far from being the earliest of Plato's dialogues, but they are the first dialogues where we encounter a full-blown theory of Forms, the overwhelming presence of beauty at all levels of existence, and the coupling of Beauty with the Good. In the treatise *On Sensible Beauty*, the historian of philosophy is confronted with the peculiarity which runs through all of Plotinus' written work. He presents even his most original ideas, as often as not, as a mere repetition, or at least a mere explication, of what had already been said by Plato. The ironic problem is that he tells us no more than we have learnt from Plato, or worse still, that Plato's dialogues already contain, with varying degrees of explicitness, ideas that he will be put forward. Plotinus' theory of beauty is a particularly good case in point, since in the course of his long and sometimes rather rambling arguments, initially directed against the Stoics, Plotinus does incorporate several ideas taken from Plato. The problem lies not in simply identifying such ideas, but in learning how to appraise the radical differences which separate those ideas, when they are presented as part of Plato's "new-found" theory of beauty, and when they are made use of as part of Plotinus' very different philosophy of the experience of beauty.

For those of us with a Kantian aesthetic already a part of our mother's milk, Plotinus' analysis of the roles of judgment and imagination offered much to Kant's aesthetics as well. In the treatise *On Sensible Beauty*, the historian of philosophy is confronted with the peculiarity which runs through all of Plotinus' written work. He presents even his most original ideas, as often as not, as a mere repetition, or at least a mere explication, of what had already been said by Plato. The ironic problem is that he tells us no more than we have learnt from Plato, or worse still, that Plato's dialogues already contain, with varying degrees of explicitness, ideas that he will be put forward. Plotinus' theory of beauty is a particularly good case in point, since in the course of his long and sometimes rather rambling arguments, initially directed against the Stoics, Plotinus does incorporate several ideas taken from Plato. The problem lies not in simply identifying such ideas, but in learning how to appraise the radical differences which separate those ideas, when they are presented as part of Plato's "new-found" theory of beauty, and when they are made use of as part of Plotinus' very different philosophy of the experience of beauty.

---

of Divinity, 155-173; Horn, *Stoische Symmetrie und Theorie des Schoenen*, 1455-1471; O'Meara, *Plotinus*, 88-99; Moreau, *Origine et expressions du beau*, 249-263; Rich, *Plotinus and the Theory of Artistic Imitation*, 233-239.

II. Imagination and Memory

A helpful way into Plotinus's notion of the experience of beauty is to proceed from its initial manifestation in intelligible matter. Intelligible matter is defined as the potentiality of indefiniteness which contains no separation of otherness. It has these characteristics because the first effluence from the One is indefinitely infinite and contains opposites:

> ... and it could be imagined as either ... But if you approach any of it as one it will appear many; and if you say that it is many, you will be wrong again; for each [part] of it is not one, all of them cannot be many. And this nature of it according to one and the other of your imagination is movement, and, according as according as imagination has arrived at it rest. And the impossibility of seeing it by itself is movement from intellect and slipping away; but that it cannot run away but is held fast from outside and all around and is not able to go on, this would be its rest; so that it is only in motion.[9]

The shape or figure of images produced by the imagination is an approximation if not the shadows of the intelligible forms. Hence *phantasia* shares characteristics common to *Nous* and *Hule* but is distinct from either. Here Plotinus affirms two souls, the irrational and rational, within which *phantasia* functions in two distinct ways, one lower; the other higher.[10] Imagination is pivotal in his philosophy of mind for in its activity the sensible and intelligible realms converge whereby a transition occurs from consciousness to self-consciousness [or in more modern parlance from being conscious to consciousness]. The lower imagination apprehends and unifies sense data representing them in image form. Here sense-perception finds its end in imagination which associates sensible objects into an intelligible, unified object.[11] As such, imagination has the power to unify sensible impressions which are retained by memory and apprehended by mind. It is this apprehensive power [*antilepsis*] of imagination that triggers the emergence of awareness [*parakolouthein*].[12]

The higher imagination apprehends the ideas or forms in spatial images transforming indivisible entities into extended mental images.

9. Plotinus, *Ennead*, VI.6.3.33-43.]

10. Plotinus defines *phantasia* as both a single and double faculty. This is owed to his notion of procession and return where each lower stage is an image of the higher and that the lower is in the higher. cf. O'Meara, 26-27.

11. Here Plotinus follows Aristotle. cf. Plotinus, *Enneads*, IV.3.2924-27; IV.4.19.4-7; IV.7.6.10-11 and *De Anima*, 426b17-19.

12. Plotinus, *Ennead*, IV.4.13.3-17.

[*Ennead* IV.3.30.15-16] underscores the necessity of the ideas conversion to images as the conditions for the possibility of self-awareness and memory. Plotinus proposes that the activity of imagination in mind [*nous*], as distinct from in soul [*psuche*] is *logos*-intuitive.[13] *Logos* "accompanies the act of intelligence" [*Ennead* IV.3.30.6] we are told by unfolding its content into *phantasia* [imagination] which apprehends it and represents it as an image.[14] *Logos* does not represent the idea or concept in picture form as is the case with sensation. Rather this higher *phantasia* is an apprehension of the dynamics in Soul and fixes its object as an image, a process which results in self-consciousness—an upward gaze into the intelligible realm. Using a mirror metaphor, Plotinus claims that this activity of the imagination permits it by virtue of *logos* to apprehend the indivisible ideas or forms by making them spatial.[15] The metaphor is important for *phantasia* does not receive *logos* or the ideas directly. Receiving their expression it represents them through spatial images. At [*Ennead* I.4.2.25-27] Plotinus insinuates that this higher form of *logos-nous* is a capacity that judges.[16] Indeed, when gazing downward the faculty of imagination is that singular faculty that receives sensations and transmits the image of such objects to mind or intellect. Here imagination receives the ideas/forms and extends them into spatial ones as mental representations.[17]

Plotinus's duplication of imagination has its correlate in a duplication of memory.[18] *Phantasia* imagines through two image-making powers.[19] Lower memory is concerned with the memories of our passions and appetites and higher memory with soul's life in the intelligible world. Thus memory of temporal events belongs to the lower irrational soul, while those memories of ideas and forms are a prior activity common to the rational soul and preclude time.[20] This means that memory of ideas is a prior activity of soul, belonging to the higher or rational soul.[21] Moreover,

13. Following Nyvlt, *Aristotle and Plotinus*, 2012, 165-171.

14. Plotinus, *Ennead*, IV.3.30.8-12.

15. Following Blumenthal, *Plotinus' Psychology*, 1971, 88.

16. It is imaginations' *logos*-capacity for judgment that constitutes a crucial link between Plotinus's *phantasia* and Kant's *Einbildungskraft*.

17. This cyclical process is one of unification and multiplication

18. Plotinus, *Ennead*. IV. 3.25-27. Both souls have a memory *Ennead*. IV.4.31. cf. Helleman-Elgersma, *Soul-Sisters*.

19. Plotinus, *Ennead*, IV.3.31.1-3.

20. *Ennead*, IV.3.24.

21. It is this imaginative-memory activity that concerns the study which follows. Although each soul remembers in representational form, there are two corresponding forms of imagination for the activity of memory presupposes the activity of

souls [higher and lower] are what they are on the basis of memory which is dependent on their respective imaginations.

Plotinus offers a correlative theory of *phantasia* as dependent and independent living beings [*zoa*].[22] What is of significance here is that he asserts that *we* experience [as *Nous*] or perceive only one image when the two images, one from the higher and the lower, are harmonious. This unanimity of perception is due to the higher soul-imaginative faculty in images copying the higher. Both souls and their activities allow for a single image to occur.[23] This means while both faculties of *phantasia* are separate, the image produced in both souls is found through the act of imagining. Thus the imagining of the lower soul does not lose itself in the higher [or the shadow remains a shadow because of the light]. There is a transition from one level of souls and its imagining to another.[24] As we shall see, this "duplicity" re-emerges in Kant's distinction between images derived from *a posteriori* sense data and those constituted *a priori* by mind. Here the Kantian transition is from the imaginative reception sense data to its intelligibility. In both cases the duplicity of the imagination is conditioned by a fundamental harmony between the activities of both imaginations.

What is significant here is that self-awareness is a consequence of the imagination's imaging of sensibles and intelligibles and its co-operation with memory which has a *logos* center. As noted earlier, the activity in Mind [*Nous*] is intuitive or non-propositional-non-discursive. It is *logos* that "accompanies the act of intelligence" [*Ennead* IV.3.30.6] that makes mind [*nous*] discursive. The point is imagination is the unique mental faculty in which sensible, intelligible, psychic, and cosmic activities converge. Moreover, in *phantasia* a non-propositional-non-discursive language emerges which allows for a contemplation of the One which is a speechless image of the One.

Thirdly, two onto-logical distinctions from Leibniz and Kant: the *a priori/a posteriori* and *analytic/synthetic* distinctions are helpful. Aristotle offers an *a posteriori* image theory of meaning where the soul pictures simple *phantasmata* and then imagines and remembers such perceptions.[25] Plotinus adds an *a priori* image theory of meaning where the soul imagines ideas. Here we initially encounter both an *a priori* and an *a posteriori* synthetic operation of the imagination. This is complemented by a language theory of meaning within which there is an *a priori* synthetic process where

---

imagination. cf. *Ennead*. IV.3.31.1-3.

22. Plotinus, *Ennead*, IV.3.31.1-10.
23. *Ennead*, IV.3.31.3-7.
24. *Ennead*, IV.3.31.13-18.
25. Aristotle, *De Interpretatione*, I.16a-3-9; *De Anima*, III.8.

the soul imagines through memory, sensory images [*phantasmata*] and their affections [*pathemata*] and an *a posteriori* process where sensations are simply imaged. Meanings of words found in memories of external objects are intelligibly imagined, sensibly imaged, and remembered through a non-propositional language which frames and constitutes the activities of imagination non-discursively.[26] In such talk about mind's images and its imagination[s] is recognition of the limits of propositional mind and discursive language. Such a move toward thinking past thinking is justified in the case of Plotinus by the nature of thinking on thinking in *Nous* and in the case of Kant by his claim that mind knows only phenomena not noumena. Hence both require an instrument that allows intellect or reason to transcend the limits of propositional-discursive thought and language. They find it in the faculty of imagination.

Summary: Plotinus's lower soul images sensibles while the higher soul images the forms and the One. Here we witness a lower imaginative *a posteriori* synthetic process and a higher imaginative *a priori* synthetic and analytic process at work. Kant's *Einbildungskraft* combines aspects of both Aristotle's and Plotinus's *phantasia*. Sense, or imaging sensations refers to the operations common to the *a posteriori* or 'lower activities' of the imagination which simply pictures or images *particulars* or sense data. Meaning signifies the operations of the *a priori* or 'higher activities' of the imagination which pictures and imagines for Kant *universals* such as the beautiful and the sublime and for Plotinus a form such as beauty or even the One in speechless images. In thinking past thinking, aesthetic intuition becomes the ultimate clue to the meaning of Plotinus's *Nous*, Kant's *Vernunft* and Hegel's *Geist*. Such Minds begin as sheer intelligibility, thinking on thinking. Later recognizing not only the limits of thinking but of language, they attain in aesthetic self-awareness a vision of the ultimate nature of Mind [and the One] in a thinking past thinking. In that intuition, at once aesthetic and intellectual, mind speaks an imaginative language that articulates Mind [and images the One].

III. On Beauty

In the preliminaries to his analysis of beauty in *Ennead* I.6.[1].1-6, Plotinus includes not only perceptual beauty, which is the beauty of nature and art that

---

26. This second theory is proposed by Modrak in *Aristotle's Theory of Language and Meaning*. If plausible Aristotle's image and language theories of meaning underlie Plotinus's own in regard to the imaginative activities of the soul.

we see and hear, but also non-perceptual beauty, which are tied to the virtues and intellect. This opening is followed by a series of provocative questions:

> Very well then, what is it which makes us imagine [*phantazesthai*] that bodies are beautiful and attracts our hearing to sounds because of their beauty. And how are things which depend on soul beautiful . . . What are this principle, then, which is present in bodies? We ought to consider this first. What is it that attracts the gaze of those who look at something, and turns and draws them to it and makes them enjoy the sight? If we find this perhaps we can use it as a stepping-stone and get a sight of the rest.[27]

Now the sheer range and detail of Plato's theory of beauty are overwhelming and cannot be examined here. What can be focused upon is Plotinus' interpretation of Plato's theory of beauty. Plotinus praises Plato because he treats beauty as a complex psychological reaction.[28] But he also tacitly corrects him: first, when he argues that beauty is not limited to sensible particulars alone but beauty is also in those particulars' intelligible archetypes; and secondly, when he reflects on the experience of beauty in the activities of judgment and imagination.

What is distinctive in Plotinus is that he takes the experience of beauty and extends it far beyond what Plato originally proposed. First, he claims that imagination and judgment are key players in the complex psychological reaction to beauty.[29] Secondly, he attributes an onto-genetic capacity to beauty. Once the soul experiences beauty, she brings higher [sensible and intelligible] worlds into existence.

Plotinus begins the discussion of such possibilities by proposing:

> So then the beautiful body comes into being by sharing in a formative power which comes from the divine forms.[30]

Next, he associates the beautiful body, which shares a power that comes from the intelligible world, with the power of judgment:

> The power ordained for the purpose recognizes this, and there is nothing more effective for judging its own subject-matter, when the rest of the soul judges along with it; or perhaps the rest of the soul too pronounces the judgment by fitting the beautiful body

---

27. Plotinus, *Ennead*, I.6.1.7-20.
28. Plato, *Symposium* 210ac; *Hippias major* 297e-298b.
29. Plotinus, *Ennead.*, I.6.1.7-20.
30. Plotinus, *Ennead*, I.6.2.28-29..

to the form in itself and using this for judging beauty as we use a ruler for judging straightness.[31]

In brief, the soul, the founding principle of the whole aesthetic enterprise, is not a phenomenal entity to be added to the objects it sees and hears. Rather it brings beautiful objects to presence and so moves in a different sphere altogether. That is to say, the soul is not only a phenomenon in the world. She brings a transcendent viewpoint to the things of the world in the very act of judging objects beautiful:

> But how do the bodily agree with that which is before body? How does the architect declare the house outside beautiful by fitting it to the form of house within him? . . . When sense perception . . . sees the form in bodies binding and mastering the nature opposed to it, which is shapeless . . . [the soul] brings it back and takes it in, now without parts, to the soul's interior and presents it to that which is within as something in tune with it and fitting it and dear to it . . . And the simple power of color comes about by shape and the mastery of the darkness in matter by the presence of light which is incorporeal and formative power and form . . . the melodies in sounds too, the imperceptible ones which make the perceptible ones, make the soul conscious of beauty in the same way.[32]

It is important to note that Plotinus proposes a division between two kinds of judgment: one perceptive [or aesthetic], another cognitive [or rational]. Although this is novel itself, the true originality of his position lies in the notion of interplay between judgment and imagination in the perception of beauty. He appears to argue that the only context within which perceptive judgment is properly meaningful is when the soul grasps the unified totality of the intelligible world with the assistance of imagination.[33]

Perceptive judgment, and the imaginative insight that accompanies it, makes the soul conscious of beauty. Such consciousness is born of a free association within the soul of these two powers. Once the soul focuses upon a sight or sound she judges and imagines them as beautiful, thereby making them and herself beautiful.

This association or free play between judgment and imagination has significant consequences. The beautiful object offers a reconciliation of the sensible and intelligible worlds, even of sensibility and concepts [eide]. This means the beautiful object grasped through the activity of judgment and

31. Plotinus, *Ennead*, I.6.3.1-5.
32. Plotinus, *Ennead*, I.6.3.5-30
33. Plotinus, *Ennead*, IV.3.29-31.

imagination is an instantiation of the whole realm of the Ideas. Indeed, a beautiful sight or sound is a symbolic trace of the One:

> ... when it sees something akin to it or a trace of its kindred reality, it is delighted and thrilled and returns to itself and remembers itself and its possessions.[34]

Plotinus suggests the experience of beauty not only constitutes a primary realm of human experience, but that the judgment itself is a non-cognitive one. The first proposition emerges when he argues that becoming beautiful enables one to approach the source of all beauty, the One.[35] He tells us that the pursuit of beauty is the pursuit of true being, and its source, the One or the Good.[36] The second suggestion appears when he proposes the artist creates beauty with a serene lack of consciousness. The artist is unable to articulate the rules of his own creation because he works at the behest of higher and deeper forces beyond and within himself.[37] That is to say, the experience of beauty fundamentally surpasses merely cognitive "horizons" of meaning.

This leads Plotinus to the position that the experience of beauty is not confined to empirical subjectivity alone. The beautiful object rests on the presence of forms, which awaken in the soul an awareness of the source of all beauty, the One. Hence, when we become conscious of beauty there is no longer any distinction for us between the sensible and the intelligible, intuition and concept, the particular and the universal. Indeed, the experience of beauty brings into reality an imaginative reconciliation of the sensible and the intelligible. The soul acquires a point of view upon the world which a divine understanding would have.[38]

How does this point of view come about? The rational and perceptive souls each have their own imaginative power. It is through the free interplay between perceptive judgment and imagination that the soul represents beauty to consciousness "as though in a mirror."[39] Briefly, *aisthesis* is nothing more than the lower soul becoming conscious of what the higher soul eternally beholds. *Phantasia* is nothing more than the presentation to the lower soul of an *antilepsis*, or sensuous perception, which permits her to identify her empirical self with her pure, true self that transcends the

---

34. Plotinus, *Ennead*, I.6.2.9-12
35. Plotinus, *Ennead*, I.6.9.7-12.
36. Plotinus, *Ennead*, I.6.7.
37. Plotinus, *Ennead*, I.6.9.
38. Plotinus, *Ennead*, I.6.2.1-12.
39. Plotinus, *Ennead*, I.6.2.1-12.

sensible. As a result of the experience of beauty the soul gains the capacity to establish unforeseen imaginative relations with the world of Ideas, and perhaps, even the One itself.[40]

Pursuing Plotinus' insights further, it appears that he proposes that the judgment of beauty is not based solely on determinate forms and concepts [or rules]. For example, when the soul perceives a beautiful object, she associates matter with form. However, association is not regulated by a concept for the interplay of judgment and imagination is quite free in that it obeys no prescribed cognitive rule. Indeed, it is impossible to "argue" about beauty as if it were a cognitive judgment. The reason for this is that even Primary Beauty itself is formless.[41] Two insights emerge here worth noting. First, experience of the beautiful is in little way cognitive, but it, nonetheless, has about it the form and structure of the rational. Plotinus describes aesthetic judgment as a kind of free-wheeling of the soul's judgmental and imaginative faculties. Aesthetic judgment is an undecidable half-way house between the uniform laws of cognition and utter indeterminacy. Secondly, what we have here is a fusion of judgment, imagination, and teleology.

Plotinus proposes the consoling thought of a world that is not after all indifferent to us, which has a regard for our mental capacities. Experience of the beautiful unites us with intellect, the ideas, and the One, but at an affective, intuitive level.[42] What brings souls together is knowledge, but perhaps more importantly, an ineffable reciprocity with beauty which is dispersed everywhere.[43] Significantly, he also suggests that the soul is at least partially modeled on a self-referential conception of beauty. If the soul is to flourish she has to extend her colonizing sway over things beautiful and stamp them with her indelible presence.[44] Indeed, when the soul finds herself in judgment of beauty, she exercises a curious form of inter-subjectivity, onto-genetically establishing within herself a link to the beautiful community of Ideas, and perhaps even through the Ideas a bridge to the One.[45]

For Plotinus then, some of the pleasure of the beautiful arises from a quick sense of the world's teleological conformity to our capacities.[46] In the experience of beauty, judgment and imagination create a purposive synthesis between soul and reality. A soul is home in the world because

---

40. Plotinus, *Ennead*, I.6.2.1-12.
41. Plotinus, *Ennead*, VI.7.33.37-38.
42. Plotinus, *Ennead*, I.6.2.28-29.
43. Plotinus, *Ennead*, VI.7.3.9-10.
44. Plotinus, *Ennead*, I.6.6.27-33.
45. Plotinus, *Ennead*, I.6.2.1-17.
46. Plotinus, *Ennead*, I.6.6.13-18; 27-33.

the world is designed to suit her aesthetic capacities.[47] Whether this is actually true or not, Plotinus cannot say, since we can know nothing of what the One is like in itself. That the soul's experience of beauty fits reality must remain a hypothesis but it is the kind of heuristic fiction which permits us a sense of purposiveness, centeredness, and significance beyond all theoretical demonstration.[48]

This is so because Plotinus had an acute sense of crisis in the multiplicity of reality and the chain of intermediaries that reached from soul to the One.[49] Beauty, and the experience of beauty functioned to erase the distinctions between the layers of the soul, and brought the ontologically distant, aesthetically present. It is, perhaps, accurate to say that for Plotinus beauty brings that which is transcendent and intelligibly distant, immanent and sensibly present. It may even be that the experience of beauty is about the joining of heaven and earth in the human soul herself.[50]

With Plotinus metaphysics and aesthetics are analogous. The soul is separated, only to be unified, in the experience of beauty. The soul inhabits simultaneously two spheres in which everything beautiful in the "One" is beautiful in the other.[51] Ultimately, then, Platonic mimesis fulfills itself with new meaning. Beauty no longer looks to the Ideas alone to make it anew. The Ideas no longer provide the only exemplary model for beauty to follow. The beautiful soul offers her own judgmental, imaginative, even exemplary model.[52] Yet, remarkably, the source to which she responds seems to be the same one to which beauty has always responded—the One.[53]

Now, there are degrees of beauty relative to the One, Mind, Soul, and Matter, and many ways of grasping beauty relative to an entity's metaphysical place or status in reality. In

[*Ennead* I.6.1] Plotinus explains how sensible beauty is encountered and experienced from the eidos or "perspective" of the embodied, sensible soul.[54]

Now from one point of view you might think that this was a fairly innocuous addition to Plato's argument, hardly more, really, than an

---

47 Plotinus, *Ennead*, I.6.9.7-12.

48. Plotinus, *Ennead*,I.6.2.9-12.

49. This was brought about by the Gnostic threat. cf. Plotinus, *Ennead*, II.8; V.8; V.5; II.9.

50. Plotinus, *Ennead.*, VI.7.3.9-10; I.6.6.13-33.

51. Plotinus, *Ennead*, I.6.2.28-29; I.6.3.1-5.

52. Plotinus, *Ennead*, I.6.6.13-18.

53. Plotinus, *Ennead*, I.6.9.40-45.

54. For the perspectives from the vantage point of intelligible beauty see Plotinus, *Ennead*, V.8.[31]; and from the One see *Ennead*, VI.7.[38].

explication of a series of ideas that Plato already put foward. But this simple step, within the framework of the Enneads, is not at all as simple as it might seem at first blush. Plotinus' soul does not derive its existence from itself. Rather soul, like Intellect, derives her existence from the One.

To quote only one sample passage from a much latter treatise, entitled by Porphyry as On the Knowing Hypostases, Plotinus writes:

> How is it that the One is the principle of all things? It is because it perceives them, having made each of them to be one [hen hekaston auton poiesasa einai]? It is also that it has brought them into existence [hupestesen auta].[55]

The One perceives and brings all things, including souls into existence, because:

> What comes to be, turned back upon the One, and was filled, and came to be by looking at the One. And this is intellect.[56]

Plotinus continues:

> Its standing toward the One made being. Its gazing towards the One made Intellect.[57]

He explains:

> Since it stood towards the One in order to see the One, it becomes at once Intellect and being.[58]

We are then told that the same is true of the production of soul from Intellect:

> Intellect pours forth much power.[59]

> This activity from the substance of Intellect—this belongs to soul.[60]

> The soul, therefore, looking back to Intellect, the Intellect from which it came to be is filled.[61]

---

55. Plotinus, *Ennead*, V.3.[49] 15.27-29.
56. Plotinus, *Ennead*, V.2 [11] 1.7-9.
57 Plotinus, *Ennead*, V.2 [11] 1.9.
58. Plotinus, *Ennead*, V.2 [11] 1.12-13.
59. Plotinus, *Ennead*, V.2.[11] 1.14.
60. Plotinus, *Ennead*, V.2 [11] 1.16.
61. Plotinus, *Ennead*, V.2 [11] 1.19-20.

The citations just quoted are dangled like pearls on a string. So much so that they hardly bear the weight of commentary heaped upon them by modern readers of Plotinus. My concern here is with two features of his description. First, is Plotinus' use of Platonic 'spectator imagery' such as "looking, "gaze" sight," to characterize the soul's ascent to Intellect and the One. The second is the use of Aristotelian terms such as "power" and "activity" to describe the ability of the soul to grasp Intellect and the One. With both in mind, let me ask one very simple question. How does soul turn back to the One?

The answer to this question lies in the soul's ability to judge beautiful objects, and imagine their relationship to the Idea of Beauty, and the One. The soul is only fulfilled when she looks upon beautiful things, and when she looks back, of herself, towards the Intellect from which she has sprung, she visualizes the form of Beauty itself, which itself is a "speechless image of the One."

At this point Plotinus can say that the soul aesthetically exists of herself, for without turning upon herself in the experience of the beautiful, and hence back to the Idea of Beauty, and the One, the soul would not be soul, since it would not be fulfilled by beauty. Indeed, if the soul were not fulfilled by looking inward, and hence backward, what would she be? She would have neither existence nor being. There are thus two 'moments' in the aesthetics of the soul: an awareness of beauty and a turning back on reflection of beauty to the soul's source in Intellect and the One. It is because of this duality that Plotinus can claim both that the soul exists when she experiences beauty, and that when she experiences beauty, she "sees things together in respect of the One,' as a "speechless image of the One."

In the first half of the third century, we find ourselves caught up in an unfolding crisis still incomplete. In a way, Plotinus had a heady impulse to "aestheticize" reality. I say "heady" because as a "systematic" yet "revolutionary" philosopher he fractured the foundations of earlier Platonic "aesthetics."[62] The results were a new late-classical aestheticism. Bit by bit, the static framework of the noetic world on which Platonic metaphysics rested was dismantled. The ineffaceable character of forms and gods, which earlier Platonists saw as the ultimate justification of a *mimesis* between the intelligible and sensible worlds, between intelligibility and sensibility has been dissolved in the apprehension of beauty. Plotinus views such experiential *mimesis* as imagining form. This usually occurs when *Nous* is confronted by the mute, yet profoundly familiar Pythagorean harmonies of form in color and sound. Later beauty is present in things whenever it succeeds

---

62. On these terms see Rorty, *Mirror of Nature*, 365-372.

in representing to the soul a configuration, an order of unity in tension, perhaps a world of its own experience of the One in miniature.

Nous thinks the One by thinking past thinking by appealing to images which hold an intermediary place between Mind and Soul. This heightens the status of images to intelligible objects [*ta noeta*] which "are satisfied with themselves by their participation in or imagination of the Good."[63] This means that imagining and speaking of or about the One takes "place" in "no place." *Phantasia* as intelligible matter is related to both non-being, a being which is beyond being, and to being or being as thinking. In Plotinus's peculiar way where imagination "thinks" takes place in a potential "place" or a place that has the potentiality of becoming defined [like the *chora* of *Tim.* 52a]. It is an empty receptacle that receives entities.[64] Thus there is the place where images of the One are pictured quasi-spatially.[65] This place or *chora* is in intelligible matter and its products are both physical entities and geometrical figures generated by imagination. It follows that *phantasia*'s imaginative images of the One would be multiple, irrational, intermediary [offer shifting images between the One, forms, sensibles, and matter], and they lack definition. They are ambiguously Here and There as images of fluctuating forms[66] and as images of Plotinus's Transcendentals—the Same and the Other.[67]

Is it possible for *Nous* to think itself and the One? Yes but only within the context of the relationship between *phantasia* and intelligible matter. As noted earlier, characterized as the potentiality of indefiniteness which contains no separation of otherness, intelligible matter is the first effluence from the One.[68] Plotinus's higher imagination has access to intelligible matter and then images shadows of the intelligible forms after which further images are modeled.[69] Consequently, *phantasia* has characteristics it shares with both Mind and intelligible matter although it is distinct from both in that it is the locus of quasi-extended mental images which picture or represents it as a plurality of intelligibles expressed in images.

---

63. Plotinus, *Ennead*, VI.8.13.46. cf. Nikunin, *Intelligible Matter in Plotinus*, 85-114. esp. 97.

64. Plotinus, *Ennead*, VI.6-9.

65. Nikunin, *Intelligible Matter*, 98.

66. For an excursus on imaginative ambiguity see, Nikunin, *Intelligible Matter*, 108.

67. See chapter six.

68. Plotinus, *Ennead*, VI.6.3.33-43.

69. See, Nikulin, *Intelligible Matter*, 96. Nyvlt, *Aristotle and Plotinus*, 174-176.

How such images are expressed by *Nous* is non-propositional and non-discursive. What such images are is described superbly by Stephen Gersh.[70]

> ... what follows as a sequence of linguistic prescriptions corresponding not to the temporal interruption of a proposition's enunciation but to certain formulae which have a relation to propositions analogous to similes which metaphors have ... this elliptical relation constitutes a psycho-linguistic expression of Intellect's thinking of Intellect and Intellect's thinking of the One.[71]

> This something higher is not the temporal interruption of proposition's enunciation nor is it captured by the relation between intention and extension. Rather we would suggest that it is something ultimately inexpressible which however can be indicated by an analogy: namely, just as a metaphor is an elliptical version of a simile, so is this something an elliptical version of a proposition.[72]

In [*Ennead* V.8.6.1-13] Plotinus proposes the pictorial analogy of hieroglyphic writing to express what such non-propositional thinking in images looks like. He also offers another analogy that assists in picturing such language. This time his focus is on how Mind thinks the One.

Plotinus initially explains this thinking past thinking within the context of what thinking on thinking the One is all about.

> We first assume a space and place [*choran kai topon*], a Kind of vast openness [*chaos*], and then, when the space is already There we bring this nature into that place which has to be or is in our Imagination, and bringing it into this kind of place, we inquire in this Way as if into whence and how it came here, and as if it was a stranger we have asked about its [One's] presence and, in a way, its substance, really just as if we thought that it had been thrown up from some depth or down from some high.[73]

Aristotle said—and when do we encounter a truth in Plotinus that is not already found in Aristotle?—that a proper work is one where there is neither too little nor too much, nothing in excess and nothing missing.[74] This is a simple but difficult measure for beauty for the soul now provides a

---

70. See, Gersh, *Neoplatonism After Derrida*, 163-168. Also see Rappe, *Non-Discursive Thinking*.
71. Rappe, *Non-Discursive Thinking*, 168.
72. Rappe, *Non-Discursive Thinking*, 164.
73. Plotinus, *Ennead*, VI.8.11.15-22.
74. Aristotle, *Nic. Ethics*, 1106b9.

speechless image of beauty. To be "speechless" does not mean that beauty has nothing to say. On the contrary, the speechlessness of beauty is really a kind of speech. It is a rich, colorful, and resplendent language whose light brightly, clearly and fluently, shines out from the One which is the:

> ... spring and origin of beauty.[75]

Summary: If we were to ask Plotinus to account for beauty—that "speechlessness" which addresses us so forcefully with its unique mute eloquence—his answer might be—such speechlessness is really a kind of speech for:

> ... no eye ever saw the sun without becoming sun-like,
> nor can a soul see beauty without becoming beautiful.[76]

Such an elliptical proposition and simile make no sense within the strictly logical sphere. They do so within the aesthetic realm where the declarative, imperative, and expressive functions of language overlap. Here Plotinus has clearly passed from thinking propositionally and discursively to thinking non-propositionally and non-discursively at the levels of Mind and Mind thinking the One. Kant offers a similar 'aesthetic turn'.

IV. An Aesthetic Turn

Kant assumed that Plato [and Plotinus] had traditionally subordinated phenomena to the intelligible world, and by means of the participation of the sensible in the intelligible, the relationship between the *phenomena* and *noumena* is explained. This contrast between the phenomenal and the noumenal explains the gulf Kant postulated between nature and the unknowable realm of freedom, the opposition between matter and form, sense and reason, chaotic material and organizing structure of the understanding.[77] Finally for Kant, the noumenal world, like the One of Plotinus, is shut off and inaccessible to propositional-discursive knowledge and language. Indeed, Kant refused to employ "transcendental deduction" to

---

75. Plotinus, *Ennead*, I.6.9.40-45. cf. Plato, *Phaedrus*, 245c9.

76. Plotinus, *Ennead*, I.6.9.30-33. Cf. Plato, *Republic*, VI 508b3; 509a1.

77. It is unlikely that Kant read Plotinus. What he knew of Plotinus was largely derived from Leibniz who knew Neoplatonism as well as any early modern philosopher. This is most clear in that for each of them knowledge is not the passive effect of experience, describing and reproducing it in a copy, but knowledge, even knowledge of beauty, is an active organization and interpretation of experience. This is because each took this world as possessing an objective structure which reason expresses in its own language. In their own way, Plotinus and Kant viewed knowledge [of beauty] as a human rendering of divine "intelligibility".

derive all the lower terms of the antithesis from the higher—until he wrote the *Critique of Judgment*.[78]

Kant regarded the third critique as his masterpiece of reconciliation. He was quite aware of the difficulties created by the antithesis of his several dualisms. This is why he tested the rigidity and absoluteness he had insisted upon in the *Critique of Pure Reason* later in the *Critique of Judgment*. He did this in the following ways. First, he examined the interplay of reason and sense outside the realm of universal and necessary scientific knowledge. As a result he brought together several issues usually regarded as quite distinct. These are the rational elements in science that are not universal and necessary, and elude deductive form and demonstrative certainty, the methods of empirical investigation with their hypotheses and regulative principles, and their relation to the a priori assumptions of the understanding.

Secondly, he raised again the problem he had contemplated in 1772 in his *Inaugural Dissertation*. In the third critique he examines the aesthetic principles of taste determining the beautiful and the sublime, and he reviews the question of the teleological and organic concepts which the treatment of living creatures demands. In brief, Kant links together diverse problems such as scientific hypotheses, of art and taste, and of teleology in the biological realm, as all belonging to the faculty of judgment.

Kant in his reflections on beauty invites us to reverse the traditional relation that exists between finiteness and the Absolute. In its apprehension of beauty the soul begins with finitude, or the beautiful object, and dialectically "goes up" toward the Absolute, or beauty. The soul is able to do this because of the activity judgment, imagination, and taste play in the apprehension and conceptualization of beauty. The consequences of Kant's reformulation are significant. Sensibility is not denigrated in favor of the intelligible or intelligibility. Most importantly, the soul is able to perceive the intelligible aesthetically through reflective judgment which is a free association of the imagination and the understanding. In sum, sensible access to intelligibility is aesthetically justified by both.

Judgment, for Kant, like the *doxa* of the *Theaetetus*, is the application of rules to individual instances:

---

78. The text and translation of Kant's *Critique of Judgment* are C. Meredith tr. Oxford: 1952, and Bernard tr. London: 1914. The German text utilized is I. Kant, *Kritik der Urteilskraft*, Philosophische Bibliothek Band 39a. Felix Meiner Verlag, Hamburg: 1974.

Studies on Kant's *Critique of Judgment* are too extensive to list. Those that merit attention include two in the Neo-Kantian tradition of exegesis. Cohen, *Aesthetik des reinen Gefuels*; Cassirer, *Commentary on Kant's Critique of Judgment*; and Natorp, *Platons Ideenlehre*.

> Judgment in general is the faculty of thinking the particular as contained under the universal... For all faculties or capacities of the soul can be reduced to three, which cannot be further derived from one common ground: the faculty of knowledge, the feeling of pleasure and pain, and the faculty of desire. For the faculty of knowledge, the understanding alone is legislative... For the faculty of desire, the reason alone is alone a priori legislative. Now between the faculties of knowledge and desire there is the feeling of pleasure, just as the Judgment is intermediate between the understanding and reason. We may therefore suppose provisionally that the Judgment likewise contains in itself an a priori principle. And as pleasure or pain is necessarily combined with the faculty of desire... we may also suppose that the Judgment will bring about a transition from the pure faculty of knowledge, the realm of natural concepts, to the realm of the concept of freedom, just as in its logical use it makes possible the transition from understanding to reason.[79]

This transition is Kant's supreme problem of reconciliation. It is his attempt to develop a theory in the critical philosophy that is analogous to the doctrine of intermediaries and of participation in the intelligible proposed by Plato and Plotinus.[80]

Kant examines the faculty of Judgment to discover whether when the mind deals with the multiplicity of individuals and particular relations, it is guided by any general principles. Nature has many concrete forms, all of which illustrate the universal structure of the categories, though they are not completely determined by it. Following Leibniz he connected geometry with the realm of *aistheta*. In the *Critique of Pure Reason* Kant describes the soul as a generatrix which "gives birth to" [*hervorbringen*] mathematical truths as the geometer must bring forth what was necessarily implied in the concepts and geometrical figures constructed. Thus, reason allows the natural scientist to generate a plan of his own to put Nature to the test:

> die Vernunft in ihrem Schosse allein diese Ideen selbst erzeugt hat [Reason has begotten her ideas in her womb alone].[81]

The procreative function of reason allows not only the soul-geometer to create a mathematical world but it also the soul-artist to imagine a beautiful world. Here Kant makes imagination central to the sensibility of knowing [or *aisthesis*]. He argues that imagination provides a schema or

---

79 Kant, *Critique of Judgment*, Bernard, tr., 17, 15-16.

80. Kant, *CJ*, V. 182.

81. Kant, *Kritik der Reinen Vernunft*, 1971. Bxii.

template for synthetically generating a multiplicity from a single representative object.[82] Thus, the individual figure constructed by the imagination is a schema, a temporal representative that unifies sensible images of the model so they conform to a unifying concept. The importance of Kant's formulation is that *aistheta* and *noeta* are no longer thought of as two separate realms, but as two aspects of the same reality. This position clearly concurs with that of Plotinus.

Kant invites us to reverse the relation that exists between finiteness and the Absolute. He begins in finitude and goes up to the Absolute. The metaphysical pretension to know the ultimate essence of reason, to demonstrate God's existence, or experience the beautiful is relativized in relation to the initial affirmation of the sensible condition which is the foundation of human consciousness. The significance of this fact is that it is no longer possible to relativize sensual knowledge as a lesser type of knowledge in comparison to intelligible knowledge. This results in autonomy for aesthetics. It is because knowledge is always tied to sensible intuition that sense-based knowledge finally acquires legitimacy. Kant pursues the consequences of this in the "Transcendental Aesthetic" in the *Critique of Pure Reason* when he goes from the "Aesthetic" to the "Dialectic and back again in his analysis of space and time as non-conceptual, as sensible and intuitive in character.

The details of Kant's analysis of space and time in the Critique of Pure Reason stand outside the scope of this paper. Nonetheless, it does frame the horizon of his analysis of aesthetic subjectivity in the *Critique of Judgment*. Here Kant focuses on "reflection" and offers an almost Plotinian distinction between determinant and reflective judgements, between judgements of cognition and judgements of taste which are "reflective" judgements.

> Judgment in general is the faculty of thinking the particular as contained under the universal. If the universal [the rule, principle, of law] is given, then the judgment which subsumes the particular under it is a determinant. [This is so even where such a judgment is transcendental and thereby provides the conditions *a priori* in conformity with which alone subsumption under that universal can be carried out.] If, however, only the particular is given and the universal has to be found for it, then the judgment is simply reflective.[83]

Aesthetic judgements are based on the passive receptivity of the mind. They state the way the mind is affected by the sensible forms of the products of

---

82. Kant, *KrV*, B177/A138-B181/A142.
83. Kant, *CJ*, Introduction, #4.

nature or of art, and the effect of purpose or organic harmony they exert upon the senses.

On the basis of this distinction Kant turns attention to beauty. The idea of beauty is not a part of our knowledge of objects but is concerned with the relation of objects to the observer, and the pleasure they generate in the mind. Aesthetic judgements are very different from those of science. They are not "objective" but "subjective" or relative to our own intellectual powers.[84] They are also "free" in that they are not determined by the concept that is employed in knowing the object, but only by its sensible form. They are also not like practical judgements for they are "disinterested."[85] Indeed, the relation of the beautiful object to any purposes of ours is irrelevant:

> Everyone must admit that a judgment about beauty, in which the least interest mingles, is very partial and is not a pure judgment of taste. We must not be in the least prejudiced in favor of the existence of things, but be quite indifferent in this respect, in order to play the judge in things of taste.[86]

Furthermore, the objects of aesthetic judgment are always individual. The faculty of judgment considers reflectively the individual object in relation to us and without adjusting it to our desires, our practical concerns, or our rules for knowing. It is an expression of our immediate experience. In nuce, beauty cannot be reduced to the agreeable or the good. It is a wholly disinterested pleasure.[87]

Such pleasure initially arises in judgements we make in contemplation of nature:

> Thus the principle of Judgment, in respect of the form of things of nature under empirical laws generally, is the purposiveness of nature in manifoldness. That is, nature is represented by means of this concept, as if some understanding contained the ground of the unity of the manifold of its empirical laws.[88]

Purposiveness or unity in the order of nature arouses in the soul a feeling of pleasure. This pleasure is subjective or aesthetic because it is not an objective element in our knowledge.[89]

---

84. Kant, *CJ*, 84.
85. Kant, *CJ*, 55.
86. Kant, *CJ*, 47-48.
87. Kant, *CJ*, 55.
88. Kant, *CJ*, 19.
89. Kant, *CJ*, 24.

> If pleasure is bound up with the mere apprehension of the form of an object of intuition, without reference to a concept for a definite cognition, then the representation is thereby not referred to the object, but simply to the subject, and the pleasure can express noting else than its harmony with the cognitive faculties which come into play in the reflective judgment... Now in this comparison the imagination as the faculty of a priori intuitions, is placed by means of a given representation undesignedly in agreement with the understanding, as the faculty of concepts, and thus a feeling of pleasure is aroused, the object must then be regarded as purposive for the reflective judgment... The object is then called "beautiful," and the faculty of judging by means of such a pleasure, and consequently with universal validity, is called taste.[90]

Here purposiveness has two aspects for Kant. As the harmony of the sensible form of the object with man's cognitive faculties, the pleasure that results is the ground for judging an object beautiful. As the harmony of that form with the concept itself, there follows no pleasure, but the idea of a final cause or teleology.

On the basis of this Kant, like Plotinus, regards natural beauty as the presentation of formal or subjective purposiveness, and natural purposiveness as the presentation of the concept of objective purposiveness. The former we judge by taste, aesthetically; the latter by understanding and reason, logically. This distinction allows Kant to speak of aesthetical and teleological judgment. The former is the faculty of judging the formal purposiveness of nature by means of pleasure or pain. The latter is real or objective purposiveness by means of understanding or reason.[91]

Beauty is based upon the feeling of pleasure, and upon immediacy. Although such feeling varies from individual to individual, Kant claims the structure of this aesthetic experience is common to every man. Pleasure is not found in the constitution of objects themselves, but in the way they act upon the mind and its powers.

The feeling of pleasure that leads us to call a thing beautiful is generated by the operation of the object upon the free play of the imagination and understanding it stimulates. Moreover, the universality of judgements of beauty comes from the formal relation of harmony and proportion it sets in motion in the human mind. Hence, the formal structure of aesthetic judgment is universal, but it is "subjectively" universal. It resides in the nature of the experiencer rather that in what is objectively experienced.

90 *Kant, CJ*, 31ff.
91. Kant, *CJ*, 36.

Beauty is the reconciliation of sensibility and intelligibility or concepts, and of nature and spirit.[92] This agreement of the sensible and intellectual faculties, caused by reflection on a beautiful object, also functions to bring into reality those ideas of reason which symbolize the reconciliation of the sensible and the intelligible. These ideas of reason include God, Freedom, and the Moral Law.

Kant appears to agree with Plotinus here. He sees in the Beautiful a symbolic "trace" of the Idea of Reason just as Plotinus sees in the Beautiful a symbolic "trace" of the One. Why this is so is that for Kant taste rests on the presence of an object which, if it is beautiful, awakens a necessary idea of reason common to humanity. The judgment of taste is not based on determinate concepts [or rules]. Nor is it confined to the pure empirical subjectivity of feeling. Borrowing Husserl's formula that taste grounds "transcendence" [objectivity and intersubjectivity] within "immanence" [without "exiting from" representations].

The judgment of taste does so because it participates in two types of association: the empirical subjective association and the conceptual objective association. The purely empirical type of association carries subjective meaning while the objective type of association, which presupposes the intervention of a concept, carries objective meaning. Kant argues that the judgment of taste participates in both without becoming identical with either. He claims that the feeling of beauty and the aesthetic pleasure that accompanies it are born of a "free" association of the imagination. When there is a perception of a beautiful object, the imagination, which is the most powerful sensible faculty, associates images without their regulation by a concept.

This free and contingent agreement between the imagination and understanding allows us to actualize a reconciliation of the sensible and intelligible corresponding to the point of view a divine understanding would have upon the world. There is an "expansion of the object," as Kant puts it that corresponds to an "expansion of the subject." The result is the subject ceases to be contained within the narrow frontiers of monadical egoism and arrives at the sphere of "the common sense." That is to say, an entirely intelligible world is realized in aesthetic reflection.

> Under the *sensus communis* we must understand the idea of sense common to all, that is, a faculty of judgment, that in its reflection takes into account in thoughts [a priori] everyone else's mode of representation, in order simultaneously to maintain its judgment within the whole of human reason, and thereby to escape the illusion that, stemming from subjective private

---

92. Kant, *CJ*, 201.

conditions which could easily be taken as objective, would have a disadvantageous influence on judgment.[93]

The reflective faculty of judgment as "expanded thinking" is to: "An der Stelle jedes anderen denken"; "To think in every other one's place" is to experience the *sensus communis*. Kant argues that neither dogmatic rationalism or empiricism aim at this common sense. The expansion of reflection that generates a common sense is conceived of in reference to reason but this reason is not determinate in any way. Rather it is indeterminate. It is the indeterminate Idea of an agreement of the sensible imagination and understanding—an Idea evoked by the emergence of natural or genial beauty. The expansion of reflection that generates a common sense is also conceived of in reference to feeling. But in contrast to what happens empirically such feeling is not to be confused with sympathy.

> The property man possesses of being able to judge the particular only in the universal is sentiment. Sympathy is entirely different: it has only to do with the particular . . . [in sympathy] we do not at all put ourselves in the Idea, but in the place of others [as simply empirical beings and not as humanity in general].[94]

Kant proposes the transcendental conditions of the possibility of a truly subjective aesthetic common sense. In the *sensus communis* particular sentiments are linked to a universal idea as operated by reflection. In this sense the common sense is itself a symbolic trace of Ideas whose results are a non-conceptually grounded communication between individuals.

Beauty for Kant, as it was for Plotinus, is a formal matter. It is the proportion, harmony, conformity, and unity in variety that generate aesthetic pleasure. The difference with Plotinus is also clear. Kant's is a "critical" formalism, locating these objects in man rather than in natural objects or Ideas. An object is judged beautiful because of the way it causes our mental powers of imagination and understanding to function.

The concrete meaning of Kant's aesthetics is clear. Through the object of a private and intimate feeling mediated by the judgment of taste, beauty awakens the Ideas of Reason present in every man and woman. The experience of beauty allows us to transcend private subjectivity and bring forth a common sense. The Ideas "awakened" by the beautiful object in common sense are common to all humanity because the beautiful object is simultaneously purely sensible yet intellectual. What we encounter in the experience

---

93. Kant, *CJ*, 40.

94. Kant, *Gesammelte Schriften*. hrsg. von der Koeniglichen Preussischen Akademie der Wissenschaften. *Kant Kritik der reinen Vernunft*, 342 = 782.

of beauty is a reconciliation of nature and mind, object and subject, transcendence and immanence.

The harmony of our mental powers that gives rise to the feeling of beauty is complex. When we experience an object that corresponds exactly to its natural end, we feel pleasure in that perfection. The idea the understanding forms agrees completely with the image the imagination constructs. If the understanding gives no idea, then the imagination freely constructs an image in the same way as when it takes part in the operation of knowing. That is to say, its activity is in accordance with the understanding but no cognitive idea is involved. Because there is accord there is finality in the image, but a "finality without an end."

> The cognitive powers are here in free play, because no definite concept limits them to a particular rule of cognition. Hence the state of mind in this representation must be a feeling of free play of the representative powers in a given representation with reference to a cognition in general... The subjective universal communicability of the mode of representation in a judgment of taste, since it is to be possible without presupposing a definite concept, can refer to nothing else than the state of mind in the free play of the imagination and the understanding [as far as they agree with each other, as is requisite for cognition in general]. We are conscious that this subjective relation, suitable for cognition in general, must be valid for everyone, and thus must be universally communicable, just as if it were a definite cognition.[95]

As such, Kant arrives at a formal definition of beauty:

> Beauty is the form of the purposiveness of an object, so far as this is perceived in it without any representation of purpose.[96]

> The beautiful is that which without any concept is cognized as the object of a necessary satisfaction.[97]

An object that stimulates the imagination and understanding in their proper harmony or proportion produces aesthetic pleasure and is judged to be beautiful. Beautiful objects are thus purposive to the understanding and are in harmonious agreement with the imagination.[98]

---

95. Kant, *Critique of Judgment*, 64.
96. Kant, *CJ*, 90.
97. Kant, *CJ.*, 96.
98. Kant, *CJ*, 162.

Judgements of taste also take the form of particular judgements about an individual object. Kant claims both nature and art affect the mind by the sensible forms of its objects and generate disinterested pleasure. However, nature is more powerful than art in rendering the soul pleasurable.

> Nature is beautiful because it looks like art; and art can only be called beautiful if we are conscious of it as art while yet it looks like nature.[99]

Here Kant moves in the atmosphere of Shaftesbury and Burke. First, nature's affects are immediate and more powerful than those of art. Secondly, since beauty [and sublimity] is a matter of feeling, not one of the rules and laws which can be reduced to intelligibility or rational knowledge has provenance, aesthetically. One has to know the object's entelechy to judge it immediately. According to Kant, such judgment is more spontaneous with natural objects than with artistic ones. In either case, aesthetically, the soul feels disinterested pleasure in nature and art.

Finally, Kant claims that pleasure are independent of any sensible or moral need:

> The beautiful is that which apart from concepts is represented as the object of a universal satisfaction.[100]

Such aesthetic amorality for Kant actually counts for a fundamental morality. Only in a satisfaction without ends is ethics possible. Thus aesthetics and ethics dialectically coincide.

In the last half of the eighteenth century, we find ourselves in an unfolding aesthetic still incomplete. In a way Kant had a heady impulse to "aestheticize" reality, and like Plotinus in doing so he fractured the foundations of an emerging rationalist and empiricist aesthetics opened by Baumgarten and Burke. This is because again like Plotinus, Kant's aesthetics does not discuss judgment without weaving it into the fabric of a wider horizon inclusive of metaphysics, epistemology, and ethics. When Kant proceeds with aesthetics his very style reflects his faith in the analytic and synthetic involvement of all the faculties of sense, sensibility, and intelligibility. Kant also claims beauty and sublimity express that aspect of reality that has an ontological immediacy as embodiment and experience. Then almost paradoxically such ontological power translates into an epistemological apathy. That is to say, reality is experienced aesthetically as disinterested pleasure,

---

99. Kant, *CJ*, 187.
100 Kant, *CJ*, 55.

satisfaction. Why this dialectic of the soul is so brings us back to the move from a pre-critical to a critical Kant.

In the wake of Leibniz, Kant tried to get back to an Aristotelian position that Plotinus also shared. He was trying to discover in experience a logical structure on which to build an aesthetics. This attempt would serve the critical Kant well, once he saw that intelligibility must come from the human mind itself; from its creative activity in judging sensible things. The results were a new aesthetics whose structure emerged in the first and third critiques. Here it was seen that knowledge contains a logical form or structure, a set of reasons why. Kant also inherited from Leibniz the notion of the activity and productivity of the soul. From Baumgarten and Hume he culls "the natural principles of the imagination." The monads drew all knowledge and willing from their own resources. They're very essence is to be active force, feeling, and intellect. The free-play of the imagination allows the soul to taste the structure of immediate rather than analytic experience. In all its work the soul exhibits a creative power. It is not a mere receptacle for sensations. It is a *Denkkraft*.

He insisted that the universe be so interpreted as to take into account all elements of human experience including the experience of beauty and sublimity. These feelings must be made intelligible, and they were. This is why, in its own and time and long after, the Critique of Judgment was the most influential of his works. It expressed all those remarkable demands which the Romantics were beginning to make, and it contributed the philosophical foundations for transcendental idealism by which the next generation was to interpret nature and art.

It is suggested that Plotinus and Kant share much in their theories of beauty and the roles judgment and imagination play in the experience of beauty. Where they part ways is equally profound and these should be mentioned briefly. Plotinus argues that the experience of beauty leads the soul to knowledge of Beauty and the Good. Kant proposes that it is the sublime that arouses the soul and makes it aware of the Good. In the sublime, whether of mathematical size or dynamic force, the imagination cannot compass its infinite end. Here the soul becomes aware of the realm of freedom.

Although Plotinus and Kant value beauty differently, they concur on how the faculties of the soul function when it apprehends beauty. Beauty attracts and calms the soul in restful contemplation. Here judgment and the imagination have finite and determinate tasks which they are able to fulfill. In the presence of beauty the soul experiences harmony, acquires moral "taste", and through such experience a bridge is provided for the soul so that it crosses the gulf between sensibility and intelligibility. Moreover, both concur that in beauty *aistheta* and *noeta* are longer thought as two separate realms. They are telescoped into one another.

This insight owes much to their reinterpretations of the venerable philosophical term *mimesis*. Plotinus views *mimesis* as imagining form. Beauty is present in things whenever it succeeds in representing to the soul a configuration, an order of unity in tension, perhaps a world of its own in miniature. This usually occurs when we are confronted by the mute, yet profoundly familiar Pythagorean harmonies of form in color and sound. Kant casts mimesis in the context of *communis sensus*, or expanded thinking. This usually occurs when the soul grasps the beautiful in reflective judgment. In that moment of agreement sensible imagination and intelligible understanding are one.

Summary: Plotinus and Kant are major forces in the transformation of their philosophical heritages. Both are key transitional figures between classical and post-classical, modern and post- modern modes of ontological thinking. This is because they propose an aesthetic of "subjectivity" whose ontological consequences are profound and problematic. The beautiful is not merely an "in-itself" but it is also a "for-itself." The beautiful is not merely "for us" but is "in us." Plotinus could justify both perspectives by his theory of intermediaries and of the participation of sense and sensibility in intelligibility. Kant's had a more difficult task. His sturdy empiricism made him accept the contrast between phenomena and noumena but his aestheticism provided a way out. He thought that in the experience of beauty the soul reconciles the subjectivization of the beautiful with the demand for objective criteria for the beautiful. Ultimately, it is in its relation to the "idea of world" that aesthetic activity becomes concrete for Kant. Since we can imaginatively invoke the idea of beauty and then concretize it, the subjectivization of the beautiful entails its objectification. His task was, to borrow Husserl's formula that of grounding "transcendence" within "immanence" without exiting from the representations of judgment, imagination, and taste which are universally shared in the *communis sensus*. Whether this is philosophically justifiable remains an open question.

Conclusion

Plotinus and Kant recall Plato's formulation of the task of philosophy: "to see things together in respect of the one."[101] If this is so, then the experience of beauty dialectically brings particulars under universals, and elicits

---

101. Plato, *Phaedrus*, 265d.

finiteness in relation to reality in new ways. What we are left with Plotinus is a speechless image of the "One" and with Kant a symbolic trace of the "Absolute." Here, in varying degrees, intelligibility gives way to sensibility, and the sensible gains autonomy in relation to the intelligible. Moreover, distancing intelligibility and increasing sensibility signals a metaphysical elevation of the aesthetic point of view. Although this is not the place to debate this celebrated "turn," the consequences and "merits" of this re-interpretation changed the landscape of modern philosophical aesthetics permanently. Because it is in the aesthetic that the limitations of language are recognized and a further need realized—that of transcending such limits. Since it is impossible to formulate in language the relation between language and reality, reality offers aesthetic hints and gestures which are judged beautiful or sublime. Such traces are enigmatic. They beckon to us. They beckon away. They beckon us toward a new dialogue, not of sayings, but of silences. Such a beckoning has redemptive as well as therapeutic consequences.

13

Fracture and Return

> But it is fit to call the one neither beautiful nor good, because of the fact that it is above the beautiful and the good...
>
> —Iamblichus, *Universal Math.* IV, 16.10–11

Précis

THIS ESSAY AIMS AT retracing two conceptual moments of a history of the soul and the self within the "horizon" of aesthetics.[1] The field of aesthetics is one in which sediments of such a history are most visible and perhaps richest in meaning. Thus the attempt is made in this study to hold on to both ends of a fragile, complex chain: initially, to recapture definitions of art, aesthetics, and the soul at the close of antiquity in Plotinus. Next to represent definitions of subjectivity where they have been most strongly formulated in our present age with Foucault. A single focus, consequently, and four problematics generally define this paper. The human subject is the focus. The problematics are the specter of the isolated subject, the relation between art and truth, the notion that we construct our ontological and axiological positions by recourse

---

1. "Horizon" is the metaphor Nietzsche used in his celebrated "God is dead" passage: "How could we drink up the sea? Who gave us the sponge to wipe away the entire horizon." cf. *The Gay Science*, 181 par. 125. It became a central philosophical concept in the phenomenological tradition associated with Husserl, Heidegger, Merlou-Ponty, and Gadamer. Here the term is used to call to attention what lies aesthetically in the backgrounds of Plotinus' view of the soul and Foucault's understanding of the self. The term also has a normative aura, for example when I speak of the aesthetic pretence underlying their respective visions of the soul and the individual. cf. Bernstein, *The New Constellation*, 10. n. 14.

to an aesthetics of the soul and of the self, and most importantly for this study, the value both Plotinus and Foucault see in art and aesthetics for the overcoming of the fallenness and isolation of the self in later antiquity and later modernity. Some brief statements on the self, the subject, and subjectivity are apposite. To avoid misunderstanding it is not my intention to provide a history, or even an outline of these concepts in antiquity and modernity. Briefly, my purpose is to point out the importance of these concerns as they impact upon the thought of Plotinus and Foucault.

I. The Self, the Subject, and Subjectivity

> There is no real blood flowing
> Through the veins of the knowing
> Subject constructed by Locke, Hume,
> and Kant, only the diluted juices
> of reason, a mere parade of thought.
>
> —Dilthey, *Selected Writings*[2]

The concern with subjectivity in antiquity begins with an interest in the problem of knowledge. In terms of the subject-object relation it is fair to say that Parmenides, Heraclitus, Plato, Aristotle, and Plotinus stress the objective aspects of this relation. Being, Logos, the ideas, substance, and Nous satisfy a normative requirement for an invariant object understood as a necessary condition of knowledge, the object that is known, and the subject that knows.

The concern with subjectivity in modernity, as part of a heightened focus on the foundations of knowledge, shifts the emphasis from the object to the subject of knowledge. Beginning with Descartes the view of the subject is dependent on the concept of the individual. Here the cogito becomes the basis of objectivity. This "turn" is subsequently heightened and refined, at least in the continental traditions, by Kant, Hegel, Husserl, and Heidegger. Here it is proposed that the subject is the condition of objective knowledge and that subjectivity is the key to objectivity.

We need merely to be reminded of Kant's transcendental unity of apperception, Hegel's substance becoming subject, Husserl's transcendental ego, and Heidegger's *Dasein*. Each of these concepts is introduced to support a claim to know not in a subjective sense, but in an objective sense. That is to say, a proposition is raised that resonates to this day in contemporary

---

2. Dilthey, *Selected Writings*, 1976,162.

philosophy—that subjectivity is the key to objectivity.[3] Now this "epistemological turn" from objectivity to subjectivity is not the concern of this essay although it impacts upon what is the focus of this study. The "aesthetic turn" has as its focus the subject and its clue to its value in the world. As such, the focus here is aesthetical and ethical. Indeed, in the case of Plotinus and Foucault it appears that the subject-object problem is an elision largely solved. The concern they primarily address is the subject-value relation.

Plotinus' theory of knowledge turns on a foundationalist conception of *Nous* as the indubitable ground of the soul and knowledge. Moreover, he argues that perception is a type of knowing whereby the soul grasps the ideas aesthetically. Furthermore, he proposes that aesthetic knowledge transforms the soul in terms of its value in the world. This insight reformulated by Baumgarten, Kant, and Hegel is reassessed by Foucault on Nietzschean and Heidegerrean terms. He proposed that to be in the world required knowledge of how to be aesthetically in the world.

The leading theme of this whole story, accordingly, is the notion of an extraordinary concept of the self as subject. This is the soul of Plotinus whose nature and ambitions are soberly ecstatic, unprecedentedly hypercosmic and the self of Foucault who is uniquely autonomous and remarkably self-constrained. The soul of Plotinus and the self of Foucault are no ordinary subjects. The soul is not merely the singular self. It is rather Self as such, the soul of humanity, whose *telos* is an imaginative, ecstatic union with a hyper-reality—the One. For Foucault the individual is the singular self as such, the individual, whose goal is the creation of an `aesthetics of existence,' which finds expression in a radical autonomy of the self.[4]

Despite remarkable differences between these `horizons of the self' one insight links Plotinus and Foucault—`the aesthetic pretence.' Fully developed this pretence has two central components: first, the remarkable inner richness and expanse of the soul or self; and secondly, the consequent right to project from the undescended and subjective structures of one's own mind to ascertain the nature of human value and the destiny of subjectivity as such. That is to say, an aesthetic pretence accompanies this self as a mode of experience fundamental to the attainment of wholeness and freedom. As such, the aesthetic structures of one's own personality establish the conditions for the possibility of ethics. Now these advocates of aesthetic pretence really thought they could change the subject, and sometimes they probably did. Indeed, an appreciation for their lack of modesty

3. For an overview of this issue in contemporary philosophy see Rockmore, *Heidegger and French Philosophy*, 40–58.

4. For a solid study of Foucault's concept of the subject see Stoekl, *Agonies of the Intellectual*, 174–98.

is essential for understanding their aesthetics and ethics. Their imaginative, if sometimes abstruse efforts aimed at changing human beings. They thought of themselves as sages and revolutionaries. In this sense, the aesthetic pretence as argued by Plotinus and Foucault is not so much about the study of knowledge as it is about the human being concerned with being, as the clue to being. Indeed, both offer dramatic stories of a philosophical self-image in which knowledge and reason play an important role in the cultivation of the self, but only alongside perception, imagination, feeling, and creativity. And as such, Plotinus and Foucault represent a minority in the history of western philosophy. That is to say, they are representative of those isolated philosophers who valorized aesthetics and marginalized reason in the cultivation of the subject.

II. Art, Aesthetics, and the Self

> Very early in my life I took
> the question of the relation of
> art to truth seriously: even now
> I stand in holy dread in the face
> of this discordance.
>
> —Nietzsche, *Nachlass*, xiv.386

A specter haunted later ancient and contemporary thought: the specter of the isolated subject.[5] In fact many aspects of ancient and contemporary culture bring forth the suspicion that the individual's relation to the world is undergoing a profound dislocation, and that the relation to the idea of an objective universe, simultaneously transcending the subject and uniting the self to others has become singularly problematic.

Moreover, the discordance of art and truth, in the face of which Nietzsche felt holy dread, is as old as philosophy itself.[6] The proposition that art stands in second relation to the true for the intelligible world is always superior to the sensible world can be traced back to the "construction" of the metaphysical Plato, with his two-world theory, his denigration of corporeality, and his celebration of eternal immutable ideas which are the erotic telos of dianoia and noesis. The realm of *aisthesis*, consequently, was the sign of the human condition, of limited knowledge.

In the wake of such a judgement Plato challenged the authority of Homer and expelled artists from the republic that was to be grounded in reason and

---

5. Ferry, *Homo Aestheticus*, 1.
6. For a review of this topic see Bernstein, *Fate of Art*, 1–16; 225–74.

truth alone. Since the cosmic order was viewed as closed, hierarchical, and purposeful by Plato, the idea of the beautiful was associated with the bringing into reality by the artist of an order where measure and proportion ruled.[7] Moreover, the beautiful object was understood as a sensible presentation (an illustration) of the true, as the transposition into the sphere of the material sensibility of a moral or intellectual truth. A work of art, subsequently, is the mere reflection of the idea of the beautiful. It is the idea of the beautiful that furnishes the work of art with its authentic meaning from without. There is a dread of art and aesthetics for two reasons: first, art is mere art, and as such it is merely a matter of taste; secondly, art and aesthetics always appear to be outside of truth, reason, and morality.

If art and aesthetics appeared as somehow more truthful than noetic or empirical truth, more rational than methodical reason, more just than liberal justice, more valuable than principled morality or utility, then the very foundations of *episteme* would crumble. That is to say, the claim that art is somehow more than reason is always disturbing. It is undemonstrable and incommensurable with what truth saying and valuing are thought of in the shadow of Plato.

As such, the discordance of art and truth, in the face of which Nietzsche felt holy dread, stands over and constitutes modernity more so than it did over Plato's utopia. Few philosophers after Plato placed art and aesthetics at the center of the constitutive, cognitive, and practical mechanisms that produce society. The reasons are not difficult to discern. Art, and the theoretical discourse that comprehends art, speaks its own voice and this voice lies outside truth, goodness, and reason. Two philosophers will challenge this perspective—Plotinus and Foucault.

III. Plotinus

> In the aesthetic mode of
> contemplation we have found two
> inseparable constituent parts—
> the knowledge of the object, not as
> individual thing but as Platonic
> idea and the self-consciousness
> of the knowing person ... as pure
> will-less subject of knowledge.
>
> —SCHOPENHAUER, *THE WORLD AS WILL AND IDEA*[8]

---

7. Plato, *Gorgias*, 503e.
8. Schopenhauer, *The World as Will and Idea*, 130.

A. Perception and Intellection

Plotinus stolidly maintained the priority and superiority of intellection over perception as laying the foundations for physics, and subsequently for psychology and epistemology.[9] Nonetheless, his view of the plastic arts is decidedly novel.[10] First, he claims that art is a visible expression of ideal beauty.[11] Second, he asserts that the ideas of beauty exist in the human soul.[12] Third, he claims that the imagination is the mental faculty through which the soul gains initial awareness of ideal beauty.[13] Fourth, this aesthetic awareness leads, eventually, to knowledge of the ideas of beauty, if not the beautiful itself.[14] Fifth, and perhaps most importantly, he claims that the arts are a means for the soul to reverse a situation of misfortune—her descent into corporeality. For through the arts and the aesthetic imagination the soul regains her awareness of her intelligible origins and, consequently, begins her ascent from sensibility to intelligibility.[15] Yet Plotinus' powerful defense of aesthetics is, accordingly, based on something far more profound than a reappraisal of the value of the plastic arts themselves. For the origin of all symbolic activity, including artistic activity emerges from the fact of the soul's descent and its ignorance of its authentic undescended state.[16] Even though the higher soul remains in the intelligible world the lower soul is unconscious of this fact.[17]

B. The Undescended Soul and the Active Intellect

Goodness and beauty are known to the higher soul but not the lower soul. For only souls motivated by intellect and illuminated by beauty know goodness.[18] These souls are exceptional and conscious of their undescended selves. The higher soul always remains united with intelligible being; the lower soul is unconscious of this link. Envoloved in the sensible world, in the tumult of the body, she is unconscious of what the upper

---

9. On Plotinus' psychology and epistemology there are many works. See, Blumenthal, *Plotinus' Psychology*, 8–66; 67–133; cf. Rist, *Plotinus*, 410–22.

10. Plotinus, *Enneads*, V.8.1; cf. I.6.2,3,5.

11. Plotinus, *Ennead*, V.8.1.

12. Plotinus, *Ennead*, I.6.2.

13. Plotinus, *Ennead*, I.6.3.

14. Plotinus, *Ennead*, I.6.5.

15. Plotinus, *Ennead*, IV.8.4,28–31; cf. I.6.3, 5.

16. On this theory in Plotinus see Rist, *Plotinus*, 1967, 410–22; Steel, *The Changing Self*, 1978, 34–38.

17. Plotinus, *Ennead*, V.1.12.

18. Plotinus, *Ennead*, IV.7.10.

part beholds.[19] Busied with carnal desires she knows nothing of her divine link. What of these souls, unconscious of their undescended selves, and ignorant of the eternal verities? For:

> living under a crust of evil ... filled with injustice and desires, torn by internal strife, full of the fears of its own cowardice and the jealousy of its meanness, busied in its thoughts about the perishable and the low, the friend of vile pleasure, it lives a life of submission to bodily desires.[20]

There is away out of this situation of misfortune. Through apprehension of aesthetic symbols the soul becomes aware of the forms and begins her tenuous ascent from unconsciousness to consciousness.[21]

Visible beauty points to soul to intelligible beauty.[22] In this sense art functions to make the soul aware of her divine source. Once conscious this soul becomes aware of her eternal, intelligible link to the divine. For through the aesthetic imagination the soul unites her disparate self and begins her ascent to the eternal verities andeventual union with the divine.[23] Consequently, art is therapeutic. It assists in the transfiguration of the soul from unconsciousness to consciousness, from an awareness of its sensibility to knowledge of its intelligibility.

For Plotinus, then, the psychological shift from unconsciousness to consciousness, from misfortune to fortune, involves the use of the imagination, the active intellect, and at times, the plastic arts. Art, thus, commits the soul to an upward passage, to an ascent from the lower to the highest divine beauty. Consequently, the various *artes* are accorded a valued place in Plotinus' system.[24] Logic, observation, and piety all reinforced this position. For Plotinus there was something grotesquely impious in the idea that the sense-world was devoid of the forms or that physical objects, even objects of art, could not awaken in the soul images of the eternal verities.

C. The Imagination and Intelligible Beauty

Plotinus' judgement is understandable, only when it is coupled to his psychology and epistemology. Plotinus rejected Plato's tripartition of the

19. Plotinus, *Ennead*, V.1.2; 4.1.8.
20. Plotinus, *Ennead*, I.6.5.
21. Plotinus, *Ennead*, V.8.1.
22. Plotius, *Ennead*, I.6.3.
23. Plotinus, *Ennead*, I.6.5.
24. Berchman, *Rationality and Ritual*, 229–68.

soul. Moreover he accepted Aristotle's view that knowledge is a function of a series of psychological faculties.[25] Although Plotinus does not settle on a definite scheme of faculties, his acceptance of Aristotle's view of the imagination plays a decisive role in his aesthetics.[26] With these concessions, Platonism finally comes to terms with the insights of Aristotelianism. Among the most important of the Aristotelian elements in Plotinus' system is the notion that an actively thinking mind is identical with its objects.[27] He also accepted Aristotle's view that sense-perception involved the reception of the forms of sense-objects without their matter.[28] As Alexander insisted the absolute certainty of knowledge springs from the fact that it has its origins in perception.[29] This is the complement of Plotinus observation that the physical world is a self-contained, cogent, and certain instantiation of the noetic world.[30] This is possible because the soul is self-moving. Always in movement she is in contact with those intelligible faculties active within her even though she is unconscious of them. The lower soul becomes conscious of her higher self when the active intellect transmits to the imagination an image of the forms. This occurs when the soul views an art form. This triggers memory of the intelligibles for the soul sees the form of beauty in the work of art.

There are two faculties of imagination. One arises in regions of the soul concerned with the body. Another emerges from the part of the soul concerned with the intellect.[31] Plotinus says that the secondary act of imagination which is opinion in the soul is caused by disturbance and shock. Thus it is the product of the lower part of the organism. Its images are a faint opinion and unexamined mental picture.[32] However, it is not secondary but primary imagination that is important in Plotinian aesthetics. The primary imagination has images of the forms passed on to it by

25. This is not to say that Plotinus merely adopts the Aristotelian psychology. As Blumenthal notes Plotinus goes to great lengths to preserve the soul's autonomy which he thought Peripateticism radically compromised, cf. Blumenthal, *Plotinus' Psychology*, 8–44.

26. On the two faculties of the imagination, cf. Aristotle, *De Anima*, 433b29; 434a5–7.

27. See, A. H. Armstrong, *Plotinus*, 393–413; cf. Merlan, *Monopsychism, Mysticism, Metaconsciousness*.

28. See, Blumenthal, *Plotinus' Psychology*, 137–45.

29. Alexander, *De Animae.*, 85; cf. 89.21–22; 90.19–20; {Wallis}. *De Intellectu.*, 112.2–4 {Bruns}.

30. Plotinus, *Ennead*, I.6.2–3.

31. On the dual imagination in Plotinus see Blumenthal, *Plotinus' Psychology*, 1971, 92–97.

32. Plotinus, *Ennead*, III.6.4,14–23.

the active intellect and the higher soul.[33] The *logos* deploys the thought and shows it to the imaginative faculty as though in a mirror. This presentation of thought to the imagination makes us aware of the intellection (*noesis*) which is always in progress. The imagination apprehends it and the persistence of the image is memory.

The imagination (*phantasia*) receives the products of thought (*logoi*) and perception (*aisthesis*).[34] These products are, then, passed on to the reasoning faculty for processing.[35] Imagination is, accordingly, based on something far more profound than an awareness of physical conditions. It carries a meaning close to the idea of consciousness.[36] This means that the imagination is a power of perceptive awareness that transcends sensation. Significantly, it refers to that mental faculty which provides knowledge of the intelligibles above and within the soul.[37] This assures for Plotinus the possibility of memory (*anamnese*)—the becoming receptive on the part of the lower soul what the higher soul eternally beholds.[38]—for image-collecting is the basis of memory.[39] Memory, in turn, plays an important role in Plotinian eschatology and psychology.

For Plotinus believed in reincarnation, and assumed the form in which the soul is reincarnated depends on its previous life and conforms to the characteristics of that life. For example, the way the soul preserves its character between reincarnations is through memory. Memory makes the soul what it is and controls its descent.[40] As noted Plotinus assumed that souls move from an unconscious to a conscious understanding of the intelligibles[41] and the way the transition is made is through memory.[42] For example, the imagination fired by its perception of a statue of a god remembers the form of the god and moves from an unconscious to a conscious awareness of the divine.[43] Thus art plays an important role in the way consciousness of the higher soul and the intelligibles is

---

33. Plotinus, *Ennead*, IV.3.30,1–5.
34. Plotinus, *Ennead*, IV.3.30,5–8.
35. Plotinus, *Ennead*, V.3.2.7–9.
36. On this see Schwyzer, *Bewusst und Unbewusst*, 1961, 343–90.
37. Plotinus, *Ennead*, 1.4.9,25–32.
38. Plotinus, *Ennead*, IV.8.4,28–31.
39. Plotinus, *Ennead*, IV.3.29,22–24.
40. Plotinus, *Ennead*, IV.3.8,5–9; cf. 3.4.2.11.
41. On the unconscious and conscious intellect in Plotinus see Merlan, *Monopsychism, Mysticism, Metaconsciousness*, 72–80.
42. This is illustrated by Blumenthal, *Plotinus' Psychology*, 94–99.
43. Plotinus, *Ennead*, I.6.3.

achieved by the lower soul.[44] For images of the forms are transmitted to the imagination through sense objects. Accepting the Aristotelian postulate that sense-perception involves the reception of the forms of sense-objects without their matter Plotinus says:

> On what principle does the architect when he finds the house standing before him correspond with his inner ideal of a house and pronounce it beautiful? Is it not that the house before him, the stones apart, is the inner idea stamped on the mass of exterior matter, the indivisible exhibited in diversity? We call something beautiful when we see something imprinted on it that we recognize as our own, by virtue of our continuity with the Ideal world, and the immanence of that world in the object where we recognize beauty.[45]

Art objects also move the soul to imagine the form of beauty. This notion is forcefully presented in his work *On the Intelligible Beauty*.[46] Plotinus describes an intelligible world in unity with the sensible world. The capacity to grasp this synthesis leads the mind to an understanding of beauty. Next, he examines the imagination and shows how it aids the soul in its ascent from sensible to intelligible knowledge. Finally, he illustrates how the craftsman and his *artes* concretely instantiate in visible form the intelligible world's truth and beauty. Plotinus describes an intelligible world whereby each member remains itself, in distinction from all others, yet simultaneously all members form a single unity. He asks us to imagine a transparent globe or sphere containing all the things of the universe. Then he asks us to correct it by imagining another sphere stripped of all magnitude and spatial differences. Next we are urged to make a synthesis wherein each is all, one undivided divine power of many facets, each sharing one existence and remaining distinct from all others.[47] This is the beautiful.

Plotinus strains to lead our minds to the higher world of the forms and argues that sensual images lead us on our ascent. To correct the conclusions we might draw from the first-level image, he asks us not to abandon imagery entirely but to imagine another sphere, one whose properties run counter to the first. The deficiencies of image-thinking are eventually corrected by bringing the sense-image to a second stage and then urging our metaphysical imaginations to leap beyond this stage as well, to the

---

44. Plotinus, *Ennead*, V.8.1.
45. Plotinus, *Ennead*, I.6.3.
46. Until publication of the *Belles Lettres Editions* on this treatise see, Brehier, *La Philosophie du Plotin* 3 1961, 17–23; Puech, *Plotin et les Gnostiques*, 161–90.
47. Plotinus, *Enneads*, 5.8.9.

desired insight into the intelligible realm. Central to this process of ascent is not of abandoning or turning away from the sensible world but of using imagery and the faculty of imagination to the point of strain and shatter. At the moment of shatter, intelligible insight occurs.[48] The ingredience of the higher in the lower world suggests the fecundity of Plotinian aesthetics. He illustrates this in his comparison of hieroglyphics and art. Both suggest non-discursive images of the intelligible world—the ideas are not propositional truths but reified beings (*onta*).[49]

Moreover the ideas are envisaged as agalmata, each bodying forth in a species of translucence the inner wealth of the intelligible world's truth and beauty. Thus the individual who has seen this world of beauty will become his true self, even in this sensible, corporeal world, a concrete embodiment, in and through which others catch the glimmerings of the transcendent splendor of the forms.[50] For Plotinus one such an agalma is the artist, another artist's creation. Thus the craftsman's task is, first, to imagine the ideal specification to which reality conforms, and then—so far as the nature of matter permits—to arrange it in conformity with its ideal specification.

A sculpture, for example, represents the creative ideas contained in the soul of the artist. With the assistance of the imagination the artist in an inward vision grasps the forms intuitively. Next the craftsman projects the intelligible beauty of the forms outwards, giving them visible form. This understanding emerges from his interpretation of Phidias' statue of Zeus. Plotinus states that:

> . . . it goes back to the ideas from which nature itself derives and adds where nature is lacking.[51]

The craftsman's work instantiates the form of beauty for it reflects the *he kallone*—the beauty of deity itself. The sculpture, then, functions to awaken in other souls an imaginative awareness of the ideas from which all else derives. Plotinus suggests that such awareness leads to psychological enlightenment for the soul is the immovable place or subject for the immutable truth of the higher world.[52]

> What do you feel in the beauty of souls? When you see that you yourself are beautiful within, what do you feel? What is this Dionysian exaltation that thrills through your being, this straining

48. Plotinus, *Ennead*, VI..4.5.
49. Plotinus, *Ennead*, VI.4.5.
50. Plotinus, *Ennead*, V.8.11, 17–19; cf. IV.4–6, 42–44.
51. Plotinus, *Ennead*, V.8.1.
52. Plotinus, *Ennead*, IV.7.

upwards of all you soul, this longing to break away from the body and live sunken within the true self? These are no other than the emotion of souls under the spell of love ... All these noble qualities are to be rever-encode and loved but what entitles them to be called ignore that sees them must admit that they have reality of being, and is not real being, really beautiful?[53]

D. Aesthetic Symbols, the Soul, and the Arts

Note carefully that Plotinus' understanding of intellectual beauty confirms a new Roman rhythm. His terminology—imagination (*phantasia*), exaltation (*ekstasis*), love (*eros*), and emotion (*pathe*)—affirms that the intelligible world and its divine source can be grasped not only noetically, but also aesthetically. In a remarkable reversal of an older aesthetic pattern divine apperception involves *patheia* not *apatheia*. Another *via sacra* opens up that involves a non-discursive, imaginative and erotic ascent to the divine. Plotinus is toying with a sweeping hypothesis.[54]

Although the theme is strongly reminiscent of the Platonic Socrates, that Silenus figure which, once opened, was seen to contain the images of the gods within him, the Plotinian Phidias and that Zeus figure are strikingly distinct.[55] Plato often returned to that mysterious, youthful experience, to that encounter with the beloved which is simultaneously an encounter with a transcendent world of value that stretches beyond the concrete person involved in the encounter.[56] Plotinus reflects and expands upon this encounter and includes within the *agalmata* that permits encounter with the intelligible world factors which Plato never countenanced—the imagination, the active intellect, and the plastic arts. The forms are communicated to the soul by the active intellect through the image making faculty of the soul in reflection on the work of art. The consequence of these assumptions propels Plotinus to propose, at least for

---

53. Plotinus, *Ennead*, I.6.5.

54. This interpretation might represent a conscious development of the insight of the *Phaedrus* 250d where Plato suggests that of all the forms beauty alone makes itself manifest to the sensuous perceiver.

55. As with Augustine see O'Connell, *Art and the Christian Intelligence in St. Augustine*, 46–47. Access to the divine Intellect within both *kosmos* and *psuche* is possible, only non-propositionally and non-discursively, via aesthetics.

56. Plato develops this theme in the *Laws* where household shrines, the aged, and the stars are proposed as concrete examples of the divine, cf. *Laws*, 930e-931a; 899b; 966e-968a. Plotinus follows suite. Plotinus, *Enn*ead, I.6 best exemplifies such divine reification.

Platonism, an unprecedented aesthetic axiology. Psychological and ontological schizophrenia are overcome aesthetically. The soul's unawareness of her higher self is reversed and her situation of misfortune overturned through imaginative, indeed, artistic perception.

Aesthetics, then is not only therapeutic, it is also a path to salvation.[57] The soul's descent into matter results in the unconscious splitting of the self. Her fall from the intelligible world also signals her separation from true reality and her embodiment in symbolic reality. This leap into matter is a function of a situation of misfortune. The imagination, the active intellect, and the arts are intimately linked to the reversal of psychological and ontological misfortune. Indeed, for Plotinus the arts present to the soul one of the greatest blessings a later Roman could obtain—full possession of the self, awareness of the forms, and ascent to the divine. Art assists the soul to leave the sensible world and terrestrial pollution and gain the intelligible world and celestial bliss.

Thus, in turning to a statue or temple the imagination sees not merely a physical object but perceives an image of the forms. This, eventually, leads to an awareness of the eternal value of nature, the human soul, and the divine like nature of both. An awareness of beauty is nothing less than recognition of the value of the physical world and of self. Through art the ontological distance between being and becoming is overcome in an epistemological and psychological act of imaginative identification. For Plotinus the human soul contains within herself the ability to gain salvation. She has the ability to willingly save herself through contemplation (*theoria*).[58] Art and the imaginative perception of its inner beauty is a mode of contemplation which leads the soul on her ascent to the intelligible world.

Although no clear doctrine of the vehicle of the soul (*pneuma-ochema*) emerges from Plotinus' writings, the philosopher was probably aware of it.[59] He appears to subscribe to belief in such a vehicle based on his theory of *pneuma*.[60] In discussing the descent of the soul Plotinus says that when the soul leaves the noetic realm it goes: "first into heaven and receives there a

---

57. Porphyry reports that after encountering a god at the temple in Isis at Rome, Plotinus wrote a treatise *On the Spirit That Allotted Itself to Us*, cf. *Vit. Plot.*, 10. Presumably this work served to explain how to differentiate between higher and lower gods and daemons upon their visible manifestation. Such knowledge certainly had therapeutic and soteriological dimensions for Plotinus and his followers.

58. Plotinus, *Ennead*, IV.4.44.

59. Dillon shows that the doctrine was known by the second century C.E. cf. Dillon, *Aisthesis noete*, 433–55. Thus, it is probable Plotinus knew of it.

60. On Plotinus' view of *pneuma* see, *Greeks and the Irrational*, Berkeley, 1951, 318; Verbeke, *L'Evolution de la doctrine du Pneuma du stoicisme a S. Augustine*, 352–63; A. Smith, *Porphyry's Place*, 152–55.

body through which it continues into more earthly bodies." As the soul descends gradations of envelops of matter attach themselves to a primary body. Consequently, Plotinus proposes that the soul must be purified from these envelopes to rise to its higher self. Then she lives peacefully with her purified *pneuma*. For Plotinus, probably following his reading of Aristotle, the vehicle is important for its imaginative function. Since the vehicle is an intermediary between bodily sensations and intellection sense impressions are impressed upon the vehicle and then processed by the soul.[61] Here Plotinus has an acute sense of the multiplicity of reality and self and a chain of intermediaries that reached, yet further still, from self to God.

Ascent is an important component in Plotinus' philosophical system when coupled to his understanding of ecstasy. Ecstasy (*ekstasis*) understood as "expansion" is a central aspect in accounts of the ascent of the soul.[62] Plotinus calls ecstasy an awakening of the soul from its physical nature. Aesthetics, thus, is closely tied to the awakening of the soul from its physical nature, its ascent to the divine ideas, and consequently to the divine. The gift of ecstasy is a divine one for Plotinus. Porphyry assumed his teacher possessed it from birth.[63] There is no evidence that Plotinus thought it could be transmitted from teacher to disciple by the laying on of hands. But an individual may become ecstatic or expansive upon entering a holy place or viewing a statue of a god.[64] This is only possible, in turn, because the mind has accredited sense-perception and the imagination with the capacity to grasp the forms with the aid of the active-intellect. As a result a new world beckons.

What may be called Plotinus' 'aesthetic shift' has its grounds in his valuation of the natural world, his concerns about the "fall" of the soul, and his desire to expand its horizons by rendering nugatory the unconsciousness of *aisthesis* and the arts. Art functions to erase the distinctions between the layers of the soul, to bring the ontologically distant epistemologically present. *Aisthesis* is nothing more than the lower soul becoming conscious of what the higher soul eternally beholds. *Phantasia* is nothing more than the presentation to the lower soul of an antilepsis which permits her to identify her

61. Plotinus, *Enn*ead, IV.3.15. From his use of the term *ocheisthai* we can, with caution, suggest that Plotinus was familiar with the term *ochema*. cf. A. Smith, *Porphyry's Place*, 153. However, a comprehensive elaboration of this doctrine comes after Plotinus. cf. Dodds, *Proclus*, 313–21.

62. Plotinus, *Ennead*, VI.4. Ekstasis involves *ektasis*, cf. Proclus, *In Platon. Alc.*, 1.92.3ff.: "The soul expands in order to get closer to god while god expands to meet the soul, without ever stepping outside, for he always remains inside himself." Although a false etymology, *ekstasis* is derived from *existasthai* and *ektasis* from *ekteinein*, it illustrates well the Neoplatonic understanding of this state.

63. Porph. *Vit. Plot.*, 10.

64. On this belief in general in late antiquity see, Heliodorus, *Aeth.*, 2.11.

empirical self with her pure, true self that transcends the sensible. Art serves to heal the disparate self. It brings that which is so noetically distant, sensibly present. It is about the joining of heaven and earth in the human soul. Thus the dangerously long distance between being and becoming consciousness and unconsciousness is overcome through an aesthetic that stresses the possibility of unanimity between subject and object. Such identification makes the soul conscious of her intelligible beauty. Such consciousness leads the soul upwards to divine beauty itself.

In nuce, the second half of the third century, we find ourselves caught up in an aesthetic transformation which is still incomplete. Plotinus fractures the foundations of earlier Platonic aesthetic theory. Bit by bit, the static framework of the noetic world, on which Platonic metaphysics rested, is dismantled. By now, the ineffaceable character of forms and gods, which earlier Platonists saw as the ultimate justification of a *mimesis* between the intelligible and sensible worlds, between intelligibility and sensibility has been dissolved aesthetically. Art—as Plotinus hints all along—no longer belongs to the sensible world alone. This discovery has three aspects. It compels Platonists to recognize the value of perception—something they might guess but before Plotinus could not prove. Secondly, it establishes the veracity of the imagination because later Platonists have come to understand the general processes by which it works: its link to the higher soul and active-intellect provides proof of its intelligibility. Thirdly, it establishes the conditions for the possibility of rendering nugatory the specter of the isolated subject and the discordance between art and truth. A central concern for any philosophy of art, whether about humanity or nature is to distinguish universal factors, operative everywhere and at all times, from conditional ones, which arise out of accident and so acquire significance only derivatively. Finally, there is the question of motivation: in philosophical culture, at any rate, paradigm shifts occur when we reconstruct for ourselves, the reasons, fears, and ambitions of humans caught up in historical events—and we do so non-propositionally and non-discursively.

IV. Kant and Foucault

> Our age is, in especial degree, the age of criticism, and to criticism everything must submit.
>
> —Kant, Preface to *The Critique of Pure Reason*[65]

---

65. Kant, *Critique of Pure Reason*, 8.

There has been an explosion about the term "post modernity" which is difficult to pin down. Heidegger called such an amorphous, elusive protean debate a *Stimmung*. Indeed, postmodernism is perhaps the most controversial intellectual movement of our times. There are those who think that it is a clever intellectual fraud, a harbinger of nihilism, a whimsical destroyer of any canons of rationality, a self-indulgent scribbling that delights in irresponsible word play, punning, parody, and even self-parody. With wit, barbs, and deft swift movements, this movement is the slayer of the tradition of western metaphysics and logo centrism. This characterization is to say the least problematic. The reasons are several. Many interpreters of postmodernism—and one should not place Foucault's thinking solely in a postmodernist context—have characterized the postmodern ethos as excluding all notions of truth, enlightenment, and self-understanding. Moreover, Foucault's genealogies of power/nowledge have been identified as exhibiting a Nietzschean scepticism with regard to truth-claims or ethical values of whatever kind.

This picture incorrectly characterizes Foucault's later philosophical positioning. Foucault's philosophical agenda is about criticism and the "decentering" of a variety of methodological and metaphysical apriora. In this sense its pedigree is an ancient one and its philosophical precursors include Socrates, Pyrrho, Sextus Empiricus, Montaigne, Voltaire, Kant, and Nietzsche. Those who read these thinkers and their heirs as merely celebrating formlessness and chaos are missing the Socratic sense, the Kantian deconstructive bite, which demands that there is no "boundary-fixing" that cannot itself be questioned. In nuce, Foucault will continue this critical approach which can be identified with Kant's and Nietzsche's own critique of foundations. Moreover, his attention is drawn to the ethics and aesthetics of these thinkers in three ways. First, Kant and Nietzsche made freedom something that is necessarily outside the province of (theoretical) knowledge. Secondly, one of the radical novelties of Kant was the notion that we construct our meaning of life through ethics because it is through this medium that we endow ourselves with purpose. Thirdly, it was Nietzsche who suggested to Foucault that 'living one's life as a work of art' is the telos of human existence.

A. Critique in the Modern Age

Kant taught us that what characterizes the enlightenment impulse is not dogmatism or the search for firm foundations, but its persistent questioning of the conditions and possibility of experience: including ethical-political experience.[66] Foucault's historical work was guided by a philosophical attitude derived from the Enlightenment values of human liberation and of autonomous human thought as an instrument of that liberation. He defined his project by comparing and contrasting it to Kant's eighteenth century critique of reason which was an attempt to make use of understanding without direction from another.[67] Kant thought that his own age was the beginning of reason's emergence as an autonomous force directing human life. Thus, reason itself required a careful assessment of its precise scope and limits. Thus, according to Foucault, Kant indicated a way out of the immaturity and the heteronomy that characterized human thought before Enlightenment. By immaturity Kant meant "a certain state of our will that makes us accept someone else's authority to lead us in areas where the use of reason is called for."[68] Its motto was *aude sapere* and it must be construed "both as a process in which men participate collectively and as an act of courage to be accomplished personally."[69] Thus Enlightenment is characterized by Kant as on ongoing process and as a task and an obligation to problematize existing readings of knowledge and truth.

Kant thought that the limits of reason derived from necessary a priori structures that defined the very possibility of our knowledge—that is, from formal structures with universal value. It is here that Foucault's project for a critique of reason differs from Kant's. Foucault is not concerned with determining the a priori, necessary conditions governing the exercise of reason but with a critical reflection on the extent to which such conditions have a contingent historical origin. Through such reflection—carried out by histories of thought—he attempts to show how we can free ourselves from the constraints of these conditions. Even free ourselves from the error of mistaking culture-specific for a priori valid truth-claims.

In this sense Foucault scarcely alters the agenda and axiology of the Kantian critique. His central concern is to articulate a critique of reason and an ethic premised on the values of autonomy, freedom, and self-determination attained through an exercise of practical will remarkably kin to Kant's own threefold question "What can I know?; What should I will?; and What may I reasonably hope for?" The crucial difference is in Foucault's way of posing these questions. He treats them in genealogical fashion as not belonging to a transcendentally certain but to a historically

---

66. Particularly in his *History of Sexuality* and in his article *What is Enlightenment?*
67. Foucault, *What is Enlightenment?* tr. Porter in Rabinow (ed.), *The Foucault Reader*, 32–50. See also, Kant, *What is Enlightenment?* and *On History*.
68. Kant, *Enlightenment*, 3.
69. Foucault, *WIE.*, 34.

delimited configuration of knowledge, discourse, and the will to truth. This shift represents an important reformulation of the cultural role played by reason. Foucault abandons the traditional philosophical goal of grounding theoretical, practical, and aesthetic knowledge in an understanding of the essential, universal structures of thought and reality. Instead he applies the philosopher's analytic and synthetic skills to the task of uncovering and dissolving contingent historical constraints on thought and action. As such Foucault abandons the venerable but empty pretension that philosophy provides a privileged access to fundamental truths. That is to say, he rejects any version of the strong universalist premise that would hold such values to be more than contingent, more than just a product of own modernist attachment to universal discourse.

In brief, Foucault inverted Kant's order of priorities. He demoted the claims of "transcendental" reason (or critique) to the status of a localized episode in the history of thought, and he identified truth with the level of contingent events or shifts in the order of power/knowledge relations that can best be revealed through his genealogical approach to thought systems. That is to say, the enlightenment project survives in Foucault in a sharply delimited form as the impetus to the kind of reasoned investigative thinking that does not characterize much of postmodernism. As such for Foucault the Kantian questions still have a capacity to provide critical reflection on the ways and means of enlightened self-knowledge that exist for us now as subjects inscribed with a culture specific discourse.

Critique needs to be recast in such a form as to exclude any notion of truth or critique as values transcending this localized context of utterance. Thus: "How are we constituted as subjects of our own knowledge? How are we constituted as subjects who exercise or submit to power relations? How are we constituted as subjects of our own actions?" This remains among the most important of enlightenment questions for Foucault.[70] These are the kinds of questions that have occupied thinkers from Kant to Habermas. But they differ that for Foucault self-knowledge can only arise through the exercise of a freedom created in the margins of an otherwise ubiquitous will to power whose watchwords are "reason," "enlightenment," and "truth." Hence the most important question for Foucault is: "how can the growth of capabilities be disconnected from the intensification of power relations?"[71] His answer is to shift the main burden from the relationship between knowledge and ethics (as developed chiefly in the first two *Critiques*) to the relationship

---

70. *WIE*, 49.
71. *WIE*, 48.

between ethics and aesthetics (as taken up in the last *Critique*). This explains Foucault's turn to an aesthetic perspective.[72]

B. The Aesthetic Turn

There are differences between Kant's and Foucault's ways of answering the question "What is Enlightenment?" For Kant it is a matter of attaining intellectual and moral maturity through the exercise of criticism in its various modes, whether applied to issues of theoretical understanding (where intuitions must be brought under adequate concepts), to questions of an ethical or political order (where practical reason supplies the rule), or to issues in the sphere of aesthetic judgement where the tribunal can only be that of an inter-subjective community of taste appealing to shared principles or criteria of value.

For Foucault this doctrine of the faculties is a "transcendental" illusion and in its place he offers an artistic and literary ethos which possesses no such universalist claims. Here the aesthetic moves to center stage as the focal point of everything that challenges, eludes, or subverts the truth-claims of a traditionally understood Enlightenment critique. Following Baudelaire and Nietzsche, Foucault argued we should not go off to discover ourselves, our secrets and hidden truths. We should try to invent ourselves by ironically "heroizing" the present moment and the scope it offers for aesthetic self-creation.[73] This turn explains Foucault's focus upon a categorical imperative of ever more inventive variations on the theme of aesthetic self-invention that leads toward an ethos of "Private" (aesthetic) fulfillment. If we are to see the significance of the question of the nature of the work of art and how this question is connected with the basic problems of philosophy for Foucault we must gain some insight into certain assumptions present in the Kantian concept of a philosophical aesthetics.[74]

It was only with the explicit restriction of Enlightenment rationalism that the autonomous right of aesthetic knowledge would be first asserted by Baumgarten.[75] With these premises in hand Kant in his third critique—specifically the *Critique of Judgment*—argued for the

---

72. *WIE*, 41.

73. *WIE*, 41–42.

74. The literature on Kant's third critique (and his aesthetics in general) is too vast and philosophically variegated to mention in detail. Two recent studies merit attention, however. Ferry, *Homo Aestheticus*, A, 77–113 and Eagleton, *The Ideology of the Aesthetic*, 1994, 70–101.

75. For an informative assessment of the influence of Baumgarten's aesthetics see Ferry, *Homo Aestheticus*, 33–77.

independence of the judgement of taste from the categories of the understanding and its regulatory concepts. Kant established the problem of aesthetics in its systematic significance. Here he discovered in the subjective universality of the aesthetic judgement of taste the powerful and legitimate claim to independence the aesthetic judgement makes against the claims of the understanding and morality.[76] Kant established the problem of aesthetics in its systematic significance. Here he discovered in the subjective universality of the aesthetic judgment of taste the powerful claim to independence the aesthetic judgment makes against claims of the understanding and morality.[77] According to Kant the taste of the observer can not be comprehended as the application of concepts, norms, or rules. The beautiful and the sublime cannot be apprehended as a knowable, determinate property of an object. Rather it manifests itself in a subjective manner—in the intensification of the "Lebensgefuehl" through the harmonious correspondence of imagination and understanding.[78]

What we experience in beauty or sublimity in nature and in art is the free interplay of our moral powers. These judgements of taste are not knowledge, yet they are not arbitrary. They involve a claim to universality that establishes the autonomy of the aesthetic realm on the basis of the subjectivity of the mind's powers.[79] For Kant the determining factor was the congruity that existed between the beauty and sublimity of nature and the subjectivity of the subject. Similarly, he understood the creative genius who transcends all rules in creating the work of art to be a favorite of nature.[80] This assumption was based on the self-evident validity of a natural order that has its ultimate foundation in the teleological idea of creation.[81]

The disappearance of a teleological grounding of aesthetics followed rapidly upon Kant. In its place there emerged a notion of radical subjectification, or the doctrine of the freedom of the genius from the horizons of rules. No longer subject to the comprehensive whole of the order of nature this artist is privileged to contrast reality and the raw prose of life. Here art—on the level of sense intuition—becomes the manifestation of the perfected concept of spirit. In the literal sense of the word art became for Schiller and Hegel an intuition of the world.[82]

76. Kant, *Critique of Judgment*, 1973, 41–227.
77. *CJ*, 41–74.
78. *CJ*, 86–89.
79. *CJ*, 90–98.
80. *CJ*, 175–83.
81. *CJ*, 20–39.
82. Eagleton, *Ideology of the Aesthetic*, 102–52; Ferry, *Homo Aesthetics*, 114–47.

Gadamer argues that "basing aesthetics on the subjectivity of the mind's powers was . . . the beginning of a dangerous process subjectification.[83] Dangerous from Gadamer's phenomenological perspective, this was the "way" of transcendental aesthetics from Kant to Cassirer. Moreover, if we wish to understand the point of departure of Foucault's aesthetics, we must keep in mind that these earlier aesthetic horizons of Kant, Schiller, and Hegel—that inscribed a special significance to nature and works of art as the organon of a nonconceptual understanding of truth—are eclipsed in Foucault's lexicon by Nietzsche and to a lesser degree by Heidegger, and Bataille.[84] It is to Foucault's aesthetics we now turn.

C. Aesthetics of the Self

Foucault suggested that such an aesthetic turn cannot be perceived or theorized by a philosophy still wedded to "transcendental" notions of reason, truth, and critique. Hence Foucault's (often misunderstood) critique of the Enlightenment humanism associated with Kant's first two *Critiques* that prevented discourse from moving beyond its subject-centered or anthropological origins.[85] This kind of humanism can be opposed Foucault thought by "the principle of a permanent critique and a permanent creation of ourselves in our autonomy: that is a principle that is at the heart of the historical consciousness that the Enlightenment has of itself."[86]

The consequence of Foucault's revisionist reading of Kant's third *Critique* is to aestheticize issues of politics, morality, and social justice to the point where they become a "transfiguring play of freedom with reality," an "aesthetic elaboration of the self," worked out by the Nietzschean strong individual in pursuit of desires, or in accordance with a private self-fashioning, that "ironic heroization of the present . . . which Baudelaire called art." In nuce, Foucault rejected a Kantian ethics grounded in the maxims and postulates of enlightened practical reason to an ethics premised on the Nietzschean will to treat existence as "justified" to the extent we can view it as an "aesthetic phenomenon." The important question now is does such an espousal of a private-aestheticist creed force Foucault to abandon the truth values of enlightened thought—of reason in its jointly

83. Gadamer, *Heidegger's Ways*, 101.

84. See, Rochliz, *The Aesthetics of Existence: Postconventional morality and the theory of power in Michel Foucault*, in Armstrong (trs.), *Michel Foucault Philosopher*, New York: Routledge, 248–59.

85. Foucault, WIE, 44.

86. WIE, 44.

epistemological and ethico-political modes? Does it compel Foucault to renounce any claim to promote and articulate the interests of autonomy, justice, and human emancipation? I suggest not. Rather it initially leads to the kind of self-delighting paradox or wished for aporia that figures so prominently in Foucault's thought. Later it culminates in discourses, practices, and technologies of the self, where individuals create their own identities through ethics and forms of aesthetic self-constitution in order to attain a certain state of happiness and purity.

Foucault states that, henceforth, criticism will "not deduce from the form of what we are what it is impossible for us to know and do." Rather it will "separate out, from the contingency that has made us what we are, the possibility of no longer being, doing, or thinking what we are, do, or think."[87] Initially, this sentence strikes one as a repudiation of Kantian thought. It appeared to support his claim that the only type of project that warrants his allegiance is an ethics/aesthetics of radical self-invention. Foucault's statement might promote this interpretation, but it also corresponds at every point to Kant's own claims in the original text "What Is Enlightenment?" Kant argued that we must think our way through and beyond these limits, those various forms of self-imposed tutelage or servitude as we exercise our powers of autonomous critical reason. If this is done autonomous judgement makes possible a critique that promotes human liberty. It also allows us to evaluate various orders of truth telling and to judge their ethical accountability in respect to their meaning, conditions, and goals.[88]

Perhaps, this explains how much was at stake in Foucault's historical studies of the origins of the human sciences and his critiques of structuralism and various (neo) Marxisms. He acknowledges the claims of certain moral imperatives. These imperatives necessarily hold whenever human liberty is endangered or compromised. Moreover, their validity cannot be relativized to this or that "phrase-regime," discourse," or cultural "form of like" (contra Lyotard). Nor can this merely be a matter of one's private "perspective" (contra Lyotard and Rorty). For Foucault ethics is a matter of autonomous, freely willed choice arrived at after a laborious, critical study of historical evidence. On the basis of empirical evidence we make aesthetic judgements on the value of such evidence. Thus, "the thread that connects Foucault to the Enlightenment is not faithfulness to its doctrinal elements, but rather the permanent reactivation of an attitude—that is of a philosophical ethos that could be

---

87. Foucault, *"Polemics, Politics, and Problematizations,"* interview with Rabinow in *The Foucault Reader*, 381–90, esp. 388.

88. Foucault, *"Polemics, Politics, and Problematizations,"* interview with Rabinow in *The Foucault Reader*, 331–90, esp. 388.

described as a permanent critique of our historical era."[89] That is to say, in keeping with Kant's critical imperative Foucault required that philosophy take nothing on trust, its own "doctrinal elements" included. Instead we should persist in the kind permanent critique of self-questioning activity that allows no privileged exemptions, no truth claims (epistemic or ethical) that cannot be justified on reasoned or principled grounds. The primary function of the philosopher then is to analyze the present and to reveal its fractures and instabilities, the ways it once limits human liberty.

In brief, freedom is not understood as the liberation of some human essence that is locked up in what we essentially are or the even liberation of some repressed human essence. Freedom is a type of detachment or suspension of judgement that opens new possibilities for thought and action. It is new possibilities of thinking and acting, of giving new impetus to the undefined work of freedom—which is immediately bound up with"aesthetics of existence" where it is imperative that we turn our lives into a work of art through self-mastery and ethical stylization.

Foucault as Kant *Redivivus?* Yes and no. Foucault argued that the Enlightenment formulated a philosophical question that remains for us to consider and a philosophical attitude that requires implementation—namely an ethos of permanent critique. Such critique abjures the "blackmail of the Enlightenment—that the acceptance that its reasoning discourses are a "final vocabulary" that progressively lead to wider and deeper modes of human emancipation. It is to this topic we now briefly turn.

D. A Perspectivism Concerning Art and Truth

We should push forward with a reflection upon the questions: "What is Enlightenment?" and "How and why does one become what one is?" These are questions raised by Kant and Foucault. Our question is linked to these. Is it valid that Foucault's critique appears to be more concerned with a deconstruction of the epistemological ideals of a foundation of all knowledge than with "normative ideals of rationality?" Clearly, Foucault holds deconstruction as a part of his agenda, but he also offers much that is constructive. Given his Enlightenment legacy this is hardly surprising.[90]

Foucault deconstructs not only the certainty of the possibility of the correspondence view of truth with its world of inherent (natural) and discoverable structures of thought which can be "represented" by thought, they also argue that the coherence view of truth with its world of comprehensible

---

89. Foucault, *WIE*, 42.
90. Foucault, *The Order of Things*, 9.

(logical) and inherent structures of thought which can be "intuited" from the form of a comprehensive account of reality is "problematic." Finally, adding insult to injury he re-affirms the validity of the pragmatic view of truth, which allows for truths as deemed true if they provide the individual with vital beliefs (or truth as a consensus established by experimental verification). Foucault argues that truth does not need a "theory" to begin with. According to the correspondence theory of truth—truth is explained in terms of a relation between beliefs and the world. According to the coherence theory, truth is explained in terms of a relation among beliefs. Truth according to this perspective is that there really is not anything about "truth" to be explained. Foucault attaches no significance to either the world or the self as "it really is." "True" is merely a form of praise we use for a belief that is presently so solidly established that we do not think that anything further inquiry is required to justify our accepting it. In brief, Foucault makes no significance to the world as it is (correspondence or coherence theories as to what it is) independent of the "perspective" from which it is conceived.

Here philosophers like Foucault fall prey to "perspectivism"—that there is no neutral language of observation—which means we must be sensitive to the possible "facticity" of views from anywhere. This means that Foucault thought that even though all discourses are self-contained languages incommensurable with each other—there are, nonetheless, languages of observation that adjudicate between competing paradigms (epistemic, scientific, political, and ethical). Moreover, such languages share two perspectives in common. They are critical and aesthethical. In this 'pragmatic sense' such languages, Foucault argues, are rational and can be represented as "true" propositions. There was no question more central to Foucault's work than "What is Enlightenment?" To paraphrase Jonathon Swift, Foucault became increasingly disposed to assert his distance from that state of perfected self-assurance that comes of being blissfully well deceived (a state not limited to postmodernist/men and women alone). It was here that Foucault took issue with the facile strain of counter-enlightenment rhetoric. For there was nothing more alien to the later Foucault than the kind of ultra-relativist orthodoxy that erects its own lack of critical and ethical resources into a terminal indifference with regard to issues of truth and ethics.

As mentioned at the beginning of this study the discordance of art and truth, in the face of which Nietzsche felt holy dread, is as old as philosophy itself. That art is not possible without the imagery of signs, and that the artist consciously manipulates the arbitrariness of the imagery of signs, is an ancient as well as modern insight. In philosophical aesthetics it has been noted that images do not refer to things (let alone things-in-themselves). Rather they have reference only within an epistemic-specific reality system, or a culture-specific language system. The issue that concerns us is that such questioning (or undermining) of the correspondence theory of the relation between signifier (word) and signified (object) is not only both complex and circumlocutionary. It also renders nugatory the possibility that art (either produced by the genius or enjoyed by an audience) is autonomous of epistemic, linguistic, and cultural constraints. In nuce, art is not objectively grounded in reason and truth. That art undermines the correspondence theory of truth is instructive for our discussion. Foucault argues that the relation of imagery to painting is an infinite relation based upon the distinction between resemblance and similitude.

Following Nietzsche, Foucault suggests that there is no mimetic correspondence (resemblance) between an image and object. Rather there exists only a discourse of similitude (similitude) between any image and the object represented by an image.[91] That is to say, there exists no single (true) correspondence (resemblance) of a work of art to an object. Similitude (similitude) is simply the result of a pragmatic decision to let a particular interpretation represent an end product, even though that "end product" is merely an (individual or collective) emblem of a relationship that exists among a number of fragmentary images.

In this respect Foucault explicitly reverses Plotinus. He advocates a separation of our aesthetics from ontology and epistemology. There is no original meaning, datum, substance, things-in-themselves, nor even any "thing" in nature that art refers to. We merely impose our will upon a work of art rendering the relationship between image and object comprehensible. That is to say, art is justified "pragmatically" if it provides an individual with vital benefits. The consequence of this reading of imagery to object is that issues of art become "aestheticized" to the point that art becomes a transfiguring play of freedom with reality, an elaboration of the self worked out by the strong individual in pursuit of desires in accordance with a private self-fashioning that results, Foucault suggests, in a "ironic heroization of the present . . . which Baudelaire called art."[92] In nuce, Foucault offers an aesthetics grounded in a Nietzschean will to treat art as justified to the extent we can view art as play, not as truth.

E. An Aesthetic Ethos.

Most philosophers agree that what we today call the artistic and aesthetic (art as a "sector of cultural activity") has little power to reveal the truth, save, or

91. *Order*, 23–24.
92. *Order*, 32.

redeem us. Indeed, art in the age of technology no longer reveals truth(s). Art has merely become a series of artworks to be enjoyed "aesthetically." Thus, for example, under the influence of Heidegger, Foucault argued that art in our time has lost its power to reveal truth (*a-letheia*).[93] In *This is Not a Pipe*, Foucault argues that it is high time to question all piety of thought that still clings to an aesthetic-mindedness that no longer guards and preserves human freedom but renders it nugatory. Foucault saw in Magritte an ally to campaign with against all forms of linguistic and representational realism. Foucault (historically/epistemically) and Magritte (visually) rejected the totality of this language/image game. In brief, in their works the arbitrariness of signs are underscored, the coherence images questioned, and the heteronomy of art and the artist methodically challenged. The reasons for their critique are not always clear but they point to the question as to whether a work of art should be organic or fragmentary. Both Foucault and Magritte privilege the fragment. Why they do so requires a brief explanation.

The question whether a work of art should be an organic unity or consist of fragments is perhaps best understood philosophically by the debate between Georg Lukacs and Theodor Adorno. Whereas Lukacs holds on to the organic work of art (realism) as an aesthetic norm, Adorno elevates avant-gardist, non-organic art to a historical norm and condemns all efforts to create a realistic art in our time. Avant-garde art is the only authentic expression of the contemporary state of the world because it is the historically necessary expression of alienation in late capitalist society. Following Adorno, Foucault (and Magritte) rejected Lukacs view that the organic work of art constitutes a type of perfection. The organic work, by its very form, promotes the illusion of a world that is whole. For Foucault and Magritte avant-garde art is a radical protest that rejects all false reconciliation with what exists. As such it is the only art form that has historical legitimacy today.

Foucault and Magritte are important for their cautious moral scepticism in warning us not only of the hidden dangers of the false "we" of organic art but also the creative "I" implicit in much avant-garde art. Organic art is self-explanatory. It is essentially narrative, historical, and conventional. Avant-garde art, on the other hand, is non-organic, fragmentary. Benjamin's concept of allegory assists in explaining non-organic works of art. The allegorist pulls an element out of the totality of the life context, isolating it, depriving it of its function (allegory is essentially a fragment, the opposite of an organic symbol). Then the allegorist joins several isolated fragments together and thereby creates meaning. It is only after art is detached from the praxis of contemporary (bourgeois) life, Foucault argued, can two things be

93. Foucault, *This is Not a Pipe*, 43–52.

seen: first, that the progressive separation of art from modern life contexts advocated by Kee, Kandinsky, and Magritte is positive; and secondly, that the crystallization of a distinctive sphere of experience—the aesthetic—is possible once this separation has occurred. The crucial question is how is this separation undertaken and accomplished?

Foucault follows in the wake of the avant-garde and their attempts to negate conventional understandings of art. First, he challenges modernist claims that works of art are acts of individual genius; secondly, he argues that notions of the unique individual and artistic individualism are ideological. Both are merely aspects of a modernist episteme. The (bourgeois) individual artist is a thing of the past. Indeed, even stylistic innovation is no longer possible. All that is left is the commercial artist, the pastiche, and the parody of dead styles. Marcel Duchamp (and later Andy Warhol) knew this well. By signing mass-produced objects both mocked a society in which the signature (signifier) meant more than the quality of work (signified). Klee, Kandinsky, and Magritte also knew this. By disassociating image (signifier) from object (signified) each parodied a culture that clings to the non-arbitrariness of the sign in most aspects of life. As such it was through the efforts of the avant-garde that the historical (narrative) succession of techniques and styles was replaced by simultaneity of the radically disparate—the fragmentation of time, objects, subjects, of society itself.

It is here that the critical bite of avant-garde criticism takes hold. The role of chance and shock became the principle of artistic intent rather than art organized around a means-ends calculus (be it political, ethical, or social). Magritte criticized schools that preceded his own as well as art as an institution. Art in bourgeois society continues to be a realm distinct from the praxis of life. Magritte's own art turns not so much against the techniques of traditional art (which he utilized), but against the status of art in bourgeois society, and the distribution apparatus on which works of art depend (as defined by bourgeois-capitalist concepts of autonomy). In brief, Magritte's protest suggests an absence of autonomy—an absence between individual "artistic" autonomy coupled to an absence of "aesthetic" consequences. It was just such self-conscious recognition of "absence" in Magritte (Klee and Kandinsky) that Foucault celebrated. He noted these artists because their critique of organic art highlighted arts "aesthetic absence." He celebrated their critique because he thought that once it was seen that art as an institution neutralized the aesthetic (liberating) effect works of art should have upon society—artists themselves would again "aestheticize" art.

What Foucault is up to is comprehensible within the context of Enlightenment notions of the sublime. A review of Kant's theory is helpful here. For Kant, the sublime is that which exceeds all our powers of representation, an experience for which we can find no adequate sensuous or conceptual mode of expression, and which differs from the beautiful in so far as it affords no sense of harmonious balance or agreement between mental faculties. The sublime figures for Kant as a means of expressing (by analogy) what would otherwise be strictly inexpressible. The Kantian sublime serves as a reminder of the gulf that opens up between truth-claims lacking any measure of justice by which to resolve their dispute. For Foucault the sublime comes to figure as an index of the radical heterogeneity that inhibits our discourses of truth and value, or the kinds of injustice that inevitably result when one such art discourse—most often the "realistic"—seeks to monopolize the whole conversation. As noted this move signals a host of problems—epistemological, ethical, social, and political. Nonetheless, he argued, such problems can be overcome aesthetically. It is almost as if Foucault thinks the "aesthetic turn" can bring us out of the wilderness, that it can overturn (ueberwinden) the violent history of reason that it can provide us with an orientation for avoiding the abyss of nihilism that he so desperately wanted to avoid. In brief, Foucault reduces all artistic truth-claims to the level of discourses. In doing so, he makes a turn toward the Kantian sublime as a means of devaluing cognitive truth-claims and elevating the notion of the unrepresentable to valorization in the aesthetical realm. (that is, intuitions cannot be brought under adequate concepts). As such, even art is "aestheticized" as a non-propositional and non-discursive language of metaphysics.

F. Aesthetics, Ethics, and the Technologies of the Self

What do aesthetics, ethics, freedom, and purposiveness have to do with each other? In his last writings Foucault was drawn to the ancient philosophical notion of life as the art of living, as a style of life, as a way of life. He described this *ethos* as practices of the self, as the care of the self, and called it 'aesthetics of existence.' Foucault taught that the only way we can be individuals is to create ourselves. He grounded his aesthetics (and ethics) on the idea of freedom. He argued that the inherently unknowable (or unreason) should be the foundation of aesthetics and ethics. Finally, he suggested that the key to understanding aesthetics and ethics is the concept of 'purposiveness.' He understood the ethics of the ancients as one of pleasure which is taken into the self.[94] Moreover, he saw in these practices of the self a conversion towards the self wherein one liberates oneself from externals, from sensual attachment to external objects and to the pleasures which these procure. Finally, he perceived in this lifestyle a self-mastery,

---

94. Foucault, *Care of the Self*, 83.

self-possession, and acquisition of happiness in internal freedom and independence. Through moderation and regulation one cares for the self. Indeed, it is the responsibility of each individual to give style, beauty, and grace to his existence. Ethics and aesthetics is the relation the individual has with himself. The notion that ethics is immediately bound up with an aesthetics of existence is central to Foucault's understanding of freedom. For Foucault ethics is the deliberative component of free aesthetic activity and the basis for a prolonged practice of the self whereby one masters oneself in order to constitute one self as a free self. That is to say, freedom is associated with a mastery of the self and its desires. As such, the subject can turn his life into a work of art through self-mastery and ethical stylization. Such a transformation leads to a certain state of happiness, purity, perfection, or immortality.[95]

While Foucault does not uncritically affirm Greek culture, his unstated "normative assumption" was that Greco-Roman ethical practice is superior to later ancient and mediaeval Christian, and modern moral systems. First, subjectivity is not viewed as a reified construct of power. Secondly, the subject is no longer determined by a functionalist system of gratuitous power whose bio-power trains bodies and regulates populations for no purpose other than its own intrinsic ends. Rather Greco-Roman ethics allow for the conditions of the possibility that a self-governing individual could create itself, and enjoy types of experience, pleasure, and desire in autonomous stylized forms which lead to a transformation of the self. In brief, for Foucault ancient philosophy offered the opportunity to promote new forms of subjectivity to counter the normalized individuality which has been imposed on us for centuries.[96] The point is that contemporary philosophers can take up the Greek philosophy again "as an experience which took place once and with regard to which one can be completely free."[97] The specter of the isolated subject in contemporary thought is overcome through Foucault's aesthetical inquiries into ancient ethics and his valorization of a form of ethical practice that is non-universalizing, non-normalizing, attentive to individual differences, attentive to individual liberty, and the larger social context of the freedom of the self.[98]

Ethics here depends not so much on moral norms as free choice based upon aesthetic criteria which bracket the subjectivizing of the individual

---

95. Foucault, *Technologies of the Self*, in Gutman and Hutton (eds.), *Technologies of the Self*, 18.

96. Foucault, *The Subject and Power* in Dreyfus and Rabinow (eds.), *Michel Foucault: Beyond Structuralism and Hermeneutics*, 216.

97. Foucault, *Final Interview*, Raritan no. 5, 1–13.

98. *Final Interview*, 12.

into a normalized, universal ethical subject. Foucault argued that the task of life is not to discover oneself but to continually produce a self as an autonomous subject.[99] That is to say, freedom is understood as an ongoing ethical practice of self-mastery and care of the self. Foucault argued that the subject is still discursively and socially conditioned, and still theorized as situated within power relations. The difference is now he sees that individuals also have the power to define their own identity, to master their body and desires, and to create a practice of freedom through 'techniques of the self.' Freedom is mastery of and power over oneself. As such, "liberty is the ontological condition of ethics and ethics as the deliberate form assumed by liberty."[100] This study began with a specter that haunts contemporary thought: the specter of the isolated subject. Foucault proposed the overcoming of isolation through the study of how individuals in Greco-Roman culture handled problems such as "questioning their own conduct, watching over and giving shape to it, and shaping themselves as ethical subjects." Foucault claims that "ethical freedom has to be practiced," that "ethics is the thoughtful practice of freedom," and that such self-mastery leads to an 'aesthetics of existence.'[101]

V. Plotinus and Foucault

> The effort to rethink the Greeks today consists not in valorizing Greek ethics as the moral domain par excellence that we need in order to think about ourselves but of doing it in such a way that European philosophy can start again from Greek philosophy as an experience once given, in relation to which we can be totally free.
>
> —FOUCAULT, LES NOVELLAS LITTERERS[102]

Although there are marked differences between the aesthetics of Plotinus and Foucault, and difficulties in Foucault's interpretation of ancient philosophical texts,[103] there exist, nonetheless, certain ideas each shares with the other. First, there is the recognition that aesthetics heal the disjointed, fractured self. Through art and aesthetics the individual overcomes isolation,

---

99. Foucault, *WIE*, 43.

100. Foucault, *The Ethic of Care for the Self as a Practice of Freedom* in Bernauer and Rasmussen (eds.), *The Final Foucault*, 4.

101. Foucault, *The Use of Pleasure*, 13.

102. Interview of May 29, 1984 in *Les Nouvelles litteraires*.

103. As noted by P. Hadot in "Reflections on the notion of 'the cultivation of the self'" in P. Hadot, *MFP*, 230.

dislocation, and rupture. Secondly, there is the claim that art and aesthetics are linked to truth, autonomy, and happiness. There is no discordance between art, aesthetics, and truth. Indeed, both appear more truthful than empirical truth, more rational than methodical reason, more valuable than normative principles of morality or utility.

The essential point for both is: cultivate yourself, create your own beautiful or sublime individuality, aestheticize your existence, and craft an *ethos* that is good and honorable. Aesthetic and non-normative, sustained by personal choice and not by legal constraint, both Plotinus and Foucault propose relationships with the self that are differentiated, whose primary purpose is the aestheticization of the self. As such the power of philosophy is drawing up a design for an ethics of the individual, an ethics of freedom, which permits the self's overcoming of rupture, fragmentation, and isolation.

A. Art and Aesthetics: Rupture and Reconciliation

The ancient subject was not able to cultivate the soul apart from the metaphysical and mythical discourses which accompanied them. Plotinus proposed that whoever practices these aesthetic exercises accedes concretely to the universality of the noetic perspective, through the marvelous grasping of the presence of intelligible beauty.

The art of living in Plotinus' philosophy was grounded on a metaphysical foundationalism. The emancipation of the individual has its locus in the domains of ethics and aesthetics. The individual achieves liberation through contemplative technologies of the self. These exercises make one aware of the undescended soul. Next they permit one to grasp intelligibles, and the One through a variety of aesthetic symbols. Plotinus reflects on the ascent of the soul and the role art and aesthetics play in going beyond the self, at thinking and acting in union with universal reason. The best part of the self is ultimately a transcendent, "undescended" self which art and aesthetic perception reveals to the subject. In grasping this eternal self, by discovering she has a reason in herself, the soul discovers she is a part of the universal reason which is within all humanity and the cosmos itself.

The contemporary self is able to practice the philosophical exercises of antiquity while separating them from the metaphysical or mythical discourses which accompany them. Indeed, Foucault argues whoever practices these aesthetic exercises sees the world with new eyes. He discovers, in the enjoyment of the present a splendor of existence which Nietzsche said allows us to say yes 'not only to ourselves but to existence.' Foucault describes with precision what he calls the practices of the self preached by

Platonists, Epicureans, and Stoics in antiquity. He saw in this care of the self a cultivation of the body and soul which leads to a conversion towards the self, a possession of the self. In mastering this contingent self, by discovering it has a value in itself, the subject forges his spiritual identity as an autonomous being.

The art of living according to Foucault is not grounded in any metaphysical foundationalism. Nonetheless, the emancipation of the individual depends upon recognition of the many relationships the subject has with the self, or of the consciousness of the self. Moreover, the individual achieves liberation through technologies of the self which manifest themselves through a variety of symbols. It is here we encounter similarities between Plotinus and Foucault.

Subjectivity for both denotes relations to the self and the critical function of philosophy is the elaboration of new subjectivities through the construction of technologies of existence. Plotinus and Foucault propose a fundamental relationship of the self (subjectivity in its broadest meaning), ethics (determination of the principles of existence), and aesthetics (the individual's attempt to care for the self). The goal of life is caring for oneself by making one's life a work of art by designing one's life with the conviction that by caring for the self the individual renders the greatest service to humanity.

What Plotinus calls the ascent of the soul to intelligible beauty and what Foucault calls the practices of the self in the ancients corresponds to a movement of conversion towards the self: one liberates oneself from externals, attachments, and the pleasures one can procure. The difference between this ancient and this 'postmodern,' however is that in Plotinus this movement of interiorization is inseparably linked to another movement in which one raises oneself to a higher psychic level in which one remembers another type of exteriorization, another relationship with the exterior, another way of being-in-the-world which consists of being aware of the self as part of universal reason.

According to Plotinus, one identifies with an 'Other' which is universal reason, which is present in each of us. According to Foucault, however, one identifies with the 'Self' which is freedom, which is present in each of us. As such in Plotinus there is a radical transformation of perspective which has a universal and cosmic dimension which Foucault does not see. That is to say, interiorization for Plotinus is going beyond the self in a way which leads to universalization.

For Foucault there is nothing apart from interiorization, a conversion toward the self which leads to a cultivation of the self.[104] The subject needs only recognition of the self to grasp the multiple forms the self can take to attain enlightenment and freedom. Indeed, for Foucault liberty becomes a certain form of relationship of the individual to the self. Hence his refusal to exteriorize: "the . . . critical function of philosophy derives . . . from Socrates' imperative: 'Know thyself': that is, base yourself on freedom, through self-mastery."[105] Freedom is located in the individual fragment which is the contemporary self. It is not located in any universal totality beyond and within the self as argued by Plotinus.

B. *Homo Aestheticus* and Old Gods Ascending

Kierkegaard has noted:

> Each age has its characteristic depravity. Our is perhaps not pleasure or indulgence or sensuality, but rather a dissolute contempt . . . for individual man.[106]

In their own times, Plotinus and Foucault affirmed the self as soul and individual. Moreover, they argued that ethics are possible through the aesthetic cultivation of the self. This soul or self are not in the world as the limit of the world or exclusively as a subject that has *episteme* and *dianoia*. They are in the world as the un-limit of the world as a self that has *eupatheia* and *phronesis*.

In a contemporary world, Foucault argues that if moral experiences centered on the subject are no longer satisfying today because they have been uncovered as subjugation, then "we are confronted by a certain number of questions posed to us in the same terms used in antiquity."[107] Indeed, because "we no longer believe ethics to be based upon religion" . . . and . . . "we do not want any legal system to intervene in our private and personal lives," "our problem today . . . is . . . somewhat similar" to what it was for the Greeks: how to base ethics on the rigorously personal choice of a style of existence. A clear result from reading Foucault is that the achievement of wholeness and

---

104. See, Hadot, *MFP*, 225–31.
105. *L'Ethique du souci de soi comme pratique de la liberte*, Interview with Fornet-Betancourt, Becker, and Gomez-Muller (Jan. 20, 1984).
106. Kierkegaard, *Concluding Unscientific Postscript*, 33.
107. *Interview* of May 29, 1984 in *Les Nouvelles litteraires*.

freedom in our age demands a return to the individuality of antiquity, and a retreat from subjectivity as moderns describe it.

In Plotinus (and Kant) the cohesion of the self rests upon transcendent (or transcendental) foundations. For Foucault cohesion rests on aesthetic interindividuality that abjures all types of transcendence provided either by a metyaphysical reality or a transcendental normalizing intersubjectivity that would be humanity's shared lot. We can now, perhaps, better understand, at the end of our story, what Foucault rejects in these enlightenment philosophies. But we can also better appreciate what he finds appealing in them. He locates freedom in the individual, he structures the quest for liberty in the arts and aesthetics. Contemporary existence can no longer be anything than an extension of the self as artist. The world is an aesthetic reality created by the subject, who is finally an autonomous, indeed ethical individual.

The ancient world considered ethics as an art which brings about in the community and the individual the order within which each individual finds the place and proportion due it. In brief, the goal of life is to achieve aristocratic excellence. This can only be achieved through the cultivation of the soul which is achieved through the care of the self. That is to say, autonomy lies in individuality, in the invention of a *homo aestheticus*. Since nothing is given and everything is constructed, ancient ethics and aesthetics provides the contemporary individual with the knowledge lacking to achieve autonomy Foucault argues. Aesthetics also provides us with a means to overcome the prison of modernity, a way to emancipate ourselves from forgetfulness, fragmentation, and rupture.

Although Foucault argues we cannot go back and there is no *arche* that is free of all forgetting of concern for the self, explicit in his later works is an appreciation for the philosophy of the ancients. In this sense he has been central in the rehabilitation of ancient philosophy among contemporary philosophers. By his critical appropriation of themes in Plato, Seneca, Marcus Aurelius, Metrodorus, and Plotinus—Foucault has argued that our `postmodern' condition, our existence in the world, is to be a creative individual. As such, it is necessary to return to the ancient sages in order to go beyond modernism. His `postmodern' road begins in the via antiqua. For Foucault this is the only consistent basis for the new departure. Antiquity offers an ethics "through which the subject postulates the form he gives to his life."[108] It proposes aesthetics as a philosophical *ethos*.

For Foucault the need to lend a voice to the silence of the "Other" is a condition for enlightenment and freedom. His reading of the Plato and the

---

108. *Interview* of May 29, 1984 in *Les Nouvelles litteraires*.

ancients lead to a remarkable discovery. It was his autonomous self. This "self" is not just another entity in the world. In a fundamental sense this self creates worlds. Moreover, in knowing itself it comes to recognize other selves, and the horizons of any and every possible self. This acquisition of an aesthetic pretence is no innocent philosophical thesis. It is a weapon of enormous power. And it could not have been uncovered without the help of old gods ascending. Foucault has called for open conversation and for the revitalization of western philosophy, a revival that must begin with the Greeks and Romans themselves. In the words of Dewey—who some might think an odd supporter of a return to Plato movement:

> Nothing could be more helpful to present philosophizing than a "Back to Plato" movement; but it would have to be a back to the dramatic, restless, cooperatively inquiring Plato of the Dialogues, trying one mode of attack after another to see what it might yield; back to the Plato whose highest flight of metaphysics always terminated with a social and practical turn, and not to the artificial Plato constructed by unimaginative commentators who treat him as the original university professor.[109]

Is it no longer possible along with Nietzsche, Heidegger, Derrida, and Rorty to link Plato and Platonism with the death of philosophy. This remains to be seen. However, Foucault has helped replace the metaphor of the Gorgon-Meduza to characterize ancient philosophy. The cliché that all post pre-Socratic philosophy prefigures the nihilistic triumph of *Gestell* (enframing) requires re-thinking. Arguably, the history of the soul and the self as traced in this study adequately challenges the association of Plato and Platonism with the "fallenness" and "forgetfulness" of Being.

Conclusion

This partial, yet it is hoped, representative survey of the aesthetics of Plotinus, Kant and Foucault, does not yield firm conclusions about the commensurability of their views of the arts and aesthetics. It does, however, suggest that their theories are not incommensurable. Therefore, it is possible to draw a few preliminary conclusions: First, Plotinus, Kant and Foucault make extensive use of aesthetic symbols and techniques for overcoming the fallenness of the soul and rupture of the self. They also affirm the concordance of art and truth. Art and aesthetics form an integral part of their strategies for the ascent of the soul and the technologies of the self.

---

109. Dewey, *From Absolutism to Experimentalism*. cf. Bernstein, *John Dewey*, 13.

In addition they reject any associations of Plato, Platonism, and ancient philosophy with oppression, repression, and the loss of being. The ancient sages offer the possibility for an 'aesthetic turn' which once taken culminates in the liberation of the self as homo aestheticus and the attainment of an 'aesthetics of existence.' Secondly, art and aesthetics are valuable for the philosophical intentions of Plotinus, Kant and Foucault. Each stands as important and independent elements within larger programs for the ascent of the soul and the liberation of the self. To view the aesthetics of Plotinus and Foucault from this perspective is to connect their theories of the arts with their proper philosophical context. Aesthetics is an affirming philosophical ethos that valorizes the individual thereby vanquishing the darkness of forgetfulness, betrayal, and nihilism. Thirdly, the aesthetic individual is the locus of value. Aesthetics so far as it springs from the desire to say something about the ultimate meaning of life argues that the absolute good cannot merely be a product of logismos. Self and value can be represented, perhaps better, as *aisthesis*. The self, the subject, and indeed subjectivity are best expressed in the words of Wittgenstein:

> the 'whereof one cannot speak, thereof one must be silent.'[110]

---

110. Wittgenstein, *Tractatus*, 7.

Conclusion

Flatland

> "...the need for philosophy arises when the power of unification disappears from the life of men."
>
> —Hegel, *Philosophy of Spirit*

Précis

OF CLOUDS AND CLOCKS—PROVIDES some context of what a 'parsing of mind, meaning and subjectivity' are about. "Clouds," a metaphor for indeterministic systems, are contrasted with "clocks" or deterministic ones. Siding with indeterminism, Popper comments—"Peirce was right in holding that all clocks are clouds to some considerable degree—even the most precise of clocks. This, I think, is the most important inversion of the mistaken determinist view that all clouds are clocks.[1] Extending this metaphor Aristotle, Origen and Plotinus suggest we are correct to think that all 'clocks' (intentionality and meaning) are 'clouds' (thought and language)—if for no other reason than clocks and clouds share marks of the mental[2]—and that 'thinking is thinking on thinking' cannot be explained by mind, matter, or a mind-matter dualism alone but also by thought, language and their intentionalities;[3] ho-

---

1. Popper, *Clouds, and Clocks,* 215.

2. Marks of the mental include (but are not exhaustive of): 1) non-spatiality (having a non-spatial space or element); 2) an ability to exist separately from bodies; 3) an inability to be identified with any object "in the world; 4) an ability to know itself incorrigibly ("privileged access"); 5) an ability to grasp universals; 6) an ability to sustain relations ("intentionality"); 7) an ability to use language; 8) an ability to act freely; and 9) an ability to form part of a social group. See, Feigl, *Mental and Physical.*

3. A theory that posits mental events and processes where 'mental' means exhibiting

lenmermism that the whole is present *as whole* in each part;[4] and synechism that reality cannot be identified with physical existence (or actuality) alone but also comprises real mental identities and relations, necessities and possibilities.[5] Origen's *logos* and *nous* carry with them kindred commitments to mentalism, holenmermism and synechism.[6]

---

intentionality. Aristotle's divine *nous* thinking itself (*kai estin he noesis noeseos noesis*) is complete and self-sufficient and that from which nothing is wanting. cf. Aristotle, *Metaphysics*, XII.9.1074b33–35. Plotinus's doctrine that every form in *Nous* contains every other form by the interiority of their relation to other Forms is based on claims that each Form is all the other Forms and each mind is identical (qualitatively) with each and every Form because the multiplicity of intellect is not spatially articulated: "Intellect and the intelligible substance; each individual Idea is not other than Intellect, but each is Intellect. And Intellect as a whole is all the Forms, and each individual Form is an individual intellect ... we must assume that the real beings have their place in the thinking subject." cf. Plotinus, *Ennead*, V.9.8.1–5; 10–12. cf. V.V.1.19–43; V.8.3.30–34; V.9.6; V.9.8.3–7.

4. Holenmermism (that 'the whole is in the part'): is based on the notion that exclusion is always posterior to inclusion. This theory arose out of attempts to think of the divine mind as unitary in its internal aspects, relations and differentiations without being sundered in to its parts. cf. Hedley, *Iconic Imagination*, 134–35. Aristotle's claim that 'the whole is in the part' is: "the sort of principle that constitutes the nature of each ... all must at least come to be dissolved into their elements ... in which all share for the good of the whole." cf. Aristotle, *Metaphysics*, XII.10.1075a23–26. Aristotle claims the perfection of divine *nous* thinking itself (*kai estin he noesis noeseos noesis*) includes knowledge of other forms including forms in nature—for to be perfect is to be complete and self-sufficient and "that from which nothing is wanting ... what is true of each particular is true of the whole as such—the whole is that of which nothing is outside." cf. Aristotle, *Physics*, III.6.207a8–15; *Metaphysics*, XII.9.1074b33–35; *Metaphysics*, XII.8.1074b33–35; XII.10.1075b21–24. cf. Berti, *Intellection*, 1978, 141–63. Plotinus argues that while a distinction can be drawn between what a thing is and the unity which makes it what it is: "all are bound together by the one (VI.9.2.20) ... it is by the one that all beings are beings" traced to its external cause in the "uniform" (VI.9.5.27) nature of *Nous* and finally to the One itself." cf. Corrigan, *Essence and Existence*, 109–10.

5. Synechism (Greek > *suneches*): is based on claims that reality is not merely mind, matter, or a mind-matter dualism and cannot be identified with existence (potentiality) but comprises actual (objective) possibilities where space and time are eternal. Aristotle proposes that although there is a formal difference between Intellect's act of thinking and its object, this does not amount to a material difference as long as the object can exist self-sufficiently without any matter. In the case of divine *nous* its *noesis* as an act of self-contemplation comprises the interiority of its relations to the whole of reality. In 'thinking itself' nothing is wanting and existence is an actual possibility. See *Metaphysics*, XII.8.1074b33–35; XII.10.1075b21–24. cf. De Konnick, *La Noesis*, 474–515. Plotinus argues that every Form in *Nous* contains every other Form by the interiority of its relations to the other Forms (V.5.1.19–43). Given the relation of a superior model to an inferior image (V.8.4.3–11), intelligible Form is reflected in the sensible world. The Forms in their mutual reflection are like images (*algamata*). (V.8.4.42–43). Also see *Enneads* V.8.3.30–34; V.9.6; V.9.8.3–7. cf. Schroeder, 344–346; Trouillard, *Logic*, 125–38.

6. Logos is in the whole and in every part; creating, sustaining and redeeming the

I. Deconstructing

A caveat remains—incommensurability. In relation to objects known epistemological realists hold knowledge to be grounded in first causes; while epistemological anti-realists view it a consequence of a privileged first-person access to epistemological foundations. The first sees rationality and self-reflection as part of a *theoria* or living contemplation; the second views subjectivity as the key to objectivity, the world a construction of consciousness, mind a mirror of reality and both a mere fact of physical processes. Revolutions introduced by mechanics and corpuscular physics, a revaluation in ideas about 'ideas,' the invention of the subjective self, 'analysis' of how minds, bodies and language 'relate,' and semantic parsings about the meaning of 'meaning' have widened the gap between them.

Analytic and deconstructionist arguments that foundationalism and its subjectivities are non-cognitive[7] or non-sensical[8] has prevailed throughout the last century. Analytic objections are four-fold: the first is based upon a rejection of substance dualism: either reality and minds are not substances; or mental substances are ontologically dependent on physical substances; or since physical states of the body are more fundamental than mental states; substance can be explained in terms of physical states. The second is that dualism claims involve a category (logical-semantic) mistake.[9] The third

---

intelligible and sensible worlds. Origen, *De Prin* I.6.2. cf. Ramelli, *Apokatastasis*, 2009, 217–63.

7. See, Schlicht, *Positivism and Realism*. The principle asserts that the meaning of a proposition its method of verification. It is a simple principle which draws a sharp distinction between cognitive and non-cognitive expressions. The former being factual, are either true or false; they set out to give us information about the world, and if they are true, they do so. The latter, being non-factual, are neither true nor false. The verifiability principle proved impossible to verify as verifiability as a method involves infinite regress. Why does P1 hold; because of P2; why does P2 hold; because of P3, why does P3 hold; because of P4; why does P4 hold; because of P5 >>>> infinite regress. It also casts doubt on its own status. How is it to be verified? It also proved impossible to frame in a form that did not admit all metaphysical sentences as meaningful. With Ayer, various repairs were attempted to salvage the principle: none has succeeded. Knowing for Aristotle and Plotinus, for example, does not necessitate an infinite regress because some knowledge does not depend on demonstration.

8. The later neo-Platonist *a* of *differance*, the not heard, that which remains silent, or secret and discreet as a tomb, is beyond mind and language awaits an onto-theological distancing from Intellect-Being initiated by Proclus and Pseudo-Dionysius to be consummated by Heidegger is assessed in Derrida. cf. Derrida, *Margins*, 1–2.

9. See, Ryle, Critics of physicalism and logical behaviorism generally argue that: (1) by insisting reality and minds cannot not be classified as substances or (2) that dualists fall into the entity-aspect category mistake, (3) physicalist-logical behaviorist arguments fall into the fallacy of 'begging the question'—they assume what they are trying to prove. Searle's arguments against identity theory suffice to illustrate both points.

rests on Frege's claim that sense (*Sinn*) and meaning/reference (*Bedeutung*) are two sorts of entities. Fourthly, Quine argues the distinction provides a justification for dismissing talk about meaning as entities altogether.[10] These claims result in a dissolution of a distinction between questions of meaning and questions of fact—which results in dismissal of the *a priori/ a posteriori*, *analytic/synthetic*, and *a se/per se* distinctions and theories of meaning derived upon such distinctions. Since each distinction lacks explanatory power from the perspective of "canonical notations"—only a small portion of reality can be described as linguistically meaningful.[11]

Deconstructionists up the ante ironically inferring from the collapse of the verifiability argument and the analytic/synthetic distinction that: first, if what can be thought or spoken of has as no transcendental signified or 'sayable,' then reality must be considered as a text whose meaning is never 'present.' ('IL n'y pas de hors texte'—there is nothing outside the text or there is no outside text); and secondly since meaning depends on linguistic interconnections, in an ever-changing web of signifiers within a multivalent terrain of what they signify, any attempt to characterize 'first philosophy' as 'foundational philosophy' is inexpressible or 'self-deceptive'—meaning is undetermined—by an ever-changing web of signifiers with no verifiable signified.[12] Four conclusions emerge from these critiques. The first is: a) if there is nothing verifiable that can be mapped from Russell's and Carnap's sense data and there is nothing that can be known or spoken of beyond Russell's and Wittgenstein's theory of descriptions: 'first philosophy' is non-cognitive. The second is: a) if there is nothing other than Heidegger's 'silence of silence;' or Derrida's interplay of signs—where there is but a 'trace' of meaning whose thought and language is never present—then are only linguistic traces to be thought of, or spoken of, or mapped, or signified at all: first-philosophy is self-deceptive.[13] The third following Quine

---

cf. Searle, *Rediscovery*, 65.

10. Quine, *Logical Point of View*, 21.

11. A kindred approach is offered by Dummet and Putnam—that the task of philosophy is not epistemology but analysis of meaning. Dummett proposes epistemological issues—if formulated correctly—address issues of linguistic meaning. cf. Dummett, *Frege's Philosophy*, 559.

12. On Derrida reading Neoplatonism see Gersh, 2007, 237–60. For attempts a dialogue within Neoplatonic, Heideggerian, and onto-theological "horizons" cf. Narbonne, *Henologie* and *Levinas*; and Gersh, *Neoplatonism and Derrida*.

13. See, Gersh, *Neoplatonism after Derrida*, 72–76; 137–82. Gersh argues that Derrida endorses a variety of non-foundationalisms based on a complex cluster tier structure tied to the polyvalence non-intentionality of texts and language contexts. Due attention is given to skeptical arguments about justification claims to either foundationalism essentialism or realism. This anti (or post) epistemological standpoint challenges

is: Aristotle and Plotinus may model or picture first principles in *a priori/ analytic/a se* ways but can do nothing more.[14]

Much of twentieth century philosophy of language was initially shaped by two problems: 1) Russell's and C.I. Lewis' claims that problems in mind, language and meaning could be resolved or dissolved by linguistic reflection.[15] The sources that underlie contemporary philosophy of language claims involve a cluster of problems initiated by Frege, discussed by Wittgenstein in the *Tractatus* and by Carnap in *Meaning and Necessity*. Here how to systematize notions of meaning and reference to take advantage of quantifactional logic, preserve our intuitions about modality and produce a clear picture of the way in which notions like truth, meaning, necessity and name fit together are emphasized. Meaning is determined by verifiability. Schlicht proposed that if what can be thought and spoken of can only be justified either on the basis of Russell's and the early Wittgenstein's truth-functional calculus, where "atomic facts" correspond with "unit propositions" of an idealized formal language or Carnap's sense data foundations, then 'first philosophy' cannot be a 'foundational philosophy.' It is not factual and utilizes 'non-cognitive' rather than 'cognitive' expressions.[16]

Thus the verifiability view that every true statement contains our contribution (in the form of the meanings of the component terms) as well as the world's (in the form of the facts of sense perception); and 2) Quine's proposal that Frege's sense/meaning distinction provides a justification for dismissing talk about meaning as entities altogether.[17] Instead of talking about meaning, we should talk about the sameness of meaning. Turning to the notion of analyticity Quine distinguishes two ways in which a statement can be true by

---

metaphysical arguments or standpoints and knowledge (*episteme*) as providing an accurate mapping mind and language into final reference vocabularies—on the basis of either correspondence or coherence theories of truth. They also reject any complete, unique and closed *epistemes* about grand narratives. Thus Aristotle's and Plotinus's claims to 'first philosophy' as 'foundational philosophy' fall under suspicion as either non-sensical or self-deceptive. It remains an open question, well outside the horizons of this enquiry, whether a compatabilism exists between the later ancient Neoplatonists and contemporary deconstructionists on challenges to any 'first philosophy' and all 'foundationalist' presuppositions.

14. A fundamental move in defense of first principles is to distinguish on the basis of property language: 1) between Ideas and First principles *a se* and *per se*—or between eternal and immutable Forms and the capacity to make universal judgments; and 2) distinctions between abstract entities with properties *per se* and abstract objects without properties *a se*.

15. See, Soames, *Philosophy of Language*.

16. Schlicht, *Positivism and Realism*.

17. Quine, *Logical Point of View*, 21.

virtue of meanings and independently of fact.[18] The claim that two expressions may have the very same extension yet not be synonymous (i.e. refer to the very same set of things) is crucial.[19] Synonymy can be explained using the notion of interchangeability. But if interchangeability holds it has to be non-accidental or necessary.[20] If neither holds meaning stands in need of an explanation. If this cannot be achieved, the distinction between analytic meanings as entities must be dropped altogether.[21]

Summary: Despite such incommensurability there remain grounds for commensurability. There are thinkers in both camps that tend toward monism (holenmermism), or neutral monism (synechism), who oppose substance dualism in its Cartesian and post- Cartesian senses, and are critics of subjectivism and constructivism. Most are property dualists and agree, despite all the efforts expended on escaping from the fly-bottle, the most dangerous and seductive of all fly-bottles is "I am and we are not a fly-bottle . . ."[22]

II. Reconstructing

Aristotelians,[23] neo-Aristotelians[24] and Neoplatonists[25] offer grounds for a contemporary reconstruction of "foundations." Whether mental or

18. Quine, *Logical Point of View*, 22–23.
19. See, Hahn and Schlipp *Philosophy of Quine*, 473.
20. Quine, *Pursuit of Truth*, 1.
21. Quine, *Pursuit of Truth*, 4.
22. Wittgenstein, *Tractatus*, 6.54.
23. For a defense of Aristotelian first principles on Aristotelian grounds on see, De Koninck, *La Noesis*, 215–18; *Aristotle on God*, 474–515; Cleary, *Aristotle's Criticisms*, 70–97; *Powers that Be*, 19–64; Berti, *Intellection*, 141–63. Also see Brinkmann, *Aristoteles Metaphysik*; Barnes, Schofield, and Sorabji, *Metaphysics*; Seidl, *Realistische Metaphysik*; and Nyvlt, *Aristotle and Plotinus*. The thesis proposed is although Aristotle and Plotinus anticipate some empirical-analytic mind, language and meaning claims, their metaphysics cannot be adequately interpreted from empirical, physicalist or linguistic perspectives alone.
24. For a defense of a neo-Aristotelian metaphysics on empirical and analytical grounds see, G.E.L. Owen, *Snares of Ontology*, and *Platonism of Aristotle*,; Lowe, *Of Being,*; *Kinds*; *Survey of Metaphysics*,; *Four-Category Ontology*; *More Kinds of Being*; Loux, *Universals and Particulars* and *Substance and Attribute*; Mandrake, *Aristotle's Language and Meaning*; Tahko, *Contemporary Aristotelian Metaphysics*; Novotný and Novák, *Metaphysics*.
25. For a defense of Aristotelian-Neoplatonic first philosophy on philological-historical-philosophical grounds see, Schroeder, *Conversion*, 185–95; *Synousia*, 677–699; *Plotinus and Language*, 336–52; Corrigan, *Essence and Existence*; Bussanich, *Metaphysics of the One*; Gerson, *Aristotle and Other Platonists*; Gersh, *Platonism After Derrida*.

linguistic, the kind of foundational philosophy that stems from Aristotle and Plotinus is kindred to those of Kant, Frege, Russell, and Husserl. The idea of philosophy as distinct from science makes little sense without the Aristotelian-Plotinian-Augustinian claim that by turning to *episteme* we find ineluctable truth. This assertion results in the Cartesian claim that by turning inward we find ineluctable truth, the Kantian-Husserelean notion that this truth imposes limits on the results of empirical enquiry, the Fregean-Russelarian proposal that philosophy is a transaction between language and reality and the Wittgensteinian-Rylean suggestion that language is a tool that uncovers the necessary conditions for the possibility of linguistic-behavioral representation. The first 'move' has to put philosophy in the position of a special knowledge of "foundations" that offers a permanent, neutral framework for all enquiries inclusive of a defense of mental causality and abstract objects.[26]

Firstly, out of foundationalism, Aristotle and Plotinus can hold to a strong version of property dualism, one insisting that mental properties are *sui generis*—that they are reducible to *Nous* if not the One. A mental substance thus causes mental events as mental properties. Here a divine Intellect is postulated in order to causally explain how and what we are as noetic-rational structures. Secondly, since *sunaisthesis* (self-reflexivity) cannot be translated as "consciousness" of the Cartesian kind that knows only its own internal mental states in its representational, phenomenalist, or constituting activities, the possibility exists for a shared conversation on mental causality and property dualism. Thirdly, deconstructionist arguments against first philosophy as foundational philosophy ultimately founder on the circularity and infinite-regress arguments.[27] Fourthly, since the *analytic/synthetic* (and *a priori/a posteriori*) distinction(s) are ultimate presuppositions they cannot be empirically justified as either true or false nor are they

---

Studies by Brisson, Dillon, Sayre, Rappe, Witt, Annas, Code, Charles, M. Cohen, Gill, Strange, and Svetla-Griffin offer a defense of first philosophy-foundational arguments of first-philosophy metaphysics with readings of Aristotle and the Aristotelian tradition from a Plotinian and Neoplatonic perspective.

26. On Aristotle see Casten, *Aristotle on Consciousness*, 751–815. On Plotinus see Schroeder, *Categories*, 115–36.

27. The first fallacy is that: a) to assume infinite regress proves what is to be proved; and the second is: b) the questions proposed do not end in infinite regress but in either self-evident beliefs or externalist truths. Plato in *Theatetus* 200d-201c defines knowledge as justified true belief or a rational explanation for belief. True opinion accompanied by reason is knowledge (202c). An infinite regress arises when we ask what the justifications for the reasons asked are. The skeptical response is if the reasons count as knowledge, they must be justified with the reasons for the reasons and so on. Thus for deconstructionists there is no foundationalism or coherentism—only a textual infinite regress.

open to propositional verification or negation. Rather they are meaningful and ultimate as a basis for propositional thinking.[28] Fifthly, since the *a se/per se* distinction is based on what is logically rather than causally possible, the existence of abstract objects is necessary (*a se*) and not contingent (*per se*).[29] Sixthly, on this basis a modal version of the ontological argument for the existence of God (or necessary existence) follows.[30]

Since Aristotle and Plotinus claim that thought, language and meaning achieve a greater or lesser degree of clarity in proportion to their proximity to *Nous* or the One, two additional claims follow: first, reality has its foundations in first principles, first causes and mental agency;[31] and secondly, language coheres within *episteme* meaningfully.[32] Perhaps here we may think of the passages in which Aristotle maps mind and language where every thought is accompanied by an image;[33] Origen where thought is imaged in prayer, and where Plotinus sees the Egyptian hieroglyphs as the perfect image of any ideal language.[34] The laws in the mind of the divine king are laid up in a heavenly script. Attempts at discursive thought and language are only partial restorations of a true language.[35] Here again a distinction between ordinary and ideal language may resonate with contemporary views.

All this may look promising but as in a late summer afternoon—storm-clouds are gathering. A defense of first philosophy metaphysics and epistemology faces a skeptical challenge. Emilsson notes that Wittgenstein's and Kripke's points against Fregean Platonism are analogous to an objection Plotinus raises against classical Platonism—ideas are extra-mental.[36]

---

28. Collingwood, *Essay*, 23–31.

29. See, Plantinga, *Warranted Christian Belief*. On the *a se/per se* distinction. If the *a se/per se* distinction holds weaker versions of the *analytic/synthetic* and *a priori/a posteriori* distinctions may as well. cf. Lowe, *Of Being*; *Survey of Metaphysics*; *Four-Category Ontology*; *Kinds of Being*.

30. The argument is seductive and obviously not flawed. Arguments about modal versions of the argument remain in full swing. cf. Loux, *Substance and Accident*; *Universals and Particulars*.

31. See Doerrie, *Denken*, 139–67.

32. On propositional and non-propositional language cf. Gersh, *Platonism After Derrida*, 153–64; 168–80.

33. Below *Nous* that thinks itself subordinate levels of thought entail a separate and distinct object of thought (*en parergo*) Aristotle, *Metaphysics*. 12.9.1074b36. cf. *Nicomachean Ethics*, IX.9.1170a32.

34. Plotinus, *Ennead.*,V.8.6.6–9.

35. See, Schroeder, *Conversion*, 336–52. Platonists and Aristotelians hold a common position concerning language that it is related to an extra-textual, nonlinguistic reality—*Nous* and the One.

36. Plotinus, *Ennead*, V.5.1.28–33. See Emilsson, *Intellect*, 299–315.

Here Ryle's critique of Cartesian consciousness as a concept of mind that is self-intimating, incapable of being delusive, and therefore incorrigible might apply to Plotinus' notion also.[37] Ryle argues such a concept of mind is a category mistake and dubbed it the ghost in the machine.[38] Gerson sees the applicability of Ryle's critique and suggests self-reflexivity (*sunaisthesis*) and not consciousness as constituting an Aristotelian and Neoplatonic concept-of-mind.[39]

Summary: One might expect Ryle to conclude that Gerson got it right—no phosphorescence conception of mind; thus no category mistake. Since most contemporary readers of Aristotle, Origen and Plotinus maintain "consciousness" as somehow constitutive, Ryle's critique continues. Simply attaining knowledge of one's own private and singular self is irremediably subjective because extrapolation from one's own case to other states of mind is impossible. The inwardness of mental states requires *sui generis* justification. In nuce, Cartesian and post-Cartesian consciousness differs from introspection and self-reflexivity. Some mental states are *de facto* unintrospectible, not self-intimating, capable of being delusive, and corrigible.[40]

III. Retrospection

Ryle and Stern-Gillet introduce retrospection, recollection and self-reflexivity as epistemically respectable processes because they do not require a concept of the mental involving privileged access.[41] In doing so, they avoid the category mistake or type error of picturing the mind and its operations as merely the inner counterparts of the soul, body and its activities (the dogma of the ghost in the machine).[42] The inner-outer or two-world Cartesian view has distinctive ontological, epistemological and semantic commitments that lead to particularly modern philosophical puzzles. Ontological commitments lead to the claim that there are two *toto caelo* distinct kinds of things—mind and body. Bodies exist in space and are subject to mechanical laws but nonetheless interact with minds leads to the mind-body problem. Aristotle, Plotinus and Ryle do not view mind and body as independent substances. The significant question is the relation of their mental and

37. Ryle, *Concept of Mind*, 158.
38. Ryle, *Concept of Mind*, 160.
39. Gerson, *Introspection*, 160–61.
40. Ryle, *Concept of Mind*, 166–67; Gerson, *Introspection*, 160–65.
41. Stern-Gillet, *Consciousness*, 1–36; esp. 3–4.
42. Ryle, *Concept of Mind*, 160.

physical properties. Aristotle and Plotinus differ from Ryle in that they do not attempt to establish a connection between mental predicates and behavior. Rather causal theories of mind and mental properties are introduced. Mental properties make a causal difference. Finding a place for the mental in the physical world is justified on the basis that abstract objects like minds, numbers, quarks and black holes carry causal efficacy.

Epistemological commitments lead to the problem of other minds. Bodily processes are external and observable but mental processes are "internal," private and known directly by the person who has them through the introspection of consciousness. The subject of the mental states is incorrigible, cannot be corrected by others and cannot be wrong about which mental states he is in (incorrigibility). Others can know them only indirectly from what the body does. Moreover, I cannot be sure there are other conscious experiences or if they occur in others at all. Given Cartesian assumptions about how language works Ryle's insights are again instructive. If mental conduct verbs pick out "occult" causes then we would not be able to apply those verbs as we do. Only privileged access to consciousness provides authentic testimony mental-conduct verbs are correctly or incorrectly applied. We can never be sure that language has any vestige of truth.[43] Such hidden-ness of the mental and semantic is deficient. It signifies only inaccessible inner processes.

Wittgenstein agrees. His arguments against consciousness and continuity are important in this context. A first impression is anyone who asserts the fact of consciousness is promising more than he can deliver. To assume the fact and origin of consciousness are a 'given' is a fly-trap, a 'fore-structure, a set of concepts and meanings provided by the interpreter.' To move beyond 'interpretive solipsism' necessitates recognition that consciousness claims must not only be mapped but justified beyond self-referential claims of its incorrigibility if for nothing more than to rule out the fact or the origin of consciousness is an opinion, a misunderstanding or a misinterpretation.

Wittgenstein argues 'there is no such thing as the soul—the subject, etc.—as it is conceived in the superficial psychology of the present day;'[44] secondly, he claims that the conceptual field which *I* bring to bear on the world is supplied by the acquisition of language alone;[45] thirdly, he notes that the grammatical *I* does not even have direct access to its own experiences;[46] and fourthly, his proposal that consciousness is a linguistic trap nourished

43. Ryle, *Concept of Mind*, 16–17.
44. Wittgenstein, *Tractatus*, 5.5421.
45. Wittgenstein, *Tractatus*, 5.6; 5.62.
46. Wittgenstein, *Blue Book*, 55 and 404.

by a mistake of grammar and thus nonsensical[47] opens a dialogue which might clarify why it is possible for mind to capture itself because as Ryle puts it—'the quarry is the hunter'[48]

Summary: Three questions arise. 1) what is the nature of ego-consciousness (the ego-centric predicament); 2) what rational basis do I have for the belief that other persons are similarly conscious and have minds (the problem of other minds); and 3) what grounds do I have that I am conscious and I have direct access to my own mind (solipsism)?

IV. From Introspection to Solipsism

Descartes' first certitude is his existence as mind but his introspective conception of the content of mental states ends with two problems: what antirealist-internalist basis may a person have for the claim that other persons are similarly self-reflexive and have minds?[49] Being aware of my internal mental states *I* know that *I* have a mind but the mental states of others are not so obvious—which is an answer grounded in a form of epistemological solipsism based on the priority of an *I* or (*ego*) access to mental states—where *I* stand in isolation from the world as a result of the epistemic priority possessed by first-person access to mental states. Whereas others have experiences, only *I* really have them—they are *my* own alone.

Wittgenstein ups the ante and proposes it might well be that the metaphysical subject is not the human body with which biology deals, or soul or self with which psychology deals, but an *I* which is in the end a grammatical subject where—"the limits of my language mean the limits of my world;" where 'the subject does not belong to the world but is the boundary of the world (not a part of it)"; where "we cannot therefore say what we cannot think"; and where "the boundary of language (the language that *I* alone understand) is the boundary of my world."[50] There is no denying Wittgenstein believed that philosophers were easily led into talking nonsense and his task was to uncover and dismantle the linguistic traps into which they fall. He thus raises the egocentric predicament to undercut Cartesian and Humean claims of the epistemic priority of first person access to my own or another's mental states. Thus 'what the solipsist is getting at (*meint*) is quite correct— 'there is no such thing as a subject that thinks or entertains ideas'—and being

---

47. Wittgenstein, *Tractatus*, 4.003.
48. Ryle, *Concept of Mind*, 198.
49. Descartes, *Meditations*, I-II.
50. Wittgenstein, *Tractatus*, 5.6; 5.61; 5.62; 5.632–33.

nothing it performs no function.[51] Shrinking to a point without extension—it is a something of which nothing can be said.[52]

Attaching importance to the distinction between a metaphysical and an experiential proposition his solipsist asks: 'how can we believe the other person has pain; what does it mean to believe this; how can I suppose, think, or imagine that someone else has what I have? I can't feel his pain' from the experiential proposition 'we can't have pains in another person's tooth' he shows that one person does not actually feel another's pain.[53] Significantly, 'if we exclude *I* have his toothache from our language, we thereby also exclude "I have or feel my toothache—*I* do not even have direct access to my own experiences'—solipsism worthy of Pyrrho indeed![54]

It is possible that Wittgenstein is being ironical when suggests that the attraction of solipsism is the temptation to say that only what one sees or feels oneself is not really seen or felt—and that consciousness of what one sees and feels is nourished on grammar. And even if his mistake is generalizing solipsism—which is not at all the same thing as claiming a special position only for oneself—his point is well taken. We have arrived at *the* itch that must be scratched—if the center is to hold: is consciousness a linguistic trap nourished by a mistake of grammar and thus nonsensical; is the grammar of—*I* think, *I* wish, *I* expect a conscious process at all or is it merely the use of the first person pronoun by those who insist on a consciousness of experience?[55]

V. Mind and Consciousness Revisited

One might think there is no more to be said but Wittgenstein is like a water diviner who detects a skeptical trap about foundationalism and epistemic justification that warrants additional attention. Abstract objects including consciousness must have real components to exist—even if they are not actually exhibited—or are even fictively assembled like a centaur. It is here that 'pre-understanding' concerning the fact of consciousness gives rise to a philosophical question—how can one think what may not be the case? If I am conscious there is a fire in my fireplace when there is no fire, the fact of such a fire does not exist. Then how can *I* be conscious of it? How can we hang a thief who doesn't exist? Wittgenstein's answer can be

- 51. Wittgenstein, *Tractatus*, 5.6.4.
- 52. Wittgenstein, *Tractatus*, 5.6.2.
- 53. Wittgenstein, *Blue Book*, 48.
- 54. Wittgenstein, *Blue Book*, 55.
- 55. Wittgenstein, *Tractatus*, 4.003.

CONCLUSION: FLATLAND 367

put in this form: *I* can't hang him when he doesn't exist; but *I* can look for him when he doesn't exist.[56]

All this Wittgenstein may be a bit much—but any claim concerning consciousness remains nonsense and fragmented unless the *fact* of consciousness is firmly established. But is there a point where *I* can go looking for consciousness—despite the fact that *I* regret that other people are opaque or that *I* am not aware of the thoughts and feelings of others as *I* should wish to be? And even if this were so and *I* were to follow what Wittgenstein's solipsist demands—that *I* change my way of speaking—would any change of notation be of any use?

Wittgenstein's challenges the assumption that there are private mental states such as ideas, sensations and beliefs. He also rejects that degree of certainty is degree of conviction and that certainty is nothing psychological but something logical. His critique of introspectivism, i.e. the view that mental states are private, also undermines phenomenalist tendencies toward solipsism and skepticism—that we know the contents of our own minds better than we know external objects. Such questioning of an inner versus outer distinction suggests Aristotle, Origen, Plotinus, Wittgenstein and Ryle might actually agree—that thinking is essentially the activity of a *We* not and not merely an *I* operating within a private world of language, signs or information.[57]

The possibility that Wittgenstein got it right—that 'the limits of my language mean the limits of my world' and that mind encompasses the limits of language (or information) opens up talk about the self and self-identity in non-psychological ways resonates.[58] If mind is not merely a biological or psychological process, but a 'sign', a product of an *existential* that Heidegger calls understanding rather than a mere private experience that carries significance. A benefit of this shift is that it diminishes the tendency to think of mind as a special category of objects. By explaining how consciousness is expressed in language one acquires what Wittgenstein calls the life of the 'sign' or its use—"don't ask for its meaning, ask for its use"[59]

56. Wittgenstein, *Blue Book*, 30–31.

57. In the case of writing the activity is performed by the hand; in speaking the mouth and larynx; but what of the cases when thought is given no overt expression? If we are tempted to say that the activity is performed by the mind do we go astray because we are resorting to metaphor? It appears very much so indeed. Consciousness is not an agent in the same sense as a hand or a mouth. But why should we not say that we think with our brains? To treat the brain as the locality of thought or not to see the question of 'what is consciousness' is again is an example of what Ryle calls a category mistake.

58. Wittgenstein, *Tractatus*, 1998, 5.641.

59. Wittgenstein, *Blue Book*, 1958, 4–5.

We see an epistemological suggestion of Plato's in the *Theatetus* that there is a difference between having knowledge in possession of it and having it at hand.[60] The mark of gaining possession of knowledge is having gained a power (*dunamis*) over possessed knowledge so one has it "at hand." While he begins with the notion of the power of having knowledge, later he gives the characterization of power to affect or to be affected as the mark of reality. Significantly, the conception of power shifts from the ability of the knowing subject of attribution to the objects of attribution themselves. On his way to a predicate ontology Plato spells out the conditions for this in the *Sophist* where the constitution of the world is understood in the mixing of its formal attributes in terms of the various kinds of blending possessed by the greatest kinds (*megista gene*) which makes the perceptual individual merely a placeholder for its attributes, much as in predicate logic the individual variable becomes a placeholder to which functions in various relations are attached. Significance has been moved to the predicate position. Aristotle adds to this a principle of constitutionality—that the parts of things and their functions cannot be understood without understanding the nature of that whole being: that the out-of-which is never a *that* but a *that-en* (e.g. never wood but wood-en). Such accounting for the individual (*tode ti*) as the unit of being and motion maintains the principle of constitutionality without violating that of compositionality.[61] By treating being in terms of properties and attributes and moving toward an understanding of its constitution in terms of *function* (and the unit of being in terms of the unit of *motion*), Aristotle ontologically anticipates of thought and language what Plotinus and Origen shall propose but of which Wittgenstein demands—"don't ask for their meaning, ask for their use."

Summary: At this stage of our discussion to use 'I know' with sense-datum statements is non-sensical. It adds nothing. In mathematics, logic and as the activity of *nous* it is not. The point is largely a logical and rational one. There are kinds of thoughts and statements that future experience cannot refute, e.g. sense-datum, mathematical, and logical statements There is also a close resemblance between mathematical, logical and theoretical statements—namely future events won't provide reasons for rejecting them either. But what must be granted from a 'first philosophy' precipice are: that mind and mental states are not merely dispositions to behave (behaviorism), or brain states (identity theory), or functional states that causally relate inner states with behavioral effects (functionalism), or do

---

60. Plato, *Theatetus*, 197c-200c.
61. Aristotle, *Physics*, VII.3.246a1–4.

not exist at all (eliminative materialism). That self-reflexivity is nothing physical, psychological or behavioral but something sentient, logical and rational; that meaning is not reducible to either semantic or behavioral pragmatism; that the a priori-a posteriori and analytic-synthetic distinction somehow holds; holenmermism and synechism are logically possible; and where in the end all "clocks are clouds."

Conclusion: Flatland

The notion that enquiry takes place within a framework isolated prior to its conclusion through a set of presuppositions discoverable *a priori* links contemporary philosophy not only to the Descartes-Lockean-Kantian traditions but also to the Platonic and Aristotelian traditions. The former tradition asserts this is an interior framework imposed by the nature of the knowing subject; while the latter claims it is an exterior reality discoverable by a knowing subject.

The story *Flatland*, about a square which lives in a two-dimensional, world allows for final reflection on why realist and anti-realist *a priori* distinctions make a difference. There are two distinct philosophical grammars—one square; the other spherical.[62] One day a square is enlightened by a sphere about the three-dimensional world. The square cannot see the sphere except as a two-dimensional projection in his flat two-dimensional world. A circle magically appears, grows, and shrinks out of existence as it moves through a plane. The clever way in which the sphere enlightens the square is with the cryptic nonsense phrase "upward not northward." In square language this is strictly nonsense for upward and northward are synonymous. Of the four possible directions of movement to flatlanders if gravity pulls southward, north is up and south is down. Thus when the sphere says "upward not northward" it is like someone saying: "come closer but do not get any nearer" which sounds like nonsense. But in the case of the sphere talking to the square, this is not nonsense but an illuminating sort of nonsense designed to turn mind in a third direction. With these questions, we enter the ring face-to-face—inside a squared circle. As "spheres", Aristotle, Origen and Plotinus direct Cartesian, Lockean, Russelian, Carnapian and Quinean "squares" beyond the limits of their worlds to see what happens when "squares" are asked to think and speak like "spheres" with—as Wittgenstein says—an illuminating sort of nonsense.[63]

---

62. Abbott, *Flatland*, 47–65.
63. Wittgenstein, *Philosophical Investigations*, 464.

One needs thus both pyramid and raft.[64] Aristotle, Origen and Plotinus picture knowledge as a pyramid having the *a priori* structure of a pyramid where justified true beliefs like the planks that make up a raft mutually support one another. Hegel and Plato are helpful here. As a raft, thinking is not an addition to experience, but its pre-condition. Thus mind, language and meaning must be defined within the totality of the concept and provide *a priori* synthetic foundations for otherwise *a posteriori* synthetic brute facts that would make no sense at all. Aristotle, Origen and Plotinus might also concur with Hegel of the impossibility of determining any single Idea by itself, independently of the totality of Ideas. Here agreeing with Plato that any turn toward the *logoi*, thought moves exclusively in the medium of the concept it follows whether "in Ideas, through Ideas, or toward Ideas" it is impossible to determine or to articulate any single Idea by itself, independently of the totality of other Ideas.[65] As Plotinus notes:

> Our country from which we came is there, our Father is there. How shall we travel to it, where is our way of escape? We cannot get there on foot: for our feet only carry us everywhere in this world, from one country to another. You must not get a carriage either or a boat ready. Let these things go and do not look. Shut your eyes and change and wake to another way of seeing which everyone has but few use.[66]

It is here that the tones of 'thinking is thinking on thinking' finally resonate like a pre-Raphaelite, perhaps better said, a Medici Gallery print of strong verticals and horizontals with a conflict of rich dark reds and Lincoln greens against fishscale greys and arctic blues. For *son-et-lumiere*, the hope is that it quickens the interest of one who contemplates a 'thinking on thinking' so few are aware of or let alone use.

---

64. Sosa, *Raft and Pyramid*, 3–25. Foundationalists hold beliefs are based on other beliefs in a hierarchy similar to bricks in the structure of a pyramid. Coherentists hold beliefs are logical interconnections between beliefs similar to planks in a raft.

65. Plato, *Phaedo*, 99e; *Republic*, 511c.

66. Plotinus, *Ennead*, I.6.8.21–27.

Bibliography

The Loeb Classical Library, Oxford Classical Texts, or Teubner editions were used for classical authors. The Corpus scriptorum ecclesiasticorum latinorum (CSEL), Corpus Christianorum series latina (CChr.SL), Sources chrétiennes (SC), Die griechischen christlichen Schriftsteller der ersten Jahrhunderte (GCS), and Migne Patrologia Graeca and Patrologia Latina (PG and PL) series were used for patristic sources. Abbreviations are from S. Schwertner, *Internationales Abkürzungsverzeichnis für Theologie und Grenzgebiete* (Berlin, 1993) supplemented by the *Journal of Biblical Literature* guidelines, the *Oxford Classical Dictionary*, and Liddell Scott Jones (LSJ).

Abbott, E. *Flatland*. In D. Kolak and R Martin, eds., *The Experience of Philosophy*. Belmont, CA: Wadsworth, 1996.
Abraham, William J. "Symeon the New Theologian." In *The Oxford Handbook of the Epistemology of Theology*, edited by William J. Abraham and Frederick D. Aquino, 382–94. Oxford: Oxford University Press, 2017.
Abraham, William J. and Frederick D. Aquino, eds. *The Oxford Handbook of the Epistemology of Theology*. Oxford: Oxford University Press, 2017.
Ackrill, J. L., trans. and ed. *Categories and De Interpretatione*. Oxford: Oxford University Press, 1963.
Addey, Crystal. *Divination and Theurgy in Neoplatonism. Oracles of the Gods*. Burlington, VT: Ashgate, 2014.
Aersten, J. *Medieval Philosophy and the Transcendentals: The Case of Thomas Aquinas*. Studien und Texte zur Geistesgeschichte des Mittelalters 52. Leiden: Brill, 1996.
———. *Medieval Philosophy as Transcendental Thought: From Philip the Chancellor (ca. 1225) to Francisco Suarez*. Studien und Texte zur Geistesgeschichte des Mittelalters 107. Leiden: Brill, 2012.
Alcinous, [John M. Dillon tr.] *The Handbook of Platonism*. Oxford: Oxford University Press. 1993.

Alexander of Aphrodisias. *De Anima liber cum mantissa.* Edited by I. Bruns. *Supplementum Aristotelicum* [SA] 2.1, 1887.

———. *In De Sensu.* Edited by P. Wendland. [*CAG* 3.1], 1901.

———. *In Metaphysica.* Edited by M. Hayduck. *Commentaria in Aristotem Graeca* I [*CAG*], 1891.

———. *The De Anima of Alexander of Aphrodisias: A Translation and Commentary.* Translated and commented on by A. P. Fotinis. Washington, DC: University Press of America, 1979.

———. *Two Aristotelian Greek Commentators on the Intellect: The de Intellectu attributed to Alexander of Aphrodisias and Themistius' Paraphrase of Aristotle De Anima 3.4–8.* Introduction, translation, commentary and notes by F. M. Schroeder and R.B. Todd. Medieval Studies in Translation 33. Toronto: Pontifical Institute of Mediaeval Studies, 1990.

Alfino, M. "Plotinus and the Possibility of Non-Propositional Thought." *Ancient Philosophy* 8 (1988) 273–84.

Allan, A. B., and J. F. Wippel, eds. *Medieval Philosophy: From St. Augustine to Nicholas of Cusa.* Readings in the History of Philosophy. New York: Free Press, 1969.

Alcinous [Albinus]. *Didaskalikos.* Edited by C. F. Hermann. *Platonis Dialogi.* 3rd. ed. Berlin, 1958.

Andresen, C. *Logos und Nomos: Die Polemik des Kelsos wider des Christentum.* Berlin: Weidemanns, 1953.

Annas, J. *Hellenistic Philosophy of Mind.* Berkeley: University of California Press, 1992.

———. "Knowledge and Language: The *Theatetus* and the *Cratylus*." In *Language and Logos: Studies in Ancient Greek Philosophy Presented to G.E.L Owen.* Edited by M. Schofield and M. C. Nussbaum. Cambridge: Cambridge University Press, 1982.

Anton, John. "Plotinus' Approach to Categorical Theory." In *The Significance of Neoplatonism,* edited by R. B. Harris, 83–100. Studies in Neoplatonism, Ancient and Modern 1. Norfolk, VA: International Society for Neoplatonic Studies, 1976.

———. "Plotinus' Conception of the Functions of the Artist." *Journal of Aesthetics and Art Criticism* 26 (1967) 91–101.

———. "Plotinus' Refutation of Beauty as Symmetry." *Journal of Aesthetics and Art Criticism,* 23 (1964) 233–37.

Aquila, R. "A New Look at Kant's Aesthetic Judgments." In *Essays in Kant's Aesthetics.* Edited by T. Cohen and P. Guyer P. Chicago: University of Chicago Press. 1982.

Aquila, Robert F. "On Plotinus on the Togetherness of Consciousness." *Journal of the History of Philosophy* 30 (1992) 7.

Archer-Hind, R.D. *The Phaedo of Plato.* London: MacMillan. 1883.

Aristotle. *Aristotle.* 23 vols. Loeb Classical Library. Cambridge: Harvard University Press, 1975.

———. *Aristotle's De Anima,* Edited by W. D. Ross. Oxford, 1956.

———. *Aristotle's Metaphysics.* Edited by W. D. Ross. 2 vols. Oxford, 1924.

———. *Aristotelis Opera.* rec. I. Bekker. vols. i–v. Berlin, 1831–1870.

Armstrong, A. Hillary. "Beauty and the Discovery of Divinity in the Thought of Plotinus." In *Kephalaion Studies,* edited by J. Mansfeld and L. de Rijk, 155–73. Assen: Van Gorcum, 1975.

———. *Plotinus.* London: Allen & Unwin,1957.

———. "The Background of the Doctrine that 'That the Intelligibles Are not Outside the Intellect." In *Plotinian and Christian Studies.* London: Variorum, 1979.

Arnou, R. *Le Desir de Dieu dans la Philosophie de Plotin.* Paris: Vrin, 1921.
Atkinson, M. *Plotinus, Ennead VI.1. On the Three Principle Hypostases.* Oxford: Oxford University Press, 1983.
Aubenque, Paul. "Plotin et Dexippe Exegetes des Categories." In *Aristotelica: Melanges Offerts A. M. De Corte,* 7–10. Brussels: Ousia, 1985.
———. "Une Occasion Manquee: La Genese Avortee de la Distinction Entre 'Etant et le Quelque Chose.'" In *Etudes sur le Sophiste de Platon,* edited by P. Aubenque, Naples: Bibliopolis, 1991.
Audi, Robert, ed. *Cambridge Dictionary of Philosophy.* Cambridge: Cambridge University Press, 1995.
Ayer, A. J. *Language, Truth and Logic.* New York: Dover, 1936.
———. *Philosophy in the Twentieth Century.* New York: Vintage, 1982.
Austin, J. L. *How to Do Things with Words.* Edited by J. O. Urmson and M. Sbisa. William James Lectures 1955. Oxford: Clarendon, 1962.
———. *Philosophical Papers.* Edited by J. O. Urmson and M. Sbisa. Oxford: Oxford University Press, 1961, 1970, 1979.
———. *Sense and Sensibilia.* Edited by G. J. Warnock. Oxford: Clarendon, 1962.
Baltzly, Dirk. "Porphyry and Plotinus on the Reality of Relations." *JNP* 6 (1988) 49–75.
Bambrough, R., ed. *Essays on Plato and Aristotle.* London: Routledge & Kegan Paul, 1965.
Barnes, Jonathan. *Aristotle: Posterior Analytics.* Clarendon Aristotle Series. Oxford: Clarendon, 1975.
———. *The Presocratic Philosophers.* Arguments of the Philosophers. London: Routledge & Kegan Paul, 1986.
Barnes, Jonathan, Michael Schofield Michael, and Richard Sorabji, eds. *Metaphysics.* Vol. 3 *Articles on Aristotle.* London: Duckworth, 1979.
Bauloye, L., and Rutten, C. "Genres e Cartegories chez Aristote, chez Plotin et chez Averoes." In *Platon et Aristote: Dialectique et Metaphysique,* edited by T. Tsimbidaros, 103–19. Brussels: Ilias, 2004.
Baumgarten, Alexander G. *Aesthetica.* Hildesheim: Olms. 1961.
Beatrice, P. F. "Porphyry's Judgment on Origen." In *Origeniana Sexta: Origène et la Bible = Origen and the Bible: Actes du Colloquium Origenianum Sextum, Chantilly, 30 Août–3 Septembre 1993.* Edited by G. Dorival and A. Le Boulluec. BETL 118. Leuven: Peeters, 1995.
Beierwaltes, Werner. *Denken des Einen.* Frankfurt: Klostermann, 1985.
———. "Die Metaphysik des Lichtes in der Philosophie Plotins." *Zeitschrift für philosophische Forschung* 15 (1961) 334–62.
———. "Epekeina: Eine Anmerkung zu Heidegger's Platon-Rezeption." *Transzendenz: Zu einem Grundwort der klassischen Metaphysik,* edited by L. Honnefelder and W. Schüsser, 39–55. Paderborn: Schöningh, 1992.
———. *Identitaet und Differenz.* Frankfurt: Klostermann, 1980.
———. *Il paradigma neoplatonico nell'interpretazione di Platone,* Naples, 1991.
———. *Pensare L'Uno. Studi sulla filosofica neoplatonica e sulla storia dei suoi influssi,* Milan, 1991.
———. *Platon über Ewigkeit und Zeit.* Frankfurt: Klostermann, 1965.
———. *Platonismus und Idealismus.* Frankfurt: Klostermann, 1972.

———. "Plotins Theorie des Schoenen und der Kunst." In *Plato Revived: Essays in Ancient Platonism in Honour of Dominic J. O'Meara*, edited by F. Karfik and E. Soong, 3–26. Berlin: de Gruyter, 2013.

———. *Selbsterkentniss und Erfahrung der Einheit: Plotins Ennead V.3*. Frankfurt: Klostermann, 1991.

Bell, D. "The Art of Judgement" *Mind* 96 (1987) 221–44.

Benacerraf, Paul. "Mathematical Truth." In *Philosophy of Mathematics: Selected Readings*, edited by P. Benacerraf and H. Putnam, 403–20. 2nd ed. Cambridge: Cambridge University Press, 1983.

Benacerraf, Paul, and Hilary Putnam, Hilary, eds. *Philosophy of Mathematics: Selected Readings*. 2nd ed. Cambridge: Cambridge University Press, 1983.

Benson, Hugh. *Socratic Wisdom: The Model of Knowledge in Plato's Early Dialogues*. New York: Oxford University Press, 2000.

Berchman, Robert M. "Arithmos and Kosmos: Arithmology as an Exegetical Tool in the *De Opificio Mundi* of Philo of Alexandria." In *Gnosticism, Platonism and the Late Ancient World: Essays in Honour of John D. Turner*, edited by K. Corrigan and T. Rasimus, 167–98. Nag Hammadi and Manichaean Studies 82. Leiden: Brill, 2013.

———. "The Categories of Being in Middleplatonism: Philo, Clement, and Origen of Alexandria." In *The School of Moses: Studies in Philo and Hellenistic Religion*, edited by John Peter Kenney, 98–140. Studia Philonica Monographs 1. Atlanta: Scholars, 1995.

———. "Commentary on Perl." In *Proceedings of the Boston Area Colloquium in Ancient Philosophy* 23 (2007) 27–40.

———. *From Philo to Origen: Middle Platonism in Transition*. Brown Judaic Studies 69. Chico: Scholars, 1984.

———. "The Language of Metaphysics Ancient and Modern." In *Platonisms: Ancient, Modern and Postmodern*. Edited by K. Corrigan and J. T. Turner. Studies in Platonism, Neoplatonism, and the Platonic Tradition 4. Leiden: Brill, 2007.

———. "Metaphors Thinking and Being in Aristotle and Plotinus." In *History of Platonism: Plato Redivivus*, edited by J. Finamore and R. M. Berchman, 69–94. New Orleans: University Press of the South, 2005.

———. "Of Clocks, Clouds and Sparrows." *Science et Esprit* 71 (2019) 261–71.

———. "Of Hunting Doves and Pigeons: Aristotle Reading Plato and Parmenides on Thinking and Being are the Same." *Science et Esprit* 72 (2020) 31–48.

———. "Origen of Alexandria." In *The Oxford Handbook of the Epistemology of Theology*, edited by W. J. Abraham and F. D. Aquino. Oxford: Oxford University Press, 2017.

———. "Origen of Alexandria: Spheres, Squares and Other Abstract Objects." In *Platonic Interpretations*, edited by J. F. Finamore and E. Perl, 30–50. Westbury, UK: Prometheus, 2019.

———. "Origen on the Categories: A Study in First Principles." In *Origeniana Quinta: Historica, Text and Method, Biblica, Philosophica, Theologica, Origenism and Later Developments*, edited by Robert J. Daly, 231–52. BETL 105. Leuven: Peeters, 1992.

———. "Rationality and Ritual in Neoplatonism." In *Neoplatonism and Indian Philosophy*, edited by P. M. Gregorios, 229–68. Studies in Neoplatonism 9. Albany: SUNY Press, 2002.

———. "Thinking on Thinking: Ultimate Presuppositions in Plotinus and Leibniz." In *Platonic Inquiries*, edited by C. D'Amico, J. F. Finamore, and N. Strok, 329-48. Farnham, UK: Prometheus, 2017.
Berkeley, George. *A Treatise Concerning the Principles of Human Knowledge*. Edited by H. Robinson. Oxford: Oxford University Press, 1996.
Bernstein, Richard J., *Beyond Objectivism and Relativism. Science, Hermeneutics, and Practice*. Cambridge: MIT Press, 1983.
———. *The Fate of Art: Aesthetic Alienation from Kant to Derrida and Adorno*, University Park, PA: Pennsylvania State University Press, 1992.
———. *The New Constellation: The Ethical-Political Horizons of Modernity/Postmodernity*. Cambridge MA: MIT Press, 1993.
Berti, Enrico. "The Intellection of Indivisibles according to Aristotle." In G. E. R. Lloyd and G. E. L. Owen, eds., *Aristotle on Mind and Senses: Proceedings of the Seventh Symposium Aristotelicum*, 141-63. Cambridge: Cambridge University Press, 1978.
Bertoldi, E. F. "Absolute Presuppositions and Irrationalism." *Southern Journal of Philosophy* 27 (1989) 157-72.
Bickel, Ernst. "Senecas Briefe 58 und 65." *Rhein. Mus.* 103 (1969) 1-20.
Blumenthal, Henry. *Aristotle and Neoplatonism in Late Antiquity*. Ithaca, NY: Cornell University Press, 1996.
———. "Aristotle in the Service of Platonism." *IPQ* 12 (1972) 340-64.
———. "Neoplatonic Elements in the 'de Anima' Commentaries." *Phronesis* 21 (1976) 64-87.
———. "Nous and Soul in Plotinus: Some Problems of Demarcation." In *Plotino e il Neoplatonismo in Oriente e in Occidente. Atti del Convergo internazionale dell'Accademia Nazionale dei Lincei*, 203-19. Rome: Accademia Nazionale del Lincei, 1974.
———. "On Soul and Intellect." In *The Cambridge Companion to Plotinus*, edited by Lloyd P. Gerson, 82-104. Cambridge Companions to Philosophy. Cambridge: Cambridge University Press, 1996.
———. *Plotinus' Psychology: His Doctrines of the Embodied Soul*. The Hague: Nijhoff, 1971.
Bobzien, Susanne. "Chrysippus and the Epistemic Theory of Vagueness." *PAS* 1998.
———. "Logic." In *The Oxford Classical Dictionary*. Edited by Simon Hornblower and Anthony Spawforth. Oxford: Oxford University Press, 1996.
———. "Logic: The Stoics." In *The Cambridge History of Hellenistic Philosophy*. Edited by Algra Keimpe. Cambridge: Cambridge University Press, 1999.
———. "Stoic Syllogistic." *Oxford Studies in Ancient Philosophy* 14 (1996).
Boehm, Thomas. "Die Unbegreiflichkeit Gottes bei Origenes und Unsagbarkeit des Einen bei Plotin." In L. Perrone, ed. *Orig. VIII*. Vol. 1, 451-65. Leuven: Peeters, 2003.
Bonitz, H., *Ueber die Kategorien des Aristoteles*. Sitzungsbericht der kaiserlischen Akademie der Wissenschaften. Phil-hist. Klasse 10. Berlin: de Gruyter, 1961.
Bos, A.P. "God as Father and Maker in Philo of Alexandria and Its Background in Aristotelian Thought." *Elenchos* 24 (2003) 311-32.
———. "Aristotle's Doctrine of the Instrumental Body of the Soul." *Philosophia Reformata* 64 (1999) 37-51.
———. *Aristotle on God's Life Generating Power and on Pneuma as Its Vehicle*. SUNY Series in Ancient Greek Philosophy. Albany: SUNY Press, 2018.

———. *Cosmic and Meta-Cosmic Theology in Aristotle's Lost Dialogues*. Brill's Studies in Intellectual History 16. Leiden: Brill, 1989.
Bostock, David. "Plato on 'Is not.'" *Oxford Studies in Ancient Philosophy* 2 (1984) 89–119.
———. *Aristotle's Metaphysics, Books Z and H*. Oxford, 1994.
Bostock. George. "Origen and the Pythagoreanism of Alexandria." In L. Perrone, ed. *Origeniana Octava*. Leuven: Peeters, 2003.
Brandl, J. "Intentionality." In L. Alberzatti, M. Libardi and R. Poli, eds. *The School of Franz Brentano*. Dortrecht: Kluwer. 2013.
Brentano, Franz. *Aristotle's Lehre vom Ursprung des menschlischen Geistes*. Leipzig: Veit, 1911.
———. *Die Psychologie des Aristotle, inbesondere seine Lehre vom Nous Poietikos*, Mainz: Verlag von Franz Kirchheims. 1867. *The Psychology of Aristotle*, Berkeley: University of California Press, 1977.
———. *Psychologie vom empirischen Standpunkt*, Leipzig: Duncker & Humboldt, 1874. (2ter enl. Oskar Krauss ed.) Leipzig: Meiner, 1924.
———. *Psychology from an Empirical Standpoint*. 2nd ed. London: Routledge, 1995
———. *Vom sinnlichen und noetischen Bewusstein*, (Psychologie vom empirischen Standpunkt, vol. 3 Oskar Krauss, ed.) Leipzig: Meiner Verlag, 1928. *Sensory and Noetic Consciousness. Psychology from an Empirical Standpoint*, III. London: Routledge, 1981.
———. *Von der mannifachen Bedeutung des Seienden nach Aristotles*. Freiburg: Herder, 1862. *On the Several Senses of Being in Aristotle*. Berkeley: University of California Press, 1975.
Brehier, Emile. *La Philosophie du Plotin* 3. Paris: Vrin, 1961.
Brinkmann, Klaus. *Aristoteles' allgemeine und spezielle Metaphysik*. Berlin: de Gruyter 1979.
———. "The Objectivity Problem in Ancient Philosophy." Klaus Brinkmann 2014.
Brisson, Luc. "Plotinus and the Magical Rites Practiced by the Gnostics." In *Gnosticism, Platonism and the Late Ancient World*, edited by K. Corrigan and T. Rasimus, eds. Nag Hammadi and Manichaean Studies 82. Leiden: Brill, 2014.
Bruns, G. *Hermeneutics Ancient and Modern*. New Haven: Yale University Press, 1992.
Burnet, John. *Early Greek Philosophy*. New York: Meridian, 1965.
Burns Dylan. *Did God Care? Providence, Dualism and Will in Later Greek and Early Christian Philosophy*. Leiden: Brill, 2020.
Burnyeat, Myles."Aristotle on Understanding Knowledge." In E. Berti ed., *Aristotle on Science: The Posterior Analytics*, 97–139. Padua: Antenoire, 1981.
———. "Idealism in Greek Philosophy: What Descartes Saw and Berkeley Missed." *Philosophical Review* 91 (1982) 3–40.
———. *The Theatetus of Plato*. Indianapolis: Hackett, 1990.
Bussanich, John. "Plotinus's Metaphysics of the One." In L. P. Gerson, ed., *The Cambridge Companion to Plotinus*, edited by Lloyd P. Gerson, 38–65. Cambridge Companions to Philosophy. Cambridge: Cambridge University Press, 1996.
———. Review of L. P. Gerson, *Aristotle and Other Platonists*, NDPR, 2006.03.13.
———. *The One and Its Relation to Intellect in Plotinus*. Leiden: Brill, 1988.
Caluori, Damian. "Plotinus on Primary Being." In *Substantia – Sic et Non: Eine Geschichte des Substanzsbegriffs von der Antike bis zur Gegenwart in Einzelbetraegen*, Frankfurt: Ontos, 2008.

———. *Plotinus on the Soul*. Cambridge: Cambridge University Press, 2015.
———. "The Essential Functions of a Plotinian Soul." *Rhizai* 2 (2005) 75–93.
Carnap, Rudolf. *The Logical Syntax of Language*. London: Keegan Paul, Trench, Tubner, 1937.
Cassirer, Ernst. *The Philosophy of Symbolic Forms*. Volumes 1–3: *The Phenomenology of Knowledge*. New Haven: Yale University Press.1955–1957.
———. *Commentary on Kant's Critique of Judgment*. London: Methuen. 1938.
Castagno, A. M. *Origene: Dizionaro, la Cultura, il Pensiero, le Opera*. Rome: Citta Nuova, 2000.
Casten, Victor. *Alexander of Aphrodisias: On Aristotle on the Soul*. London: Duckworth, 2011.
———. "Aristotle on Consciousness." *Mind* 111 (2002).
Cavini, W. "Chrysippus on Speaking Truly and the Liar." In K. Doering and T. Ebert eds., *Dialektiker und Stoiker*. Stuttgart: Steiner, 1993.
Chalmers, David. *The Conscious Mind*. Oxford: Oxford University Press, 1996.
Chase. F. H. "The Lord's Prayer in the Early Church." In J. Robinson and J. Armitage, 42–58. Piscataway, NJ: Gorgias, 2004.
Chase, Michael. "Porphyry on the Cognitive Process." *Ancient Philosophy* 30 (2010) 383–405.
Cherniss, Harold. "Parmenides and the Parmenides of Plato." *American Journal of Philology* 53 (1932) 122–38.
———. "The Characteristics and Effects of Presocratic Philosophy." In D. J. Furley and R.E. Allen, eds. *Studies in Presocratic Philosophy*. Vol. 1 New York: Routledge & Kegan Paul, 1970.
Chiaradonna, R. "Le Categorie in Plotino: Tra Logica e Physica: Il Caso della Sostanza (Enn. VI.3.8.12–37)." In *Metapfisca Logica Filosofia della Natura: I Termini delle Categorie Aristoteliche dal Mondo Antico All'eta Moderna*, C. Eugenio, ed., 137–54. Saranza: Agora, 2004.
———. The Categories and the Status of the Physical World: Plotinus and the Neoplatonic Commentators." In *Philosophy, Science and Exegesis in Greek, Arabic and Latin Commentaries*. Vol. 1 London: ICS University of London Press, 2004.
———. "Plotinus' Account of the Cognitive Powers of the Soul." *TOPOI* 31 (2012) 191–207.
———. *Sostanza Movimento Analogia. Plotino Critico di Aristotele*. Naples: Bibliopolis, 2002.
Chrudzimski, A. *Brentano and Aristotle on the Ontology of Intentionality*. Leiden: Brill, 2004.
Clark, Stephen R. L. "Plotinus: Body and Soul." In *The Cambridge Companion to Plotinus*, edited by Lloyd P. Gerson, 275–91. Cambridge Companions to Philosophy. Cambridge: Cambridge University Press, 1996.
Cleary, John. *Aristotle and Mathematics: Aporetic Method in Cosmology and Metaphysics*. PA 67. Leiden: Brill, 1995.
———. *Aristotle on the Many Senses of Priority*. Carbondale, IL, 1988.
———. "Aristotle's Criticisms of Plato's First Principles." In *Pensee de l'Un dans l'Histoire de la Philosophie: Etudes en Hommage au Professor Weiner Beierwaltes*, edited by J.-M. Narbonne and A. Reckermann, 70–97. Laval, 2004.
———. "Nous as the Ground of Aristotle's Metaphysics." *SAGPNL* 164 (1993). https://orb.binghampton.edu/sagp/164.

———. "'Powers that Be': The Concept of Potency in Plato and Aristotle." *Methexis* 11 (1998) 19–64.

———, ed. The *Perennial Tradition of Neoplatonism*. Ancient and Medieval Philosophy, series 1, 24. Leuven: Leuven University Press, 1997.

Cleary, John, and Gary Gurtler. *Proceedings of the Boston Area Colloquium in Ancient Philosophy*. Vol. 22. Leiden: Brill, 2006.

Clement of Alexandria. *Clemens Alexandrinus, Stromata Buch I-VI., Die Griechische Christliche, Schriftsteller der ersten drei Jahrhundert* [GCS], O. Staehlin, ed. Leipzig, 1906–1909. 3rd ed. Berlin, 1960.

———. *Extraits de Theodote*. F. Sagnard, ed. Paris, 1948.

Cobb, H. "Consciousness and the Self in the Philosophy of Plotinus and Its Relation to Greek Thought." PhD diss. Yale University, 1936.

Cohen, Hermann. *Aesthetik des reinen Gefuels*. Berlin: Weidemann, 1925.

Collette, B. *Dialectique et Henologie chez Plotin*. Cahiers de philosophie ancienne 18. Brussels: Ousia, 2002.

Collingwood, R. G. *An Autobiography*. London: Oxford University Press, 1939.

———. *Essay on Metaphysics*. Oxford: Clarendon, 1940.

———. *The Idea of History*. Edited and with a Preface by T. M. Knox. Oxford: Clarendon, 1946.

Cooper, J. M. "Plato on Sense Perception and Knowledge: *Theatetus* 184–186." *Phronesis* 15 (1970).

Cornford, Francis M. "Mathematics and Dialectic in the *Republic* VI-VII." *Mind* 41 (1932).

———. *Plato and Parmenides*. New York. Liberal Arts, 1957.

———. *Plato's Cosmology*. Indianapolis: Hackett, 1952.

Corrigan, Kevin. "Body's Approach to Soul: An Examination of a Recurrent Theme in the Enneads." *Dionysius* 9 (1985) 37–52.

———. "Divine and Human Freedom: Plotinus' New Understanding of Creative Agency." In *Causation and Creation in Late Antiquity*, edited by A. Marmodoro and B. D. Prince, 131–49. Cambridge: Cambridge University Press, 2015.

———. "Enneads 5, 4 [7] 2 and Related Passages: A New Interpretation of the Status of the Intelligible Object." *Hermes* 114 (1986).

———. "Essence and Existence in the Enneads." In *The Cambridge Companion to Plotinus*, edited by Lloyd P. Gerson, 105–29. Cambridge Companions to Philosophy. Cambridge: Cambridge University Press, 1996.

———. *Plotinus' Theory of Matter-Evil and the Question of Substance: Plato, Aristotle and Alexander of Aphrodisias*. Leuven: Peeters, 1997.

———. "The Sources and Structures of Power and Activity in Plotinus." In *Divine Powers in Late Antiquity*, A. Mamodoro and A.-J. Viltonioti, 17–37. Oxford: Oxford University Press, 2017.

Corrigan, Kevin, and Tuomas Rasimus, eds. *Gnosticism, Platonism and the Late Ancient World Essays in Honour of John D. Turner*, 443–58. Nag Hammadi and Manichaean Studies 82. Leiden: Brill Academic, 2013.

Corrigan, Kevin, and John D. Turner, eds. *Platonisms: Ancient, Modern, and Postmodern*. Studies in Platonism, Neoplatonism, and the Platonic Tradition 4. Leiden: Brill, 2007.

Costa, Cristina D'Ancona. "'*Amphoron kai Aneideon*': Causalite des Forms et causalite de l'un chez Plotin." *Revue de philosophie ancienne* 10 (1992) 69–113.

———. "Modeles de causalite chez Plotin." *Les Etudes philosophiques* 90 (2009) 361–85.

———. "Plotinus and Later Platonic Philosophers on the Causality of the First Principle." In *The Cambridge Companion to Plotinus*, edited by Lloyd P. Gerson, 356–85. Cambridge Companions to Philosophy. Cambridge: Cambridge University Press, 1996.

Courcelle, Pierre. "*Connais toi-meme* de Socrate a saint Bernard." Vol. 1. Paris: *Etudes augustiniennes*, 1974–1975.

Craig, W. Lane, "A Nominalist Perspective on God and Abstract Objects." *Philosophia Christi* 13 (2011) 305–18.

Crouzel, Henri. *La Connaissance*. Paris: Vrin, 1964.

———. "Le Dieu d'Origene et le Dieu de Plotin." In *Origeniana Quinta*, edited by Robert J. Daly, 406–17. Leuven: Peeters, 1992.

———. *Origene et la "Connaissance mystique."* Museum Lessianum, Section theologique 56. Paris: Deschee de Brouer: 1961.

———. "Qu'a voulu faire Origene en composant le Traite des Principes." *Bull. Litt. Eccl.* 76 (1975) 161–86.

Crowther, P. *The Kantian Sublime*. Oxford: Clarendon Press. 1989.

Crystal, I. "Plotinus on the Structure of Self-Intellection." *Phronesis* 43 (1998) 264–86.

Curd, Patricia. *The Legacy of Eleatic Monism and Later Presocratic Thought*. Las Vegas, 2004.

Daly, Robert J. *Origeniana Quinta*. Leuven: Peeters, 1992.

D'Amico, Claudia, John F. Finamore, and Natalia Strok. *Platonic Interpretations*. Wiltshire, UK: Prometheus Trust Press, 2017.

Davidson, Donald. *Essays on Actions and Events*. Oxford: Clarendon, 1980.

———. "Thinking Causes." In *Mental Causation*, edited by J. Heil and A. Mele, 3–17. Oxford: Clarendon, 1993.

Dancy, R. M. *Two Studies in the Early Academy*. SUNY Series in Ancient Greek Philosophy. Albany: SUNY Press, 1991.

Danielou, Jean. *Origene et la Philosophie*. Aubier: Paris, 1962.

Davidson, Donald. *Plato's Philebus*. New York: Garland, 1990.

Debbins, William, ed. *Essays in the Philosophy of History by R. G. Collingwood*. Austin: University of Texas Press, 1965.

De Filippo. J. "Thinking of Thinking in Metaphysics Lambda." *JHP* 33 (1995) 543–62.

De Keyser. E. *La Signification de l'art dans les Enneades de Plotin*. Leuven: Peeters, 1955.

De Koninck, Thomas. "Aristotle on God as Thought Thinking Itself." *Review of Metaphysics* 47 (1994) 474–515.

———. "La noesis et L'indivisible selon Aristote." In *La naissance de la raisonen Grece: Acts du Congres de Nice Mai 1987*, edited by J. F. Mattei, ed., 215–18. Paris: Presses Universitaires de France, 1990.

De Lubac, Henri. *History and Spirit: The Understanding of Scripture according to Origen*. San Francisco: Ignatius. 2007.

Derrida, Jacques. "Differance." In *Margins of Philosophy*. Translated by Alan Bass. Chicago: University of Chicago Press, 1982.

———. *Of Grammatology*. Translated by Gayatri Chakravorty Spivak. Baltimore: Johns Hopkins University Press, 1997.

———. "The Double Session." In *Dissemination*. Translated by Barbara Johnson. Chicago: University of Chicago Press, 1981.

Descartes, Rene. *The Philosophical Writings of Descartes.* Vol. 1. Translated by J. Cotting-ham, R. Stoothoff, D. Murdoch, and A. Kenney. Cambridge: Cambridge University Press, 1988.
Detienne, Marcel. *The Masters of Truth in Archaic Greece.* Translated by Janet Lloyd. New York: Zone, 1996.
Devereux, Daniel T. "Separation and Immanence in Plato's Theory of Forms." *OSAP* 12 (1994) 63–90.
Dewey, John. "From Absolutism to Experimentalism." In *John Dewey: On Experience, Nature, and Freedom.* Edited by R. J. Bernstein ed. New York: Library of Liberal Arts, 1990.
Dilthey, Wilhelm. *Selected Writings.* Edited, translated, and introduced by H. P. Rickman. London: MacMillan, 1976.
Dillon, John. "*Aisthesis noete*: A Doctrine of Spiritual Exercises in Plotinus and Origen." In *Hellenica et Judaica: Hommage à Valentin Nikiprowetzky*, edited by A. Caquot, M. Hadas-Lebel, and J. Riaud, 443–55. Collection de la Revue des études juives 3. Leuven: Peeters, 1986.

———. *Iamblichi Chalcidensis in Platonis Dialogos Commentariorum Fragmenta.* Leiden: Brill, 1971.

———. "Image, Symbol and Analogy: Three Basic Concepts of Neoplatonic Allegorical Exegesis." In *The Significance of Neoplatonism*, edited by R. B. Harris, 247–62. Studies in Neoplatonism, Ancient and Modern 1. Norfolk, VA: International Society for Neoplatonic Studies, 1976.

———. *The Handbook of Platonism.* Oxford: Oxford University Press, 1993.

———. "Plotinus and the Transcendental Imagination." In J. P. Mackey, ed., *Religious Imagination*, 55–64. Edinburgh: Edinburgh University Press, 1986.

———. *The Middle Platonists.* Ithaca, NY: Cornell University Press, 1977.

Dodds, E. R. *Proclus. The Elements of Theology.* Oxford: Oxford University Press, 1963.

———. *The Greeks and the Irrational.* Berkeley: University of California Press, 1951.

———. "The Parmenides of Plato and the Origins of the Neoplatonic One." *CQ* (1928) 136ff.

Di Vona, P. *Spinoza ei i transcendentali.* Naples: Morano, 1977.
Doerrie, Heinrich. "Denken ueber das Sprechen hinaus. Unteresuchungen zu den Denkund Sprachgewohnheiten der platonischen Philosophen des 2.-4 Jahrhunderts nach Christus,." In *Collectanea Philologica: Festschrift für Helmut Gibber*, edited by G. Heintz und P. Schmitter, 139–67. Saecula Spiritalia 14–15. Baden-Baden: Koerner, 1985.

———. *Les Sources de Plotin: Entretiens sur l'Antiquite Classique V.* Geneva: Vandoeuvres, 1960.

———. "Porphyre" *Entretiens sur l'Antiquite Classique* XII. Geneva: Vandoeuvres, 1966.

Donini, P. "Plotino e la Tradizione dei Neoplatonici e dei Commentatori Aristotelici." In *Plotino e L'ontologia*. Edited by Matteo Bianchetti. Studi 7. Milan: Albo Vesorio. 2006.
D'Oro, G. *Collingwood and the Metaphysics of Experience.* London: Routledge. 2002.

———. "The Gap Is Semantic not Epistemological." *Ratio* 20 (2007) 168–78.

Dorival, Gilles. "L'Apport d'Origene pour la connaissance de la philosophie grecque." In *Orgeniana Quinta*, Robert J. Daly, ed., 189–216. Peeters: Leuven, 1992.

Dorival, Gilles and Alain Le Boulluec, eds. *Origène et la Bible = Origen and the Bible: Actes du Colloquium Origenianum Sextum, Chantilly, 30 août-3 septembre 1993*. BETL 118. Leuven: Peeters, 1995.
Doyle, J. P. *On the Borders of Being and Knowing: Late Scholastic Theory of Supertranscendental Being*. Leuven: Leuven University Press, 2012.
Dufour, R. "Plotin et les Stoiciens." *Etudes Platoniciennes* 3 (2006) 177–94.
Dummett, Michael. *Frege's Philosophy of Language*. London, 1973.
———. "What Is a Theory of Meaning?" In *Mind and Language*. Edited by S. Guttenplan. Oxford: Oxford University Press, 1975.
During, I., and G. E. L. Owen, eds. *Aristotle and Plato in the Mid-Fourth Century*. Studia Graeca et Latina Gothoburgensia 11. Goteborg: Acta Universitatis Gothoburgensis, 1960.
Dykstra, Vergil H. "Philosophers and Presuppositions." *Mind* 69 (1960) 63–68.
Eagleton, Terry. *The Ideology of the Aesthetic*. Oxford: Blackwell, 1994.
Edelstein, Ludwig. "Plato's Seventh Letter." *Philosophia Antiqua* Vol. 14. Leiden: Brill, 1966.
Edwards, Mark J. "Christians against Matter: A Bouquet for Bishop Berkeley." In *Gnosticism, Platonism and the Late Ancient World*, edited by K. Corrigan and T. Rasimus, 569–80. Nag Hammadi and Manichaean Studies 82. Leiden: Brill, 2013.
———. *Origen against Plato*. New York: Routledge, 2002.
Emilsson E. K. "Cognition and its Object." In *The Cambridge Companion to Plotinus*, edited by Lloyd P. Gerson, 217–49. Cambridge Companions to Philosophy. Cambridge: Cambridge University Press, 1996.
———. *Plotinus on Intellect*. Oxford. Oxford University Press, 2007.
———. *Plotinus on Sense Perception*. Cambridge. Cambridge University Press, 1988.
———. "Plotinus and Soul-Body Dualism." In *Psychology*. Edited by S. Everson. Companions to Ancient Thought 2. Cambridge: Cambridge University Press, 1991.
Evangeliou, Christos. *Aristotle's Categories and Porphyry*. Philosophia Antiqua 48. Leiden: Brill, 1988.
———. "The Ontological Basis of Plotinus's Criticism of Aristotle's Theory of Categories." In *The Structure of Being: A Neoplatonic Approach*, edited by R. B. Harris, 73–82. Studies in Neoplatonism 4. Norfolk, VA: International Society for Neoplatonic Studies, 1982.
Feigl, Herbert. *The "Mental and the "Physical": The Essay and a Postscript*. Minneapolis: University of Minnesota Press, 1967.
Ferejohn, M. T. "Aristotle on Focal Meaning and the Unity of Science." *Phronesis* 25 (1980) 117–28.
Ferry, Luc. *Homo Aestheticus*. Chicago: University of Chicago Press, 1993.
Festugiere, A.-J. *La revelation D'Hermes Trismegiste*. Vol. IV, 22. Paris: Vrin, 1954.
Field, H. H. *Realism, Mathematics and Modality*. Oxford: Blackwell, 1989.
Filler, J. "Relationality as the Ground of Being: The One as Pure Relation in Plotinus." *IJPT* 13 (2019) 1–23.
Finamore, John F., and Robert M. Berchman, eds. *History of Platonism: Plato Redivivus*. New Orleans: University Press of the South, 2005.
Finamore, John F. and Danielle A. Layne, Danielle, eds. *Platonic Pathways: Selected Papers from the Fourteenth Annual Conference of the International Society for Neoplatonic Studies* . Hockley, UK: Prometheus Trust. 2018.

Findlay, John N. "Hegel." In *A Critical History of Western Philosophy*. Edited by D. J. O'Connor. New York: Macmillan, 1964.
———. *Hegel: A Re-examination*. London: Colliers, 1958.
———. "Hegelianism and Platonism." In *Hegel and the History of Philosophy*, 62–76. The Hague: Nijhoff, 1974.
———. *Plato: The Written and Unwritten Doctrines*. London: Routledge & Kegan Paul, 1974.
Fine, Gail. "Knowledge and Logos in the *Theatetus*." *PR* 88 (1979) 366–97.
Finkelberg, A. "Being, Truth and Opinion in Parmenides." *AGP* 81 (1999) 233–48.
Flanagan, O., and T. Honderich, eds. *The Oxford Companion to Philosophy*. Oxford: Oxford University Press, 1995.
Fodor, Jerry. A. "Making Mind Matter More." *PT* 17 (1989) 59–79.
———. "Methodological Solipsism Considered as a Research Strategy." *Cognitive Psychology in Brain and Behavioral Sciences* 3 (1980) 63–109.
Foucault, Michel. *Beyond Structuralism and Hermeneutics*. Chicago: University of Chicago Press, 1982.
———. *Care of the Self*. New York: Vintage, 1988.
———. "The Ethic of Care for the Self as a Practice of Freedom." In *The Final Foucault*, edited by J. Bernauer and D. Rasmussen. Cambridge: MIT Press, 1988.
———. L'Ethique du souci de soi comme pratique de la liberte." Interview with R. Fornet-Betancourt, H. Becker, and A. Gomez-Muller. Jan. 20, 1984.
———. "Final Interview." *Raritan* 5 (1982).
———. "Polemics, Politics, and Problematizations." Interview with Paul Rabinow in *The Foucault Reader*, edited by Paul Rabinow. New York: Pantheon, 1984.
———. *The Order of Things: A Archaeology of the Human Sciences*. New York: Pantheon, 1970.
———. "The Subject and Power,." In *Michel Foucault: Beyond Structuralism and Hermeneutics*. Edited by H. L. Dreyfus and Paul Rabinow. Chicago: University of Chicago Press, 1982.
———. "Technologies of the Self." In *Technologies of the Self*. Edited by L. Martin, H. Gutman, and P. H. Hutton. Amherst: University of Massachusetts Press, 1988.
———. *This Is not a Pipe*. Translated and edited by James Harkness. Berkeley: University of California Press, 1982.
———. *The Use of Pleasure*. The History of Sexuality 2. Translated by Robert Hurley. New York: Vintage, 1986.
Frede, Michael. *Essays in Ancient Philosophy*. Minneapolis: University of Minnesota Press, 1987.
———. "The Stoic Notion of a Lekton." In *Cambridge Companion to Ancient Thought* 3: *Language*, 109–28. Cambridge: Cambridge University Press, 1994.
Frede, Michael, and Myles Burnyeat. *The Pseudo-Platonic Seventh Letter*. Edited by D. Scott, ed. Oxford: Oxford University Press, 2015.
Frege, Georg. *The Foundations of Arithmetic*. Oxford: Blackwell, 1953.
———. *Translations from the Philosophical Writings of Gottlob Frege*. Edited by P. Geach and M. Black. Oxford: Blackwell, 1980.
Fronterotta, F. "La critique plotinienne de la causalite finale dans le traite VI.7 (38) des Enneades (chap. 1–3 et 25)." *Chora* 12 (2014) 47–66.
Furley, David J., and R. E. Allen. *Studies in Presocratic Philosophy*. Vol. 1. ILPSM. New York: Routledge & Keegan Paul, 1970.

Furth, Montgomery. "A Philosophical Hero? Anaxagoras on the Eleatics." *Oxford Studies in Ancient Philosophy* 9 (1991) 95–129.
Gadamer, Hans-Georg. *Heidegger's Ways*. Translated by John W. Stanley. SUNY Series in Contemporary Continental Philosophy. Albany: SUNY Press, 1994.
———. *Reason in the Age of Science*. Translated by Frederick G. Lawrence. Studies in Contemporary German Social Thought. Cambridge: MIT Press, 1984.
———. *Relevance of the Beautiful and Other Essays*. Edited by Robert Bernascone. Translated by Nicholas Walker. Cambridge: Cambridge University Press. 1986.
———. *Truth and Method*. 2nd ed. Translated by Joel Weinsheimer and Donald G. Marshall. New York: Crossroad, 1989.
Gasparro, G. S. "Eguaglianza di natura e differenza di condizioni dei logikoi: la soluzione origeniana nel contesto delle formule anthropologiche e demonologiche greche del II e III sec." In *Origeniana Quinta*, edited by Robert J. Daly. Leuven: Peeters, 1992.
Gavirlyuk, Paul L., and Sarah Coakley, eds. *The Spiritual Senses: Perceiving God in Western Christianity*. Cambridge: Cambridge University Press, 2011.
Geach, P. T. *Mental Acts*. London: Routledge & Kegan Paul, 1956.
Genequand, Charles. *Alexander of Aphrodisias: On the Cosmos*. London: Duckworth. 2001.
George, R. "Brentano's Relation to Aristotle." *Grazer Philosophische Studien* 5 (1978) 249–66.
Gersh, Stephen. "Derrida Reads (Neo-) Platonism." In *Platonisms: Ancient, Modern, and Postmodern*, edited by K. Corrigan and J. D. Turner. Studies in Platonism, Neoplatonism, and the Platonic Tradition 4. Leiden: Brill, 2007.
———. *Middle Platonism and Neoplatonism: The Latin Tradition*. Vol. 1. South Bend: University of Notre Dame Press, 1986.
———. *Neoplatonism after Derrida: Parallelograms*. Studies in Platonism, Neoplatonism, and the Platonic Tradition 3. Leiden: Brill: 2006.
Gerson, Lloyd. P., ed., *Aristotle and Other Platonists*. Ithaca, NY: Cornell University Press, 2005.
———. "Being and Knowing in Plotinus." In *Neoplatonism and Indian Thought*. Edited by P. M. Gregorios. Ithaca, NY: Cornell University Press, 2002.
———, ed. *The Cambridge Companion to Plotinus*. Cambridge Companions to Philosophy. Cambridge University Press, Cambridge, 1996.
———. *From Plato to Platonism*. Ithaca, NY: Cornell University Press, 2013.
———. *God and Greek Philosophy: Studies in the Early History of Natural Theology*. London: Routledge, 1990.
———. "Introspection, Self-Reflexivity and the Essence of Thinking." In *The Perennial Tradition of Neoplatonism*, edited by J. Cleary, 153–73. Ancient and Medieval Philosophy, series 1, 24. Leuven: Leuven University Press, 1997.
———. *Plotinus*. The Arguments of the Philosophers. London: Routledge, 1994.
———. "Review of Blumenthal Aristotle and Neoplatonism in Late Antiquity. Interpretations of the De Anima." *Journal of the History of Philosophy* 36 (1988).
———. "The Unity of Intellect in Aristotle's *De Anima*." *Phronesis* 49 (2004) 350–69.
———. "What Is Platonism?" *Journal of the History of Platonism* 43 (2005) 253–76.
Gill, M. L. *Aristotle on Substance. The Paradox of Unity*. Princeton: Princeton University Press, 1989.

———. "Division and Definition in Plato's Sophist and Statesman." In *Definition in Greek Philosophy*, edited by D. Charles, 172–99. Oxford: Oxford University Press, 2010.

———. "Method and Metaphysics in Plato's Sophist and Statesman." In *Stanford Encyclopedia of Philosophy*, 2005/2015.

Ginsborg, H. "On the Key to Kant's Critique of Taste." *Pacific Philosophical Quarterly* 72 (1991) 290–313.

———. *The Role of Taste in Kant's Theory of Cognition*. New York: Garland. 1990.

Gonzalez, Francisco J. "Plato's Dialectic of Forms." In *Plato's Forms*, edited by William A. Welton, 31–84. Lanham, MD: Lexington, 2002.

———. Review of Franco Trabbatoni. *Scrivere nell'anima: verita, dialectica e persuasione in Platone and Oralita e scrittura in Platone*. *JHS* 38 (2000) 269–71.

Goodman, Nelson. *Languages of Art: An Approach to a Theory of Symbols*. 2nd ed. Indianapolis: Bobbs-Merrill, 1976.

———. *Ways of Worldmaking*. Indianapolis: Hackett. 1978.

Gorez, Jean. *De ebrietate*. In *Oeuvres de Philon d'Alexandrie*. Vol. 11. Paris: Cerf, 1962.

Gould, P. "The Problem of God and 'Abstract Objects.'" *Philosophia Christi* 13 (2011) 255–74.

Graeser, A. *Plotinus and the Stoics: A Preliminary Study*. Philosophia Antiqua 22. Leiden: Brill, 1972.

Greco, J. "Knowledge of God." In *The Oxford Handbook of The Epistemology of Theology*. Edited by W. J. Abraham and F. D. Aquino. Oxford: Oxford University Press, 2017.

———. "The Value Problem." In *Social Epistemology*. Edited by A. Haddock, A. Millar and D. Pritchard. Oxford: Oxford University Press, 2010.

Gregorios, Paulos Mar, ed. *Neoplatonism and Indian Thought*. Studies in Neoplatonism: Ancient and Modern 9. Albany: SUNY Press, 2002.

Green, Thomas H. *Collected Works of T. H. Green, 1885–1888*. Edited by R. L. Nettleship. 3 vols. London: Longmans, 1968.

Gurtler, Gary. *Ennead IV.4.30–45 & IV.5* Translation, Introduction Commentary. Las Vegas: Parmenides. 2015.

———. "Plotinus and the Alienation of the Soul." In *The Perennial Tradition of Neoplatonism*. Edited by J. Cleary. Ancient and Medieval Philosophy, series 1, 24. Leuven: Leuven University Press, 1997.

———. *Plotinus: The Experience of Unity*. Bern: Lang, 1988.

———. "Plotinus: Self and Consciousness." In *History of Platonism: Plato Redivivus*, edited by J. F. Finamore and R. M. Berchman, 113–30. New Orleans: University of the Press of the South, 2005.

———. Review *IJPT* 4 (2010) 83–85. 2010.

———. "The Origin of Genera: *Ennead* VI.2. [43].20." *Dionysius* 12 (1988) 3–15.

Guthrie, W. K. C. *The Later Plato and the Academy*. Cambridge. Cambridge University Press, 1987.

Haas, F. A. J de. "Context and Strategy of Plotinus' Treatise on *Genera of Being* (*Enn.* VI.1–3 [42–44])." In *Aristotle e i Suoi Esegeti Neoplatonici: Logica e Ontologia nell Interpretatzioni Greche e Arabe*, edited by Vincenza Celluprica and Cristina D'Ancona Costa, 39–53. Rome: Bibliopolis, 2004.

———. "Did Plotinus and Porphyry Disagree on Aristotle's Categories?" *Phronesis* 46 (2001) 492–526.

Hackforth, Robert. *Plato's Phaedrus*. Indianapolis: Bobbs-Merrill, 1945.

Haddock, A., A. Millar, and D. Pritchard, eds. *The Nature and Value of Knowledge: Three Investigations*. Oxford: Oxford University Press. 2010.
Hadot, I. *Arts Liberaux et Philosophie dans le Pensee Antique*. Leuven: Brepols, 1984.
Hadot, Pierre. "Etre, vie, pensee chez Plotin et avant Plotin." In *Les sources de Plotin*, 107–41. Entretiens sur l'Antiquité classique 5. Vandoeuvres-Geneve: Fondation Hardt, 1960.

———. *Exercises spirituels et philosophiqueAntique*. Paris: Micel, 2002.

———. "L'harmonie des Philosophies de Plotin et D'Aristote selon Porphyre dans le Commentaire de Dexippe sur les Categories." In *Plotino e Neoplatismo in Oriente e Occidente*. Rome: Accademeia nazionale dei Lincei, 1974.

———. "Histoire de la Pensee hellenistique et romaine." *Annuaire du College de France* 1982/83.

———. *Plotin, ou la simplicite du regard*. Paris: Gallimard, 1997.

———. *Porphyre et Victorinus*. Paris: Etudes Augustiniennes, 1968.

———. "Reflections on the Notion of 'the Cultivation of the Self.'" In *MFP*.

———. "Revue of Harder." *Revue Belge de Philologie et d'Histoire* 36 (1959) 158–59.

———. "Revue of H-S2." *Revue Belge de Philologie et d'Histoire* 164 (1963) 92–96.

———. "Structure et themes du Traite 38 [VI.7] de Plotin." In *ANRW* II.36.1, 624–76. Berlin: de Gruyter, 1987.

———. "L'union de l'ame avec i'intellect divin dans l'experience mystique plotinenne." In *Proclus et son influence: actes du colloque de Neuchatel*. Edited by G. Boss and C. Steel. Zurich: Grand Midi, 1987.

———. *Wittgenstein et le Limites du Language*. Paris: Vrin, 1998.

Hager, F. P. "Die Aristotlesinterpretation des Alexander von Aphrodisias und die Aristoteskritik Plotinus bezueglich der Lehre von Geist."*AGP* 46 (1964) 174–87.
Hahn, L. E. and P. A. Schlipp, eds. *The Philosophy of Quine*, La Salle, IL: Open Court, 1986.
Hamlyn, D. W. "Focal Meaning." *Proceedings o f the Aristotelian Society* 78 (1977–78) 1–18.
Hankey, Wayne. "'Knowing as We Are Known' in Confessions 10 and Other Philosophical, Augustinian and Christian Obedience to the Delphic Gnothi Seauton from Socrates to Modernity." *Augustinian Studies* 34 (2003) 23–48.
Hankinson, R. J. "Parmenides and the Metaphysics of Changelessness." In *Presocratic Philosophy: Essays in Honor of Alexander Mourelatos*, edited by V. Caston and D. W. Graham. Burlington, VT: Ashgate, 2002.
Hansen, M.J. "Parmenides B6.1–2 without a Modal Fallacy." *Aporia* 21 (2011).
Harte, V. *Plato on Parts and Wholes: The Metaphysics of Structure*. Oxford. Oxford University Press, 2002.
Hartmann, Nicolai. *Zur Grundlegung der Ontologie*. Berlin: de Gruyter, 1935.
Hatzimichali, Myrto. *Potamo of Alexandria and the Emergence of Eclecticism in Late Hellenistic Philosophy*. Cambridge: Cambridge University Press, 2015.
Hedley, Douglas R. *The Iconic Imagination*. London: Bloomsbury, 2016.
Hegel, G. F. W. *Hegel: The Letters*. Translated by Clark Butler and Christiane Seiler. Bloomington: Indiana University Press, 1984.

———. *Introductory Lectures on Aesthetics*. Translated by Bernard Bosanquet. Edited with an introduction and commentary by Michael Inwood. Penguin Classics. New York: Penguin, 1993.

———. *Lectures on the History of Philosophy: Plato and the Platonists.* Vol. 2. Translated by E. S. Haldane and F. H. Simson. Lincoln: University of Nebraska Press, 1995.
———. *Philosophy of History.* Translated by J. Sibree. New York: Dover, 1956.
———. *Philosophy of Mind.* Translated by A. V. Miller. Oxford: Clarendon, 1971.
———. *Philosophy of Right.* Translated by T. M. Knox. Oxford: Oxford University Press, 1952.
———. *Phenomenology of Spirit.* Translated by A.V. Miller. Oxford: Clarendon.1977.
———. *Saemtliche Werke: Jubilaeumsausgabe.* Edited by H. Glockner. 20 vols., 1927.
———. *Science of Logic.* Translated by A.V. Miller. London: Allen & Unwin, 1969.
Heide, Daniel. "Heresy, Hermeneutics, and the Hellenization of Christianity: A Reappraisal of Embodiment in Origen's *De Principiis.*" *Journal of the School of Religious Studies, McGill University* 44 (2016) 41–59.
Heidegger, Martin. *Being and Time.* Translated by John Macquarie and Edward Robinson. New York: Harper & Row, 1962.
———. *Poetry, Language, Thought.* New York: Harper & Row, 1971.
———. "Zur Sache des Denkens." In *Discourse on Thinking.* Translated by J. Anderson and E. H. Freund. New York: Harper & Row, 1966.
Heinaman, R. "Aristotle and the Mind-Body Problem." *Phronesis* 35 (1990) 83–102.
Heine, Ronald E. "The Introduction to Origen's Commentary on John Compared with the Introductions of Ancient Philosophical Commentaries on Aristotle." In In *Origeniana Sexta: Origène et la Bible = Origen and the Bible: Actes du Colloquium Origenianum Sextum, Chantilly, 30 août–3 septembre 1993,* edited by G. Dorival and A. Le Boulluec, 3–12. BETL 118. Leuven: Peeters, 1995.
Helleman-Elgersma, C. *Soul-Sisters: A Commentary on Enneads IV.3 [27].* Amsterdam: Nijhoff, 1988.
Hendrix, John Shannon. "Plotinus and the Artistic Imagination." docs@rwu 2015.
———. "Plotinian Aesthetics." In *Platonic Architectonics: Platonic Studies and the Visual Arts.* New York: Lang, 2004.
———. "The Symposium and the Aesthetics of Plotinus." In *Aesthetics & the Philosophy of Spirit: From Plotinus to Schelling and Hegel.* New York: Lang, 2005.
Henry, P. "Tois apories orales de Plotin sur les Categories d'Aristote." *Zetesis Album Amicorum* (1973) Antwerp, 234–65.
———. "Une Comparaison chez Aristote, Alexander et Plotin." In *Les Sources de Plotin.* Vol. V. Vadoeuvres-Geneve: Foundation Hardt, 1960.
Hintikka, J. "Parmenides' Cogito Argument." *Ancient Philosophy* 1 (1980) 5–16.
———. "The Phenomenological Dimension." In B. Smith and D. W. Smith, eds., *The Cambridge Companion to Husserl.* Cambridge: Cambridge University Press,1999.
Hobbes, Thomas. *The Leviathan.* Edited by J. C. A. Gaskin. Oxford: Oxford University Press, 1996.
Hogan, John P. *Collingwood and Theological Hermeneutics.* College Theological Society Studies in Religion. New York: University Press of America, 1989.
Horn, H.-J. "Stoische Symmetrie und Theorie des Schoenen in der Kaiserzeit." In *ANRW* II.36.3 (1979) 1455–71.
Huby, P. M. "Socrates and Plato." In *A Critical History of Western Philosophy,* edited by D. J. O'Connor. Free Press Textbooks in Philosophy. New York: Free Press, 1964.
Hume, David. *An Enquiry Concerning Human Understanding.* Edited by T. L. Beauchamp. Oxford: Clarendon, 2000.

———. *Essays: Moral, Political and Literary*. Edited by T. H. Greene and T. H. Grose. London: Longmans, Green, 1875.

Hunt, D. P. "Contemplation and Hypostatic Procession in Plotinus." *Apeiron* 15.2 (1981) 71–79.

Husserl, Edmund. *Cartesian Meditations*. Translated by D. Cairns. Dortrecht: Kluwer, 1988.

———. *Crisis*, Chicago: Northwestern University Press, 1970.

———. *Ideas Pertaining to a Pure Phenomenology and to a Phenomenological Philosophy*. Translated by T. E. Klein and W. E. Pohl. Dortrecht: Kluwer, 1980.

———. *Ideen zu einer reinen Phänomenologie und phänomenologischen Philosophie*. In *JPpF*, 1913.

———. *On the Phenomenology of the Consciousness of Internal Time (1893–1917)*. Translated by J. B. Brough. Dortrecht: Kluwer, 1994.

Hutardo, Larry W. *At the Origins of Christian Worship: The Context and Character of Early Christian Devotion*. Grand Rapids: Eerdmans, 1999.

Hutchinson, Donald M. "Apprehension of Thought in Ennead 4.3.30." *IJPT*. Leiden: Brill, 2011.

———. *Plotinus on Consciousness*. Cambridge: Cambridge University Press, 2018.

Igal, J. "La Genesis de la Intelligencia en un Pasage de las Eneadas de Plotino V.1.7.4–35." *Emerita* 39 (1971) 129–57.

Insole, J. C. "Realism and Anti-Realism." In *The Oxford Handbook of the Epistemology of Theology*, edited by W. J. Abraham and F. D. Aquino. Oxford: Oxford University Press, 2017.

Irwin, Terrence .H. "Aristotle's Concept of Signification." In *Language and Logos*, edited by M. Schofield and M. C. Nussbaum, 241–66. Cambridge: Cambridge University Press, 1982.

———. *Aristotle's First Principles*. Oxford: Clarendon, 1988.

Johnson, F. "Epiphenomenal Qualia." *PQ* 32 (1982) 127–36.

Judovitz, D. *Subjectivity and Representation in Descartes*. Cambridge: Cambridge University Press, 1988.

Kahn, Charles. "Being in Parmenides and Plato." *La parola del passato* 43 (1988) 237–61.

———. "The Greek Verb 'to Be' and the Concept of Being." *Foundations of Language* 2 (1966) 245–65.

———. "Language and Ontology in the *Cratylus*." In *Exegesis and Argument: Studies in Greek Philosophy Presented to Gregory Vlastos*. Edited by E. N. Lee, A. P. D. Mourelatos, and R. M. Rorty. Phronesis Supplements 1. Assen: Van Gorcum, 1973.

———. "Linguistic Relativism and the Greek Project of Ontology." In *The Question of Being: East-West Perspective*. Edited by Mervyn Sprung. University Park: Pennsylvania State University Press, 1978.

———. "Myles Burnet and Michael Frede The Pseudo-Platonic Seventh Letter." *NDPR* 11.09.2015.

———. "The Role of *Nous* in the Cognition of First Principles in *Posterior Analytics* II.19." In *Aristotle on Science: "The Posterior Analytics."* Proceedings of the Eighth Symposium Aristolelicum, edited by E. Berti, 385–414. Studia aristotelica 9. Padua: Antenore, 1981.

———. "Sensation and Consciousness in Aristotle's Psychology." *Archiv für Geschichte der Philosophie* 48 (1960) 43–81.

———. "Why Existence Does not Emerge as a Distinct Concept in Greek Philosophy." *Archiv für Geschichte der Philosophie* 58 (1976) 323–34.
Kant, Immanuel. *Critique of Judgment*. Translated by J. C. Meredith. Oxford: Oxford University Press, 1952.
———. *Critique of Pure Reason*. Translated by N. Kemp-Smith. New York: Macmillan, 1975.
———. *Gesammelte Schriften*, ed. PAS. 22 vols. 1900–1942.
———. *Kritik der reinen Vernunft*. Hamburg: Meiner, 1971.
———. *Metaphysical Foundations of Natural Science*. Translated by J. W. Ellington. New York: Hackett, 1985.
Karamanolis, George. "Early Christian Philosophers on Aristotle." In *The Brill Companion to the Reception of Aristotle*, edited by A. Falcon, 460–79. Leiden: Brill, 2016.
Kennedy, George, A. "Language and Meaning in Archaic and Classical Greece." In *The Cambridge History of Literary Criticism*. Vol. I, *Classical Criticism*, edited by G. A. Kennedy. Cambridge: Cambridge University Press, 1989.
Kenney, John Peter, ed., "*Proschresis* Revisited: An Essay in Numenian Theology." In *Origeniana Quinta*, edited by Robert J. Daly, 217–30. Leuven: Peeters, 1992.
———, ed. *The School of Moses: Studies in Philo and Hellenistic Religion*. Studia Philonica Monographs 1. Atlanta: Scholars, 1995.
Kenny, Anthony. "Descartes on Ideas." In *Descartes: A Collection of Critical Essays*, edited by W. Doney. Garden City, NY: Doubleday, 1967.
Ketchum, R. "Names, Forms and Conventionalism: *Cratylus*, 383–95." *Phronesis* 24, (1979).
Kierkegaard, Soren. *Concluding Unscientific Postscript*. Princeton: Princeton University Press, 1973.
Kneale W., and M. Kneale. *The Development of Logic*. Oxford: Oxford University Press, 1961.
Kern, Iso. *Husserl und Kant*. The Hague: Nijhof, 1964.
Ketner, K. L. *An Emendation of R.G. Collingwood's Doctrine of Absolute Presuppositions*. Texas Tech University Graduate Studies 4. Lubbock: Texas Tech Press, 1973.
de Keyser, E. *La Signification de l'art dans les Enneades de Plotin*. Leuven: Peeters, 1955.
King, R. A. H. *Aristotle and Plotinus on Memory*. Berlin: de Gruyter. 2009.
Kirwan, C. *Aristotle Metaphysics, Books Γ, Δ and E*. 2nd ed. Oxford: Oxford University Press, 1993.
Koch, Hal. *Pronoia und Paideusis: Studien ueber Origenes und sein Verhaeltniss zum Platonismus*. Berlin: Weidemann, 1932.
Knuutilla, S. and Kaerkkaeinen, P. *Theories of Perception in Medieval and Early Modern Philosophy*. Hamburg: Springer, 2008.
Kraemer, Hans Joachim. "Epekeina tes ousias. Zu Platon, Politeia 509b." *AGP* (1969) 1–30.
———. *Der Ursprung der Geistmetaphysik: Untersuchungen zur Geschichte des Platonismus zwischen Platon und Plotin*. Amsterdam: Nijhof, 1964.
Krausz, Michael. "The Logic of Absolute Presupposition." In *Critical Essays on the Philosophy of R. G. Collingwood*. Edited by Michael Krausz. Oxford: Clarendon, 1972.
Krayle, Jill. "Aristotle's God and the Authenticity of *De Mundo*: An Early Modern Controversy." *JHP* 28 (1990) 339–58.

Kripke, Saul. *Wittgenstein on Rules and Private Language.* Cambridge: Harvard University Press, 1982.
Kuebel, Paul. "Zum Aufbau von Origenes De Principiis {PERI ARCHON}." *VC* 25 (1971) 31-39.
Kvanvig, Jonathon, L. "Understanding." In *The Oxford Handbook of the Epistemology of Theology*, edited by W. J. Abraham and F. D. Aquino, 175-89. Oxford: Oxford University Press, 2017.

———. *The Value of Knowledge and the Pursuit of Understanding.* Cambridge: Cambridge University Press. 2003.

Lagerlund, Henrik, Mikko Yrjoensuuri et. al., eds. *Studies in the History of Philosophy of Mind: Forming the Mind.* Vol. 5. Hamburg: Springer, 2008.
Langerbeck, Hans. "Die Verbindung aristotelischer und christlicher Elemente in der Philosophie des Ammonius Saccas." *AAWG* 69 (1957) 146-66.
Lavecchia, Salvatore. *Agathological Realism: Searching for the Good beyond Subjectivity and Objectivity or On the Importance of Being Platonic*, Etica & Politica / Ethics & Politics 16 (2014), 533-49 (also in G. De Anna-R. Martinelli, eds., *Moral Realism and Political Decisions*, 29-50. Bamberg: University of Bamberg Press, 2015.

———. *Creatività come agatopoièsi L'esperienza della formatività Agathologie. Denken als Wahrnehmung des Guten oder: Auf der Suche nach dem offenbarsten Geheimnis*, Perspektiven der Philosophie 38 (2012) *nella filosofia di Platone*, in A. Bertinetto-A. Martinengo, eds., *Rethinking Creativity*, Tròpos 5 (2012), 11-25.

———. "Das Gute als Quelle der Selbstbewegung: Betrachtungen zum nous und zum Selbstbewusstein in Platons Philosophie." In *Selbstbewegung und Lebendigkeit: Die Seele in Platons Spätwerk*, edited by M. Abbate, J. Pfefferkorn, and A. Spinelli, 19-32. Berlin: de Gruyter, 2016.

———. *Generare la luce del bene. Incontrare veramente Platone.* Bergamo: Moretti & Vitali, 2015.

———. "Höchste Erkenntnis als königliche Kunst. Zur demiurgischen Dimension der Philosophie in Platons Politeia." In *Art, Intellect and Politics: A Diachronic Perspective*, G. M. A. Margagliotta and A. A. Robiglio, 177-91. Leiden: Brill, 2013.

———. "*Idéa tou agathoú-agathòn epékeina tes ousías*: Überlegungen zu einer platonischen Antinomie." *Bochumer Philosophisches Jahrbuch für Antike und Mittelalter* 10 (2005) 1-20.

———. "La luce del Bene: l'essere e la coscienza, la materia e lo spirito: Su ciò che Platone tralascia nell'analogia fra il Bene e il sole." *Chôra* 15-16 (2017-2018) 445-56.

———. *Oltre l'uno ed i Molti. Bene ed Essere nella filosofia di Platone.* Milan: Mimesis, 2010.

———. "Poesia e cosmopoièsi. Sulle fonti della scrittura filosofica in Platone." In L. Battezzato and G. B. D'Alessio, eds., Κόσμος ἐπέων: *Studi offerti a Franco Ferrari, Materiali e discussioni per l'analisi dei testi classici* 76 (2016) 171-83.

———. "Saggio. Luce a se stessa trasparente," *Eudia* Anno 11, 2017 24 Maggio.

Lear, Jonathon. *Aristotle: The Desire to Understand.* Cambridge: Cambridge University Press, 1988.
Leibniz, G. W. *Hauptschriften zur Grundlegung der Philosophie.* Edited by A. Buchenau und E. Cassirer. Philosophische Bibliothek 107, 108. Leipzig: Meiner, 1924.

———. *Leibniz: Philosophical Writings.* Edited by ed. G. Parkinson New York: Roman & Littlefield,1973.

———. *New Essays on Human Understanding*. Edited by P. Remnant and J. Bennett. Cambridge: Cambridge University Press, 1982.

———. *Philosophical Papers and Letters*. Edited by Leroy E. Loemker. Dordrecht: Reidel, 1969.

———. *Philosophische Schriften von Gottfried Wilhelm Leibniz*. Edited by C. J. Gerhardt. Berlin, 1875–1900.

———. *Theodicy*. Translated by E. M. Huggard. London: Open Court, 1985.

Leszl, Walter. *Logic and Metaphysics in Aristotle*. Padua: Antenore, 1970.

Lilla, Salvatore. "Aristotelianism." In *Encyclopedia of Ancient Christianity*. Vol. 1, edited by A. Di Berardino et al., 228–35. Downer Grove: IVP Academic, 2014.

———. *Clement of Alexandria: A Study in Christian Platonism and Gnosticism*. Oxford: Oxford University Press, 1971.

Limone, Vito. *Origene e la filosofia greca*. Brecia: Morcellina, 2018.

Llewelyn, John. "Collingwood's Doctrine of Absolute Presuppositions." *Philosophical Quarterly* 11 (1961) 49–60.

Lloyd, A. C. *The Anatomy of Neoplatonism*. Oxford: Oxford University Press, 1990.

———. *Form and Universal in Aristotle*. ARCA, Classical and Medieval Texts, Papers, and Monographs 4. Liverpool: Cairns, 1981.

———. "The Later Neoplatonists." In *The Cambridge History of Later Greek and Early Medieval Philosophy*, edited by A. H. Armstrong, 287–93. Cambridge: Cambridge University Press, 1967.

———. "Non-Discursive Thought—an Enigma of Greek Philosophy." In *Proceedings of the Aristotelian Society* 70 (1969–1970) 261–74.

———. "Non-Propositional Thought in Plotinus." *Phronesis* 31 (1986) 258–65.

———. "*Nosce Tepsium* and *Conscientia*." *Archiv für Geschichte der Philosophie* 46 (1964) 188–200.

———. "The Principle that the Cause is Greater than the Effect." *Phronesis* 21 (1976) 146–56.

Lloyd, G. E. R., and G. E. L. Owen, eds. *Aristotle on Mind and Senses: Proceedings of the Seventh Symposium Aristotelicum*. Cambridge. Cambridge University Press, 1978.

Locke, John. *An Essay Concerning Human Understanding*. Edited by P. H. Nidditch. Oxford: Clarendon, 1975.

Lonergan, Bernard. *Method in Theology*. New York: Herder & Herder, 1972.

Long, A. A., ed. *The Cambridge Companion to Early Greek Philosophy*. Cambridge Companions to Philosophy. Cambridge. Cambridge University Press, 1999.

———. "Parmenides on Thinking Being." *BACAP* 12 (1996) 125–62.

Long, A. A., and David M. Sedley, eds. *The Hellenistic Philosophers*. 2 vols. Cambridge: Cambridge University Press, 1987.

Longuenesse, B. "Kant's Leading Thread in the Analytic of the Beautiful." In *Aesthetics and Cognition in Kant's Critical Philosophy*. Edited by R. Kukla. Cambridge: Cambridge University Press. 2006.

———. "Kant's Theory of Judgment and Judgments of Taste" *Inquiry* 46 (2003) 146–63.

Lorimer, W. L. *The Text Tradition of Ps-Aristotle De Mundo together with an Appendix Containing the Text of the Mediaeval Latin Versions*. Oxford: Oxford University Press, 1927

Loux, M. J. *Substance and Attribute*. Hamburg: Springer, 1978.

———. *Universals and Particulars*. New York: Doubleday 1970; reissued South Bend: Notre Dame University Press, 1977.

Lowe, E. J. *The Four-Category Ontology* Oxford: Oxford University Press, 2006.
———. *Kinds: The Possibility of Metaphysics*. Oxford: Oxford University Press, 1998.
———. *More Kinds of Being*. Malden, MA: Wiley-Blackwell, 2009.
———. *Of Being*. London: Blackwell, 1989.
———. *A Survey of Metaphysics*. Oxford: Oxford University Press, 2002
Lundin, R. "Hermeneutics." In *Contemporary Literary Theory: A Christian Appraisal*. Edited by Clarence Walhout and Leland Ryken. Grand Rapids: Eerdmans, 1991.
Makkai, K. "Kant on Recognizing Beauty" *European Journal of Philosophy* 18 (2010) 385–413.
Makkreel, R. *Imagination and Interpretation in Kant*. Chicago: University of Chicago Press. 1990.
Malcom, J. *Plato on the Self-Predication of Forms*. Oxford: Clarendon, 1991.
———. "Semantics and Self-Predication in Plato." *Phronesis* 26 (1981) 286–94.
Malcolm, Norman. "Anselm's Ontological Arguments." *PA* 69 (1960) 143–49.
Malekin, P. *Time, Consciousness and Writing*. Leiden: Brill/Rodopi, 2019.
Maloney, T. S. *Three Treatments of Universals by Roger Bacon*. MRTS. Binghampton, 1989.
Mallarme, Stephane. *Correspondance 1862–1871*. Paris: Gallimard, 1959.
Manchester, Peter. *The Syntax of Time: The Phenomenology of Time in Greek Physics and Speculative Logic from Iamblichus to Anaximander*. Studies in Platonism, Neoplatonism, and the Platonic Tradition 2. Leiden: Brill, 2005.
———. "Time and the Soul in Plotinus." *Dionysius* 2 (1978) 101–36.
Mandrake, D. K. W. *Aristotle's Theory of Language and Meaning*. Cambridge: Cambridge University Press, 2001.
Martin, Ralph P. *Worship in the Early Church*. Grand Rapids: Eerdmans, 1964.
Mates, Benson. "Identity and Predication in Plato." *Phronesis* 24 (1979) 211–29.
Mathen, Mohan."Forms and Participants in Plato's *Phaedo*." *Nous* 18 (1984) 281–98.
———. "Plato's Treatment of Relational Statements in the *Phaedo*." *Phronesis* 24 (1979) 211–29.
Matson, W. "Why Isn't the Mind–Body Problem Ancient?" In *Mind, Matter and Method: Essays in Philosophy and Science in Honor of Herbert Feigl*, edited by P. Feyerabend and G. Maxwell, 92–102. Minneapolis: University of Minnesota Press: Minneapolis, 1966.
Marx, Werner. *The Meaning of Aristotle's 'Ontology'*. The Hague: Nijhoff, 1954.
Mastrocinque, A. "The Divinatory Kit from Pergamon and Greek Magic in Late Antiquity." *JRA* 13 (2013) 173–88.
McAllister, L. L., ed. *The Philosophy of Brentano*. London: Duckworth, 1976.
McCabe, M.M. "Unity in the *Parmenides*: The Unity of the *Parmenides*." In *Form and Argument in Late Plato*. Edited by C. Gill and M. M. McCabe. Oxford: Oxford University Press, 1996.
McDowell, John. "Knowledge and the Internal." *Philosophy and Phenomenological Research* 55 (1995) 877–93.
McGuckin, John Anthony. "Pre-Existence and Mystical Thought." In *The Westminster Handbook to Origen*, edited by John Anthony McGuckin. Westminster Handbooks to Christian Theology. Louisville: Westminster John Knox, 2004.
Merlan, Philip. "Greek Philosophy from Plato to Plotinus." In *The Cambridge History of Later Greek and Early Medieval Philosophy*. Edited by A. H. Armstrong. Cambridge: Cambridge University Press, 1967.

———. *From Platonism to Neoplatonism*. The Hague: Nijhof, 1953.
———. *Monopsychism, Mysticism, Metaconsciousness: Problems of the Soul in the Neoaristotelian and Neoplatonic Traditions*. The Hague: Nijhoff, 1963.
Metzger, Bruce M. *Historical and Literary Studies: Pagan, Jewish and Christian*. Leiden: Brill, 1968.
Mink, Louis O. *Mind, History, and Dialectic: The Philosophy of R. G. Collingwood*. Bloomington: Indiana University Press, 1969.
Modrak, Deborah K. W. *Aristotle's Theory of Language and Meaning*. New York: Cambridge University Press: 2001.
Moran, Richard. "Kant, Prout and the Appeal to Beauty." *Critical Inquiry*. 38 (2012) 298–329.
Moravcsik, Julius. *Plato and Platonism*. Oxford: Blackwell, 1992.
———. "Understanding and Knowledge in Plato's Philosophy." *Neue Hefte für Philosophie* 15 (1979) 53–69.
Moraux, Paul. *Der Aristotelismus bei den Griechen, Von Andronikos bis Alexander von Aphrodisias*. Berlin: de Gruyter, 2001.
Moreau, Jean. "Origine et expressions du beau suivant Plotin." In *Neoplatonisme: Melanges offert a Jean Trouillard*, 249–63. Cahiers de Fontenay. Fontenay-aux-Roses: Ecole Normal Superieure, 1981.
Morrison, D. "The Evidence for Degrees of Being in Aristotle." *Classical Quarterly* 37, (1987) 382–401.
Mortley, R. *From Word to Silence II. The Way of Negation, Christian and Greek*. Bonn: Hannstein, 1986.
Mosse-Bastide, R.-M. *Bergson et Plotin*. Paris: Presses Universitaires de France, 1959.
Mourelatos, A. P. D. *The Route of Parmenides: A Study of Word, Image and Argument in the Fragments*. New Haven: Yale University Press, 1970.
———. "Two Analytical Approaches to Parmenides' Metaphysical-Cosmological Poem." DOI 10.15.15/rhiz.2016–0013. 2016.
Mueller-Vollmer, K. *The Hermeneutics Reader: Texts of the German Tradition from the Enlightenment to the Present*. New York: Continuum, 1992.
Murphy, D. J. "Origin of Intentionality." MA thesis, University of Guelph, 2005.
Nagel, Thomas. "Panpsychism." In *Mortal Questions*. Edited by Thomas Nagel. Cambridge: Cambridge University Press, 1979.
Narbonne, Jean-Marc. *Henologie, ontologie et Ereignis: Plotin, Proclus, Heidegger*. Paris, 2001.
———. *Levinas et l'heritage grec*. Paris: Vrin, 2004.
Narbonne, Jean-Marc, and Wayne Hankey, eds. *Cent ans de Neoplatonisme en France: Une breve histoire philosophique*. Paris: Vrin, 2004.
Natorp, Paul. *Platons Ideenlehre*. Hamburg: Meiner, 1961.
Naugle. D. "R. G. Collingwood and the Hermeneutic Tradition." Online pub., 1993.
Nikunin, D. "Intelligible Matter in Plotinus." *Dionysius* 14 (1988) 85–114.
Norman, R. "Aristotle's Philosopher-God." *Phronesis* 14 (1969) 63–65.
Novotný, D. and Novák, L., eds. *Metaphysics: Aristotelian, Scholastic, Analytic*. Routledge Studies in Metaphysics. London: Routledge, 2013.
Nozick, Robert. *Philosophical Explanations*. Cambridge: Harvard University Press, 1981.
Nussbaum, Martha. *Logic, Science and Dialectic*. London: Duckworth, 1986.
Nyvlt, Mark. *Aristotle and Plotinus on the Intellect*. Lanham, MD: Lexington, 2012.

O'Brien, Denis. "Plotinus on Matter and Evil." In *The Cambridge Companion to Plotinus*, edited by Lloyd P. Gerson, 171–95. Cambridge: Cambridge University Press, 1996.

O'Cleirigh, Padraig. "Theology in Origen and Plotinus." In *The Perennial Tradition of Neoplatonism*. Edited by J. Cleary. Ancient and Medieval Philosophy, series 1, 24. Leuven: Leuven University Press, 1977.

———. "*Topoi* of Invention in Origen's Homilies." In *Origène et la Bible = Origen and the Bible: Actes du Colloquium Origenianum Sextum, Chantilly, 30 août–3 septembre 1993*, edited by G. Dorival and A. Le Boulluec, 277–86. BETL 118. Leuven: Peeters, 1995.

O'Connell, Robert J. *Art and the Christian Intelligence in St. Augustine*. Cambridge: Cambridge University Press, 1978.

O' Daly, G. J. P. *Plotinus' Philosophy of the Self*. Shannon: Irish University Press, 1976.

———. "The Presence of the One in Plotinus." In *Plotino e il Neoplatonismo in Oriente e in Occidente*, 159–69. Rome: Accademia Nazionale dei Lincei, 1974.

Oehler, K. *Subjektivitaet und Selbstbewusstsein in der Antike*. Wuerzburg: Neumann, 1997.

Olsen, Eric T. *What Are We? A Study in Personal Ontology*. Oxford: Oxford University Press, 2007.

Olshewsky, Thomas M. "The Dynamics of *Dunamis*." *Review of Metaphysics* 71 (2018) 501–16.

O'Meara, Dominic John. "Intentional Objects in Later Neoplatonism." In *Ancient and Medieval Theories of Intentionality*, edited by D. Perler, 115–25. Leiden: Brill, 2001.

———. *Plotinus*. Oxford: Oxford University Press, 1995.

———. "Plotinus on How Soul Acts on Body." In *Platonic Investigations*, edited by D. J. O'Meara, 262–72. Studies in Philosophy and History of Philosophy. Washington, DC: CUAP, 1985.

———. "The Hierarchical Reordering of Reality." In *The Cambridge Companion to Plotinus*. Edited by Lloyd P. Gerson. Cambridge: Cambridge University Press, 1996.

O'Meara, J. J., ed. *Prayer and Exhortation to Martyrdom*. Ancient Christian Writers: The Works of the Fathers in Translation 19. Westminster, MD: Newman, 1954.

Origen of Alexandria. *Contra Celsum*. Edited by P. Koetschau. GCS 2–3. Berlin, 1913.

———. *Origen's Commentary on the Gospel of John*. Introduction and translated by A. Menzies. ANF 10. Reprint, Grand Rapids: Eerdmans, 1980.

———. *Origene. Commentaire sur. S. Jean I-V*. SC 120.157.222.290.385. Edited by C. Blanc. Paris, 1966–1992.

———. *Origenes. Der Johanneskommentar*. GCS 10. Edited by E. Preuschen. Berlin, 1903.

———. *Origen on First Principles*. Translated by G. W. Butterworth. London: SPCK, 1936.

———. *Origenes: Vier Buecher von den Prinzipien*. Edited by H. Gorgemanns and H. Karpp. Darmstadt: Wissenschaftliche Buchgesellschaft, 1985.

———. *Origenes Werke, De Principiis*. GCS 22, ed., P. Koetschau, Leipzig: Hinrichs, 1913.

Osborne, C. *Rethinking Early Greek Philosophy: Hippolytus of Rome and the Presocratics*. Ithaca, NY: Cornell University Press, 1987.

Osborn, Eric. *The Beginnings of Christian Philosophy*. Cambridge: Cambridge University Press, 1981.

———. "Clement and the Bible." In *Origeniana Sexta: Origène et la Bible = Origen and the Bible: Actes du Colloquium Origenianum Sextum, Chantilly, 30 août–3 septembre 1993*, edited by G. Dorival and A. Le Boulluec, 121–32. BETL 118. Leuven: Peeters, 1995.

Owen, G. E. L. "Aristotle on the Snares of Ontology." In *Essays on Plato and Aristotle*, edited by R. Bambrough, 69–75. London: Routledge & Kegan Paul, 1965.

———. "Eleatic Questions." In M. Nussbaum, ed., *Logic, Science and Dialectic: Collected Papers in Greek Philosophy*. Ithaca, NY: Cornell University Press, 1986.

———. "Logic and Metaphysics in Some Earlier Works of Aristotle." In *Aristotle and Plato in the Mid-Fourth Century*, edited by I. During and Owen, G. E. L. Owen, 163–90. Goteborg, 1960.

———. "The Platonism of Aristotle." *Proceedings of the British Academy* 51 (1966) 125–50.

Owens, John. *The Doctrine of Being in the Aristotelian Metaphysics*. Toronto: PIM, 1951.

———. "The Physical World of Parmenides." In *Essays in Honour of Anton Charles Pegis*. Edited by J. R. O'Donnell. Toronto: PIMS, 1974.

Palmer, Richard E., *Hermeneutics: Interpretation Theory in Schleiermacher, Dilthey, Heidegger, and Gadamer*. Northwestern University Studies in Phenomenology and Existential Philosophy. Evanston, IL: Northwestern University Press, 1969.

Palmer, John. *Parmenides and Presocratic Philosophy*. Oxford: Oxford University Press, 2009.

Parfit, Derek. *Reasons and Persons*. Oxford: Clarendon, 1984.

Passmore, J.A. *One Hundred Years of Philosophy*. London: Duckworth, 1957.

———. "The Idea of a History of Philosophy." *History and Theory* Supplement 5 (1965) 1–32.

Peirce, Charles Sanders. *The Collected Papers of Charles Sanders Peirce*. Edited by C. Hartshorne, P. Weiss, and A. Burks. Cambridge: Harvard University Press, 1931–1958.

———. "Immortality and Synechism." In *Collected Papers*, vol. 7, paragraphs 565–78. Harvard: Harvard University Press, 1931.

———. "Synechism." In *Baldwin's Dictionary of Philosophy and Psychology*, vol. 2 (1911) 657. Reprinted in *Collected Papers*, vol. 6, 169–73.

Penner, Hans H. "Rationality, Ritual and Science." In *Religion, Science and Magic in Concert and in Conflict*. New York: Oxford University Press, 1989.

Pepin. Jean. "Elements pour une histoire de la relation entre l'intelligence et l'intelligible chez Platon et dans le neoplatonisme." *Revue philosophique* 146 (1956) 100–106.

———. "Linguistique et theologie dans la tradition platonicienne." *Languages* 65 (1982) 91–116.

Perl, Eric D. "The Presence of the Paradigm; immanence and Transcendence in Plato's Theory of Forms." *RM* 53 339–362, 1999.

———. "The Togetherness of Thought and Being: a Phenomenological Reading of Plotinus' Doctrine 'That the Intelligibles Are not Outside the Intellect.'" In *BACAP*, edited by John Cleary and Gary Gurtler, 1–26. Leiden: Brill, 2006.

Perler, D., ed. *Ancient and Medieval Theories of Intentionality*. Leiden: Brill, 2001.

Perrone, Leone. *La Preghiera secondo Origene*. Brecia: Morcelliana, 2011.

Peters, T. "The Nature and Role of Presuppositions: An Inquiry into Contemporary Hermeneutics." *International Philosophical Quarterly* 14 (1974) 128–35.

Philipse, H. "Transcendental Idealism." In *The Cambridge Companion to Husserl*, 239–322. Cambridge: Cambridge University Press, 1995.
Philo of Alexandria. *Indices ad Philonis Alexandrini opera*. Edited by I. Leisegang. Berlin, 1896–1930. 2nd ed., 1962.
———. *Philonis Alexandrini opera quae supersunt*. 7 vols. Edited by L. Cohn, P. Wendland, and S. Reiter. Berlin, 1896–1930. 2nd ed., 1962.
Philo. Loeb Classical Library. 12 vols. Edited by F. H. Colson and G. H. Whittaker. Cambridge: Harvard University Press, 1921.
Pillow, K. *Sublime Understanding: Aesthetic Reflection in Kant and Hegel*. Cambridge: MIT Press. 2000.
Plantigna, A. *Does God Have a Nature?* Milwaukee: Marquette University Press, 1980.
———. *Warranted Christian Belief.* Oxford: Oxford University Press, 2000
Plato. *Platonis Opera*. Edited by J. Burnet. 4 vols. Oxford, 1900–1907, 1950–1952.
———. *Plato*, Loeb Classical Library. 12 vols. Cambridge: Harvard University Press, 1970.
Plezia, M. *De Andronici Rhodii Studiis Aristotelicis*. Cracow: Archiwum Filologiczne 20, 1946.
Plotinus. *Plotini Opera*. Edited by P. Henry and H.-R. Schwyzer. 3 vols. Leiden, 1951–1973.
———. *Plotinus*. 7 vols. Translated by A. H. Armstrong. Loeb Classical Library. Cambridge: Harvard University Press, 1966–1988.
Popper, Karl. "Back to the Presocratics." *Proceedings of the Aristotelian Society* 59 (1958/59).
———. *Objective Knowledge: An Evolutionary Approach*. Oxford: Clarendon, 1972.
Pritchard, R. "Knowledge and Understanding." In *The Nature and Value of Knowledge: Three Investigations*. Edited by A. Haddock, A. Millar, and D. Pritchard. Oxford: Oxford University Press. 2010.
Pseudo-Aristotle. *De Mundo* in *Aristotle the Complete Works*. Edited by J. Barnes. 2 vols. Princeton: Princeton University Press, 1985.
Puech, H.-C ."Plotin et les Gnostiques." *Entretiens Hardt V*, 1960.
Putnam, Hilary. *Mind, Language and Reality*. Cambridge: Cambridge University Press, 1975.
———. "Why There Isn't a Ready Made World." In *Realism and Reason* in *Philosophical Papers*. Vol. 3 Cambridge: Cambridge University Press, 1983.
Quine, W. V. O. *From a Logical Point of View*. Cambridge: Harvard University Press, 1953.
———. *Ontological Relativity*. New York: Columbia University Press, 1969.
———. *Pursuit of Truth*. Cambridge: Harvard University Press, 1992.
Rahner, Karl. "The Spiritual Senses in Origen." *Theological Investigations* vol. 16: 81–103, 1979.
Ramelli, Illaria. *The Christian Doctrine of Apokatastasis: A Critical Assessment from the New Testament to Eriugena*. Oxford: Oxford University Press, 2009.
———. "Origen, Patristic Philosophy, and Christian Platonism. Rethinking the Christianization of Hellenism." *VC* (2009) 217–63.
Randall, John Hermann. *Aristotle*. New York: Columbia University Press, 1965.
Rapp, Christof. "Intentionalitaet und *phantasia* bei Aristoteles." In D. Perler, ed., *Ancient and Medieval Theories of Intentionality*, 63–96. Leiden: Brill, 2001.

Rappe, Sara. *Reading Neoplatonism: Non-Discursive Thinking in the Texts of Plotinus, Proclus and Damascius.* Cambridge: Cambridge University Press, 2000.

———. "Self-Knowledge and Subjectivity in the *Enneads.*" In L. P. Gerson, ed., *The Cambridge Companion to Plotinus,* edited by Lloyd P. Gerson, 250–74. Cambridge: Cambridge University Press, 1996.

Raven, J. E. *Pythagoreans and Eleatics.* Cambridge: Cambridge University Press, 1948.

Reale, Giovani. "I fondamenti della metafisca di Plotino e la strattora della processione." In *Grateful Reason: Essays in Ancient and Medieval Philosophy Presented to Joseph Owens,* edited by Lloyd P. Gerson, 153–75. Toronto: TPIMS, 1983.

Remes, Paulina. *Plotinus on Self: The Philosophy of the We.* Cambridge: Cambridge University Press, 2007.

Rich, A. "Plotinus and the Theory of Artistic Imitation." *Mnemosyne* 13 (1960) 233–39.

Rist, John. "The Indefinite Dyad and Intelligible Matter in Plotinus." *CQ* 12 (1967) 99–107.

———. "The One of Plotinus and the God of Aristotle." *Review of Metaphysics* 27 (1973) 75–87.

———. *Plotinus: The Road to Reality.* Cambridge: Cambridge University Press, 1967.

———. "Tracking Alexander of Aphrodisias." *Archiv für Geschichte der Philosophie,* Berlin, 1966.

Robinson, H. M., ed. *Objections to Physicalism.* Oxford: Oxford University Press, 1993.

Robinson, T. M. "Parmenides on Ascertainment of the Real." *CJP* 4 (1975).

Rochliz, R. "The Aesthetics of Existence: Post-conventional Morality and the Theory of Power in Michel Foucault." In T. J. Armstrong, trans., *Michel Foucault Philosopher.* New York: Routledge, 1992.

Roecklin, Robert J. *Plato versus Parmenides.* Lanham, MD: Lexington, 2011.

Rockmore, Thomas. *Heidegger and French Philosophy.* London: Routledge, 1995.

Rorty, Richard. *Objectivism, Relativism, and Truth: Philosophical Papers.* Vol. I. Cambridge: Cambridge University Press, 1991.

———. *Philosophy and the Mirror of Nature.* Princeton: Princeton University Press, 1979.

Roskam, Gert. "Aristotle in Middle Platonism: The Case of Plutarch of Chaeronea." In *Plato, Aristotle or Both? Dialogues between Platonism and Aristotelianism in Antiquity.* Edited by T. Benatouil, E. Maffi, and F. Trabbatoni. Hildesheim: Olms, 2011.

Rubinoff, L. *Collingwood and the Reform of Metaphysics: A Study in the Philosophy of Mind.* Toronto: University of Toronto Press, 1970.

Ruis-Camps, J. "*El dinamsimo trinitario en la digitization de los seres rationales segun Origenes.* Rome, 1970.

Runciman, W. G. *Plato's Later Epistemology.* Cambridge. Cambridge University Press, 1962.

Runia, David. "Festugiere Revisited: Aristotle in the Greek *Patres.*" *VigChr* 43.1 (1989) 1–34.

———. *Philo of Alexandria and the Timaeus of Plato.* Amsterdam: Nijhof, 1983.

Russell, Bertrand. "Knowledge by Acquaintance and Knowledge by Description." *PAS* 11 (1911) 108–28.

Rutten, C. "La doctrine des duex actes dans la philosophie de Plotin." In *Revue philosophique de la France et de l'étranger* 146 (1956) 100–106.

Ryle, Gilbert. "Categories." *PAS* 38 (1938) 189–206.

———. "Knowing How and Knowing That." *PAS* 46 (1941).
———. "Plato's Parmenides." *Mind* 48 (1939) 129–51, 303–25.
———. "Logical Atomism and Plato's *Theatetus.*" *Phronesis* 35 (1990) 21–46.
———. *The Concept of Mind.* Chicago: University of Chicago Press, 1949/2002.
Santoprete, Luciana, Gabriela Soares, and Philippe Hoffmann, eds. *Langage des dieux, langage des demons, langage des homes dans l'Antiquite.* Turnhout: Brepols, 2017.
Schenkeveldt, D.M. "Stoic and Peripatetic Kinds of Speech Act and the Distinction of Grammatical Moods." *Mnemsoyne* 37 (1984) 291–351.
Schlicht, Moritz. "Positivism and Realism." In *Logical Positivism.* Edited by A. J. Ayer. New York: Free Press, 1959.
Schofield, Michael. "The Antinomies of Plato's Parmenides." *Classical Quarterly* 27 (1977) 139–58.
———. "The Denouemont of the Cratylus." In M. Schofield and M. C. Nussbaum, eds., *Language and Logos: Studies in Ancient Greek Philosophy Presented to G. E. L. Owen.* Cambridge: Cambridge University Press, 1982.
Schopenhauer, Arthur. *The World as Will and Idea.* New York: Dover, 1969.
Schroeder, Frederic M. "The Analogy of the Active Intellect to Light in the 'de Anima' of Alexander of Aphrodisias." *Hermes* 109 (1981) 215–25.
———. "Aseity and Connectedness in the Plotinian Philosophy of Providence." In *Gnosticism and Later Platonism,. Themes, Figures and Texts,* edited by J. D. Turner and R. Majercik, 303–13. Atlanta, SBL Press, 2000.
———. "*Avocatio*, Rhetoric, and the Technique of Contemplation in Plotinus." *Dionysius* 30 (2012) 147–60.
———. "The Categories and Plotinian Aesthetics." In *Science et Esprit* 71/72 115–136 2020.
———. "Conversion and Consciousness in Plotinus, `Enneads' 5.1 [10], 7." *Hermes* 114 (1986) 185–95.
———. *Form and Transformation. A Study in the Philosophy of Plotinus.* Montreal: McGill-Queen's Press. 1992.
———. "From Alexander of Aphrodisias to Plotinus" In *Routledge Handbook of Neoplatonism,* edited by S. Slaveva-Griffin and P. Remes, 293–309. London: Routledge, 2014.
———. "The Hermeneutics of Unity in Plotinus." In J.-M. Narbonne and A. Reckermann, eds., *Pensees de l'Un dans l'histoire de la philosophie: Etudes en hommage au Professeur Werner Beierwaltes,* 108–22. Paris: Vrin, 2004.
———. "Plotinus and Interior Space." In P. M. Gregorios, ed., *Neoplatonism and Indian Thought,* 83–96. Ithaca, NY: Cornell University Press, 2002.
———. "Plotinus and Language." In *The Cambridge Companion to Plotinus,* edited by Lloyd P. Gerson, 336–52. Cambridge Companions to Philosophy. Cambridge: Cambridge University Press, 1996.
———. "The Potential or Material Intellect and the Authorship of the *de Intellectu*: A Reply to B.C. Bazan." *Symbolae Osloenses* 57 (1982) 115–25.
———. "*Synousia, Synaisthesis,* and *Synesis*: Presence and Dependence in the Plotinian Philosophy of Consciousness." In *ANRW* (1987) 677–99.
———. "The Vigil of the One and Plotinian Iconoclasm." In *Neoplatonism and Western Aesthetics.* Edited by A. Alexandrakis. Albany: SUNY Press 2002, 147–59.
Schwyzer, H-R. *Bewusst und Unbewusst bei Plotin: Les sources de Plotin.* Geneva: Foundation Hardt, 1960.

Searle, John. *Intentionality.* Cambridge: Cambridge University Press 1983.

———. *The Rediscovery of the Mind.* Cambridge: MIT Press, 1992.

Sedley, David. *The Midwife of Platonism: Text and Subtext in Plato's Theaetetus.* Oxford: Oxford University Press, 2004.

———. "Parmenides and Melissus." In *The Cambridge Companion to Early Greek Philosophy*, edited by A. A. Long,, 113-33. Cambridge Companions to Philosophy. Cam-bridge: Cambridge University Press, 1999.

Seidl, Horst. *Der Begriff des Intellekts bei Aristotles.* Hildesheim: Olms, 1971.

———. *Realistische Metaphysik: Stellungsnahme zu Moderner Kritik an der Traditionellen Metaphysik.* Philosophische Texte und Studien 83. Hildesheim: Olms, 2006.

Sellars, Wilfrid. *Science, Perception and Reality.* London: Routledge, 1963.

Sharples, Robert. W. *Alexander of Aphrodisias: Supplement to on the Soul.* London: Duckworth. 2004.

———. *Aristotelian Philosophy.* Studies in Philo of Alexandria 5. Leiden: Brill, 2008.

———. "Philo and Post-Aristotelian Peripatetics." In *Philo of Alexandria and Post-Aristotelian Philosophy*, edited by F. Alesse, 55-74. Studies in Philo of Alexandria 5. Leiden: Brill, 2008.

Silverman, A. "Plato's *Cratylus*: The Nature of Naming and the Naming of Nature." *Oxford Studies in Ancient Philosophy* 10 (1992) 25-71.

Slavena-Griffin, Svetla. *Plotinus on Number.* Oxford: Oxford University Press, 2009.

Smith, A. *Porphyry's Place in Neoplatonism.* Leiden: Brill, 1974.

———. "Potentiality and the Problem of Plurality in the Intelligible World." In *Neoplatonism and Early Christian Thought.* Edited by H. J. Blumenthal and R. A. Markus. London: Blackwell, 1981.

———. "Unconsciousness and Quasiconsciousness in Plotinus." *Phronesis* 23 (1978) 292-302.

Smith, B., and D. W. Smith, eds. *The Cambridge Companion to Husserl.* Cambridge. Cambridge University Press.1995.

Soames, S. *Philosophy of Language.* Princeton: Princeton University Press, 2012.

Solomon, Robert C. *From Hegel to Existentialism.* Oxford: Oxford University Press, 1987.

Somerville, James, "Collingwood's Logic of Question and Answer." *Monist* 72 (1989) 526-41.

Sorabji, Richard. "The Ancient Commentators on Aristotle." In The Transformation of Aristotle's Physics and Theology." In *Aristotle Transformed: The Ancient Commentators and their Influence*, edited by R. Sorabji, 1-30. London: Duckworth, 1990.

———. "Body and Soul in Aristotle." *AA* 4 (1972) 49-53.

———. "From Aristotle to Brentano: the Development of the Concept of Intentionality." In *Oxford Studies in Philosophy* (Supplementary Volume), 227-59. Oxford: Oxford University Press, 1991.

———. "Gregory of Nyssa: The Origins of Idealism." In *Time Creation, and the Continuum*, 287-96. Ithaca, NY: Cornell University Press, 1983.

———. "Infinite Power Impressed: The Transformation of Aristotle's Physics and Theology." In *Aristotle Transformed: The Ancient Commentators and their Influence*, edited by R. Sorabji, 181-98. London: Duckworth, 1990.

———. *Philoponus and the Rejection of Aristotelian Science.* Ithaca, NY: Cornell University Press, 1987.

———. *Time, Creation, and the Continuum*. Ithaca, NY: Cornell University Press, 1983.
———. "Why the Neoplatonists did not have Intentional Objects of Intellection." In *Ancient and Medieval Theories of Intentionality*, edited by D. Perler, 105–14. Leiden: Brill, 2001.
Sosa, E. *Epistemology*. Princeton: Princeton University Press, 2017.
———. "The Raft and the Pyramid: Coherence versus Foundations in Theory of Knowledge." *Midwest Studies in Philosophy* 5 (1980).
Spiegelberg, H. "'Intention' and 'Intentionality' in the Scholastics, Brentano, and Husserl,." In *The Philosophy of Brentano*, edited by L. L. McAlister, 108–27. Atlantic Highland, NJ, 1976.
Stead, G. C. *Divine Substance*. Oxford: Oxford University Press, 1977.
Stern-Gillet, Suzanne. *Consciousness and Introspection in Plotinus and Augustine*, PBACAP 22(1) *Colloquium* 5 (2007) 1–33.
———. "Plotinus and the Problem of Consciousness." In *Consciousness and the Great Philosophers: What Would They Have Said about Our Mind-Body Problem?*, edited by S. Leach and S Tartaglia, 19–27. New York: Routledge, 2016.
Steidele, B. "Neue Untersuchungen zu Origenes *Peri Archon*." *ZNW* 40 (1941) 236–43.
Stoekl, A. *Agonies of the Intellectual*. Lincoln: University of Nebraska Press, 1992.
Strange, Stephen. "Plotinus, Porphyry and the Neoplatonic Interpretation of the Categories." In *ANRW* 36 (1987) 955–74.
———. "Plotinus Account of Participation in Ennead VI.4–5." *Journal of the History of Philosophy* 30 (1992) 479–96.
Stoicorum Veterum Fragmenta [SVF]. Edited by H. F. A. von Arnim. 4 vols. Leipzig: Teubner, 1903–1924/1964.
Suppe, F. *The Structure of Scientific Theories*. Urbana: University of Illinois Press, 1977.
Szlezak, Thomas A. *Platon und Aristotles in der Nuslehre Plotins*. Stuttgart: Schwabe, 1979.
———. Review of K. Wurm, *Substanz und Qualitaet. Ein Beireag zur Interpretation der plototinischen Traktate VI. 1.2 und 3*." *Goettingische Gelehrte Anzeigen* 227 (1975) 216–25.
Tahko, T. E., ed. *Contemporary Aristotelian Metaphysics*. Cambridge: Cambridge University Press, 2013.
Taran, Leonardo. *Parmenides*. Princeton: Princeton University Press, 1965.
Tardieu, M., A. Van den Kerchove, and M. Zago, M., eds. *Nomes barbares 1: Formes et contexts d'une pratique magique*. Bibliotheque de l'Ecole des Hautes Etudes Sciences religieuses 162. Turnhout: Brepols. 2013.
Taylor, A. E. *A Commentary on Plato's Timaeus*. Oxford. Oxford: University Press, 1928.
———. *Plato*. Cleveland:Meridian, 1964.
Tazzolio, T. T. "Le probleme de la causalite du Principe chez Plotin." *Revue philosophique de Louvain* 102 (2004) 59–71.
Textor, M. "Brentano [and some Neo-Brentanians] on Inner Consciousness." *Dialectica* 60 (2006) 411–31.
Theiler, Willy. *Zur Geschichte der teleologischen Naturbetrachtung bei Aristotles*. Leipzig: Klostermann, 1965.
Thom, Johan.C. ed. *Pseudo-Aristotle, Cosmic Order and Divine Power*. Tuebingen: Mohr/Siebeck. 2014.
Thomasson, A. "After Brentano: A One Level Theory of Consciousness." *European Journal of Philosophy* 8 (2006) 190–209.

Tiomkin, Andrei. "Causality of the First Principle and Two Activities in Plotinus *Enn* [V.4 [7]]." In *Platonism and Its Legacy*. Edited by J. F. Finamore and T. Nejeschleba. Bream, Lydney: Prometheus Trust Press, 2019.

Tiomikin, Andrei, and John Dillon, John, eds. *Neoplatonic Prayer*. Leiden: Brill, 2015.

Torjeson, Karen Jo. "Influence of Rhetoric on Origen's Old Testament Homilies." *Origène et la Bible* = *Origen and the Bible: Actes du Colloquium Origenianum Sextum, Chantilly, 30 août–3 septembre 1993*, edited by G. Dorival and A. Le Boulluec, 13–26. BETL 118. Leuven: Peeters, 1995.

Trabattoni, Franco. *Platone*. Rome: Carocci, 1998.

Trouillard, Jean. "The Logic of Attributions in Plotinus." *IPQ* 1 (1961) 125–38.

Turnball, Robert. *The Parmenides and Plato's Late Philosophy*. Toronto: University of Toronto Press, 1998.

Turner, John D., and Ruth Majercik, eds. *Gnosticism and Later Platonism: Themes, Figures and Texts*. Atlanta: SBL Press, 1998.

Yu, Jiyuan, "Is There a Focal Meaning of Being in Aristotle?" *Society for Ancient Greek Philosophy Newsletter* 192 (1999).

Van Gulick, R. "Consciousness." *SEP* (2014).

Vandenabeele, B. "The subjective universality of aesthetic judgments revisited" *British Journal of Aesthetics* 64 (2008) 254–58.

Veldsman, D. P. 2017. "The Place of Metaphysics in the Science-Religion Debate." *HTS* 73.3 [7]. Online pub.

Ventureyra, Scott D. G. *On the Origin of Consciousness*. Eugene, OR: Wipf & Stock, 2018.

Verbeke, G. *L'Evolution de la doctrine du Pneuma du stoicisme a S. Augustine*. Paris-Louvain, 1945.

Vescovini, G. F., ed. *Le probleme des Transcendentaux du XIVe au XVIIe siecle*. Bibliotheque d'Histoire de la Philosophie. Paris: Vrin, 2001.

Viellard-Baron, J.-L. *Platon et l'idealismus allemand* [1770–1830]. Paris: Vrin, 1979.

Violette, E. "Les forms de la conscience chez Plotin." *Revue des Etudes Grecques* 107 (1994).

Vlastos, Gregory. "Self-Predication and Self-Predication in Plato's Later Period." *PR* 78 (1969) 74–78.

Von Fritz, Karl. "*Nous, Noein* and Their Derivatives in Pre-Socratic Philosophy [Excluding Anaxagoras]." In Mourelatos, ed., *Studies in Presocratic Philosophy*. New York: Humanities Press, 1993.

Wachterhauser, B. R., ed., *Hermeneutics and Modern Philosophy*. Albany: SUNY Press, 1986.

Wagner, Michael. "Realism and the Foundation of Science in Plotinus." *AP* 5 (1985) 269–92.

———. "Veridical Causation in Plotinus." In *The Structure of Being*, edited by R. B. Harris, 51–72. Albany: SUNY Press, 1982.

Warren, E. "Consciousness in Plotinus." *Phronesis* 9 (1964) 83–97.

Waugh, Joanne B. and Wilkinson, Lisa. "Fleshing Out the Form of Beauty: Socrates, Dialogue and the Forms." In *Plato's Forms: Varieties of Interpretation*, edited by William A. Welton, ed., , 221–37. Lanham, MD: Lexington, 2002.

Wedin, Michael V. "auta ta isa and the Argument of *Phaedo* 74b7–c5." *Phronesis* 23 (1978) 191–205.

———. *Parmenides' Grand Deduction: A Logical Reconstruction of the Way of Truth.* Oxford: Oxford University Press, 2014.
Whittaker, John. "EPEKEINA NOU KAI OUSIAS." *VC* 23 (1969) 91–104.
Wicks, R. *Routledge Philosophy Guidebook to Kant on Judgment.* London: Routledge. 2007.
Wilkes, J. "Is Consciousness Important?" In *BJPS* 35 (1984) 223–43.
———. "Losing Consciousness." In T. Metzinger, ed., *Conscious Experience*. Paderborn: Schoeningh, 1995.
———. "Yishi, Duo, Us and Consciousness." In *Consciousness in Cottemporary Science.* Edited by A. Marcel and E. Bisiach. Oxford: Oxford University Press, 1988.
Wittgenstein, Ludwig. *Tractatus,* Mountain View, CA: Mayfield, 1998.
———. *The Blue Book.* London: Blackwell, 1958.
———. *Philosophical Investigations.* Oxford: Oxford University Press, 1953.
Wolinski, J. "Le Recours aux *EPINOIAI* du Christ dans le Commentaire sur Jean d'Origene." In *Origeniana Sexta: Origène et la Bible = Origen and the Bible: Actes du Colloquium Origenianum Sextum, Chantilly, 30 août–3 septembre 1993,* Edited by G. Dorival and A. Le Boulluec, 465–94. Bibliotheca Ephemeridum theologicarum Lovaniensium 118. Leuven: Peeters, 1995.
Wolterstorff, N. *On Universals: An Essay in Ontology.* Chicago: University of Chicago Press, 1970.
Wood, Kelsey. *Troubling Play: Meaning and Entity in Plato's Parmenides.* Albany: SUNY Press. 2005.
Wurm, Karl. *Substanz und Qualitaet. Ein Beitrag zur Interpretation der Plotinischen Traktate VI 1, 2 und 3.* Berlin: de Gruyter, 1973.
Zahavi, D. "Back to Brentano." *Journal of Consciousness Studies* 11 (2004) 66–87.
———. "Two Takes on a One-Level Account of Consciousness." *Psyche* 12 [2] (2006). Online pub.
Zalta, Edward. "Frege's Theorem and Foundations of Arithmetic." In *Stanford Encyclopedia of Philosophy*. Stanford: Stanford University Press, 2013.
———. "Natural Numbers and Natural Cardinals as Abstract Objects: A Partial Reconstruction of Frege's *Grundgesetze* in Object Theory" Journal of Philosophical Logic 28 (6): 619–660. 1999.
Zhyrkova, A. "The Doctrine of Categories in Neoplatonism." In *Being or Good? Metamorphoses of Neoplatonism.* Lublin: Wydawnnictwo: KUL.
Zinkin, M. "Intensive Magnitudes and the Normativity of Taste." In *Aesthetics and Cognition in Kant's Critical Philosophy.* Edited by R. Kukla.Cambridge: Cambridge University Press. 2. 2006.

Index of Names

Abbott E., xxvn19, 369n62
Abraham, William J., 71n1
Ackrill, J. L., 60n23
Addey, Crystal, 68n40, 69n41, 80n53, 198n218
Adorno, Theodor, 344
Aersten, J., 146n3, 148n21
Alcinous [Albinus], 37n87, 124–25, 129, 129n100, 135–36n140, 141, 166, 166n30, 175, 185
Alexander of Aphrodisias, 37n87, 102, 102n72, 124, 124n49, 124n76, 126n64, 126n69, 127–29, 129n94, 166, 168, 168n38, 171, 174n82, 184n153, 185, 201, 201n3, 201n4, 219, 252n112, 256, 256n130, 267, 267n35, 282, 282n115
Alexander of Halles, 146n3
Alfino, M., 46n117, 78n43
Ambrose, 84
Ammonius Saccas, 126, 126n64, 128–29
Andresen, C., 126n66
Andronicus, 1n2, 121, 122n33, 122n38
Annas, J., 73n5, 118n7, 230n21, 361n25
Anselm, 44, 224
Antiochus, 122
Anton, John, 145n2, 261n1, 270n56, 276n86, 291n8
Aquinas, 1n2
Aquino, Frederick D., 71n1
Archer-Hind, R. D., 102n67
Archimedes, 23–24n41

Aristotle, xv–xvi, xvn1, xviii–xxv, xxn17, xxiin18, xxvn21, xxvin22, xxvin23, 1n2, 2–10, 2n3, 5n14, 14–16, 15n137, 16n40, 17n44, 19n8, 23–24, 26n60, 27–32, 27n61, 27n62, 27n63, 27n64, 27n65, 27n66, 28n68, 29n70, 29n71, 35, 37, 37n87, 40, 41n97, 42–44, 42n101, 47–50, 47n123, 48n124, 48n125, 54–66, 57n14, 58n16, 58n17, 60n22, 60n23, 63–65, 63n30, 64n31, 64n32, 66n37, 68–69, 72, 72n4, 74n22, 84n73, 88, 88n5, 90n18, 91–92, 91n27, 97, 99, 102–16, 102n69, 102n70, 102n71, 102n73, 103n74, 104n77, 105n80, 105n83, 106n87, 106n88, 107n89, 108n96, 111n116, 112n122, 112n123, 112n124, 118n5, 120–23, 121n27, 121n29, 121n30, 122n35, 122n36, 122n39, 124n43, 124n45, 124n46, 126n67, 127n71, 136, 136n145, 138n159, 145n2, 146n3, 146n6, 146n11, 147n12, 147n13, 147n14, 147n15, 152–55, 153n37, 154n38, 154n40, 155n41, 155n42, 155n43, 155n44, 155n45, 155n46, 155n47, 155n48, 159, 162–68, 162n4, 164n18, 165n20, 165n21,

INDEX OF NAMES

Aristotle *(continued)*, 166n29, 167n35, 168n37, 169n42, 171, 173n71, 174–75, 174n77, 174n81, 180, 180n135, 185–86, 185n158, 189–190, 189n184, 190n190, 192–93n201, 194, 195n212, 200–201, 201n1, 201n2, 203–7, 210–14, 211n30, 211n31, 212n32, 214n39, 214n40, 214n41, 214n42, 214n43, 214n45, 214n46, 216–226, 216n53, 216n55, 218n60, 220n65, 220n66, 220n67, 220n68, 220n69, 220n70, 221n72, 222n73, 223n74, 224n80, 228, 228n4, 232n31, 233–242, 234n39, 234n40, 236n49, 237n50, 237n51, 237n52, 240n62, 240n63, 241n67, 241n68, 241n69, 242n70, 242n72, 244–260, 244n79, 245n81, 246–47n89, 246n86, 246n87, 246n88, 250n106, 251n107, 252n112, 253n115, 253n116, 254n117, 254n118, 254n119, 254n120, 254n121, 255n128, 256n129, 257n141, 257n142, 257n143, 258–260, 258n144, 260n150, 260n151, 267, 278, 278n97, 282, 288n140, 295, 295n25, 305–6, 305n74, 320, 326–27, 326n26, 356n3, 356n4, 357n7, 359, 359n13, 361–64, 362n33, 367–370, 368n61
Armstrong, A. Hillary, 145, 180n131
Atkinson, M., 175–78, 176n102, 177n104, 178n113, 180n131, 182–83, 183n150, 184n152
Aubenque, Paul, 145n2
Audi, Robert, 14n35
Augustine, 2, 115, 115n131, 162n4, 186, 201, 202n7, 238n53
Ayer, A. J., 50, 52, 163, 229, 229n12, 232, 357n7

Baltzly, Dirk, 145n2

Barnes, Jonathan, xv, 60n22, 89n8, 94n39, 360n23
Bataille, Georges, 339
Baudelaire, Charles, 337, 339, 343
Bauloye, L., 146n4
Baumgarten, Alexander G., 290–91, 290n2, 291n3, 315–16, 321, 337, 337n75
Beierwaltes, Werner, 52n37, 66n37, 84n73, 183n148, 217n59, 241n68, 246n87, 252, 253n114, 256n131, 261n1, 276n86
Berchman, Robert M., 29n70, 32n79, 41n95, 46n114, 46n117, 54n11, 63n30, 72n4, 80n53, 106n84, 119n8, 124n48, 125n54, 127n77, 129n97, 130n108, 135n140, 136n141, 168n40, 185n159, 198n217, 233n32, 325n24
Berkeley, George, 6–7, 13–16, 29, 29n70, 30–32, 54, 67, 163, 195n212, 202–4, 206–7, 223n78, 331n60
Bernstein, Richard J., 319n1, 332n6, 353n109
Berti, Enrico, xvn1, xxvin22, 112n122, 164n15, 228n4, 356n4, 360n23
Bertoldi, E. F., 22, 22n27
Bickel, Ernst., 133n126
Blumenthal, Henry, 114n129, 118n5, 146n3, 150n33, 162n6, 166n25, 166n26, 166n27, 167n32, 239n59, 261n2, 266n25, 267n34, 281n112, 282n113, 282n114, 283n127, 324n9, 326n25, 326n28, 326n31, 327n42
Bobzien, Susanne, 94n40, 247n92
Bos, A.P., xv, 121n24, 121n25, 127n76, 128n90
Bostock, George, 75n29, 76n31, 210n29
Brehier, Emile, 284n131, 328n46
Brentano, Franz, xix, 50, 54, 57, 57n14, 61–66, 61n26, 63n30, 197–98n215
Brinkmann, Klaus, xv, 162n9, 162n10, 164n19, 166n28, 360n23
Brisson, Luc, 46n117, 361n25
Brontius, 126n69

INDEX OF NAMES   405

Burke, Edumud, 315
Burnet, John, 89n10, 91n22
Burnyeat, Myles, xxn17, 14, 14n32,
    14n34, 14n36, 18n3, 66n37,
    75n23, 88n5, 162n3, 202,
    202n10, 230n21, 233n35
Bussanich, John, xvn1, 42n101, 105n83,
    113n128, 176n96, 176n102, 177,
    177n105, 177n106, 178n120,
    179n121, 179n124, 180n130,
    180n131, 181, 182n143,
    183n150, 360n25

Caluori, Damian, 162, 169, 171, 171n63,
    171n64, 172, 172n65, 172n66,
    172n67
Carnap, Rudolf, 21n24, 21n26, 24n41,
    26n56, 26n58, 152n35, 154n39,
    163, 229, 358–59, 369
Cassirer, Ernst, 291n7, 307n78, 339
Castagno, A. M., 71n2, 71n3
Casten, Victor, 162n5, 167n32, 167n33,
    199, 199n221, 361n26
Cavini, W., 247n93
Celsus, 126–28
Chalmers, David, 205n18
Charles,, 361n25
Chase, Michael, 118n4
Chase. F. H., 82n62
Cherniss, Harold, 92n30, 97–98n52
Chiaradonna, R., 145n2, 168n41,
    170n48
Chrudzimski, A., 61n26
Chrysippus, 247, 249
Cleary, John, xvn1, 165, 194n204,
    216n51, 216n52, 223n79,
    224n81, 360n23
Clement of Alexandria, 77, 77n38,
    77n39, 86, 88, 88n6, 125,
    125n56, 126, 132, 132n121,
    133, 133n127, 133n128, 135,
    135n140, 141
Coakley, Sarah, 71n1, 80n51
Code,, 361n25
Cohen, Hermann, 307n78
Cohen, M., 361n25
Collette, B., 145n2

Collingwood, Robin George, xix, 19–26,
    19n10, 20n13, 20n16, 20n17,
    20n18, 20n20, 21n21, 21n22,
    21n24, 21n25, 21n26, 22n28,
    22n29, 22n30, 22n31, 22n32,
    22n33, 22n34, 22n35, 23n36,
    23n37, 23n39, 23n40, 23n41,
    24n45, 25n48, 25n49, 25n50,
    25n52, 25n53, 25n54, 26n56,
    26n57, 26n58, 47–48, 48n130,
    159, 159n62, 197n215, 198n216,
    200, 362n28
Cooper, J. M., 73n5
Cornford, Francis M., 89n8, 98n54,
    193n202, 216n51
Corrigan, Kevin, xvn1, xxvin22, 108n99,
    146n3, 150n33, 172n68, 173n72,
    174n78, 175, 175n88, 175n89,
    176n94, 182n141, 183n149,
    256n134, 356n4, 360n25
Costa, Cristina D'Ancona, xviiin15,
    46n117, 108n99
Courcelle, Pierre, 252n111
Craig, W. Lane, 195n211
Crouzel, Henri, 71n2, 79n45, 118n4,
    126n63, 128n84
Crystal, I., 185, 186n162
Curd, Patricia, 89n9
Cusanus, Nicolaus, 116

D'Amico, Claudia, 329–330
Dancy, R. M., 180n134
Davidson, Donald, 180, 180n132,
    194n206
De Filippo. J., xvn1
de Keyser, E., 291n8
De Koninck, Thomas, xv, 41n98,
    166n23, 241n68, 246n87,
    360n23
De Lubac, Henri, 82n65
Derrida, Jacques, xviii, 19n8, 353,
    357n8, 358, 358–59n13, 358n12
Descartes, Rene, xviii, xxii–xxiii, 1–8,
    3n10, 4n12, 7n19, 10–12, 15, 28,
    28n69, 29n70, 31–36, 31n75,
    32n80, 48, 48n132, 54, 57n14,
    65–67, 67n38, 76, 148–49, 152,
    159, 159n64, 162–63, 163n11,

Descartes, Rene *(continued)*, 169, 169n43, 189, 191, 191n195, 192n197, 195n213, 199–200, 202, 204, 204n14, 206–7, 206n20, 223n78, 240–42, 245, 247, 253, 290, 290n2, 320, 361, 365, 365n49, 369
Detienne, Marcel, 2n6, 119n12
Dewey, John, 353, 353n109
di Vona, P., 146n7
Dillon, John, 32n81, 71n1, 81n55, 120n15, 120n16, 121n20, 122n38, 127n70, 163n12, 166n28, 262n3, 269n49, 331n59, 361n25
Dilthey, Wilhelm, 320, 320n2
Dodds, E. R., 127n70, 280n105, 281n111, 288n141, 332n61
Doerrie, Heinrich, 125n58, 362n31
Donini, P., 145n2
Dorival, Gilles, 72n3, 118n4, 126n63, 128n84, 129n97
D'Oro, G., 20n14
Doyle, J. P., 146n8
Duchamp, Marcel, 345
Dufour, R., 145n2
Dummett, Michael, 194n207, 358n11
Duns Scotus, 146n3

Eagleton, Terry, 337n74, 338n82
Edelstein, Ludwig, 75n23
Edwards, Mark J., 71n2, 118n4, 126n66, 202, 202n10
Emilsson, E. K., 14n33, 15n36, 66n37, 108n96, 108n99, 109n103, 156n55, 162, 167n32, 170n48, 170n50, 170n51, 172n67, 174n79, 175n87, 186n167, 187n171, 190–91, 190n185, 190n187, 190n189, 191n191–94, 192, 223n76, 223n78, 251n109, 261n2, 362, 362n36
Empiricus, Sextus, 119n13, 185
Epiphanius, 117
Eudorus, 125, 127
Eusebius, 117, 126n64
Evangeliou, Christos, 145n2

Feigl, Herbert, xxvn20, 228n6, 355n2
Ferejohn, M. T., 60n22
Ferry, Luc., 322n5, 337n74, 337n75, 338n82
Festugiere, A.-J., 127n73
Fichte,, 116n132
Field, H. H., 195n213
Filler, J., 108n95
Findlay, John N., 149n25, 194n205
Fine, Gail, 230n21
Finkelberg, A., 102n73
Fodor, Jerry. A., 152n35, 153–54n38, 154n39, 180n133
Foucault, Michel, xxv, 319–323, 319n1, 321n4, 333–353, 335n67, 335n69, 339n85, 340n87, 340n88, 341n89, 341n90, 344n93, 346n94, 347n96, 347n97, 348n99, 348n100, 348n101
Frede, Michael, 75n23, 247n91, 248n100
Frege, Georg, 74n8, 74n19, 74n22, 194, 197n215, 358, 359, 361
Fronterotta, F., 108n99
Furth, Montgomery, 89n9

Gadamer, Hans-Georg, xvin2, xvi, xviii–xix, 1n1–2, 2, 6, 6n16, 20n14, 20n15, 24, 24n46–47, 47n122, 48, 48n130, 159, 159n62, 197–98n215, 200, 319n1, 339, 339n83
Galen,, 118n7
Gasparro, G. S., 72n3
Gavirlyuk, Paul L., 71n1, 80n51
Geach, P. T., 158n59
Gersh, Stephen, xvin5, 45n107, 305, 305n70, 358n12, 358n13, 360n25, 362n32
Gerson, Lloyd P., xvn1, 14n33, 89n12, 97n51, 102n69, 106n86, 107, 107n92, 108n95, 145n2, 146n3, 150n33, 162n4, 162n6, 166n25, 166n26, 167n32, 176, 181, 181n139, 186n163, 199, 199n221, 224, 224n83, 261n2, 360n25, 363, 363n39, 363n40

INDEX OF NAMES   407

Gill, M. L., 150n33, 361n25
Gonzalez, Francisco J., 98n55
Gorgias, 91
Gould, P., 43n104, 194n207
Graeser, A., 183n148
Greco, J., 48n127, 48n128, 48n129
Green, T. H., 5, 5n15, 8-9, 8n22, 9n23,
    30, 30n74, 31, 31n77, 32n78,
    204-5, 204n13, 205n16, 205n17
Gregory, 202
Gregory of Nyssa, 86
Gregory the Great, 146n3, 164
Gurtler, Gary, 36n84, 37n88, 59n18,
    76n30, 118n5, 145n2, 146n3,
    162n6, 167n32, 168n41,
    170n48, 187n173, 192n200, 199,
    199n220, 199n221, 256n133
Guthrie, W.K.C., 97n52, 98n52

Haas, F. A., 145n2
Hackforth, Robert, 263n9
Hadot, I., 80n53
Hadot, Pierre, 175-76, 178, 178n112,
    180n131, 181-83, 181n138,
    183n145, 183n146, 183n148,
    252, 252-53n114, 252n114,
    348n103
Hager, F. P., 124n49, 129n91, 166n25
Hahn, L. E., 360n19
Hamlyn, D. W., 60n22
Hankey, Wayne, 75, 75n28
Hankinson, R. J., 91n22, 91n25
Hansen, M.J., 95n41, 96n46
Harte, V., 76n8, 98n54
Hartmann, Nicolai, 26, 26n59
Hatzimichali, Myrto, 122n33
Hedley, Douglas R., xxvin22, 32n82,
    43n103, 163n13, 193n202,
    198n219, 225n87, 356n4
Hegel, G.F.W., xvi, xviii, xix, xxi-xxii,
    1-7, 5n13, 13-16, 23, 28n68,
    29n70, 29n71, 34, 37, 39-40,
    48-49, 54, 66, 116, 116n132,
    145-154, 146n3, 146n7, 146n8,
    147n16, 147n17, 147n18,
    148n20, 148n21, 148n24,
    149n25, 149n26, 149n29,
    150n30, 150n31, 153n37,
    154n38, 156-160, 158n59,
    169n42, 171, 195n212, 296,
    320-21, 338-39, 355, 370
Heide, Daniel, 118n4
Heidegger, Martin, xvi, 39n91, 86,
    86n81, 279, 290, 319n1, 320,
    334, 339, 344, 353, 357n8, 367
Helleman-Elgersma, C., 294n18
Hempel, C. G., 163
Hendrix, John Shannon., 262n5, 262n7
Henry, P., 175, 176n93, 178n118
Heraclitus, 18, 89n13, 320
Hermippus of Smyrna, 128
Hermogenes, 73
Hierocles, 126n64
Hintikka, J., 5n13, 12, 12n30, 13n31,
    101n64
Hippolytus, 125
Hoffmann, Philippe, 69n41
Hogan, John P., 23n36
Homer, 89n13
Horn, H.-J., 291-92n8
Hume, David, 2, 5-10, 7n21, 29-32,
    29n70, 54, 161-63, 169, 169n43,
    191, 191n195, 195n213, 202-4,
    206-7, 206n21, 316, 320
Hunt, D. P., 182, 184, 184n156, 184n157
Husserl, Edmund, xix, 2-7, 5n13,
    12-14, 12n27, 12n28, 12n29,
    16, 28n67, 29, 29n70, 31, 49,
    49n133, 50, 54, 57, 57n12,
    57n13, 57n14, 61-66, 63n29,
    63n30, 65n34, 147n16, 152n35,
    154n38, 158-59, 159n65,
    169n42, 169n45, 197-98n215,
    203-4, 206, 236n48, 245n81,
    312, 317, 319n1, 320, 361
Hutchinson, Donald M., 162, 169-170,
    170n46, 170n47, 170n49,
    170n50, 170n52, 170n53,
    170n54, 189n182, 192n200

Iamblichus, 48, 69, 319
Igal, J., 175-78, 176n99, 176n102,
    177n109, 177n110, 178n113,
    182-83, 184n151, 184n153
Insole, J. C., 67n39
Irwin, Terrence .H., 60n22

INDEX OF NAMES

Jerome, 84, 117
Johnson, F., 205n18
Justin, 125–26
Justinian, 117, 117n1, 139, 139n166

Kahn, Charles, 74n17, 74n20, 75n23, 87–88, 87n1, 87n2, 88n3, 89n9, 91n23, 94n39, 120n14, 135n135
Kandinsky, Wassily, 345
Kant, Immanuel, xxii, xxiv–xxv, 2–7, 9–16, 11n24, 11n25, 29, 29n70, 31–32, 32n78, 32n79, 48, 48n132, 54, 66–67, 66n36, 116, 116n132, 146–150, 147n14, 148n19, 148n22, 152, 157–59, 159n64, 163, 169, 169n42, 169n44, 189, 191, 191n195, 194n206, 195n212, 203–6, 205n17, 259n149, 264, 291–92, 294n16, 295–96, 306–18, 306n77, 307n78, 308n79, 308n80, 308n81, 309n82, 309n83, 310n84, 310n85, 310n86, 310n87, 310n88, 310n89, 311n90, 311n91, 312n92, 313n93, 313n94, 314n95, 314n96, 314n97, 314n98, 315n98, 315n100, 320–21, 333–348, 333n65, 335n67, 335n68, 337n74, 338n76, 352–54, 361
Karamanolis, George, 129n92
Kennedy, George, A., 2n6, 119n12
Kenney, John Peter, 123n41
Kern, Iso, 12n26, 169n45
Ketchum, R., 73n12
Ketner, K. L., 20n12, 24n44
Kierkegaard, Soren, 351, 351n106
Kirwan, C., 60n22
Koch, Hal, 126n66
Kraemer, Hans Joachim, 127n71, 127n73
Krayle, Jill, 121n22, 121n24, 128n90
Kripke, Saul, 362
Kuebel, Paul, 129n95
Kvanvig, Jonathon, L., 48n127

Laertius, Diogenes, 120

Langerbeck, Hans, 128n85
Lavecchia, Salvatore, 261n2, 289, 289n143
Leibniz, G. W., xxiii, 10, 23, 29n71, 32–36, 38–40, 39n89, 39n90, 40n92, 40n93, 66, 83n66, 90n17, 106, 116n132, 162–63, 194, 195n213, 197n215, 207n23, 235n42, 243n73, 290n2, 295, 306n77, 308, 316
Lewis, C. I., 359
Lilla, Salvatore, 126n63, 126n66, 128n84
Limone, Vito, 71n2, 72n3, 75n29, 121n21
Lloyd, A. C., 17n41, 75, 75n28, 85n78, 108n99, 175, 178, 178n114, 179n124, 180n134, 183n149, 202, 202n8
Locke, John, xxii–xxiii, 2–10, 3n10, 4n11, 12, 15, 29n70, 30–32, 40, 54, 57n14, 65–66, 67n38, 149, 158, 158n58, 162–63, 169, 169n43, 202–7, 223n78, 230, 242, 247, 369
Lorimer, W. L., 128n90
Loux, M. J., 360n24, 362n30
Lowe, E. J., 195n208, 360n24, 362n29
Lukacs, Georg, 344

Magritte, René, 344–45
Malcolm, Norman, 224, 224n84, 225n88
Mallarme, Stephane, xviii, xviiin16
Manchester, D.K.W., 360n24
Manchester, Peter, 45n109, 45n110, 48, 48n126, 50n1, 89n11, 92n28, 93n34, 162, 162n7, 162n8
Marcus Aurelius, 352
Mastrocinque, A., 69n41
Mates, Benson, 98n55
McCabe, M.M., 73n8, 98n54
McDowell, John, 2n5, 119n12
McGuckin, John Anthony., 81n55
Melissus of Samos, 91, 253n116
Merlan, Philip, 127n70, 127n71, 282n113, 326n27, 327n41
Merlou-Ponty, Maurice, 319n1
Methodius, 117
Metrodorus, 352

INDEX OF NAMES   409

Metzger, Bruce M., 82n62
Mink, Louis O., 20n19, 23n38, 25n51
Moderatus, 125, 127
Modrak, Deborah K. W., 296n26
Montesquieu, 290n2, 334
Moore, G. E., 197n215
Moraux, Paul, 124n49, 129n91
Moravcsik, Julius, 195n208
Moreau, Jean, 291–92n8
Morrison, D., 62n27
Mourelatos, A. P. D., 89n8, 94n39

Narbonne, Jean-Marc, 108n99, 358n12
Natorp, Paul, 358n12
Naugle, D., 19n11, 24n43
Nemesius, 126n64, 128n86, 129
Nicholas of Cusa, 146n3
Nietzsche, Friedrich, 319n1, 322–23,
    334, 337, 339, 342–43, 349, 353
Nikunin, D., 304n63, 304n65, 304n66
Norman, R., 223n75
Novak, L., 360n24
Novotny, D., 360n24
Numenius, 125–27, 141
Nyvlt, Mark, xvn1, 41n98, 166n28,
    173n73, 174n78, 175n85,
    176n92, 176n95, 178n118,
    182n142, 182n143, 184n153,
    185n160, 185n161, 216n51,
    291n6, 294n13, 304n69, 360n23

O'Brien, Denis, 110n113, 148n24,
    149n28
O'Cleirigh, Padraig, 81n56
O'Connell, Robert J., 330n55
O'Daly, Gerard J.P., 162, 175–77, 181
Oehler, K., 153n37
O'Meara, Dominic John., xvn1, 42n101,
    105n83, 167n36, 195n209,
    195n210, 212n35, 215n50,
    252n111, 291–92n8, 293n10
O'Meara, J. J., 81n57
Origen of Alexandria, xv–xvi, xx,
    xxi, xxv, 2–4, 45–46, 45n108,
    46n113, 46n116, 46n117,
    47n118, 47n120, 47n121, 71–72,
    71n1, 72n2, 72n3, 72n4, 75–79,
    75n23, 75n25, 75n29, 76n33,
    76n34, 76n35, 76n36, 77n37,
    77n40, 77n41, 78n43, 78n44,
    79n46, 79n48, 80–86, 80n51,
    80n52, 80n53, 80n54, 81n55,
    81n56, 81n58, 81n59, 81n60,
    82n61, 82n62, 82n63, 82n64,
    83n67, 83n68, 83n69, 83n70,
    83n71, 83n72, 84n73, 84n74,
    84n75, 85n76, 85n77, 85n80,
    117–125, 118n4, 125–144,
    125n57, 126n61, 126n64,
    127n78, 127n79, 127n80,
    127n81, 128n82, 128n83,
    128n85, 128n86, 128n87,
    128n88, 128n91, 129n98,
    129n99, 130n104, 130n106,
    130n109, 130n110, 130n111,
    130n112, 131n113, 131n114,
    131n115, 131n116, 131n117,
    131n118, 131n119, 132n124,
    132n125, 133n127, 133n128,
    134n129, 134n130, 134n131,
    134n132, 134n133, 134n134,
    135n136, 135n140, 136n142,
    136n143, 136n144, 136n146,
    136n147, 137n148, 137n149,
    137n150, 137n153, 137n154,
    137n155, 137n156, 138n157,
    138n158, 138n160, 138n161,
    139n162, 139n163, 139n164,
    139n166, 140n167, 140n168,
    140n169, 140n170, 140n171,
    140n172, 141n173, 141n174,
    141n176, 141n177, 141n178,
    142n179, 142n181, 142n182,
    200, 225, 355–56, 357n6, 362–
    63, 367–370
Owen, G.E.L., 51–52, 51n2, 51n3, 51n4,
    51n5, 58–60, 58n15, 60n20,
    60n22, 72n4, 88n4, 89n8, 91n23,
    94n39, 103, 103n75, 103n76,
    220n71, 360n24
Owens, John, xvn1, 102n73

Palmer, John, xxn17, 88n5
Palmer, Richard E., 95n42
Pamphilius, 117

410 INDEX OF NAMES

Parmenides, xx, xxn17, xxi, 39n91, 50–51, 73–74, 88, 88n5, 90n18, 94–103, 108–9, 116, 218, 253n116, 320
Pascal, 29on2
Passmore, J. A., 28n67, 123n42
Pasternak, Boris, 87
Peirce, Charles Sanders, 228n7, 259n149, 355
Penner, Hans H., 26n57
Pepin, Jean, 47n119, 75n27, 102n67
Phidias, 285, 329–330
Philip the Chancellor, 148n21
Philip the Chanchellor, 146n3
Philipse, H., 6, 6n16
Philo of Alexandria, 76n32, 119n13, 120, 120n17, 120n18, 121n20, 125–26, 125n54, 127n70, 132–33, 132n120, 132n122, 133n127, 135, 135n140, 141
Philoponus, 202, 267
Plantinga, Alvin, 44, 90n17, 106, 224–25, 224n85, 225n88
Plato, xv–xviii, xvii, xviin6, xviin7, xviin8, xviin9, xviin10, xviin11, xviin12, xviin14, xxn17, xx–xxi, 2–5, 7–10, 15–16, 15n37, 15n38, 18n1, 18n2, 18n3, 18n4, 19n5, 19n6, 35, 37n87, 48n131, 53n9, 53n10, 54, 58, 66n37, 72–75, 72n3, 73n5, 73n7, 73n10, 73n12, 73n13, 73n14, 74n16, 74n18, 74n19, 74n20, 74n21, 74n22, 75n23, 75n24, 78n42, 79n47, 88, 88n5, 89n13, 89n14, 90n18, 91–92, 92n29, 92n30, 96n49, 97–103, 97n51, 98n56, 99n57, 100n59, 101n60, 101n61, 101n62, 101n63, 101n64, 106–11, 107n89, 113–15, 116n133, 117, 118n4, 118n5, 120–21, 120n18, 121n23, 121n26, 122n34, 125, 125n54, 125n59, 126n61, 127n80, 128n83, 136n140, 146, 146n3, 146n5, 146n10, 147n15, 149–150, 150n33, 159, 159n63, 168, 168n39, 179n126, 181, 185, 186n169, 190, 192n201, 193, 193n202, 193n203, 206, 209–10, 209n24, 209n25, 209n26, 209n27, 210n28, 216n51, 224, 227–230, 227n1, 227n2, 230n18, 230n19, 230n21, 231n23, 231n24, 232–33, 232n25, 232n26, 232n27, 232n28, 233n32, 233n33, 233n34, 233n35, 233n36, 233n37, 233n38, 235, 235n44, 235n45, 235n46, 238n54, 240, 240n61, 242n72, 244–45, 244n76, 244n77, 244n78, 245n82, 249–250, 250n104, 250n105, 255–56, 255n126, 256n131, 259n147, 259n148, 261, 262–64, 263n8, 263n10, 266, 266n24, 271, 271n58, 276, 278n98, 278n99, 280, 280n103, 280n104, 280n105, 285, 285n136, 286n139, 288–89, 291–92, 291n4, 297, 297n28, 301–2, 306, 306n75, 306n76, 308, 317, 317n101, 320, 322–23, 323n7, 325–26, 330, 330n54, 330n56, 352–54, 361n27, 368, 368n60, 370, 370n65
Plezia, M., 122n33
Pliny, 50
Plotinus, xv–xvii, xviin14, xix–xxv, xx, xxn17, xxi–xxiv, xxv–xxvin21, xxvin22, xxvin23, xvn1, 2–5, 8–10, 14–17, 15n137, 17n43, 17n44, 17n45, 19n8, 23–24, 28n68, 29n70, 29n71, 33–38, 36n84, 36n85, 36n86, 37n87, 40, 40n93, 41n94, 42–43, 42n99, 42n101, 43n105, 45, 45n108, 45n110, 48–49, 57n14, 59, 59n18, 61, 63–65, 63n30, 65n33, 66n37, 69, 71n1, 74n22, 75n23, 84n73, 85n79, 88–97, 88n5, 89n13, 90n18, 92n31, 93n31, 97, 99, 105n83, 106, 108–16, 108n94, 108n97, 108n98, 109n101, 109n102, 109n103, 109n104, 109n105, 109n106,

INDEX OF NAMES 411

109n107, 110n108, 110n109, 110n110, 110n111, 110n112, 111n114, 111n115, 111n116, 111n117, 111n118, 111n119, 111n120, 112n121, 112n125, 113n126, 113n127, 115n130, 118n5, 122n37, 125n58, 126n64, 128n86, 128n91, 130n105, 145–46, 145n2, 146n3, 146n5, 146n9, 147n16, 148–152, 148n21, 150–54, 150n33, 153n37, 154n38, 156–57, 156n50, 156n51, 156n52, 156n53, 156n54, 156n55, 157n56, 159, 162–63, 162n4, 165–179, 166n31, 167n32, 168n39, 169n42, 170n52, 171n58, 172n65, 173n69, 173n70, 173n71, 173n74, 174n75, 174n76, 174n80, 174n83, 175n84, 175n86, 175n90, 176n93, 176n100, 177n107, 177n108, 179n121, 179n122, 179n125, 179n128, 179n129, 181–194, 181n136, 181n137, 184n154, 184n155, 186n165, 186n166, 186n168, 186n169, 187n170, 187n172, 188n175, 188n176, 188n177, 188n178, 188n179, 188n180, 189n181, 189n183, 190n185, 190n188, 190n190, 195n212, 200, 201–7, 202n5, 202n6, 202n8, 212–226, 212n33, 212n34, 212n35, 213n36, 213n37, 214n47, 215n49, 215n50, 216n56, 217n57, 217n58, 218n61, 219n62, 219n63, 224n80, 228, 228n5, 233n31, 234n41, 238n54, 238n55, 238n56, 238n57, 239n58, 239n60, 240–42, 240n64, 241n67, 246n86, 250n106, 251n108, 251n109, 252–56, 252n110, 252n111, 252n112, 252n113, 252n114, 254n122, 255n123, 255n124, 255n125, 256n133, 256n135, 256n136, 256n137, 256n138, 256n139, 257n140, 258–260, 258n145, 258n146, 260n152, 260n153, 262–288, 262n4, 262n5, 262n6, 263n11, 264n12, 264n13, 265n14, 265n15, 265n16, 265n17, 265n18, 265n20, 266n22, 266n23, 266n26, 266n27, 266n28, 266n29, 266n30, 266n31, 267n32, 267n33, 267n36, 267n37, 268n38, 268n39, 268n40, 268n41, 268n42, 268n43, 268n44, 268n45, 269n46, 269n47, 269n48, 269n51, 270n53, 270n54, 270n55, 271n57, 271n59, 271n60, 272n61, 272n62, 272n63, 273n64, 273n65, 273n66, 273n67, 273n68, 274n69, 274n70, 274n71, 274n72, 274n73, 274n74, 275n75, 275n76, 275n77, 275n78, 275n79, 275n80, 275n81, 275n83, 276n84, 276n85, 276n86, 276n87, 276n88, 276n89, 277n90, 277n91, 277n92, 277n93, 277n94, 277n95, 277n96, 278n98, 281n106, 281n107, 281n108, 281n109, 281n110, 281n111, 282n116, 282n117, 282n118, 283n119, 283n120, 283n122, 283n123, 283n124, 283n125, 283n127, 283n128, 283n129, 284n130, 284n132, 285n133, 285n134, 285n135, 286n137, 286n138, 288n141, 288n142, 291–317, 291n144, 293n9, 293n11, 293n12, 294n18, 294n19, 295n22, 295n23, 297n27, 297n29, 297n30, 298n31, 298n32, 298n33, 299n34, 299n35, 299n36, 299n37, 299n38, 299n39, 300n40, 300n41, 300n42, 300n43, 300n44, 300n45, 300n46, 301n47, 301n48, 301n49, 301n50, 301n51,

412 INDEX OF NAMES

Plotinus *(continued)*, 301n52, 301n53, 301n54, 302n55, 302n56, 302n57, 302n58, 302n59, 302n60, 302n61, 304n63, 304n64, 304n68, 305n73, 306n75, 306n76, 306n77, 319n1, 320–333, 324n11, 324n12, 324n13, 324n14, 324n15, 324n17, 324n18, 325n19, 325n20, 325n21, 325n22, 325n23, 326n25, 326n30, 326n32, 327n33, 327n34, 327n35, 327n37, 327n38, 327n39, 327n40, 327n43, 328n44, 328n45, 328n47, 329n48, 329n49, 329n50, 329n51, 329n52, 330n53, 330n56, 331n57, 331n58, 332n61, 332n62, 348–353, 352–55, 356n3, 356n5, 357n7, 359, 359n13, 360n23, 361–64, 362n34, 362n36, 367–370, 370n66

Plutarch of Chaeronea, 132

Popper, Karl, 89n10, 91n22, 228n7, 355, 355n1

Porphyry of Tyre, 164, 202, 276–77, 279–280, 302, 331n57, 332

Potamon of Alexandria, 120

Proclus, 202, 279–280

Protagoras, 73–74, 230

Puech, H.-C., 284n131, 328n46

Putnam, Hilary, 152n35, 153n36, 154n39, 164n14, 194, 194n206, 358n11

Pyrrho, 249, 334

Pythagorean imagery, 77

Quine, W.V.O., xvi, xvin3, 194n206, 196n213, 196n214, 197n215, 198, 358–360, 358n10, 359n17, 360n18, 360n20, 360n21, 369

Rahner, Karl, 80n53

Ramelli, Illaria, 71n2, 118n4, 126n66, 357n6

Rappe, Sara, 14n33, 85n79, 151n34, 256n132, 305n70, 305n71, 305n72, 361n25

Raven, J. E., 89n8

Remes, Paulina, 162, 169–171, 170n46, 170n55, 170n56, 171n57, 171n58, 171n59, 171n60, 171n61, 171n62, 192n200

Rich, A., 292n8

Rist, John, 124n49, 128, 128n91, 175, 176n100, 178, 178n115, 178n120, 183n149, 281n111, 281n112, 291n8, 324n9, 324n16

Robinson, H. M., 162n2

Robinson, T. M., xxn17, 88n5, 95n42, 96n46

Rochliz, R., 339n84

Rockmore, Thomas, 321n3

Roecklin, Robert J., xxn17, 88n5, 93n35, 249n103

Rorty, Richard, xvi, 2n5, xvin4, 7, 7n17, 7n18, 9, 31n76, 32n82, 119n11, 119n12, 163n13, 204n14, 204n15, 204n19, 242n71, 247n90, 279n100, 303n62, 340, 353

Roskam, Gert, 121n20

Rubinoff, L., 23n38

Rufinus, 117

Ruis-Camps, J., 79n45

Runciman, W. G., 98n53

Runia, David, 121n25, 123n42, 126n63, 128n84, 129n92

Russell, Bertrand, 20n20, 21n24, 24n41, 25n52, 26n56, 26n58, 28n68, 50, 52, 85, 158, 358–59, 361, 369

Rutten, C., 108n99, 146n4

Ryle, Gilbert, 21n24, 26n56, 29, 29n72, 50, 52, 54, 68, 98n53, 149, 158, 158n60, 163, 191–92, 191n195, 192n199, 200, 203, 203n11, 208, 229–231, 229n10, 229n13, 230n14, 230n15, 236n48, 244n75, 245n81, 245n83, 357n9, 361, 363–65, 363n37, 363n38, 363n40, 363n42, 364n43, 365n48, 367, 367n57

Santoprete, Luciana, 69n41
Sappho, 145
Sartre, Jean-Paul, 158
Sayre,, 361n25
Schenkeveldt, D.M., 249n101
Schiller, Friedrich, 338–39
Schleiermacher, Friedrich, xviii, 1
Schlicht, Moritz, 129n212, 357n7, 359, 359n16
Schlipp, P. A., 360n19
Schofield, Michael, xvn1, 74n21, 98n54, 360n23
Schopenhauer, Arthur, 261, 323, 323n8
Schroeder, Frederic M., xvn1, xviin13, xxvin23, 45n107, 61, 61n24, 61n25, 71n1, 78n43, 84n73, 106n85, 113n127, 118n5, 122n37, 124n49, 145, 145n1, 145n2, 146n3, 166n28, 167n33, 175–78, 176n94, 176n100, 177n104, 178n116, 178n117, 178n119, 179n127, 181n140, 182–83, 183n147, 183n149, 184n151, 189n183, 191n193, 201n4, 218n61, 219, 219n64, 228n5, 232n30, 255n127, 256n132, 261n1, 275n82, 276n86, 286n139, 356n5, 360n25, 361n26, 362n35
Schwyzer, H-R, 170n49, 172, 175–78, 176n94, 176n97, 178n111, 189n182, 265, 265n19, 283n121, 283n126, 327n36
Searle, John, 200, 357–58n9
Sedley, David, 89n12
Seidl, Horst, xvn1, 360n23
Seneca, 120, 125, 133, 352
Sextus Empiricus, 334
Shaftesbury, Third Earl of, 315
Shakespeare, William, 227
Sharples, Robert. W., 121n20, 126n63, 129n97
Silverman, A., 74n18
Simplicius, 202, 231
Smith, A., 85n79, 151n34, 269n50, 281n111, 288n141, 331n60, 332n61
Smith, Jonathon, 342

Soames, S., 359n15
Socrates, 10, 18, 18n3, 23n41, 53, 230–32, 334, 351
Solomon, Robert C., 149n27, 150n32, 153n37, 157n57
Sorabji, Richard, xvn1, 14n32, 17n42, 17n44, 46n115, 62n28, 66n37, 162n3, 162n7, 164n17, 166n24, 201n4, 202, 202n9, 202n10, 213n38, 214, 214n44, 360n23
Sosa, E., xxvn20, 65n35, 370n64
Speusippus, 127
Spinoza, Baruch, xviii, 2, 11, 66, 162, 222
Stead, G. C., 135n135
Steidele, B., 129n95
Stern-Gillet, Suzanne, 162n4, 168n41, 191n194, 192n200, 363, 363n41
Stoekl, A., 321n4
Strange, Stephen, 145n2, 361n25
Suarez, 146n3
Suppe, F., 26n58, 198n218
Svelta-Griffin, Svetla, 361n25
Syrian, 126n69
Szlezak, Thomas A., 109n103, 145n2, 190n185

Tahko, T. E., 360n24
Taran, Leonardo, 88n7, 89n8, 94n39
Tardieu, M., A. Van den Kerchove, 69n41
Taylor, A. E., 102n67, 164n14, 249n103
Tazzolio, T. T., 108n99
Theiler, Willy, 120n15, 127n72, 133n126, 179n129
Theophrastus, 102, 121
Thomas of Aquinas, 1n2, 146n3
Tiomkin, Andrei, 81n55, 108n96, 109n100
Trouillard, Jean, xxvin23, 113n127, 228n5, 326n5
Turnball, Robert, 98n53

Van Gulick, R., 168n40
Varro, Marcus Terentius, 132, 133
Veldsman, D. P., 1n2
Ventureyra, Scott D. G., 168n40
Verbeke, G., 269n50, 331n60

Vescovini, G. F., 146n7
Vlastos, Gregory, 98n55
Voltaire, 334

Wagner, Michael, 59n19, 166n26
Warhol, Andy, 345
Waugh, Joanne B., 2n4, 119n9, 119n10
Wedin, Michael V., xxn17, 88n5, 95n42, 96n46
Whittaker, John, 125n53
Wilkes, J., 161n1
Wilkinson, Lisa, 2n4, 119n9, 119n10
Wippel, J. F., 146n3
Witt, Charlotte, 361n25
Wittgenstein, Ludwig, 2-4, 2n7, 3n8, 3n9, 15, 16n40, 19n8, 28n68, 29, 29n70, 29n73, 50, 52-54, 52n6, 53n7, 53n8, 68-69, 71, 73, 73n11, 85-86, 85n80, 86n81, 88n5, 93n35, 149, 155, 155n49, 163-64, 191-92, 191n195, 191n196, 192n198, 197n215, 203, 203n12, 229-232, 229n8, 229n9, 229n11, 230n15, 230n16, 230n17, 231n23, 241n67, 246n86, 332n61, 354-55, 354n110, 358-59, 360n22, 364-69, 364n44, 364n45, 364n46, 365n47, 365n50, 366n51, 366n52, 366n53, 366n54, 366n55, 367n56, 367n58, 367n59, 369n63
Wolinski, J., 79n45
Wolterstorff, N., 8n22, 42n100, 105n82, 108n93, 224, 224n82
Wood, Kelsey, 73n9, 98n53
Wurm, Karl, 130n105

Xenophanes, 253n116

Yu, Jiyuan, 58n15

Zago, M., 69n41
Zalta, Edward, 196n213
Zeno, 247
Zeus, 329-330
Zhyrkova, A., 145n2

Index of Subjects

absolute presuppositions
    actuality, preceding potentiality, 180n134
    Aristotle on, 26–32
    description of, 26
    interpretation and, 20
    logical efficacy and, 25
    meaning of a 'text,' 22
    methodological solipsism, xix, 47–48
    overview, xix, 19–24
    Plotinus on, 26–32
    primary and secondary principles, 19n7
    question and answer logic, 22–26, 24n42
    relative presuppositions distinctions, 23
    similes in the *Theaetetus*, 18–19
    synthetic a priori function, 23n38
absolute solipsism, xxii
abstract objects, 193–98, 193n201, 216–225
Academic skepticism, 119–120n11
active intellect, 55–56, 62, 108, 201, 264–270, 324–25
active reason, 56, 62
actuality, preceding potentiality, 19n7, 33–37, 180n134
aesthetic cognition, 261
aesthetic exercises, 349–350
aesthetic philosophy, 288–89
aesthetic symbols, 330–33

aesthetics
    art and, 349–351
    beauty and, 283–87, 296–306
    epistemology of, 291, 291n3
    ethics and, 346–352
    ethos of, 343–46
    horizons, 291–92
    imagination (*See* imagination)
    Kant on, 306–17
    memory and, 291–92
    overview, xxiv, 290–91
    turn in, 306–17
aisthesis
    the soul and, 268, 274, 279–281, 286
    term usage, 79n47, 299, 322
alethic modality, 95
algamata, 285
analytic *a priori*, 34
anti-constitutive realism, 16
antilepsis
    imagination and, 293
    lower soul of, 268, 274, 279, 287
    term usage, 189, 299–300
anti-realism, 65–67, 118n6, 241n65, 245n84
Aristotelian category theory, xxi, 118, 118n5, 120–21, 133n140, 135, 135–36n140, 143–46, 143n3
art
    aesthetics and, 349–351
    aesthetics of soul and, xxiv, 264–270, 332–33
    expression of ideal beauty, xxiv

art *(continued)*
   hieroglyphics and, 284, 305, 329, 362
   nature and, 264
   perspectivism and, 341–43
aseity argument, 42–43, 42n100
avant-garde art, 344–45
aviary simile, 18–19, 18n4, 193, 227–28, 227–28n2, 227n1, 233, 249–250

bad infinite, 171
beauty
   aesthetic emerging, 283–87
   aesthetic philosophy, 288–89
   defined as, 314
   degrees of, 301
   imagination and, 270–75, 291–92, 294n21, 314
   intelligible beauty, 325–330
   judgement, 273–75
   Kant on, 310–12
   meaning of, xvii
   memory, 282–83
   mind ascending to, xxiv
   overview, 261–62
   Plato's writings on, 262–63
   Plotinus' analysis of, 270–72
   Plotinus' writings on, 262–64, 323–333
   reification, 279–281
   seeing in respect of the One, 262–64
   soul and, xxiv, 264–272, 277–79, 298–305
   speechless of, 278
   symmetry and the One, 275–77
   turning toward the One, 277–79
behaviorism, 163–64, 164n14, 357n9
being
   Aristotle on, 59–61, 102–3, 210
   divine, 141–43
   and existence in, 50–52, 88n4
   imagination and, 282–83
   intellect and, 108–9
   Kahn on, 87–88
   knowing and, 88–93
   levels of, 123–25
   mapping of, 50–52
   non-being and, 50–51, 100, 111, 114, 146, 209–10
   primary being, 59, 105n82
   thinking and, 213–15
   thinking as same as, 100–102, 116n132
   unity and, 98–101
being divine, 141–43
belief, in other minds, 233–36
bundle theories, 202–3

Cartesianism, xviin2, 29–30, 32n78, 36–37, 202
categories
   being divine, 141–43
   category mistakes, 29n72, 203n11, 236n48, 244–45, 245n81
   as classification of being, 143
   degrees of divinity, 73n11, 123–24, 129–132, 139–141
   degrees of reality, 133–35, 139–141
   divine transcendence, 125–29
   foundations, 120–23
   horizons, 119–120
   intelligible categories, 135n139, 136
   naming to meaning, 60
   ontology, 123–25
   rethinking of, xxi, 117–19, 135–39
   as symbols or signs, 119
Categories (Aristotle), 110–11, 122
causal possibility, 19n7, 28, 80, 84n74, 187
causality
   of intelligible realities, 108
   mental, 29, 164–69, 172
   transference theory of, 165, 172
   transmission theory of, 180n134
Cogito (Descartes), 3–4, 6–7, 12, 15, 31n75, 48, 67, 148, 159, 204n14
cognition, 165, 247–49
cognitive expressions, 357n7
cognitive impression, 247
coherentism, 248
Commentary on John (Origen), 125, 135
Commentary on Samuel (Origen), 138
Commentary on the Song of Songs (Origen), 80
complexity theory of identity, 63–65

INDEX OF SUBJECTS   417

compound proposition, 52, 229–230
conceivability argument, 82, 196–97,
    197n215, 207, 209–13, 243,
    244n75
concepts, intuitions and, 206
conceptualism, 107n91
Confessions (Augustine), 2
conflicting appearances argument,
    118n7
consciousness
    beauty and, 273
    continuity and, 364
    covering both sense and intellect,
        30–32
    features of, 168–69
    introspection and, 162n4, 363–64,
        363–66
    inventing, 169–172
    levels of, 170
    mind and, xxii–xxiii, 162–64, 172,
        366–69
    mind as, 206–7
    of objects, 198n215
    phenomena of, 162n4
    term usage, 161–62
    transcendental foundation of, 13, 32
    unconsciousness and, 265, 268–270
    unidentifiable character of, 13
constitutionality principle, 368
contact language, 214
contemplation, 114, 114n129, 188, 239,
    258
contemplative prayer, xx, 46–47, 72, 75,
    80–85
continuity principle, 33–34, 37–41
contraries, 111, 151
Copernican revolution, 11
Cratylus (Plato), 53, 73–74, 119n11
criticism, 97n52, 98, 333–37, 340
Critique of Judgment (Kant), 307, 309,
    316, 337, 339
Critique of Pure Reason (Kant), 307,
    308, 309

De Anima III (Aristotle), 16, 55–56,
    221, 237
De Emendatione Intellectus (Spinoza), 11

De Mundo, 121, 128n90
deconstructionist arguments, 357–360,
    357n7
Demiurge and the Forms, 102n66,
    102n67, 120
Demiurge and World Soul, 122, 125,
    130
Demiurge/Logos, 120, 131, 135
differences, 38–41
distinctions
    discursive, 45–47
    family resemblances, 2–3
    idealism, 14–16
    language of metaphysics, 2–5
    overview, xviii–xix, 1–2
    phenomenalism, 5–10
    phenomenological reduction, 4–5,
        10–13, 15
    realism, 14–16
    representationalism, 5–10
divine
    abstract objects and, 223–25
    being, 141–43
divine intellect, 58, 107, 109, 112, 208
divine levels, 131
divine transcendence, 125–29
divinity, degrees of, 73n11, 123–24,
    129–132, 139–141
double activity (*energeia*), 188
double-aspect theory, 66
double-self, 36–37, 36n86
doubt, 8, 15, 207

EE (Aristotle), 58
ego-consciousness, 365
ego-identity, 236–39
egoistic solipsism, 154
eikon, term usage, 84n75
Eleatic modal logic, 94n40
Eleatic parsings, 93–94
Eleaticism, 51, 87, 91–94
elementary propositions, 52, 53, 85,
    229, 231
Enlightenment, 334–37, 339–341
Enneads (Plotinus), xv, xxi, 14, 17, 33,
    35, 38–39, 183
enquiry, xviii, 19, 119–120

418 INDEX OF SUBJECTS

entity criteria, 246–47n89
episteme
    to have knowledge, xv, xvii, xviin8
    meaning and, 27–28, 58, 79n47
    method of knowledge, xvi
    Plato on, 72
epistemic regress argument, 235, 244–45, 250–51
ethics, aesthetics and, 346–352
Eucharist, 82–83
exact similarity, 90n16
excluded middle, law of, 93–94
exclusion, posterior to inclusion, xxvi, 112, 112n122
existence, non-existence and, 51, 95–96
existential being, 87–88
Extensional-Intensional thesis, 197n215
externalists, 153n36, 241n67, 246n86, 361n27
extrinsic properties, 90n16

false judgment, xvii, 18, 227–28n2, 233, 244
false knowledge, xviin8, 18n4, 233n36, 235, 244
false statements, 200–221
falsity-truth distinction, 251, 253–54, 254n121
family resemblances, 2–4, 15–16
First Alcibiades (Plato), 36
first philosophy, xxv, 2n3
Flatland (story), 369
focal meaning, xix, 58–59, 72, 79n47, 103, 113–15
Forms
    being and, 100–102
    Intellect and the One (See Intellect and the One)
    Nous and, xxviin23, 109–12
    Platonic unity of intellect, xxiii, xxv–xxviin21
    plurality of, 64
    sources of intentionality meaning, xix–xx, 61
    universals and, 106–8, 107n89
fracture, return and
    Foucault on, 333–353
    Kant on, 333–348

    overview, xxv, 319–320
    Plotinus on, 323–333, 348–353
    self and aesthetics, 322–23
    self and subjectivity, 320–22
freedom, 341, 346–48, 351

Geist, 49, 54, 147–49, 151–52, 157–58, 160, 296
God
    divine transcendence, 125–29
    existence of, 44–47
    within and likeness to, 75–80
    ousia of, xxi, 82–83, 118, 137, 141–44
    substance and, 121–26
God, Son of, xxi, 46, 81–83, 131–37, 137n155, 139–142, 144
God the Father, xxi, 45–46, 130–33, 130n105, 134n130, 135, 137–142, 144
good
    idea of, Plato, 262
    light of, Plato, 288–89
    the One and, 33, 38, 97, 273
goodness, 324–25
Greco-Roman ethics, 347–48
Greek *De Mundo*, 128n90
Grossschrift (Plotinus), 262

heaven, 121n26
Hecate's left hip, 279–281
helmsman-guardian, 130, 130n104, 131–33
hierarchism, 123
hieroglyphics, art and, 284, 305, 329, 362
holenmermism. See the whole is in the part
Holy Spirit, 131–33, 135–142, 137n155, 144
Homilies on Leviticus (Origen), 80
homo aestheticus, 351–53
homoiosis theo principle, 77
"horizon" of aesthetics, 319n1
hupostasis, term usage, 215
hyper-noetic awareness, 188
hyper-noetic faculty, 181
hyper-noetic intelligence, 181

INDEX OF SUBJECTS 419

hyper-noetic *Nous*, 178
hyper-noetic One, 175
hypothetical-deductive model of rationality, 198, 198n218

Ich Denke (Kant), xxiv, 11, 48, 116n132, 147, 159, 169
Idea of the Good (Plato), 262
idealism, 11, 14–16, 66n36
identity
  complexity theory of, 63–65
  conceivability argument and, 207, 209–13
  ego-identity, 236–39
  intentionality and, 64–65
  numerical (*See* numerical identity)
  participation and, 257–58
  principle of, xx–xxi, 33–34, 37–41, 39n91
  qualitative, 90n16, 97, 113–15
  term usage, 90n16
  of thinking and being, xx–xxi, 88–93, 104–6
identity theory, 207, 243
illumination, 84n73, 217, 219–221, 255–57
image, as imitative artifice, 119, 119n11
imagination
  beauty and, 270–75, 291–92, 294n21, 314
  being and, 282–83
  intelligible beauty and, 325–330
  Kant on, 308–9, 314
  phantasia and, 179, 268, 283, 294–96
immanence-immanence intentionality thesis, 198n215
immaterial being, 212–13
immaturity, 335
impressions, 247–49
  See also inner representations
imprinting, 203
Inaugural Dissertation (Kant), 307
inchoate intellect, 176n100
inchoate *nous*, 175–180
inclusion, anterior to exclusion, xxvi, 112, 112n122
incognitive impression, 248

indeterministic systems, 228n7
indispensability argument, 195, 195–96n213
indubitability, 8, 15, 207
inferential intuitions, 96n50, 104n79
infinite regress argument, 167, 167n34, 240, 251, 361, 361n27
inner representations, 4, 8–9, 10, 30–31, 203
innocence, of modern notions, 8, 29–30, 203
intellect
  active (*See* active intellect)
  activity of thought toward objects, 56–57
  being and, 108–9, 258
  generation of, 183–84
  inchoate *nous*, 175–180
  intentionality and, 63, 63n30
  life of, 17
  mind as, 6, 206–7
  passive intellect, 56, 108
  Platonic unity of, xxiii, xxv–xxvin21
  Plotinus' *Enneads*, xv, 35, 183
  plurality in, 175
  powers of, 181
  the soul and, 302–3
  thinking and, 238–39
  thought and, 56–57, 251–52
Intellect and the One, xxiv, 17, 99, 105n82, 112, 114–15
intellection, perception and, 324
intelligibility, 164–65
intelligible architecture, 145
intelligible beauty, 325–330
intelligible categories, 135n139, 136
intelligible matter, 174–75, 179, 293, 304
intentionality
  Aristotle on, 54–56
  complexity theory of, 63
  direction and, 61–62, 63
  irreducible feature of mental phenomena, 61–62
  meaning in naming objects, 52–54
  mental states, 243
  overview, xix–xx
  property of mental states, 207–8
  types of, 56–57

420 INDEX OF SUBJECTS

interpretation, 48, 159
introspection, 162n4, 363–64
   consciousness and, 363–64
   mental states and, 365
intuitions, 206
is, meaning of, 91–92, 120n14, 121, 210
isomorphic similarity, 90n16

Jesus Christ. *See* God, Son of
judgement
   beauty and, 273–75
   Kant on, 307–12
   types of, 298–300
justifiable true belief, 249–252

Kantian categories, 145–46
"know thyself" meaning of, 36
knowledge
   by acquaintance, 158
   aviary simile and (*See* aviary simile)
   defined as, 361n27
   false knowledge, xviii8, 18n4, 233n36, 235, 244
   goal of, xv
   to have (*episteme*), xvii
   as identity with objects, 247–49
   language and, 27–29
   mental states and, 30–31
   of phenomena, 205n17
   philosophizing and, 151–52
   possession of, xvii, 368
   power and, 368
   as a pyramid, 248
   questioning and, 20n20, 21n23, 21n26, 26n55
   of reality, 75
   spectator theory of, xviii–xix, 2, 118–19
   thinking abstract objects, 216
Kritik der reinen Vernunft (Kant), 11

language
   approaches to, 19n8
   articulating truth and reality, 35
   as boundary of my world, 203n12
   clarity, degree of, 362
   compositionality of, 74n19
   contact language, 214
   contradictory aspect of, 91
   family resemblances, 2–4
   knowledge and, 27–29
   limits of, xx, 29n71, 72, 365–67
   of metaphysics, 2–5, 35
   of prayer, 81–83, 85–86, 85n80
   reality and, 35, 362
   as share of being, 90–91
   of spiritual sensation, 71–72
   Stoic theory on, 248, 248n100
   term usage, 28n66
   thought and, 119, 204
Language (*Sprache*) thesis, 197n215
Leibniz's Law, 40n93, 83n66, 195n213, 197n215, 207n23, 235n42, 243n73
Life-Form (*Lebensform*) thesis, 197n215
light, substantiality, not mere metaphor, 84n73
Light of the Good (Plato), 288–89
linguistic intentionality, 56–57
linguistic solution, 209–10
logical atomism, 232
logical behaviorism, 357n9
logical efficacy, of a presupposition, 20, 25
logical positivists, 195n212, 229
logical possibility, 19n7, 23, 80, 84n74, 92–93, 93n32, 94n39, 104n78, 175n91, 177, 194n207, 197n215
Logos, 4

mathematical objects, 194n205
meaning
   focal meaning, xix, 58–59, 72, 79n47, 103, 113–15
   overview, xix–xx
   subjectivity and, xvii–xviii
meaningfulness, described, 195n212
Meditations (Descartes), 11
megista gene, Plato's categories, xxii
memory, 282–83
mental
   events and processes, 355–56n3
   exhibiting intentionality, xxvn21
   marks of, xxvn20, 228n6, 355n2
   priority of, 33–47
mental acts, 107n90

mental agency, 172–75
mental causality, 29, 164–69, 172, 180
mental event types, 153–54n38
mental properties, 361, 364
mental states, 162n4, 365
   causal theories of mind, 29
   as distinct from perceptions, 7
   divine intellect and, 235n42
   identity and conceivability
      arguments, 208
   as internal to a mind, xxii, xxiii
   knowledge and, 30–31
   physical states, xv, xxii, xxiii
   self-conscious states, xxiii, 29
   subjective, xxiv, 203–4
   as transcendental, 11
metaphysics
   language of, 2–5
   models, 120–23
   of prepositions, 120, 133–35
   pseudo-metaphysics, 22
   as pure being, 21n24, 23–24n41, 26n56
   term usage, 1–2, 1n2
Metaphysics (Aristotle), 14, 16, 26, 54–55, 237
methodological solipsism, xix, xxii, 47–49, 152–58, 153n35
Middle Platonic philosophy, 118, 118n5, 120, 125, 130–31
mimesis, xviii, 264, 275–77, 279, 287, 301, 303, 317, 333
mind
   ascending to beauty, xxiv
   beauty and, 264–270
   body and, 363–64
   causal theories of, 29
   as consciousness, 206–7
   consciousness and, xxii–xxiii, 9, 162–64, 206–7, 366–69
   as immaterial thinking substances, 207
   as intellect, 6, 206–7
   as prior to matter, 35
   term usage, 28–29, 28–29n70
   See also other minds
misfortune, shift to fortune, 268–270
modal arguments, 116, 225

modal logic, xx, 88, 94n39, 104, 104n78, 194
modalism, 123
modality
   identity of thinking and being, 104–6
   necessary and possibility, 88n5
   overview, xxi, xxn17
   Parmenides' arguments, 94–97
modus ponens argument, 242–43
Monadology (Leibniz), 38, 39
monism, 91, 91n26
movement, 216–17, 216n56
multiplicity, unity and, 151–52

naming
   being and existence in, 50–52
   descriptions and, 53–54
   intentionality and meaning in, 52–54, 67–68
   overview, xix–xx
   reference and meaning in, 54
   use and, 53–54
natural things, 136
necessary being, 59, 93–97
necessary existence, xxi, 92, 94n39, 97, 104, 194, 224n85, 225n88
necessity
   as modal modifier, xxn17, 88n5, 95–97
   preeminent form of, 99–100, 109
nominalism, 107n91
non-being, being and, 50–51, 100, 111, 114, 146, 209–10
non-cognitive expressions, 357n7
non-existence, existence and, 51, 95–96
non-immanence intentionality thesis, 198n215
noon, term usage, 73n11, 88, 89n13
noumenal/phenomenal contrast, 306
Nous
   defined as, 41, 105
   emerging, 180–85
   Forms and, xxvin23, 109–12
   generation of, 183
   inchoate *nous*, 175–180
   the One and, xxiii
nous-identity, 236–39

INDEX OF SUBJECTS

numerical identity
    in an *a se* relation, 94, 100, 103, 105–6, 113–15, 185
    of thinking and being, xx–xxi, 88, 90n16, 97

objects
    abstract objects, 193–98, 193n201, 216–225
    activity of thought toward, 56–57
    meaning in naming of, 52–54
    object of thought, 173
    ordinary empirical objects, 90
Of Clouds and Clocks (Popper), 355
On Intelligible Beauty (Plotinus), 262, 263–64
On Prayer (Origen), 80–81
On Sensible Beauty (Plotinus), 262, 292
On the Intelligible Beauty (Plotinus), 328
On the Knowing Hypostases (Porphyry), 276–77, 302
On the Spirit That Allotted Itself to Us (Plotinus), 331n57
ontological commitment argument, 196, 196–97n214
ontological monism, 91
ontology, categories, 123–25
organic work of art, 344
Organon (Aristotle), 58
other minds
    aviary simile (*See* aviary simile)
    foundation of, 233–36
    horizons, 229–232
    identity and, 236–39
    justifiable true belief, 249–252
    knowledge as identity with objects, 247–49
    overview, xxiii–xxiv
    problems of, 240–47
    thinking and, 252–58
    the whole is in the part, 229–232
ousia
    complexity of, 100–101
    divine transcendence and, 125–131
    forms of, 210–15, 212n32
    of God, xxi, 82–83, 118, 137, 141–44

Parmenides (Plato), xx, 73, 74, 97–98, 100, 101

participation, 257–58
passive intellect, 56, 108
passive reason, 56
per se and *se*, distinction, 41–44, 41n96
perceptible substances, 202–3
perceptions, 7, 30, 204, 324
Peripatetic thought, 102–3, 128–29
perspectivism, 341–43
petitionary prayer, 81
Phaedo (Plato), 101
Phaedrus (Plato), xvii, 262–63, 292
phantasia
    cognitive impression, 247
    faculties of, 286–87, 293–94, 293n10
    image-making faculty, 170
    imagination and, 179, 268, 283, 294–96
    sense perception, 187, 274, 279
    term usage, 274, 293n10, 299
phenomenal properties of consciousness, 63–64, 63n30, 169
phenomenalism, 4–5n13, 5–10, 62–63, 162n4
phenomenal/noumenal contrast, 306
phenomenological reduction, 4–5, 10–13, 15
phenomenological residuum, 57n12
phenomenological synthesis, 66
Phenomenology (Hegel), 150
phenomenology of consciousness, 170
Philosophical Investigations (Wittgenstein), 2
philosophy, aim of, 27, 28n67
Philosophy of Law (Hegel), 39
physicalism, 357n9
picture theory, of language, 2
Platonic realism, xviii–xix
Platonic unity of intellect, xxiii, xxv–xxvin21
plurality
    duality of subject, 173
    of Forms, 64
    in intellect, 175
    object of thought, 173
    of ordinary empirical objects, 90
    of the self, 174
    of things, 106
    unity and, 99, 102, 130

INDEX OF SUBJECTS 423

pneuma, theory of, 269
Politeia (Plato), 288–89
possibility, xxn17, 88n5, 104, 104n77
    See also causal possibility; logical possibility
Posterior Analytics (Aristotle), 216
postmodernism, 334
potentiality, actuality and, 35–37
power, knowledge and, 368
prayer
    contemplative (*See* contemplative prayer)
    language of, 81–83, 85–86, 85n80
    places for, 84
    silent prayer, 84–86
    soul and, 81–83, 85n77
    types of, 81
prepositions, metaphysics of, 120, 133–35
Presuppositional thesis, 197–98n215
primary being, 59, 105n82
primary substances, 122, 136–37, 192–93n201
principles, meanings of, 117–19
prior simplicity principle, xix, xxii, 16, 19n7, 33, 35, 37–41, 63–64, 110, 146
privacy, 158
procession-return-image model., 182
properties, 90n16, 107n91, 181–82, 187–88
property dualism, 165, 167, 190, 190n186, 205, 361–62
propositional distinction, 45–47
propositional logic, 20n20, 21, 24n41, 25n52, 26n56, 26n58, 28n68, 229–230
pseudo-metaphysics, 22
psychological solipsism, 155
public language argument, 241n67, 246n86
pure being theory, 21n24, 23–24n41, 26n56
pyramid analogy, 370
Pyrrhonism, 119–120n11

qualia, term usage, 205–6, 205n18
qualitative identity, 90n16, 97, 113–15

questioning. *See* absolute presuppositions
Quine-Putnam indispensability argument, 42n102, 195–96n213

realism, 14–16, 65–67, 107n91, 119, 241n65, 245n84
reality
    degrees of, 133–35, 139–141
    knowledge of, 75
    language and, 35, 362
    mapping of, 151–52
    as productive process, 188, 188n174
    term usage, 356n5
reason
    idea of, 312–13
    Kant on, 307–9, 335–36
reconciliation (*Versoehnung*), 49, 160, 171
reconstruction, 360–63
reductionism, 198n215
reflection, 256–57
    See also illumination
Refutation of Idealism (Kant), 11
reification, 279–281
reincarnation, 283, 327
relation
    overview, xxi
    term usage, 90n17
relational intentionality, 56–57
relative presuppositions, 19–20, 23, 25
relativism, 198n215
representational language, 2, 2n5
representationalism
    imprinting, 203
    phenomenalism and, 5–10
    term usage, 2, 119
    thought and language, 119, 204
    types of, 184–85, 184n157
Republic (Plato), 181, 292
retrospection, 363–65
ritual, 67–68, 69

se and *per se*, distinction, 41–44, 41n96
Second Fragment (Parmenides), 50–51
secondary substances, 122, 136–37, 192–93n201
seeing, xxiii, 101, 216–19, 221–23

self
  aesthetics and, 339–341
  art and aesthetics, 322–23
  senses of, 170–71
  soul and, 319–320
  subjectivity and, 29, 36, 201–2
  technologies of, 346–350
self-conscious states, xxiii, 29
self-contemplation, xxvin23, 46, 105,
    166–67, 185, 223, 356n5
self-identity
  consciousness, mind as, 206–7
  horizons, 202–6
  intellect, mind as, 206–7
  overview, 201–2
  self-knowledge and, 189–193
  subjectivity and, 207–15
self-knowledge, 75–76, 189–193,
    225–26
self-reflexivity, 76, 78, 166–67, 187–89
  See also sunaisthesis (self-reflexivity)
self-thought, xxiii, 109–10
semantic solipsism, 155
sensations, 204
Seventh Letter (Plato), 75, 75n23
signification, 60, 60n22, 60n23
signs (sema), 119
silent prayer, 84–86
simplicity, 38–42
skepticism, 118n7, 119–120n11, 249
solipsism
  absolute, xxii
  epistemological, 192–93, 365–66
  methodological, xix, xxii, 47–49,
    152–58, 153n35, 193
Sophist (Plato), 100, 101, 109–11, 146n9,
    209–10, 215, 368
soul
  aesthetics and, 331–32, 332n62
  beauty and, xxiv, 264–272, 277–79,
    298–305
  contemplation and, 114n129
  development of, 76–77
  dimensions of, 265–69, 293
  harmony of, 76
  as immutable, 115
  intellect and, 302–3
  prayer and, 81–83, 85n77

self and, 319–320
two powers of, 166
undescended, 324–25
use of body, 33, 36–38, 37n87, 40,
  271–72
spectator imagery, 277, 303
spectator theory of knowledge, xviii–
  xix, 2, 118–19
speechless, image of beauty, 278
spiritual senses, 80
square analogy, 369
Stoic modal logic, 94n40
subjectivity
  consciousness and, 169
  meaning and, xvii–xviii
  self and, 320–22
  self-identity and, 207–15
  self-knowledge and, 225–26
substance, 121–22, 202
successions of apprehensions, 205
sunaisthesis (self-reflexivity), 170, 178,
  187–89, 246, 252, 287, 363
Symposium (Plato), 262, 291
synechism, xxvin23, 356n5
synthetic a posteriori, 34

taste, judgement of, 309–17, 337–38
technologies of the self, 346–350
the One
  beauty and, 262–64, 275–79, 299–
    300, 302
  generates Nous, xxiii, 175–180
  God the Father and, 45
  On the Good and, 33, 38, 97, 273
  good and, 33, 38, 97, 273
  Intellect and, xxiv, 17, 99, 105n82,
    112, 114–15
  seeing in respect of, 262–64
  simplicity and, 41–42
  speechless image of, xxiv, 264, 278,
    295–96, 303, 306, 318
  symmetry and, 275–77
  turning toward, 277–79
  virtue of identity and, 39
Theaetetus (Plato), xvii, xviin8, 15n38,
  18–19, 18n4, 72, 101, 119n11,
  227–29, 233
Theatetus (Plato), 250, 361n27, 368

INDEX OF SUBJECTS 425

thinking
    as activity of the mind, 367, 367n57
    being and, 213–15
    as being of or about something, 79n47
    forms and, 106–8
    identity of being and, xx–xxi, 88–93, 104–6
    meaning and, 58–59
    other minds and, 252–58
    past thinking, 305
    pointing toward primary being, 57
    as same as being, 100–102, 116n132
    thought thinking itself, xv–xvi
thought
    expression of, 68–69
    intellect and, 56–57
    limits of, xx
    self-thought, xxiii
thought experiments, 150–52
thought thinking itself, xv–xvi, 185–87
Timaeus (Plato), 102, 109
to on, term usage, 89n14
touching
    illumination and, 219–221
    seeing and, xxiii, 101, 217–18, 221–23, 248
touch-thinking, 253–55
traces/flatland, xxv
transcendent subjectivity, xxiii
"Transcendental Aesthetic" (Kant), 309
transcendental deduction, 11
transcendental ego, 12
transcendental reduction, 5, 12
transcendentals
    divine transcendence, 125–29
    foundation of, 13, 32
    horizons, 146–48
    overview, xxi–xxii
    Plotinus/Hegel comparison, 148–150

thought experiments, 150–52
transference theory of causality, 165, 172
transmission theory of causality, 180n134
trinity. *See* God, Son of; God the Father; Holy Spirit
true belief, 233–34
truth-falsity distinction, 251, 253–54, 254n121
truths, 4, 6, 25, 25n52, 200–221, 341–43

ultimate presuppositions, 24n41, 29n71, 33–35, 38, 197–98, 197n215
ultimate principle, 34, 38, 124
understanding, happening of, xvi
unity
    being and, 98–101
    multiplicity and, 151–52
    Parmenides' arguments, 97–100
    plurality and, 99, 102–3, 130
universals, 3, 6, 106–8, 107n89, 223–24
Unmoved Mover, 121, 124, 167, 221–22

veridical being, 87–88, 118–120, 120n14
verifiability argument, 358–59
verifiability principle, 195n212
Versoehnung (reconciliation), 49, 160, 171

the whole is in the part
    Aristotle on, xxvin22, 112–16, 112n122, 228n4, 259–260, 356n4
    objects of knowledge, 229–232
    Plotinus on, 113n127, 228n5, 356n4
words
    importance of knowledge of, 74n20
    as labels, 73, 73n11

www.ingramcontent.com/pod-product-compliance
Lightning Source LLC
Chambersburg PA
CBHW071223290426
44108CB00013B/1273